Radical Feminism

RADICAL FEMINISM

A Documentary Reader

EDITED BY

Barbara A. Crow

New York University Press

NEW YORK AND LONDON

NEW YORK UNIVERSITY PRESS
New York and London

Library of Congress Cataloging-in-Publication Data
Radical feminism : a documentary reader / edited by Barbara A. Crow.
p. cm.
Includes bibliographical references and index.
ISBN 0-8147-1554-0 (cl. : alk. paper) — ISBN 0-8147-1555-9 (pa. : alk. paper)
1. Feminism — United States — History — 20th century — Sources.   2. Radicalism — United
States — History — 20th century — Sources.   I. Crow, Barbara A.
HQ 1426.R325 2000
305.42'0973 21 — dc21   99-044846

New York University Press books are printed on acid-free paper,
and their binding materials are chosen for strength and durability.

Manufactured in the United States of America

10 9 8 7 6 5 4 3 2 1

Contents

Acknowledgments

I am a feminist who is a beneficiary of and has been influenced by the theoretical and activist work of United States radical feminism in the late sixties and early seventies. This edited collection is the result of teaching women's studies at a number of institutions in the United States and Canada. In my women's studies classes, I have tried to convey my own passion for early radical feminism and the powerful influence that it and the women's movement have played in shaping feminist politics. When I introduced students—both women of color and white women—to radical feminism, they were either indifferent, dismissive, or outright hostile. They thought of radical feminists as "just a bunch of dykes" who "hate men," "just a bunch of white middle-class women with nothing better to do," and they declared: "You thought burning your bras was radical; we don't even wear them."

Many students are persuaded by the promises of postmodern analyses of feminism, postcolonial studies, cultural studies, and queer theory. They challenged me to represent and contextualize radical feminism to mean something to them. Why did they respond this way? Why has radical feminism been constructed as archaic? What are the implications of its representation in women's studies, if it is represented at all as maligned or misguided? Who benefits from this silence and absence? Is there something to be gained from reexamining radical feminism in the context of identity politics? How did radical feminists get represented as having lost their engagement with these crucial concerns? Can revisiting these texts assist us with current theoretical and activist practices? Does it offer us any insights on how to avoid erasing histories and identities?

These questions shaped my selections in this collection. I want to thank the radical feminists who provided material, insights, and suggested readings. While some surviving radical feminists were skeptical about having their work reproduced, others were excited. Those who work on contemporary feminist theory know how difficult it is to represent the contemporary women's movement when the authors are still alive. I hope that my representation of these works is respectful of them.

Many individuals have assisted in the production of this book. First, I would like to thank Polly Thistlethwaite of Lesbian Herstory Archives and Barbara Grier of Naiad Press for helping me identify and locate many of the authors in this collection; the Redstockings Women's Liberation Archives and the Women's Educational Center, Inc.; my research assistants, Barbara MacDonald, Susan Harris, and Shoaib Nasir; The Barnard Center for Research on Women Associate spring–summer 1994; my colleagues Jeanne Perreault and Susan Rudy at the University of Calgary; a Starter

Research Grant from the University of Calgary and the support of my dean, Michael McMordie; Cecelia Cancellaro, who started the project at Routledge and supported its initial development; I would like to thank the staff at NYU Press—Eric Zinner, Daisy Hernandez, Alice Calaprice, and Despina Papazoglou Gimbel for their professionalism, support, patience, and editorial suggestions.

I also have a long list of family and friends who have supported and endured the production of this book from its beginnings in 1993 to its completion in July 1999. I am grateful to be surrounded and loved by these individuals: Jamie Bennett, Nancy Bennett, James Brown, Kim Croffot-Suede, Lance Croffot-Suede, Barry Crow, Timothy Daum, Brian Dorscht, Debbie Egan, Leslie Gash, Lise Gotell, Paige Hamilton-Platten, Geoffrey Hendricks, Beverly Longford, Kimberly Longford, Graham Longford, Sydney Longford, Susan Minette, Susan Prentice, Kathryn Rowan, Kimberly Sawchuk, Paul Sheardown, Melanie Sinclair, Patty Smith, Rae Staseson, Allison Weir, and Mike Woods.

I would like to thank all of the authors who agreed to have their work reprinted. It was difficult to locate many of them and I have done my best to secure the appropriate permissions. Many radical feminists have died of breast cancer, live in poverty, or have been institutionalized, but many others are successful journalists and scholars; these histories need to be known to understand the risks these women took for us and how these risks have affected their life journeys.

Finally, I would like to thank my long-term partner, Michael Longford, and my son, Elijah Michael Crow-Longford. Michael has supported me, prodded me, and celebrated the production of this book with me, and Eli has provided me with a new way of knowing the world.

Again, my thanks to all these individuals who made this edited collection possible.

Introduction
Radical Feminism

Many young women today are dismissive of radical feminism, and are quite sure it has nothing to teach them that might be of use in their lives. Some of this is due to years of distorted and caricatured portrayals of radical feminism in mass culture[1] and secondary scholarship, and some is the result of a perhaps inevitable "taken-for-grantedness" that young women affect toward achievements of women's movements. A result of more than thirty years of "second wave" feminism is a comfortable cushion of freedoms; but that cushion also mutes and distances the struggles that created those freedoms. The obvious path toward reconnecting with the origins of radical feminism would be a search for the original sources, but even here there is no easy recourse. Often, libraries do not carry the texts, many of the early radical feminist anthologies are out of print, and they are virtually impossible to find in archives unless you live in a major city. To understand where the women's movement is now and to fairly acknowledge and assess the attitudes, values, and practices of radical feminism, these radical feminist documents must be made easily available.

This collection is just the beginning of the kind of work that still needs to be done in the area of radical feminism. It is an attempt to provide some historical material that acknowledges that some radical feminists did make connections between sex, gender, race, class, sexual orientation, age, religious beliefs, region, children, and physical and mental abilities.[2] It brings together many of the original documents that have defined, contested, and shaped radical feminism in the United States from 1967 to 1975.[3] The material derives largely from the work I conducted at the Lesbian Herstory Archives, the Redstockings Archives, and the Barnard College Special Collections, and thus it has a particular regional focus on the East Coast. Other forms of radical feminism will certainly have evolved in other regions. I am aware that significant radical feminist activity occurred in other communities and cities.[4]

From these various sources, ranges of definitions of radical feminism emerge, including the following:

> [W]e must eradicate the sexual division of labour on which our society is based. Only then do men and women have a hope of living together as human beings (Kreps 1972, p. 75).

> Radical feminism is working for the eradication of domination and elitism in all human relationships. This would make self-determination the ultimate good and require the downfall of society as we know it today (Ware in this collection).

I believe that sexism is the root oppression, the one which until and unless we *uproot* it, will continue to put forth branches of racism, class hatred, ageism, competition, ecological disaster, and economic exploitation (Morgan 1977, p. 9).

Women are a class, and the terms that make up that initial assumption must be examined (Atkinson 1970, pp. 32–33)

If we women are to get basic, then surely the first job is to find out what liberation for ourselves means, what work it entails, what benefits it will yield (Cade in this collection).

While these selections reveal the diversity of radical feminism, the key distinguishing feature of radical feminism is its refusal to accept the traditional category of "women" as it has been defined in the West.

So, what makes radical feminism distinct?[5] While radical feminism has been hailed for everything from increased rates of female juvenile delinquency[6] to its liberatory politics, many terms, practices, and movements signify radical feminism.[7] However, I have selected pieces for this collection that convey the unique contributions of radical feminism. First, individual women, and groups of them, have named and defined themselves as radical feminists. Its theory and practice are unique to a particular time frame (1967–1975)[8] and nation.[9] Second, radical feminism saw women's oppression as the first, the oldest, and the primary form of oppression (see Willis in this collection) to which all other forms of oppression are related and connected (see Ware in this collection). Third, its method of transformation was consciousness-raising (see Allen in this collection). And finally, it recognized the limitations and efficacy of a wide range of political strategies.

In its early configuration, radical feminists referred to themselves as radical women for fear that their concerns would not be taken seriously by the left (Dixon 1969, 1970, Koedt 1968, Willis 1969, Burris 1973). The shift from radical women to radical feminists occurred on October 17, 1968, when a group of feminists designated themselves as "The Feminists" with organizing principles set out on June 13, 1969.[10] Radical feminism named and associated itself with "women's liberation" as opposed to "women's rights" and saw themselves as part of a movement rather than a specialized interest group.[11] Much of the work associated with radical feminism was publicized through radical feminist groups such as the Women's Liberation Movement, Cell 16, the Furies, the Feminists—New York, the Redstockings, and Radical Feminist 28.[12] In Ware's (1970) *Women Power*, she identifies the influence of the male left on the first radical feminist group (p. 19). However, Morgan (1977), Carden (1974), and Deckard (1983) identify unrest by women in the Student Non-Violent Coordinating Committee (SNCC) as early as 1964 in Chicago. Ruby Doris Smith Robinson[13] wrote about women's inferior position in the SNCC eliciting the infamous response by Stokely Charmichael: "The only position for women in SNCC is prone" (Freeman 1975, p. 57). A number of women presented other papers at various events: Heather Booth and Naomi Weisstein held a seminar on women's issues at the free university in Chicago (Deckard 1983, p. 327), while others continued to put women's issues on the platform of SNCC and the Students for a Democratic Society (SDS), but they were met with disapproval. As a result of these activities, Joreen Freeman started the first women's liberation newsletter at the 1967 National Convention of New Politics in Chicago. Shulamith Firestone joined this group in September and later left with Pamela Allen to start a women's liberation group in New York (Ware 1970, pp. 20–21). After Firestone and Allen moved to New York, two events "marked the emergence of an independent Women's Liberation movement" (Carden 1974, p. 61). The first was an anti-Vietnam protest march organized by the Jeannette Rankin Brigade[14] in Washington in January 1968. During this march, an "alternative action" was held at the Arlington National Cemetery where Kathie (Sarachild) Amatniek gave the speech, "Funeral Oration for the Burial of Traditional Womanhood" (Firestone 1968, pp. 20–22). The second public protest was held a year later at an inaugural counter-demonstration in Washington. At this protest, Marilyn Salzman-Webb spoke about women's issues and was booed off the stage with comments like, "Take her off the stage and fuck her" (Carden 1974, p. 62). These two events confirmed for these women that they would have to organize separately.

Radical feminist groups[15] used mimeographs, meeting minutes, pamphlets, newsletters, journals, and newspaper and magazine articles to get their views out (see Appendix 1). A growing demand produced edited collections such as Toni Cade's *The Black Woman* (1970), Robin Morgan's *Sisterhood is Powerful* (1970), Sookie Stambler's *Women's Liberation* (1970), Leslie Tanner's *Voices from Women's Liberation* (1970), Edith Hoshino Altbach's *From Feminism to Liberation*, (1971), Vivian Gornick and Barbara Moran's *Women in Sexist Society* (1971), Cellestine Ware's *Woman Power* (1970), Anne Koedt, Ellen Levine, and Anita Rapone's *Radical Feminism* (1973), and single-authored books such as Shulamith Firestone's *The Dialectic of Sex* (1970), Kate Millet's *Sexual Politics* (1970), Ti-Grace Atkinson's *Amazon Odyssey* (1974), and Jill Johnston's *Lesbian Nation* (1973)

Within feminist scholarship and practice, radical feminism has sometimes been characterized by its essentialist construction of the category of women, its universalization of the category of women, and its sole focus on women's oppression (Jaggar 1983, Lorde 1984, Spelman 1988, Tong 1994). While I do not want this introduction or collection to valorize radical feminism, I do want to reinsert in the developing narrative in women's studies the contributions, contradictory positions, and complexity of U.S. radical feminism of this time period, to reflect on the legacy of radical feminism, and to ask ourselves why some of the issues that were raised by radical feminists have been ignored, submerged, and denied. Some radical feminists, in their construction of women's oppression as the first form of oppression, argued that women could attain autonomy only by separating themselves, their energy, and their commitment, from men; lesbians offered a role model (Zimmerman 1974, p. 11). Other radical feminists believed that only through seeing the interconnections among all women's political struggles could social change emerge (see Weathers in this collection). For these radical feminists, class, sex, race, age, and sexuality were intertwined and interrelated. We need to acknowledge these contributions and revisit their history before we, yet again, make radical feminism's contributions invisible.

What kinds of issues did radical feminists raise, explore, denounce, and develop? From my archival work, secondary readings, and interviews, it seems evident to me that radical feminists covered questions about paid work, domesticity, heterosexuality, family, lesbianism, bisexuality, racism, poverty, class, war, violence, abortion, reproductive freedom, children, international politics, colonialism, and friendship. Some radical feminist positions saw these issues as interrelated (see Ware and Cornwell in this collection) and some saw them as issues onto themselves (see Firestone and Johnston in this collection). But why were some issues emphasized over others? What kinds of tools did radical feminists have available to them to shape their analyses? For example, there were few historical texts for feminists to consult that articulated women's oppression,[16] nor was there much popular sentiment that women were disadvantaged in American public consciousness. Moreover, in some of their publications, they tried to locate themselves within a U.S. radical labor history. They did some of the work to reclaim women's participation in this history and to make explicit links to their questions, issues, and analyses (Firestone 1968, Morgan 1970, Koedt, Levine, and Rapone 1973).

Race

While radical feminists attempted to work against racism with the tools that were available to them at the time, white women had yet to learn how central racism was to the struggle for social change. Two features of radical feminism have been erased in the rewriting of the U.S. women's movement. First, bell hooks's *Feminist Theory from Margin to Center* (1984, p. 6) argues that radical feminism was developed and practiced by women of colour[17] *and* white women, and second, white women were interested in combating racism. What happened? How did the women's movement get represented as losing its interest in racism? Part of the explanation lies in the fracturing of the radical feminist movement; part of it can be explained by the changing economics and politics of the 1970s; and part of it lies with the professionalization and institutionalization of the U.S. women's movement. While many radical feminists continued to work against racism (Bell and Klein 1996), radical feminism had been so tainted by representations in the mainstream and popular press that many women attracted to the ideas espoused by radical feminists gravitated to the more liberal and less tainted feminist groups.

Racism and sexism were articulated differently by white women and by African American women. White women often constructed race as the "other," with little reflection on whiteness. They did acknowledge racism as an institutional and systemic practice, with its focus on women's oppression as the primary oppression, and racism was seen as an extension of sexism (Firestone 1970, p. 108). Indeed, many radical feminists constructed and understood race and sex as separate categories, while some privileged sex as the primary, biologically based difference (Willis 1969).

Many of the earlier books and edited collections were authored by African American women. The relationship between race and sex was articulated as follows: "If women of both races see their problems as originating in female dependency on men and in their self-contempt, then women will make a revolution in our social and economic order" (Ware 1970, pp. 98–99). Others spoke to African American women's hesitancies:

What do black women feel about Women's Lib? Distrust. It is white, therefore suspect. In spite of the fact that liberating movements in the black world have been catalysts for white feminism, too many movements and organizations have made deliberate overtures to enroll blacks and have ended up by rolling them. They don't want to be used again to help somebody gain power—a power that is carefully kept out of their hands. They look at white women and see them as the enemy—for they know racism is not confined to white men, and there are more white women than men in this country (Morrison in this collection).

These articulations have affected the legacy of the analysis of race and sex.

Lesbianism

Because of its focus on women, radical feminism is often associated with lesbianism.[18] The familiar and misrepresented quote, "feminism is the theory; lesbianism is the practice," attributed to Ti-Grace Atkinson (Koedt 1971, 1973, p. 246) has occupied much of the contemporary construction of radical feminism.[19] However, while a significant part of radical feminist theory and practiced was concerned with lesbianism, it was framed by analyses of heterosexuality, sexuality, marriage, and children (see Radicalesbians in this collection).

Anti-lesbianism, as an ultimate form of misogyny, continues to be a strategy which deters and detracts women and men from seeing the potential of radical feminism (see Abbott and Love in this collection). Lesbians raised the important point, just like issues of race, that radical feminism could not universalize the category of women: "To end the oppression of the lesbian is to admit of a wider range of being and acting under the generic name 'woman'" (Abbott and Love in this collection).

The Furies, in their analysis of the inefficacy of capitalism, racism, and imperialism (Berson 1972a, p. 2) devoted much of their newsletter to understanding lesbianism (its subtitle was *lesbian/feminist monthly*). For the Furies, "relationships between men and women were essentially political," lesbianism was not a matter of sexual preference, but rather was a deliberate political choice (see Bunch in this collection). Lesbianism critiqued heterosexuality as an institution that keeps women oppressed. Abbott and Love and the Furies also discussed bisexuality and its implications for the heterosexual nexus and lesbianism.[20]

Another area integrally related to sexuality was childbearing and children. Many radical feminists wrote about women and children. The journal *Women: A Journal of Liberation* dedicated a whole issue to women and children (vol. 4, no. 3, 1976), arguing that "[u]nless men and women can come to share the responsibilities—and the joys—of child care and household work neither women nor children will be much freer" (see Babcox in this collection). Rosalyn Baxandall (1970) recounted the work involved in establishing a cooperative nursery which they called the "Liberation Nursery." Baxandall discusses the membership of the nursery and specifically the conflict of values that precluded African American women's participation. This was one of the first attempts to make a child-care collective and integrate its practices with women's liberation issues.

Class

As mentioned earlier in discussing the genesis of radical feminism, many of its participants were involved with the SDS, which had explicit analyses of class.[21] Hence, it is not surprising that many radical feminist writings were influenced by these class analyses and not unlike their analyses of race made analogies between sex as class and the relationship between class and women's oppression "that their enemies are our enemies, and their fight our fight" (see D'Amico in this collection). Also, related to issues of class were the politics of housework. *Women: A Journal of Women's Liberation* had Giuliana Pompei's "Wages for Housework" translated, and Pat Mainardi in the "Politics of Housework" argued that "participatory democracy begins at home" (see Mainardi in this collection).

As radical feminists began to privilege women's oppression as primary and lost their faith in the left's ability to integrate women's issues, class issues became less important but not absent. Most of the radical feminist anthologies and many of the journals produced at the time included some kind of analysis of class. However, while some radical feminist analyses focussed on women as a class and/or the uneven distribution of unpaid and paid labor, little attention was given to the ways in which class separated and differentiated women.

Organization

This book is organized into three sections. The first section focuses on radical "Feminist Theories of Women's Oppression"; the articles in this section reflect the range of conceptualizations of women's oppression in radical feminist thought. Some essays reflect on women as a class and on racism and heterosexism. Many of these analyses of women's oppressions emerged from a range of radical feminist groups such as Cell 16, the Furies, the Feminists, and the Women's Liberation Movement.

The second section focuses on manifestos and methods. The manifestos were a popular form for early radical feminist positions. They were called manifestos to acknowledge their engagement and challenges to the Communist Manifesto, and their methods were shaped by the Maoist revolutionary practice of "speaking bitterness" (Freeman 1975, p. 118).[22] These manifestos are polemical, bold, visionary, and contradictory. Radical feminists key analytic method was consciousness-raising. It was through this practice that radical feminists were able to construct and delineate the principle of the "personal as the political."[23] In this method, small groups of women came together to "rap," discuss, and share their personal experiences. Some consciousness-raising groups invoked certain kinds of guidelines that not only allowed for personal expression and its politicization, but also as an opportunity to develop skills.[24] This method was not easily transported to larger-sized groups and presented dilemmas for radical feminist organizing. Moreover, at times it remained constrained by what Freeman (1973) articulated as "the tyranny of structurelessness."

Finally, I end with sites of contestation to reveal the ways in which radical feminists were engaged with a range of interrelated questions of separatism, lesbianism, heterosexuality, children, race, and class. The selection of writings reveals the ways in which many radical feminists viewed these questions as interrelated.

Radical feminism developed theoretical frameworks and practices that started from women's experiences. They began from a place that implicitly valued women and tried to understand and develop strategies to change the power relations between men and women and between and among women. It was radical not only as it pertained to "getting at the roots" of women's oppression, but also radical in its ability to develop a theoretical framework and practice emanating from women's bodies and experiences. We need to critically reinsert this history into contemporary feminist practice and women's studies.

I hope that *Radical Feminism* is able to convey the diversity, complexity, paradoxical, and sometimes singular vision of radical feminism. I invite feminist scholars to continue, and to extend this work to other countries and parts of North America.

NOTES

1. When I ask students what they think radical feminism is, they often cite the "bra burning" event at the Miss America pageant. A group of radical feminists organized a protest during the Miss America pageant in September 1968. The event received nationwide coverage. One of the most infamous stories associated with the protest was that the participants "burned their bras"—an event that never happened.

See Lindsay Van Gelder's article "The Truth about Bra-Burners" (1992). In this article, Van Gelder reveals how the myth of the "bra burning" was created.

2. A number of books and articles that were widely circulated at the time and mentioned in various minutes and articles herein include Simone de Beauvoir's *The Second Sex* (1952), Betty Friedan's *The Feminine Mystique* (1963), Juliet Mitchell's "Women: The Longest Revolution" (1966), Margaret Benston's "The Political Economy of Women's Liberation" (1969), Mary Daly's *The Church and the Second Sex* (1968), and Andrea Dworkin's *Woman Hating* (1974).

3. Radical feminism does not start at one particular time in the mid-1960s nor does it end in 1975. I have confined the collection to these years because of the intense activity at this time. Radical feminism, much like its predecessors and often with modifications, is still practiced in most Western countries. For its current manifestations, see the collection, *Radically Speaking: Feminism Reclaimed*, edited by Diane Bell and Renate Klein (1996).

4. See Nancy Whittier's *Feminist Generations: The Persistence of the Radical Women's Movement* (1995) focusing on women in Columbus, Ohio. There are archives across the United States that have material pertaining to radical feminist activity across the country. For example, the Archives Distribution Project, Gainesville, Florida; Laura X's Women's History Research Center, Berkeley, California; the Lesbian History Archives, Brooklyn, New York; and the Women's Liberation Research Network at Duke University (http://www.dukeu.edu/~ginnyd/wlrndir2.html).

5. There has been significant feminist debate about the categorization of feminisms

(Jaggar 1983, Eisenstein 1983, Tong 1994). Generally, the categories are distinguished as radical feminism, liberal feminism, socialist feminism, cultural feminism, Marxist feminism, psychoanalytic feminism, postmodern feminism, anti-racist feminism, multiracial feminism, and lesbian feminism. Many feminist scholars have pointed out how feminist analyzes and practices overlap (Freeman 1975, Bunch 1987, Bacchi 1990, Vickers, Rankin, and Appelle 1993).

6. During the mid- to late seventies, numerous articles were published in psychology journals focusing on the effects of women's liberation. These articles suggested that women's liberation was responsible for the decrease in childbirth rates (Schmelz 1976, Shea 1983), increased juvenile delinquency among girls (Siassi and Wesner 1974, 1975, Terry 1979, Baldwin 1983), role conflicts (Stollof 1973, Bayes Whisnante and Wilk 1977, Baker 1982), and some studies even suggested that there was a relationship between physical attractiveness and women's participation in the liberation movement (Johnson et al. 1978, Beaman and Klentz 1983).

7. For example, King (1994) argues that radical feminism is represented by a range of terms:

Questions about definitions suggest something of the flux and shift of tendencies becoming political objects, metamorphosing [sic] from one possibility to another, and dissolving or budding with time. These terms overlay each other: women's liberation, women's liberation movement, radical women, radical feminists, radical feminism, women's liberationists, feminists, WLM, feminist radicals, radical feminists, radical feminism, white women's movement. (p. 11)

8. I use this date because this is when consensus emerges about the concept and is often cited as its origin (Echols 1989).

9. Radical feminism was developed and practiced in other western nations including Australia, Canada, Italy, the United Kingdom. As Judith Allen (1990) argues, it is important that we contextualize and acknowledge that there are various ways in which feminism manifests itself in a particular culture—"comparative studies of feminism permit due recognition of the fact that feminism emerged relatively contiguously across western countries in response to relatively common international characteristics of transformations in sexual patternings and sexual cultures" (p. 17).

10. The term "radical feminism" first appeared in *Notes from the Second Year* (Firestone 1970).

11. Often this distinction was made in reference to Betty Friedan's earlier publication of *The Feminine Mystique* (1963) and the development of the United States' first national women's organization, the National Organization of Women (NOW). Radical feminists in the women's liberation movement characterized advocates of "women's rights" worked within the system and used male standards as the norm. However, Freeman (1975) argued (as Bacchi does about first-wave feminism's "maternal" and "egalitarian" feminism) that "women's rights" and "women's liberation" strategies overlap and that there are similarities between the two groups (pp. 50–51).

12. Also, some radical feminists were self-conscious about their history, and there are a number of articles about the origins of radical feminism. See Dixon 1969, 1970, Altbach 1971, Freeman 1975, Willis 1984, Baxandall 1994, and Hanisch's self-published collection of writings *frankly feminist* (New York: truthtellers, 1996).

13. Ruby Doris Smith Robinson was a black woman and the founder of SNCC.

14. The Jeannette Rankin Brigade was a coalition of women's peace groups.

15. Some of the more influential radical feminist groups included Bread and Roses, Cell 16, the Chicago Women's Liberation Union, the Class Workshop, Chicago Women's Libera-

tion, DC Women's Liberation, the Feminists, the Furies, New York Radical Feminists, New York Radical Women, the Redstockings, the Westside Group, Women's Majority Union, and WITCH (Women's International Terrorist Conspiracy from Hell).

16. A few radical feminists make reference to the importance of Simone de Beauvoir's *The Second Sex*, translated and made available for a U.S. audience by Knopf publishers in 1952. However, Simons (1983) and Dietz (1992) argued that while radical feminists such as Shulamith Firestone and Mary Daly acknowledge the importance of de Beauvoir, their analyses are not necessarily reflected in their work.

The first feminist edited collection, and still a very popular one, that put together a historical set of readings by feminists was Alice Rossi's *The Feminist Papers* (1973). Also, *Voices from Women's Liberation* edited by Leslie Tanner (1970) included a section, "Voices from the Past," to start its collection of radical feminist papers.

17. Not only were African American women writing about radical feminism, as this collection illustrates, but, as recent scholarship by Polatnick (1994, 1996) argues, African American women were also active in it.

18. For a good discussion and overview of lesbianism and radical feminism, see Carol Anne Douglas, *Love and Politics: Radical Feminist and Lesbian Theories* (1990).

19. King (1994) argues that:

Atkinson did not use the phrase this way herself. Instead it dates from a 1970 talk to the New York Chapter of the Daughters of Bilitis (DOB), in which she asserted that lesbians and feminists were different groups, that perhaps could not work together at all. She said, "Feminism is a theory; but Lesbianism is a practice." Not "the" but "a"; not connected with "and" but distinguished by "but." The value is on "theory" here, as politically transformatory, not on "practice," which is enacted without revolutionary reflection. (p. 125)

20. "Bisexual women, who have been caught on both sides and in the middle of heterosexual/homosexual argument, have a unique contribution to make to open discussion on sexuality in the movement. Their experience is nearly as hidden and difficult to weigh as a factor as that of the possibly prevalent asexuality in the movement (Abbott and Love 1972, p. 156)." Also see L. Ulmschneider 1973.

21. See Mitchell 1966, Benston 1969, Dixon 1969, 1970.

One way in which the women's movement differs from prior protests in American history is in its concern with consciousness-raising not as a preliminary to other group activity, but often as the [*sic*] significant political act. Previous movements have utilized consciousness-raising techniques, but mainly as preparation from concerted group action; such methods, for example, were employed by the Communists in the 1930s in order to get people into the party, after which they took up things.

There is some of this kind of *agitprop* in the use of consciousness-raising among feminists, but for many radical women, the practice of sharing experiences and feelings, with the goal of heightened consciousness as women in a particular political environment, is the full extent of their activism. Yet despite the quiet quality of the efforts to expand one another's sights, many women consider such activity a revolutionary undertaking. (McWilliams 1974, p. 162)

23. The first article to articulate the personal as political was Carol Hanisch's "The Personal Is the Political" (1970) in *Notes from the Second Year*.

24. Some consciousness-raising groups used a variety of strategies to destabilize and challenge hierarchical relations in organizations. These strategies included the lot system, the distribution of tokens or chips, and/or rotating chairs.

Political Statements and Processes
An Introduction

Most of the key radical feminist groups formed in the late 1960s and early 1970s, including the Furies (Washington, DC), the Feminists (New York, NY), Radical Feminists 28 (Kansas, MO), the Redstockings (New York, NY), Cell 16 (Boston, MA), New York Radical Women (New York, NY), WITCH (Women's International Terrorist Conspiracy from Hell, New York) and Women's Liberation drew their membership from disaffected student, civil rights, and anti-war activists (as well as from already extant feminist groups). These organizations provided community, places to organize political activities, and forums to think and write about women's oppression. As a result, most of the important theoretical work which shaped radical feminism emerged from these groups.

The pieces I have selected were reproduced and distributed in a variety of formats and collections, from meeting minutes, pamphlets, and newsletters, to collections such as *Sisterhood Is Powerful* and *Women's Liberation*. I have attempted to represent the diversity and depth of radical feminist thought and activity, and also the range of genres, in which this work was made available. One of the most important position papers that traveled across the United States was Beverly Jones's and Judith Brown's *Toward a Female Liberation Movement*, commonly referred to as the "Florida Paper." The two parts of the "Florida Paper" are a response to the Women's Manifesto prepared by the female caucus of the SDS and published in the *New Left Notes*, July 1967. In the first part, Jones details the manifesto and argues that it does not adequately address women's oppression and that the only way women can attain this political end is to "start fighting primarily for the liberation and independence of women" (see Jones and Brown in this collection). In the second part, Brown begins by sarcastically outlining the exclusionary practices of the SDS and their stereotypes about radical women and female liberation. She criticizes the institution of marriage and the family, and then provides a set of strategies and practices to attain women's liberation. In "a personal summary," Jones ends her reflection on "female liberation" with the following:

> "I am my brother's keeper" is the cautious altruism of those who are themselves enchained. Rather: "I Am My Brother's Brother, My Sister's Sister." Women together, sustaining each other politically, restored to an affection for each other, and unburdening themselves of their struggle with men, must move to take that Savage Society apart. (See Jones and Brown in this collection)

At the same time that the "Florida Paper" was in circulation, the New York Radical Women were producing *Notes from the First Year*, followed by *Notes from the Second Year*, and *Notes from the Third Year*. In its first edition, Anne Koedt outlines why women have chosen to organize separately and what makes them radical in "Women and the Radical Movement."[1] As mentioned in the introduction, before radical feminism and the women's liberation movement were embraced, these activists referred to themselves as radical women in relation to radical men in the various youth, student, civil rights, and antiwar movements. Koedt argues that the kind of liberation being made by "radical men" maintains the "dominant/submissive relationship between men and women" (Koedt 1968, p. 27). In other newspapers such as *Rat* and *Ramparts*,[2] a number of radical feminists raised questions about their exclusion from "revolutionary" politics. Marlene Dixon's "Why Women's Liberation" argues that "[m]ale supremacy, marriage and the structure of wage labour—each of these aspects of women's oppression has been crucial to the resurgence of the women's struggle" (see Dixon in this collection). Ti-Grace Atkinson's "Radical Feminism," appeared in *Notes from the Second Year* and later became a more expanded version as a chapter in her book *Amazon Odyssey*. Atkinson argued that "those individuals who are today defined as women must eradicate their own definition. Women must, in a sense, commit suicide, and the journey from womanhood to a society of individuals is hazardous. . . . We must create, as no other group in history has been forced to do, from the very beginning" (See Atkinson in this collection).

On the other hand, Cellestine Ware, in *Woman Power*, is wary of universalizing the category of women. She articulates some of the discomfort women of color have with a politics that wants to eradicate definition. Ware argues instead that the connections between racism and sexism need to be addressed in order for the movement to be successful.

While the above selections provide a range of ways in which radical feminists understood and articulated women's oppression, one of the popular formats for presenting these ideas was the manifesto.[3] Several manifestos were produced across the United States, raising issues about race, class, sexuality, work, and heterosexuality. Blunt, straightforward, passionate, and angry, they convey a sense of urgency, a theoretical understanding of women's oppression, and, most importantly, make calls for action. All of the manifestos included here were produced by radical feminist groups, except for Valerie Solanas's *S.C.U.M.* manifesto. While Solanas was not active in any organized radical feminist group, this work was widely circulated and discussed.

While the manifesto provided a set of guidelines, analyses, and calls for action, the process to enact and achieve women's liberation was through consciousness-raising (CR). For many radical feminists, CR was a process by which to give voice to women's personal experiences of oppression. The political slogan "the personal is political" captures this process (see Hanisch in this collection). Consciousness-raising groups developed across the United States, and Vivian Gornick's piece from the *New York Times Magazine* introduces us into this process.

CR groups were composed of a small group of women, from as few as three to as many as twenty. A number of strategies were invoked to encourage women to speak, such as the "lot" and "disk" system (Morgan 1970, p. xxxi). Not only were strategies invoked to get women to speak, but CR groups also functioned as a way to teach women how to speak in public, chair meetings, and/or write. Moreover, many women involved with CR groups moved from their articulation of the personal to political action. Some CR groups organized women's centers, shelters for battered women, and provided rape crisis phone lines.

CR groups, however, were not without their critics, most notably radical feminist Joreen Freeman. In the "Tyranny of Structurelessness," Freeman warned of the "impotence" of structurelessness and its "diffusion" of power. She argued that "[I]f the movement continues to keep power as diffuse as possible because it knows it cannot demand responsibility from those who have it, it does prevent any group or person from totally dominating. But it simultaneously insures that the movement is as ineffective as possible" (1973, p. 297). Freeman wanted the women's liberation movement to produce some kind of structure that would allow for informal CR groups to be part of a movement (p. 297). Indeed, CR groups began to dissipate in the early seventies largely not because of the "tyranny of structurelessness," but as shelters, services, and groups became more widely available for women.

NOTES

1. This was originally a speech given at the Free University of New York City, February 17, 1968 (Koedt, Levine, Firestone and Rapone 1973, p. 318). It was then published in *Notes from the First Year* (1968) and is again in the edited collection *Radical Feminism* (Koedt, Levine, and Rapone 1973).

2. *RAT* and *Ramparts* were underground radical newspapers produced in New York City and San Francisco, respectively in the early 1960s and 1970s.

3. As stated earlier, many radical feminists were active in other social movements at the time. Some of the movements were influenced by class analyses and Marx and Engel's *Communist Manifesto* (1848), and hence there was a double entendre to their use of the manifesto. First, many radical feminists wanted to acknowledge the importance of class, but they also wanted to demonstrate that the *Communist Manifesto* did not address women's oppression.

A. Why Women Are Oppressed

Chapter One

Toward A Female Liberation Movement

Beverly Jones and Judith Brown

PART I, BY BEVERLY JONES

Women's steady march onward, and her growing desire for
a broader outlook, prove that she has not reached her
normal condition, and that society has not yet conceded all
that is necessary for its attainment.

> —(Introduction, *A History of Women Suffrage*, 1889)

The Manifesto

For a middle-aged female accustomed to looking to militant youth for radical leadership it was a shock to read the Women's Manifesto which issued from the female
caucus of the national SDS convention last summer (1967; Manifesto printed in *New
Left Notes* of 10 July 1967). Here were a group of 'radical women' demanding respect
and leadership in a radical organization and coming on with soft-minded NAACP
logic and an Urban League list of grievances and demands. One need only substitute
the words 'white' and 'black' for 'male' and 'female' respectively, replace references
to SDS with the city council, and remember all the fruitless approaches black groups
made and are still making to local white power groups to realize how ludicrous this
manifesto is.

To paraphrase accordingly,

1. Therefore we demand that our brothers on the city council recognize that they
   must deal with their own problems of white chauvinism in their personal,
   social, and political relationships.

"Toward a Female Liberation Movement" was written by Beverly Jones and Judith Brown in Gainesville, Florida, and was published as a pamphlet and distributed by Gainesville Women's Liberation in
1968. It is reprinted by permission of Gainesville Women's Liberation. This article, as well as other
writings from the 1960s rebirth years of feminism and by current women's liberation organizers, is
available from Redstockings Women's Liberation Archives Distribution Project, P.O. Box 2625, Gainesville, FL 32602-2625. Please enclose a self-addressed stamped envelope with inquiries.

2. It is obvious from this meeting of the city council that full advantage is not being taken of the abilities and potential contributions of blacks. We call upon the black people to demand full participation in all aspects of local government from licking stamps to assuming leadership positions.

3. People in leadership positions must be aware of the dynamics of creating leadership and are responsible for cultivating all of the black resources available to the local government.

4. All University administrations must recognize that campus regulations discriminate against blacks in particular and must take positive action to protect the rights of black people.

And so on. The caucus goes on to charge *New Left Notes* with printing material on the subject, developing bibliographies, and asks the National Council to *set up a committee to study* the subject and report at a future date!

There is also a rather pathetic attempt on the part of the caucus to prove its credentials by mimicking the dominant group's rhetoric on power politics. Thus there ensues some verbiage about the capitalist world, the socialist world, and the third world in which it is implied that women are somehow better off under socialism.

It must have been disappointing indeed to the women who drew up the 'analysis of women's role' and insisted it be printed verbatim in *New Left Notes* to find Castro quoted the following month in the *National Guardian* to the effect that he is assuredly grateful to the women of Cuba for having fought in the hills and otherwise aided the revolution, but now all that is past and women's place is once again servant to husband and children, in the home.

In a plea to the Women's Federation to hold down its goals of female integration into the greater Cuban society, he said, 'But who will do the cooking for the child who still comes home for lunch? Who will nurse the babies or take care of the preschool child? Who will cook for the man when he comes home from work? Who will wash and clean and take care of things?'

The Women's Manifesto ends, and again we will substitute 'white' for male and 'black' for female:

'We seek the liberation of all human beings. The struggle for the liberation of blacks must be part of the larger fight for freedom. (A line which could better have been uttered by the city commission.) We recognize the difficulty our brothers will have in dealing with white chauvinism and we assume our full responsibility (as blacks) in helping to resolve the contradiction.'

And lest the men get upset by all this wild talk, or even think of taking it seriously, the woman add a reassuring note.

'Freedom now! We love you!'

What lessons are to be learned from this fantastic document, the discrimination which preceded it, and the unchanging scene which followed? I think the lessons are several and serious. I'd like to list them first and discuss each one separately.

1. People don't get radicalized (engaged with basic truths) fighting other people's battles.

2. The females in SDS (at least those who wrote the Manifesto) essentially reject

an identification with their own sex and are using the language of female power in an attempt to advance themselves personally in the male power structure they are presently concerned with.

3. That for at least two reasons radical females do not understand the desperate condition of women in general. In the first place, as students they occupy some sexy, sexless, limbo area where they are treated by males in general with less discrimination than they will ever again face. And in the second place, few of them are married or if married have children.

4. For their own salvation and for the good of the movement, women must form their own group and work primarily for female liberation.

1. People Don't Get Radicalized Fighting Other People's Battles

No one can say that women in the movement lack courage. As a matter of fact they have been used, aside from their clerical role, primarily as bodies on the line. Many have been thrown out of school, disowned by their families, clubbed by the cops, raped by the nuts, and gone to jail with everyone else.

What happened to them throughout the movement is very much what happened to all whites in the early civil rights days. Whites acted out of moral principles, many acted courageously, and they became liberalized but never radicalized. Which is to say, they never quite came to grips with the reality of anybody's situation. It is interesting to speculate on why this should be the case. At least one reason, it seems to me, is that people who set about to help other people generally manage to maintain important illusions about our society, how it operates, and what is required to change it. It is not just that they somehow manage to maintain these illusions, they are compelled to maintain them by their refusal to recognize the full measure of their own individual oppression, the means by which it is brought about, and what it would take to alter their condition.

Any honest appraisal of their own condition in this society would presumably lead people out of logic, impulse, and desire for self preservation, to shoot at the guys who are shooting at them. Namely, first of all, to fight their own battles. No one thinks that poor whites can learn about their own lives by befriending black people, however laudable that action may be. No one even thinks that poor whites can help black people much, assuming some might want to, until they first recognize their own oppression and oppressors. Intuitively we grasp the fact that until poor whites understand who their enemies are and combine to fight them they can not understand what it is going to take to secure their freedom or anyone else's. And no one seriously doubts that if and when the light dawns upon them collectively, it will be, in the first instance, their battle they will fight.

We understand this intuitively but white students in the early civil rights days would not have done so. They thought they were really getting a thorough education in the movement, that they were really helping, that they knew in what limited ways the society needed changing and what was necessary to obtain those limited changes, and they were thoroughly shaken by Black Power, which said in effect: you don't understand anything. They also thought in those dim days of the past, that they as white students had no particular problems. It was more or less noblesse oblige. Enlightenment soon followed, at least for some white male students.

One of the best things that ever happened to black militants happened when they got hounded out of the stars-and-stripes, white-controlled civil rights movement, when they started fighting for blacks instead of the American Dream. The best thing that ever happened to potential white radicals in civil rights happened when they got thrown out by SNCC and were forced to face their own oppression in their own world. When they started fighting for control of the universities, against the draft, the war, and the business order. And the best things that may yet happen to potentially radical young women is that they will be driven out of both of these groups. That they will be forced to stop fighting for the 'movement' and start fighting primarily for the liberation and independence of women.

Only when they seriously undertake this struggle will they begin to understand that they aren't just ignored or exploited—they are feared, despised, and enslaved.

If the females in SDS every really join the battle they will quickly realize that no sweet-talking list of grievances and demands, no appeal to male conscience, no behind-the-scenes or in-the-home maneuvering is going to get power for women. If they want freedom, equality, and respect, they are going to have to organize and fight for them realistically and radically.

2. Radical Females Essentially Reject an Identification with Their Sex and Use the Language of Female Liberation in an Attempt to Advance Themselves in the Male Power Structure of the Movement

It is hard to understand the women's manifesto in any other way. It reeks of the bourgeois black who can't quite identify with the lame and mutilated casualties of the racist system; who doesn't really see himself as an accidental oversight but as a genetic mutation; who takes it upon himself to explain problems he doesn't understand to a power structure that could care less; who wants to fight for blacks but not very hard and only as a member of the city council or perhaps one of its lesser boards.

If the women in SDS want study committees on the problems of women, why don't they form them? If they want bibliographies, why don't they gather them? If they want to protest University discrimination against women, why don't they do so? No one in SDS is going to stop them. They can even use SDS auspices and publish in *New Left Notes*, for a while anyway.

But that isn't what they want. They want to be treated like 'white people' and work on the problems important to white people like planning, zoning, and attracting industry, or in this case the war, the draft, and university reform.

The trouble with using the language of black or female liberation for *this* purpose—essentially demanding a nigger on every committee—is twofold. In the first place it is immoral—a Tom betrayal of a whole people. In the second place, it won't work. There is an almost exact parallel between the role of women and the role of black people in this society. Together they constitute the great maintenance force sustaining the white American male. They wipe his ass and breast feed him when he is little, they school him in his youthful years, do his clerical work and raise his and their replacements later, and all through his life in the factories, on the migrant farms, in the restaurants, hospitals, offices, and homes, they sew for him, stoop for him, cook for him, clean for him, sweep, run errands, haul away his garbage, and nurse him when his frail body falters.

Together they send him out into his own society, shining and healthy, his mind freed from all concern with the grimy details of living. And there in that unreal world of light and leisure he becomes bemused and confused with ideas of glory and omnipotence. He spends his time saving the world from dragons, or fighting evil knights, proscribing and enforcing laws and social systems, or just playing with the erector sets of manhood—building better bridges, computers, and bombs.

Win or lose on that playground, he likes the games and wants to continue playing—unimpeded. That means that the rest of the population, the blacks and females, who maintain this elite playboy force, must be kept at their job.

Oh, occasionally it occurs to one or another of the most self-conscious, self-confident, and generous white man that the system could be changed. That it might be based on something other than race or sex. But what? Who would decide? Might not the change affect the rules of the game or even the games themselves? And where would his place be in it all? It becomes too frightening to think about. It is less threatening and certainly less distracting simply to close ranks, hold fast, and keep things the way they are.

This is done by various techniques, some of which are: sprinkling the barest pinch of blacks and women over the playground to obscure the fact that it is an all white male facility; making a sacred cow out of home and family; supporting a racist and antifeminist church to befuddle the minds of the support force and to divert what little excess energy is available to it; and most importantly, developing among white men a consensus with regard to blacks and females and a loyalty to each other which supercedes that to either of the other groups or to individual members of them, thus turning each white man into an incorruptible guard of the common white male domain.

The gist of that consensus which is relevant to the point at issue here is,

1. Women and blacks are of inherently inferior and alien mentality. Their minds are vague, almost inchoate, and bound by their personal experiences (scatter-brained, or just dumb). They are incapable of truly abstract, incisive, logical, or tactical thinking.

2. Despite or perhaps because of this inferior mentality, women and blacks are happy people. All they ask out of life is a little attention, somebody to screw them regularly, secondhand Cadillacs, new hats, dresses, refrigerators, and other baubles.

3. They do not join mixed groups for the stated purposes of the groups but to be with whites or to find a man.

3. Radical Women Do Not Really Understand the Desperate Conditions of Women in General—As Students, They Occupy Some Sexy, Sexless Limbo Where They Are Treated by Males with Less Discrimination Than They Will Ever Again Face

It may seem strange, but one of the main advantages of a female student, married or unmarried, with or without children, is that she is still public. She has in her classes, in her contacts on campus, the opportunity to express her ideas publicly to males and females of all rank. Indeed, she is expected to do so—at least in good schools, or in good seminars. Anyway, she has this opportunity on an equal basis with men.

Moreover, her competition with men, at least scholastically, is condoned—built into the system. This creates in the girl an illusion of equality and harmony between the sexes very much as a good integrated school (where students visit each other's homes even for week ends and are always polite) creates in the black the illusion of change and the faith in continued good relations upon graduation.

These female illustrations are further nurtured by the social life of students. Since many live in dorms or other places where they can not entertain members of the opposite sex, most social intercourse of necessity takes place in public. I mean that people congregate in coffeehouses, pubs, movies, or at parties of the privileged few with off-campus apartments or houses. And since most students are unmarried, unsure of themselves, and lonely, they are constantly on the make. Thus they dance with each other and talk with each other. The conversation between the sexes is not necessarily serious or profound but it takes place, and, as we have said, takes place, in the great main, publicly. Each tries to find out more about the other, attempts to discover what future relations might be possible between them, tries to impress the other in some way.

So that the female student feels like a citizen, like an individual among others in the body politic, in the civil society, in the world of the intellect. What she doesn't understand is that upon graduation she is stripped of her public life and relegated to the level of private property. Enslavement is her farewell present. As things stand now, she is doomed to become someone's secretary, or someone's nurse, or someone's wife, or someone's mistress. From now on if she has some contribution to make to society she is expected to make it privately through the man who owns some part of her.

If as a secretary she has a criticism of the firm she works for and a money-making idea of improvement for the company, she certainly doesn't express her view publicly at the board meeting of the firm, though she may be there taking minutes. Nor does she speak to her boss about it at an office party or in any other public place. She is expected rather to broach him in private, in a self-effacing manner, indicating that she probably doesn't really know what she is talking about but it seems to her . . .

He then proposes the idea to the board and receives both the credit and the raise or promotion. And the peculiar twist is that this holds equally true even if in passing he mentions that the idea was brought to him by his secretary. For in the eyes of the board, as in the eyes of all male society, the female employee has no independent identity. She belongs to the boss as a slave belongs to his master. If slaves are exceptionally productive, the slaves holder is given credit for knowing how to pick them and how to work them. Slaves aren't promoted to free men and female secretaries aren't promoted to executive positions.

But slavery is an intricate system. As an institution it cannot be maintained by force alone. Somehow or other slaves must be made to conceive of themselves as inferior beings and slave holders must not be permitted to falter in the confidence of their superiority. That is why female secretaries are not permitted to offer public criticism. How long, after all, could the system survive if in open *public* exchange some women even in their present downtrodden position, turned out to be smarter than the men who employ them?

What is feared most is that woman, looking out at their natural surroundings, will suffer a reversal of perspective like that one experiences looking at optically balanced drawings where background suddenly becomes subject. That one day looking at men and women in full-blown stereotype a woman will suddenly perceive individuals of varying ability, honesty, warmth, and understanding. When that day comes her master stands before her stripped of his historical prerogative—just another individual with individual attributes. That has ponderous implications for their relationship, for all of society.

In the world of the graduated and married, this situation is forestalled in perhaps the most expeditious way. Men simply refuse to talk to women publicly about anything but the most trivial affairs: home, cooking, the weather, her job, perhaps a local school board election, etc. In these areas they are bound to be able to compete and if they fail—well, men aren't supposed to know anything about those things anyway. They're really just trying to give the girls a little play.

But even that routine has its dangers. Women are liable to change the topic, to get to something of substance. So generally to be absolutely safe men just don't talk to women at all. At parties they congregate on one side of the room, standing up as befits their condition and position (desk workers in the main), and exhausted women (servants and mothers) are left propped up by girdles, pancake make-up, and hair spray, on the couch and surrounding chairs. If the place is big and informal enough, the men may actually go into another room, generally under the pretext of being closer to the liquor.

Of course, most women don't understand this game for what it is. The newcomer to it often thinks it is the women who withdraw and may seek out what she imagines to be the more stimulating company of the men. When she does, she is quickly disillusioned. As she approaches each group of men the conversation they were so engrossed in usually dies. The individual members begin to drift off—to get a refill, to talk with someone they have just noticed across the room, etc. If she manages to ensnare a residual member of the group in conversation, he very soon develops a nervous and distressed look on his face as though he had to go to the bathroom; and he leaves as soon as possible, perhaps to make that trip.

There is another phenomenon not to be confused here. Namely, men being stimulated to show off in the presence of an attractive female, to display in verbal exchange what they imagine to be their monstrous cleverness. But the rules of this game require the women to stand by semi-mute, just gasping and giggling, awed, and somewhat sexually aroused. The verbal exchange is strictly between the men. Any attempt on the woman's part to become a participant instead of a prize breaks up the game and the group.

This kind of desperate attempt by men to defend their power by refusing to participate in open public discussion with women would be amusing if it were not so effective. And one sees the beginnings of it even now, while still students, in SDS meetings. You are allowed to participate and to speak, only the men stop listening when you do. How many times have you seen a woman enter the discussion only to have it resume at the exact point from which she made her departure, as though she had never said anything at all? How many times have you seen men get up and actually walk out of a room while a woman speaks, or begin to whisper to each other as she starts?

In that kind of a hostile, unresponsive atmosphere, it is difficult for anyone to speak in an organized, stringent manner. Being insulted, she becomes angry, in order to say what she wanted to say and not launch an attack upon the manners of her 'audience', she musters the energy to control her temper, and finally she wonders why she is bothering at all since no one is listening. Under the pressure of all this extraneous stimulation she speaks haltingly, and if she gets to the point at all hits it obliquely.

And thus the male purpose is accomplished. Someone may comment, 'Well, that is kind of interesting but it is sort of beside the main point here.' Or, whoever is in charge may just look at her blankly as if, 'What was that all about?' The conversation resumes and perhaps the woman feels angry, but she also feels stupid. In this manner the slave relationship is learned and reinforced.

Even if the exceptional case is involved—the woman who does sometimes get up front—the argument holds. I know whom you are thinking about. You are thinking about the girl who has thirty IQ points over almost anyone in the group and therefore can't be altogether put down. She is much too intelligent, much too valuable. So she is sometimes asked by the male leadership to explain a plan or chair a meeting and since it is obvious that she is exercising *male*—delegated authority and because she is so bright people will sometimes listen to her. But have you ever known the top dog in an SDS group to be a woman, or have you ever known a woman to be second in command? Have you ever seen one argue substance of tactics with one of the top males *in front* of the full group? She may forget her place and do so, but if she does she receives the same treatment as all other females. The rules may and sometimes have to be stretched for the exceptional, but never at the price of male authority and male control.

Of course, being a student, having not as yet come under the full heel of male domination, and not identifying with woman in general, you may view SDS group dynamics somewhat differently. You may grant the male domination but think it is a function of the particular males in command, or you may grant its existence but blame the women for not asserting themselves.

With regard to the first assumption, let me point out that almost all men are involved in the male mystique. No matter how unnecessary it may be, particularly for the bright and most able among them, each rests his ego in some measure on the basic common denominator, being a man. In the same way white people, consciously or unconsciously, derive ego support from being white and Americans from being American.

Allowing females to participate in some group on the basis of full equality presents a direct threat to each man in that group. And though an individual male leader may be able to rise above this personal threat he cannot deviate from the rules of the game without jeopardizing his own leadership and the group itself. If he permits the public disclosure in an irrefutable manner of the basic superiority of half of the women to half the men, of some of the men, he breaks the covenant and the men will not follow him. Since they are not obliged to, they will not suffer this emasculation and the group will fall apart.

To think that women, by asserting themselves individually in SDS, can democratize it, can remove the factor of sex, is equally silly. In the first place, the men will not permit it, and in the second place, as things stand now, the women are simply incapable of that kind of aggressive individual assertion. The socialization process has gone too far, they are already scrambled. Meeting after meeting their silence bears witness to their feelings of inferiority. Who knows what they get out of it? Are they listening, do they understand what is being said, do they accept it, do they have reservations? Would urging them to speak out have any effect other than to cut down their numbers at the next meeting?

The Limbo

Though female students objectively have more freedom than most older married women, their life is already a nightmare. Totally unaware they long ago accepted the miserable role male society assigned to them: help-mate and maintenance worker. Upon coming to college they eagerly and 'voluntarily' flood the great service schools— the college of education, the college of nursing, the department of social work, physical therapy, counseling, and clinical psychology. In some places they even major in home economics.

Denied most of them forever is the great discovery, the power and beauty of logic and mathematics, the sweeping syntheses, the perspective of history. The academic education in these service schools varies from thin to sick—two semester courses in history of Western civilization, watered down one-quarter courses on statistics for nurses, and the mumbo-jumbo courses on psychoanalysis.

It is no wonder that women who may have come to college with perfect confidence in themselves begin to feel stupid. They are being systematically stupefied. Trying to think without knowledge is just a cut above trying to think without language. The wheels go around but nothing much happens.

The position of these women in college is very much like the position of black kids in the black public schools. They start out with the same IQ and achievement scores as their white counterparts but after the third year they begin to lag further and further behind in both measurements. Those blacks still around to graduate from high school usually measure at least two years below graduating whites. Of course, black kids blame the discrepancy on the schools, on the environment, on all kinds of legitimate things. But always there is the gnawing doubt. It is hard to believe the schools could be so different; white women, being at the same school and from the same families, understand that they are simple, though individually inferior.

But that is not the only reason female students are scrambled. They are also in a panic, an absolutely frenzy, to fulfill their destiny: to find a man and get married. It is not they that have all been brainwashed by the media to want a husband, split level house, three children, a dog, a cat, and a station wagon. Many just want out from under their parents. They just can't take the slow slaughter any more but they don't have the courage to break away. They fear the wrath of the explosion but even more they fear the ensuing loneliness and isolation.

Generally a single girl's best friend is still her family. They are the only people she can rely upon for conversation, for attention, for concern with her welfare, no matter how misdirected. And everyone needs some personal attention or they begin to experience a lack of identity. Thus the big push to find the prince charming who will replace the chains with a golden ring.

But that is not as simple as it may seem. It is not proper for women to ask men out. They are never permitted the direct approach to anything. So women must set traps and, depending upon their looks and brains, that can be terribly time-consuming, nerve-racking, and disappointing. Thus the great rash of nose jobs, the desperate dieting, the hours consumed in pursuit of the proper attire. There is skin care, putting up one's hair each night, visits to the hairdressers, keeping up with, buying, applying, and taking off make-up, etc. The average American woman spends two hours a day in personal grooming, not including shopping or sewing. That is one-twelfth of her whole life and one-eighth of the time she spends awake. If she lives to be eighty, a woman will have spent ten whole years of her time awake in this one facet of the complex business of making herself attractive to men. It is staggering to think what that figure would be if one were to include the endless hours spent looking through fashion magazines, shopping and window shopping, discussing and worrying about clothes, hair style, diet, and make-up. Surely one-forth of a woman's waking time would be a conservative estimate here. Twenty years of wakeful life!

So, one-fourth of a female student's day goes down the drain in this manner, another one-fourth to one-half is spent getting brainwashed in school and studying for the same end. What does she do with the rest of the time? Often, she must work to support herself and she must eat, clean, wash clothes, date, etc. That leaves her just enough time to worry about her behaviour on her last date and her behavior on her next one. Did she say and do the right thing, should she change her approach? Does he love her or does he not? To screw or not to screw is often a serious question. It is taken for granted amongst the more sophisticated that it helps to nail a man if one sleeps with him. Still, it is no guarantee and there are only so many men with whom a woman can cohabit in the same circle and still expect a proposal. Movement men seem prone to marry the 'purer' non-movement types. And at that age and stage, when girls are worried about being used, about pregnancy and privacy, still ignorant of the potentials of their bodies, and hung-up by the old sexual code which classifies so much as perversion and then demands it, sex usually offers only minimal gratification anyway. Given the girls' hang-ups and the insecurity and ineptness of young men, even that gratification is more often psychological than sexual.

Sex becomes the vehicle for momentary exchanges of human warmth and affection. It provides periods in which anxiety is temporarily allayed and girls feel wanted and appreciated, periods in which they develop some identity as an individual. It is ironic indeed that a woman attains this sense of identity and individuality through performing an act common to all mankind and all mammals. It bespeaks her understanding that society as it is presently organized will not permit her to function at all except through some male. The church used to say that 'husband and wife are as one, and that one is the husband,' or, 'The husband and wife are as one body and the husband is the head.' As though fulfilling a prophesy unmarried women go about like chickens with their heads cut off.

In this terrible delirium between adolescence and marriage the friendship of female to female all but disappears. Girls, because they are growing duller, become less interesting to each other. As they slip into the role of submissiveness or respondent to male initiative, male intelligence, they also become increasingly uneasy with one another. To be the benefactor of female intelligence and to respond with warmth and affection brings with it anxieties of 'homosexual tendencies.' To initiate, direct, or dominate brings with it the same apprehension. To insure a female for every male (if he wants one), to insure his freedom and his power through the enslavement of our sex, males have made of homosexuality *the* abomination. Everyone knows what happens to them: they go crazy and get buried at some intersection. It is too terrible to think about; it can only be feared.

And that fear, initiated by men, is reinforced by both men and women. Perform a simple spontaneous act like lighting another woman's cigarette with the same match you've just lit your own and there is panic on all sides. Women have to learn to inhibit these natural, asexual gestures. And any close and prolonged friendship between women is always suspect.

So women use each other as best they can under the circumstances, to keep out the cold. And the blood-pacts of childhood where one swore not to reveal a secret on penalty of death turn into bargains about not leaving each other until both are lined up for marriage. Only these later pacts are never believed or fulfilled. No woman trusts another because she understands the desperation. The older a woman becomes the more oppressive the syndrome. As one by one her contemporaries marry she begins to feel the way old people must when one by one their friends and relatives die. Though an individual in the latter condition is not necessarily burdened with a sense of failure and shame.

So there you have the typical coed—ignorant, suffering from a sense of inferiority, barely perceiving other woman except as mindless, lonely, and terrified. Hardly in any condition to aggressively and individually fight for her rights in SDS. It seems, in a way, the least of her problems. To solve them all she is fixated on marriage. Which brings us to the second arm of this discussion, the point we raised earlier.

4. Radical Women Do Not Really Understand the Desperate Conditions of Women in General—Because So Few Are Married, or If Married Have No Children

No one would think to judge a marriage by its first hundred days. To be sure there are cases of sexual trauma, of sudden and violent misunderstandings, but in general all is happiness; the girl has finally made it, the past is but a bad dream. All good things are about to come to her. And then reality sets in. It can be held off a little as long as they are both students and particularly if they have money, but sooner or later it becomes entrenched. The man moves to insure his position of power and dominance.

There are several more or less standard pieces of armament used in this assault upon wives, but the biggest gun is generally the threat of divorce or abandonment. With a plucky woman a man may actually feel it necessary to openly and repeatedly toy with this weapon, but usually it is sufficient simply to keep it in the house undercover somewhere. We all know the bit, we have heard it and all the others I am about to mention on television marital comedies and in night club jokes; it is supposed to be funny.

The husband says to the wife who is about to go somewhere that doesn't meet with his approval, 'If you do, you need never come back.' Or later, when the process is more complete and she is reduced to frequent outbreaks of begging, he slams his way out of the house claiming that she is trying to destroy him, that he can no longer take these endless, senseless scenes; that 'this isn't a marriage, it's a meat grinder.' Or he may simply lay down the law that, God damn it, her first responsibility is to her family and he will not permit or tolerate something or other. Or if she wants to maintain the marriage she is simply going to have to accommodate herself.

There are thousands of variations on this theme and it is really very clever the way male society creates for women this pre-marital hell so that some man can save her from it and control her ever after by the threat of throwing her back. Degrading her further, the final crisis is usually averted or postponed by a tearful reconciliation in which the wife apologizes for her shortcomings, namely the sparks of initiative still left to her.

The other crude and often open weapon that a man uses to control his wife is the threat of force or force itself. Though this weapon is not necessarily used in conjunction with the one described above, it presupposes that a woman is more frightened of returning to an unmarried state than she is of being beaten about one way or another. How can one elaborate on such a threat? At a minimum it begins by a man's paling or flushing, clenching his fists at his sides or gritting his teeth, perhaps making lurching but controlled motions or wild threatening ones while he states his case. In this circumstance it is difficult for a woman to pursue the argument which is bringing about the reaction, usually an argument for more freedom, respect, or equality in the marital situation. And of course, the conciliation of this scene, even if he has beat her, may require his apology, but also hers, for provoking him. After a while the conditioning becomes so strong that a slight change of color on his part, or a slight stiffening of stance, nothing observable to an outsider, suffices to quiet her or keep her in line. She turns off or detours mechanically, like a robot, not even herself aware of the change, or only momentarily and almost subliminally.

But these are gross and vulgar techniques. There are many more subtle and intricate ones which in the long run are even more devastating. Take for instance the ploy of keeping women from recognizing their intelligence by not talking to them in public, which we mentioned earlier. After marriage this technique is extended and used on a woman in her own home.

At breakfast a woman speaks to her husband over or through the morning paper, which he clutches firmly in his hands. Incidentally, he reserves the right to see the paper first and to read the sections in order of his preference. The assumption is, of course, that he has a more vested interest in world affairs and a superior intelligence with which to grasp the relevance of daily news. The Woman's Section of the paper is called that, not only because it contains the totality of what men want women to be concerned with, but also because it is the only section permitted to women at certain times of the day.

I can almost hear you demur. Now she has gone too far. What super-sensitivity to interpret the morning paper routine as a deliberate put-down. After all, a woman has the whole day to read the paper and a man must get to work. I put it to you that this same situation exists when they both work or when the wife works and the husband is still a student, assuming he gets up for breakfast, and on Sundays. What we are describing here is pure self-indulgence. A minor and common, though nonetheless enjoyable, exercise in power. A flexing of the male perogative.

Perhaps the best tip-off to the real meaning of the daily paper act comes when a housewife attempts to solve the problem by subscribing to two papers. This is almost invariably met with resistance on the part of the man as being an unnecessary and frivolous expense, never mind whether they can afford it. And if his resistance doesn't actually forestall the second subscription he attempts to monopolize the front sections of both papers! This is quite a complicated routine, but, assuming the papers are not identical, it can be done and justified.

However, we were talking about conversation and noted that it was replaced by the paper in the morning. In the evening men attempt to escape through more papers, returning to work, working at home, reading, watching television, going to meetings, etc. But eventually they have to handle the problem some other way because their wives are desperate for conversation, for verbal interchange. To understand this desperation you have to remember that women before marriage have on the whole only superficial, competitive, and selfish relationship with each other. Should one of them have a genuine relationship it is more likely with a male than a female. After marriage a woman stops courting her old unmarried or married female side-kicks. They have served their purpose, to tide her over. And there is the fear, often well founded, that these females will view her marriage less as a sacrament than a challenge, that they will stalk her husband as fair game, that they will outshine her, or in some other way lead to the disruption of her marriage.

Her husband will not tolerate the hanging around of any past male friends, and that leaves the woman isolated. When, as so often happens, after a few years husband and wife move because he has graduated, entered service, or changed jobs, her isolation is complete. Now all ties are broken. Her husband is her only contact with the outside world, aside, of course, from those more or less perfunctory contacts she has at work, if she works.

So she is desperate to talk with her husband because she must talk with *someone* and he is all she has. To tell the truth, a woman doesn't really understand the almost biologic substructure to her desperation. She sees it in psychological terms. She thinks that if her husband doesn't talk to her he doesn't love her or doesn't respect her. She may even feel that this disrespect on his part is causing her to lose her own self-respect (a fair assumption since he is her only referrant). She may also feel cheated and trapped because she understood that in return for all she did for him in marriage she was to be allowed to live vicariously, and she cannot do that if he will not share his life.

What she does not understand is that she cannot go on thinking coherently without expressing those thoughts and having them accepted, rejected, or qualified in some manner. This kind of feedback is essential to the healthy functioning of the human mind. That is why solitary confinement is so devastating. It is society's third-rung 'legal deterrent,' ranking just below capital punishment and forced wakefulness, or other forms of torture that lead to death.

This kind of verbal isolation, this refusal to hear a woman, causes her thought process to turn in upon itself, to deteriorate, degenerate, to become disassociated from reality. Never intellectually or emotionally secure in the first place, she feels herself slipping beyond the pale. She keeps pounding at the door.

And what is her husband's response? He understands in some crude way what is happening to her, what he is doing to her, but he is so power-oriented that he cannot stop. Above all, men must remain in control; it's either him or her. The worse she becomes the more convinced he is the coin must not be turned. And from thence springs anew his fear of women, like his fear of blacks.

We tend to forget that witches were burned in our own country not too long ago, in those heroic days before the founding fathers. That each day somewhere in our country women are raped or killed just for kicks or out of some perverted sense of retribution. And we never even consider the ten thousand innocent women annually murdered by men who refuse to legalize abortion. The fear and hatred must be deep indeed to take such vengeance.

But back to the husband. We all know that marriage is far from solitary confinement for a woman. Of course, the husband talks to her. The questions are, how often, what does he say, and how does he say it? He parries this plea for conversation, which he understands thoroughly, until bedtime or near it and then exhausted and exasperated he slaps down his book or papers, or snaps off the TV, or flings his shoe to the floor if he is undressing and turns to his wife, saying, 'Oh, for Christ sake, what is it you want to talk about?'

Now he has just used all of his big guns. He has showed temper which threatens violence. He has showed an exasperated patience which threatens eventual divorce. He has been insulting and purposely misunderstanding. Since she is not burning with any specific comments, since she is now frightened, hurt, angry, and thoroughly miserable, what is she to say? I'll tell you what she does say: 'Forget it. Just forget it. If that's the way you are going to respond I don't want to talk with you anyway.'

This may bring on another explosion from him, frightening her still further. He may say something stupid like, 'You're crazy, just crazy. All day long you keep telling me you've got to talk to me. O.K., you want to talk to me, talk. I'm listening. I'm not reading. I'm not working. I'm not watching TV. I'm listening.'

He waits sixty silent seconds while the wife struggles for composure and then he stands up and announces that he is going to bed. To rub salt in the wound, he falls to sleep blissfully and instantly.

Or, playing the part of both cops in the jailhouse interrogation scene he may, after the first explosion, switch roles. In this double-take he becomes the calm and considerate husband, remorseful, apologizing, and imploring her to continue, assuring her he is interested in anything she has to say, knowing full well the limitations of what she can say under the circumstances. Predictably, done in by the tender tone, she falls in with the plot and confesses. She confesses her loneliness, her dependence, her mental agony, and they discuss *her* problem. Her problem, as though it were some genetic defect, some personal shortcoming, some inscrutable psychosis. Now he can comfort her, avowing how he understands how she must feel, he only wished there were something he could do to help.

This kind of situation if continued in unrelieved manner has extreme consequences. Generally the marriage partners sense this and stop short of the brink. The husband, after all, is trying to protect and bolster his frail ego, not drive his wife insane or force her suicide. He wants in the home to be able to hide from his own inner doubts, his own sense of shame, failure, and meaninglessness. He wants to shed the endless humiliation of endless days parading as a man in the male world. Pretending a power, control, and understanding he does not have.

All he asks of his wife, aside from hours of menial work, is that she not see him as he sees himself. That she not challenge him but admire and desire him, soothe and distract him. In short, make him feel like the kind of guy he'd like to be in the kind of world he thinks exists.

And by this time the wife asks little more, really, than the opportunity to play that role. She probably never aspired to more, to an egalitarian or reality-oriented relationship. It is just that she cannot do her thing if it is laid out so badly; if she is to be denied all self-respect, all self-development, all help and encouragement from her husband.

So generally the couple stops short of the brink. Sometimes, paradoxically enough, by escalating the conflict so that it ends in divorce, but generally by some accommodation. The husband encourages the wife to make some girlfriends, take night courses, or have children. And sooner or later, if she can, she has children. Assuming the husband has agreed to the event, the wife's pregnancy does abate or deflect the drift of their marriage, for a while, anyway.

The pregnancy presents to the world visible proof of the husband's masculinity, potency. This visible proof shores up the basic substructure of his ego, the floor beyond which he cannot now fall. Pathetically, his stock goes up in society, in his own eyes. He is a man. He is grateful to his wife and treats her, at least during the first pregnancy, with increased tenderness and respect. He pats her tummy and makes noises about mystic occurrences. And since pregnancy is not a male thing and he is a man, since this is cooperation, not competition, he can even make out that he feels her role is pretty special.

The wife is grateful. Her husband loves her. She is suffused with happiness and pride. There is at last something on her side of the division of labor which her husband views with respect, and delight of delights, with perhaps a twinge of jealousy.

Of course, it can't last. After nine months the child is bound to be born. And there we are back at the starting gate. Generally speaking, giving birth must be like a bad trip with the added feature of prolonged physical exhaustion.

Sometimes it takes a year to regain one's full strength after a messy caesarian. Sometimes women develop post-parturational psychosis in the hospital. More commonly, after they have been home awhile they develop a transient but recurring state called the 'Tired Mother Syndrome.' In its severe form it is, or resembles, a psychosis. Women with this syndrome complain of being utterly exhausted, irritable, unable to concentrate. They may wander about somewhat aimlessly, they may have physical pains. They are depressed, anxious, sometimes paranoid, and they cry a lot.

Sound familiar? Despite the name one doesn't have to be a mother to experience the ailment. Many young wives without children do experience it, particularly those who, without an education themselves, are working their husband's way through college. That is to say, wives who hold down a dull eight or nine hour a day job, then come, home, straighten, cook, clean, run down to the laundry, dash to the grocery store, iron their own clothes plus their husband's shirts and jeans, sew for themselves, put up their hair, and more often than not type their husband's papers, correct his spelling and grammar, pay the bills, screw on command, and write the inlaws. I've even known wives who on top of this load do term papers or laboratory work for their husbands. Of course, it's insanity. What else could such self-denial be called? Love?

Is it any wonder that a woman in this circumstance is tired? Is it any wonder that she responds with irritability when she returns home at night to find her student husband, after a day or half day at home, drinking beer and shooting the bull with his cronies, the ring still in the bathtub, his dishes undone, his clothes where he dropped them the night before, even his specific little chores like taking out the garbage unaccomplished?

Is it any wonder that she is tempted to scream when at the very moment she has gotten rid of the company, plowed through some of the mess, and is standing in a tiny kitchen over a hot stove, her husband begins to make sexual advances? He naively expects that these advances will fill her with passion, melting all anger, and result not only in her forgetting and forgiving but in gratitude and renewed love. Ever hear the expression, 'A woman loves the man who satisfies her'? Some men find that delusion comforting. A couple of screws and the slate is wiped clean. Who needs to pay for servants or buy his wife a washing machine when he has a cock?

And even the most self-deluded woman begins to feel depressed, anxious, and used, when she finds that her husband is embarrassed by her in the company of his educated, intellectual, or movement friends. When he openly shuts her up saying she doesn't know what she is talking about or emphasizes a point by saying it is so clear or so simple even his wife can understand it.

He begins to confuse knowledge with a personal attribute like height or a personal virtue like honesty. He becomes disdainful of and impatient with ignorance, equating it with stupidity, obstinacy, laziness, and in some strange way, immorality. He forgets that his cultivation took place at his wife's expense. He will not admit that in stealing from his wife her time, energy, leisure, and money he also steals the possibility of her intellectual development, her present, and her future.

But the working wife sending her husband through school has no monopoly on this plight. It also comes to those who only stand and wait—in the home, having kiddy after kiddy while their husbands, if they are able, learn something, grow somewhere.

In any case, we began this diversion by saying that women who are not mothers can also suffer from the 'Tired Mother Syndrome.' Once a mother, however, it takes on a new dimension. There is a difference of opinion in the medical and sociological literature with regard to the genesis of this ailment. Betty Friedan, in the sociological vein, argues that these symptoms are the natural outgrowth of restricting the mind and body of these women to the narrow confines of the home. She discusses the destructive role of monotonous, repetitive work which never issues in any lasting, let alone important, achievement. Dishes which are done only to be dirtied the same day; beds which are made only to be unmade the same day. Her theory also lays great emphasis on the isolation of these women from the larger problems of society and even from contact with those concerned with things not domestic, other than their husbands. In other words, the mind no more than the body can function in a straitjacket, and the effort to keep it going under these circumstances is indeed tiring and depressing.

Dr. Spock somewhat sides with this theory. The main-line medical approach is better represented by Dr. Lovshin, who says that mothers develop the 'Tired Mother Syndrome' because they are tired. They work a 16-hour day, 7 days a week. Automation and unions have led to a continuously shortened day for men but the work day of housewives with children has remained constant. The literature bears him out. Oh, it is undoubtedly true that women have today many time-saving devices their mothers did not have. This advantage is offset, however, by the fact that fewer members of the family help with housework and the task of child care, as it is organized in our society, is continuous. Now the woman puts the wash in a machine and spends her time reading to the children, breaking up their fights, taking them to the playground, or otherwise looking after them. If, as is often said, women are being automated out of the home, it is only to be shoved into the car chauffeuring children to innumerable lessons and activities, and that dubious advantage holds only for middle and upper class women who generally can afford not only gadgets but full or part-time help.

One of the definitions of automation is a human being acting mechanically in a monotonous routine. Now as always the most automated appliance in a household is the mother. Because of the speed at which it's played, her routine has not only a nightmarish but farcical quality to it. Some time ago the *Ladies Home Journal* conducted and published a forum on the plight of young mothers. Ashley Montague and some other professionals plus members of the *Journal* staff interviewed four young mothers. Two of them described their morning breakfast routine.

One woman indicated that she made the breakfast, got it out, left the children to eat it, and then ran to the washing machine. She filled that up and ran back to the kitchen, shoved a little food in the baby's mouth and tried to keep the others eating. Then she ran back to the machine, put the clothes in a wringer and started the rinse water.

The other woman stated they had bacon every morning, so the first thing she did was to put the bacon on and the water for coffee. Then she went back to her room and made the bed. 'Generally, I find myself almost running back and forth. I don't usually walk. I run to make the bed.' By that time the pan is hot and she runs back to turn the bacon. She finishes making the children's breakfast and if she is lucky she gets to serve it before she is forced to dash off to attend to the baby, changing him and sitting him up. She rushes back, plops him in a little canvas chair, serves the children if she has not already done so, and makes her husband's breakfast. And so it goes through the day. As the woman who runs from bed to bacon explains, 'My problem is that sometimes I feel there aren't enough hours in the day. I don't know whether I can get everything done.'

It's like watching an old-time movie where for technical reasons everyone seems to be moving at three times normal speed. In this case it is not so funny. With the first child it is not as severe.

What hits a new mother the hardest is not so much the increased work load as the lack of sleep. However unhappy she may have been in her childless state, however desperate, she could escape by sleep. She could be refreshed by sleep. And if she wasn't a nurse or airline stewardess she generally slept fairly regular hours in a seven to nine hour stretch. But almost all babies returning from the hospital are on something like a four-hour food schedule, and they usually demand some attention in between feedings. Now, children differ, some cry more, some cry less, some cry almost all of the time. If you have never, in some period of your life, been awakened and required to function at one in the morning and again at three, then maybe at seven, or some such schedule, you can't imagine the agony of it.

All of a woman's muscles ache and they respond with further pain when touched. She is generally cold and unable to get warm. Her reflexes are off. She startles easily, ducks moving shadows, and bumps into stationary objects. Her reading rate takes a precipitous drop. She stutters and stammers, groping for words to express her thoughts, sounding barely coherent—somewhat drunk. She can't bring her mind to focus. She is in a fog. In response to all the aforementioned symptoms she is always close to tears.

What I have described here is the severe case. Some mothers aren't hit as hard but almost all new mothers suffer these symptoms in some degree and what's more, will continue to suffer them a good part of their lives. The woman who has several children in close succession really gets it. One child wakes the other, it's like a merry-go-round, intensified with each new birth, each childhood illness.

This lack of sleep is rarely mentioned in the literature relating to the Tired Mother Syndrome. Doctors recommend to women with newborn children that they attempt to partially compensate for this loss of sleep by napping during the day. With one child that may be possible; with several small ones it's sort of a sick joke. This period of months or years of forced wakefulness and 'material' responsibility seems to have a long-range if not permanent effect on a woman's sleeping habits. She is so used to listening for the children she is awakened by dogs, cats, garbage men, neighbors' alarm clocks, her husband's snoring. Long after her last child gives up night feedings she is still waking to check on him. She is worried about his suffocating, choking, falling out of bed, etc. Long after that she wanders about opening and closing windows, adjusting the heat or air conditioning, locking the doors, or going to the bathroom.

If enforced wakefulness is the handmaiden and necessary precursor to serious brainwashing, a mother—after her first child—is ready for her final demise. Too tired to comprehend or fight, she only staggers and eventually submits. She is embarrassed by her halting speech, painfully aware of her lessened ability to cope with things, of her diminished intellectual prowess. She relies more heavily than ever on her husband's support, helping hand, love. And he in turn gently guides her into the further recesses of second-class citizenship.

After an extended tour in that never-never land, most women lose all capacity for independent thought, independent action. If the anxiety and depression grow, if they panic, analysis and solution elude them.

The Return from the Never-Never Land

Women who would avoid or extricate themselves from the common plight I've described, and would begin new lives, new movements, and new worlds, must first learn to acknowledge the reality of their present condition. They have got to reject the blind and faulty categories of thought foisted on them by a male order for its own benefit. They must stop thinking in terms of 'the grand affair,' of the love which over-comes, or substitutes for, everything else, of the perfect moment, the perfect relationship, the perfect marriage. In other words, they must reject romanticism. Romance, like the rabbit of the dog track, is the illusive, fake, and never-attained reward which for the benefit and amusement of our masters keeps us running and thinking in safe circles.

A relationship between a man and a woman is no more or less personal a relationship than is the relationship between a woman and her maid, a master and his slave, a teacher and his student. Of course, there are personal, individual qualities to a particular relationship in any of these categories, but they are so overshadowed by the class nature of the relationship, by the volume of class response as to be almost insignificant.

There is something horribly repugnant in the picture of women performing the same menial chores all day, having almost interchangeable conversations with their children, engaging in standard television arguments with their husbands, and then in the late hours of the night, each agonizing over what is considered her personal lot, her personal relationship, her personal problem. If women lack self-confidence, there seems no limit to their egotism. And unmarried women cannot in all honesty say their lives are in much greater measure distinct from each other's. We are a class, we are oppressed as a class, and we each respond within the limits allowed us as members of that oppressed as a class. Purposely divided from each other, each of us is ruled by one or more men for the benefit of all men. There is no personal escape, no personal salvation, no personal solution.

The first step, then, is to accept our plight as a common plight, to see other women as reflections of ourselves, without obscuring, of course, the very real differences intelligence, temperament, age, education, and background create. I'm not saying let's now create new castes or classes among our own. I just don't want women to feel that the movement requires them to identify totally with and, moreover, love every other woman. For the general relationship, understanding and compassion should suffice.

We who have been raised on pap must develop a passion for honest appraisal. The real differences between women and between men and women are the guideposts within and around which we must dream and work.

Having accepted our common identity the next thing we must do is to get in touch with each other. I mean that absolutely literally. Women see each other all the time, open their mouths and make noises, but communicate on only the most superficial level. We don't talk to each other about what we consider our real problems because we are afraid to look insecure, because we don't trust or respect each other, and because we are afraid to look or be disloyal to our husbands and benefactors.

Each married woman carries around in her a strange and almost identical little bundle of secrets. To take, as an example, perhaps the most insignificant, she may be tired of and feel insulted by her husband's belching or farting at the table. Can you imagine her husband's fury if it got back to him that she told someone he farted at the table? Because women don't tell these things to each other the events are considered personal, the woman may fantasize remarriage to mythical men who don't fart, the man feels he has a personal but minor idiosyncrasy, and maledom comes out clean.

And that, my dear, is what this bit of loyalty is all about. If a man made that kind of comment about his wife, he might be considered crude or indiscreet; she's considered disloyal—because she's subject, he's king, women are dominated and men are the instruments of their domination. The true objective nature of men must never become common knowledge lest it undermine in the minds of some males—but most particularly in ours—the male right-to-rule. And so we daily participate in the process of our own domination. For God's sake, let's stop!

I cannot make it too clear that I am not talking about group therapy or individual catharsis (we aren't sick, we are oppressed). I'm talking about movement. Let's get together to decide in groups of women how to get out of this bind, to discover and fight the techniques of domination in and out of the home. To change our physical and social surroundings to free our time, our energy, and our minds—to start to build for ourselves, for all mankind, a world without horrors.

Women involved in this struggle together will come to respect, love, and develop deep and abiding friendships with each other. If these do not thoroughly compensate for losses that may be ours, they will carry us through. For different ages and different stages there are different projects. Young married or unmarried women without children are sympathetic to the problems of mothers but do not pretend to fully understand them. In all honesty, as a middle-aged mother I cannot really grasp the special quality of life of an unmarried young woman in this generation. Her circumstance is too distinct from mine, and my memories of youth are by this time too faded to bridge the gap. Youth has available to it perspectives and paths not destined to be shared by many in the older generation. We must work together but not presuppose for each other. It is, then, the younger author who will speak to the young. Before this part of the paper is ended, however, I would like to mention briefly projects I think women my age must undertake as part of the overall movement. If they have any relevancy for young women, so much the better.

1. Women must resist pressure to enter into movement activities other than their own. There cannot be real restructuring of this society until the relationships between the sexes are restructured. The inegalitarian relationship in the home is perhaps the basis of all evil. Men can commit any horror, or cowardly suffer any mutilation of their souls and retire to the home to be treated there with awe, respect, and perhaps love. Men will never face their true identity or their real problems under these circumstances, nor will we.

If movement men were not attempting to preserve their perogative as men while fighting 'the system,' they would welcome an attack launched upon that system from another front. That they do not shows how trapped they are in the meshes of the very system they oppose. Our vision must not be limited by theirs. We must urge in speech and in print that women go their own way.

2. Since women in great measure are ruled by the fear of physical force, they must learn to protect themselves. Women who are able ought to take jujitsu or karate until they are proficient in the art. Certainly they ought to organize and enroll their daughters in such courses. Compare the benefits young girls would derive from such courses with those they attain from endless years of ballet. As an extra added goodie, we could spare ourselves the agony of those totally untalented recitals, and later, the sleepless nights worrying about our daughter's safety.

3. We must force the media to a position of realism. Ninety percent of the women in this country have an inferiority complex because they do not have turned-up noses, wear a size ten or under dress, have 'good legs,' flat stomachs, and fall within a certain age bracket. According to television no man is hot for a middle-aged woman. If she is his wife he may screw her but only because he is stuck with her. More important than that, women are constantly portrayed as stupid. The advertisements are the worst offenders. Blacks used to be left out of TV altogether except for occasional Tom roles. Women are cast on every show and always Tom. From such stuff is our self-image created, the public and accepted image of women. The only time my daughter saw a woman on TV who gave her pride in being a woman was when she saw Coretta King speak to the poor people's march. And as my son said, 'It was almost like he had to die before anyone could know she existed.' Let's not

simply boycott selected products; let's break up those television shows and refuse to let them go on until female heroines are portrayed in their total spectrum. And let's make sure that every brilliant heroine doesn't have a husband who is just an eentsy teentsy bit more brilliant than she is.

4. Women must share their experiences with each other until they understand, identify, and explicitly state the many psychological techniques of domination in and out of the home. These should be published and distributed widely until they are common knowledge. No woman should feel befuddled and helpless in an argument with her husband. She ought to be able to identify his stratagems and to protect herself against them, to say, you're using the two-cop routine, and premature apology, the purposeful misunderstanding, etc.

5. Somebody has got to start designing communities in which women can be freed from their burdens long enough for them to experience humanity. Houses might be built around schools to be rented only to people with children enrolled in the particular school, and only as long as they were enrolled. This geographically confined community could contain cheap or cooperative cafeterias and a restaurant so that mothers would not have to cook. This not only would free the woman's time but would put her in more of a position of equality with Daddy when he comes from work. The parents could both sit down and eat at the same time in front of and with the children, a far different scene from that of a conversing family being served by a harassed mother who rarely gets to sit down and is usually two courses behind. These geographic school complexes could also contain full-time nurseries. They could offer space for instrument, dance, and self-defense lessons. In other words, a woman could live in them and be relieved of cooking, child care for the greater part of the day, and chauffeuring. The center might even have nighttime or overnight babysitting quarters. Many women will be totally lost to us and to themselves if projects like this are not begun. And the projects themselves, by freeing a woman's time and placing her in innumerable little ways into more of a position of equality, will go a long way toward restructuring the basic marital and parental relationships.

6. Women must learn their own history because they have a history to be proud of and a history which will give pride to their daughters. In all the furor over the *Ramparts* article, I have heard women complain of the photographs and offer unlikely stories of trickery. I've heard them voice resentment toward coalitions like the Jeanette Rankin Brigade and toward *Ramparts* for pushing them. But I have yet to hear a cry of outrage to the real crime of that article. It purposely, maliciously, and slanderously rewrote, perverted, and belittled our history—and most of us weren't even aware of it. What defense is there for a people so ignorant they will believe anything said about their past? To keep us from our history is to keep us from each other. To keep us from our history is to deny to us the group pride from which individual pride is born. To deny to us the possibility of revolt. Our rulers, consciously, unconsciously, perhaps intuitively, know these truths. That's why there is no black or female history in high school texts, *Ramparts'* reference to its location there notwithstanding. Courageous women brought us out of total bondage to our

present improved position. We must not forsake them but learn from them and allow them to join the cause once more. The market is ripe for feminist literature, historic and otherwise. We must provide it.

7. Women who have any scientific competency at all ought to begin to investigate the real temperamental and cognitive differences between the sexes. This area has been hexed with a sort of liberal taboo like the study of race differences. Presumably, we and blacks were being saved from humiliation by a liberal establishment which was at least in pretense willing to grant that aside from color and sexual anatomy we differed from white men in no significant aspect. But suppose we do? Are we to be kept ignorant of those differences? Who is being saved from what?

8. Equal pay for equal work has been a project poo-pooed by the radicals but it should not be because it is an instrument of bondage. If women, particularly women with children, cannot leave their husbands and support themselves decently, they are bound to remain under all sorts of degrading circumstances. In this same line, college entrance discrimination against females, and job discrimination in general, must be fought, no matter what we think about the striving to become professional. A guaranteed annual income would also be of direct relevance to women.

9. In what is hardly an exhaustive list, I must mention abortion laws. All laws relating to abortion must be stricken from the books. Abortion, like contraceptives, must be legal and available if women are to have control of their bodies, their lives, and their destiny.

PART II, BY JUDITH BROWN

> We are determined to foment a rebellion, and will not hold ourselves bound to obey any laws in which we have no voice or representation.
> —(Abigail Adams, to her husband, John Adams, then in the Continental Congress, 1776)

5. For Their Own Salvation, and for the Good of the Movement, Women Must Form Their Own Groups and Work for Female Liberation

In the previous sections we have attempted to refute the erroneous assumptions of the female caucus at the 1967 SDS Convention. We have emphasized the plight of the married woman in her relationship with a power-oriented representative of the master caste. Here, we will take up the situation in which the younger, typical radical female finds herself, and talk about some of the hassles in the emerging liberation movement.

We do not wish to belabor the classic statements in the literature which affirm the slave status of women in Western culture. There is sufficient evidence of our economic, political, psychological, and physiological subjugation. For radical women we will propose radical solutions; let the fainthearted cling to the 'desegregation' model.

First, it requires only a cursory glance at history to recall that men have played the games of war, racial taboo, mastery, and conspicuous production and consumption for thousands of years. While we do not question the courage of radical men who now confront most of the manifestations of imperialism, we do recognize that, like their brave predecessors in other eras, they expect and require that women—*their* women—continue to function as black troops—kitchen soldiers[1]—in *their* present struggle. Radical men are not fighting for female liberation, and in fact, become accountably queasy when the topic is broached. Regrettably the best—radical men and their black counterparts—do not even have a political interest in female liberation.[2]

And indeed, this is not peculiar. We cannot expect them to relinquish, by our gentle persuasion, the power their sex knows and takes for granted. They do not even know how. Few can say, 'The only honorable course, when confronted with a just revolt against yourself or political territory in which you have a vested interest, is to yield gracefully.' Yet we, like radical men, have only one life we know of. It is a serious question whether we should live it as slaves to the rhetoric, the analysis, and the discipline of the movement we have come to be a part of, if that movement, that analysis, and that discipline systematically deprive us of our pride, genuine relationships with free women, equal relationships with men, and a sense that we are using our talents and dedication to a committed life as fully and as freely as possible.

The SDS Experience—A Female View

For a moment it will be helpful to review the experience of a young woman who enters a radical movement, unmarried, in order to appreciate her position against the backdrop of male movement behavior. For we should recognize clearly the conditions under which we live as oppressive in order to identify ourselves with other women in a common struggle.

The typical 'radical' woman goes to college and is well endowed intellectually, physically, and sexually. She has most likely excelled somewhere in high school, whether as a scholar, politico, or artist. She is fully capable of competing with men in college work, and simultaneously, she has already learned that it pays to restrain those overt displays of her competency which men feel no shame in exercising. In exclusively female circles she has held leadership positions and felt bored there, and she has remarked, at least once in her life, that she 'prefers the more stimulating company of men.' She is not a homosexual, and she usually echoes the fraternity brand of contempt for 'fags' and 'dikes.' She thinks she is turned off to women and is secretly relieved that she passed through the 'stage' of homosexuality without 'becoming one.' Yet, she may quietly recognize that she has loved at least one woman somewhere along the way.

At the same time, she is unusually adroit at the sophisticated forms of putting down men, and more than once she watched a movement male explaining tactics or leading a demonstration with personal knowledge that he is a bad screw or privately panders to his parents. Her nearly subliminal review of these failings would stop at mere insight were it not also true that she has, on occasions she can recall, savored her knowledge and derived malicious pleasure from it. It is this idle malicious pleasure, which in adult life finds fuller expression in a petty, indirect, consistent, and fruitless attack on men, which should be the litmus for why the woman ought to concern herself with female liberation first.

Because she knows that equality between the sexes in the movement is nonexistent. She knows, as we have said, that women are silent at meetings, or if they speak, it is slightly hysterical and of little consequence to all the others. Men formally or informally chair the meeting. Women, like all good secretaries, take notes, circulate lists, provide ashtrays, or prepare and serve refreshments. They implement plans made by men through telephoning, compiling mailing lists, painting picket signs, etc. In some quarters, now that written analysis seems to have supplanted organizing as the status movement work, women are promoted to fill that void. More often than not, however, radical women sit through meetings in a stupor, occasionally patting or plucking at 'their' men and receiving, in return, a patronizing smile, or as the case may be, a glare. In demonstrations they are conspicuously protected, which does not always mean, however, that they are spared the club or the jailhouse, but they are spared *responsibility* for having made the direct confrontation.

In the jailhouse, they experience perhaps the only taste of independent radical female expression given them. There, they are segregated by sex, and the someone who always assumes leadership is this time a woman. They find out about each other, probably for the first time. They learn that the others, like themselves, are generally brave, resourceful, and militant. If they stay in jail long enough, they begin to organize themselves and others in the cell-block for prison reform, etc. They get up petitions, smuggle out protest letters and leaflets, mount hunger strikes, and other forms of resistance. They manage very adequately to sustain the abuses, self-imposed disciplines, the loss of status, and the fear, which their brothers face. Outside, of course, jailhouse reminiscence is dominated by the men. And the women desegregate themselves, recalling only rarely a faint affection for their former cell-mates. It is little wonder then that for some women, jail may be the first time that they know their sisters and work with them in radical organizing *where they're at*. A very militant white woman remarked to me that after 34 years, a husband, and three children, an earlier two-month stint in jail was the first time she felt at home in organizing.

The radical woman lives off-campus, away from her parents, and often openly with one man or another. She thinks this is 'freedom.' But if she shares a place with a man, she 'plays marriage,' which means that she cooks, cleans, does the laundry, and generally serves and waits. Hassles with parents or fear of the Dean of Women help to sustain the excitement—the romantic illusions about marriage she brought to the domicile.

If she shares an apartment with other women, it is arranged so that each may entertain men for extended visits with maximum privacy. Often, for the women, these apartments become a kind of bordello; for the men, in addition to that, a good place to meet for political discussion, to put up campus travelers, to grab a free meal, or sack out. These homes are not centers for female political activity; and rather than being judged for their interior qualities—physical or political—they are evaluated by other women in terms of the variety and status of the radical men who frequent them.

But women in general are becoming healthier, better educated, more independent, and as the years go by, more experienced movement personnel. The movement itself is growing up. The one-time single female organizer marries, and her younger sisters are beginning to see that movement participation will not save them from essentially the same sexual and marital styles they reject in their parents. The older, now married radical woman goes on trips—to visit the parents; may live in a larger, less free apartment; or may even live in a home she and her husband buy. She is 'protected' by her husband, and generally she stays at home when he goes out to move the world. The marital pattern sets in, and he lapses from a sloppy courtship to ordering her to get the drinks, cut the grass, etc. The tremendous political investments made by the older radical women (now 25–30) didn't make a way for the younger; newcomer female radicals have fewer illusions these days about what is in store for them anyway, and the life-styles of their predecessors offer little inspiration. Is it surprising then that we read in radical journals that they are dropping out of the movement in droves?

The female radical, or old-timey civil rights activist, is soon 'cooled out' of the movement in one of several ways and for several reasons: (1) if she is too competent and threatens male dominance (perhaps her credentials are too impeccable), she is given a high-level secretarial post (forceably ejected), or she is co-opted and perhaps even impregnated by a male honcho; (2) if she has suffered for several years, consistently being handed menial tasks, she may find, since she has been around so long, that she is one of the 'old guard,' and she wonders why she isn't invited to steering committee meetings—she quietly drops out; (3) some men are more direct; in squelching a paper questioning the role of black women, Stokely Carmichael said, 'The only position for women in SNCC is prone.' Most women are not long-suffering for the movement; they never really get in, and their brief passing is hardly noted. The radical female is cooled out, very simply, because she is not wanted politically, and she cannot proffer her secretarial skills as payment for inclusion in traditionally male activity—political decision-making.

More sophisticated male leadership, a year or two ago, began to sense the rumblings of discontent. An effort was made to buy off female militants. They were included in some photographs of the 'leadership,' given titles in the organization, or consistently laid by the second in command. Those who were married were advised by their husbands to take a year off and do research into the problems of women (meaning take off), or urged to enter one of the new, female 'coalition' groups. The last resort, winningly argued, is the We Need You; and, of course, everybody knows that those who fight for peace are the best, anyway. It parallels the Johnsonian whine to blacks, and it goes like this: there is a war; radical men are being cut down on all sides; we know there must be merit in what you say, but for the *good of the movement*, we ask you to wait, to defer to the higher aim of draft resistance; besides, if you will fight along with us in our battles, you will receive equality when we return from the serious front.

The weak position paper of the 1967 female caucus brought an anonymous response (*New Left Notes*, 4 December 67) from a male, a response we are still hearing and from both sexes. He suggested (and see how this would sound if the word 'black' were substituted) that: (1) there is danger in placing an underdeveloped woman in a position of leadership because her certain failure would only reinforce her sense of innate inferiority; (2) it is not possible for females to separate themselves from the oppressor class; (3) women must be more accepting and understanding than men; (4) women must first educate themselves and develop their capabilities; and finally, (5) when they marry, they should keep their maiden names. Translation: Nigger, you can't be an officer in our white civil rights group until you are properly educated; if you intend to challenge white racists, best do it lovingly, you have no identity of your own, so forget combinations in your own interests; but, we do think an Afro would be advisable.

In Southern plantations in the 'days of slavery,' each member of a wealthy white family had attached to him, often for life, at least one black person who 'did for him.' In turn, the black derived from the master a commensurate status. Our analysis should be that it is the destiny of most women—no less the radical—to become, finally, some man's nigger. If these be harsh words they only bespeak a desperate future for the young radical female.

She is dehumanized and politically turned off and turned out. The *Ramparts* issue on Woman Power featured exceptional niggers who had attained positions of power formerly held by men. If one imagines a substitution of that article for one in *Ebony* on successes of black businessmen, our objection is clear. *Ramparts* on female liberation is Urban League logic.

Marilyn Webb's article in *New Left Notes* ('Women: We Have a Common Enemy,' 10 June 68) deserves more space. It is dangerous because in its description of the female's lot in the movement it hits the mark perfectly, which only makes its damaged conclusion the more tempting. Marilyn tells it like it is with respect to women in the movement but she refuses to name the representatives of the sexual domination system, refuses to acknowledge that for a time at least, men are the enemy, and that radical men hold the nearest battle position. Instead, she emphasizes that 'In building a woman's movement, we clearly see that we have to be active within other, co-ed (if you will) movement organizations and action.' She attacks the mini-culture correctly because 'We are forced to view ourselves as commodities to be "sold" sexually,' but she hastens to add that we aren't masculine, but instead we are attired in the 'colorful dress of a turned-on generation'—the movement has baubles too. She is dismayed that movement marriages rarely last more than two years, but cannot elucidate the obvious reason. Lots of marriages last less than two years, and we assume that radical women catch on a little more quickly to the game, just at that crucial juncture when it's time to 'begin raising a family'; they want out before it's too late.

Finally, she invokes the experience of Vietnamese women as her only real programmatic suggestion—the Third World Hang-up, with which we will deal later; to paraphrase: they have their 'freedom' because they took up arms to support an ideology they never developed, a political framework in which they never participated, and—get this—because they 'could not identify (their struggle) with the common struggle for liberation.' Remember Fidel!

A movement of women which speaks to their needs, and which can mobilize their full political energies, may very well, as we shall propose, look quite different from SDS, SNCC, or the NLF. Any thorough radical analysis would, of course, incorporate a stance vis-à-vis the war, racism, and the Savage Society. But it may be a long and dark passage before ours should risk co-educational alliances or actions.

So the young radical woman does her secretarial tour of duty for the movement, drops out, or, finding that she is getting older, marries. If she marries out of the movement, she's in a position similar to that described in Part I. If she marries within the movement, she is faced with a comparable life style except that (1) she thinks she is already liberated by virtue of marriage to a movement guy, and (2) the movement man has, in addition to the standard male ploys, some extra, even more oblique, confusing, and 'convincing'. Since they married, in good part, on the basis of a shared and serious commitment, the movement itself then becomes reason for male domination. A radical woman, after all, is more likely to give in when the issue is draft resistance than when it is impressing the boss, although some of that goes on too. It may take two years before she ceases to hand out rhetoric about a 'liberated marriage which began several years before the license' and recognizes that the style of her days is more like that of her non-movement sisters than like her husband's. And female liberation literature, so far, offers her no alternative way to go.

Women Must Work for Female Liberation First, and Now

A respectable canon of new left philosophy to which we turn is that central theme that human beings, by combining in organizations, by seeking to participate in decision-making which affects their lives, can achieve a democratic society, and hence, a life-experience perhaps approximating their potentiality.

> Social life imposes on the consanguineous stocks of mankind an incessant traveling back and forth, and family life is little else than the expression of the need to slacken the pace at the crossroads and to take a chance to rest.
>
> (Levi-Strauss)

We want to make a few tentative comments about the form of the marriage institution, for we hope that radical women will begin to turn from psychiatry to anthropology for insight about their oppressive sexual relationships. Family arrangements, as we all know, vary from culture to culture. While the female has a biological requirement for some support immediately after childbirth, anthropology suggests that the form of this support is not always that which we find institutionalized in the West—namely, one man providing economic aid so that one female can be a full-time mother, with this relationship extended then, perhaps for a lifetime.

The institution of marriage, given us in the United States, was the pawn of other, more powerful, institutions. It is a potent instrument for maintaining the status quo in American Society. It is in the family that children learn so well the dominance-submission game, by observation and participation. Each family, reflecting the perversities of the larger order and split off from the others, is powerless to force change on other institutions, let alone attack or transform its own. And this serves the Savage Society well.

The family owes its characteristic features to the economic necessities of frontier America (nation building), its monogamous form to a statistical and cultural happenstance (monogamy seems to prevail where the sex ratio is about 50/50 and there is a pretense to democracy), and the monogamy is sustained by the Puritan ethic. The particular division of labor was designed to contribute to the industrial revolution, a requirement of the most powerful national institution. Levi-Strauss suggests that 'like the form of the family, the division stems more from social and cultural considerations than from natural ones.' He recalls the 'Nambikwara father nursing his baby and cleaning it when it soils itself' as a contrast to the European nobleman who rarely sees his children. And he notes that the 'young concubines of the Nambikwara chieftain disdain domestic activities and prefer to share in their husband's adventurous expeditions.' In the absence of household servants, most American émigré men first subdued one woman, and with her aid produced a family of servants sufficient at least to manage the homestead and offer him the leisure to participate in town politics and even revolutions.

Now, with birth control, higher education for women, and the movement itself, it is becoming clear to some women that the marriage institution, like so many others, is an anachronism. For unmarried women it offers only a sanctional security and the promise of love. The married woman knows that love is, at its best, an inadequate reward for her unnecessary and bizarre heritage of oppression. The marriage institution does not free women; it does not provide for emotional and intellectual growth; and it offers no political resources. Were it not for male-legislated discrimination in employment, it would show little economic advantage.

Instead, she is locked into a relationship which is oppressive politically, exhausting physically, stereotyped emotionally and sexually, and atrophying intellectually. She teams up with an individual groomed from birth to rule, and she is equipped for revolt only with the foot-shuffling, head-scratching gestures of 'feminine guile.' We conceptualize the significance of the marriage institution this way:

$$\frac{\text{Marriage}}{\text{Integration}} \qquad \frac{\text{Women}}{\text{Blacks}}$$

Marriage, as we know it, is for women as integration is for blacks. It is the atomization of a sex so as to render it politically powerless. The anachronism remains because women won't fight it, because men derive valuable benefits from it and will not give them up, and because, even given a willingness among men and women to transform the institution, it is at the mercy of the more powerful institutions which use it and which give it its form.

We would return to our relational model and suggest that some women will have to remove themselves totally from the marriage arrangement which insists that they love, in a predetermined style, their own personal masters. And married women will have to do this periodically to revitalize their commitment to their sex and to the liberation movement.

All-Female Communes for Radical Women

Many younger, unmarried women live in all-female groups now. The problem, as we have mentioned earlier, is that these domiciles are not self-consciously arranged to serve political as well as personal needs. They are not a temporary stopping off place for women who need to re-evaluate their lives. They are no sanctuary from destructive male-female encounters. They are no base for female liberation work.

Some radical women, in deciding to live together, ought to fashion homes which have definite political goals. A woman, married or unmarried, could move into such a center for a period of time and be relieved of the terrible compulsion to one-up her sisters in dating, grooming, etc. The commune should decide on house rules, experiment with sexual relationships on an equal basis with men (that is, remove the bordello element from the place). The commune should be a center for women to live during decision periods in their lives. We all know about these crisis periods; most of the time we manage to suffer through them while at the same time carrying all the burdens of 'keeping face,' maintaining some sexual life, etc. The commune would define itself as a female place. Innumerable experiments in living, political forays and serious and uninterrupted thinking could center in the commune.

While sexual and emotional alliances with men may continue to be of some benefit, the peculiar domestic institution is not. Only women can define what 'womanhood' might best be, and likewise men might better redefine themselves in the absence of a daily reminder of their unwarranted experience of masterdom. Theoretically, such women and men might, in the future, liberated from this master-slave hang-up, meet and work out a new domestic institution which better serves the interest of free men and free women. We do not feel compelled to offer any Utopian model for that institution, but we are certain that it will be designed most rapidly, and most reasonably, by liberated souls. Some women, then, and perhaps some men, will have to reject the present domestic model given us, destroy it, and build another.

And we consider this operation worthy of the time of radical women. Let us review briefly why this program at least parallels in importance the anti-draft, anti-imperialistic movements we all know. (1) People Get Radicalized Fighting Their Own Battles. For women, these are her chains, and she will ultimately invest more energy and in the process become radicalized, breaking them than attacking the other forms of colonialism men urge us to fight. (2) Pace of History Making. Men have accelerated their rate of history-making beyond humane proportions. With their slaves secure at home, they have the time to play abstractly and inhumanly with their technology and to make history more rapidly than they can effectively comprehend or control. Robbed of a faithful custodial class (women, blacks, etc.), they will be less effective, and time may finally overtake them so that where they're at is also where it's at. Women who organize other women to slow male history-making are functioning, in this country, at their political best. (3) Benefits Accrue to the Movement. The goal of the new left is to dismantle worn-out institutions and replace them with better arrangements. Presently, the energies of radical women are not wholeheartedly with this effort because it has no program which speaks to their needs. Women mobilized where they stand against the nearest oppressor, will make their most effective contribution to this process.

We cannot cover all the bases in such a paper. A few, perhaps the most pressing, deserve attention here.

Long-Term Goals vs. Short-Term Tactics

One of the serious flaws in most radical male thinking is the substitution of goals for tactics. The Columbia sit-ins, with all of their attendant anti-feminism, were guerrilla plays. It was a good show, and we all applauded from in front of our television sets. It lacked a tone, however, an important tone and thrust, which should accompany any such further operations. Women make the same mistake when they perform guerrilla theater at SDS conventions, and so it is important to look for a moment at the Columbia scene.

Everybody inside the buildings knew that they remained there only because the administration hesitated, foolishly, to mount its police attack. Nobody thought the students would actually hold Columbia, and subsequently administrators have dropped the guise of dialogue and moved in immediately with their troops. The action was groovy, but the retrospective analysis is misleading. That operation at Columbia cannot be cast parallel with sieges on Saigon, etc. But most movement men are unable to see it as merely a 'royal finger' given the establishment. Instead, they talk about occupation and sieges. And because they up the ante on their behavior, attempt to make it look like something it was not, women are pulled along as support troops, taken in by the rhetoric. A play is a play however you cut it. And if the men cannot admit that the movement cannot take tangible territory, women shouldn't fall into the trap. In radical journals, the tone of analysis should be: 'Well, we really shook them up for a while—they fell for our revolutionary language and provided a good forum. The next operation, however, can't take the same form because they're on to our game.' A lot of movement men would prefer a Columbia 'siege' to telling their parents when to shove it. And I imagine that most of the women who perform guerrilla theater protests against male chauvinism would find it far more scary to, let us say, refuse to perform their traditional domestic tasks for movement men. Demonstrations in this country are still limited to two functions: (1) radicalizing the participants, and (2) getting a point across to the media or a constituency. As long as we remember this, men in the movement won't claim the perogatives of participation in a real 'third world' battle, and women won't feel obligated, by falling into the analogy, to limit themselves to loading the metaphorical guns.

From looking around these days, it becomes obvious that the radicals of the early '60s do grow older. Most of them are still alive, much to their own surprise. And the wiser men among them are beginning to talk about programs which will keep the older troops in touch and in action. Women must do the same. When we begin to go about organizing, we will have to recognize that we are dealing with a number of constituencies and design our tactics accordingly. A radical confrontation for one group would be an unavailable option to another. I would like to cover briefly some topics which may serve in the overall strategy for female liberation.

Integration: The Central Problem

Most women are integrated with men in an ongoing institutionalized setup. One or two all-female meetings, or even one a month, will not begin to solve our problems or guide our programming intelligently. The particular need to get together is shared by the youngest and the older, married women who have children. We are all separated from each other. This does not mean that the constituency should meet together—there is no little hostility among older women toward what they imagine to be their more liberated younger sisters, and the problems differ. The tactics will differ. But both groups need to plan programs in which women can meet for extended periods to talk about the political issues of female liberation. And this meeting, this talking, in itself, is more difficult than we had imagined.

But women are beginning to meet, and they are beginning to talk to each other. That some of these discussions produce ideas or actions at which male radicals giggle, and Aunt Thomasinas cat-call, is a measure of what we are up against.

Children

The big push to have children, whether we are married or not, should be viewed as one of the strong links in the chain which enslaves us. Biological arguments are romantically blown out of proportion by men and their 'Dr. Joyce Brothers' spokesmen in the female ghetto of the mind. We have plenty of so-called biological needs which we have learned to control or rechannel for political purposes. Let us remember that many of us have been willing to exchange, for principle, what are bound to be even more basic needs: food, during hunger strikes; and our lives, in police battles and the more extended confrontations on dirt roads in the civil rights South. We were willing to face being shot-gunned to death for black voter registration; I think we can defer dropping children on cultural command for our own thing, if we think that necessary. I am not making a call for eternal celibacy, but for intelligent birth control and a rethinking of the compulsion to have children, a compulsion, I am sure, which still troubles even the most 'liberated' of women. The same radical woman who thinks draft resistance is more important than female liberation ends up having a baby, and then she is immobilized for both battles. If we take seriously our role-in history, we will plan to have or not have children on a political basis.

Sexuality and Celibacy

Control over our own sexuality is another short-term goal. We all believe in birth control and legalized abortion. However, there is little talk of periodic, self-imposed celibacy. We are brainwashed by the media with sexy commercials and talk in the movement about screwing as often as possible; many of us have already been on the pill for longer than we can medically afford. And a good many of us, I would suspect, are desperately screwing some guy because we think we should and wonder what our friends would think if we didn't at all for a while. Celibacy has always been a tool for those who wish, for a time, to 'stop the world and get off.' It requires, from an unmarried woman, a lot more time to maintain a sexual relationship than it does for her male partner; many of these relationships are mind-blows as well. Radical women could gain a lot in time, energy, and getting themselves together if they would avail themselves of this tactic occasionally. We must stop being pawns in the media's sexuality game and reconsider the whole scene.

Emergency Tactics for Non-Separatists

Those radical females already married, but without children, should be prepared to make a decision about how they will live their lives in order to have time for their political activities. Regardless who is working, going to school, etc., you should demand equal time for your own things. This requires your husband to assume half of the burden of maintaining a home: in terms of cooking, cleaning, laundering, entertaining, etc. If he can't do these things now, you can teach him. If you plan to live with your husband, you will have to begin making changes in the marital pattern. And the chances are that unless he has a radical analysis which is pretty thorough, your marriage will end in divorce if you take this route.

If you have children already, the most devastating pattern of the male-female relationship has set in long ago. If you are serious about political activity and female liberation, you may have to make important adjustments in your life. Presently you work from daybreak until the time when your husband falls asleep. He will have to assume enough of the child-caring and housekeeping chores so that you each have equal time off during each day. His posture of dominance will be threatened, his time consumed, and his ability to live in 'maleville' decimated by such a plan. Stop-gap measures such as communal evening-care centers and communal eating are short-term tactics which serve the long-term goal of freeing women up for first-class personal and political behavior. What is central to our problem is our complete alienation from other women. We will have to get out of our houses and meet with them on serious issues. The most serious for the moment is not the war, the draft, the presidency, the racial problem, but our own problem. We will need each other's support and advice to achieve liberation. We will need time to read, to study, to write, to debate, among ourselves. And when we act politically, we will need time for organizing, etc.

No woman can go this alone. The territory ahead is new, frightening, and appears lonely. We must begin by forming organizations which will provide emotional support and an intellectual base for framing action. If we are to enter the struggle, and in addition, attempt to preserve our marriages, it will require group approaches. It will require a realistic appraisal of the history of women, which we must research and compile. It may require new programs for economic self-help, in anticipation of male retribution.

Underlying much of the evasiveness, the apparent lack of self-confidence, and even the downright silliness among women when confronted with the possibility of a female liberation movement, is the big male gun—the charge of homosexuality. Before turning to some current hassles in our movement, many of which at least partially derive from this question, we want to begin an open discussion of homosexuality in the hope that future conferences and private thinking will consider the issue.

Homosexuality

The radical woman, for very specific reasons, is probably more uptight about homosexuality than other women. This is one of the curious paradoxes in the movement; in many ways, movement people tend to maintain some Puritan mores to excess. Most of us entered the movement on the basis of simple, middle-class, idealistic hangups. Our parents taught us all the tenets of 'clean living,' including equality for the races and humanity among men, and when we got to college we recognized that this was science fiction. Our minds were momentarily blown, we went to a meeting somewhere, got involved, and a few of us got radicalized along the way. While younger radicals tend to be more cynical, perhaps have freer life-styles, all of us have a heritage which is essentially Puritanical. Homosexuality is 'wrong.'

There are political considerations. Those who are actually organizing disapprove of drug use which becomes so extensive that the user drops out politically. We look upon homosexuals who will not protest openly against mores as cop-outs. And while we are willing to combat the social order, while we accept ostracism from our families and live in that twilight zone which is at once inside and outside of the system, for self-protection we have learned a thousand tricks to forestall the ultimate bust— legal or psychological. Homosexuality, we imagine, would be too much to add to an already strained relationship with the society in which we dwell.

And there are practical considerations. We don't carry with us, as part of our movement baggage, an understanding of homosexual technique, so our childhood excursions appear bland in comparison with even the clumsiest heterosexual referrent.

The movement places no premium on homosexuality. While everybody clamors for more meaningful relationships, more self-expression, more affection, and less inhibition in our social styles, nobody suggests in radical journals that we mean homosexuality. Anything but that; what we say is that we wish people would not define as homosexual the new human forms of relationship we want to enjoy. This must have been what the SDS men were playing at the convention when they complained to radical women that they 'aren't supposed to cry or to express their love for each other physically' (*Guardian*, 28 June 68). For once they were caught in their own bag.

Women who turn from men for a time, to look to each other for political relationships, movement thinking, and an organizational milieu, are bound to see here and there someone they love. The slightest measure of female liberation will bring with it an ability to perceive again the precise qualities and degree of responsivity which inhere in other women. For those in serious communes or political trenches, a continued fear of homosexuality may be the one last strand by which the male order can pull us back into tow. It has been our past error to repress the political attraction we have for our own kind. It would be equally wrong to turn female communes into anything less than a tentative experiment with a new domestic arrangement; political content will not suffice to fill the need every human has for that place where one 'slackens the pace at the crossroads, and takes a chance to rest.' It will be in these communes, or their less rigorous counterparts in female rediscovery, that we may learn to design new living arrangements which will make our coexistence with men in the future all the more equal and all the more humane. And exploring the possibilities of non-elitist, non-colonial love may teach us forms of political strength far more valuable than guerrilla theater.

We have got to stop throwing around terms like 'fag,' 'pimp,' 'queer,' and 'dike' to reassure men of our absolute loyalty to them. This is the language which helps to insure that each man has his female slave, and that each woman eventually becomes one.

Indirect male sniping, insinuating homosexuality is a horror which is bound to attend female liberation activity, has some interesting analogies in our movement experience. It's like the signals southern whites put out: 'If you leave a white and a black alone for five minutes, there's no telling what might happen.' And it's a lot like red-baiting. Our answers to red-baiting will serve us well here. The charge of homosexuality—which will be more openly voiced by non-movement males—stands for a fear of something greater, as did the charge of communism against southern blacks and whites getting together: that they might get together. An indigenous movement of any people determined to gain their liberation is a more serious threat than 'communism' or 'homosexuality,' and the charge is merely a delaying tactic to obstruct organization.

We should begin to talk about homosexuality; be prepared to defend against male sniping on the issue. Most importantly, we should not couch the issue in the language of 'affection' until we can define affection through the experience of our liberation and then stand by our knowledge, whatever that may come to be.

6. Some Current Hassles in the Development of the Movement

The Co-ed Model

Several thoughtful writers have recently suggested that all-female groups be organized to fight corporate liberalism on the early Black Power model. That is, these new groups formed to attack the draft, racism, etc., would be distinguishable from traditional movement groups only in their all-female composition. Presumably, these groups would negotiate with others on a coalition, or as Marilyn Webb puts it, a co-ed basis. If there is any need at all for solely female political groups, this purposeful segregation by sex must then mean that some women consider themselves—if not an oppressed class—at least different from men in a politically relevant way. If men are to be permitted to continue defining the movement for us while we operate in these co-ed arrangements, why segregate at all, since we all agree that they do their thing better than we do, for now, anyway. I suspect that even the formation of such groups as Coretta King's implies something about the female condition other than anatomy.

Women should combine politically and define for themselves their enemy and describe the machinery of their oppression. We should not promise in advance that we will join any specific issue. We think that well organized women, supportive of each other, will carry their share.

The Third World Analogy

The Third World analogy has caused plenty of trouble in the radical male left. Looking to revolutionary movements in underdeveloped countries has encouraged a sort of one-one-upmanship desperation to act; and, much to its detriment, the left usually only mimics in what are essentially theatrical performances, the real lifeblood and guts scene of revolutionary movements in action.

What is so important for women is that we not become trapped in this frenzied, often irrational behavior. The Third World Analogy is inappropriate to us. First, the conditions under which people live in ongoing revolutions are simply different from ours and call for different activity. Second, radical women who invoke the Third World Analogy are unaware of the role women have actually played in the Cuban, Vietnamese, and Algerian struggles; or, if they describe these roles accurately, they then romanticize, misquote, and generally push them off as something desirable, when in fact these roles are pawns of a historical circumstance—imperialism—not chosen by those in revolt.

In female liberation literature we hear about three groups of women who allegedly 'won their freedom' or are winning equality by picking up guns and fighting for the national liberation of one or another country. Cuba, the most often cited case, did use women as troops, much as they are used in SDS. In the war, women had much the same status as the female in SDS, and now that the Cuban revolution has moved into its cultural phase, we know what Castro wants them to do: go home, cook, take care of the kids. It is true that many women are becoming doctors (Russia has more female physicians than male; this is the highest rank in the 'caring for' professions). Certainly a few are executives in the nationalized Ford Motors to the South. But the largest female group, the Women's Federation, 'does not crusade for the emancipation of Women.' Of course, 'its main function is to implement government work policies' ('Cuban Women,' by Mary Nelson, *Voice of the Women's Liberation Movement*, June 1968). Mary Nelson, who has just returned, tells us that nothing basic has changed in patterns of dominance between the sexes. OEO may provide public nurseries for working women before Castro gets hep [sic]. What's the big hangup with Cuba? Men still run it their own way, for their own ends.

Socialism, or even a commitment to socialism, is viewed by many American women as the panacea for their problems. Why doesn't anybody ever talk about the plight of women in the socialized Mid-Eastern or African nations?

Now Marilyn Webb is cool. She can strain the analogy between the US left and the NLF just enough to make it look reasonable for the American women, who can't be in the black thing, and want to do something, to think of themselves as Vietnamese. What we have got to recognize is that women living in Viet Nam face very different circumstances than our own. Their children, and they themselves, are being murdered daily, and a third of the population goes about missing a limb. Under constant military attack, it is necessary to defer designing new institutions in order to preserve life itself; Vietnamese women have no choice. We should admit that we are not in the same position. We who support draft resistance are not being literally shelled out of existence. And more to the point, women who *merely* support draft resistance are not doing all they can in what is an essentially devolutionary movement. In the United States, women ought to be organizing women, as their proper constituency, to add to the growing number of disaffected quarters. In a country which is on the offensive in the world, our job is to reorganize our institutions so that they are no longer viable instruments of colonialism and war. Marilyn tells us that Vietnamese women found out that the only way they can get equality is to participate in the national political struggle. The strict analogy between Viet Nam and the United States is more realistically phrased: American women would get a lot more equality if they gave militant support to our *national* struggle: to colonize, to murder, to enslave. The most proper third world analogy I have heard is the 'eerie, high pitched wail of the Algerian women.' That is already our own.

Male Chauvinism

Somebody very courageously put this phrase into the female manifesto at last year's SDS Convention, and ever since, women have been taking it back or redefining it to spare the male ego. There is great value in naming your enemy. The definition of the phrase goes: Surname of Nicholas Chauvin, soldier of Napoleon I, notorious for his bellicose attachment to the lost imperial cause: militant, unreasoning devotion to one's race, sex, etc., with contempt for other races, the opposite sex, etc.: as, male chauvinism. The phrase makes some sense, and if you apply it to men in general, rather than to the nice guy you're living with (this comes later), that's more or less where it's at.

The argument over terminology really stands for a much more important proposition, one to which Carl Oglesby addressed himself some time ago. He presented a very significant speech in which he kept repeating to this effect: Let's stop talking about General Motors, the Poverty Program, or the Justice Department; let's call it by its name; it has a name, and that name is the System. We're not going to solve the problem by attacking General Motors; the system is the enemy, let's call it by its name. The drive for domination, be it genetic or learned, which so aptly characterizes the male sex, finds larger expression in our national posture. We may decide later, as the female liberation movement matures, that our real job is to dethrone the king—an entire sex bred for mastery—and replace it with an order which more closely corresponds with the traditional female approach: attention to personal needs, caring for others, making decisions on the basis of a multitude of human data. If this be our goal, we must, as must all oppressed people, assume for a time an adversary stance (unaccustomed for women) toward our oppressors. Since such a stance places a premium on winning, we are going to have to name what it is that we want to win, and against whom; that requires naming goals and the enemy.

In the life of each woman, the most immediate oppressor, however unwilling he may be in theory to play that role, is 'the man.' Even if we prefer to view him as merely a pawn in the game, he's still the foreman on the big plantation of maleville. And that plantation has a name. While 'male chauvinism' isn't sacred, if we're searching for a better name for the enemy, let's not de-escalate.

So-called Female Elitism and Male Liberation Groups

It turns out that men at the SDS convention this summer got hacked off having to drink beer waiting for the women to return from political discussion. They started talking about the oppressive aspects of the male roles given them. Like when a white person first realizes that racism hurts him too. Well, fine, if men want to form male liberation groups, they should go ahead. But what we must understand is that in the area of sex, a male liberation group *could* be to female liberation what 'SPONGE' is to the black revolution. That is, I wonder if these male groups will focus on support-ing us, when we want them, in our attacks on the male order; or, will they attempt to liberate themselves at our further expense. From Susan Sutheim's report ("Women Shake Up SDS Session," *Guardian*, 28 June 68), the impulse for male liberation groups sounds reactionary, and in our community, when the term is used, it is often accompanied by a particularly vengeful smirk.

However, as we have already suggested, with a separation of the sexes, real or political, some men might come to a more humane understanding of what it means to be a man. And if this is the program the men intend to pursue, let them go it alone. We must remember that there is a great difference between an organization of the dominant and an organization of the oppressed, whatever sweet language attempts to fuse the two (as, for example, Johnson's grunting out 'We Shall Over-come').

Susan Sutheim, who wants to invite men to female liberation meetings, and who supports the idea of male liberation groups, assumes that the problem is limited to psychological flaws in sexual roles; in fact, the problem is political and does not call for desegregated soul searching. We don't need T-groups. And as one of the Cana-dian women has observed, men will not participate democratically in decision-making that disrupts their lives.

The hysterical and reactionary responses of men at the SDS convention this summer—the charges of female elitism and the call for male liberation groups—will serve their function with women who insist upon an NAACP approach to their condition: half-assed attempts to recapture some half-assed female territory.

6. *Some Urgent Priorities*

As we begin talking to women about female liberation, most of them accept our description of our lot with little argument. But they do come on with honest fears about engaging in the movement, and they tell us how incompetent (inferior) they feel, how they lack self-confidence (have been brainwashed), how they don't have much time (got a lot of custodial tasks on the home front), and most important how they're scared.

Being afraid has been a genuine response of oppressed people to their initial encounter with a vision of liberation. As is always the case, discipline and organization are the antidote, the means by which the exploited are drawn out of the routine of their ghettos. We cannot meet fear with rhetoric or statistics. We must become ready to organize, support, and act.

As radical women, we must set the tone, and there are several things we can begin doing now. We can discuss the problems of organizing uncommitted women and designing for them support facilities which will free them up for political behavior. We can get clear about our own history. We should elevate our own, and there really are some groovy women in the movement. We can begin to think about our proper relationships to our derivative movements, to the men we know and to men as a class. The professionals among us can look into legal discrimination and the lies about our history. We can support the newsletter and the journal and write out and exchange our thoughts in these media. And, we can begin to think about organizing projects, pacing and fashioning them, so that they speak to American women about their condition and encourage them to join the movement.

A good US newsletter, *Voice of the Women's Liberation Movement*, has already started. It serves well the functions of rapid communication, morale-building, and reporting of organizational activity. Dee Ann Pappas has begun a journal which offers a forum for larger organizational issues, studies on women, the history of women, and female art. Marilyn Webb and others have already initiated some fascinating organizing projects.

A PERSONAL SUMMARY

June 17, 1968

I had saved this particular evening for reviewing our paper, perhaps to add and change a word or two. But I cannot approach the task properly, because today I witnessed once more that sort of oppression which drives one back into the thick of the movement. And as I sit here in poorly controlled rage, I realize that there is one thing we have omitted from our paper which I must try to fill in now.

The media warn us daily of a national and even international Apocalypse. We who have experienced the movement—even as troops in the battles of others—know so well that for many people the Day of Doom has been the measure of their years and the only Revelation of their lives. Political and emotional devastation are the weird bread and wine—the vinegared communion-of the Damned. Our experience attunes us to these people, their lives, but they move among us, except when we know rage, only as metaphors for our understanding of the social order.

And in our paper we have not yet spoken of that indignation, that rage—perhaps the essence of militancy—which almost never finds it way into movement writing but which surely must be the impetus of our commitment. Tonight I am with the rage, an old friend now. And since for me, at any rate, that rage has always been the maelstrom in which I come to recall again my own alienation, my own political powerlessness, the peculiar prison of my female days, as well as my passion for my comrades, I want to share it in this context.

The occasion is one we all have known. I was writing earlier of a friend who had spent several months in jail. This morning I watched while a southern judge racked her again on another charge, and this one carrying a big penalty. No bail, no appeal—off to the prison-house with one of the best and most beautiful of my generation and my sex. Can we allow this to be our Coda?

We gathered up her children and sent them to safety, out of reach of the greedy juvenile officers. My husband and I reordered her now silent house, locked the doors again. Because this rare, rare, white woman had become a sort of Che in another land than her own, the black community will pop off tonight. But we worry very little about our safety now, for this kind of rage makes one brave and negligent of the usual curious defenses. Carol Thomas felt it so often, herself moving with the doomed, was brave so often, was enraged so often, and now is racked by the Savage Society, as she so often had been before. Carol, my sister, they have got you again in that ugly place they build as a refuge from themselves.

We have not conned ourselves into political paralysis as an excuse for inaction—we are a subjugated caste. We need to develop a female movement, most importantly, because we must fight this social order with all of the faculties we have got, and those in full gear. And we must be liberated so that we can turn from our separate domestic desperation—our own Apocalypse of the Damned—toward an exercise of social rage against each dying of the light. We must get our stuff together, begin to dismantle this system's deadly social and military toys, and stop the mad dogs who rule us every place we're at.

'I am my brother's keeper' is the cautious altruism of those who are themselves enchained. Rather: 'I Am My Brother's Brother, My Sister's Sister.' Women together, sustaining each other politically, restored to an affection for each other, and unburdening themselves of their struggle with men, must move to take that Savage Society apart.

NOTES

1. 'It was in Fayerweather that a male leader asked for girls to volunteer for cooking duty and was laughed down . . . ,' in "The Siege of Columbia," *Ramparts,* 15 June 68.

2. In response to what is hopefully the last stand of women *in* SDS, at the 1968 National Convention, June 13: 'The feeling in the room was, well, those Women have done their silly little thing again.' *Guardian,* 28 June 68.

Chapter Two

Toward a Radical Movement

Heather Booth, Evi Goldfield, and Sue Munaker

Ours is an age of promise. Technology and abundance have made it clear that a decent life might at least be easily within the reach of all. Self-determination, freedom seem like real possibilities. More than this, though, it is an age of promise denied. Under the banner of freedom, atrocities are committed. With all the rhetoric of economic development, the majority of the earth's people are hungry, exploited, powerless.

Not only the impoverished, but many others, are learning that no one is really free in our society; that while some groups are much more oppressed than others, ordinary individuals have little ability to live the life or bring about the changes they desire. Among these others are groups of women, angered at the society that relegates them to a secondary and servile position.

The movement for social change taught women activitists about their own oppression. Politically, women were excluded from decision-making. They typed, made leaflets, did the shitwork. The few women who attained leadership positions had to struggle against strong convention.

Also, women in the movement were in a unique situation. As some got married, they found that there were no models for a marriage in which both man and woman were politically active. Was the once active woman now to assume a supportive role, to stay at home with the kids or get an unwanted job to support her activist husband? Were both partners' interests to have equal weight in determining what kind of work they would do, where they would live?

In December 1965, at a national conference of the Students for a Democratic Society, the subject of women's role in society and in the movement was openly discussed. The discontent of the women activists was brought to the surface, therein initiating a radical women's movement.

The problems discussed were not just those of political activists, but of all contemporary women.

Women had been integrated into the labor work force during the war, doing what they felt was useful, purposive work. When the men came home, though, women were either pushed into the lower sectors of the labor force or moved back into the home. Women's image began to change in the popular magazines; domesticity was glorified, frills were again in vogue, drudgery was made glamorous.

Women who returned to the domestic setting found that things were not quite the same as before. New labor-saving devices gave them free time. This freedom made a vacuum in their lives; they had nothing meaningful to fill it with. The housewife role, offered up as the most fulfilling for women, was expanded, elaborated, filled up with trivia so that each labor-saving device could be compensated for by a new task. Women joined clubs and charity organizations in vast numbers. They took enrichment courses and dabbled in the arts. Shopping became a major occupation; an incredible amount of energy was expended on finding those items which would adorn the house and the woman, expressing her identity. Yet, none of this really satisfied. It was not serious, not involving; it merely whittled away the long endless hours.

Many women remained in the labor force, although often displaced from the jobs they held during the war. More women than in preceding generations began to work outside the home, but not on equal basis with men. With their taste of economic independence came also the taste of exploitation both as women and as workers. As workers they learned that rights can be won through collective union action, as women the lesson was not learned so quickly.

The new generation of women sense the boredom and bitterness of their mothers. They do not need to be confined to the same roles. They are trying to understand why it is that women are still expected to play subordinate roles.

Myths

There have always been myths which defined as the essence of the 'true woman' her natural passivity and her maternal instincts. While today's elaboration of them may be more subtle, they are still unfounded, haunting women as they are invoked to justify today's norms.

Woman's nature is usually explained in terms of her biology. She is passive in her sexual role; she receives the penis. Therefore, she desires to encircle and enclose, rather than to extend to and to strive. Man's sex, on the other hand, is activity itself, the symbol of strength, potency, and dominance. Too often this metamorphic passivity is taken as 'literal truth.' Freudian psychology and its popularly understood implications assume that what was thought, though not proven, true for Victorian German upper-middle class women is universally true. Freud's concept of penis envy tells us that women are motivated primarily by the fact that they are not men. Erik Erikson, a favorite of social psychologists, describes ' . . . the basic modes of feminine inception and maternal inclusion preparing women for the perceptive and acceptant traits of future motherhood' (*Childhood and Society*, pp. 88–90). Only as people began to suspect that the 'truths' were unsubstantiated did they begin to find that in fact women are sexually as non-passive as men (see the Masters-Johnson study, *Human Sexual Response*).

And then, why should function follow form? Even if women were by nature sexually passive, it hardly follows that they should be passive in other realms. But social institutions, historically created by men, have perpetuated the functional myths to justify their own position.

The Judaic-Christian Church teaches that to the extent that women are sexual creatures that are unclean, foul, 'the doorway to the devil.' Yet, by regarding sex only as a duty, the pure chaste woman can attain a holiness denied to men. Embodying these myths are the harlot, the virgin (the latter to become a respectable woman). Both of them are socially useful, each subordinate to men, serving their needs.

Today's new family has institutionalized the myth of whore and saint with a new slant. The real woman is wife, mother, mistress—the playboy's dream. She is to comfort and serve man under the guise of the 'modern free woman' that releases the man from his guilt. She is still his woman, weak, gentle, submissive, emotionally sensitive, intuitive, unable to cope with the world without a man. She attains her identity through her husband and later through her children, whom she treats like private property; she's hurt when they leave home because they are denying her of her identity.

Historically, there may have been an excuse for this role as part of a division of labor. Continuous pregnancies kept women physically weak and less mobile than men. Now that the pill enables people to control the timing and number of children they will have, the incessant childbearing role is a lame excuse for confining women to domestic chores.

Educational institutions further perpetuate the myths. The liberal arts education legitimates, for men, their right to control and manage the society. For women, it is a waiting period in which they can find a husband and make themselves educated companions of introspective victims. As women are irrelevant to the decisions made in society, so this education they receive is irrelevant for preparing them to make such decisions. The situation is perpetuated because women are either excluded from academic consideration or else presented in shallow characterizations.

Evolving from the sexual myths and reinforcing them are the limiting and stereo-typed ideas of masculine and feminine. A woman who does not conform to the notions of feminine as servile and supportive is deviant: masculine, castrating, shrew-ish, sluttish, frustrated or worse. Thus, nonconformist women are labeled and put in their place. As long as artificially constructed, mythically based images of masculine and feminine are the only alternative, both men and women are going to find conflict between their imposed sexual identity and their goals as human beings.

New myths are being created. They say that women are better off than they have ever been, that a New Woman is emerging. She is middle class and liberated. She is able to have a family; yet, because of labor-saving devices she has much leisure time to devote to meaningful activity. A wide variety of consumer goods enable her to enjoy life on a scale never enjoyed before. These are the myths; what is the reality?

Realities

Although a large number of women do work, it is usually in service occupations. And, even if women considered their jobs worthwhile, the jobs pay less than men's and are low in status. According to statistics gathered by the Department of Labor in 1964, women are paid $5–$10 less per week for the same job as men. The median annual income for white working men is $6497, for white women, $3859, for non-white men, $4285, for non-white women, $2674. Only 1% of these women make more than $10,000 per year and one-quarter of those women own estates. While a radical movement does not aim to integrate women into the male job structure, even less to encourage women to become business executives, weapons experts, or advertising writers, it is important to note where discrimination exists. With the exception of those few who 'make it in a man's world,' women are systematically excluded from science, business, medicine, law, and academia. Most working women are low paid factory workers, maids, waitresses, secretaries, elementary school teachers, social workers, or nurses. Some are in high paying occupations which exploit their femininity, such as models, playboy bunnies, or exotic dancers.

The career woman image does not apply to the bulk of women workers who are stuck in low paying, tedious, dead-end positions. Neither does it apply to middle-class, white-collar women workers who are idealized by the media. We are supposed to believe that a career is glamorous because a woman dresses sytlishly and serves men in such jobs as airline stewardess or New York secretary. The justification for channeling women into service occupations is that women are better servants. The excuse for keeping them out of high-status occupations is that women are bad risks: they will marry and have kids. These are self-fulfilling prophecies. Women are raised to believe that they should serve and that they can't have both a career and a family. Then, the smart thing to do is to find a man to support them. Society reinforces these conditions by not providing enough child-care centers, public all-day nurseries, paid pregnancy leaves, shorter work days, etc.

Why is there a new myth? The mystique of the idealized New Woman has been generated in order to sell a lot of unnecessary products to a lot of bored, insecure, passive, frustrated women. Clothing and make-up are not just adornments, but become expressions of one's very essence—which is constantly being manipulated by the mass media. Miss Clairol says:

> Have you found the real you? Some women never do. In fact, many women never make the most exciting discovery of all: they should have been born blond.

A host of other advertisers echo her statement.

Styles change constantly; 'new' products flood the market. Women must be made to want—no, need—more and more things. The New Freedom for women is the freedom to buy and thereby support our market economy. The new leisure time is time for consuming. Irrationally changing clothing styles would not be accepted in a society where priorities centered on human needs rather than on profit-making. In the United States, priority is put on automobiles and military equipment—goods which will produce the most profits—rather than on something socially necessary from a humane point of view, such as low-cost housing for poor people. Passive, docile, accepting women are therefore important to this system since their tasks as consumers can be manipulated. As long as work for most people is meaningless and unfulfilling and as long as women are not expected to DO anything, women will have to gain identity from what they buy, what they own, and how they look.

What about sexual liberation? It would be nice if the mini-skirted girl in gay colors and way-out makeup really were a symbol for a new, sexually liberated woman. Since women have been thought of primarily as sexual beings, it would be expected that their liberation would come through sex, but those who have been 'sexually liberated' have often merely adapted men's attitudes towards sex. Women are still seen and see themselves as sexual objects and treat men in kind, taking pride in the number of conquests they make. This attitude is at best one of revenge for women's own sexual exploitation. Women cannot liberate themselves through sex while in other important respects their social role remains unchanged.

Program

The initial work of any new radical women's group is to understand the realities and myths which relegate women to a subordinate role. Women come into the movement with two perspectives: either with a primary concern for women's issues such as abortion, child-care centers or the desire to research and discuss in greater depth women's position in society, or with a more general concern about political issues such as racism and the war. There is no contradiction between women's issues and political issues, for the movement for women's liberation is a step toward changing the entire society. Women are not seeking equality in an unjust society, rather from an understanding of the basis of their own oppression they are developing programs for overall social change.

The common understanding, whichever the perspective, is that part of the way women are oppressed is that they see their problems as personal ones and thus blame themselves. The first step in building a movement is to see that the problems are that men as individuals are not 'the enemy'; rather, 'the enemy' is those social institutions and expectations perpetuated by and constraining members of both sexes. Radical women are not forming groups for the purpose of segregating themselves from men, but in order to focus on the means by which women can come to terms with those institutions.

There are now about 35 small radical women's groups concentrated in a few cities. The programs develop according to the interests of the members. In groups where most of the women are in the radical movement, the first discussion often center on their role in the movement. From these talks comes the realization that as women they have been non-radical, playing passive political roles as secretaries or administrative help rather than as strategic planners.

Though the original groups were just of young radical New Left women, there are now groups of once non-political housewives, women now married to movement men who previously had no politics of their own, college students, high school students. They want to share their understanding of their problems as women with other women. As they see the nature of other types of oppression—of the poor, of black people; and other movements of liberation—NLF, Black Power, etc.

Groups are undertaking action projects such as leafletting women factory workers about the war, high prices, and women's wages. Some are fighting to change abortion laws and practices, setting up communal child care centers, forming drug and consumer co-ops. One university group is planning a student-run course on women, for women. Others are setting up seminars on imperialism and other political issues. By discussing these serious political and intellectual questions in small groups with other women, inhibitions about females using their minds can be overcome. Several groups are talking about running guerrilla theater in stores and shopping centers to dramatize the war, high prices, and women's role as consumer and servant.

Some are looking for ways to relate to the anti-war movement that will not be auxiliary. Women may set up and run coffee shops near army bases to talk with the GIs, to see how they feel about the war, and to pose alternatives to them. Women may also try to organize wives of servicemen and women in the service or other women in towns where bases are located. Some women are going door-to-door to talk with wives of working-class men about the war, racism, and the presidential election. Many are planning for some activity around the Democratic Convention.

Talking about common problems in the context of the need for social change is in itself liberating. Creating programs such as these allows for the development of self-confidence, leadership, and an analysis which widens the possible alternatives seen for women. Working on such issues, one develops a vision of and a movement for a society in which all people can define themselves without the awkward imposition of social roles.

Conclusion

The roots of the movement for women's liberation were in the contradiction between the promise held out and the existence lived. The promise was for freedom and justice now. Instead there was oppression and injustice for all but a few. Once it seemed as though reforms such as civil rights bills, anti-draft legislation, the end of the war in Vietnam, would in themselves bring justice. But unlike the feminists of the 1800s, women now realize that America's problems must be attacked at their root. For justice to come to black people there must be black economic and political self-determination. For an end to militarism there must be an end to control of society by business which profits only with the suppression of national wars of independence. For the true freedom of all women, there must be restructuring of the institutions which perpetuate the myths and the subservience of their social situation.

It is the explicit consciousness of these hopes and analysis which lead us to fight for women's liberation and the liberation of all people.

April 1968

Chapter Three

Women and the Radical Movement

Anne Koedt

Within the last year many radical women's groups have sprung up throughout the country. This was caused by the fact that movement women found themselves playing secondary roles on every level—be it in terms of leadership, or simply in terms of being listened to. They found themselves (and others) afraid to speak up because of self-doubts when in the presence of men. They ended up concentrating on food-making, typing, mimeographing, general assistance work, and serving as a sexual supply for their male comrades after hours.

As these problems began being discussed, it became clear that what had at first been assumed to be a personal problem was in fact a social and political one. We found strong parallels between the liberation of women and the black power struggle—we were both being oppressed by similar psychological/economic dynamics. And the deeper we analyzed the problem and realized that all women suffer from this kind of oppression, the more we realized that the problem was not just confined to movement women.

It became necessary to go to the root of the problem, rather than to become engaged in solving secondary problems arising out of that condition. Thus, rather than storming the Pentagon as women, or protesting the Democratic Convention as women, we must begin to expose and eliminate the *causes* of our oppression as women. Our job is not only to improve the conditions of movement women any more than it is only to improve the conditions of professional working women. Both are reformist if thought of only as ends in themselves; and such an approach ignores the broader concept that one cannot achieve equality for some members of one's group while the rest are not free.

In choosing to fight for women's liberation it is not enough, either, to explain it only in general terms of "the system." For the system oppresses many groups in many ways. Women must learn that the technique used to keep a woman oppressed is to convince her that she is at all times secondary to man, and that her life is

Speech given at a city-wide meeting of radical women's groups at the Free University in New York City on February 17, 1968. First printed in *Notes From the First Year* (New York, 1968). The speech is representative of the early attempts to define the relationship between the new left and the beginning feminist consciousness. The word *feminist* then was scarcely if ever used for fear that women's oppression would not be considered "radical." By 1971 the critique of the left was more sharply delineated, cf., *The Fourth World Manifesto*.

defined in terms of him. We cannot speak of liberating ourselves until we free ourselves from this myth and accept ourselves as primary.

In our role as radical women we are confronted with the problem of assuring a female revolution within the general revolution. And we must begin to distinguish real from apparent freedoms.

Radical men may advocate certain freedoms for women when they overlap with their own interests, but these are not true freedoms unless they spring out of the concept of male and female equality and confront the issue of male supremacy. For example, men may want women to fight in the revolution because they need every able bodied person they can get. And they may need women to join the work force under a socialist economic system because they cannot afford, like capitalism, to have an unemployed (surplus) labor force not contributing work and being supported by the state. And men may therefore advocate state nurseries so that mothers are not kept from work. But has the fundamental concept of women changed? Do these changes mean that men have renounced the old supremacy relationship, wherein women must always be defined in terms of men? Has the basic domination changed?

It is important to analyze the history of revolutions in terms of special interest groups. The American Revolution was a white male bourgeois revolution. The issues were self-government and the right to make a profit without England's interference; the Declaration of Independence was specifically written to justify independence from England. It was a document which guaranteed rights neither to blacks nor to women. Crispus Attucks, one of the first black men to lose his life for the revolution, was fighting in a vicarious revolution—the white revolution. Betsy Ross sewing the flag was participating vicariously in a male revolution. The rights gained were not for her.

It is always true of an oppressed group that the mere fact of their existence means that to a certain extent they have accepted their inferior-colonial-secondary status. Taught self-hatred, they identify instead with the oppressor. Thus such phenomena as blacks bleaching their skin and straightening their hair, and women responding with horror at the thought of a woman president.

The economic revolution—i.e., change from capitalism to socialism—can also be viewed in terms of male interest. Under capitalism, the majority of men were exploited and controlled by a few men who held the wealth and power. By changing the economic structure to socialism, this particular economic exploitation was largely eradicated. Women in the Soviet Union fought for and supported such a revolution. But whether out of a genuine hope that non-exploitation would be applied as liberally to them, or worse, out of a lack of even a minimum awareness that they themselves were important, the Soviet revolution remained a male power revolution, although many new benefits fell to women. The Soviet Union is still primarily male governed; women's integration into the labor force meant simply that she transferred her auxiliary, service relationship with men into the area of work. Soviet women are teachers, doctors, assistants, food handlers. And when they come home from work they are expected to continue in their submissive role to men and do the housework, cooking and take primary responsibility for child rearing.

It is important for radical women to learn from these events. The dominant/submissive relationship between men and women was not challenged. Not confronted. We were asked by them instead to equate our liberation with theirs—to blame our inferior conditions on the economic structure rather than confront the obvious male interest in keeping women "in their place." We never insisted upon as explicit a program for freeing women as men had demanded for freeing themselves from economic exploitation. We never confronted men and demanded that unless they give up their domination over us, we would not fight for their revolution, work in their revolution. We never fought the primary cause, hoping instead that changing the secondary characteristics would win us freedom. And we ended up with a revolution that simply transferred male supremacy, paternalism, and male power to the new economy. A reformist revolution that only improved upon our privileges but did not change the basic structure causing our oppression.

A black male revolutionary today would not be satisfied knowing only that the economic structure went from private to collective control; he would want to know about racism. And you would have to show him how white power and supremacy would be eliminated in that revolution before he would join you.

Until we make such similar demands, revolution will pass us by.

Chapter Four

What Is Liberation?

Women: A Journal of Liberation

The words which movements use to describe themselves often suggest the terms of their struggle. In the early part of this century and before, women described themselves as "suffragettes" or "abolitionists"—the very words showed the limitation of their struggle: to gain the vote or to end slavery. These limited goals were not enough to achieve full equality for women or for black people. It is significant that the common phrase which describes the present women's movement is the word, "liberation." This word implies a deep consciousness of the significance of our struggle: Women are asking for nothing less than the total transformation of the world.

Before discussing the meaning of liberation, it is necessary to explore three basic concepts: (1) the material conditions for liberation, (2) the problem of alienation, and (3) the method of dialectic thought.

The Material Conditions for Liberation

When we discuss liberation, we are not talking about an abstract "idea"; we are talking about a potential that is firmly rooted in reality. We are talking about actual possibilities. The possibility for liberation exists because the material conditions of the world have evolved enough that our oppression and secondary status are no longer necessary. By "material conditions" we mean technology, scientific discoveries, industrialization, and the economic system which defines the way human beings relate to each other. For example, the full liberation of women was not possible until humanity evolved to the stage where reproduction could be controlled. The oppression of women began in primitive times when the biological nature of women severely limited their mobility. Now that women have a choice about reproduction in advanced industrial countries, one of the crucial fetters to our liberation has been removed.

We are not blaming women's oppression *only* on material conditions. Something more than technology or reproduction must explain the kind of myths and attitudes which have devalued women. For example, many religions perpetuate abusive concepts: the myth that Eve caused the fall of man, or that the Orthodox Jew in a morning prayer thanks God that he was not born a woman.

Alienation

In a capitalist society alienation has three forms. People are alienated from their work because they do not receive the full benefits produced by their labor. People are alienated from each other because they must compete for survival and success. The alienation between the sexes is a key aspect of this social alienation in which people see themselves as isolated units and women are viewed as objects of pleasure. Humans cannot feel a genuine comfort in the world in which they are forced to conceive of others as competitors and of the opposite sex as dominant or inferior. Finally, there is an alienation from nature. Instead of using the resources of nature for the benefit of all people, they are ravaged for the benefit of a few.

Dialectic Thought

Contradiction exists in the process of development of all things. In the process of development there exists a conflict of opposites. For example, in personality development we are both being and becoming. At the moment of conception we begin to die as well as grow. This formulation comes not from a deductive assumption, but it follows from a scientific observation of nature and human behavior. All processes involve change or motion, and change occurs through the interaction of contradictions. Dialectic thought, another mode of thinking, helps us understand the realities of change. Change occurs because a given concept is challenged by its opposite until a synthesis occurs which is unlike either conflicting idea. History has progressed because humans have acquired new knowledge and technology which contradicts earlier formulations and the struggle between the old and the new result in different understandings of the world.

With these three concepts in mind, it is possible to discuss liberation.

Liberation: A Linguistic Definition

The linguistic function of the word "liberation" carries within it the dynamics of struggle. The word means "to set free," and thus implies that we must know both the oppressed and the liberated state. Within the word is the understanding that one is struggling *against* some oppression in order *to do* something else. When applie to women's oppression, liberation is the struggle *against* the limitations of our reproductive function which minimizes our personal potential, against the concepts which make us solely responsible for raising children, against the rigid social mores which limit our contribution to the world. But the word also suggests that we want liberation in order *to define* new social relationships, in order *to find* meaningful work, in order *to discover* new self concepts.

Liberation: An Evolving Process

Liberation is an evolving concept which proceeds in stages: (1) survival, (2) greater comforts and civil liberties, and (3) non-alienation (happiness). Before the Industrial Revolution most people spent most of their lives struggling for survival. Since the Industrial Revolution certain classes of people have reaped the benefits of technology. Middle class and upper class people live comfortable lives and have guarantees of civil liberties from their governments. Clearly, masses of people, even in the modern world, still subsist at the survival level. But the important point is that because of the existence of technology, these people can perceive the contradiction between their own impoverished conditions and the affluent, highly industrialized world around them. The implications are that people do not necessarily proceed from stage to stage. Once the possibility for liberation exists in the material conditions for some people, it becomes possible for all. At this stage in history, people are beginning to perceive the possibilities of living in a world in which people are no longer alienated from their work, from each other and from nature. The women's liberation movement is adding a crucial dimension to the vision of the non-alienated state.

Liberation: A Widening of Choices

Liberation means choice among alternatives, something which has consistently been denied women. Women have been conditioned to accept passive roles in which all major decisions are made by nature or by men. The major choice in a woman's life is who her husband will be, and he then will determine all future choices. In another way, marriage can be seen as a way of avoiding the difficult and serious human choice of establishing an identity and purpose in life. To achieve liberation, each person must discover herself as an individual with significance in her own right. A woman cannot fulfill herself through her children or through her husband; she must do it alone. Identity comes only through making choices and liberation is the process of obtaining ever-wider choices for people.

Liberation: Happiness

We do not mean the glib, syrupy concept of happiness which suggests that we will be happy if we buy this car or that deodorant, or if we find someone to marry. Happiness is more than the end emotion of gratified desire. That conception of happiness serves the outmoded capitalist system. It is our belief that true happiness is living in a non-alienated world. We are not fully capable at this stage of history to conceive of all the dynamics of happiness, but we do know that if a person is suffering, there is a cause. And if all the causes of unnecessary suffering could be removed—like the isolation of the individual, the inequality of the sexes, meaningless work—we could begin to comprehend what the potential life state of mankind could be.

Dialectics of Struggle

Our definitions of liberation reveal to us the evolutionary nature of human progress and provide us with a vision of the future. The issues taken up in this volume of the magazine—abortion, birth control, childcare, education, self-defense, and work are the problems which oppress women in the second stage of human history. We believe: 1) that these problems cannot be solved until basic economic relationships are altered in society, and 2) that women's liberation involves the solution of these problems and the end to human alienation. As we see it, the women's liberation movement is the key in the struggle for more advanced social relationships.

When we look at the material potential (technology, etc.) for life in this century, we can only be awed at the great benefits all humans could receive. All people could at least be clothed, fed, and housed decently. In spite of this great possibility and hope, we discover that the treasures of the earth, and the labors of workers are being exploited by an outmoded economic system which benefits a few. Capitalism, or the present ordering of human relationships, does not allow for the full realization of human potential. We must think of profit being used for all the people. We must begin to conceive of human relationships in cooperative rather than competitive ways.

On the face of it, abortion, child care, education, etc. appear to be reforms. Can the present system meet these demands? If we consider the problem of abortion, it is clear that even if the laws are liberalized, the problem of cost remains. Unless abortions are free, the poor woman who needs one will not be helped. Until hospitals, doctors, and the medical system are free from the profit motive, these reforms are meaningless. Child care, as we envision it, could not be provided by this system unless priorities are reordered to place children's growth and mothers' freedom as of primary importance. This would require providing large portions of manpower and funds for this purpose, which this society is unable to do without destroying the profit motive. Any attempt to reform the schools, where young girls are conditioned to passive roles and low-paying jobs, would encounter the needs of the system for women to serve their husbands and the society as a whole.

It is clear that the present system is not equipped to handle the full demands for abortion, childcare and education. The conclusion we reach is that women must work against all of these specific oppressions, but in a special way. We must realize that although specific problems can be eased, we must be aware that the full solution for all people is not possible under capitalism.

Chapter Five

Why Women's Liberation?

Marlene Dixon

The 1960s has been a decade of liberation; women have been swept up by that ferment along with blacks, Latins, American Indians and poor whites—the whole soft underbelly of this society. As each oppressed group in turn discovered the nature of its oppression in American society, so women have discovered that they too thirst for free and fully human lives. The result has been the growth of a new women's movement, whose base encompasses poor black and poor white women on relief, working women exploited in the labor force, middle class women incarcerated in the split level dream house, college girls awakening to the fact that sexiness is not the crowning achievement in life, and movement women who have discovered that in a freedom movement they themselves are not free. In less than four years women have created a variety of organizations, from the nationally-based middle class National Organization of Women (NOW) to local radical and radical feminist groups in every major city in North America. The new movement includes caucuses within nearly every New Left group and within most professional associations in the social sciences. Ranging in politics from reform to revolution, it has produced critiques of almost every segment of American society and constructed an ideology that rejects every hallowed cultural assumption about the nature and role of women.

As is typical of a young movement, much of its growth has been underground. The papers and manifestos written and circulated would surely comprise two very large volumes if published, but this literature is almost unknown outside of women's liberation. Nevertheless, where even a year ago organizing was slow and painful, with small cells of six or ten women, high turnover, and an uphill struggle against fear and resistance, in 1969 all that has changed. Groups are growing up everywhere with women eager to hear a hard line, to articulate and express their own rage and bitterness. Moving about the country, I have found an electric atmosphere of excitement and responsiveness. Everywhere there are doubts, stirrings, a desire to listen, to find out what it's all about. The extent to which groups have become politically radical is astounding. A year ago the movement stressed male chauvinism and psychological oppression; now the emphasis is on understanding the economic and social roots of women's oppression, and the analyses range from social democracy to Marxism. But the most striking change of all in the last year has been the loss of fear. Women are no longer afraid that their rebellion will threaten their very identity as women. They are not frightened by their own militancy, but liberated by it. Women's Liberation is an idea whose time has come.

The old women's movement burned itself out in the frantic decade of the 1920's. After a hundred years of struggle, women won a battle, only to lose the campaign: the vote was obtained, but the new millennium did not arrive. Women got the vote and achieved a measure of legal emancipation, but the real social and cultural barriers to full equality for women remained untouched.

For over 30 years the movement remained buried in its own ashes. Women were born and grew to maturity virtually ignorant of their own history of rebellion, aware only of a caricature of blue stockings and suffragettes. Even as increasing numbers of women were being driven into the labor force by the brutal conditions of the 1930's and by the massive drain of men into the military in the 1940's, the old ideal remained: a woman's place was in the home and behind her man. As the war ended and men returned to resume their jobs in factories and offices, women were forced back to the kitchen and nursery with a vengeance. This story has been repeated after each war and the reason is clear: women form a flexible, cheap labor pool which is essential to a capitalist system. When labor is scarce, they are forced onto the labor market. When labor is plentiful, they are forced out. Women and blacks have provided a reserve army of unemployed workers, benefiting capitalists and the stable male white working class alike. Yet the system imposes untold suffering on the victims, blacks, and women, through low wages and chronic unemployment.

With the end of the war the average age at marriage declined, the average size of families went up, and the suburban migration began in earnest. The political conservatism of the '50s was echoed in a social conservatism which stressed a Victorian ideal of the woman's life: a full womb and selfless devotion to husband and children.

As the bleak decade played itself out, however, three important social developments emerged which were to make a rebirth of the women's struggle inevitable. First, women came to make up more than a third of the labor force, the number of working women being twice the prewar figure. Yet the marked increase in female employment did nothing to better the position of women, who were more occupationally disadvantaged in the 1960's than they had been 25 years earlier. Rather than moving equally into all sectors of the occupational structure, they were being forced into the low paying service, clerical and semi-skilled categories. In 1940, women had held 45 per cent of all professional and technical positions; in 1967, they held only 37 per cent. The proportion of women in service jobs meanwhile rose from 50 to 55 per cent.

Second, the intoxicating wine of marriage and suburban life was turning sour; a generation of women woke up to find their children grown and a life (roughly 30 more productive years) of housework and bridge parties stretching out before them like a wasteland. For many younger women, the empty drudgery they saw in the suburban life was a sobering contradiction to adolescent dreams of romantic love and the fulfilling role of woman as wife and mother.

Third, a growing civil rights movement was sweeping thousands of young men and women into a moral crusade—a crusade which harsh political experience was to transmute into the New Left. The American Dream was riven and tattered in

Mississippi and finally napalmed in Viet-Nam. Young Americans were drawn not to Levittown, but to Berkeley, the Haight-Ashbury and the East Village. Traditional political ideologies and cultural myths, sexual mores and sex roles with them, began to disintegrate in an explosion of rebellion and protest.

The three major groups which make up the women's movement—working women, middle class married women and students—bring very different kinds of interests and objectives to women's liberation. Working women are most concerned with the economic issues of guaranteed employment, fair wages, job discrimination and child care. Their most immediate oppression is rooted in industrial capitalism and felt directly through the vicissitudes of an exploitative labor market.

Middle class women, oppressed by the psychological mutilation and injustice of institutionalized segregation, discrimination and imposed inferiority, are most sensitive to the dehumanizing consequences of severely limited lives. Usually well educated and capable, these women are rebelling against being forced to trivialize their lives, to live vicariously through husbands and children.

Students, as unmarried middle class girls, have been most sensitized to the sexual exploitation of women. They have experienced the frustration of one-way relationships in which the girl is forced into a "wife" and companion role with none of the supposed benefits of marriage. Young women have increasingly rebelled not only against passivity and dependency in their relationships but also against the notion that they must function as sexual objects, being defined in purely sexual rather than human terms, and being forced to package and sell themselves as commodities on the sex market.

Each group represents an independent aspect of the total institutionalized oppression of women. Their differences are those of emphasis and immediate interest rather than of fundamental goals. All women suffer from economic exploitation, from psychological deprivation, and from exploitive sexuality. Within women's liberation there is a growing understanding that the common oppression of women provides the basis for uniting across class and race lines to form a powerful and radical movement.

Racism and Male Supremacy

Clearly, for the liberation of women to become a reality it is necessary to destroy the ideology of male supremacy which asserts the biological and social inferiority of women in order to justify massive institutionalized oppression. Yet we all know that many women are as loud in their disavowal of this oppression as are the men who chant the litany of "a woman's place is in the home and behind her man." In fact, women are as trapped in their false consciousness as were the mass of blacks 20 years ago, and for much the same reason.

As blacks were defined and limited socially by their color, so women are defined and limited by their sex. While blacks, it was argued, were preordained by God or nature, or both, to be hewers of wood and drawers of water, so women are destined to bear and rear children, and to sustain their husbands with obedience and compassion. The Sky-God tramples through the heavens and the Earth/Mother-Goddess is always flat on her back with her legs spread, putting out for one and all.

Indeed, the phenomenon of male chauvinism can only be understood when it is perceived as a form of racism, based on stereotypes drawn from a deep belief in the biological inferiority of women. The so-called "black analogy" is no analogy at all; it is the same social process that is at work, a process which both justifies and helps perpetuate the exploitation of one group of human beings by another.

The very stereotypes that express the society's belief in the biological inferiority of women recall the images used to justify the oppression of blacks. The nature of women, like that of slaves, is depicted as dependent, incapable of reasoned thought, childlike in its simplicity and warmth, martyred in the role of mother, and mystical in the role of sexual partner. In its benevolent form, the inferior position of women results in paternalism; in its malevolent form, a domestic tyranny which can be unbelievably brutal.

It has taken over 50 years to discredit the scientific and social "proof" which once gave legitimacy to the myths of black racial inferiority. Today most people can see that the theory of the genetic inferiority of blacks is absurd. Yet few are shocked by the fact that scientists are still busy "proving" the biological inferiority of women.

In recent years, in which blacks have led the struggle for liberation, the emphasis on racism has focused only upon racism against blacks. The fact that "racism" has been practiced against many groups other than blacks has been pushed into the background. Indeed, a less forceful but more accurate term for the phenomenon would be "social Darwinism." It was the opinion of the social Darwinists that in the natural course of things the "fit" succeed (i.e. oppress) and the "unfit" (i.e. the biologically inferior) sink to the bottom. According to this view, the very fact of a group's oppression proves its inferiority and the inevitable correctness of its low position. In this way each successive immigrant group coming to America was decked out in the garments of "racial" or biological inferiority until the group was sufficiently assimilated, whereupon Anglo-Saxon venom would turn on a new group filling up the space at the bottom. Now two groups remain, neither of which has been assimilated according to the classic American pattern: the "visibles"—blacks and women. It is equally true for both: "it won't wear off."

Yet the greatest obstacle facing those who would organize women remains women's belief in their own inferiority. Just as all subject populations are controlled by their acceptance of the rightness of their own status, so women remain subject because they believe in the rightness of their own oppression. This dilemma is not a fortuitous one, for the entire society is geared to socialize women to believe in and adopt as immutable necessity their traditional and inferior role. From earliest training to the grave, women are constrained and propagandized. Spend an evening at the movies or watching television, and you will see a grotesque figure called woman represented in a hundred variations upon the themes of "children, church, kitchen" or "the chick sex-pot."

For those who believe in the "rights of mankind," the "dignity of man," consider that to make a woman a person, a human being in her own right, you would have to change her sex: imagine Stokely Carmichael "prone and silent"; imagine Mark Rudd as a Laugh-In girl; picture Rennie Davis as Miss America. Such contradictions as these show how pervasive and deep-rooted is the cultural contempt for women, how difficult it is to imagine a woman as a serious human being, or conversely, how empty and degrading is the image of woman that floods the culture.

Countless studies have shown that black acceptance of white stereotypes leads to mutilated identity, to alienation, to rage and self-hatred. Human beings cannot bear in their own hearts the contradictions of those who hold them in contempt. The ideology of male supremacy and its effect upon women merits as serious study as has been given to the effects of prejudice upon Jews, blacks, and immigrant groups.

It is customary to shame those who would draw the parallel between women and blacks by a great show of concern and chest beating over the suffering of black people. Yet this response itself reveals a refined combination of white middle class guilt and male chauvinism, for it overlooks several essential facts. For example, the most oppressed group within the feminine population is made up of black women, many of whom take a dim view of the black male intellectual's adoption of white male attitudes of sexual superiority (an irony too cruel to require comment). Neither are those who make this pious objection to the racial parallel addressing themselves very adequately to the millions of white working class women living at the poverty level, who are not likely to be moved by this middle class guilt-ridden one-upmanship while having to deal with the boss, the factory, or the welfare worker day after day. They are already dangerously resentful of the gains made by blacks, and much of their "racist backlash" stems from the fact that they have been forgotten in the push for social change. Emphasis on the real mechanisms of oppression—on the commonality of the process—is essential lest groups such as these, which should work in alliance, become divided against one another.

White middle class males already struggling with the acknowledgment of their own racism do not relish an added burden of recognition: that to white guilt must soon be added "male." It is therefore understandable that they should refuse to see the harshness of the lives of most women—to honestly face the facts of massive institutionalized discrimination against women. Witness the performance to date: "Take her down off the platform and give her a good fuck," "Petty Bourgeois Revisionist Running Dogs," or in the classic words of a Berkeley male "leader," "Let them eat cock."

Among whites, women remain the most oppressed—and the most unorganized—group. Although they constitute a potential mass base for the radical movement, in terms of movement priorities they are ignored; indeed they might as well be invisible. Far from being an accident, this omission is a direct outgrowth of the solid male supremacist beliefs of white radical and left-liberal men. Even now, faced with both fact and agitation, leftist men find the idea of placing any serious priority upon women so outrageous, such a degrading notion, that they respond with a virulence far out of proportion to the modest requests of movement women. This only shows that women must stop wasting their time worrying about the chauvinism of men in the movement and focus instead on their real priority: organizing women.

Marriage: Genesis of Women's Rebellion

The institution of marriage is the chief vehicle for the perpetuation of the oppression of women; it is through the role of wife that the subjugation of women is maintained. In a very real way the role of wife has been the genesis of women's rebellion throughout history.

Looking at marriage from a detached point of view one may well ask why anyone gets married, much less women. One answer lies in the economics of women's position, for women are so occupationally limited that drudgery in the home is considered to be infinitely superior to drudgery in the factory. Secondly, women themselves have no independent social status. Indeed, there is no clearer index of the social worth of a woman in this society than the fact that she has none in her own right. A woman is first defined by the man to whom she is attached, but more particularly by the man she marries, and secondly by the children she bears and rears—hence the anxiety over sexual attractiveness, the frantic scramble for boyfriends and husbands. Having obtained and married a man the race is then on to have children, in order that their attractiveness and accomplishments may add more social worth. In a woman, not having children is seen as an incapacity somewhat akin to impotence in a man.

Beneath all of the pressures of the sexual marketplace and the marital status game, however, there is a far more sinister organization of economic exploitation and psychological mutilation. The housewife role, usually defined in terms of the biological duty of a woman to reproduce and her "innate" suitability for a nurturant and companionship role, is actually crucial to industrial capitalism in an advanced state of technological development. In fact, the housewife (some 44 million women of all classes, ethnic groups and races) provides, unpaid, absolutely essential services and labor. In turn, her assumption of all household duties makes it possible for the man to spend the majority of his time at the workplace.

It is important to understand the social and economic exploitation of the married woman, since the real productivity of her labor is denied by the commonly held assumption that she is dependent on her husband, exchanging her keep for emotional and nurturant services. Margaret Benston, a radical women's liberation leader, points out: "In sheer quantity, household labor, including child care, constitutes a huge amount of socially necessary production. Nevertheless, in a society based on commodity production, it is not usually considered even as 'real work' since it is outside of trade and the marketplace. This assignment of household work as the function of a special category 'women' means that this group *does* stand in a different relationship to production. . . . The material basis for the inferior status of women is to be found in just this definition of women. In a society in which money determines value, women are a group who work outside the money economy. Their work is not worth money, is therefore valueless, is therefore not even real work. And women themselves, who do this valueless work, can hardly be expected to be worth as much as men, who work for money."

Women are essential to the economy not only as free labor, but also as consumers. The American system of capitalism spends for its survival on the consumption of vast amounts of socially wasteful goods, and a prime target for the unloading of this waste is the housewife. She is the purchasing agent for the family, but beyond that she is eager to buy because her own identity depends on her accomplishments as a consumer and her ability to satisfy the wants of her husband and children. This is not, of course, to say that she has any power in the economy. Although she spends the wealth, she does not own or control it—it simply passes through her hands.

In addition to their role as housewives and consumers, increasing numbers of women are taking outside employment. These women leave the home to join an exploited labor force, only to return at night to assume the double burden of housework on top of wage work—that is, they are forced to work at two full-time jobs. No man is required or expected to take on such a burden. The result: two workers from one household in the labor force with no cutback in essential female functions—three for the price of two, quite a bargain.

Frederick Engels, now widely read in women's liberation, argues that, regardless of her status in the larger society, within the context of the family the woman's relationship to the man is one of proletariat to bourgeoisie. One consequence of this class division in the family is to weaken the capacity of men and women oppressed by the society to struggle together against it.

In all classes and groups, the institution of marriage functions to a greater or lesser degree to oppress women; the unity of women of different classes hinges upon our understanding of that common oppression. The 19th century women's movement refused to deal with marriage and sexuality, and chose instead to fight for the vote and elevate the feminine mystique to a political ideology. That decision retarded the movement for decades. But 1969 is not 1889. For one thing, there now exist alternatives to marriage. The most original and creative politics of the women's movement has come from a direct confrontation with the issue of marriage and sexuality. The cultural revolution—experimentation with life-styles, communal living, collective child-rearing—have all come from the rebellion against dehumanized sexual relationships, against the notion of women as sexual commodities, against the constriction and spiritual strangulation inherent in the role of wife.

Lessons have been learned from the failures of the earlier movement as well. The feminine mystique is no longer mistaken for politics, nor gaining the vote for winning human rights. Women are now all together at the bottom of the work world, and the basis exists for a common focus of struggle for all women in American society. It remains for the movement to understand this, to avoid the mistakes of the past, to respond creatively to the possibilities of the present.

Women's oppression, although rooted in the institution of marriage, does not stop at the kitchen or the bedroom door. Indeed, the economic exploitation of women in the workplace is the most commonly recognized aspect of the oppression of women.

Most women who enter the labor force do not work for "pin money" or "self-fulfillment." Sixty-two per cent of all women working in 1967 were doing so out of economic need (i.e., were either alone or with husbands earning less than $5000 a year). In 1963, 36 per cent of American families had an income of less than $5000 a year. Women from these families work because they must; they contribute 35 to 40 per cent of the family's total income when working full-time, and 15 to 20 per cent when working part-time.

Despite their need, however, women have always represented the most exploited sector of the industrial labor force. Child and female labor were introduced during the early stages of industrial capitalism, at a time when most men were gainfully employed in crafts. As industrialization developed and craft jobs were eliminated, men entered the industrial labor force, driving women and children into the lowest categories of work and pay. Indeed, the position of women and children industrial workers was so pitiful, and their wages so small, that the craft unions refused to organize them. Even when women organized themselves and engaged in militant strikes and labor agitation—from the shoemakers of Lynn, Massachusetts, to the International Ladies' Garment Workers and their great strike of 1909—male union-ists continued to ignore their needs. As a result of this male supremacy in the unions, women remain essentially unorganized, despite the fact that they are becoming an ever larger part of the labor force.

The trend is clearly toward increasing numbers of women entering the work force: women represented 55 per cent of the growth of the total labor force in 1962, and the number of working women rose from 16.9 million in 1957 to 24 million in 1962. There is every indication that the number of women in the labor force will continue to grow as rapidly in the future.

Job discrimination against women exists in all sectors of work, even in occupations which are predominantly made up of women. This discrimination is reinforced in the field of education, where women are being short-changed at a time when the job market demands higher educational levels. In 1962, for example, while women con-stituted 53 per cent of the graduating high school class, only 42 per cent of the entering college class were women. Only one in three people who received a B.A. or M.A. in that year was a woman, and only one in ten who received a Ph.D was a woman. These figures represent a decline in educational achievement for women since the 1930's, when women received two out of five of the B.A. and M.A. degrees given, and one out of seven of the Ph.Ds. While there has been a dramatic increase in the number of people, including women, who go to college, women have not kept pace with men in terms of educational achievement. Furthermore, women have lost ground in professional employment. In 1960 only 22 per cent of the faculty and other professional staff at colleges and universities were women—down from 28 per cent in 1949, 27 per cent in 1930, 26 per cent in 1920. 1960 does beat 1919 with only 20 per cent—"you've come a long way, baby"—right back to where you started! In other professional categories: 10 per cent of all scientists are women, 7 per cent of all physicians, 3 per cent of all lawyers, and 1 per cent of all engineers.

Even when women do obtain an education, in many cases it does them little good. Women, whatever their educational level, are concentrated in the lower paying occupations. The figures in Chart A tell a story that most women know and few men will admit: most women are forced to work at clerical jobs, for which they are paid, on the average, $1600 less per year than men doing the same work. Working class women in the service and operative (semi-skilled) categories, making up 30 per cent of working women, are paid $1900 less per year on the average than are men. Of all

CHART A

Comparative Statistics for Men and Women in the Labor Force, 1960

Occupation	Percentage of working women in each occupation category	Income of Year Round Full Time Workers		Numbers of Workers in Millions	
		Women	Men	Women	Men
Professional	13%	$4358	$7115	3	5
Managers, Officials and Proprietors	5	3514	7241	1	5
Clerical	31	3586	5247	7	3
Operatives	15	2970	4977	4	9
Sales	7	2389	5842	2	3
Service	15	2340	4089	3	3
Private Household	10	1156	—	2	—

SOURCES: U.S. Department of Commerce, Bureau of the Census: "Current Population Reports," P-60, No. 37, and U.S. Department of Labor, Bureau of Labor Statistics and U.S. Department of Commerce, Bureau of the Census.

working women, only 13 per cent are professionals (including low-pay and low-status work such as teaching, nursing and social work), and they earn $1600 less per year than do professional men. Household workers, the lowest category of all, are predominantly women (over 2 million) and predominantly black and third world, earning for their labor barely over $1000 per year.

Not only are women forced onto the lowest rungs of the occupational ladder, they are in the lowest income levels as well. The most constant and bitter injustice experienced by all women is the income differential. While women might passively accept low status jobs, limited opportunities for advancement, and discrimination in the factory, office and university, they choke finally on the daily fact that the male worker next to them earns more, and usually does less. In 1965 the median wage or salary income of year-round full-time women workers was only 60 per cent that of men, a 4 per cent loss since 1955. Twenty-nine per cent of working women earned less than $3000 a year as compared with 11 per cent of the men; 43 per cent of the women earned from $3000 to $5000 a year as compared with 19 per cent of the men; and 9 per cent of the women earned $7000 or more as compared with 43 per cent of the men.

What most people do not know is that in certain respects, women suffer more than do non-white men, and that black and third world women suffer most of all.

Women, regardless of race, are more disadvantaged than are men, including non-white men. White women earn $2600 less than white men and $1500 less than non-white men. The brunt of the inequality is carried by 2.5 million non-white women, 94 per cent of whom are black. They earn $3800 less than white men, $1900 less than non-white men, and $1200 less than white women.

There is no more bitter paradox in the racism of this country than that the white man, articulating the male supremacy of the white male middle class, should provide the rationale for the oppression of black women by black men. Black women constitute the largest minority in the United States, and they are the most disadvantaged group in the labor force. The further oppression of black women will not liberate black men, for black women were never the oppressors of their men—that is a myth

CHART B
Median Annual Wages for Men and Women
by Race, 1960

Workers	Median Annual Wage
Males, White	$5137
Males, Non-White	$3075
Females, White	$2537
Females, Non-White	$1276

SOURCE: U.S. Department of Commerce, Bureau of the Census. Also see: President's Commission on the Status of Women, 1963.

of the liberal white man. The oppression of black men comes from institutionalized racism and economic exploitation: from the world of the white man. Consider the following facts and figures.

The percentage of black working women has always been proportionately greater than that of white women. In 1900, 41 per cent of black women were employed, as compared to 17 per cent for white women. In 1963, the proportion of black women employed was still a fourth greater than that of whites. In 1960, 44 per cent of black married women with children under six years were in the labor force, in contrast to 29 per cent for white women. While job competition requires even higher levels of education, the bulk of illiterate women are black. On the whole, black women—who often have the greatest need for employment—are the most discriminated against in terms of opportunity. Forced by an oppressive and racist society to carry unbelievably heavy economic and social burdens, black women stand at the bottom of that society, doubly marked by the caste signs of color and sex.

The rise of new agitation for the occupational equality of women also coincided with the re-entry of the "lost generation"—the housewives of the 1950's—into the job market. Women from middle class backgrounds, faced with an "empty nest" (children grown or in school) and a widowed or divorced rate of one-fourth to one-third of all marriages, returned to the workplace in large numbers. But once there they discovered that women, middle class or otherwise, are the last hired, the lowest paid, the least often promoted, and the first fired. Furthermore, women are more likely to suffer job discrimination on the basis of age, so the widowed and divorced suffer particularly, even though their economic need to work is often urgent. Age discrimination also means that the option of work after child-rearing is limited. Even highly qualified older women find themselves forced into low-paid, unskilled or semi-skilled work—if they are lucky enough to find a job in the first place.

The realities of the work world for most middle class women—that they become members of the working class, like it or not—are understandably distant to many young men and women in college who have never had to work, and who tend to think of the industrial "proletariat" as a revolutionary force, to the exclusion of "bourgeois" working women. Their image of the "pampered middle class woman" is factually incorrect and politically naive. It is middle class women forced into working class life who are often the first to become conscious of the contradiction between the "American Dream" and their daily experience.

Faced with discrimination on the job—after being forced into the lower levels of the occupational structure—millions of women are inescapably presented with the fundamental contradictions in their unequal treatment and their massive exploitation. The rapid growth of women's liberation as a movement is related in part to the exploitation of working women in all occupational categories.

Male supremacy, marriage, and the structure of wage labor—each of these aspects of women's oppression has been crucial to the resurgence of the women's struggle. It must be abundantly clear that radical social change must occur before there can be significant improvement in the social position of women. Some form of socialism is a minimum requirement, considering the changes that must come in the institutions of marriage and the family alone. The intrinsic radicalism of the struggle for women's liberation necessarily links women with all other oppressed groups.

The heart of the movement, as in all freedom movements, rests in women's knowledge, whether articulated or still only an illness without a name, that they are not inferior—not chicks, nor bunnies, nor quail, nor cows, nor bitches, nor ass, nor meat. Women hear the litany of their own dehumanization each day. Yet all the same, women know that male supremacy is a lie. They know they are not animals or sexual objects or commodities. They know their lives are mutilated, because they see within themselves a promise of creativity and personal integration. Feeling the contradiction between the essentially creative and self-actualizing human being within her, and the cruel and degrading less-than-human role she is compelled to play, a woman begins to perceive the falseness of what her society has forced her to be. And once she perceives this, she knows that she must fight.

Women must learn the meaning of rage, the violence that liberates the human spirit. The rhetoric of invective is an equally essential stage, for in discovering and venting their rage against the enemy—and the enemy in everyday life is men—women also experience the justice of their own violence. They learn the first lessons in their own latent strength. Women must learn to know themselves as revolutionaries. They must become hard and strong in their determination, while retaining their humanity and tenderness.

There is a rage that impels women into a total commitment to women's liberation. That ferocity stems from a denial of mutilation; it is a cry for life, a cry for the liberation of the spirit. Roxanne Dunbar, surely one of the most impressive women in the movement, conveys the feelings of many: "We are damaged—we women, we oppressed, we disinherited. There are very few who are not damaged, and they rule. . . . The oppressed trust those who rule more than they trust themselves, because self-contempt emerges from powerlessness. Anyway, few oppressed people believe that life could be much different. . . . We are damaged and we have the right to hate and have contempt and to kill and to scream. But for what? . . . Do we want the oppressor to admit he is wrong, to withdraw his misuse of us? He is only too happy to admit guilt—then do nothing but try to absorb and exorcize the new thought. . . . That does not make up for what I have lost, what I never had, and what all those others who are worse off than I never had. . . . Nothing will compensate for the irreparable harm it has done to my sisters. . . . How could we possibly settle for anything remotely less, even take a crumb in the meantime less, than total annihilation of a system which systematically destroys half its people. . . ."

Chapter Six

Radical Feminism

Ti-Grace Atkinson

Almania Barbour, a black militant women in Philadelphia, once pointed out to me: "The women's movement is the first in history with a war on and no enemy." I winced. It was an obvious criticism. I fumbled about in my mind for an answer: surely the enemy must have been defined at some time. Otherwise, what had we been shooting at for the last couple of years? Into the air? Only two responses came to me, although in looking for those two I realized that it was a question carefully avoided. The first and by far the most frequent answer was "society." The second, infrequently and always furtively, was "men". If "society" is the enemy, what could that mean? If women are being oppressed, there's only one group left over to be doing the oppressing: men. Then why call them "society"? Could "society" mean the "institutions" that oppress women? But institutions must be maintained, and the same question arises: by whom? The answer to "who is the enemy?" is so obvious that the interesting issue quickly becomes "why has it been avoided?" The master might tolerate many reforms in slavery but none that would threaten his essential role as master. Women have known this, and since "men" and "society" are in effect synonymous, they have feared confronting him. Without this confrontation and detailed understanding of what *his* battle strategy has been that has kept us so successfully pinned down, the "women's movement" is worse than useless: it invites backlash from men, and no progress for women.

There has never been a feminist analysis. While discontent among women and the attempt to resolve this discontent have often implied that women form a class, no political or *causal* class analysis has followed. To rephrase my last point, the persecution of women has never been taken as the starting point for a political analysis of society.

Considering that the last massing of discontent among women continued some 70 years (1850–1920) and spread the world and that the recent accumulation of grievances began some three years ago here in America, the lack of a structural understanding of the problem is at first sight incomprehensible. It is the understanding of the *reasons* for this devastating omission and of the *implications* of the problem that forces one to "radical feminism."

Women who have tried to solve their problems as a class have proposed not solutions but dilemmas. The traditional feminists want equal rights for women with men. But on what grounds? If women serve a different *function* from men in society, wouldn't this necessarily affect women's "rights"? For example, do *all* women have the "right" not to bear children? Traditional feminism is caught in the dilemma of demanding equal treatment for unequal functions, because it is unwilling to challenge political (functional) classification by sex. Radical women, on the other hand, grasp that women as a group somehow fit into a political analysis of society, but err in refusing to explore the significance of the fact that women form a class, the uniqueness of this class, and the implications of this description to the system of political classes. Both traditional feminists and radical women have evaded questioning any part of their *raison d'etere*: women are a class, and the terms that make up that initial assumption must be examined.

The feminist dilemma is that it is as women—or "females"—that women are persecuted, just as it was as slaves—or "blacks"—that slaves were persecuted in America: in order to improve their condition, those individuals who are today defined as women must eradicate their own definition. Women must, in a sense, commit suicide, and the journey from womanhood to a society of individuals is hazardous. The feminist dilemma is that we have the most to do, and the least to do it with; we must create, as no other group in history has been forced to do, from the very beginning.

The "battle of the sexes" is a commonplace, both over time and distance. But it is an inaccurate description of what has been happening. A "battle" implies some balance of powers, whereas when one side suffers all the losses, such as in raids (often referred to as the "rape" of an area), that is called a *massacre*. Women have been massacred as human beings over history, and this destiny is entailed by their definition. As women begin massing together, they take the first step from *being* massacred to *engaging in* battle (resistance) and, hopefully, eventually to negotiations—in the very far future—and peace.

When any person or group of persons is being mistreated or, to continue our metaphor, is being attacked, there is a succession of responses or investigations:

1. Depending on the severity of the attack (short of an attack on life), the victim determines how much damage was done and what it was done with.
2. Where is the attack coming from?—from whom?—located where?
3. How can you win the immediate battle?—defensive measures?—holding actions?
4. Why did he attack you?
5. How can you win (end) the war?—offensive measures.—moving within his boundaries.

These first five questions are necessary but should be considered diplomatic maneuvers. They have never been answered by the so-called "women's movement," and for this reason I think one cannot properly call that movement "political," it could not have had any direction relevant to women as a class.

If diplomacy fails, that is, if your enemy refuses to stop attacking you, you must force him to stop. This requires a strategy, and this strategy requires a map of the relevant landscape, including such basic information as

1. Who is the enemy?
2. Where is he located?
3. Is he getting outside support?—material?—manpower?—from whom?
4. Where are his forces massed?
5. What's the best ammunition to knock them out?
6. What weapons is he using?
7. How can you conteract them?
8. What is your plan of attack on him to force diplomatic negotiations?—program of action (including priorities).—techniques.

I am using some military terminology, and this may seem incongruous. But why should it? We accept the phrase "battle of the sexes." It is the proposal that *women* fight *back* that seems incongruous; it was necessary to program women's psychic structure to non-resistance on their own behalf—for obvious reasons: they make up over half the population of the world.

Without a programmatic analysis, the "women's movement" has been as if running blindly in the general direction of where they *guess* the last missle that just hit them was based. For the first two years of the last organizing, I was very active in this running-blind approach. It's true that we were attacking evils, but why *those* particular evils. Were they the central issues in the persecution of women? There was no map so I couldn't be sure, but I could see no reason to believe that we knew what the key issues were, much less that we were hitting them. It became increasingly clear to me that we were incorporating many of our external problems (e.g., power hierarchies) into our own movement, and in understanding this and beginning to ask myself some of the obvious questions I've listed above, I came to the conclusion that at this time the most radical action that any woman or group of women could take was a feminist analysis. The implications of such analysis is a greater threat to the opposition to human rights for women than all the actions and threatened actions put together up until this time by women.

With this introduction to the significance of a feminist analysis, I will outline what we have so far.

As I mentioned before, the *raison d'etre* of all groups formed around the problem of women is that women are a class. What is meant by that? What is meant by "women" and what is meant by "class"? Does "women" include all women? Some groups have been driven back from the position of *all* women to some proposed "special" class such as "poor" women and eventually concentrated more on economic class than sexual class. But if we're interested in women and how women *qua* women are oppressed, this class must include *all* women. What separates out a particular individual from other individuals as a "woman"? We recognize it's a sexual separation and that this separation has two aspects, "sociological" and "biological." The term for the sociological function is "woman" "wif-man"); the term for the biological function is "female" (to suckle): both terms are descriptive of functions in the interests of someone other than the possessor.

And what is meant by "class"? We've already covered the meaning as the characteristic by which certain individuals are grouped together. In the "women's movement" or "feminism," individuals group together to *act* on behalf of women as a class in opposition to the *class* enemies of women. It is the interaction between classes that defines political action. For this reason I call the feminist analysis a *causal class analysis*.

We have established that women are a political class characterized by a sexual function. It is clear that women, at the present time at any rate, have the *capacity* to bear children. But the question arises: "How did this biological classification become a political classification": how or why did this elaborate superstructure of coercion develop on top of a capacity (which normally implies choice)?

It is generally agreed that women were the first political class. (Children do not properly constitute a political class since the relevant characteristic of its members is unstable for any given member by definition). "Political" classes are usually defined as classes treated by other classes in some special manner distinct from the way other classes are treated. What is frequently omitted is that "political" classes are *artificial*; they define persons *with* certain capacities *by* that capacity, changing the contingent to the necessary, thereby appropriating the *capacity* of an individual as a *function* of society. Df. of "political class"—individuals grouped together by other individuals as a function of grouping individuals, depriving the grouped individuals of their human status. A "function" of society cannot be a free individual: exercising the minimum human rights of physical integrity and freedom of movement.

If women were the first political class and political classes must be defined by individuals outside that class, who defined them, and why, and how? It is reasonable to assume that at some period in history the population was politically undifferentiated; let's call that mass "mankind" (generic). The first dichotomous division of this mass is said to have been on the grounds of sex: male and female. But the genitals per se would be no more grounds for the human race to be divided in two than skin color or height or hair color. The genitals, in connection with a particular activity, have the *capacity* for the initiation of the reproductive process. But, I submit, it was because one half the human race bears the *burden* of the reproductive *process* and because man, the "rational" animal, had the wit to take advantage of that, that the childbearers, or the "beasts of burden," were corraled into a political class: equivocating the biologically contingent burden into a political (or necessary) penalty, thereby modifying these individuals' definition from the human to the functional, or animal.

There is no justification for using any individual as a function of others. Didn't *all* members of society have the right to decide if they even *wanted* to reproduce? Because one half of humanity was and still is forced to bear the burden of reproduction at the will of the other half, the first political class is defined not by its sex—sexuality was only relevant originally as a means to reproduction—but by the function of being the *container* of the reproductive process.

Because women have been taught to believe that men have protective feelings towards women (men have protective feelings towards their functions (property) *Let* other human beings!), we women are shocked by these discoveries and ask ourselves *why* men took and continue to take advantage of us. Some people say that men are naturally, or biologically, aggressive. But this leaves us at an impasse. If the values of society are power oriented, there is no chance that men would agree to be medicated into an humane state. The other alternative that has been suggested is to eliminate men as biologically incapable of humane relationships and therefore a menace to society. I can sympathize with the frustration and rage that leads to this suggestion, but the proposal as I understand it is that men constitute a social disease, and that by "men" is meant those individuals with certain typical genital characteristics. These genital characteristics are held to determine the organism in every biochemical respect thus determining the psychic structure as well. It may be that as in other mental derangements, and I do believe that men behave in a mentally deranged manner towards women, there is a biochemical correspondence but this would be utlimately behaviorally determined not genetically.

I believe that the sex roles of both male and female must be destroyed, not the individuals who happen to possess either a penis or a vagina, or both, or neither. But many men I have spoken with see little to choose between the two positions and feel that without the role they'd just as soon die. Certainly it is the master who resists the abolition of slavery, especially when he is offered no recompense in power. I think that the *need* men have for the role of oppressor is the source and foundation of all human oppression: they suffer from a disease peculiar to mankind which I call "metaphysical cannibalism," and men must at the very least cooperate in curing themselves.

Date (April 1969)

Perhaps the pathology of oppression begins with just that characteristic which distinguishes mankind from the other species: rationality. It has been proposed before that the basic condition of man is Angst: the knowledge and constant awareness that he will die and is thus trapped by existence in an inescapable dilemma. My proposal is more fundamental.

Man is not aware of the possibility of death until he is able to put together certain abstractions, e.g., descriptions of events, and with the relevant descriptive connectives. It requires a fairly sophisticated intellect to be able to extrapolate from the description of an event to one's own condition, that is, from another person's *experience* to one's own essential definition. If instead of asking ourselves what particular conclusion rationality might arrive at, we ask what the nature of this distinguishing human characteristic is, we come to a more fundamental question.

The distinction between the nature of the animal and human brain seems to be that while an animal can imagine, that is, can mentally image some object before its eyes in some familiar situation, an animal cannot *construct* with its imagination. An animal cannot imagine a new situation made up of ingredients combined together for the first time with each initiating consequences for the other ingredients to produce the new situation.

Man's rationality is distinguished by its "constructive imagination," and this constructive imagination has been a mixed blessing. The first experience of Man in His existence is usually called "awareness" or "consciousness"; we are *sensible*; our senses are operating unrestricted by external coercions; (so far our description is also true of animals). What probably is first *known* to us as a distinct thing is our own body, since it is the object most consistently within our perception. As we see other objects with parts similar to our first object of perception, I think we can observe our first operation of rationality: we "imagine" that the second observation has *consequences* for the first observation. We see another human being as physically complete and autonomous (powerful) and ourselves as abbreviated thus incomplete (powerless). We can never see ourselves as fleshly integral units; we feel and sense and analogize that we are each independent units, but we can never completely perceive *ourselves* as such. Each of us begins with this initial insecurity.

Rational action (intention) requires some sense of individual autonomy. We have choice only to the degree that we are physically free, and every Man by His nature feels ambiguity on this point. In addition, Man realizes early in His maturity that there is an enormous gap between what He can do and what He can *imagine* done. The powers of His body and the powers of His mind are in conflict within one organism; they are mockeries of each other. This second factor adds frustration to the first factor of insecurity.

We now posit Man as insecure and frustrated. He has two needs: (1) substance, as autonomous body—necessarily outside Himself, and (2) the alleviation of His frustration (the suppression of feeling) through anger—*oppression*. When we understand these two consequences peculiar to Man's nature, we can begin to understand the nature of "politics."[1]

Man feels the need of something like Himself, an "extension." This presents a problem since *all* Men suffer this same need: all Men are looking for potency—the substantive power to close the gap between their bodily and mental powers. It seems clear that, once the resolution takes this external direction, some Men—ideally half (thus, one for each)—would have to catch *other* Men in some temporary depression of consciousness (when matured, rationality or constructive imagination) and at some physical disadvantage. This temporary depletion of Self provides the opportunity to simultaneously devour the mind of a member of the selected class and to appropriate their substance to oneself. It is this process that I call "metaphysical cannibalism." It is to eat one's own kind, especially that aspect considered most potent to the victim while alive, and to destroy the evidence that the aggressor and the victim are the Same. The principle of metaphysical cannibalism seemed to meet both needs of Man: to gain potency (power) and to vent frustration (hostility).

Some psychic relief was achieved by one half the human race at the expense of the other half. Men neatly decimated mankind by one half when they took advantage of the *social* disability of those men who bore the burden of the reproductive process; men invaded the being of those individuals now defined as functions, or "females," appropriated their human characteristic and occupied their bodies. The original "rape" was political, the robbing of one half of Mankind of its Humanity; the sexual connotations to the term no doubt grew out of the characterizations made later of the Men in the original action. This rape in its essential features has been reenacted and rationalized and justified ever since. Firstly, those Men called women have been anchored to their position as victim by men devising numerous direct variations on women's capture, consolidating women's imprisonment. Secondly, men have devised indirect variations on the original crime via the principle of oppression against other men. But all of these variations—what we call class systems and their supportive institutions—are motivated by Man's nature, and all political change will result in nothing but other variations on metaphysical cannibalism—rape—until we find a human and equitable alternative to Man's dilemma.

The male-female distinction was the beginning of the role system, wherein some persons function for others. This primary distinction should properly be referred to as the Oppressor (male)—Oppressed (female) distinction, the first political distinction. Women were the first political class and the beginning of the class system.

Certainly in the pathology of oppression, it is the agent of oppression who must be analyzed and dealt with: he is responsible for the cultivation and spread of the disease. Still a question arises: how is it that, once the temporary susceptibility to disease (aggression) has passed, the patient does not spontaneously recover? It must be that the external attack aggravates in the victim a latent disorganization which grows and flourishes in response to and finally in tandem with the pathology imposed from outside. The disease drawn out and cultivated from within can finally maintain the original victim in a pathological state with fewer external pressures. I propose that the latent disorganization in "females" is the same disorganization—dilemma— from which "males" opted for metaphysical cannibalism. The role of the Oppressor (the male role) is to attempt to resolve his dilemma at the expense of others by destroying their humanity (appropriating the rationality of the Oppressed). The role of the Oppressed (the female-woman role) is to resolve her dilemma by self-destruction (bodily destruction or insanity). Given an Oppressor—the will for power—the natural response for its counterpart, the Oppressed (given any shade of remaining Self-consciousness), is self-annihilation. Since the purpose and nature of metaphysical cannibalism is the appropriation of and extension *to* substance, bodily self-destruction is uncommon in comparison with mental escapes. While men can "cannibalize" the consciousness of women as far as human self-construction for the woman is concerned, men get no direct use from this except insofar as they *believe* it gives them magic powers. But rationality imprisoned must destroy itself.

Metaphysical cannibalism does not solve the dilemma posed by human rationality for either the Oppressor or the Oppressed. The Oppressor can only whet his appetite for power by external measures (like drugs to dull the symptom of pain) and thus increases his disease and symptoms; the Oppressed floats in a limbo of unconsciousness driven there by the immobilization of her vital organ-rejecting life but not quite dead—sensible enough to still feel the pain.

The most common female escape is the psycho-pathological condition of love. It is a euphoric state of fantasy in which the victim transforms her oppressor into her redeemer: she turns her natural hostility towards the aggressor against the remnants of herself—her Consciousness—and sees her counterpart in contrast to herself as all-powerful (as he is by now at her expense). The combination of his power, her self-hatred, and the hope for a life that is self-justifying—the goal of all living creatures—results in a yearning for her stolen life—her self—that is the delusion and poignancy of love. "Love" is the natural response of the victim to the rapist. What is extremely difficult and "unnatural," but necessary, is for the Oppressed to cure themselves (destroy the female role), to throw off the Oppressor, and to help the Oppressor to cure himself (to destroy the male role). It is superhuman, but the only alternative—the elimination of males as a biological group—is subhuman.

Politics and political theory revolve around this paradigm case of the Oppressor and the Oppressed. The theory and the practices can be divided into two parts: those institutions which directly reinforce the paradigm case of oppression, and those systems and institutions which reinforce the principle later extrapolated from this model.

(May 1969)

NOTE

1. While I cannot go into it here in detail, I want to make clear that we must use our constructive imagination to devise a moral alternative. Such an alternative must provide an internal solution to the feelings of inadequacy. The solution would probably depend upon just that faculty that initiated the original dilemma, the human imagination. Rationality will have to construct the substance sufficient for individual autonomy from the inside. This would resolve both the problem of substantive incompleteness and the reconciliation of mind and body.

Chapter Seven

The Dialectic of Sex

Shulamith Firestone

Sex class is so deep as to be invisible. Or it may appear as a superficial inequality, one that can be solved by merely a few reforms, or perhaps by the full integration of women into the labor force. But the reaction of the common man, woman, and child—"*That?* Why you can't change *that!* You must be out of your mind!"—is the closest to the truth. We are talking about something every bit as deep as that. This gut reaction—the assumption that, even when they don't know it, feminists are talking about changing a fundamental biological condition—is an honest one. That so profound a change cannot be easily fit into traditional categories of thought, e.g., "political," is not because these categories do not apply but because they are not big enough: radical feminism bursts through them. If there were another word more all-embracing than *revolution* we would use it.

Until a certain level of evolution had been reached and technology had achieved its present sophistication, to question fundamental biological conditions was insanity. Why should a woman give up her precious seat in the cattle car for a bloody struggle she could not hope to win? But, for the first time in some countries, the preconditions for feminist revolution exist—indeed, the situation is beginning to *demand* such a revolution.

The first women are fleeing the massacre, and, shaking and tottering, are beginning to find each other. Their first move is a careful joint observation, to resensitize a fractured consciousness. This is painful: No matter how many levels of consciousness one reaches, the problem always goes deeper. It is everywhere. The division yin and yang pervades all culture, history, economics, nature itself; modern Western versions of sex discrimination are only the most recent layer. To so heighten one's sensitivity to sexism presents problems far worse than the black militant's new awareness of racism: Feminists have to question, not just all of *Western* culture, but the organization of culture itself, and further, even the very organization of nature. Many women give up in despair: if *that's* how deep it goes they don't want to know. Others continue strengthening and enlarging the movement, their painful sensitivity to female oppression existing for a purpose: eventually to eliminate it.

Before we can act to change a situation, however, we must know how it has arisen and evolved, and through what institutions it now operates. Engels' "[We must] examine the historic succession of events from which the antagonism has sprung in order to discover in the conditions thus created the means of ending the conflict." For feminist revolution we shall need an analysis of the dynamics of sex war as comprehensive as the Marx-Engels analysis of class antagonism was for the economic revolution. More comprehensive. For we are dealing with a larger problem, with an oppression that goes back beyond recorded history to the animal kingdom itself.

In creating such an analysis we can learn a lot from Marx and Engels: Not their literal opinions about women—about the condition of women as an oppressed class they know next to nothing, recognizing it only where it overlaps with economics—but rather their analytic *method*.

Marx and Engels outdid their socialist forerunners in that they developed a method of analysis which was both *dialectical* and *materialist*. The first in centuries to view history dialectically, they saw the world as process, a natural flux of action and reaction, of opposites yet inseparable and interpenetrating. Because they were able to perceive history as movie rather than as snapshot, they attempted to avoid falling into the stagnant "metaphysical" view that had trapped so many other great minds. (This sort of analysis itself may be a product of the sex division.) They combined this view of the dynamic interplay of historical forces with a materialist one, that is, they attempted for the first time to put historical and cultural change on a real basis, to trace the development of economic classes to organic causes. By understanding thoroughly the mechanics of history, they hoped to show men how to master it.

Socialist thinkers prior to Marx and Engels, such as Fourier, Owen, and Bebel, had been able to do no more than moralize about existing social inequalities, positing an ideal world where class privilege and exploitation should not exist—in the same way that early feminist thinkers posited a world where male privilege and exploitation ought not exist—by mere virtue of good will. In both cases, because the early thinkers did not really understand how the social injustice had evolved, maintained itself, or could be eliminated, their ideas existed in a cultural vacuum, utopian. Marx and Engels, on the other hand, attempted a scientific approach to history. They traced the class conflict to its real economic origins, projecting an economic solution based on objective economic preconditions already present: the seizure by the proletariat of the means of production would lead to a communism in which government had withered away, no longer needed to repress the lower class for the sake of the higher. In the classless society the interests of every individual would be synonymous with those of the larger society.

But the doctrine of historical materialism, much as it was a brilliant advance over previous historical analysis, was not the complete answer, as later events bore out. For though Marx and Engels grounded their theory in reality, it was only a *partial* reality. Here is Engels' strictly economic definition of historical materialism from *Socialism: Utopian or Scientific:*

> Historical materialism is that view of the course of history which seeks the *ultimate* cause and the great moving power of all historical events in the economic development of society, in the changes of the modes of production and exchange, in the consequent division of society into distinct classes, and in the struggles of these classes against one another. (Italics mine)

Further, he claims:

> ... that all past history with the exception of the primitive stages was the history of
> class struggles; that these warring classes of society are always the products of the modes
> of production and exchange—in a word, of the economic conditions of their time; that
> the *economic* structure of society always furnishes the real basis, starting from which we
> can alone work out the *ultimate* explanation of the whole superstructure of juridical
> and political institutions as well as of the religious, philosophical, and other ideas of a
> given historical period. (Italics mine)

It would be a mistake to attempt to explain the oppression of women according to
this strictly economic interpretation. The class analysis is a beautiful piece of work,
but limited: although correct in a linear sense, it does not go deep enough. There is
a whole sexual substratum of the historical dialectic that Engels at times dimly
perceives, but because he can see sexuality only through an economic filter, reducing
everything to that, he is unable to evaluate in its own right.

Engels did observe that the original division of labor was between man and woman
for the purposes of child-breeding; that within the family the husband was the owner,
the wife the means of production, the children the labor; and that reproduction of
the human species was an important economic system distinct from the means of
production.[1]

But Engels has been given too much credit for these scattered recognitions of the
oppression of women as a class. In fact he acknowledged the sexual class system only
where it overlapped and illuminated his economic construct. Engels didn't do so well
even in this respect. But Marx was worse: There is a growing recognition of Marx's
bias against women (a cultural bias shared by Freud as well as all men of culture),
dangerous if one attempts to squeeze feminism into an orthodox Marxist
framework—freezing what were only incidental insights of Marx and Engels about
sex class into dogma. Instead, we must enlarge historical materialism to *include* the
strictly Marxian, in the same way that the physics of relativity did not invalidate
Newtonian physics so much as it drew a circle around it, limiting its application—
but only through comparison—to a smaller sphere. For an economic diagnosis
traced to ownership of the means of production, even of the means of reproduction,
does not explain everything. There is a level of reality that does not stem directly
from economics.

The assumption that, beneath economics, reality is psychosexual is often rejected
as ahistorical by those who accept a dialectical materialist view of history because it
seems to land us back where Marx began: groping through a fog of utopian hypotheses, philosophical systems that might be right, that might be wrong (there is no way
to tell), systems that explain concrete historical developments by *a priori* categories
of thought; historical materialism, however, attempted to explain "knowing" by
"being" and not vice versa.

But there is still an untried third alternative: We can attempt to develop a
materialist view of history based on sex itself.

The early feminist theorists were to a materialist view of sex what Fourier, Bebel,
and Owen were to a materialist view of class. By and large, feminist theory has been

as inadequate as were the early feminist attempts to correct sexism. This was to be expected. The problem is so immense that, at first try, only the surface could be skimmed, the most blatant inequalities described. Simone de Beauvoir was the only one who came close to—who perhaps has done—the definitive analysis. Her profound work *The Second Sex*—which appeared as recently as the early fifties to a world convinced that feminism was dead—for the first time attempted to ground feminism in its historical base. Of all feminist theorists De Beauvoir is the most comprehensive and far-reaching, relating feminism to the best ideas in our culture.

It may be this virtue is also her one failing: she is almost too sophisticated, too knowledgeable. Where this becomes a weakness—and this is still certainly debatable— is in her rigidly existentialist interpretation of feminism (one wonders how much Sartre had to do with this). This in view of the fact that all cultural systems, including existentialism, are themselves determined by the sex dualism. She says:

> Man never thinks of himself without thinking of the Other; he views the world under the sign of duality *which is not in the first place sexual in character*. But being different from man, who sets himself up as the Same, it is naturally to the category of the Other that woman is consigned; the Other includes woman. (Italics mine)

Perhaps she has overshot her mark: Why postulate a fundamental Hegelian concept of Otherness as the final explanation—and then carefully document the biological and historical circumstances that have pushed the class "women" into such a category—when one has never seriously considered the much simpler and more likely possibility that this fundamental dualism sprang from the sexual division itself? To posit *a priori* categories of thought and existence—"Otherness," "Transcendence," "Immanence"—into which history then falls may not be necessary. Marx and Engels had discovered that these philosophical categories themselves grew out of history.

Before assuming such categories, let us first try to develop an analysis in which biology itself—procreation—is at the origin of the dualism. The immediate assumption of the layman that the unequal division of the sexes is "natural" may be well-founded. We need not immediately look beyond this. Unlike economic class, sex class sprang directly from a biological reality: men and women were created different, and not equally privileged. Although, as De Beauvoir points out, this difference of itself did not necessitate the development of a class system—the domination of one group by another—the reproductive *functions* of these differences did. The biological family is an inherently unequal power distribution. The need for power leading to the development of classes arises from the psychosexual formation of each individual according to this basic imbalance, rather than, as Freud, Norman O. Brown, and others have, once again overshooting their mark, postulated, some irreducible conflict of Life against Death, Eros vs. Thanatos.

The *biological family*—the basic reproductive unit of male/female/infant, in whatever form of social organization—is characterized by these fundamental—if not immutable—facts:

1. That women throughout history before the advent of birth control were at the continual mercy of their biology—menstruation, menopause, and "female ills,"

constant painful childbirth, wetnursing and care of infants, all of which made them dependent on males (whether brother, father, husband, lover, or clan, government, community-at-large) for physical survival.

2. That human infants take an even longer time to grow up than animals, and thus are helpless and, for some short period at least, dependent on adults for physical survival.

3. That a basic mother/child interdependency has existed in some form in every society, past or present, and thus has shaped the psychology of every mature female and every infant.

4. That the natural reproductive difference between the sexes led directly to the first division of labor at the origins of class, as well as furnishing the paradigm of caste (discrimination based on biological characteristics).

These biological contingencies of the human family cannot be covered over with anthropological sophistries. Anyone observing animals mating, reproducing, and caring for their young will have a hard time accepting the "cultural relativity" line. For no matter how many tribes in Oceania you can find where the connection of the father to fertility is not known, no matter how many matrilineages, no matter how many cases of sex-role reversal, male housewifery, or even empathic labor pains, these facts prove only one thing: the amazing *flexibility* of human nature. But human nature is adaptable *to* something, it is, yes, determined by its environmental conditions. And the biological family that we have described has existed everywhere throughout time. Even in matriarchies where woman's fertility is worshipped, and the father's role is unknown or unimportant, if perhaps not on the genetic father, there is still some dependence of the female and the infant on the male. And though it is true that the nuclear family is only a recent development, one which, as I shall attempt to show, only intensifies the psychological penalties of the biological family, though it is true that throughout history there have been many variations on this biological family, the contingencies I have described existed in all of them, causing specific psychosexual distortions in the human personality.

But to grant that the sexual imbalance of power is biologically based is not to lose our case. We are no longer just animals. And the Kingdom of Nature does not reign absolute. As Simone de Beauvoir herself admits:

> The theory of historical materialism has brought to light some important truths. Humanity is not an animal species, it is a historical reality. Human society is an antiphysis—in a sense it is against nature; it does not passively submit to the presence of nature but rather takes over the control of nature on its own behalf. This arrogation is not an inward, subjective operation; it is accomplished objectively in practical action.

Thus, the "natural" is not necessarily a "human" value. Humanity has begun to outgrow nature: we can no longer justify the maintenance of a discriminatory sex class system on grounds of its origins in Nature. Indeed, for pragmatic reasons alone it is beginning to look as if we *must* get rid of it.

The problem becomes political, demanding more than a comprehensive historical analysis, when one realizes that, though man is increasingly capable of freeing himself from the biological conditions that created his tyranny over women and children, he has little reason to want to give this tyranny up. As Engels said, in the context of economic revolution:

> It is the law of division of labor that lies at the basis of the division into classes [Note that this division itself grew out of a fundamental biological division]. But this does not prevent the ruling class, once having the upper hand, from consolidating its power at the expense of the working class, from turning its social leadership into an intensified exploitation of the masses.

Though the sex class system may have originated in fundamental biological conditions, this does not guarantee once the biological basis of their oppression has been swept away that women and children will be freed. On the contrary, the new technology, especially fertility control, may be used against them to reinforce the entrenched system of exploitation.

So that just as to assure elimination of economic classes requires the revolt of the underclass (the proletariat) and, in a temporary dictatorship, their seizure of the means of *production,* so to assure the elimination of sexual classes requires the revolt of the underclass (women) and the seizure of control of *reproduction:* not only the full restoration to women of ownership of their own bodies, but also their (temporary) seizure of control of human fertility—the new population biology as well as all the social institutions of childbearing and childrearing. And just as the end goal of socialist revolution was not only the elimination of the economic class *privilege* but of the economic class *distinction* itself, so the end goal of feminist revolution must be, unlike that of the first feminist movement, not just the elimination of male *privilege* but of the sex *distinction* itself: genital differences between human beings would no longer matter culturally. (A reversion to an unobstructed *pansexuality*—Freud's "polymorphous perversity"—would probably supersede hetero/homo/bisexuality.) The reproduction of the species by one sex for the benefit of both would be replaced by (at least the option of) artificial reproduction: children would be born to both sexes equally, or independently of either, however one chooses to look at it; the dependence of the child on the mother (and vice versa) would give way to a greatly shortened dependence on a small group of others in general, and any remaining inferiority to adults in physical strength would be compensated for culturally. The division of labor would be ended by the elimination of labor altogether (cybernation). The tyranny of the biological family would be broken.

And with it the psychology of power. As Engels claimed for strictly socialist revolution:

> the existence of not simply this or that ruling class but of any ruling class at all [will have] become an obsolete anachronism.

That socialism has never come near achieving this predicated goal is not only the result of unfulfilled or misfired economic preconditions, but also because the Marxian analysis itself was insufficient: it did not dig deep enough to the psychosexual roots of class. Marx was onto something more profound than he knew when he observed that the family contained within itself in embryo all the antagonisms that later develop on a wide scale within the society and the state. For unless revolution uproots the basic social organization, the biological family—the vinculum through which the psychology of power can always be smuggled—the tapeworm of exploitation will never be annihilated. We shall need a sexual revolution much larger than— inclusive of—a socialist one to truly eradicate all class systems.

I have attempted to take the class analysis one step further to its roots in the biological division of the sexes. We have not thrown out the insights of the socialists; on the contrary, radical feminism can enlarge their analysis, granting it an even deeper basis in objective conditions and thereby explaining many of its insolubles. As a first step in this direction, and as the groundwork for our own analysis we shall expand Engels' definition of historical materialism. Here is the same definition quoted above now rephrased to include the biological division of the sexes for the purpose of reproduction, which lies at the origins of class:

> Historical materialism is that view of the course of history which seeks the ultimate cause and the great moving power of all historic events in the dialectic of sex: the division of society into two distinct biological classes for procreative reproduction, and the struggles of these classes with one another; in the changes in the modes of marriage, reproduction and childcare created by these struggles; in the connected development of other physically-differentiated classes [castes]; and in the first division of labor based on sex which developed into the [economic-cultural] class system.

And here is the cultural superstructure, as well as the economic one, traced not just back to (economic) class but all the way back to sex:

> All past history [note that we can now eliminate "with the exception of primitive stages"] was the history of class struggle. These warring classes of society are always the product of the modes of organization of the biological family unit for reproduction of the species, as well as of the strictly economic modes of production and exchange of goods and services. The sexual-reproductive organization of society always furnishes the real basis, starting from which we can alone work out the ultimate explanation of the whole superstructure of economic, juridical and political institutions as well as of the religious, philosophical and other ideas of a given historical period.

And now Engels' projection of the results of a materialist approach to history is more realistic:

> The whole sphere of the conditions of life which environ man and have hitherto ruled him now comes under the dominion and control of man who for the first time becomes the real conscious Lord of Nature, master of his own social organization.

In the following chapters we shall assume this definition of historical materialism, examining the cultural institutions that maintain and reinforce the biological family (especially its present manifestation, the nuclear family) and its result, the power psychology, an aggressive chauvinism now developed enough to destroy us. We shall integrate this with a feminist analysis of Freudianism: for Freud's cultural bias, like that of Marx and Engels, does not invalidate his perception entirely. In fact, Freud had insights of even greater value than those of the socialist theorists for the building of a new dialectical materialism based on sex. We shall attempt, then, to correlate the best of Engels and Marx (the historical materialist approach) with the best of Freud (the understanding of the inner man and woman and what shapes them) to arrive at a solution both political and personal yet grounded in real conditions. We shall see that Freud observed the dynamics of psychology correctly in their immediate social context, but because the fundamental structure of that social context was basic to all humanity—to different degrees—it appeared to be nothing less than an absolute existential condition which it would be insane to question—forcing Freud and many of his followers to postulate *a priori* constructs like the Death Wish to explain the origins of these universal psychological drives. This in turn made the sicknesses of humanity irreducible and uncurable—which is why his proposed solution (psychoanalytic therapy), a contradiction in terms, was so weak compared to the rest of his work, and such a resounding failure in practice—causing those of social/political sensibility to reject not only his therapeutic solution, but his most profound discoveries as well.

NOTE

1. His correlation of the interdevelopment of these two systems in *Origin of the Family, Private Property and the State* on a time scale might read as in the following chart:

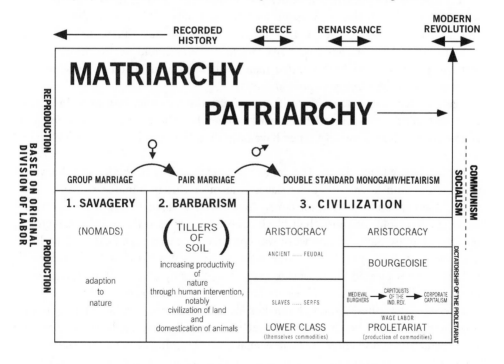

Chapter Eight

The Relationship of Black Women to the Women's Liberation Movement

Cellestine Ware

The Women's Liberation Movement is a multitude of white women with an only occasional black sister to lend color to the meetings. At this point in American history there are many forces divisive of black-white political coalitions, but the oppression of women has induced rivalries that intensify these separations.

Any analysis of the current hostility and/or indifference to feminism among black women must begin with a consideration of the old reality of black imitation of whites and the resulting self-contempt. In ways subtle and obvious, our society socializes women into narcissism. Fashion magazines tout the desirable woman much as advertisements glorify the high-salaried man. Girls soon learn to rate themselves according to their desirability to boys and men.

Black society has patterned itself closely on white people, but since blackness connotes ugliness and evil to whites, black women have been despised as coarse and animal-like in their sensuality. They have been despised both by whites and by their own people.

Under slavery blacks learned to value, revere even, white aesthetics and the white ethos. They soon learned that the slaves who most closely imitated whites in language, manners and, most importantly, looks, were favored by the masters. "Part-white children sold for more than black children. They used them for house girls," reminisced an ex-slave.[1] House work was considerably easier than field work and the house servants and concubines thought themselves better than the "field niggers." Indeed where it pleased the master to assert his power by keeping those slaves most like himself for his pleasure and leisure hours, many benefits came to them.

After abolition, these lighter-skinned ex-slaves maintained their ascendancy in the wage-earning world. Being better educated, they were more likely to acquire advanced educations and enter the professional fields. Forming an elite, they sometimes lived in their own towns in the South, and darker-skinned blacks were unwelcome. They had separate churches, clubs, and social customs that closely imitated those of white society.

A dark-skinned man who became successful would seek one of the light-skinned elites to solidify his status. Caucasoid features as the visible badge of respectability and worthiness were admired as blacks sought to become as white as possible. A good complexion was a light skin. Good hair was straight or curly, but never kinky. Black was bad; black was ugly.

As late as the mid-1960's, black sororities in the South were known to reject prospective pledges for their dark complexions. Sometimes dark-skinned girls already in sororities would blackball dark-skinned pledges. All blacks rejected their own blackness. Consequently, color-conscious was a frequent epithet; dark-skinned people watched lighter-skinned people closely for signs of rejection, and they often didn't have to look very hard. Robbed of their culture and deprived of their identity, the pre-civil rights movement blacks sought to escape their awful blackness, stigma of their fall from grace. Black militance is a healthy effort to reclaim the black man's rightful self-acceptance and identity.

The black middle class has not joined the militant movement. As a class, it has closely identified itself with white America. Up until now it has been a conservative force in the black community. This middle class, largely descended from the lighter-skinned slaves, has been the segment of black society that has benefited most from things as they are. They have preferred the advantages they know to the mere possibilities of the black revolution.

Black bourgeois women are the most closely mimetic of all blacks. In black culture, they have been the almost-desirable ones. Their conventionality usually demands the full panoply of middle-class acquisitions. They are the perfect consumers, and as such, the perfect mates for ambitious black men.

Ebony magazine advertises in the *New York Times* that the black bourgeoisie is a more avaricious consumer class than whites with comparable incomes. Of course in black families, as in all American families, the wife is the high priestess of consumption. However, as black families entertain more in their homes (they are uncertain of their welcome in places of public entertainment), wives bear a larger responsibility for creating a sheltering environment.

At a time when middle-class white youths are rebelling against parental mores and ethics, the young black bourgeoisie continue in their passion for propriety. While some young black males are to be seen in the bohemian ghettos, black females are rare, and middle-class black females even rarer. It is seldom that you will find a college-educated black girl living with her boyfriend. Black girls believe, and not without some cause, that middle-class black males don't marry black females who have been promiscuous.

Not surprisingly, these young, almost entirely conservative black women have seldom joined the Women's Liberation Movement, for they are usually apolitical. They constitute that part of the black community that has remained the longest outside the mainstream of the sixties. It is as if their mimetic interaction with the white community were located back in the fifties. Many black bourgeois families disapprove of the Afro hairdo. Black women of Katharine Cleaver's background are rarely seen in public life. Middle-class black women remain in the home, in the private lives of the community.

Even more rarely encountered than bourgeoises in women's liberation are poor black women. Lower-class black women have joined the black militant movement so it is not that they are apolitical. Furthermore the Black Panthers are considered the vanguard of Leftist politics in America, and all female liberation groups profess empathy with blacks as a kindred oppressed group. It is remarkable then that feminists often cite the political strategy of the black movement and encourage themselves with black precedents while they are seemingly unable to attract black women to the female liberation cause.

One reason that women's liberation doesn't or won't attract black women is that blacks are suspicious of whites who might coopt their support, energy and drive. Feminists are perceived as whites before they are seen to be oppressed. Secondly, black lower-class women are presently emphasizing their independence of, and prideful difference from, white women. Thirdly, poor black women are too occupied struggling for essentials: shelter, food and clothing to organize themselves around the issue of women's rights.

Fourthly, lower-class black women have deliberately submerged their identities in the struggle for racial equality. This is in tune with the collective spirit of the sixties. In black radical politics, individual concerns are superseded by the needs of the group or party. In this context, it is possible to view an autonomous women's drive for rights as an obstacle to radical changes. Black feminism would thus be another attempt by the power structure to divide black men and women. Feminist goals, like abortion on demand and easily obtainable birth control, are viewed with paranoid suspicion by some black militants at a time when they are literally fighting for their lives and looking everywhere to increase their numbers.

Lower-class black women have received little satisfaction from the identities allowed them by society, which were the identities based on close imitation of whites, a charade at which they were pre-destined to fail. Joining the Women's Liberation Movement may seem at this time like a re-entry into the old farce of pretending to be white. They are therefore not drawn by the feminists' cry for self-determination. Rather, they seek black militant movements, whether male-dominated or female and organized around specific grievances such as housing, for the self-respect and pride through group identity that they offer.

To women's liberation groups, marriage and the family are the roots of women's oppression, while to black women of the middle class, this thought is abhorrent, and to black lower-class women, their oppression is completely racial. Yet black women are the largest and most oppressed minority group in the United States. Their oppression by whites is clearly discernible, but their oppression by men is not recognizable to most people.

In the past, the analogy between the oppression of slaves and the oppression of women was easily seen. Nineteenth-century feminists had only to substitute the word wife for the word slave to understand the nature of man's tyranny over woman. The nineteenth-century woman had no redress against a husband who wasted her property, consorted with other women, beat her and beat their children and she could easily empathize with female slaves. As Maria Child wrote in *An Appeal in Favour of the Class of Americans Called Africans:* "(the slave) is the property of her master, and her daughters are his property. . . . They must be entirely subservient to the will of their owner, on pain of being whipped as near unto death as will comport with his interest, or quite to death if it suit his pleasure." As Andrew Sinclair makes clear: "Any woman who feared rape herself could identify with the female slave and transfer her hatred from the plantation owner to the whole male sex. . . . In that way then, the wrongs inflicted on Negro women were the wrongs of womankind."[2]

Today the oppression of women is more subtly prosecuted. Without consciousness-raising, the ways in which they are controlled are generally unclear to women. Moreover the inferior position of women is of such long tradition that it has remained unquestioned even by radical thinkers, that is by male radical thinkers.

Just as black militants expect black women to sink their abilities into the movement and fulfill their interests by fighting for racial equality, so abolitionists demanded that nineteenth-century feminists turn away from the "woman question" lest they harm the fight to free the slaves. The Grimke sisters who linked the fight for women's rights with the anti-slavery fight were told they could most benefit humanity by working against slavery. This is really social feminism: the idea that it is woman's duty to be selflessly enrolled in working for a higher cause. Certainly Theodore Weld's accusation to Angelina Grimke might well come from the mouths of black nationalists or other blacks who see black women's problems only as the result of the economic position of black men.

"Your woman's rights! You put the cart before the horse; you drag the tree by the top in attempting to push your *woman's* rights until human rights have gone ahead and broken the *path*," declared Mr. Weld.

Angelina Grimke's answer might well be used by black women today if black race is substituted for slave. "The slave may be freed and woman be where she is, but woman can not be freed and the slave remain where he is."[3]

It is not only militants who ignore the black woman's right to self-determination. Dorothy Height, President of the National Council of Negro Women, has said: "Negro women have the same problems and hopes as other women, but they cannot take the same things for granted." Her analysis then led her to the same arguments as those voiced by the abolitionists in accusing woman's rights of putting the cart before the horse: "If the Negro woman has a major underlying concern, it is the status of the Negro man and his position in the community and his need for feeling himself an important person, free and able to make his contribution in the whole society in order that he may strengthen his home."[4] Mrs. Height's analysis, like that of the black radicals, stops short of the inequities between men and women. Black men doubtless see women's oppression as inconsequential compared to blacks' sufferings.

Black women have the same needs for self-determination as all people have. They have been made to feel some guilt at the thought of acting in their own interests rather than in those of their race, where these seem to diverge in the minds of black males. The inferior position of women is not due to economics or race; otherwise, in socialist countries, or in racially homogeneous countries, women would enjoy a functional equality and not just improved status. The real basis of the oppression of women is man's psychological need for dominance. Men need women to make them feel good. A typical remark from an untypically honest male is: "If women weren't weaker than men, I'd just as soon sleep with men." As Gore Vidal, among many, has commented, sexual congress is a power relationship.

The rejection of black women by black men is a phenomenon best explained by the need to dominate that underlies male-female relations. As such, this rejection is an excellent study for feminists. The strength of the resistance to women's independence is shown by the strong epithets directed against black women. The black male's reaction is the forerunner of what all feminists will face as they grow in strength. As women begin to assume positions of equality with men, they will meet virulent abuse, much like that endured by black women now. They will also discover that men will reject them for more "feminine" women.

Black sociologist Calvin Hernton's *Sex and Racism in America* is filled with examples of the defamation and rejection now subtle, now blatant, that are the lot of black women. For example: "It is no mystery why white society is now tending to accept the black woman more readily than the black male. First of all, the Negro woman, like the white woman, does not represent to the white world as much of an aggressor against the present power structure as does the Negro man." It hasn't been true any time in the sixties that black women were hired before black men. On the contrary black women got little benefit from the drive to find black talent.

The rare black woman who has achieved a position of prominence was bitterly resented by black males. Black personnel men have been known to lose the résumés of promising black women. One such administrator at a famous radio and television station told a black woman applicant: "We already have enough sisters in the communications industry. It's time the brothers got ahead."

"In the executive talent shortage of the 1960's, some organizations encouraged women in the patronizing way they had encouraged promotable Negroes when the Negro rights movement was popular, but the efforts to see that qualified women were promoted were much more half-hearted than those promoting Negroes. In 1967, for instance, 15% of a group of companies queried by the Bureau of National Affairs said they had undertaken aggressive recruiting of promotable Negroes in response to Title VII, but only one company reported an aggressive policy of recruiting women.

" 'I'm not ready for a woman,' a frank management consultant confessed in 1966 when a woman executive recommended a woman for a job he had open. 'But boy, would I love to get hold of a good Negro!' "[5] In the business world, sex is more of a barrier than race.

Another example from Mr. Hernton's book is: "When it comes to women, the Negro male, like the white male, is a product and victim of male supremacy, and he becomes disgruntled and difficult to get along with when 'his women' are in a position where they no longer have to honor his claim to superiority. In addition to the crisis occurring in contemporary race relations, a more specific crisis is ensuing in the relations between Negro men and Negro women—and I suspect it will become more intense as time goes on unless Negro women (I say women because, in this regard, I doubt the capacity of the men) to initiate measures to resolve it."[6]

What he is doing here, other than lightly criticizing male supremacists, is to place on women the burden and full responsibility for reconciling their achievements with male vanity. He cagily ends the chapter at this point without suggesting just what she is to sacrifice to this peacemaking mission. Men such as Hernton believe that women alone can save the human race through their superior virtues. Doubtless he is opposed to the oppression of women, but he would object to full equality for them as likely to bring them down to the level of men.

Yet history has made black women more independent than most American women. "Although the African matriarchal pattern" (actually not a true matriarchy as only lineage was traced through the mother, and authority and disciplinary powers were invested in the mother's brother) "had been largely destroyed, slave life itself gave the Negro woman a unique status. It was not only that, in the constant flux of slave relations, her relationship to the children was clear while the father's was often not, but also, that, in addition to her capacity as a worker, the owner profited from her child-bearing and rearing her young. She was, therefore, less apt to be sold out of hand than the male and was the more stable element in what little there was of slave family life.

"As a rule, the Negro woman as wife and mother was the mistress of her cabin, and, save for the interference of the overseer, her wishes in regard to mating and family matters were paramount. Neither economic necessity nor tradition had instilled in her the spirit of subordination to masculine authority."[7]

Because of this failure to develop subserviency to the male. black women are belittled by both middle-and lower-class black men. The middle-class black man, such as Mr. Hernton, sees the black woman as domineering and castrating. To wit: "Repeatedly I have witnessed Negro women virtually dominating their white husbands. There may be fights, but she capitalizes on her Negroness and on her sex image by wielding a sort of *Amazon mastery* (italics mine) over the white male. In all but a few black woman-white man relationships, it is the man who must do the adjusting—and what he must adjust to is nothing less than what is referred to as the Negro's mode of existence or the Negro's conceptualization of life in the United States."[8]

Mr. Hernton is displaying common anxieties and fears in his emotionally charged statement about the "Amazon mastery" that he says black women develop over their white husbands. His translation of circumstantial necessity into a deliberate attempt at oppression ignores social realities: Discrimination and intolerance invariably force interracial couples to live in black communities, or at least in well-integrated ones.

The lower-class black male sees black women as bitches. The welfare check has made the poor black woman economically independent of the men who come and go in her life, and on whom she cannot rely. Poor black males complain of being told to "Get out! And don't bring your ass back here until you've got a job!" There is antagonism between black males and females, especially in the poorest segments of the community. The women are contemptuous of the men for not being able to keep jobs, or not being able to find work and provide for their families, or for throwing their money away on gambling, other women, and drinking. The women belittle the men for not taking care of business. The men curse the women for not being feminine and comforting.

The mistake that sociologists are making and that black men seem to be making is the assumption that these women have chosen to be heads of their families. They have become heads of households by default—as the only responsible adults in their families. It is interesting to note that the state menaces and subordinates these women in much the same way that the salary-earning male head of the household does his wife. Protection has its price.

It is the pressures of poverty and slum life that grind down the black family and destroy the role of the black male as father-protector. It is these pressures, not black women, that make the confidence man the ghetto hero. In Harlem, in Watts, in Hough, the admired man beats the game: dresses sharp, has a string of girlfriends, and doesn't have a steady job. He gets by doing a little of this and a little of that. For the poor black man, there is no ego aggrandizement in the traditional role of head of the house. Economic and social racism force him to be inadequate in such a role. And so the black bitch was created to justify the confidence man.

"A dark-skinned woman is discriminated against by Negroes as well as whites. 'A yellow woman may be low-down, but a black one is evil,' goes the saying among Negroes. She is not born evil but her chances of being genteel, loving, and personable are virtually impossible in a world that sees nothing but her color. Here Mr. Hernton is actually concurring in the existence of the mythical black bitch.

To continue: "This is why many black women in the North have developed what I call 'black woman chauvinism.' They have a genuine hatred for white women and the Negro men who pursue them; they hate the sight of a light-skinned Negro woman. After all, black women are females, and they have the desires that all females have—for attention, for sexual gratification, for respect, for reverence, for sexual self-esteem. And if they do not realize such desires, like any other women, they tend to become 'difficult personalities,' 'evil'."[9] Black women are evil, and it's understandable that they should be, says Hernton. He assumes that women are estimable to the extent that they can attract men. Obviously these women are pitiable, perhaps contemptible because of their lack of allure.

Abbey Lincoln, according to Fletcher Knebel, first verbalized the current black female unrest (it is as yet unorganized) in the face of this kind of rejection. "We are the women," she declared, "...whose nose is 'too big,' whose mouth is 'too big and loud,' whose behind is 'too big and broad,' whose feet are 'too big and flat,' whose face is 'too black and shiny'...who's just too damned much for everybody." She was referring to Sapphire, the Amazon of the black male imagination.

Implied by Mr. Hernton's book is the failure of black women to sustain black men. By their own involvement with being black, black women have not been able to take the nurturing role that men look for in women. "The point is that many of the darker Negro men who pursue white mates do so because their own women have rejected them because they are 'black and ugly'.... Whereas white women... can live with a so-called 'black and ugly' Negro without constantly making the Negro secretly despise himself for the way he happens to look...Thus we hear some Negro men proclaiming that such and such a white woman treats them better than the females of their own race."[10] He adds parenthetically that the same applies to Negro women, but obviously their needs are secondary. Once again women are being valued for their ability to make men happy.

Further bias is evident in Mr. Hernton's conclusion that "The deeper meaning in the practice of Negro women in the South of beating their children (especially boys) to a point of sheer exhaustion is to be found somewhere in the pent-up rage that black women have in their hearts against white women and against a sociosexual morality that denies black women the right to be beautiful, loving and idealized by black and white men alike."[11] This practice of excessive punishment of their children by Southern (usually) blacks is capable of at least two other interpretations.

One: the authors of *Black Rage*, William Grier and Price Cobbs, theorized that black mothers punished and demoralized their male children to make them subservient to whites. The mothers did this for the survival of their children. Two: It is not only the mother who beats the children in the Southern family, the father also figures in accounts as an administrator of the razor strap. This refers of course to the generation of fathers and mothers, now in their late forties and fifties, whose own parents were the children and grandchildren of former slaves. The customary brutality of slave beatings, the fear, expectation and acceptance of them, has become part of the psychic building blocks of the black family.

Listen to these accounts from ex-slaves:

"His (the master's) wife or children could git mad with you, and if they told him anything they always beat you. Most times he beat slaves when they had done nothing a-tall.... He put her in what us called the swing, and beat her till she couldn't holler. ... Whenever your master had you swinging up, nobody wouldn't take you down. Sometimes a man would help his wife, but most times he was beat afterwards."

"Before my father (the master) gave me to his sister, I was tied and strapped and whipped like a beast by my father, till I was unconscious, and then he left me strapped to a tree all night in cold and rainy weather.... When Missy took that bell offen me, I think I in Heaven 'cause I could lie down and go to sleep. When I did I couldn't wake up for a long time, and when I did wake up I'd be scared to death I'd see my father with his whip and that old bell."

"When he go to whip a nigger he make him strip to the waist and take a cat-o'-nine-tails and bring the blisters, and then bust the blister with a wide strap of leather fastened to a stick handle. I seen the blood running outen man's back, all the way from the neck to the waist."

"Many times a nigger git blistered and cut up so that we have to git a sheet and grease it with lard and wrap 'em up in it, and they have to wear a greasy cloth wrapped around they body under the shirt for three-four days after they git a big whipping."[12]

It is not unlikely that people used to such treatment would beat their children to discipline them.

The distortions that underlie the transformation of the black mother into a witchlike figure with magical powers to destroy are obviously found in the educated as well as the ignorant. In a recent quote a black educator said: "For the black man, the black woman is too much like his mother. He sees her as domineering, bossy, a woman who runs things. He wants a desirable, easy sex companion, and he finds her in the white woman." What will happen when this desirable doll becomes a real woman? Perhaps she will be rejected for an easygoing Oriental?

An admissions official at Columbia University criticizes black women in these terms: "Too often black American women fail to free themselves from the psychological impediments imposed by their overprotective mothers. As a result, they fail to develop the self-confidence and self-assuredness necessary to achieve full womanhood in a market where the company of the black male is becoming more and more competitive." "We kind of *fear* (italics mine) the middle-class black girl we meet around school. She's snobbish, uppity and inclined to sneer at a black man unless he excels at something. White girls, for a lot of reasons, are easier, less Victorian, and let's face it, they have their own money."

It is the fear and anxiety of the black male that lead to the construction of the "evil" black female. By now, the superstructure of the "black bitch" bears as little relation to the real black woman as any myth to the reality. The preceding quotes suggest that the men speaking have no honest contact with women of either race. The magical approach of the male to the female is an ancient orientation toward women as the aliens of the human world.

The complaint that black women challenge black men is further proof of the threatening nature of female independence to most men. Philip Roth's indictment of the Jewish mother may soon seem mild as black men achieve more power. It seems significant that the literature of the omnipotent Jewish mother with her all devouring love has become a familiar theme of our literature just as the Jews have been assimilated into the power centers of American life. Although the parallels in the black and Jewish traditions are slight, both cultures are now remarkable for the vehemence of the attack on their women. I suggest that black literature will increasingly consist of virulent attacks on the evil black mother as black men move into positions of power.

When black men attain power and approximate the status of the white male of the higher classes, they tend to reject their own women for not conforming to WASP standards of femininity. Black women and Jewish women are being fitted to the Procrustean bed of the WASP female's behavior and personality.

"Uppity Women Unite" is a motto of the Women's Liberation Movement. As all women achieve self-determination, white women will cease to be preferred. The power conflict that informs sexual congress will be revealed, as condemnations of women as castrating, aggressive, snobbish, uppity, difficult and evil rise from men. But black women are still captive to the idea that to be attractive to men is the only way to be a fine woman. They are still dependent on men for feelings of self-worth.

The new black man (I'm black, and I'm proud!) is certainly attractive to white women. His defiance has made him a compelling figure. Still his self-acceptance is often only superficial. It is still possible to hear remarks such as this one made by two dashiki-clad youths, as Miss Black Teenage America went by: "Why did they have to choose someone so black?" Such men and boys choose white women out of self-loathing. Any white skin is better than any black one. Surprisingly enough, these attitudes can be found in quite sophisticated men: Afro heads and processed minds.

The black civil rights movement of the sixties, with its growing militancy and heightened racial self-confidence, generated a rejection of the self-hatred projected onto black people in America. Suddenly black is beautiful. Black is beautiful, and your (black) bird can sing. Black women were asked to legitimize the motto that Black Is Beautiful by wearing their hair natural and adopting African clothes, and, it was implied, by only dating black men. Black women were even told not to wear pants. Naturalism, in the minds of many, became confused with a return to a world defined and ruled by men. Some black men wish, by becoming militant, to assume the powers of white men in an earlier, simpler century.

In the age of the Organization Man and middle-class anonymity, some black men would be supermales. Their aggressiveness identifies them as such to themselves and to white females. The white female sees the black male as he wishes to be seen—that is, as far as his public presentation goes.

Black men pursue white women not simply as the most beautiful women and easy, but also as the symbols of the white man's privileges. White women and black women have been accepting this without criticism, but now black women are becoming increasingly vocal in their anger at this manipulation. Most white women still are not aware of the nature of black man's desire for them.

To feminists, the male aggressive attitude that a woman is to sleep with as a hole is to dig is objectionable. Many of the phrases used in slang indicate that women are seen as objects: "gash," "pussy," and "cunt." The black man is the chief victim of this supermale psychology. He accepts the myth as projected onto him, plays the part and is irresistible to white women.

Black men often can date white women who wouldn't have anything to do with them if they had the same personal characteristics but were white. Their blackness immediately makes them the peak of masculinity. Those white females who prefer black males say that white males don't even know how to smile at you; they don't know how to rap; they act as if they don't know what a woman is for! They like black life—the blues life, the jazz tradition. Dating black men, they have all the advantages (glamor) of blackness and elude the oppression.

Black women are chiefly angered by black men's pursuit of white women without understanding it. Fletcher Knebel quoted a letter from a black woman to *Ebony:* "I, as a black woman, realize that our men have been brainwashed to believe their women are nothing, but just as they are being awakened to the fact that they are beautiful, why can't they also be taught how to treat us? Our men seem to feel that as part of the black, we are beautiful, but as women, they don't even really see us."

"Many black women who saw the Broadway hit *The Great White Hope*, came away depressed," noted Mr. Knebel. "They could not forget that the play's real Jack Johnson, once the world's heavyweight champion, found no solace in black women, and that he had three white wives. Nor could they forget that Jones (who acted Jack Johnson), had himself married a white woman."

Mr. Knebel's assumption that woman is to solace man is, of course, unacceptable, but what is more depressing is the black women's self-castigation because Jack Johnson had married white women. As the play clearly shows, Johnson treated his wives badly, and his having *three* indicates the difficulties of living with him. These women are wounded by a conception of women as successful only if they have husbands.

Women of both races are being manipulated by their fear of losing or of never winning a husband. The anxiety to please and to be nice to men, to make them feel good, is inculcated on females from infancy and increasingly forced on them as they enter puberty.

The results of this are sexual jealousy and envy among women. All over New York, there have been actual battles between white women and black women over black men. Usually this sexual hostility is soft-pedaled, but whether it is spoken or silent, it is a poor background for black-white coalition in the feminist movement.

New York radio station WBAI's Julius Lester states very calmly that if he dies an unnatural death, it will probably be at the hands of a black woman enraged by his having a white wife.

A recent forum at the N.Y.U. Law School is indicative of the amount of resentment between the races. Fannie Lou Hamer and some friends of hers, well-wishers and supporters, had been invited to speak to law school students. Also invited were three women from the Women's Liberation Movement in New York City. After the feminists told something about the aims and purpose of women's liberation, the meeting was thrown open for questions from the audience.

The black women in the audience, most of whom were supporters of Fannie Lou Hamer, although some were law students, dominated the discussion period. Their first question was: "How many black women are there in the Women's Liberation Movement?" The answer, Not many, but we are working to reach more, was met by: "That's right! because black women aren't sick. Black women don't hate sex. You white women don't know how to make a man happy!" "White women can't cook." "You hate men!" The feeling grew even stronger after that. Most of the audience seemed incapable of listening to what the feminists had to say, but it was the black women who crystallized the fear and resentment by giving it a racist slant.

Some black men date and marry white women because they have fallen in love with particular individuals, but on the street, it is difficult to distinguish these men from the black men who reject any black woman as ugly. Also white women sometimes flaunt their black men as prizes they have won in the competition with black women.

The sexual competition between black and white women will diminish as women learn to value themselves as people, independent of their relationships to men. White women will not then be flattered by the pursuit of black men when these men only see in them the appanage of white power; nor will black women panic and feel betrayed at the sight of black men with white women.

Black women find in the black movement the collective identity of the sixties. Women's liberation has offered them nothing like this. The black movement is so gratifying to these newly realized needs for group pride that black women have stayed in the black movement despite many injustices. Women in black, radical organizations have sometimes found that they are constitutionally barred from holding office. If they are elected to office, they are figureheads. The Black Panthers have hitherto allowed women little significant voice in strategy and communications. But the Panther men are now often in jails or in graveyards and, for the first time in many chapters, women are now as prominent as men. This is due to an emergent situation much as in any country in time of war. But Panther membership comes largely from the poorest segments of the ghettos—those people to whom no white radical movement offers any hope or self-acceptance. A young woman organizing a Black Panther free breakfast program for children was not surprised when her two male assistants said that she should cook the breakfasts and do the dishes while they should rap to the children. She countered strongly by reversing the roles, but she succeeded only with difficulty, and expects the resistance to keep recurring on other questions.

Black militant politics offers women association with men as women's liberation does not. The black male, newly proud and assertive of his ability to take care of his women, is saying with you behind me, we'll win; and when we do, you'll be my queen, my better half, my lady on a pedestal. Through black power, you'll get the white woman's status (and the black male will win dominance over the female).

Few black women speak up in public for the woman's right to control her own body, but few of the black women who are best informed about, and most familiar with, the pill and the diaphragm are in the black radical movement.

College-age black women have been actively involved in the actions on campus, but again they have taken the traditional feminine role. In the takeover at Cornell, it was a source of pride to black male students to protect the girls who had been threatened and abused by some of the white fraternity men on campus. These same girls wound up frying chicken for the boys at the barricades.

A reliable source in the Harvard Organization of Black Unity (OBU) asserts that whenever a black girl becomes too articulate and aggressive at the meetings, a boy from the group is assigned to seduce her, and then, as his conquest, keep her in a more traditional position within the organization.

It will be interesting to see if the black female graduates of this year's campus actions will be willing to breed for black power. It is not unlikely that five years from now a wave of lower-class and college-educated black women, disillusioned by their oppression in the black militant movement (much like the white women from radical student organizations in feminism now) will be coming into the feminist movement.

While the black militant movement offers black women and black men a proud group identity, women's liberation works for abortion and equal opportunities for hiring and advancement, which the black woman sees as already having cost her black men. While it will soon no longer be true, in 1965, more black women had attended college and held college degrees than black men. It left the black college-educated woman without a man of similar background. Emphasis has been placed on winning the men education and middle-class employment, but this has been urged at the expense of the women. Black women have been urged to step back and let the men catch up. Originally black women were given more education to give them the chance for employment away from predatory white men. Black women working as domestics, particularly in the South, were invariably subject to and had little protection from the advances of male employers and of other men in the town.

By educating girls in the family to higher status, the black family was acting to protect them from this.

Black women have special problems that women's liberation has not focused on. The percent of black women in the labor force has always been higher than that of whites. In 1900, 41% of black women were employed as compared with 17% of whites. In 1963, black women still made up 25% more of the female working force than did white. About two-thirds of black women workers are in the lowest paid service occupations.

These women are not usually covered by social security, medical insurance or disability or old-age benefits. The President's Commission on the Status of Women urged the federal government to take further steps to enforce compliance with the law requiring social security for these women and to educate the Negro household worker on her rights and benefits under this program.

Black women generally want to move up out of their low-status, and thus undesirable, occupations as domestics. Women's liberation should concentrate in helping the generation of women now trapped in these jobs by working to upgrade skills in these jobs to the professional level and by improving employment conditions. Furthermore, as few Americans can afford to pay domestic workers a good salary on a full-time basis, domestic work should be reorganized to be done by contractors— professional workers would arrive in the home at the stipulated time to do the contracted duties, which would be clearly delineated and enforced. Modern equipment and training would be given the domestic professionals with certificates awarded on completion of studies.

Such a program would be a two-fold benefit. All housewives could be freed of this task which is particularly onerous for the working woman, who is usually held responsible for keeping the household as well.

There should also be training available for domestic professionals to move into other fields when they desire.

Black and Puerto Rican women are often trapped in domestic or factory jobs because they are barred from white-collar jobs. According to a report of the President's Commission on the Status of Women: "A major means of entering the secretarial field is through graduation from a recognized business or secretarial school. Many of these schools, however, do not admit Negroes. Yet they are granted licenses to operate and have such advantages as tax exemption and indirect federal funds through veterans' programs." Women's liberation has not focused its energies on these problems of minority women.

In 1964, white men who worked full time earned a median income of $6,497; black men $4,285; white women $3,859; and black women $2,674. In 1960, 44% of black married women with children under six years old were working full-time. The children of these mothers are often not cared for properly during their mother's working hours. Women's liberation should press for an enormous increase in community childcare facilities.

Women's liberation has directed itself to the impediments to the aspirations of college-educated women. There was an outcry against this at the northeastern Congress to Unite Women. A great many of the 3.8 million illiterate women in the United States are non-white. Adult education programs and vocational training programs suitable for the uneducated woman should become priorities of women's liberation if it is to attract black and Puerto Rican women.

Statistics have shown that proportionately more black women are heads of families than whites. "The tendency (for black families to be matriarchal) has continued because of the inability of many Negro men to get a decent job and earn a sufficient wage to carry their responsibilities of family life. Thus the Negro wife is forced into the labor market where she often earns more than her husband and sometimes becomes the only earner for the family. Therefore, not by choice, she may become the head of the household. Because of the barriers to education and better-paying jobs encountered by men, the Negro woman frequently has had to assume additional social and economic burdens."

Scant attention has been paid in women's liberation to problems of women who head households.

Minority women have other problems that receive little attention in the movement. In a recent article in *The New York Times*, Paul Montgomery wrote: "A study of births in New York City in 1967 showed that 5.3% of births among whites were illegitimate ... The figures for blacks were 24 per cent in 1957 and 38.3 per cent in 1967, and for Puerto Ricans 10.7 per cent in 1957 and 21.9 per cent in 1967. For Central Harlem in 1967, the illegitimacy rate was 54.2 per cent." While women's liberation is working for the right to abortion on demand, illegitimate birth rates among New York Puerto Ricans doubled within a decade. More than half of the children born in Central Harlem are illegitimate, yet women's liberation has not spoken to the problems of unwed mothers. Furthermore it has been noted that "while few white unwed mothers keep their babies, two-thirds of black and Puerto Ricans mothers do." There is a welfare rights organization, dominated by black women with a few Puerto Ricans, but this organization remains outside the women's liberation group.

There has been no effort from within the movement to work on these issues. There is a nascent black women's liberation group, formed as a caucus of the welfare rights organization, on the Lower East Side. Hopefully this group will confront the problems of single-parenthood. Women's liberation has generally left the minorities to deal with their particular problems themselves. This, then, is the explanation of why there are few minority women in feminism.

Black and white women can work together for women's liberation if the movement changes its priorities to work on issues that affect the lives of minority-group women. If raised consciousness shows white women that black men are pursuing them as symbols of white achievements; if black women currently in the black radical movement in the cities and on campus become disillusioned with their oppression by the Left; if women are educated to value themselves for their independent identities; if women of both races see their problems as originating in female dependency on men and in their self-contempt, then women will make a revolution in our social and economic order.

NOTES

1. *Lay My Burden Down*, ed. B. A. Botkin, p. 55.

2. Andrew Sinclair, *The Better Half* (New York, 1965), p. 43.

3. *Ibid.*, p. 46.

4. *The Report of the President's Commission on the Status of Women* (New York, 1965), p. 227.

5. Calvin C. Hernton, *Sex and Racism in America* (New York, 1965), p. 167.

6. *Ibid.*, p. 168.

7. E. Franklin Frazier, *The Negro Family in the United States* (Chicago, 1939), p. 125.

8. Hernton, *op. cit.*, p. 162.

9. *Ibid.*, p. 144.

10. *Ibid.*, pp. 83–84.

11. *Ibid.*, pp. 135–136.

12. *Botkin*, ed., *op. cit.*, pp. 59–107.

Chapter Nine

The Personal Is Political

Carol Hanisch

For this paper I want to stick pretty close to an aspect of the Left debate commonly talked about—namely "therapy" vs. "therapy and politics." Another name for it is "personal" vs. "political" and it has other names, I suspect, as it has developed across the country. I haven't gotten over to visit the New Orleans group yet, but I have been participating in groups in New York and Gainesville for more than a year. Both of these groups have been called "therapy" and "personal" groups by women who consider themselves "more political." So I must speak about so-called therapy groups from my own experience.

The very word "therapy" is obviously a misnomer if carried to its logical conclusion. Therapy assumes that someone is sick and that there is a cure, e.g., a personal solution. I am greatly offended that I or any other woman is thought to *need* therapy in the first place. Women are messed over, not messed up! We need to change the objective conditions, not adjust to them. Therapy is adjusting to your bad personal alternative.

We have not done much trying to solve immediate personal problems of women in the group. We've mostly picked topics by two methods: In a small group it is possible for us to take turns bringing questions to the meeting (like, Which do/did you prefer, a girl or a boy baby or no children, and why? What happens to your relationship if your man makes more money than you? Less than you?). Then we go around the room answering the questions from our personal experiences. Everybody talks that way. At the end of the meeting we try to sum up and generalize from what's been said and make connections.

I believe at this point, and maybe for a long time to come, that these analytical sessions are a form of political action. I do not go to these sessions because I need or want to talk about my "personal problems." In fact, I would rather not. As a movement woman, I've been pressured to be strong, selfless, other-oriented, sacrificing, and in general pretty much in control of my own life. To admit to the problems in my life is to be deemed weak. So I want to be a strong woman, in movement terms, and not admit I have any real problems that I can't find a personal solution to (except those directly related to the capitalist system). It is at this point a political action to tell it like it is, to say what I really believe about my life instead of what I've always been told to say.

So the reason I participate in these meetings is not to solve any personal problem. One of the first things we discover in these groups is that personal problems are political problems. There are no personal solutions at this time. There is only collective action for a collective solution. I went, and I continue to go to these meetings because I have gotten a political understanding which all my reading, all my "political discussions," all my "political action," all my four-odd years in the movement never gave me. I've been forced to take off the rose-colored glasses and face the awful truth about how grim my life really is as a woman. I am getting a gut understanding of everything as opposed to the esoteric, intellectual understandings and *noblesse oblige* feelings I had in "other people's" struggles.

This is not to deny that these sessions have at least two aspects that are therapeutic. I prefer to call even this aspect "political therapy" as opposed to personal therapy. The most important is getting rid of self-blame. Can you imagine what would happen if women, blacks, and workers (my definition of worker is anyone who *has* to work for a living as opposed to those who don't. All women are workers) would stop blaming ourselves for our sad situations? It seems to me the whole country needs that kind of political therapy. That is what the black movement is doing in its own way. We shall do it in ours. We are only starting to stop blaming ourselves.

We also feel like we are thinking for ourselves for the first time in our lives. As the cartoon in *Lilith* puts it, "I'm changing. My mind is growing muscles." Those who believe that Marx, Lenin, Engels, Mao, and Ho have the only and last "good word" on the subject and that women have nothing more to add will, of course, find these groups a waste of time.

The groups that I have been in have also not gotten into "alternative life-styles" or what it means to be a "liberated" woman. We came early to the conclusion that all alternatives are bad under present conditions. Whether we live with or without a man, communally or in couples or alone, are married or unmarried, live with other women, go for free love, celibacy or lesbianism, or any combination, there are only good and bad things about each bad situation. There is no "more liberated" way; there are only bad alternatives.

This is part of one of the most important theories we are beginning to articulate. We call it "the pro-woman line." What it says basically is that women are really neat people. The bad things that are said about us as women are either myths (women are stupid), tactics women use to struggle individually (women are bitches), or are actually things that we want to carry into the new society and want men to share too (women are sensitive, emotional). Women as oppressed people act out of necessity (*act* dumb in the presence of men), not out of choice. Women have developed great shuffling techniques for their own survival (look pretty and giggle to get or keep a job or man) which should be used when necessary until such time as the power of unity can take its place. Women are smart not to struggle alone (as are blacks and workers). It is no worse to be in the home than in the rat race of the job world. They are both bad. Women, like blacks, workers, must stop blaming ourselves for our "failures."

It took us some ten months to get to the point where we could articulate these things and relate them to the lives of every woman. It's important from the standpoint of what kind of action we are going to do. When our group first started, going by majority opinion, we would have been out in the streets demonstrating against marriage, against having babies, for free love, against women who wore makeup, against housewives, for equality without recognition of biological differences, and god knows what else. Now we see all these things as what we call "personal solutionary." Many of the actions taken by "action" groups have been along these lines. The women who did the anti-woman stuff at the Miss America Pageant were the ones who were screaming for action without theory. The members of one group want to set up a private day care center without any real analysis of what could be done to make it better for little girls, much less any analysis of how that center hastens the revolution.

That is not to say, of course, that we shouldn't do action. There may be some very good reasons why women in the group don't want to do anything at the moment. One reason that I often have is that this thing is so important to me that I want to be very sure that we're doing it the best way we know how, and that it is a "right" action that I feel sure about. I refuse to go out and "produce" for the movement. We had a lot of conflict in our New York group about whether or not to do action. When the Miss America Protest was proposed there was no question but that we wanted to do it. I think it was because we all saw how it related to our lives. We *felt* it was a good action. There were things wrong with the action; but the basic idea was there.

This has been my experience in groups that are accused of being "therapy" or "personal." Perhaps certain groups may well be attempting to do therapy. Maybe the answer is not to put down the method of analyzing from personal experiences in favor of immediate action, but to figure out what can be done to make it work. Some of us started to write a handbook about this at one time and never got past the outline. We are working on it again, and hope to have it out in a month at the latest.

It's true we all need to learn how to better draw conclusions from the experiences and feelings we talk about and how to draw all kinds of connections. Some of us haven't done a very good job of communicating them to others.

One more thing: I think we must listen to what so-called apolitical women have to say—not so we can do a better job of organizing them but because together we *are* a mass movement. I think we who work full-time in the movement tend to become very narrow. What is happening now is that when non-movement women disagree with us, we assume it's because they are "apolitical," not because there might be something wrong with *our* thinking. Women have left the movement in droves. The obvious reasons are that we are tired of being sex slaves and doing shitwork for men whose hypocrisy is so blatant in their political stance of liberation for everybody (else). But there is really a lot more to it than that. I can't quite articulate it yet. I think "apolitical" women are not in the movement for very good reasons, and as long as we say "you have to think like us and live like us to join the charmed circle," we will fail. What I am trying to say is that there are things in the consciousness of "apolitical" women (I find them very political) that are as valid as any political consciousness we think we have. We should figure out why many women don't want to do action. Maybe there is something wrong with the action or something wrong with why we are doing the action or maybe the analysis of why the action is necessary is not clear enough in our minds.

Chapter Ten

The Enemy Within

Susan Brownmiller

When I was 11 years old and talking in the schoolyard one day with a bunch of girlfriends from class, the discussion came around, as it did in those days, to "What are you going to be when you grow up?" At least three of us wanted to be actresses or models. Two had their sights already set on marriage, motherhood, and a house in the country. But one girl said *she* was going to go to medical school and be a doctor. This announcement was greeted with respectful silence (all those additional years of school!) until Martha, fat, bright, and at the head of the class, said solemnly, "I'd never go to a woman doctor. I just wouldn't have *confidence* in a woman doctor."

"Not even to deliver your baby?" I remember inquiring.

"Nope," Martha replied. "Especially not to deliver my baby. That's too important. Men doctors are better than women doctors."

It has been many years since that schoolyard discussion and I can't even recall the name or the face of the girl who had the ambitions, but I hope she wasn't sidetracked somewhere along the line. But I remember Martha. Calm, the best student, everybody's friend, more advanced physically than the rest of us—she had breasts, we didn't—and utterly positive at that tender age that men did things better than women. I will never forgive her for being the first person of my sex whom I ever heard put down women. I considered it traitorous then in the schoolyard, and I consider it traitorous now. Since that time, I have done a lot of observing of that strange phenomenon, have been guilty of it myself, I think, and have come to the conclusion that woman is often her own worst enemy—the enemy within.

One of the hardest things for a woman with aspirations to do in our society is to admit, first to herself and then to others, that she has ambitions that go beyond the routine—a good marriage, clever children. Early on, we learn that men don't take kindly to the notion of a woman entering the competitive lists. It is in the nature of power and position that those who have it do not relinquish it graciously, as all colonial peoples and all minority groups discover at a certain stage in their development. Well, O.K., so be it. But infinitely more damaging to our psyche is the realization that our ambitions are met with equal hostility—poohpoohed, sniffed at, scoffed at, ignored, or worse, not taken seriously—by mothers, sisters, cousins, aunts and friends, who won't believe that we have set our sights on a different sort of goal than *they* have envisioned, preferring instead to believe that our ambition is merely a "passing phase"—which, unfortunately, it often is because of lack of encouragement.

Psychologists talk a great deal about the importance of the approbation or approval of a peer group upon the individual. It is human nature to want to fit in. The senior at college who sends away for law-school catalogues while her dormitory mates down the corridor are sending away for catalogues of silver patterns is already conscious of swimming against the tide. (How different the atmosphere must be in a man's dormitory!) The magazine researcher who took her job as a steppingstone to becoming a writer, but discovers that girl researchers are not encouraged to write by the magazine's male editors, will find little sympathy and understanding from other researchers who have taken the job to mark time until their proper engagements are properly announced in *The New York Times*. The peer group pressure on a young woman in her 20s—as opposed to the pressure on a young man in his 20s—is decidedly against career.

I don't mean to imply that the force is necessarily insidious—although it sometimes is, and I intend to get around to discussing that aspect. I spent a wonderfully noncompetitive, warm, and friendly two years at *Newsweek* in the company of my "fellow" researchers in 1963–64 until I abruptly quit one day, wrenched myself out of the womb, because I finally realized that the warmth, the friendship, the long lunches, the joint shopping excursions to Saks Fifth Avenue, and the pleasant lack of direction among "the girls" had effectively smothered my own sense of direction. I was not the first *Newsweek* girl to break out of the researcher mold, and I will not be the last. But more heartening than individual breakthroughs is the news that has lately reached me from that sunny vineyard on Madison Avenue—the rumblings of insurrection among those very researchers who appeared so content with their lot just a few years ago.

There were two full-fledged women writers at *Newsweek* during the time I was there. One did her job quietly and went about unnoticed, but the other, an attractive, sexy young lady, was rather noticeable. We hated her. Among the grievances we held against this young woman was the fact that she never deigned to talk with us researchers. Considered herself superior, we thought. Got her job through unholy machinations, we believed. Dressed terribly, we agreed. *Couldn't really write*, we fervently hoped. It took me a few years after leaving the magazine to realize what this hostility toward someone we hardly knew was all about. She was where *we* wanted to be. When she walked through the halls she was L., the writer, not L., a researcher. There may have been 50 male writers who daily crossed our path at the magazine, but we spared them our collective resentment because, after all, they were men and we weren't. But L.—how dare she! She threatened our collective existence! Two years later, when I was working as a television newswriter at ABC (again, there were only two of us women writers), I experienced some of this collective cattiness from the ABC researchers and understood it perfectly. I also discovered that it's quite natural for writers to pal around with other writers and not with researchers. It has to do with field of interest and not with snobbery at all. L. knew it, and I discovered it.

There was a small item in the news not long ago about the first woman editor-in-chief of the University of Pennsylvania's daily student newspaper. The editor, Judith Teller, a junior at the University's Wharton School of Business, was quoted as saying, "I generally find women basically incompetent, and in general I deal with men." A harsh quote from Miss Teller, to be sure, and not designed to win her any women friends, but at the age of 20 Miss Teller, an obvious careerist, wants to be where the action is, and for that I can't blame her.

Women are *not* "basically incompetent," but so much of their energy goes into pretending incompetence when there are attractive men around who may be watching that the result is often the same. Schooled by their mothers to "let the man win" at ping-pong or tennis, how can they develop a good game? They can't, of course, and the game becomes not an exercise of skill but a minuet of manners. The ping-pong-and-tennis syndrome affects a woman's performance in practically all areas of her life. The idea is not to win. "Women is Losers," wails Janis Joplin in a repetitive, powerful lamentation. Losing has been equated with femininity for so long in our culture that it has become a virtual definition of the female role. The way to lose is not to try very hard to win, to convince oneself that personal achievement—if one is a woman—doesn't really matter at all. This peculiar attitude, which flies in the face of every success homily in *Poor Richard's Almanack*, is as unnatural as it is destructive. It has its parallels in the attitudes of the hardcore unemployed who have stripped away personal ambition and belief in their own abilities to a point where they are actually incapable of functioning. We are all familiar with the sexual double standards that men employ, but here is a sexual double standard that women hold on to for dear life: *admire individual achievement in men, but deny it for yourself.* The corollary to this dictum, by the way, is *marry the achiever.* Either way, it is a terrible denial of self-worth.

I have seen women who *admit* to small hankerings of personal ambition (usually expressed by a modest "I'd like to do more at work") throw up unbelievable psychological barriers to their own success. Two conversations I once had in the space of two days with a couple of young ladies who work in television will illustrate what I mean. Both women had neatly resolved their stymied careers with the oddest excuses I have ever heard. One thought she never could rise to a producer because she found the temperature in the film-editing rooms "too cold." The other said she never felt comfortable "near machines." To the first I answered, "Get a sweater." The second rendered me speechless. Of course, what these women were really saying was that their *femininity*—not the fact that they were female—somehow made them unfit for the tough world of television production.

The risk of losing that intangible called femininity weighs heavily on many women who are afraid to compete with men for better jobs. This sad state of affairs has come about because of arbitrary and rigid definitions of what is masculine and what is feminine that our culture has relied on for a variety of complex reasons. We can thank the hippie revolution for knocking down some of the old criteria, particularly external ones like the length of hair and form of dress. But as long as such qualities as self-assertion, decision making, and leadership are considered masculine—and conversely, unfeminine—a woman who worries about her femininity will never make a go of it in terms of career.

It was men who made the arbitrary rules of masculine/feminine that we suffer under, but it is women who continue to buy the stereotypes. At the early women's-liberation meetings that I attended, I was struck with how all of us were unwilling to assume leadership roles, and how often a sensible comment or brilliant new insight was couched between giggles and stutters or surrounded by self-disparaging phrases and gestures. Clearly, we were women who were unused to speaking forthrightly—without the frills and fur belows of "feminine" roundabout logic designed to make a point as gently as possible for fear of offending. Since we had nobody to offend but ourselves, this namby-pambying ceased to some extent with the passage of time.

But a women's-liberation meeting is a very special crucible. In the world outside, the stereotype of the aggressive, castrating bitch is still posted as a warning to us. If a woman believes in the existence of this mythical creature—and believes in her own potential transmogrification—her ease is hopeless. It astounds me that so many women remain convinced that a woman who functions in high gear in business, politics, or in the professions loses something intrinsic that is worth preserving. Personally, I have always felt that true femininity was rather indestructible. One look at the Irish revolutionary Bernadette Devlin should settle the matter once and for all. I suspect that this "castrating bitch" propaganda, a big lie, really, is perpetuated not only by insecure men but also by do-nothing women, the magpies who busy them-selves with nothing more than nest-building. There is no getting around the uncom-fortable truth that the militant stay-at-homes, the clinging vines, dislike and distrust their liberated sisters. I know exactly what I lost when I gave up pretending that passivity was a virtue and entered the competitive arena—some personality distor-tions which made me pirouette in concentric circles when I could have simply walked a straight line. And I know what I gained—self-esteem and a stretching of creative muscles and an exercising of a mind which had grown flaccid from disuse since the halcyon days of college.

A major tragedy of the female sex is that friendship and respect between women has never been highly regarded. During the dating years, girls are notoriously quick to ditch an appointment with a girlfriend at the sound of a male voice on the telephone. With marriage and family comes the suspicion that all other women are potentially "the other woman." In an early episode of *The Forsythe Saga* on TV, Irene the adulteress tells Young Jolyon's daughter, "Don't you know that women don't have friends? They have a lover, and they have people that they meet." How pathetic, but how historically accurate.

There is nothing in women's chemical or biological makeup that should preclude deep loyalty to those of the same sex. The sensitivity is certainly there, as is the capacity for warmth and love and fidelity. But until women cease to see themselves strictly in terms of men's eyes and to value men more highly than women, friendship with other women will remain a sometime thing, an expedient among competitors of inferior station that can be lightly discarded. I, for one, would much rather compete with men than for them. This affliction of competition between women for the attention of men—the only kind of women's competition that is encouraged by society—also affects the liberated women who managed to secure an equal footing with men in this man's world. Watch a couple of strong women in the same room and notice the sparks fly. Many women who reject the "woman is inferior" psychology for themselves apply it unsparingly to others of the same sex. An ambitious woman frequently thinks of herself as the only hen in the barnyard, to reverse a common metaphor. *She* is the exception, she believes. Women must recognize that they must make common cause with *all* women. When women get around to really liking—and respecting—other women, why then, we will have begun.

Chapter Eleven

Theory of Sexual Politics

Kate Millet

The three instances of sexual description we have examined so far were remarkable for the large part which notions of ascendancy and power played within them. Coitus can scarcely be said to take place in a vacuum; although of itself it appears a biological and physical activity, it is set so deeply within the larger context of human affairs that it serves as a charged microcosm of the variety of attitudes and values to which culture subscribes. Among other things, it may serve as a model of sexual politics on an individual or personal plane.

But of course the transition from such scenes of intimacy to a wider context of political reference is a great step indeed. In introducing the term "sexual politics," one must first answer the inevitable question "Can the relationship between the sexes be viewed in a political light at all?" The answer depends on how one defines politics.[1] This essay does not define the political as that relatively narrow and exclusive world of meetings, chairmen, and parties. The term "politics" shall refer to power-structured relationships, arrangements whereby one group of persons is controlled by another. By way of parenthesis one might add that although an ideal politics might simply be conceived of as the arrangement of human life on agreeable and rational principles from whence the entire notion of power *over* others should be banished, one must confess that this is not what constitutes the political as we know it, and it is to this that we must address ourselves.

The following sketch, which might be described as "notes toward a theory of patriarchy," will attempt to prove that sex is a status category with political implications. Something of a pioneering effort, it must perforce be both tentative and imperfect. Because the intention is to provide an overall description, statements must be generalized, exceptions neglected, and subheadings overlapping and, to some degree, arbitrary as well.

The word "politics" is enlisted here when speaking of the sexes primarily because such a word is eminently useful in outlining the real nature of their relative status, historically and at the present. It is opportune, perhaps today even mandatory, that we develop a more relevant psychology and philosophy of power relationships beyond the simple conceptual framework provided by our traditional formal politics. Indeed, it may be imperative that we give some attention to defining a theory of politics which treats of power relationships on grounds less conventional than those to which we are accustomed.[2] I have therefore found it pertinent to define them on grounds of personal contact and interaction between members of well-defined and coherent groups: races, castes, classes, and sexes. For it is precisely because certain groups have no representation in a number of recognized political structures that their position tends to be so stable, their oppression so continuous.

In America, recent events have forced us to acknowledge at last that the relationship between the races is indeed a political one which involves the general control of one collectivity, defined by birth, over another collectivity, also defined by birth. Groups who rule by birthright are fast disappearing, yet there remains one ancient and universal scheme for the domination of one birth group by another—the scheme that prevails in the area of sex. The study of racism has convinced us that a truly political state of affairs operates between the races to perpetuate a series of oppressive circumstances. The subordinated group has inadequate redress through existing political institutions, and is deterred thereby from organizing into conventional political struggle and opposition.

Quite in the same manner, a disinterested examination of our system of sexual relationship must point out that the situation between the sexes now, and throughout history, is a case of that phenomenon Max Weber defined as *herrschaft*, a relationship of dominance and subordinance.[3] What goes largely unexamined, often even unacknowledged (yet is institutionalized nonetheless) in our social order, is the birthright priority whereby males rule females. Through this system a most ingenious form of "interior colonization" has been achieved. It is one which tends moreover to be sturdier than any form of segregation, and more rigorous than class stratification, more uniform, certainly more enduring. However muted its present appearance may be, sexual dominion obtains nevertheless as perhaps the most pervasive ideology of our culture and provides its most fundamental concept of power.

This is so because our society, like all other historical civilizations, is a patriarchy.[4] The fact is evident at once if one recalls that the military, industry, technology, universities, science, political office, and finance—in short, every avenue of power within the society, including the coercive force of the police, is entirely in male hands. As the essence of politics is power, such realization cannot fail to carry impact. What lingers of supernatural authority, the Deity, "His" ministry, together with the ethics and values, the philosophy and art of our culture—its very civilization—as T. S. Eliot once observed, is of male manufacture.

If one takes patriarchal government to be the institution whereby that half of the populace which is female is controlled by that half which is male, the principles of patriarchy appear to be two fold: male shall dominate female, elder male shall dominate younger. However, just as with any human institution, there is frequently a distance between the real and the ideal; contradictions and exceptions do exist within the system. While patriarchy as an institution is a social constant so deeply entrenched as to run through all other political, social, or economic forms, whether of caste or class, feudality or bureaucracy, just as it pervades all major religions, it also exhibits great variety in history and locale. In democracies,[5] for example, females have often held no office or do so (as now) in such minuscule numbers as to be below even token representation. Aristocracy, on the other hand, with its emphasis upon the magic and dynastic properties of blood, may at times permit women to hold power. The principle of rule by elder males is violated even more frequently. Bearing in mind the variation and degree in patriarchy—as say between Saudi Arabia and Sweden, Indonesia and Red China—we also recognize our own form in the U.S. and Europe to be much altered and attenuated by the reforms described in the next chapter.

I Ideological

Hannah Arendt[6] has observed that government is upheld by power supported either through consent or imposed through violence. Conditioning to an ideology amounts to the former. Sexual politics obtains consent through the "socialization" of both sexes to basic patriarchal polities with regard to temperament, role, and status. As to status, a pervasive assent to the prejudice of male superiority guarantees superior status in the male, inferior in the female. The first item, temperament, involves the formation of human personality along stereotyped lines of sex category ("masculine" and "feminine"), based on the needs and values of the dominant group and dictated by what its members cherish in themselves and find convenient in subordinates: aggression, intelligence, force, and efficacy in the male; passivity, ignorance, docility, "virtue," and ineffectuality in the female. This is complemented by a second factor, sex role, which decrees a consonant and highly elaborate code of conduct, gesture and attitude for each sex. In terms of activity, sex role assigns domestic service and attendance upon infants to the female, the rest of human achievement, interest, and ambition to the male. The limited role allotted the female tends to arrest her at the level of biological experience. Therefore, nearly all that can be described as distinctly human rather than animal activity (in their own way animals also give birth and care for their young) is largely reserved for the male. Of course, status again follows from such an assignment. Were one to analyze the three categories one might designate status as the political component, role as the sociological, and temperament as the psychological—yet their interdependence is unquestionable and they form a chain. Those awarded higher status tend to adopt roles of mastery, largely because they are first encouraged to develop temperaments of dominance. That this is true of caste and class as well is self-evident.

II Biological

Patriarchal religion, popular attitude, and to some degree, science as well[7] assumes these psycho-social distinctions to rest upon biological differences between the sexes, so that where culture is acknowledged as shaping behavior, it is said to do no more than cooperate with nature. Yet the temperamental distinctions created in patriarchy ("masculine" and "feminine" personality traits) do not appear to originate in human nature, those of role and status still less.

The heavier musculature of the male, a secondary sexual characteristic and common among mammals, is biological in origin but is also culturally encouraged through breeding, diet and exercise. Yet it is hardly an adequate category on which to base political relations *within civilization*.[8] Male supremacy, like other political creeds, does not finally reside in physical strength but in the acceptance of a value system which is not biological. Superior physical strength is not a factor in political relations—vide those of race and class. Civilization has always been able to substitute other methods (technic, weaponry, knowledge) for those of physical strength, and contemporary civilization has no further need of it. At present, as in the past, physical exertion is very generally a class factor, those at the bottom performing the most strenuous tasks, whether they be strong or not.

It is often assumed that patriarchy is endemic in human social life, explicable or even inevitable on the grounds of human physiology. Such a theory grants patriarchy logical as well as historical origin. Yet if as some anthropologists believe, patriarchy is not of primeval origin, but was preceded by some other social form we shall call pre-patriarchal, then the argument of physical strength as a theory of patriarchal *origins* would hardly constitute a sufficient explanation—unless the male's superior physical strength was released in accompaniment with some change in orientation through new values or new knowledge. Conjecture about origins is always frustrated by lack of certain evidence. Speculation about prehistory, which of necessity is what this must be, remains nothing but speculation. Were one to indulge in it, one might argue the likelihood of a hypothetical period preceding patriarchy.[9] What would be crucial to such a premise would be a state of mind in which the primary principle would be regarded as fertility or vitalist processes. In a primitive condition, before it developed civilization or any but the crudest technic, humanity would perhaps find the most impressive evidence of creative force in the visible birth of children, something of a miraculous event and linked analogically with the growth of the earth's vegetation.

It is possible that the circumstance which might drastically redirect such attitudes would be the discovery of paternity. There is some evidence that fertility cults in ancient society at some point took a turn toward patriarchy, displacing and downgrading female function in procreation and attributing the power of life to the phallus alone. Patriarchal religion could consolidate this position by the creation of a male God or gods, demoting, discrediting, or eliminating goddesses and constructing a theology whose basic postulates are male supremacist, and one of whose central functions is to uphold and validate the patriarchal structure.[10]

So much for the evanescent delights afforded by the game of origins. The question of the historical origins of patriarchy—whether patriarchy originated primordially in the male's superior strength, or upon a later mobilization of such strength under certain circumstances—appears at the moment to be unanswerable. It is also probably irrelevant to contemporary patriarchy, where we are left with the realities of sexual politics, still grounded, we are often assured, on nature. Unfortunately, as the psycho-social distinctions made between the two sex groups which are said to justify their present political relationship are not the clear, specific, measurable and neutral ones of the physical sciences, but are instead of an entirely different character— vague, amorphous, often even quasi-religious in phrasing—it must be admitted that

many of the generally understood distinctions between the sexes in the more significant areas of role and temperament, not to mention status, have in fact, essentially
cultural, rather than biological, bases. Attempts to prove that temperamental dominance is inherent in the male (which for its advocates, would be tantamount to
validating, logically as well as historically, the patriarchal situation regarding role and
status) have been notably unsuccessful. Sources in the field are in hopeless disagreement about the nature of sexual differences, but the most reasonable among them
have despaired of the ambition of any definite equation between temperament and
biological nature. It appears that we are not soon to be enlightened as to the existence
of any significant inherent differences between male and female beyond the bio-
genital ones we already know. Endocrinology and genetics afford no definite evidence
of determining mental-emotional differences.[11]

Not only is there insufficient evidence for the thesis that the present social distinctions of patriarchy (status, role, temperament) are physical in origin, but we are
hardly in a position to assess the existing differentiations, since distinctions which we
know to be culturally induced at present so outweigh them. Whatever the "real"
differences between the sexes may be, we are not likely to know them until the sexes
are treated differently, that is alike. And this is very far from being the case at present.
Important new research not only suggests that the possibilities of innate temperamental differences seem more remote than ever, but even raises questions as to the
validity and permanence of psycho-sexual identity. In doing so it gives fairly concrete
positive evidence of the overwhelmingly *cultural* character of gender, i.e. personality
structure in terms of sexual category.

What Stoller and other experts define as "core gender identity" is now thought to
be established in the young by the age of eighteen months. This is how Stoller
differentiates between sex and gender:

> Dictionaries stress that the major connotation of *sex* is a biological one, as for example,
> in the phrases *sexual relations* or *the male sex*. In agreement with this, the word *sex*, in
> this work will refer to the male or female sex and the component biological parts that
> determine whether one is a male or a female; the word *sexual* will have connotations of
> anatomy and physiology. This obviously leaves tremendous areas of behavior, feelings,
> thoughts and fantasies that are related to the sexes and yet do not have primarily
> biological connotations. It is for some of these psychological phenomena that the term
> gender will be used: one can speak of the male sex or the female sex, but one can also
> talk about masculinity and femininity and not necessarily be implying anything about
> anatomy or physiology. Thus, while *sex* and *gender* seem to common sense inextricably
> bound together, one purpose this study will be to confirm the fact that the two realms
> (sex and gender) are not inevitably bound in anything like a one-to-one relationship,
> but each may go into quite independent ways.[12]

In cases of genital malformation and consequent erroneous gender assignment at
birth, studied at the California Gender Identity Center, the discovery was made that
it is easier to change the sex of an adolescent male, whose biological identity turns
out to be contrary to his gender assignment and conditioning—through surgery—
than to undo the educational consequences of years, which have succeeded in making
the subject temperamentally feminine in gesture, sense of self, personality and inter-

ests. Studies done in California under Stoller's direction offer proof that gender identity (I am a girl, I am a boy) is the primary identity any human being holds—the first as well as the most permanent and far-reaching. Stoller later makes emphatic the distinction that sex is biological, gender psychological, and therefore cultural: "*Gender* is a term that has psychological or cultural rather than biological connotations. If the proper terms for sex are "male" and "female," the corresponding terms for gender are "masculine" and "feminine"; these latter may be quite independent of (biological) sex."[13] Indeed, so arbitrary is gender, that it may even be contrary to physiology: ". . . although the external genitalia (penis, testes, scrotum) contribute to the sense of maleness, no one of them is essential for it, not even all of them together. In the absence of complete evidence, I agree in general with Money, and the Hampsons who show in their large series of intersexed patients that gender role is determined by postnatal forces, regardless of the anatomy and physiology of the external genitalia."[14]

It is now believed [15] that the human fetus is originally physically female until the operation of androgen at a certain stage of gestation causes those with *y* chromosomes to develop into males. Psychosexually (e.g., in terms of masculine and feminine, and in contradistinction to male and female) there is no differentiation between the sexes at birth. Psychosexual personality is therefore postnatal and learned.

> . . . the condition existing at birth and for several months thereafter is one of psychosexual undifferentiation. Just as in the embryo, morphologic sexual differentiation passes from a plastic stage to one of fixed immutability, so also does psychosexual differentiation become fixed and immutable—so much so, that mankind has traditionally assumed that so strong and fixed a feeling as personal sexual identity must stem from something innate, instinctive, and not subject to postnatal experience and learning. The error of this traditional assumption is that the power and permanence of something learned has been underestimated. The experiments of animal ethologists on imprinting have now corrected this misconception.[16]

John Money, who is quoted above, believes that "the acquisition of a native language is a human counterpart to imprinting," and gender first established "with the establishment of a native language."[17] This would place the time of establishment at about eighteen months. Jerome Kagin's[18] studies in how children of pre-speech age are handled and touched, tickled and spoken to in terms of their sexual identity ("Is it a boy or a girl?" "Hello, little fellow," "Isn't she pretty," etc.) put the most considerable emphasis on purely tactile learning which would have much to do with the child's sense of self, even before speech is attained.

Because of our social circumstances, male and female are really two cultures and their life experiences are utterly different—and this is crucial. Implicit in all the gender identity development which takes place through childhood is the sum total of the parents', the peers', and the culture's notions of what is appropriate to each gender by way of temperament, character, interests, status, worth, gesture, and expression. Every moment of the child's life is a clue to how he or she must think and behave to attain or satisfy the demands which gender places upon one. In adolescence, the merciless task of conformity grows to crisis proportions, generally cooling and settling in maturity.

Since patriarchy's biological foundations appear to be so very insecure, one has some cause to admire the strength of a "socialization" which can continue a universal condition "on faith alone," as it were, or through an acquired value system exclusively. What does seem decisive in assuring the maintenance of the temperamental differences between the sexes is the conditioning of early childhood. Conditioning runs in a circle of self-perpetuation and self-fulfilling prophecy. To take a simple example: expectations the culture cherishes about his gender identity encourage the young male to develop aggressive impulses, and the female to thwart her own or turn them inward. The result is that the male tends to have aggression reinforced in his behavior, often with significant anti-social possibilities. Thereupon the culture consents to believe the possession of the male indicator, the testes, penis, and scrotum, in itself characterizes the aggressive impulse, and even vulgarly celebrates it in such encomiums as "that guy has balls." The same process of reinforcement is evident in producing the chief "feminine" virtue of passivity.

In contemporary terminology, the basic division of temperamental trait is marshaled along the line of "aggression is male" and "passivity is female." All other temperamental traits are somehow—often with the most dexterous ingenuity—aligned to correspond. If aggressiveness is the trait of the master class, docility must be the corresponding trait of a subject group. The usual hope of such line of reasoning is that "nature," by some impossible outside chance, might still be depended upon to rationalize the patriarchal system. An important consideration to be remembered here is that in patriarchy, the function of norm is unthinkingly delegated to the male—were it not, one might as plausibly speak of "feminine" behavior as active, and "masculine" behavior as hyperactive or hyperaggressive.

Here it might be added, by way of a coda, that data from physical sciences has recently been enlisted again to support sociological arguments, such as those of Lionel Tiger[19] who seeks a genetic justification of patriarchy by proposing a "bonding instinct" in males which assures their political and social control of human society. One sees the implication of such a theory by applying its premise to any ruling group. Tiger's thesis appears to be a misrepresentation of the work of Lorenz and other students of animal behavior. Since his evidence of inherent trait is patriarchal; history and organization, his pretensions to physical evidence are both specious and circular. One can only advance genetic evidence when one has genetic (rather than historical) evidence to advance. As many authorities dismiss the possibility of instincts (complex inherent behavioral patterns) in humans altogether, admitting only reflexes and drives (far simpler neural responses),[20] the prospects of a "bonding instinct" appear particularly forlorn.

Should one regard sex in humans as a drive, it is still necessary to point out that the enormous area of our lives, both in early "socialization" and in adult experience, labeled "sexual behavior," is almost entirely the product of learning. So much is this the case that even the act of coitus itself is the product of a long series of learned responses—responses to the patterns and attitudes, even as to the object of sexual choice, which are set up for us by our social environment.

The arbitrary character of patriarchal ascriptions of temperament and role has little effect upon their power over us. Nor do the mutually exclusive, contradictory, and polar qualities of the categories "masculine" and "feminine" imposed upon human personality give rise to sufficiently serious question among us. Under their aegis each personality becomes little more, and often less than half, of its human potential. Politically, the fact that each group exhibits a circumscribed but complementary personality and range of activity is of secondary importance to the fact that each represents a status or power division. In the matter of conformity patriarchy is a governing ideology without peer; it is probable that no other system has ever exercised such a complete control over its subjects.

III Sociological

Patriarchy's chief institution is the family. It is both a mirror of and a connection with the larger society; a patriarchal unit within a patriarchal whole. Mediating between the individual and the social structure, the family effects control and conformity where political and other authorities are insufficient.[21] As the fundamental instrument and the foundation unit of patriarchal society the family and its roles are prototypical. Serving as an agent of the larger society, the family not only encourages its own members to adjust and conform, but acts as a unit in the government of the patriarchal state which rules its citizens through its family heads. Even in patriarchal societies where they are granted legal citizenship, women tend to be ruled through the family alone and have little or no formal relation to the state.[22]

As co-operation between the family and the larger society is essential, else both would fall apart, the fate of three patriarchal institutions, the family, society, and the state are interrelated. In most forms of patriarchy this has generally led to the granting of religious support in statements such as the Catholic precept that "the father is head of the family," or Judaism's delegation of quasi-priestly authority to the male parent. Secular governments today also confirm this, as in census practices of designating the male as head of household, taxation, passports etc. Female heads of household tend to be regarded as undesirable; the phenomenon is a trait of poverty or misfortune. The Confucian prescription that the relationship between ruler and subject is parallel to that of father and children points to the essentially feudal character of the patriarchal family (and conversely, the familial character of feudalism) even in modern democracies.[23]

Traditionally, patriarchy granted the father nearly total ownership over wife or wives and children, including the powers of physical abuse and often even those of murder and sale. Classically, as head of the family the father is both begetter and owner in a system in which kinship is property.[24] Yet in strict patriarchy, kinship is acknowledged only through association with the male line. Agnation excludes the descendants of the female line from property right and often even from recognition.[25] The first formulation of the patriarchal family was made by Sir Henry Maine, a nineteenth-century historian of ancient jurisprudence. Maine argues that the patriarchal basis of kinship is put in terms of dominion rather than blood; wives, though outsiders, are assimilated into the line, while sister's sons are excluded. Basing his definition of the family upon the *patria potestes* of Rome, Maine defined it as follows:

"The eldest male parent is absolutely supreme in his household. His dominion extends to life and death and is as unqualified over his children and their houses as over his slaves."[26] In the archaic patriarchal family "the group consists of animate and inanimate property, of wife, children, slaves, land and goods, all held together by subjection to the despotic authority of the eldest male."[27]

McLennon's rebuttal[28] to Maine argued that the Roman *patria potestes* was an extreme form of patriarchy and by no means, as Maine had imagined, universal. Evidence of matrilineal societies (preliterate societies in Africa and elsewhere) refute Maine's assumption of the universality of agnation. Certainly Maine's central argument, as to the primeval or state of nature character of patriarchy is but a rather naïf[29] rationalization of an institution Maine tended to exalt. The assumption of patriarchy's primeval character is contradicted by much evidence which points to the conclusion that full patriarchal authority, particularly that of the *patria potestes* is a late development and the total erosion of female status was likely to be gradual as has been its recovery.

In contemporary patriarchies the male's *de jure* priority has recently been modified through the granting of divorce[30] protection, citizenship, and property to women. Their chattel status continues in their loss of name, their obligation to adopt the husband's domicile, and the general legal assumption that marriage involves an exchange of the female's domestic service and (sexual) consortium in return for financial support.[31]

The chief contribution of the family in patriarchy is the socialization of the young (largely through the example and admonition of their parents) into patriarchal ideology's prescribed attitudes toward the categories of role, temperament, and status. Although slight differences of definition depend here upon the parents' grasp of cultural values, the general effect of uniformity is achieved, to be further reinforced through peers, schools, media, and other learning sources, formal and informal. While we may niggle over the balance of authority between the personalities of various households, one must remember that the entire culture supports masculine authority in all areas of life and—outside of the home—permits the female none at all.

To insure that its crucial functions of reproduction and socialization of the young take place only within its confines, the patriarchal family insists upon legitimacy. Bronislaw Malinowski describes this as "the principle of legitimacy" formulating it as an insistence that "no child should be brought into the world without a man—and one man at that—assuming the role of sociological father."[32] By this apparently consistent and universal prohibition (whose penalties vary by class and in accord with the expected operations of the double standard) patriarchy decrees that the status of both child and mother is primarily or ultimately dependent upon the male. And since it is not only his social status, but even his economic power upon which his dependents generally rely, the position of the masculine figure within the family—as without—is materially, as well as ideologically, extremely strong.

Although there is no biological reason why the two central functions of the family (socialization and reproduction) need be inseparable from or even take place within it, revolutionary or utopian efforts to remove these functions from the family have been so frustrated, so beset by difficulties, that most experiments so far have involved a gradual return to tradition. This is strong evidence of how basic a form patriarchy is within all societies, and of how pervasive its effects upon family members. It is perhaps also an admonition that change undertaken without a thorough understanding of the socio-political institution to be changed is hardly productive. And yet radical social change cannot take place without having an effect upon patriarchy. And not simply because it is the political form which subordinates such a large percentage of the population (women and youth) but because it serves as a citadel of property and traditional interests. Marriages are financial alliances, and each household operates as an economic entity much like a corporation. As one student of the family states it, "the family is the keystone of the stratification system, the social mechanism by which it is maintained."[33]

IV Class

It is in the area of class that the castelike status of the female within patriarchy is most liable to confusion, for sexual status often operates in a superficially confusing way within the variable of class. In a society where status is dependent upon the economic, social, and educational circumstances of class, it is possible for certain females to appear to stand higher than some males. Yet not when one looks more closely at the subject. This is perhaps easier to see by means of analogy: a black doctor or lawyer has higher social status than a poor white sharecropper. But race, itself a caste system which subsumes class, persuades the latter citizen that he belongs to a higher order of life, just as it oppresses the black professional in spirit, whatever his material success may be. In much the same manner, a truck driver or butcher has always his "manhood" to fall back upon. Should this final vanity be offended, he may contemplate more violent methods. The literature of the past thirty years provides a staggering number of incidents in which the caste of virility triumphs over the social status of wealthy or even educated women. In literary contexts one has to deal here with wish-fulfillment. Incidents from life (bullying, obscene, or hostile remarks) are probably another sort of psychological gesture of ascendancy. Both convey more hope than reality, for class divisions are generally quite impervious to the hostility of individuals. And yet while the existence of class division is not seriously threatened by such expressions of enmity, the existence of sexual hierarchy has been re-affirmed and mobilized to "punish" the female quite effectively.

The function of class or ethnic mores in patriarchy is largely a matter of how overtly displayed or how loudly enunciated the general ethic of masculine supremacy allows itself to become. Here one is confronted by what appears to be a paradox: while in the lower social strata, the male is more likely to claim authority on the strength of his sex rank alone, he is actually obliged more often to share power with the women of his class who are economically productive; whereas in the middle and upper classes, there is less tendency to assert a blunt patriarchal dominance, as men who enjoy such status have more power in any case.[34]

It is generally accepted that Western patriarchy has been much softened by the concepts of courtly and romantic love. While this is certainly true, such influence has also been vastly overestimated. In comparison with the candor of "machismo" or oriental behavior, one realizes how much of a concession traditional chivalrous behavior represents—a sporting kind of reparation to allow the subordinate female certain means of saving face. While a palliative to the injustice of woman's social position, chivalry is also a technique for disguising it. One must acknowledge that the chivalrous stance is a game the master group plays in elevating its subject to pedestal level. Historians of courtly love stress the fact that the raptures of the poets had no effect upon the legal or economic standing of women, and very little upon their social status.[35] As the sociologist Hugo Beigel has observed, both the courtly and the romantic versions of love are "grants" which the male concedes out of his total powers.[36] Both have had the effects of obscuring the patriarchal character of Western culture and in their general tendency to attribute impossible virtues to women, have ended by confining them in a narrow and often remarkably conscribing sphere of behavior. It was a Victorian habit, for example, to insist the female assume the function of serving as the male's conscience and living the life of goodness he found tedious but felt someone ought to do anyway.

The concept of romantic love affords a means of emotional manipulation which the male is free to exploit, since love is the only circumstance in which the female is (ideologically) pardoned for sexual activity. And convictions of romantic love are convenient to both parties since this is often the only condition in which the female can overcome the far more powerful conditioning she has received toward sexual inhibition. Romantic love also obscures the realities of female status and the burden of economic dependency. As to "chivalry," such gallant gesture as still resides in the middle classes has degenerated to a tired ritualism, which scarcely serves to mask the status situation of the present.

Within patriarchy one must often deal with contradictions which are simply a matter of class style. David Riesman has noted that as the working class has been assimilated into the middle class, so have its sexual mores and attitudes. The fairly blatant male chauvinism which was once a province of the lower class or immigrant male has been absorbed and taken on a certain glamour through a number of contemporary figures, who have made it, and a certain number of other working-class male attitudes, part of a new, and at the moment, fashionable life style. So influential is this working-class ideal of brute virility (or more accurately, a literary and therefore middle-class version of it) become in our time that it may replace more discreet and "gentlemanly" attitudes of the past.[37]

One of the chief effects of class within patriarchy is to set one woman against another, in the past creating a lively antagonism between whore and matron, and in the present between career woman and housewife. One envies the other her "security" and prestige, while the envied yearns beyond the confines of respectability for what she takes to be the other's freedom, adventure, and contact with the great world. Through the multiple advantages of the double standard, the male participates in both worlds, empowered by his superior social and economic resources to play the estranged women against each other as rivals. One might also recognize subsidiary status categories among women: not only is virtue class, but beauty and age as well.

Perhaps, in the final analysis, it is possible to argue that women tend to transcend the usual class stratifications in patriarchy, for whatever the class of her birth and education, the female has fewer permanent class association than does the male. Economic dependency renders her affiliations with any class a tangential, vicarious, and temporary matter. Aristotle observed that the only slave to whom a commoner might lay claim was his woman, and the service of an unpaid domestic still provides working-class males with a "cushion" against the buffets of the class system which incidentally provides them with some of the psychic luxuries of the leisure class. Thrown upon their own resources, few women rise above working class in personal prestige and economic power, and women as a group do not enjoy many of the interests and benefits any class may offer its male members. Women have therefore less of an investment in the class system. But it is important to understand that as with any group whose existence is parasitic to its rulers, women are a dependency class who live on surplus. And their marginal life frequently renders them conservative, for like all persons in their situation (slaves are a classic example here) they identify their own survival with the prosperity of those who feed them. The hope of seeking liberating radical solutions of their own seems too remote for the majority to dare contemplate and remains so until consciousness on the subject is raised.

As race is emerging as one of the final variables in sexual politics, it is pertinent, especially in a discussion of modern literature, to devote a few words to it as well. Traditionally, the white male has been accustomed to concede the female of his own race, in her capacity as "his woman" a higher status than that ascribed to the black male.[38] Yet as white racist ideology is exposed and begins to erode, racism's older protective attitudes toward (white) women also begin to give way. And the priorities of maintaining male supremacy might outweigh even those of white supremacy; sexism may be more endemic in our own society than racism. For example, one notes in authors whom we would now term overtly racist, such as D. H. Lawrence—whose contempt for what he so often designates as inferior breeds is unabashed—instances where the lower-caste male is brought on to master or humiliate the white man's own insubordinate mate. Needless to say, the female of the non-white races does not figure in such tales save as an exemplum of "true" womanhood's servility, worthy of imitation by other less carefully instructed females. Contemporary white sociology often operates under a similar patriarchal bias when its rhetoric inclines toward the assertion that the "matriarchal" (e.g. matrifocal) aspect of black society and the "castration" of the black male are the most deplorable symptoms of black oppression in white racist society, with the implication that racial inequity is capable of solution by a restoration of masculine authority. Whatever the facts of the matter may be, it can also be suggested that analysis of this kind presupposes patriarchal values without questioning them, and tends to obscure both the true character of and the responsibility for racist injustice toward black humanity of both sexes.

V Economic and Educational

One of the most efficient branches of patriarchal government lies in the agency of its economic hold over its female subjects. In traditional patriarchy, women, as non-persons without legal standing, were permitted no actual economic existence as they could neither own nor earn in their own right. Since women have always worked in patriarchal societies, often at the most routine or strenuous tasks, what is at issue here is not labor but economic reward. In modern reformed patriarchal societies, women have certain economic rights, yet the "woman's work" in which some two thirds of the female population in most developed countries are engaged is work that is not paid for.[39] In a money economy where autonomy and prestige depend upon currency, this is a fact of great importance. In general, the position of women in patriarchy is a continuous function of their economic dependence. Just as their social position is vicarious and achieved (often on a temporary or marginal basis) though males, their relation to the economy is also typically vicarious or tangential.

Of that third of women who are employed, their average wages represent only half of the average income enjoyed by men. These are the U.S. Department of Labor statistics for average year-round income: white male, $6704, non-white male $4277, white female, $3991, and non-white female $2816.[40] The disparity is made somewhat more remarkable because the educational level of women is generally higher than that of men in comparable income brackets.[41] Further, the kinds of employment open to women in modern patriarchies are, with few exceptions, menial, ill paid and without status.[42]

In modern capitalist countries women also function as a reserve labor force, enlisted in times of war and expansion and discharged in times of peace and recession. In this role American women have replaced immigrant labor and now compete with the racial minorities. In socialist countries the female labor force is generally in the lower ranks as well, despite a high incidence of women in certain professions such as medicine. The status and rewards of such professions have declined as women enter them, and they are permitted to enter such areas under a rationale that society or the state (and socialist countries are also patriarchal) rather than woman is served by such activity.

Since woman's independence in economic life is viewed with distrust, prescriptive agencies of all kinds (religion, psychology, advertising, etc.) continuously admonish or even inveigh against the employment of middleclass women, particularly mothers. The toil of working-class women is more readily accepted as "need," if not always by the working-class itself, at least by the middle-class. And to be sure, it serves the purpose of making available cheap labor in factory and lower-grade service and clerical positions. Its wages and tasks are so unremunerative that, unlike more prestigious employment for women, it fails to threaten patriarchy financially or psychologically. Women who are employed have two jobs since the burden of domestic service and child care is unrelieved either by day care or other social agencies, or by the co-operation of husbands. The invention of labor-saving devices has had no appreciable effect on the duration, even if it has affected the quality of their drudgery.[43] Discrimination in matters of hiring, maternity, wages and hours is very great.[44] In the U.S. a recent law forbidding discrimination in employment, the first and only federal legislative guarantee of rights granted to American women since the vote, is not enforced, has not been enforced since its passage, and was not enacted to be enforced.[45]

In terms of industry and production, the situation of women is in many ways comparable both to colonial and to pre-industrial peoples. Although they achieved their first economic autonomy in the industrial revolution and now constitute a large and underpaid factory population, women do not participate directly in technology or in production. What they customarily produce (domestic and personal service) has no market value and is, as it were, pre-capital. Nor, where they do participate in production of commodities through employment, do they own or control or even comprehend the process in which they participate. An example might make this clearer: the refrigerator is a machine all women use, some assemble it in factories, and a very few with scientific education understand its principles of operation. Yet the heavy industries which roll its steel and produce the dies for its parts are in male hands. The same is true of the typewriter, the auto, etc. Now, while knowledge is fragmented even among the male population, collectively they could reconstruct any technological device. But in the absence of males, women's distance from technology today is sufficiently great that it is doubtful that they could replace or repair such machines on any significant scale. Woman's distance from higher technology is even greater: large-scale building construction; the development of computers; the moon shot, occur as further examples. If knowledge is power, power is also knowledge, and a large factor in their subordinate position is the fairly systematic ignorance patriarchy imposes upon women.

Since education and economy are so closely related in the advanced nations, it is significant that the general level and style of higher education for women, particularly in their many remaining segregated institutions, is closer to that of Renaissance humanism than to the skills of mid-twentieth-century scientific and technological society. Traditionally patriarchy permitted occasional minimal literacy to women while higher education was closed to them. While modern patriarchies have, fairly recently, opened all educational levels to women,[46] the kind and quality of education is not the same for each sex. This difference is of course apparent in early socialization, but it persists and enters into higher education as well. Universities, once places of scholarship and the training of a few professionals, now also produce the personnel of a technocracy. This is not the case with regard to women. Their own colleges typically produce neither scholars nor professionals nor technocrats. Nor are they funded by government and corporations as are male colleges and those co-educational colleges and universities whose primary function is the education of males.

As patriarchy enforces a temperamental imbalance of personality traits between the sexes, its educational institutions, segregated or co-educational, accept a cultural programing toward the generally operative division between "masculine" and "feminine" subject matter, assigning the humanities and certain social sciences (at least in their lower or marginal branches) to the female—and science and technology, the professions, business and engineering to the male. Of course the balance of employment, prestige and reward at present lie with the latter. Control of these fields is very eminently a matter of political power. One might also point out how the exclusive dominance of males in the more prestigious fields directly serves the interests of patriarchal power in industry, government, and the military. And since patriarchy encourages an imbalance in human temperament along sex lines, both divisions of learning (science and the humanities) reflect this imbalance. The humanities, because not exclusively male, suffer in prestige: the sciences, technology, and business, be- cause they are nearly exclusively male reflect the deformation of the "masculine" personality, e.g., a certain predatory or aggressive character.

In keeping with the inferior sphere of culture to which women in patriarchy have always been restricted, the present encouragement of their "artistic" interests through study of the humanities is hardly more than an extension of the "accom- plishments" they once cultivated in preparation for the marriage market. Achieve- ment in the arts and humanities is reserved, now, as it has been historically, for males. Token representation, be it Susan Sontag's or Lady Murasaki's does not vi- tiate this rule.

VI Force

We are not accustomed to associate patriarchy with force. So perfect is its system of socialization, so complete the general assent to its values, so long and so universally has it prevailed in human society, that it scarcely seems to require violent implemen- tation. Customarily, we view its brutalities in the past as exotic or "primitive" custom. Those of the present are regarded as the product of individual deviance, confined to pathological or exceptional behavior, and without general import. And yet, just as under other total ideologies (racism and colonialism are somewhat analogous in this respect) control in patriarchal society would be imperfect, even inoperable, unless it had the rule of force to rely upon, both in emergencies and as an ever-present instrument of intimidation.

Historically, most patriarchies have institutionalized force through their legal sys- tems. For example, strict patriarchies such as that of Islam, have implemented the prohibition against illegitimacy or sexual autonomy with a death sentence. In Af- ghanistan and Saudi Arabia the adulteress is still stoned to death with a mullah presiding at the execution. Execution by stoning was once common practice through the Near East. It is still condoned in Sicily. Needless to say there was and is no penalty imposed upon the male correspondent. Save in recent times or exceptional cases, adultery was not generally recognized in males except as an offense one male might commit against another's property interest. In Tokugawa Japan, for example, an elaborate set of legal distinctions was made according to class. A samurai was entitled, and in the face of public knowledge, even obliged, to execute an adulterous wife, whereas a chōnin (common citizen) or peasant might respond as he pleased. In cases of cross-class adultery, the lower-class male convicted of sexual intimacy with his employer's wife would, because he had violated taboos of class and property, be beheaded together with her. Upper-strata males had, of course, the same license to seduce lower-class women as we are familiar with in Western societies.

Indirectly, one form of "death penalty" still obtains even in America today. Patriarchal legal systems in depriving women of control over their own bodies drive them to illegal abortions; it is estimated that between two and five thousand women die each year from this cause.[47]

Excepting a social license to physical abuse among certain class and ethnic groups, force is diffuse and generalized in most contemporary patriarchies. Significantly, force itself is restricted to the male who alone is psychologically and technically equipped to perpetrate physical violence.[48] Where differences in physical strength have become immaterial through the use of arms, the female is rendered innocuous by her socialization. Before assault she is almost universally defenseless both by her physical and emotional training. Needless to say, this has the most far-reaching effects on the social and psychological behavior of both sexes.

Patriarchal force also relies on a form of violence particularly sexual in character and realized most completely in the act of rape. The figures of rapes reported represent only a fraction of those which occur,[49] as the "shame" of the event is sufficient to deter women from the notion of civil prosecution under the public circumstances of a trial. Traditionally rape has been viewed as an offense one male commits upon another—a matter of abusing "his woman." Vendetta, such as occurs in the American South, is carried out for masculine satisfaction, the exhilarations of race hatred, and the interests of property and vanity (honor). In rape, the emotions of aggression, hatred, contempt, and the desire to break or violate personality, take a form consummately appropriate to sexual politics. In the passages analyzed at the outset of this study, such emotions were present at a barely sublimated level and were a key factor in explaining the attitude behind the author's use of language and tone.[50]

Patriarchal societies typically link feelings of cruelty with sexuality, the latter often equated both with evil and with power. This is apparent both in the sexual fantasy reported by psychoanalysis and that reported by pornography. The rule here associates sadism with the male ("the masculine role") and victimization with the female ("the feminine role").[51] Emotional response to violence against women in patriarchy is often curiously ambivalent; references to wife-beating, for example, invariably produce laughter and some embarrassment. Exemplary atrocity, such as the mass murders committed by Richard Speck, greeted at one level with a certain scandalized, possibly hypocritical indignation, is capable of eliciting a mass response of titillation at another level. At such times one even hears from men occasional expressions of envy or amusement. In view of the sadistic character of such public fantasy as caters to male audiences in pornography or semi-pornographic media, one might expect that a certain element of identification is by no means absent from the general response. Probably a similar collective *frisson* sweeps through racist society when its more "logical" members have perpetrated a lynching. Unconsciously, both crimes may serve the larger group as a ritual act, cathartic in effect.

Hostility is expressed in a number of ways. One is laughter. Misogynist literature, the primary vehicle of masculine hostility, is both an hortatory and comic genre. Of all artistic forms in patriarchy it is most frankly propagandistic. Its aim is to reinforce both sexual factions in their status. Ancient, Medieval, and Renaissance literature in the West has each had a large element of misogyny.[52] Nor is the East without a strong tradition here, notably in the Confucian strain which held sway in Japan as well as China. The Western tradition was indeed moderated somewhat by the introduction of courtly love. But the old diatribes and attacks were coterminous with the new idealization of woman. In the case of Petrarch, Boccaccio, and some others, one can find both attitudes fully expressed, presumably as evidence of different moods, a courtly pose adopted for the ephemeral needs of the vernacular, a grave animosity for sober and eternal Latin.[53] As courtly love was transformed to romantic love, literary misogyny grew somewhat out of fashion. In some places in the eighteenth century it declined into ridicule and exhortative satire. In the nineteenth century its more acrimonious forms almost disappeared in English. Its resurrection in twentieth-century attitudes and literature is the result of a resentment over patriarchal reform, aided by the growing permissiveness in expression which has taken place at an increasing rate in the last fifty years.

Since the abatement of censorship, masculine hostility (psychological or physical) in specifically *sexual* contexts has become far more apparent. Yet as masculine hostility has been fairly continuous, one deals here probably less with a matter of increase than with a new frankness in expressing hostility in specifically sexual contexts. It is a matter of release and freedom to express what was once forbidden expression outside of pornography or other "underground" productions, such as those of De Sade. As one recalls both the euphemism and the idealism of descriptions of coitus in the Romantic poets (Keats's *Eve of St. Agnes*), or the Victorian novelists (Hardy, for example) and contrasts it with Miller or William Burroughs, one has an idea of how contemporary literature has absorbed not only the truthful explicitness of pornography, but its anti-social character as well. Since this tendency to hurt or insult has been given free expression, it has become far easier to assess sexual antagonism in the male.

The history of patriarchy presents a variety of cruelties and barbarities: the suttee execution in India, the crippling deformity of footbinding in China, the lifelong ignominy of the veil in Islam, or the widespread persecution of sequestration, the gynacium, and purdah. Phenomenon such as clitoroidectomy, clitoral incision, the sale and enslavement of women under one guise or another, involuntary and child marriages, concubinage and prostitution, still take place—the first in Africa, the latter in the Near and Far East, the last generally. The rationale which accompanies that imposition of male authority euphemistically referred to as "the battle of the sexes" bears a certain resemblance to the formulas of nations at war, where any heinousness is justified on the grounds that the enemy is either an inferior species or really not human at all. The patriarchal mentality has concocted a whole series of rationales about women which accomplish this purpose tolerably well. And these traditional beliefs still invade our consciousness and affect our thinking to an extent few of us would be willing to admit.

VII Anthropological: Myth and Religion

Evidence from anthropology, religious and literary myth all attests to the politically expedient character of patriarchal convictions about women. One anthropologist refers to a consistent patriarchal strain of assumption that "woman's biological differences set her apart . . . she is essentially inferior," and since "human institutions grow from deep and primal anxieties and are shaped by irrational psychological mechanisms . . . socially organized attitudes toward women arise from basic tensions expressed by the male."[54] Under patriarchy the female did not herself develop the symbols by which she is described. As both the primitive and the civilized worlds are male worlds, the ideas which shaped culture in regard to the female were also of male design. The image of women as we know it is an image created by men and fashioned to suit their needs. These needs spring from a fear of the "otherness" of woman. Yet this notion itself presupposes that patriarchy has already been established and the male has already set himself as the human norm, the subject and referent to which the female is "other" or alien. Whatever its origin, the function of the male's sexual antipathy is to provide a means of control over a subordinate group and a rationale which justifies the inferior station of those in a lower order, "explaining" the oppression of their lives.

The feeling that woman's sexual functions are impure is both world-wide and persistent. One sees evidence of it everywhere in literature, in myth, in primitive and civilized life. It is striking how the notion persists today. The event of menstruation, for example, is a largely clandestine affair, and the psycho-social effect of the stigma attached must have great effect on the female ego. There is a large anthropological literature on menstrual taboo; the practice of isolating offenders in huts at the edge of the village occurs throughout the primitive world. Contemporary slang denominates menstruation as "the curse." There is considerable evidence that such discomfort as women suffer during their period is often likely to be psychosomatic, rather than physiological, cultural rather than biological, in origin. That this may also be true to some extent of labor and delivery is attested to by the recent experiment with "painless childbirth." Patriarchal circumstances and beliefs seem to have the effect of poisoning the female's own sense of physical self until it often truly becomes the burden it is said to be.

Primitive peoples explain the phenomenon of the female's genitals in terms of a wound, sometimes reasoning that she was visited by a bird or snake and mutilated into her present condition. Once she was wounded, now she bleeds. Contemporary slang for the vagina is "gash." The Freudian description of the female genitals is in terms of a "castrated" condition. The uneasiness and disgust female genitals arouse in patriarchal societies is attested to through religious, cultural, and literary proscription. In preliterate groups fear is also a factor, as in the belief in a castrating *vagina dentata*. The penis, badge of the male's superior status in both preliterate and civilized patriarchies, is given the most crucial significance, the subject both of endless boasting and endless anxiety.

Nearly all patriarchies enforce taboos against women touching ritual objects (those of war or religion) or food. In ancient and preliterate societies women are generally not permitted to eat with men. Women eat apart today in a great number of cultures, chiefly those of the Near and Far East. Some of the inspiration of such custom appears to lie in fears of contamination, probably sexual in origin. In their function of domestic servants, females are forced to prepare food, yet at the same time may be liable to spread their contagion through it. A similar situation obtains with blacks in the United States. They are considered filthy and infectious, yet as domestic they are forced to prepare food for their queasy superiors. In both cases the dilemma is generally solved in a deplorably illogical fashion by segregating the act of eating itself, while cooking is carried on out of sight by the very group who would infect the table. With an admirable consistency, some Hindu males do not permit their wives to touch their food at all. In nearly every patriarchal group it is expected that the dominant male will eat first or eat better, and even where the sexes feed together, the male shall be served by the female.[55]

All patriarchies have hedged virginity and defloration in elaborate rites and interdictions. Among preliterates virginity presents an interesting problem in ambivalence. On the one hand, it is, as in every patriarchy, a mysterious good because a sign of property received intact. On the other hand, it represents an unknown evil associated with the mana of blood and terrifyingly "other." So auspicious is the event of defloration that in many tribes the owner-groom is willing to relinquish breaking the seal of his new possession to a stronger or older personality who can neutralize the attendant dangers.[56] Fears of defloration appear to originate in a fear of the alien sexuality of the female. Although any physical suffering endured in defloration must be on the part of the female (and most societies cause her—bodily and mentally— to suffer anguish), the social interest, institutionalized in patriarchal ritual and custom, is exclusively on the side of the male's property interest, prestige, or (among preliterates) hazard.

Patriarchal myth typically posits a golden age before the arrival of women, while its social practices permit males to be relieved of female company. Sexual segregation is so prevalent in patriarchy that one encounters evidence of it everywhere. Nearly every powerful circle in contemporary patriarchy is a men's group. But men form groups of their own on every level. Women's groups are typically auxiliary in character, imitative of male efforts and methods on a generally trivial or ephemeral plane. They rarely operate without recourse to male authority, church or religious groups appealing to the superior authority of a cleric, political groups to male legislators, etc.

In sexually segregated situations the distinctive quality of culturally enforced temperament becomes very vivid. This is particularly true of those exclusively masculine organizations which anthropology generally refers to as men's house institutions. The men's house is a fortress of patriarchal association and emotion. Men's houses in preliterate society strengthen masculine communal experience through dances, gossip, hospitality, recreation, and religious ceremony. They are also the arsenals of male weaponry.

David Riesman has pointed out that sports and some other activities provide males with a supportive solidarity which society does not trouble to provide for females.[57] While hunting, politics, religion, and commerce may play a role, sport and warfare are consistently the chief cement of men's house comradery. Scholars of men's house culture from Hutton Webster and Heinrich Schurtz to Lionel Tiger tend to be sexual patriots whose aim is to justify the apartheid the institution represents.[58] Schurtz believes an innate gregariousness and a drive toward fraternal pleasure among peers urges the male away from the inferior and constricting company of women. Notwithstanding his conviction that a mystical "bonding instinct" exists in males, Tiger exhorts the public, by organized effort, to preserve the men's house tradition from its decline. The institution's less genial function of power center within a state of sexual antagonism is an aspect of the phenomenon which often goes unnoticed.

The men's house of Melanesia fulfill a variety of purposes and are both armory and the site of masculine ritual initiation ceremony. Their atmosphere is not very remote from that of military institutions in the modern world: they reek of physical exertion, violence, the aura of the kill, and the throb of homosexual sentiment. They are the scenes of scarification, headhunting celebrations, and boasting sessions. Here young men are to be "hardened" into manhood. In the men's houses boys have such low status they are often called the "wives" of their initiators, the term "wife" implying both inferiority and the status of sexual object. Untried youths become the erotic interest of their elders and betters, a relationship also encountered in the Samurai order, in oriental priesthood, and in the Greek gymnasium. Preliterate wisdom decrees that while inculcating the young with the masculine ethos, it is necessary first to intimidate them with the tutelary status of the female. An anthropologist's comment on Melanesian men's houses is applicable equally to Genet's underworld, or Mailer's U.S. Army: "It would seem that the sexual brutalizing of the young boy and the effort to turn him into a woman both enhances the older warrior's desire of power, gratifies his sense of hostility toward the maturing male competitor, and eventually, when he takes him into the male group, strengthens the male solidarity in its symbolic attempt to do without women."[59] The derogation of feminine status in lesser males is a consistent patriarchal trait. Like any hazing procedure, initiation once endured produces devotees who will ever after be ardent initiators, happily inflicting their own former sufferings on the newcomer.

The psychoanalytic term for the generalized adolescent tone of men's house culture is "phallic state." Citadels of virility, they reinforce the most saliently power-oriented characteristics of patriarchy. The Hungarian psychoanalytic anthropologist Géza Róheim stressed the patriarchal character of men's house organization in the preliterate tribes he studied, defining their communal and religious practices in terms of a "group of men united in the cult of an object that is a materialized penis and excluding the women from their society."[60] The tone and ethos of men's house culture is sadistic, power-oriented, and latently homosexual, frequently narcissistic in its energy and motives.[61] The men's house inference that the penis is a weapon, endlessly equated with other weapons, is also clear. The practice of castrating prisoners is itself a comment on the cultural confusion of anatomy and status with weaponry. Much of the glamorization of masculine comradery in warfare originates in what one might designate as "the men's house sensibility." Its sadistic and brutalizing aspects are disguised in military glory and a particularly cloying species of masculine sentimentality. A great deal of our culture partakes of this tradition, and one might locate its first statement in Western literature in the heroic intimacy of Patroclus and Achilles. Its development can be traced through the epic and the saga to the *chanson de geste*. The tradition still flourishes in war novel and movie, not to mention the comic book.

Considerable sexual activity does take place in the men's house, all of it, needless to say, homosexual. But the taboo against homosexual behavior (at least among equals) is almost universally of far stronger force than the impulse and tends to effect a rechanneling of the libido into violence. This association of sexuality and violence is a particularly militaristic habit of mind.[62] The negative and militaristic coloring of such men's house homosexuality as does exist, is of course by no means the whole character of homosexual sensibility. Indeed, the warrior caste of mind with its ultravirility, is more *incipiently* homosexual, in its exclusively male orientation, than it is *overtly* homosexual. (The Nazi experience is an extreme case in point here.) And the heterosexual role-playing indulged in, and still more persuasively, the contempt in which the younger, softer, or more "feminine" members are held, is proof that the actual ethos is misogynist, or perversely rather than positively heterosexual. The true inspiration of men's house association therefore comes from the patriarchal situation rather than from any circumstances inherent in the homo-amorous relationship.

If a positive attitude toward heterosexual love is not quite, in Seignebos' famous dictum, the invention of the twelfth century, it can still claim to be a novelty. Most patriarchies go to great length to exclude love as a basis of mate selection. Modern patriarchies tend to do so through class, ethnic, and religious factors. Western classical thought was prone to see in heterosexual love either a fatal stroke of ill luck bound to end in tragedy, or a contemptible and brutish consorting with inferiors. Medieval opinion was firm in its conviction that love was sinful if sexual, and sex sinful if loving.

Primitive society practices its misogyny in terms of taboo and mana which evolve into explanatory myth. In historical cultures, this is transformed into ethical, then literary, and in the modern period, scientific rationalizations for the sexual politic. Myth is, of course, a felicitous advance in the level of propaganda, since it so often bases its arguments on ethics or theories of origins. The two leading myths of Western culture are the classical tale of Pandora's box and the Biblical story of the Fall. In both cases earlier mana concepts of feminine evil have passed through a final literary phase to become highly influential ethical justifications of things as they are.

Pandora appears to be a discredited version of a Mediterranean fertility goddess, for in Hesiod's *Theogony* she wears a wreath of flowers and a sculptured diadem in which are carved all the creatures of land and sea.[63] Hesiod ascribes to her the introduction of sexuality which puts an end to the golden age when "the races of men had been living on earth free from all evils, free from laborious work, and free from all wearing sickness."[64] Pandora was the origin of "the damnable race of women—a plague which men must live with."[65] The introduction of what are seen to be the evils of the male human condition came through the introduction of the female and what is said to be her unique product, sexuality. In *Works and Days* Hesiod elaborates on Pandora and what she represents—a perilous temptation with "the mind of a bitch and a thievish nature," full of "the cruelty of desire and longings that wear out the body," "lies and cunning words and a deceitful soul," a snare sent by Zeus to be "the ruin of men."[66]

Patriarchy has God on its side. One of its most effective agents of control is the powerfully expeditious character of its doctrines as to the nature and origin of the female and the attribution to her alone of the dangers and evils it imputes to sexuality. The Greek example is interesting here: when it wishes to exalt sexuality it celebrates fertility through the phallus; when it wishes to denigrate sexuality, it cites Pandora. Patriarchal religion and ethics tend to lump the female and sex together as if the whole burden of the onus and stigma it attaches to sex were the fault of the female alone. Thereby sex, which is known to be unclean, sinful, and debilitating, pertains to the female, and the male identity is preserved as a human, rather than a sexual one.

The Pandora myth is one of two important Western archetypes which condemn the female through her sexuality and explain her position as her well-deserved punishment for the primal sin under whose unfortunate consequences the race yet labors. Ethics have entered the scene, replacing the simplicities of ritual, taboo, and mana. The more sophisticated vehicle of myth also provides official explanations of sexual history. In Hesiod's tale, Zeus, a rancorous and arbitrary father figure, in sending Epimetheus evil in the form of female genitalia, is actually chastising him for adult heterosexual knowledge and activity. In opening the vessel she brings (the vulva or hymen, Pandora's "box") the male satisfies his curiosity but sustains the discovery only by punishing himself at the hands of the father god with death and the assorted calamities of postlapsarian life. The patriarchal trait of male rivalry across age or status line, particularly those of powerful father and rival son, is present as well as the ubiquitous maligning of the female.

The myth of the Fall is a highly finished version of the same themes. As the central myth of the Judeo-Christian imagination and therefore of our immediate cultural heritage, it is well that we appraise and acknowledge the enormous power it still holds over us even in a rationalist era which has long ago given up literal belief in it while maintaining its emotional assent intact.[67] This mythic version of the female as the cause of human suffering, knowledge, and sin is still the foundation of sexual attitudes, for it represents the most crucial argument of the patriarchal tradition in the West.

The Israelites lived in a continual state of war with the fertility cults of their neighbors; these latter afforded sufficient attraction to be the source of constant defection, and the figure of Eve, like that of Pandora, has vestigial traces of a fertility goddess overthrown. There is some, probably unconscious, evidence of this in the Biblical account which announces, even before the narration of the fall has begun—"Adam called his wife's name Eve; because she was the mother of all living things." Due to the fact that the tale represents a compilation of different oral traditions, it provides two contradictory schemes for Eve's creation, one in which both sexes are created at the same time, and one in which Eve is fashioned later than Adam, an afterthought born from his rib, peremptory instance of the male's expropriation of the life force through a god who created the world without benefit of female assistance.

The tale of Adam and Eve is, among many other things, a narrative of how humanity invented sexual intercourse. Many such narratives exist in preliterate myth and folk tale. Most of them strike us now as delightfully funny stories of primal innocents who require a good deal of helpful instruction to figure it out. There are other major themes in the story: the loss of primeval simplicity, the arrival of death, and the first conscious experience of knowledge. All of them revolve about sex. Adam is forbidden to eat of the fruit of life or of the knowledge of good and evil, the warning states explicitly what should happen if he tastes of the latter: "in that day that thou eatest thereof thou shalt surely die." He eats but fails to die (at least in the story), from which one might infer that the serpent told the truth.

But at the moment when the pair eat of the forbidden tree they awake to their nakedness and feel shame. Sexuality is clearly involved, though the fable insists it is only tangential to a higher prohibition against disobeying orders in the matter of another and less controversial appetite—one for food. Róheim points out that the Hebrew verb for "eat" can also mean coitus. Everywhere in the Bible "knowing" is synonymous with sexuality, and clearly a product of contact with the phallus, here in the fable objectified as a snake. To blame the evils and sorrows of life—loss of Eden and the rest—on sexuality, would all too logically implicate the male, and such implication is hardly the purpose of the story, designed as it is expressly in order to blame all this world's discomfort on the female. Therefore it is the female who is tempted first and "beguiled" by the penis, transformed into something else, a snake. Thus Adam has "beaten the rap" of sexual guilt, which appears to be why the sexual motive is so repressed in the Biblical account. Yet the very transparency of the serpent's universal phallic value shows how uneasy the mythic mind can be about its shifts. Accordingly, in her inferiority and vulnerability the woman takes and eats, simple carnal thing that she is, affected by flattery even in a reptile. Only after this does the male fall, and with him, humanity—for the fable has made him the racial type, whereas Eve is a mere sexual type and, according to tradition, either expendable or replaceable. And as the myth records the original sexual adventure, Adam was seduced by woman, who was seduced by a penis. "The woman whom thou gavest to be with me, she gave me of the fruit and I did eat" is the first man's defense. Seduced by the phallic snake, Eve is convicted for Adam's participation in sex.

Adam's curse is to toil in the "sweat of his brow," namely the labor the male associates with civilization. Eden was a fantasy world without either effort or activity, which the entrance of the female, and with her sexuality, has destroyed. Eve's sentence is far more political in nature and a brilliant "explanation" of her inferior status. "In sorrow thou shalt bring forth children. And thy desire shall be to thy husband. And he shall rule over thee." Again, as in the Pandora myth, a proprietary father figure is punishing his subjects for adult heterosexuality. It is easy to agree with Róheim's comment on the negative attitude the myth adopts toward sexuality:

"Sexual maturity is regarded as a misfortune, something that has robbed mankind of happiness . . . the explanation of how death came into the world."[68]

What requires further emphasis is the responsibility of the female, a marginal creature, in bringing on this plague, and the justice of her suborned condition as dependent on her primary role in this original sin. The connection of woman, sex, and sin constitutes the fundamental pattern of western patriarchal thought thereafter.

VIII Psychological

The aspects of patriarchy already described have each an effect upon the psychology of both sexes. Their principal result is the interiorization of patriarchal ideology. Status, temperament, and role are all value systems with endless psychological ramifications for each sex. Patriarchal marriage and the family with its ranks and division of labor play a large part in enforcing them. The male's superior economic position, the female's inferior one have also grave implications. The large quantity of guilt attached to sexuality in patriarchy is overwhelmingly placed upon the female, who is, culturally speaking, held to be the culpable or the more culpable party in nearly any sexual liaison, whatever the extenuating circumstances. A tendency toward the reification of the female makes her more often a sexual object than a person. This is particularly so when she is denied human rights through chattel status. Even where this has been partly amended the cumulative effect of religion and custom is still very powerful and has enormous psychological consequences. Woman is still denied sexual freedom and the biological control over her body through the cult of virginity, the double standard, the prescription against abortion, and in many places because contraception is physically unavailable to her.

The continual surveillance in which she is held tends to perpetuate the infantilization of women even in situations such as those of higher education. The female is continually obliged to seek survival or advancement through the approval of males as those who hold power. She may do this either through appeasement or through the exchange of her sexuality for support and status. As the history of patriarchal culture and the representations of herself within all levels of its cultural media, past and present, have a devastating effect upon her self image, she is customarily deprived of any but the most trivial sources of dignity or self-respect. In many patriarchies, language, as well as cultural tradition, reserve the human condition for the male. With the Indo-European languages this is a nearly inescapable habit of mind, for despite all the customary pretense that "man" and "humanity" are terms which apply equally to both sexes, the fact is hardly obscured that in practice, general application favors the male far more often than the female as referent, or even sole referent, for such designations.[69]

When in any group of persons, the ego is subjected to such invidious versions of itself through social beliefs, ideology, and tradition, the effect is bound to be pernicious. This coupled with the persistent though frequently subtle denigration women encounter daily through personal contacts, the impressions gathered from the images and media about them, and the discrimination in matters of behavior, employment, and education which they endure, should make it no very special cause for surprise that women develop group characteristics common to those who suffer minority status and a marginal existence. A witty experiment by Philip Goldberg proves what everyone knows, that having internalized the disesteem in which they are held, women despise both themselves and each other.[70] This simple test consisted of asking women undergraduates to respond to the scholarship in an essay signed alternately by one John McKay and one Joan McKay. In making their assessments the students generally agreed that John was a remarkable thinker, Joan an unimpressive mind. Yet the articles were identical: the reaction was dependent on the sex of the supposed author.

As women in patriarchy are for the most part marginal citizens when they are citizens at all, their situation is like that of other minorities, here defined not as dependent upon numerical size of the group, but on its status. "A minority group is any group of people who because of their physical or cultural characteristics, are singled out from others in the society in which they live for differential and unequal treatment."[71] Only a handful of sociologists have ever addressed themselves in any meaningful way to the minority status of women.[72] And psychology has yet to produce relevant studies on the subject of ego damage to the female which might bear comparison to the excellent work done on the effects of racism on the minds of blacks and colonials. The remarkably small amount of modern research devoted to the psychological and social effects of masculine supremacy on the female and on the culture in general attests to the widespread ignorance or unconcern of a conservative social science which takes patriarchy to be both the status quo and the state of nature.

What little literature the social sciences afford us in this context confirms the presence in women of the expected traits of minority status: group self-hatred and self-rejection, a contempt both for herself and for her fellows—the result of that continual, however subtle, reiteration of her inferiority which she eventually accepts as a fact.[73] Another index of minority status is the fierceness with which all minority group members are judged. The double standard is applied not only in cases of sexual conduct but other contexts as well. In the relatively rare instances of female crime too: in many American states a woman convicted of crime is awarded a longer sentence.[74] Generally an accused woman acquires a notoriety out of proportion to her acts and due to sensational publicity she may be tried largely for her "sex life." But so effective is her conditioning toward passivity in patriarchy, woman is rarely extrovert enough in her maladjustment to enter upon criminality. Just as every minority member must either apologize for the excesses of a fellow or condemn him with a strident enthusiasm, women are characteristically harsh, ruthless and frightened in their censure of aberration among their numbers.

The gnawing suspicion which plagues any minority member, that the myths propagated about his inferiority might after all be true often reaches remarkable proportions in the personal insecurities of women. Some find their subordinate position so hard to bear that they repress and deny its existence. But a large number will recognize and admit their circumstances when they are properly phrased. Of two studies which asked women if they would have preferred to be born male, one found that one fourth of the sample admitted as much, and in another sample, one half.[75] When one inquires of children, who have not yet developed as serviceable techniques of evasion, what their choice might be, if they had one, the answers of female children in a large majority of cases clearly favor birth into the elite group, whereas boys overwhelmingly reject the option of being girls.[76] The phenomenon of parents' prenatal preference for male issue is too common to require much elaboration. In the light of the imminent possibility of parents actually choosing the sex of their child, such a tendency is becoming the cause of some concern in scientific circles.[77]

Comparisons such as Myrdal, Hacker, and Dixon draw between the ascribed attributes of blacks and women reveal that common opinion associates the same traits with both: inferior intelligence, an instinctual or sensual gratification, an emotional nature both primitive and childlike, an imagined prowess in or affinity for sexuality, a contentment with their own lot which is in accord with a proof of its appropriateness, a wily habit of deceit, and concealment of feeling. Both groups are forced to the same accommodational tactics: an ingratiating or supplicatory manner invented to please, a tendency to study those points at which the dominant group are subject to influence or corruption, and an assumed air of helplessness involving fraudulent appeals for direction through a show of ignorance.[78] It is ironic how misogynist literature has for centuries concentrated on just these traits, directing its fiercest enmity at feminine guile and corruption, and particularly that element of it which is sexual, or as such sources would have it, "wanton."

As with other marginal groups a certain handful of women are accorded higher status that they may perform a species of cultural policing over the rest. Hughes speaks of marginality as a case of status dilemma experienced by women, blacks, or second-generation Americans who have "come up" in the world but are often refused the rewards of their efforts on the grounds of their origins.[79] This is particularly the case with "new" or educated women. Such exceptions are generally obliged to make ritual, and often comic, statements of deference to justify their elevation. These characteristically take the form of pledges of "femininity," namely a delight in docility and a large appetite for masculine dominance. Politically, the most useful persons for such a role are entertainers and public sex objects. It is a common trait of minority status that a small percentage of the fortunate are permitted to entertain their rulers. (That they may entertain their fellow subjects in the process is less to the point.) Women entertain, please, gratify, satisfy and flatter men with their sexuality. In most minority groups athletes or intellectuals are allowed to emerge as "stars," identification with whom should content their less fortunate fellows. In the case of women both such eventualities are discouraged on the reasonable grounds that the most popular explanations of the female's inferior status ascribe it to her physical weakness or intellectual inferiority. Logically, exhibitions of physical courage or agility are indecorous, just as any display of serious intelligence tends to be out of place.

Perhaps patriarchy's greatest psychological weapon is simply its universality and longevity. A referent scarcely exists with which it might be contrasted or by which it might be confuted. While the same might be said of class, patriarchy has a still more tenacious or powerful hold through its successful habit of passing itself off as nature. Religion is also universal in human society and slavery was once nearly so; advocates of each were fond of arguing in terms of fatality, or irrevocable human "instinct"— even "biological origins." When a system of power is thoroughly in command, it has scarcely need to speak itself aloud; when its workings are exposed and questioned, it becomes not only subject to discussion, but even to change. Such a period is the one next under discussion.

NOTES

1. The American Heritage Dictionary's fourth definition is fairly approximate: "methods or tactics involved in managing a state or government." *American Heritage Dictionary* (New York: American Heritage and Houghton Mifflin, 1969). One might expand this to a set of strategems designed to maintain a system. If one understands patriarchy to be an institution perpetuated by such techniques of control, one has a working definition of how politics is conceived in this essay.

2. I am indebted here to Ronald V. Samson's *The Psychology of Power* (New York: Random House, 1968) for his intelligent investigation of the connection between formal power structures and the family and for his analysis of how power corrupts basic human relationships.

3. "Domination in the quite general sense of power, i.e. the possibility of imposing one's will upon the behavior of other persons, can emerge in the most diverse forms." In this central passage of *Wirtschaft und Gesellschaft* Weber is particularly interested in two such forms: control through social authority ("patriarchal, magisterial, or princely") and control through economic force. In patriarchy as in other forms of domination "that control over economic goods, i.e. economic power, is a frequent, often purposively willed, consequence of domination as well as one of its most important instruments." Quoted from Max Rheinstein's and Edward Shil's translation of portions of *Wirtschaft und Gesellschaft* entitled *Max Weber on Law in Economy and Society* (New York: Simon and Schuster, 1967), pp. 323–24.

4. No matriarchal societies are known to exist at present. Matrilineality, which may be, as some anthropologists have held, a residue or a transitional stage of matriarchy, does not constitute an exception to patriarchal rule, it simply channels the power held by males through female descent—, e.g. the Avunculate.

5. Radical democracy would, of course, preclude patriarchy. One might find evidence of a general satisfaction with a less than perfect democracy in the fact that women have so rarely held power within modern "democracies."

6. Hannah Arendt, "Speculations on Violence," *The New York Review of Books*, Vol. XII No. 4, February 27, 1969, p. 24.

7. The social, rather than the physical sciences are referred to here. Traditionally, medical science had often subscribed to such beliefs. This is no longer the case today, when the best medical research points to the conclusion that sexual stereotypes have no bases in biology.

8. "The historian of Roman laws, having very justly remarked that neither birth nor affection was the foundation of the Roman family, have concluded that this foundation must be found in the power of the father or husband. They make a sort of primordial institution of this power; but they do not explain how this power was established, unless it was by the superiority of strength of the husband over the wife, and of the father over the children. Now,

we deceive ourselves sadly when we thus place force as the origin of law. We shall see farther on that the authority of the father or husband, far from having been the first cause, was itself an effect; it was derived from religion, and was established by religion. Superior strength, therefore, was not the principle that established the family." Numa Denis Fustel de Coulanges, *The Ancient City* (1864). English translation by Willard Small (1873), Doubleday Anchor Reprint, pp. 41–42. Unfortunately Fustel de Coulanges neglects to mention how religion came to uphold patriarchal authority, since patriarchal religion is also an effect, rather than an original cause.

9. One might also include the caveat that such a social order need not imply the domination of one sex which the term "matriarchy" would, by its semantic analogue to patriarchy, infer. Given the simpler scale of life and the fact that female-centered fertility religion might be offset by male physical strength, pre-patriarchy might have been fairly egalitarian.

10. Something like this appears to have taken place as the culture of Neolithic agricultural villages gave way to the culture of civilization and to patriarchy with the rise of cities. See Louis Mumford, *The City in History* (New York: Harcourt, Brace, 1961), Chapter One. A discovery such as paternity, a major acquisition of "scientific" knowledge might, hypothetically, have led to an expansion of population, surplus labor and strong-class stratification. There is good reason to suppose that the transformation of hunting into war also played a part.

11. No convincing evidence has so far been advanced in this area. Experimentation regarding the connection between hormones and animal behavior not only yields highly ambivalent results but brings with it the hazards of reasoning by analogy to human behavior. For a summary of the arguments see David C. Glass (editor), *Biology and Behavior* (New York: Rockefeller University and the Russell Sage Foundation, 1968).

12. Robert J. Stoller, *Sex and Gender* (New York, Science House, 1968), from the preface, pp. viii–ix.

13. *Ibid.*, p. 9.

14. *Ibid.*, p. 48.

15. See Mary Jane Sherfey, "The Evolution and Nature of Female Sexuality in Relation to Psychoanalytic Theory," *Journal of the American Psychoanalytic Association*, vol. 14, January 1966, no. 1 (New York, International Universities Press Inc.), and John Money, "Psychosexual Differentiation," in *Sex Research, New Developments* (New York, Holt, 1965).

16. Money, op cit., p. 12.

17. *Ibid.*, p. 13.

18. Jerome Kagin, "The Acquisition and Significance of Sex-Typing," in *Review of Child Development Research*, ed. M. Hoffman (New York, Russell Sage Foundation, 1964).

19. Lionel Tiger, *Men in Groups* (New York, Random House, 1968).

20. Through instinct subhuman species might undertake the activity of building a complex nest or hive; through reflex or drive a human being might simply blink, feel hunger, etc.

21. In some of my remarks on the family I am indebted to Goode's short and concise analysis. See William J. Goode, *The Family* (Englewood Cliffs, New Jersey, Prentice Hall, 1964).

22. Family, society, and state are three separate but connected entities: women have a decreasing importance as one goes from the first to the third category. But as each of the three categories exists within or is influenced by the overall institution of patriarchy, I am concerned here less with differentiation than with pointing out a general similarity.

23. J. K. Folsom makes a convincing argument as to the anomalous character of patriarchal family systems within democratic society. See Joseph K. Folsom *The Family and Democratic Society* (New York, John Wiley, 1934, 1943).

24. Marital as well as consanguine relation to the head of the family made one his property.

25. Strict patriarchal descent is traced and recognized only through male heirs rather than through sister's sons etc. In a few generations descendants of female branches lose touch. Only those who "bear the name," who descend from male branches, may be recognized for kinship or inheritance.

26. Sir Henry Maine, *Ancient Law* (London, Murray, 1861), p. 122.

27. Sir Henry Maine, *The Early History of Institutions* (London, 1875), pp. 310–11.

28. John McLennon, *The Patriarchal Theory* (London, Macmillan, 1885).

29. Maine took the patriarchal family as the cell from which society evolved as gens, phratry, tribe, and nation grew, rather in the simplistic manner of Israel's twelve tribes descending from Jacob. Since Maine also dated the origin of patriarchy from the discovery of paternity, hardly a primeval condition, this too operates against the eternal character of patriarchal society.

30. Many patriarchies granted divorce to males only. It has been accessible to women on any scale only during this century. Goode states that divorce rates were as high in Japan during the 1880s as they are in the U.S. today. Goode, *op. cit.*, p. 3.

31. Divorce is granted to a male for his wife's failure in domestic service and consortium: it is not granted him for his wife's failure to render him financial support. Divorce is granted to a woman if her husband fails to support her, but not for his failure at domestic service or consortium. But see Karczewski versus Baltimore and Ohio Railroad, 274 F. Supp. 169.175 N.D. Illinois, 1967, where a precedent was set and the common law that decrees a wife might not sue for loss of consortium overturned.

32. Bronislaw Malinowski, *Sex, Culture and Myth* (New York, Harcourt, 1962), p. 63. An earlier statement is even more sweeping: "In all human societies moral tradition and the law decree that the group consisting of a woman and her offspring is not a sociologically complete unit." *Sex and Repression in Savage Society* (London, Humanities, 1927), p. 213.

33. Goode, *op. cit.*, p. 80.

34. Goode, *op. cit.*, p. 74.

35. This is the gist of Valency's summary of the situation before the troubadours, acknowledging that courtly love is an utter anomaly: "With regard to the social background, all that can be stated with confidence is that we know nothing of the objective relationships of men and women in the Middle Ages which might conceivably motivate the strain of love-poetry which the troubadours developed." Maurice Valency, *In Praise of Love* (Macmillan, New York, 1958), p. 5.

36. Hugo Beigel, "Romantic Love," *The American Sociological Review*, Vol. 16, 1951, p. 331.

37. Mailer and Miller occur to one in this connection, and Lawrence as well. One might trace Rojack's very existence as a fictional figure to the virility symbol of Jack London's Ernest Everhard and Tennessee William's Stanley Kowalski. That Rojack is also literate is nothing more than an elegant finish upon the furniture of his "manhood" solidly based in the hard oaken grain of his mastery over any and every "broad" he can better, bludgeon, or bugger.

38. It would appear that the "pure flower of white womanhood" has at least at times been something of a disappointment to her lord as a fellow-racist. The historic connection of the Abolitionist and the Woman's Movement is some evidence of this, as well as the incident of white female and black male marriages as compared with those of white male and black female. Figures on miscegenation are very difficult to obtain: Goode (*op. cit.*, p. 37) estimates

the proportion of white women marrying black men to be between 3 to 10 times the proportion of white men marrying black women. Robert K. Merton "Intermarriage and the Social Structure" *Psychiatry*, Vol. 4, August 1941, p. 374, states that "most intercaste sex relations—not marriages—are between white men and Negro women." It is hardly necessary to emphasize that the more extensive sexual contacts between white males and black females have not only been extramarital, but (on the part of the white male) crassly exploitative. Under slavery it was simply a case of rape.

39. Sweden is an exception in considering housework a material service rendered and calculable in divorce suits etc. Thirty-three to forty per cent of the female population have market employment in Western countries: this leaves up to two thirds out of the market labor force. In Sweden and the Soviet Union that figure is lower.

40. U. S. Department of Labor Statistics for 1966 (latest available figures). The proportion of women earning more than $10,000 a year in 1966 was 7/10 of 1%. See Mary Dublin Keyserling "Realities of Women's Current Position in the Labor Force" in *Sex Discrimination in Employment Practices*, a report from the conference (pamphlet) University extension, U.C.L.A. and the Women's Bureau, September 19, 1968.

41. See *The 1965 Handbook on Women Workers*, United States Department of Labor, Women's Bureau: "In every major occupational group the median wage or salary income of women was less than that of men. This is true at all levels of educational attainment." A comparison of the income received by women and men with equal amounts of schooling revealed that women who had completed four years of college received incomes which were only 47% of those paid to men with the same educational training; high school graduates earned only 38%, and grade school graduates only 33%.

42. For the distribution of women in lower income and lower status positions see *Background Facts on Working Women* (1968 pamphlet) U.S. Department of Labor, Women's Bureau.

43. "For a married woman without children the irreducible minimum of work probably takes between fifteen to twenty hours a week, for a woman with small children the minimum is probably 70–80 hours a week." Margaret Benston, "The Political Economy of Women's Liberation," *Monthly Review*, Vol. XXI, September 1969.

44. See the publications of the Women's Bureau and particularly *Sex Discrimination in Employment Practices* (op. cit.) and Carolyn Bird, *Born Female* (New York, McKay, 1968).

45. Title VII of the 1964 Civil Rights Act. The inclusion of "sex" in the law upholding the civil right of freedom from discrimination in employment was half a joke and half an attempt on the part of Southern congressmen to force Northern industrial states to abandon passage of the bill.

46. We often forget how recent an event is higher education for women. In the U.S. it is barely one hundred years old; in many Western countries barely fifty. Oxford did not grant degrees to women on the same terms as to men until 1920. In Japan and a number of other countries universities have been open to women only in the period after World War II. There are still areas where higher education for women scarcely exists. Women do not have the same access to education as do men. The Princeton Report stated that "although at the high school level more girls than boys receive grades of "A," roughly 50% more boys than girls go to college." *The Princeton Report to the Alumni on Co-Education* (pamphlet), Princeton, N.J. 1968, p. 10. Most other authorities give the national ratio of college students as two males to one female. In a great many countries it is far lower.

47. Since abortion is extralegal, figures are difficult to obtain. This figure is based on the estimates of abortionists and referral services. Suicides in pregnancy are not officially reported either.

48. Vivid exceptions come to mind in the wars of liberation conducted by Vietnam, China, etc. But through most of history, women have been unarmed and forbidden to exhibit any case defense of their own.

49. They are still high. The number of rapes reported in the city of New York in 1967 was 2432. Figure supplied by Police Department.

50. It is interesting that male victims of rape at the hands of other males often feel twice imposed upon, as they have not only been subjected to forcible and painful intercourse, but further abused in being reduced to the status of a female. Much of this is evident in Genet and in the contempt homosexual society reserves for its "passive" or "female" partners.

51. Masculine masochism is regarded as exceptional and often explained as latently homosexual, or a matter of the subject playing "the female role"—e.g., victim.

52. The literature of misogyny is so vast that no summary of sensible proportions could do it justice. The best reference on the subject is Katherine M. Rogers, *The Troublesome Helpmate, A History of Misogyny in Literature* (Seattle, University of Washington Press, 1966).

53. As well as the exquisite sonnets of love, Petrarch composed satires on women as the "De Remediis utriusque Fortunae" and *Epistolae Seniles*. Boccaccio too could balance the chivalry of romances (Filostrato, Ameto, and Fiammetta) with the vituperance of Corbaccio, a splenetic attack on women more than medieval in violence.

54. H. R. Hays, *The Dangerous Sex, the Myth of Feminine Evil* (New York: Putnam, 1964). Much of my summary in this section is indebted to Hays's useful assessment of cultural notions about the female.

55. The luxury conditions of the "better" restaurant affords a quaint exception. There is not only the cuisine but even the table service is conducted by males, at an expense commensurate with such an occasion.

56. See Sigmund Freud, *Totem and Taboo*, and Ernest Crawley, *The Mystic Rose* (London, Methuen, 1902, 1927).

57. David Reisman, "Two Generations," in *The Woman in America*, edited by Robert Lifton (Boston, Beacon, 1967). See also James Coleman. *The Adolescent Society*.

58. Heinrich Schurtz, *Altersklassen und Männerbünde* (Berlin, 1902), and Lionel Tiger, *op. cit.*

59. Hays, *The Dangerous Sex*, p. 56.

60. Géza Róheim, "Psychoanalysis of Primitive Cultural Types," *International Journal of Psychoanalysis* Vol. XIII, London, 1932.

61. All these traits apply in some degree to the bohemian circle which Miller's novels project, the Army which never leaves Mailer's consciousness, and the homosexual subculture on which Genet's observations are based. Since these three subjects of our study are closely associated with the separatist men's house culture, it is useful to give it special attention.

62. Genet demonstrates this in *The Screens*; Mailer reveals it everywhere.

63. Wherever one stands in the long anthropologists' quarrel over patriarchal versus matriarchal theories of social origins, one can trace a demotion of fertility goddesses and their replacement by patriarchal deities at a certain period throughout ancient culture.

64. Hesiod, *Works and Days*, translated by Richmond Lattimore (University of Michigan, 1959), p. 29.

65. Hesiod, *Theogony*, translated by Norman O. Brown (Indianapolis, Liberal Arts Press, 1953), p. 70.

66. Hesiod, *Works and Days*, phrases from lines 53–100. Some of the phrases are from Lattimore's translation, some from A. W. Mair's translation (Oxford, 1908).

67. It is impossible to assess how deeply embedded in our consciousness is the Eden legend

and how utterly its patterns are planted in our habits of thought. One comes across its tone and design in the most unlikely places, such as Antonioni's film *Blow-Up*, to name but one of many striking examples. The action of the film takes place in an idyllic garden, loaded with primal overtones largely sexual, where, prompted by a tempter with a phallic gun, the female again betrays the male to death. The photographer who witnesses the scene reacts as if he were being introduced both to the haggard knowledge of the primal scene and original sin at the same time.

68. Géza Róheim, "Eden," *Psychoanalytic Review*, Vol. XXVII, New York, 1940. See also Theodor Reik, *The Creation of Woman*, and the account given in Hays, *op. cit.*

69. Languages outside the Indo-European group are instructive. Japanese, for example, has one word for man (*otōko*), another for woman (*ōnna*) and a third for human being (*ningen*). It would be as unthinkable to use the first to cover the third as it would be to use the second.

70. Philip Goldberg, "Are Women Prejudiced Against Women?" *Transaction*, April 1968.

71. Louis Wirth, "Problems of Minority Groups," in *The Science of Man in the World Crisis*, ed. by Ralph Linton (New York, Appleton, 1945), p. 347. Wirth also stipulates that the group see itself as discriminated against. It is interesting that many women do not recognize themselves as discriminated against; no better proof could be found of the totality of their conditioning.

72. The productive handful in question include the following: Helen Mayer Hacker, "Women as a Minority Group," *Social Forces*, Vol. XXX, October 1951. Gunnar Myrdal, *An American Dilemma*, Appendix 5 is a parallel of black minority status with women's minority status. Everett C. Hughes, "Social Change and Status Protest: An Essay on the Marginal Man," *Phylon*, Vol. X, First Quarter, 1949. Joseph K. Folsom, *The Family and Democratic Society*, 1943. Godwin Watson, "Psychological Aspects of Sex Roles," *Social Psychology, Issues and Insights* (Philadelphia, Lippincott, 1966).

73. My remarks on the minority status of women are summarized from all the articles listed, and I am particularly indebted to an accomplished critique of them in an unpublished draft by Professor Marlene Dixon, formerly of the University of Chicago's Department of Sociology and the Committee on Human Development, presently of McGill University.

74. See The Commonwealth v. Daniels, 37 L.W. 2064, Pennsylvania Supreme Court, 7/1/68 (reversing 36 L.W. 2004).

75. See Helen Hacker, *op. cit.*, and Carolyn Bird, *op. cit.*

76. "One study of fourth graders showed ten times as many girls wishing they could have been boys, as boys who would have chosen to be girls," Watson, *op. cit.*, p. 477.

77. Amitai Etzioni, "Sex Control, Science, and Society," *Science*, September 1968, pp. 1107–12.

78. Myrdal, *op. cit.*, Hacker, *op. cit.*, Dixon, *op. cit.*

79. Hughes, *op. cit.*

Chapter Twelve

Double Jeopardy
To Be Black and Female

Frances Beal

In attempting to analyze the situation of the black woman in America, one crashes abruptly into a solid wall of grave misconceptions, outright distortions of fact and defensive attitudes on the part of many. The system of capitalism (and its afterbirth—racism) under which we all live has attempted by many devious ways and means to destroy the humanity of all people, and particularly the humanity of black people. This has meant an outrageous assault on every black man, woman and child who resides in the United States.

In keeping with its goal of destroying the black race's will to resist its subjugation, capitalism found it necessary to create a situation where it was impossible for the black man to find meaningful or productive employment. More often than not, he couldn't find work of any kind. The black woman likewise was manipulated by the system, economically exploited and physically assaulted. She could often find work in the white man's kitchen, however, and sometimes became the sole breadwinner of the family. This predicament has led to many psychological problems on the part of both man and woman and has contributed to the turmoil found in the black family structure.

Unfortunately, neither the black man nor the black woman understood the true nature of the forces working upon them. Many black women accepted the capitalist evaluation of manhood and womanhood and believed, in fact, that black men were shiftless and lazy, that otherwise they would get a job and support their families as they ought to. Personal relationships between black men and women were torn asunder, and one result has been the separation of husband from wife, mother from child, etc.

America has defined the roles to which each individual should subscribe. It has defined "manhood" in terms of its own interests and "femininity" likewise. An individual who has a good job, makes a lot of money and drives a Cadillac is a real "man," and conversely, an individual who is lacking in these "qualities" is less of a man. The advertising media in this country continuously inform the American male of his need for indispensable signs of his virility—the brand of cigarettes that cowboys prefer, the whiskey that has a masculine tang or the label of the jock strap that athletes wear.

The ideal model that is projected for a woman is to be surrounded by hypocritical homage and estranged from all real work, spending idle hours primping and preening, obsessed with conspicuous consumption, and limited in function to simply a sex role. We unqualitatively reject these models. A woman who stays at home caring for children and the house often leads an extremely sterile existence. She must lead her entire life as a satellite to her mate. He goes out into society and brings back a little piece of the world for her. His interests and his understanding of the world become her own and she cannot develop herself as an individual, having been reduced to a biological function. This kind of woman leads a parasitic existence that can aptly be described as "legalized prostitution."

Furthermore, it is idle dreaming to think of black women simply caring for their homes and children like the middle-class white model. Most black women have to work to help house, feed and clothe their families. Black women make up a substantial percentage of the black working force from the poorest black family to the so-called "middle-class" family.

Black women were never afforded such phony luxuries. Though we have been browbeaten with this white image, the reality of the degrading and dehumanizing jobs that were relegated to us quickly dissipated this mirage of womanhood. The following excerpt from a speech that Sojourner Truth made at a Women's Rights Convention in the 19th century shows us how misleading and incomplete a life this model represents for us:

> . . . Well, chilern, whar dar is so much racket dar must be something out o'kilter. I tink dat 'twixt de niggers of de Souf and de women at de Norf all a talkin' 'bout rights, de white men will be in a fix pretty soon. But what's all dis here talkin' 'bout? Dat man ober dar say dat women needs to be helped into carriages, and lifted ober ditches, and to have de best place every whar. Nobody ever help me into carriages, or ober mud puddles, or gives me any best places, . . . and ar'nt I a woman? Look at me! Look at my arm! . . . I have plowed, and planted, and gathered into barns, and no man could head me—and ar'nt I a woman? I could work as much as a man (when I could get it), and bear de lash as well—and ar'nt I a woman? I have borne five chilern and I seen 'em mos' all sold off into slavery, and when I cried out with a mother's grief, none but Jesus heard—and ar'nt I a woman?

Unfortunately, there seems to be some confusion in the Movement today as to who has been oppressing whom. Since the advent of black power, the black male has exerted a more prominent leadership role in our struggle for justice in this country. He sees the system for what it really is for the most part, but where he rejects its values and mores on many issues, when it comes to women, he seems to take his guidelines from the pages of the *Ladies' Home Journal.* Certain black men are maintaining that they have been castrated by society but that black women somehow escaped this persecution and even contributed to this emasculation.

The black woman in America can justly be described as a "slave of a slave." Since the black man in America was reduced to such abject oppression, the black woman had no protector and was used, and is still being used in some cases, as the scapegoat for the evils that this horrendous system has perpetrated on black men. Her physical image has been maliciously maligned; she has been sexually molested and abused by the white colonizer; she has suffered the worst kind of economic exploitation, having been forced to serve as the white woman's maid and as wet nurse for white offspring while her own children were, more often than not, starving and neglected. It is the depth of degradation to be socially manipulated, physically raped, used to undermine your own household, and to be powerless to reverse this situation.

It is true that our husbands, fathers, brothers and sons have been emasculated, lynched and brutalized. They have suffered from the cruelest assault on mankind that the world has ever known. However, it is a gross distortion of fact to state that black women have oppressed black men. The capitalist system found it expedient to enslave and oppress them and proceeded to do so without consultation or the signing of any agreements with black women.

It must also be pointed out at this time that black women are not resentful of the rise to power of black men. We welcome it. We see in it the eventual liberation of all black people from this corrupt system of capitalism. However, it is fallacious to think that in order for the black man to be strong, the black woman must be weak.

Those who are exerting their "manhood" by telling black women to step back into a domestic, submissive role are assuming a counterrevolutionary position. Black women, likewise, have been abused by the system, and we must begin talking about the elimination of all kinds of oppression. If we are talking about building a strong nation, capable of throwing off the yoke of capitalist oppression, then we are talking about the total involvement of every man, woman, and child, each with a highly developed political consciousness. We need our whole army out there dealing with the enemy, not half an army.

There are also some black women who feel that there is no more productive role in life than having and raising children. This attitude often reflects the conditioning of the society in which we live and is adopted from a bourgeois white model. Some young sisters who have never had to maintain a household or to accept the confinement which this entails tend to romanticize (along with the help of a few brothers) the role of housewife and mother. Black women who have had to endure this function are less apt to have such utopian visions.

Those who portray in an intellectual manner how great and rewarding this role will be, and who feel that the most important thing that they can contribute to the black nation is children, are doing themselves a great injustice. This reasoning completely negates the contributions that black women such as Sojourner Truth, Harriet Tubman, Mary McLeod Bethune, and Fannie Lou Hamer have historically made to our struggle for liberation.

We live in a highly industrialized society, and every member of the black nation must be as academically and technologically developed as possible. To wage a revolution, we need competent teachers, doctors, nurses, electronics experts, chemists, biologists, physicists, political scientists, and so on. Black women sitting at home reading bedtime stories to their children are just not going to make it.

Economic Exploitation of Black Women

Capitalism finds it expedient to reduce women to a state of enslavement. They often serve as a scapegoat for the evils of this system. Much in the same way that the poor white cracker of the South, who is equally victimized, looks down upon blacks and contributes to the oppression of blacks, so, by giving to men a false feeling of superiority (at least in their own homes or in their relationships with women), the oppression of women acts as an escape valve for capitalism. Men may be cruelly exploited and subjected to all sorts of dehumanizing tactics on the part of the ruling class, but at least they're not women.

Women also represent a surplus labor supply, the control of which is absolutely necessary to the profitable functioning of capitalism. Women are systematically exploited by the system. They are paid less for the same work that men do, and jobs that are specifically relegated to women are low-paying and without the possibility of advancement. Statistics from the Women's Bureau of the U.S. Department of Labor show that in 1967, the wage scale for non-white women was the lowest of all:

White Males $6,704

Non-White Males $4,277

White Females $3,991

Non-White Females $2,861

Those industries which employ mainly black women are the most exploitative. Domestic and hospital workers are good examples of this oppression, as are the garment workers in New York City. The International Ladies Garment Workers Union (ILGWU) whose overwhelming membership consists of black and Puerto Rican women has a leadership that is nearly all lily white and male. This leadership has been working in collusion with the ruling class and has completely sold its soul to the corporate structure.

To add insult to injury, the ILGWU has invested heavily in business enterprises in racist, apartheid South Africa—with union funds. Not only does this bought-off leadership contribute to our continued exploitation in this country by not truly representing the best interests of its membership, but it audaciously uses funds that black and Puerto Rican women have provided to support the economy of a vicious government that is engaged in the economic rape and murder of our black brothers and sisters in our Motherland, Africa.

The entire labor movement in the United States has suffered as a result of the super-exploitation of black workers and women. The unions have historically been racist and chauvinist. They have upheld racism in this country and have failed to fight the white skin privileges of white workers. They have failed to fight or even make an issue against the inequities in the hiring and pay of women workers. There has been virtually no struggle against either the racism of the white worker or the economic exploitation of the working woman, two factors which have consistently impeded the advancement of the real struggle against the ruling class.

This racist, chauvinist and manipulative use of black workers and women, especially black women, has been a severe cancer on the American labor scene. It therefore becomes essential for those who understand the workings of capitalism and imperialism to realize that the exploitation of black people and women works to everyone's disadvantage and that the liberation of these two groups is a stepping stone to the liberation of all oppressed people in this country and around the world.

Bedroom Politics

I have briefly discussed the economic and psychological manipulation of black women, but perhaps the most outlandish act of oppression in modern times is the current campaign to promote sterilization of non-white women in an attempt to maintain the population and power imbalance between the white haves and the non-white have-nots.

These tactics are but another example of the many devious schemes that the ruling class elite attempts to perpetrate on the black population in order to keep itself in control. A massive campaign for so-called "birth control" is presently being promoted not only in the underdeveloped non-white areas of the world, but also in black communities here in the United States. However, what the authorities in charge of these programs refer to as "birth control" is in fact nothing but a method of surgical genocide.

The United States has been sponsoring sterilization clinics in non-white countries, especially in India, where already some 3 million young men and boys in and around New Delhi have been sterilized in makeshift operating rooms set up by American Peace Corps workers. Under these circumstances, it is understandable why certain countries view the Peace Corps not as a benevolent project, not as evidence of America's concern for underdeveloped areas, but rather as a threat to their very existence. This program could more aptly be named "The Death Corps."

The vasectomy; which is performed on males and takes only six or seven minutes, is a relatively simple operation. The sterilization of a woman, on the other hand, is admittedly major surgery. This operation (salpingectomy)* must be performed in a hospital under general anesthesia. This method of "birth control" is a common procedure in Puerto Rico. Puerto Rico has long been used by the colonialist exploiter, the United States, as an experimental laboratory for medical research before allowing certain practices to be imported and used here. When the birth control pill was first being perfected, it was tried out on Puerto Rican women and selected black women (poor), using them like guinea pigs to evaluate its effect and its efficiency.

The salpingectomy has now become the most common operation in Puerto Rico, more common than an appendectomy or a tonsillectomy. It is so widespread that it is referred to simply as "la operación." *On the Island, 20 percent of the women between the ages of 15 and 45 have already been sterilized.*

Now, as previously occurred with the pill, this method has been imported into the United States. Sterilization clinics are cropping up around the country in the

---

*Salpingectomy: through an abdominal incision, the surgeon cuts both Fallopian tubes and ties off the separated ends, so that there is no way for the egg to pass from the ovary to the womb.

black and Puerto Rican communities. These so-called "Maternity Clinics," specifically outfitted to purge black women and men of their reproductive possibilities, are appearing more and more in hospitals and clinics across the country.

A number of organizations have been formed to popularize the idea of sterilization, such as The Association for Voluntary Sterilization and The Human Betterment (!!!?) Association for Voluntary Sterilization, Inc., which has its headquarters in New York City. Front Royal, Virginia, has one such "Maternity Clinic" in Warren Memorial Hospital. The tactics used in the clinic in Fauquier County, Virginia, where poor and helpless black mothers and young girls are pressured into undergoing sterilization, are certainly not confined to that clinic alone.

Threatened with the cut-off of relief funds, some black welfare women have been forced to accept this sterilization procedure in exchange for a continuation of welfare benefits. Mt. Sinai Hospital in New York City performs these operations on many of its ward patients whenever it can convince the women to undergo this surgery. Mississippi and some of the other Southern states are notorious for this act. Black women are often afraid to permit any kind of necessary surgery because they know from bitter experience that they are more likely than not to come out of the hospital without their insides. Both salpingectomies and hysterectomies are performed.

We condemn this use of the black woman as a medical testing ground for the white middle class. Reports of ill effects, including deaths, from the use of the birth control pill only started to come to light when the white privileged class began to be affected. These outrageous Nazi-like procedures on the part of medical researchers are but another manifestation of the totally amoral and dehumanizing brutality that the capitalist system perpetrates on black women. The sterilization experiments carried on in concentration camps some twenty-five years ago have been denounced the world over, but no one seems to get upset by the repetition of these same racist tactics today in the United States of America—land of the free and home of the brave. This campaign is as nefarious a program as Germany's gas chambers and, in a long term sense, as effective and with the same objective.

The rigid laws concerning abortions in this country are another vicious means of subjugation and, indirectly, of outright murder. Rich white women somehow manage to obtain these operations with little or no difficulty. It is the poor black and Puerto Rican woman who is at the mercy of the local butcher. Statistics show that the non-white death rate at the hands of unqualified abortionists is substantially higher than for white women. Nearly half of the child-bearing deaths in New York City are attributed to abortion alone, and out of these, 79 percent are among non-white and Puerto Rican women.

We are not saying that black women should not practice birth control. Black women have the right and the responsibility to determine when it is in the interest of the struggle to have children or not to have them and this right must not be relinquished to anyone. It is also the black woman's right and responsibility to determine when it is in her own best interest to have children, how many she will have, and how far apart. Forced sterilization practices, abortion laws, and the un-availability of safe birth control methods are all symptoms of a decadent society that jeopardizes the health of black women (and thereby the entire black race) in its attempts to control the very life processes of human beings. These are symptoms of a society that believes it has the right to bring political factors into the privacy of the bedchamber. The elimination of these horrendous conditions will free black women for full participation in the revolution and, thereafter, in the building of the new society.

Relationship to White Movement

Much has been written recently about the white women's liberation movement in the United States, and the question arises whether there are any parallels between this struggle and the movement on the part of black women for total emancipation. While there are certain comparisons that one can make, simply because we both live under the same exploitative system, there are certain differences, some of which are quite basic.

The white women's movement is far from being monolithic. Any white group that does not have an anti-imperialist and anti-racist ideology has nothing in common with the black woman's struggle. In fact, some groups come to the incorrect conclusion that their oppression is due simply to male chauvinism. They therefore have an extremely anti-male tone. Black people are engaged in a life and death struggle and the main emphasis of black women must be to combat the capitalist, racist exploitation of black people. While it is true that male chauvinism has become institutionalized in American society, one must always look for the main enemy— the fundamental cause of the condition of females.

Another major differentiation is that the white women's liberation movement is basically middle class. Very few of these women suffer the extreme economic exploitation that most black women are subjected to day by day. This is the factor that is most crucial for us. It is not an intellectual persecution alone, it is not an intellectual outburst for us; it is quite real. We as black women have got to deal with the problems that the black masses deal with, for our problems in reality are one and the same.

If the white groups do not realize that they are in fact fighting capitalism and racism, we do not have common bonds. If they do not realize that the reasons for their condition lie in the system and not simply that men get a vicarious pleasure out of "consuming their bodies for exploitative reasons" (this reasoning seems to be quite prevalent in certain white women's groups), then we cannot unite with them around common grievances or even discuss these groups in a serious manner because they're completely irrelevant to the black struggle.

The New World

The black community and black women especially must begin raising questions about the kind of society we wish to see established. We must note the ways in which capitalism oppresses us and then move to create institutions that will eliminate these destructive influences.

The new world that we are attempting to create must destroy oppression of every type. The value of this new system will be determined by the status of the person who was lowest on the totem pole. Unless women in any enslaved nation are completely liberated, the change cannot really be called a revolution. If the black woman has to retreat to the position she occupied before the armed struggle, the whole movement and the whole struggle will have retreated in terms of truly freeing the colonized population.

A people's revolution that engages the participation of every member of the community, including man, woman, and child, brings about a certain transformation in the participants as a result of this participation. Once we have caught a glimpse of freedom or experienced a bit of self-determination, we can't go back to old routines that were established under a racist, capitalist regime. We must begin to understand that a revolution entails not only the willingness to lay our lives on the firing line and get killed. In some ways, this is an easy commitment to make. To die for the revolution is a one-shot deal; to live for the revolution means taking on the more difficult commitment of changing our day-to-day life patterns.

This will mean changing the traditional routines that we have established as a result of living in a totally corrupting society. It means changing how one relates to one's wife, husband, parents and co-workers. If we are going to liberate ourselves as a people, it must be recognized that black women have very specific problems that have to be spoken to. We must be liberated along with the rest of the population. We cannot wait to start working on those problems until that great day in the future when the revolution somehow, miraculously, is accomplished.

To assign women the role of housekeeper and mother while men go forth into battle is a highly questionable doctrine for a revolutionary to maintain. Each individual must develop a high political consciousness in order to understand how this system enslaves us all and what actions we must take to bring about its total destruction. Those who consider themselves to be revolutionary must begin to deal with other revolutionaries as equals. So far as I know, revolutionaries are not determined by sex.

Old people, young people, men and women must take part in the struggle. To relegate women to purely supportive roles or to purely cultural considerations is dangerous. Unless black men who are preparing themselves for armed struggle understand that the society which we are trying to create is one in which the oppression of *all members* of that society is eliminated, then the revolution will have failed in its avowed purpose.

Given the mutual commitment of black men and black women alike to the liberation of our people and other oppressed peoples around the world, the total involvement of each individual is necessary. A revolutionary has the responsibility not only to topple those who are now in a position of power, but to create new institutions that will eliminate all forms of oppression. We must begin to rewrite our understanding of traditional personal relationships between man and woman. All the resources that the black community can muster must be channeled into the struggle. Black women must take an active part in bringing about the kind of society where our children, our loved ones, and each citizen can grow up and live as decent human beings, free from the pressures of racism and capitalist exploitation.

Chapter Thirteen

Beyond Male Power . . .

Ginny Berson for the Furies

In the second issue of THE FURIES we introduced the idea of a national party in the article "Leadership vs. Stardom." We did it in a fairly offhand way without acknowledging the difficult questions which are unanswered, both in the article and in our own minds. We know that any mention of a party requires long and serious discussions and that there can be no "final" solution at this or possibly any other time. What we can do is put out our vision of what might be possible in the near future, and raise the questions which will have to be answered before we proceed to different stages of development.

When we say "party" we mean a national organization which can plan, organize, coordinate, and communicate. We mean an organization which does institutionalize power and hierarchy among people or offices, but which allows leaders, and not stars, to lead.

We envision groups of women across the country (and their size is not at issue) getting together in various stages of political development. They want to further their development and they want to figure out how to put an end to the sexist, classist, racist system which oppresses them and keeps them from controlling their lives. These women will define their direction and their goals and their strategies to meet those goals. And their commitment to each other will come from arriving at those decisions together and from having a common political base and direction. They will deal, with each other and among other groups in their area, with questions of class and race. They will begin to discuss the political thought they have been developing about ideology and program with other similar groups all across the country.

They will know that whatever strategies they develop for local use will not, by themselves, end sexism because the institutions of sexism, the governmental, economic, and social structures which uphold male supremacy and capitalism and racism are not local, but national and even worldwide. It is not a question of "our community needs a new reservoir and you folks need a new bridge; let's work together on both." That is fine in a post-revolutionary state in which women have control over their lives. The fact is that at this time we don't have control and we do not have the freedom to build a new reservoir. We don't have the freedom because we don't have the power.

White, ruling class male power is a fact of life which surrounds us and to a very large degree controls us. It is to this fact that we must speak when we talk about "party"—how do we insure that we are able to take control of our lives, to build the reservoirs when we need them, to feed ourselves, to be lesbians. When we talk about taking control of our lives we are talking about taking power, away from the men who have it, and for (not on behalf of) the people who don't have it.

Individual lesbians can and do carve out little niches for themselves in which they are as "free" as possible and in as little contact with their oppressor as possible. But, by themselves, they do nothing to change the balance of power. They do nothing to change the basic system which oppresses them and forces them into that solution. Small groups, acting on their own, with no national coordination or agreed upon action do a little more. They expand the base of the niche and can improve the lot of large numbers of women. But their effectiveness is limited by their size and the degree to which they can coordinate their actions and their understandings with other groups. They still do not threaten the balance of power; they still do not bring about a major redistribution of power. They may be able to destroy power within their own group (and even this is doubtful), but having destroyed it does not give them a basis on which to fight their enemy. Because he still has power.

We do not believe that we can totally destroy power; but we can and must redistribute it so that every woman has as much control over her life as is possible. To this end, we must at some point organize ourselves into a national party which can build a power base and which can therefore threaten the power of the oppressor.

The question then is, how can we create an organization capable of building that power base which does not institutionalize power among its offices or leaders? What is the basis for membership? How do you build an organization in a classist, racist society that doesn't reflect those same oppressions? How do you insure that women constantly change and struggle? Do you have to depend on local groups struggling for years before you build a national organization? Groups have power over their own members only because the members depend on the success of the group to reach their goals. This power is given voluntarily. But what power does an organization have over non-members? Is the promise of future success enough to make women want to change their lives? Is it enough to make men want to change their lives?

How are decisions made by the organization? What structures are employed which can both build the kind of women we need to make a revolution and make the revolution? Will we have to compromise one of *these* goals? How much is an "ideal" organization possible in a pre-revolutionary society? Where does leadership come from? How is it recognized? Does everybody get together every time a decision needs to be made? Do we have representational democracy with majority rule?

We don't want an organization filled with people who refuse to deal with their class or race privilege. We don't want an organization controlled by white, middle-class women who are into power for its own sake. Nor do we want an organization filled with passive followers who will spout the correct line as if it were a catechism and worship "leaders" only because they are "leaders." We want an organization filled with women who have the same basic understandings about sexism, class, race and who are committed with their lives to acting on that understanding. The first issues of THE FURIES have explained what our beginning analysis is. We are not the only people putting that analysis together, and we hope, through the newspaper and in other ways to increase the numbers of those who are working on it. Of course, not everybody wants to develop ideology, and there are many other tasks to be done. But everybody can and must decide by herself or in groups whether she agrees with that ideology and then decide whether she wants to be part of an organization that is trying to act on it. We are talking about an organization which has a firm ideological basis, and which arises out of people's needs to act on their political understandings. We do not think that now is the time for that organization to begin for a number of reasons. First, there has not been enough ideology produced for us to have a strategy upon which to base a national organization. Second, the movement is at this time largely white and middle class. Third, there are too many unanswered questions about what form the organization should take in its initial stages.

Why will we need any organization? First, because the system we are attacking is national and cannot be brought down by individual, uncoordinated little thrusts. Second, because the world we want to build involves women taking control of their lives, and they cannot do this if we do not organize into a unit that can give us power. Third, because outside of our own groups we have little power. Even our ability to communicate with each other depends on male good will or ignorance: we use their media, or their post office, or their telephones. Establishment newspapers long ago stopped publishing stories about bank burnings in California; they will probably not tell us about events that are even more threatening to them, like a general women's strike.

We will need an organization because everyone will need to know, in advance, what we can expect from each other and from groups, who we can count on; in other words, who shares our ideology. And we will know that by knowing who is in our organization, because the people in the organization will be deciding on their goals and strategies together, as part of the function of the organization.

We do not need a party to insure that leaders lead. We need common politics to do that. Those politics don't happen because there is a party; a party is created because there are those politics: because we cannot achieve our goals without one. And those politics happen because there is a need for them, because people are oppressed and see in those politics the key to their liberation.

We did not mean to imply that a small group is a T group. We are a small group and we are urging other people to form and be in small groups in order to develop their political direction. We apologize for the misues of the word "anarchy" and for its equation with emotionalism, cowardice, and individualism. We do not think that anarchists are necessarily dupes of the middle class, and the use of "anarchy" to describe individualism, classism, lack of discipline, and anti-leadership attitudes was wrong. "Anarchy" is a noun, not an adjective. It is a political philosophy with which we have some agreements and some disagreements, and those disagreements need to be discussed in political terms, and not brushed away with emotional rhetoric. For this mistake, we apologize.

It should also be clear that we are not defending the Marxist/Leninist parties which are in power. Some of them are classist and all of them are sexist. There is a huge difference between that type of party and the type we are discussing. We are not in favor of a bureaucratic, hierarchical organization which controls people. We are in favor of creating whatever structures are necessary to achieve our goal. We know how difficult that will be. But our goal is to create a world in which people have control over their lives. A strategy which is based primarily on substituting one form of control for another is not suited to that end. We want to build a movement of strong women who are willing and able to change their lives and help create the space for other people to do the same.

Chapter Fourteen

The New Misandry

Joanna Russ

Gee, isn't it awful for women to hate men?

Of course lots of men despise women, but that's different; woman-hating isn't serious—at worst it's eccentric, at best sort of cute. Woman-haters (many of whom are women) can express themselves all over the place, as the latest cartoon about women drivers reminds me, but man-haters have fewer opportunities. Man-hating takes self-control. Besides, man-haters are in the minority; for every Valerie Solanas, how many rapists, how many male murderers are there? What male reviewer found Hitchcock's "Frenzy" one-20th as revolting as Solanas's "Scum Manifesto?" Of course Solanas went out and did it, but then so do many, many men—in the small town I live in there were several incidents of rape last year, and a common response to them was laughter.

Alas, it's nothing new for the oppressed to be solemnly told that their entry to Heaven depends on not hating the oppressor; labor is supposed to hate management and black is not supposed to hate white because hatred is bad. It's a fine case of double-think. Watch:(1) You do something nasty to me. (2) I hate you. (3) You find it uncomfortable to be hated. (4) You think how nice it would be if I didn't hate you. (5) You decide I ought not to hate you because hate is bad. (6) Good people don't hate. (7) Because I hate I am a bad person. (8) It is not what you did to me that makes me hate you, it is my own bad nature. *I—not you—am the cause of my hating you.*

For some reason misandry (a fancy word for man-hating) is a very loaded topic. People even talk as if hating men meant murdering all of them right away—as if there were no difference between feelings and acts. Man-haters are people who feel a certain way (not even all the time, believe it or not); they aren't Instant Murderesses. If misandrists were the uncontrolled, ravening wild beasts they are supposed to be, they would've been strangled in their cradles. Surely very few of us are seriously afraid that battalions of ardent feminist misandrists will come marching out of the sunrise to castrate every man between here and California—though the jokes that are told seem to indicate we think so. Does Betty Friedan really think this will happen? Obviously not. Does Jill Johnston? Hardly. Yet Jill Johnston provokes such extraordinarily virulent abuse that she must be hitting a nerve of some sort and Betty

Friedan recently accused Gloria Steinem (of all people) of—what? *Hating men.* A serious charge.

Feminists who want feminism to be respectable are afraid the "radicals" will go "too far." That is, man-hating gives the show away—we aren't merely liberals; our complaints are drastic; we're demanding not asking; we're breaking the mold in the most thorough way possible; *we really mean it.* (That is why "Man-hating" is used as a red herring—it's such a loaded charge.) Movement women who come down hard in public on misandry are afraid of male backlash. They want men's (and women's) cooperation, they want acceptance, they want popularity.

Second, there are women who feel that their own choice of a life-style (living with a man, sleeping with a man, working with men, loving a man) is somehow inpugned or rendered invalid by women who hate men. The second group, of course, feels exactly the same way about the first group—but *that's* been going on for years. The novelty is that the conventional, socially approved choice is now open to question at all. Americans seem to be acting this way lately; we don't love ourselves enough to value our choices without some kind of outside sanction. So we deprecate others lest they deprecate us, even by implication.

Perhaps the most important cause of the fear of misandry is the awfulness of facing the extent to which misandry and misogyny are an inescapable part of the texture of our lives. It is all right to joke about "the battle of the sexes" but we must not take it seriously for the paradoxical reason that it is too serious—every man is a misogynist, how can he help it? and every woman is a misandrist, how can she help it? The misandry, of course, is far far worse than the misogyny—thus giving us a clue as to who the aggressor is in the "battle." While every woman is not Valerie Solanas, Solanas is Everywoman—this means that nobody can escape the general situation. True, some employers are nicer than others. But a job is still a job. True, the enemy isn't shooting at Yossarian in particular. But they're still shooting at him.

We are all, to a very large and uncomfortable degree, prisoners of the institutions in which we live. Being forced to endure awful things is bad enough; we are forced to *feel* awful things, too—it is truly horrible to realize how much stunting and deformation has been forced upon us. It's so much easier to say that everything (as Perelman puts it) is leeches and cream, that all women really love men, that only "sick" women hate men. It is even getting so that to say something is the "wrong" thing to do in a practical, tactical sense, carries overtones of moral condemnation. (Hence Friedan's condemnation of Steinem, et al.) If you are to accept there are women who do indeed openly hate men and that they hate men either because they have hit extreme (but characteristic) circumstances or because they are more clear-sighted than the rest of us, that means you must accept misandry as a possibility for all women. If you are a woman, that means you must accept misandry as a possibility *for yourself.* (If you are a man, this acceptance means you must accept the possibility of women's hatred as a rational response to a bad situation and that you must not get aggrieved at it.) To accept misandry is to perceive what dreadful messes are made of our lives even if we are lucky enough to escape the worst effects of our social structure. There are two kinds of women who never hate men: the very lucky and the very blind.

I think we ought to decide that man-hating is not only respectable but honorable. To be a misandrist a woman needs considerable ingenuity, originality, and resilience. A misogynist requires no such resources. Our men are brought up to hate us; it is the unconventional, intelligent, sensitive, truthful, original man who can get out from under that tyranny and love women. We are brought up to love our men— uncritically and in fear of the consequences if we don't. (I am not talking about this or that particular man, but men as a group. The doctrine that men ought to be accepted or rejected as individuals is a life-saver to women who are horrified by man-hating. But these very women know perfectly well that the issue is a class issue— they themselves argue that "men" are wonderful, that "men" are good, i.e., they almost always accept the class terms of the argument until some other person gets them off the hook by bringing in the individualist argument that people must be judged singly and then sliding imperceptibly into the stand that people do not belong to groups or classes at all.) It is the unconventional, truthful, sensitive, intelligent, original woman who can get out from under *that* tyranny and see clearly that to be discriminated against, patronized, belittled, frustrated, limited, treated without re- spect, and taught that one is not important are hardly breeding grounds for Love.

It's possible to reject misandry as a tactic, or even choose to suppress it in oneself, and yet to accept the misandrists themselves. This would involve recognizing misan- dry as a permanent possibility in every woman's situation and therefore in her life. It would mean not being nervous about what men would think of those awful, man- hating women. It would mean criticizing man-haters—if at all—in private.

Women's situation with respect to men isn't just oppressive; it's terribly confusing. As Virginia Woolf says, neither flattery, affection, ease in her company, nor love will prevent a woman from being put in her place. (Bad things happen not only when the subordinate gets uppity but when the superior gets irritable and wants somebody to take it out on—we all admire the delicate realism of the cartoon in which Boss yells at Husband, Husband yells at wife, and wife yells at Child. That Child had better have a Dog.)

That bad things are done to you is bad enough; worse is the double-think that follows. The man insists—often semi-sincerely, though he has some inkling of his motives because if you question them, he gets mad—that (1) he didn't do anything, you must be hallucinating; (2) he did it but it's trivial and therefore you're irrational ("hysterical") to resent it or be hurt; (3) it's important but you're wrong to take it personally because he didn't mean it personally; (4) it's important and personal but you provoked it, i.e., it's your fault and not his. Worse still, he often insists on all of them at once. In this sort of ideologically mystified situation, clarity is crucial. Let us get several things clear: hurting people makes them angry, anger turns to hate when the anger is chronic and accompanied by helplessness, and although you can bully or shame people into not showing their anger, the only way to stop the anger is to stop the hurt. The cure for hate is power—not power to hurt the hurter, but *power to make the hurter stop.*

It is a mistake to think that man-hating is a delicate self-indulgence; it's very unpleasant. Nor is it a pathological rarity; nothing could be more common. Go look at popular art meant for women: romance magazines, "women's" movies, modern

Gothics. Where there is no disguised revenge (as there is in the presentation of the stupid, feeble males of the old radio soaps) there is abundant helplessness, pain, and self-hatred. I find hating others morally preferable to hating oneself; it gives the human race a backbone. It is the first of all the biological virtues, self-preservation, and it takes more bravery than you might think. And before you sneer at self-preservation and declare that self-immolation is wonderful (especially for women) remember that self-sacrifice is a virtue *always* forced on oppressed groups. (Some women twist the "virtue" of self-sacrifice and Love into weapons for themselves: i.e., the guilt-making "I sacrificed everything for you" and the more-loving-than-thou crowd, who treat a spontaneous emotion as if it were a cultivated moral characteristic. They are very snotty to women who don't love as much as they do.)

Why is man-hating so dreadful? Because it is easier for everybody, male and female, to demand saintly purity of the oppressed than to tee off on the oppressor. It's about time we stopped worrying about whether feminists are saints: they're not, quite predictably. And it's also time to scotch that perennial silliness about avoiding Change because Change will provoke a Backlash. Change always provokes a backlash. If you meet with no resistance, you're not doing your political job. As Philip Slater says in "The Pursuit of Loneliness," "backlash" is what happens when people find out that change means change. Pious statements that feminism is really very moderate and harmless aren't going to deceive anybody for long. The radicalism of a cause doesn't come from the individual wishes of a few well-known leaders but from the situation in which large, large numbers of people find themselves. Feminism is radical. Those who don't want to be "that" radical are finding themselves either outstripped or ignored; they become (sadly) the darlings of an Establishment which likes them for all the wrong reasons.

To condemn misandry is to have higher standards of conduct for women than for men. It is to be so frightened about feminism per se that not a taint of ordinary human corruption can be allowed into it. It is to accept the idea of oppression only on the condition that the real, ugly effects of oppression be denied. It is to consider feminism a moral movement and not a political movement—men are okay but we've got to be better.

Isn't that what we were trying to get away from in the first place?

Chapter Fifteen

Male Supremacy

Lynn O'Connor

Women's Liberation has made it increasingly clear to many women both in and out of the women's movement that the horrendous experiences and grim conditions of their day-to-day lives are not theirs alone, but the collective condition of women as a group. Removing some of the self-blame allowed many of us to grow in new directions with the hope that changes in our behavior would change the way in which we were treated. And many of us have gone through some profound personal changes, but nothing real has changed; our condition remains the same. Too often, we have interpreted the condition of women as the result of an erroneous and unfair idea system or male chauvinism. Cheerfully, women continue to talk about teaching their men to think differently about women, as if their oppression were based on some unfortunate mistake that men would happily rectify, given time and a more sound moral education. But the exploitation and oppression of women is no mysterious, cruel accident of history that somehow happened when no one was looking. Righteous thinking or good intentions are pernicious forms of self-protective deception that flow out of the mouths of those who benefit from the oppression of women but don't want to openly admit it, which at this point means most men. The poor old ordinary man tells his wife of his love for her out of one side of his mouth, apologizes for his bad moral education and faulty ideas about women from the other side, all the while reaping the benefits of her work as a "good" woman, and beating her up in one way or another if she steps out of line. There has been no mistake, sisters, and persuasive education is a waste of time. Male supremacy cares not one whit about anyone's state of mind.

Male Supremacy: The Economic System

For eight thousand years the relationships between men and women have been nothing more than antagonistic class relationships. Since early agricultural societies, human economic organization has been based on the class division between the

This paper is the result of one year's work and talk with Ann Fury, Dare Struggle, Laura X, Pat Mialocq, Geri Shifs, Sharon, other incredible feminists, and Nicholo Leo Caldararo.

sexes, with men in the position of the ruler or owning class and women in the position of the oppressed or exploited class. The system insures that, with very few exceptions, every individual man has greater access to scarce goods and resources than any individual woman. All women must perform some kind of labor for a man or for men in order to survive. The alienation of female labor forms the framework for the system. This primary class contradiction between the sexes has served as a model for the many subsidiary forms of organization in which a few men alienate the labor of other men, creating the antagonistic class relationships that have been a major preoccupation for most male social scientists. The exploitative framework grows into a multifaceted edifice that has no boundaries; a social cancer determined to grow, no matter what the cost to the earth and all its other inhabitants.

In both cases, the value of the woman means something very real in terms of the allocation of resources, goods, and energy. The man uses that value to his own material benefit. No one questions his rights of ownership; his rights are assumed and sacred. No other group subjected to slavery has been so completely viewed as a commodity. While black slaves were certainly seen as private property, they often lived separate from their masters, in their own quarters, which allowed them to have some sense of group identity. But women have been defined only in terms of their owners, and have been divided from one another along those lines. With no group identity, there have developed hierarchies between women that reflect the hierarchies of their owners. Women owned by ruling-class men think that they're better than women owned by working-class men, who in turn hate the so-called ruling-class women. Neither the maid nor the lady of the house has anything to do with controlling the means of production, and both are treated as invisible by the man, yet a thick wall separates them and silently they view one another as enemies. Enemies don't engage in collective struggle against oppressors.

Historically, male supremacy has gone through many stages. In most of these, (for example, slavery, feudalism, capitalism) a few men have dominated other men as well as women. Monopoly-capitalism-imperialism is the current stage of male supremacy in our society, and socialism as it is in Cuba, the Soviet Union, and China is a more advanced stage of male supremacy in which the means of production are collectively owned by all men. While the fluctuating patterns of dominance and exploitation between men have been numerous and complex, the basic economic system has remained remarkably stable for centuries with little need to resort to mass violence. The burning of the witches is one of the few historical examples in which men moved violently against large groups of women who were challenging their class position.

The technological changes that put women in the mills early in the industrial revolution broke the chain of total economic dependency on the private male owner or family. Acting in the short run interests of capitalist profits, the man planted the seeds of his own destruction.

The kind of labor that any particular woman must perform has always depended on the economic relationship of her owner to other men, and has reflected her value as a commodity. Women owned by "ruling class" men have a high exchange value but a low use value. Ruling-class man gives his daughter to another ruling-class man in exchange for large economic rewards. While the relationship between monopolistic mergers and marriage has not been studied in great detail, it is common knowledge that marriages between ruling-class families are accompanied by shifts in ownership of large corporations, and sometimes whole networks that include many corporations. The value of the "ruling class" woman is totally tied up in this exchange. Once the transaction has taken place she is of little use to anyone. But there is a special kind of labor awaiting her in marriage, though it could easily be done by hired help. She must maintain an environment in which her owner can conduct business transactions that will add to his wealth. This means she must put aside all of the human qualities that would make her cry, scream out in rage, or even have a relaxed intimate conversation with a friend. Her humanity is replaced by a perpetual tight-lipped grin for the ever-present company, a series of patterned verbal responses that pass as language, and some organizational skill in distributing the work required to maintain the home. Women owned by "working class" men have very little value in terms of exchange, but a great deal of use value. The kind of labor that they must perform is primarily maintenance work, and occupies about fourteen hours per day if they are very efficient. Cooking, cleaning, shopping, washing, raising the children, and, more and more frequently, earning a supplementary income outside of the home, are some of the obvious tasks, most of which are not rewarded with wages. As wage earners, women have access only to the lowest-paying jobs and even when they are doing the same work as men they are paid less.

A great deal of the work that has been done in traditional academic disciplines has been concerned with tightening the loose ends of the ideology. For example, in the field of biology men developed concepts of "instinct" and "natural" to justify their position of power. Distorting a great deal of evidence from the non-human animal world, they went so far as to claim that social behavior is "instinctive," that is, permanent and unchangeable. It's simple to jump from such an idea to the idea that women are "by nature" passive, less intelligent, and numerous other inhibiting characteristics, which they subsequently happily applied to men whom they stole for the slave trade as well as to women. The fact that all animal social behavior is learned is irrelevant, because the scientific ideologues were never really concerned with the truth, but with protecting their power from a possible rebellion.

The so-called science of psychology is one of the most pernicious forms of chauvinist thought ever. Driving us into private cells, the psychological mind talk brings the bars of our prison so close to each of us that we become completely paralyzed. It assumes that there is an "instinctive" or "natural" way to feel and behave, and proceeds to explain that people who act in some way differently from what is natural (which we have seen, is of course, determined by men) are sick, and should be changed. The psychologists go after two enemies whom they claim produce the illness: mother, and the sick individual. The man, of course, remains innocent, eager to "cure." In fact, mother has no control over her own life so she can hardly be responsible, and the idea that people willingly make themselves sick is patently absurd. The convenience of such a system is obvious. A woman rebels against her owner. He sends her to one of his allies, a professional ideologue who specializes in cures for rebellious slaves. He informs the woman of the costs of rebellion, perhaps a lengthy stay in a hospital. Only the most obstinate rebel sticks to her guns under such a threat.

The forms of various institutions created by the ideology have changed in accordance with the needs of the system. And then those changes have been falsely interpreted by male social scientists in order to obfuscate the real purpose of the new forms. For example, the isolated nuclear family in industrialized countries has been analyzed as a result of that tendency of the capitalist mode of production to move men around like movable capital so that a man has to go from place to place in the course of his life and can at best take his wife and children with him. But the extended family has broken down and been replaced by the isolated nuclear family in countries industrialized by the socialist mode of production where men are not considered movable capital. Neither technology nor urban life demands that people live in small isolated units. But as we have seen, when women became wage earners and thus not completely dependent on the private male owner for survival, male supremacy was threatened. To compensate, the isolated nuclear family was institutionalized as the norm because that insured that a woman's living community, at least, became limited to the man to whom she belonged and their children. With little opportunity to talk to women at work, and total isolation at home, the threat that women would use their new independence to engage in a collective uprising was reduced.

Sometimes subcultures spring up in the midst of the mainstream of supremacy. Usually they try to pass themselves off as different; they claim they possess an alternative ideology and way of life. Their so-called alternative generally seems to be an even more oppressive expression of supremacy, chauvinism taken to new and higher levels of contempt for women. Dear to the broken heart of many feminist women is our contemporary hippy subculture. It is based on an eclectic conglomeration of every reactionary tendency in American thought. Conservation (interpreted as a back-to-"nature," primitive lifestyle), intense consumerism, sexual "freedom," rigidly defined sex roles, are all wrapped up in Freudian theory and the cult of individualism. Its effects on women are devastating. A primitive lifestyle combined with rigid sex roles means that women are not allowed to take advantage of any of the appliances and products that modern technology offers to ease their work load. One doesn't have to look far to find a woman washing clothes by hand in water heated on an outdoor stove, and that's just one of her innumerable chores on the groovy hip country commune. And a woman who objects to the feminine role is immediately rejected as a sick and disgusting creature. Free love is another oppressive shuck perpetuated by hip culture. Women are supposed to be able to have easygoing sexual relationships with many men. Jealousy or possessiveness are against the rules. Modesty is a "hang-up." Concern with commitment is a sure sign of an uptight chick, and receives nothing but contempt. Free love really means women are free for the taking. The hip man does not need to pay for his sexual objects in any way. A sense of responsibility is totally out of the question, and in fact, a sick thing to even think about. The music and various artifacts of the culture reinforce the ideology in every way. Women are the scum of the earth. The tragedy of the situation is that it has rapidly spread everywhere and can hardly be considered a subculture anymore.

It traps women at puberty, long before they know what's happening. A fourteen-year-old high school girl has no choice but to acquiesce or be a total social reject.

Male Dominance: The Nitty-Gritty of Oppression

Many men would like us to believe that oppression takes place in some vague and amorphous abstraction called institutions, over which they have no control. They just don't want to take any responsibility for their so-called accidental position of power; they don't want to be a target when the slaves revolt. And it is possible to discuss the oppression of women in generalized abstracted terms but only because it takes place in every relationship between a man and a woman and is therefore, a class affair. Against the backdrop of the male supremacist economy which insures the dependency of women on men and maintains a powerful army ready to move if needed, the nitty-gritty of oppression occurs in the one to one relationship, most often in the form of non-verbal communication.

All primates regularly communicate with one another through series of patterned gestures that include facial expressions, body positions, and vocalizations. These gestures are learned in childhood, modeled after the adults of the group and practiced in playgroups until perfected around the time of adolescence. Many of these gestures are directed towards creating and maintaining social hierarchies or ranking. If a dominant chimpanzee wants to sit down on a log occupied by a less dominant chimp, he will give a gesture of dominance, which may consist of a direct stare, some branch waving, or a backward jerk of the head. The less dominant animal responds with a gesture of submission, usually some variation of "presenting," and quickly moves aside. Should she or he fail to make this response, the dominant animal will quickly resort to physical violence. Thus gestures of dominance are actually patterned or ritualized threats of violence, and gestures of submission are responses designed to reduce the dominant animal's aggression and avoid a confrontation. In most primate groups, particularly in terrestrial or land-dwelling species, the most dominant members serve as watchdogs for the group, constantly on the lookout for predators when the animals are not in safe territory. They do not use their dominance to alienate the labor of other members of the group.

Many species of primates have special physical features that increase the importance of certain gestures. For example, in some, special coloration of parts of the body used in displays of dominance make the displays more obvious from a distance. Our own species provides a clear example in the large area of white around the dark part of the eyes. This coloration makes a direct stare very clear and threatening, and in fact, the direct stare or glare is a common human gesture of dominance. Women use the gesture as well as men, but often in a modified form. While looking directly at a man a woman usually has her head slightly tilted, implying the beginning of a presenting gesture or enough submission to render the stare ambivalent if not actually submissive. Our cultural artifacts greatly affect our use of gestures. For example, eye makeup which women have used on and off throughout history in order to appear "more attractive" to men has the effect of modifying the direct stare and reducing its threatening effect. Women's clothing has often served to make it impossible to assume certain bodily postures that are required in some gestures of dominance.

Although there have been no systematic studies of the gestures of dominance and submission in human groups, the most casual observation will show their crucial role in the day-to-day mechanics of oppression. An example should clarify.

A husband and wife are at a party. The wife says something that the husband does not want her to say. (Perhaps it indirectly reveals something about him that might threaten his ranking with other men.) He quickly tightens the muscles around his jaw, and gives her a rapid but intense direct stare. Outsiders don't notice the interaction, though they may have a vaguely uncomfortable feeling that they are intruding on something private. The wife, who is acutely sensitive to the gestures of the man on whom she is dependent, immediately stops the conversation, lowers or turns her head slightly, averts her eyes, or gives off some other gesture of submission which communicates acquiescence to her husband and reduces his aggression. Peace is restored, the wife has been put in her place. If the wife does not respond with submission, she can expect to be punished. When gestures of dominance fail, the dominant animal usually resorts to violence. We all know about stories of husbands beating up their wives after the party when they have reached the privacy of their home. Many of us have experienced at least a few blows from husbands or lovers when we refuse to submit to them. It is difficult to assess the frequency of physical attacks within so-called love relationships, as women rarely tell even one another when they have taken place. By developing a complicated ethic of loyalty (described above in terms of privacy), men have protected themselves from such reports leaking out and becoming public information. Having already been punished for stepping out of role, the woman is more than a little reluctant to tell anyone of the punishment because it would mean violating the loyalty code which is an even worse infraction of the rules and most likely would result in further and perhaps more severe punishment.

Another common punishment that men inflict on women who step out of line is abandonment. They depart, leaving her with children, no money, and little access to jobs that would enable her to comfortably support the family. Poverty is cruel and prolonged violence. On the job, women are subjected to the same kinds of interactions as in the family. A secretary who doesn't smile sweetly at her boss as she serves him his morning coffee (which involves a whole series of submissive gestures) receives warning gestures of dominance, and if she still does not submit, she is fired regardless of her competence as a secretary. Since women serve as a huge army of reserve labor, she is easily replaced by another woman who types well and smiles and shuffles as expected. We scab on each other all the time because we have to. Nor do women in the professions escape the system. First of all, very few are allowed to enter professional jobs at all, and those who do are not paid salaries equal to their male counterparts. Universities still tell women in private interviews, "sorry we don't hire women." Should a woman be fortunate enough to receive a faculty appointment, it will be short lived if she does not display appropriate gestures of submission in her interactions with male faculty members. The sprinkling of humor, the charm that she exhibits at faculty meetings, reassure the men that she does not take herself or her work too seriously. Charm is nothing more than a series of gestures (including vocalizations) indicating submission. Enough charm and she might keep her job.

In some relationships between men and women the mode of oppression is very devious and can fool even the cleverest woman into believing she has found a man who regards her as an equal or even superior to himself. (That she still feels miserable does not matter; she blames herself. At first glance, the gestures appear to be reversed in the passive man—aggressive woman syndrome. The man gives off gestures of submission and claims dependency on the woman though she is materially dependent on him as usual. And she gives off what look like gestures of dominance. But when a woman displays dominance gestures they are not backed up by force and are meaningless. She is passed off as a "castrating bitch," a "nag" or as a "kook" or "character." Lucille Ball gives fierce direct stares and everyone laughs with delight. However, sometimes things do get really serious in the passive man—aggressive woman syndrome, and she insists on pursuing her own development. Through clever use of submissive gestures, the passive man quickly gets control of the situation. First he slips into a severe depression with the implication that the castrating bitch is depriving him of his manhood, of his meaning and position in life. If this silent temper tantrum doesn't work and she still refuses to put on the brakes to her development, he may go so far as to act "crazy." The sick-crazy man routine inevitably brings on submission in the form of maternal, care-giving behavior, if for no other reason than the woman knows very well that it would be difficult to support the family with him in a mental hospital. The whole sequence doesn't look violent but it is. The ruling class is full of such tricks. This particular variation of the class relationship between men and women is rarely seen in the workplace, where men who use passivity as a vehicle of oppression are not likely to be in the position of boss.

Women who use gestures of dominance are sometimes subjected to heavy taming campaigns on the part of aggressive men. The honcho (super-pig supremacist) sees such a woman as a challenge, and he may go to great efforts to put her in her place. To capture and domesticate a particularly wild and rebellious animal is a good way to improve one's position among men. Sometimes the honcho does this by being more aggressive and more tyrannical than other men, and she submits in fear. Sometimes he comes on as an adoring admirer and she submits in relief, thinking she has found a nonoppressive man. As soon as she is tamed, that is, acting in an appropriate slave manner, he loses his special interest in her and treats her as he treats other slaves.

Men have conveniently interpreted and labeled all of the dominance and submission interactions between men and women so that no one sees them for what they are. When men use gestures of dominance they are called manly, brave, strong, paternal, protective, and powerful. Women who use such gestures are nagging, shrews, bitches, domineering, mean, lesbians, and, of course, unfeminine. When women use gestures of submission they are nice, sweet, lovely, and charming, but men are weak, womanly, and dull. When a man and a woman relate in the typical pattern but magnified, it is called love. So love is male dominance evoking female submission, which, as we have seen, is a form of reducing the man's aggression. In other words, love is fear. The forms of female behavior that our contemporary ideologues have called "internalized self-hate" or masochism are usually just a logical response to a man's gesture of dominance. Women have spent years on the psychiatrist's couch hunting down a nonexistent internal enemy. Should a woman actually succeed in cutting through the male interpretation of events, the loyalty ethic prevents her from sharing her information.

Women and Women: The Prison Guards

The relationships between women under male supremacy are pure tragedy. First of all, we are divided according to the class of the man who owns us, with women owned by wealthier men living in less adverse conditions in terms of material comfort. This separation is almost impossible to transcend. Then, within each subgroup, we are pitted against each other in competition for the highest-ranking owner available to our particular group. Those of us who are most ambitious (or would be were we male) are particularly eager to connect up with an aggressive high-ranking male because that's the only expression permitted and our only means to prestige. Furthermore, we are expected to act as prison guards for one another by virtue of our internal competition. Women's gossip, which has always been the exchange of real social information, has a specialized function in the guard system. First of all, by involving itself in the relative ranking of various men, it keeps the competition and thus the hostility between women going full force. You pass on negative information about someone else's men. This reduces his rank in the eyes of other men who received the information from their women. With his rank lowered, you have protected or maybe even increased the rank of your own man, and vicariously, yourself. Secondly, gossip directly reports on women who have stepped out of line. You pass on information about other women who have misbehaved in some manner and thus proved themselves less desirable (i.e., less feminine) than you. Knowing that other women will slander you in a similar manner should you really try to break out, you are locked in a pernicious system that lowers rather than increases the ranking of everyone, except men who remain pure and innocent in the public eye. This control system between women does not utilize gestures of dominance at all. As we have seen, such gestures are considered ludicrous when used by women. Instead, it relies heavily on an extreme and twisted use of gestures of submission. Presenting like mad, women slander one another behind the smile of silver-sweet sisterhood, a most deceptive kind of mind fuck.

The ruling class always lies behind these terrible fights between women. In fact, the fighters are often carrying out the orders of their men without being aware of it. In the women's movement, we have had some unique opportunities to observe this with greater clarity than is usually possible. Some sisters in the women's movement are still under the control of left-wing movement men, who hassle them continuously about the insignificance of the slavery of white women compared to the third world struggle. These so called revolutionary men don't want their women concentrating too heavily on themselves because they would begin to realize what their true condition is and begin to struggle at home. As we have seen, the ruling class prefers to avoid resorting to violence because it wastes their energy, and any real struggle at home would quickly lead to violence. So, in the quiet of their living rooms, they inform their women of the "counter-revolutionary" and selfish nature of women rising up for their own sake. These living room briefings follow the usual dominance-submission routine with its implied threats of violence or abandonment, and most sisters feel forced to submit. They continue to put most of their effort into the male dominated counter-left organizations, somehow incorporating women's issues here and there. But the men aren't satisfied with that. Knowing very well that as long as there are feminist women challenging their class position, they are in danger of an uprising, they want to destroy these women or at least remove them from the public eye. If they offend the feminist women themselves, they would reveal their class interests too openly and polarize the situation right into class warfare. Instead, they subtly instruct their women to engage in the "gossipslander" and ultimately cat-fight routine. And we end up with shameful public fights between women, while the men sit back, titillated laughing pigs with shiny pink innocent faces. They force us to act as gestapo informers on one another, and finally as their private gestapo henchmen, and we get absolutely nothing out of it except more oppression and slavery.

Recently, a new dimension has been added to the male initiated, male directed cat fight. Early in any struggle, there is a certain amount of confusion on the part of the oppressed people and the ruling class. Neither is sure how far the thing will go or what it would take to quiet it down. The ruling class hesitates a short while before bringing in the troops because violence would polarize the situation and intensify the struggle before they are sure that it's necessary. So, while getting ready to move against the rebels, they simultaneously offer a few symbolic gifts to prove their peaceful intentions. Today, the ruling class is dangling a few inviting morsels in front of our eyes, in the form of prestigious jobs, published books, acknowledgment in the media and other things that they think might trick us into false consciousness, that is, thinking that we can make it after all. Then they sit back and watch us fight to be the first co-opted. And, of course, since we are in the struggle to change the conditions of our lives, we want those morsels very badly. At the moment, everyone in the women's movement is fighting to be co-opted, and the ruling class is going about it's ordinary pig-business. A few of us will be able to obtain slightly better jobs, or some short-lived *Life* magazine revolutionary heroine status, and that would be fine if we weren't wasting so much energy fighting for their gifts that mean nothing in the long run. For most of us nothing real has changed, and we need all of our energy to bring about real changes.

Breaking the Shackles: The Feminist Revolution

No behavioral system with which animals organize their social and economic lives is instinctive or God given. Such systems are always a temporary matter of adaptation to the environmental conditions of the place and the time. As the conditions change, so must the system, if the animals are to survive. Long ago, when the forests receded, many species of primates were forced to live on the ground. Away from the safety of the tree tops, a previously insignificant potential for larger, more aggressive males became a meaningful adaptation. Male dominance was a useful specialization for groups sometimes attacked by predators; men were more expendable than women and children if the group were to survive for generation after generation. The economic system of these primate groups was, and is, a kind of democratic or communal gathering. No individual exploits or alienates the labor of any other individual. The social customs (which includes internal use of dominance gestures) and family structure of the animals varies from group to group and place to place, and are passed on to new generations through social learning that takes place until adolescence. The particular customs of any group are determined by the conditions of their environment; all behavior is adaptation.

Some behavioral systems become so overspecialized that members of the species cannot adjust to changes in environmental conditions. Overspecialization is maladaptive; it interferes with adaptation which is the goal and meaning of life. At some point in human history, around the time of early agricultural settlements, the behavioral system of male dominance became further specialized. Men, trained from childhood to aggressively defend the group, began to use that aggression against members of the group in order to have control over the available resources and over the energy potential of the members themselves. Men alienated female labor for their own material benefit and developed the system that we know as male supremacy. Male supremacy is a mal-adaptive system that has clearly led our species to a dangerous edge. Male behavior is over-specialized; it has lost its capacity to adapt to environmental changes. Greed and lust for power have driven men to rape the land and women, to exploit other men, and to create a dangerous world of death-trap highways, inhuman prisons, endless wars, and poisonous air and water. The system that developed a technology that could free so many is trapped by male behavior; the technology is a tool for male destruction instead of for freedom. The system must change rapidly if the species is to survive. And women must be the agents of change. The eternal peasants, the slaves, the unpaid workers of the world who alone have not been behaviorally specialized into rigid patterns leading to a grim and violent species death; it rests on us to overthrow male supremacy. Power must be removed from every man and placed in the hands of women, who with their flexibility and capacity to adapt will use it to reorganize society in a way that allows the human animal to live in nondestructive interaction with the earth and all its inhabitants.

It would be nice to think that the feminist revolution could be a peaceful event, that women could seize power gently. But our evidence points to the contrary. It is astounding how quickly men resort to violence when we ask for a little drop of power, or even to be heard. We asked the psychiatrists at the annual American Psychiatric Association convention to hear us. They responded with jeers, lunges, threatening fists, and displays that bordered on violence. A so-called brother on the counter-left was planning to publish a pornographic magazine. We explained the relationship between pornography and the exploitation of women. He did not hear a word until he realized we were prepared to move against him physically if he did not agree to cancel the publication. We went down to the topless-bottomless hippy-free-love oppression belt of San Francisco to let men know that women were rising up angry. We were ridiculed, shoved around, pushed, pinched, and slandered. Men respond to women's demands with laughter that rapidly turns to brutality when they realize that we are serious.

The women's movement is still a liberal movement. The surprise that we feel each time our demands are ignored, or laughed at, or met with physical brutality, is a pathetic righteous indignation. By this time we should not be surprised or indignant, and if our feelings began to match our intellectual awareness of the class antagonism between men and women we would expect such behavior from our class enemy and be prepared for it. But it would be a mistake to think that our liberalism was a personal problem or individual weakness just as we were mistaken when we thought our personal pain was an individual matter. In fact, at this point our liberalism protects us from martyrdom. With so few of us organized, any form of armed struggle would be suicide. We need many sisters with us before we let go of those liberal responses. A moderate passivity, that is; control of our rage in many of our interactions with men, is still necessary.

Our movement is going through a difficult time. We discovered our oppression and we discovered our enemy, but we don't have enough forces to successfully make a feminist revolution and overthrow male supremacy. In frustration some sisters are taking refuge in various kinds of counter-institutions, what they hope will be pickets of freedom. Women's communes; women's co-ops; women's underground papers; women's culture; all are doomed and will create more frustration because we do not have access to resources or to the means of production. We can't exist independently outside of the economic system because we are in fact dependent on it for our survival. Nothing is free in Amerika. And covering up our unhappiness with idealism and dreams of a perfect and pure sisterhood will lead to even more frustration. All of our tactics and all of our analysis have to be based on what's real even if what's real is grimy and mean and ugly. If it were possible to achieve our goals inside of the system, or if it were possible for reality to in any way match our ideals inside of the system then we wouldn't need to make a revolution at all. But it is not. We aren't going to get happier, or freer, or less crazy under supremacy. The more we struggle, the more pain we will experience, which will make us struggle even more. When there are enough of us up against the wall, desperate and in rage, we will begin the offensive. Our job now is to reach as many women as possible; we need everyone with us. Our second job is to begin training ourselves in the skills that armed struggle requires. This is our time to grow and to learn.

Some Practical Conclusions: Pigs Hiding under the Rocks

Anyone who has been involved in the women's movement for more than ten minutes has been warned by one or another so called revolutionary group that their activities, be they weekly small group meetings, abortion workshops, daycare programs, guerrilla style consciousness raising actions, or anything else that women are doing for their own liberation, are reformist, racist, or some other variation of counter-revolutionary. These warnings come in the form of pseudo-intellectual questions (feminist baiting, "but what are the goals of your activities, where are you going?" etc.) or overtly nasty accusations. They are nothing more than the efforts of men to stop us. As usual, they try to use women as their mouthpieces, so that it sounds as if one group of women is attacking the activities of another. But look behind any of the accusations, be they open or sneaky, and you will find the male pig origin.

The first often heard phrase is "reformist." How could any effort on the part of an oppressed class be reformist? Do they want us to go on dying of illegal abortions in greater numbers than they die in Viet Nam until the great moment, the REVO-LUTION? Hand in hand with the reformist attack comes the warning about co-optation. Watch out or you will be co-opted they tell us. Well that's good. When people can't get well paid enough to support their families are they supposed to refuse a pay increase and watch their kids go without meat all winter so that some male pig god will judge them pure after they're all dead and although the final judgement day of REVOLUTION has arrived? Only a ruling class with enough to eat and a nice warm secure future can afford the luxury of purity. Women clearly can not, particularly if they have broken away from the private male owner and fall in the freed slave category.

After eight thousand years of devoting their class life to the selfless care of others, it is no surprise that women are susceptible to guilt about other oppressed peoples. Our enemies, eager to try all tricks in their efforts to stop the movement for female liberation, prey on that guilt by frequently comparing the oppression of women to the oppression of third world people. The result is a sliding scale of oppression designed to stop women wherever they are, since there is always someone in worse shape. Black people in Amerika may as well stop struggling too, according to this logic, since brown peasants in Peru are hungrier than the poorest residents of the Amerikan black ghetto. This kind of comparative-competitive oppression contest leads to a lot of female breast beating, moaning, and other gestures with which women hope to relieve their guilt for worrying about themselves for a change. The breast beating reeks of paternalism which one expects from white men but is absurd coming from women.

Despite what they say, there is nothing wrong with women fighting for themselves. An altruistic intellectual revolutionary is not to be trusted beyond the cops-and-robbers Hollywood hero stage, which is at best little white boys playing out an apparently endless adolescence. Morals, love for all the poor oppressed peoples, or any other kind of altruistic motivations are meaningless in the face of a grim and unglorious day-to-day struggle.

We must fight for ourselves, sisters; we cut across traditional class lines, race lines, national lines. And we must fight wherever we are, at whatever level is organic to us. A small group in the middle of an L.A. suburb, a guerrilla witch group in the city, a day-care center on the campus, an underground group in the phone company, any woman fighting for her own liberation is creating the feminist revolution.

Chapter Sixteen

Psychology Constructs the Female

or The Fantasy Life of the Male Psychologist (with Some Attention to the Fantasies of His Friends, the Male Biologist and the Male Anthropologist)

Naomi Weisstein

It is an implicit assumption that the area of psychology which concerns itself with personality has the onerous but necessary task of describing the limits of human possibility. Thus when we are about to consider the liberation of women, we naturally look to psychology to tell us what is 'true' liberation would mean: what would give women the freedom to fulfill their own intrinsic natures.

Psychologists have set about describing the true natures of women with a certainty and a sense of their own infallibility rarely found in the secular world. Bruno Bettelheim, of the University of Chicago, tells us (1965) that

> We must start with the realization that, as much as women want to be good scientists or engineers, they want first and foremost to be womanly companions of men and to be mothers.

Erik Erikson of Harvard University (1964), upon noting that young women often ask whether they can 'have an identity before they know whom they will marry, and for whom they will make a home,' explains somewhat elegiacally that.

> Much of a young woman's identity is already defined in her kind of attractiveness and in the selectivity of her search for the man (or men) by whom she wishes to be sought
> . . .

Mature womanly fulfillment, for Erikson, rests on the fact that a woman's

> . . . somatic design harbors an 'inner space' destined to bear the offspring of chosen men, and with it, a biological, psychological, and ethical commitment to take care of human infancy.

Some psychiatrists even see the acceptance of woman's role by women as a solution to societal problems. 'Woman is nurturance . . . ,' writes Joseph Rheingold (1964), a psychiatrist at Harvard Medical School, ' . . . anatomy decrees the life of a woman . . . When women grow up without dread of their biological functions and without subversion by feminist doctrine, and therefore enter upon motherhood with a sense of fulfillment and altruistic sentiment, we shall attain the goal of a good life and a secure world in which to live it.' (p. 714)

These views from men who are assumed to be experts reflect, in a surprisingly transparent way, the cultural consensus. They not only assert that a woman is defined by her ability to attract men, they see no alternative definitions. They think that the definition of a woman in terms of a man is the way it should be; and they back it up with psychosexual incantation and biological ritual curses. A woman has an identity if she is attractive enough to obtain a man, and thus, a home; for this will allow her to set about her life's task of 'joyful altruism and nurturance.'

Business certainly does not disagree. If views such as Bettelheim's and Erikson's do indeed have something to do with real liberation for women, then seldom in human history has so much money and effort been spent on helping a group of people realize their true potential. Clothing, cosmetics, home furnishings, are multi-million dollar businesses: if you don't like investing in firms that make dollar weaponry and flaming gasoline, then there's a lot of cash in 'inner space'. Sheet and pillowcase manufacturers are concerned to fill this inner space:

> Mother, for a while this morning, I thought I wasn't cut out for married life. Hank was late for work and forgot his apricot juice and walked out without kissing me, and when I was all alone I started crying. But then the postman came with the sheets and towels you sent, that look like big bandana handkerchiefs, and you know what I thought? That those big red and blue handkerchiefs are for girls like me to dry their tears on so they can get busy and do what a housewife has to do. Throw open the windows and start getting the house ready, and the dinner, maybe clean the silver and put new geraniums in the box. *Everything to be ready for him when he walks through that door.* (Fieldcrest 1965; emphasis added.)

Of course, it is not only the sheet and pillowcase manufacturers, the cosmetics industry, the home furnishings salesmen who profit from and make use of the cultural definitions of man and woman. The example above is blatantly and overtly pitched to a particular kind of sexist stereotype: the child nymph. But almost all aspects of the media are normative, that is, they have to do with the ways in which beautiful people, or just folks, or ordinary Americans, or extraordinary Americans, should live their lives. They define the possible; and the possibilities are usually in terms of what is male and what is female. Men and women alike are waiting for Hank, the Silva Thins man, to walk back through that door.

It is an interesting but limited exercise to show that psychologists and psychiatrists embrace these sexist norms of our culture, that they do not see beyond the most superficial and stultifying media conceptions of female nature, and that their ideas of female nature serve industry and commerce so well. Just because it's good for business doesn't mean it's wrong. What I will show is that it *is wrong*; that there isn't the tiniest shred of evidence that these fantasies of servitude and childish dependence have anything to do with women's true potential; that the idea of the nature of human possibility which rests on the accidents of individual development of genitalia, on what is possible today because of what happened yesterday, on the fundamentalist myth of sex organ causality, has strangled and deflected psychology so that it is relatively useless in describing, explaining or predicting humans and their behavior. It then goes without saying that present psychology is less than worthless in contributing to a vision which could truly liberate—men as well as women.

The central argument of my paper, then, is this. Psychology has nothing to say about what women are really like, what they need and what they want, essentially because psychology does not know. I want to stress that this failure is not limited to women; rather, the kind of psychology which has addressed itself to how people act and who they are has failed to understand, in the first place, why people act the way they do, and certainly failed to understand what might make them act differently.

The kind of psychology which has addressed itself to these questions divides into two professional areas: academic personality research, and clinical psychology and psychiatry. The basic reason for failure is the same in both these areas: the central assumption for most psychologists of human personality has been that human behavior rests on an individual and inner dynamic, perhaps fixed in infancy, perhaps fixed by genitalia, perhaps simply arranged in a rather immovable cognitive network. But this assumption is rapidly losing ground as personality psychologists fail again and again to get consistency in the assumed personalities of their subjects (Block, 1968). Meanwhile, the evidence is collecting that what a person does and who she believes herself to be, will in general be a function of what people around her expect her to be, and what the overall situation in which she is acting implies that she is. Compared to the influence of the social context within which a person lives, his or her history and 'traits', as well as biological make-up, may simply be random variations, 'noise' superimposed on the true signal which can predict behavior.

Some academic personality psychologists are at least looking at the counter evidence and questioning their theories; no such corrective is occurring in clinical psychology and psychiatry: Freudians and neo-Freudians, Nudic-marathonists and Touchy-feelies, classicists and swingers, clinicians and psychiatrists, simply refuse to look at the evidence against their theory and practice. And they supply their theory and practice with stuff so transparently biased as to have absolutely no standing as empirical evidence.

To summarize: the first reason for psychology's failure to understand what people are and how they act is that psychology has looked for inner traits when it should have been looking for social context; the second reason for psychology's failure is that the theoreticians of personality have generally been clinicians and psychiatrists, and they have never considered it necessary to have evidence in support of their theories.

Theory without Evidence

Let us turn to this latter cause of failure first: the acceptance by psychiatrists and clinical psychologists of theory without evidence. If we inspect the literature of personality, it is immediately obvious that the bulk of it is written by clinicians and psychiatrists, and that the major support for their theories is 'years of intensive clinical experience'. This is a tradition started by Freud. His 'insights' occurred during the course of his work with his patients. Now there is nothing wrong with such an approach to theory formulation, a person is free to make up theories with any inspiration that works: divine revelation, intensive clinical practice, a random numbers table. But he/she is not free to claim any validity for his/her theory until it has been tested and confirmed. But theories are treated in no such tentative way in ordinary clinical practice. Consider Freud. What he thought constituted evidence violated the most minimal conditions of scientific rigor. In *The Sexual Enlightenment of Children* (1963), the classic document which is supposed to demonstrate empirically the existence of a castration complex and its connection to a phobia, Freud based his analysis on the reports of the father of the little boy, himself in therapy, and a devotee of Freudian theory. I really don't have to comment further on the contamination in this kind of evidence. It is remarkable that only recently has Freud's classic theory on the sexuality of women—the notion of the double orgasm—been actually tested physiologically and found just plain wrong. Now those who claim that fifty years of psychoanalytic experience constitute evidence enough of the essential truths of Freud's theory should ponder the robust health of the double orgasm. Did women, until Masters and Johnson (1966), believe they were having two different kinds of orgasm? Did their psychiatrists badger them into reporting something that was not true? If so, were there other things they reported that were also not true? Did psychiatrists ever learn anything different than their theories had led them to believe? If clinical experience means anything at all, surely we should have been done with the double orgasm myth long before the Masters and Johnson studies.

But certainly, you may object, 'years of intensive clinical experience' is the only reliable measure in a discipline which rests for its findings on insight, sensitivity, and intuition. The problem with insight, sensitivity, and intuition, is that they can confirm for all time the biases that one started out with. People used to be absolutely convinced of their ability to tell which of their number were engaging in witchcraft. All it required was some sensitivity to the workings of the devil.

Years of intensive clinical experience is not the same thing as empirical evidence. The first thing an experimenter learns in any kind of experiment which involves humans is the concept of the 'double blind.' The term is taken from medical experiments, where one group is given a drug which is presumably supposed to change behavior in a certain way, and a control group is given a placebo. If the observers or the subjects know which group took which drug, the result invariably comes out on the positive side for the new drug. Only when it is not known which subject took which pill is validity remotely approximated. In addition, with judgments of human behavior, it is so difficult to precisely tie down just what behavior is going on, let alone what behavior should be expected, that one must test again and again the reliability of judgments. How many judges, blind, will agree in their observations? Can they replicate, their own judgments at some later time? When, in actual practice, these judgment criteria are tested for clinical judgments, then we find that the judges cannot judge reliably, nor can they judge consistently: they do no better than chance in identifying which of a certain set of stories were written by men and which by women; which of a whole battery of clinical test results are the products of homosexuals and which are the products of heterosexuals (Hooker, 1957), and which, of a battery of clinical test results *and* interviews (where questions are asked such as 'Do you have delusions?' Little & Schneidman, 1959) are products of psychotics, neurotics, psychosomatics, or normals. Lest this summary escape your notice, let me stress the implications of these findings. The ability of judges, chosen for their clinical expertise, to distinguish male heterosexuals from male homosexuals on the basis of three widely used clinical projective tests—the Rorschach, the TAT, and the MAP—was *no better than chance*. The reason this is such devastating news, of course, is that sexuality is supposed to be of fundamental importance in the deep dynamic of personality; if what is considered gross sexual deviance cannot be caught, then what are psychologists talking about when they, for example, claim that at the basis of paranoid psychosis is 'latent homosexual panic'? They can't even identify what homosexual anything is, let alone 'latent homosexual panic'.[1] More frightening, expert clinicians cannot be consistent on what diagnostic category to assign to a person, again on the basis of both tests and interviews; a number of normals in the Little & Schneidman study were described as psychotic, in such categories as 'schizophrenic with homosexual tendencies' or 'schizoid character with depressive trends'. But most disheartening, when the judges were asked to rejudge the test protocols some weeks later, their diagnoses of the same subjects on the basis of the same protocol differed markedly from their initial judgments. It is obvious that even simple descriptive conventions in clinical psychology cannot be consistently applied; if clinicians were as faulty in recognizing food from non-food, they'd poison themselves and starve to death. That their descriptive conventions have any explanatory significance is therefore, of course, out of the question.

As a graduate student at Harvard some years ago, I was a member of a seminar which was asked to identify which of two piles of clinical test, the TAT, had been written by males and which by females. Only four students out of twenty identified the piles correctly, and this was after one and a half months of intensively studying the differences between men and women. Since this result is below chance—that is, this result would occur by chance about four out of a thousand times—we may conclude that there *is* finally a consistency here; students are judging knowledgeably within the context of psychological teaching about the differences between men and women; the teachings themselves are simply erroneous.

You may argue that the theory may be scientifically 'unsound' but at least it cures people. There is no evidence that it does. In 1952, Eysenck reported the results of what is called an 'outcome of therapy' study of neurotics which showed that, of the patients who received psychoanalysis the improvement rate was 44%; of the patients who received psychotherapy the improvement rate was 64%; and of the patients who received no treatment at all the improvement rate was 72%. These findings have never been refuted; subsequently, later studies have confirmed the negative results of the Eysenck study (Barron & Leary, 1955; Bergin, 1963; Cartwright and Vogel, 1960; Truax, 1963; Powers and Witmer, 1951). How can clinicians and psychiatrists, then, in all good conscience, continue to practice? Largely by ignoring these results and being careful not to do outcome-of-therapy studies. The attitude is nicely summarized by Rotter (1960) (quoted in Astin, 1961): 'Research studies in psychotherapy tend to be concerned more with psychotherapeutic procedure and less with outcome.... To some extent, it reflects an interest in the psychotherapy situation as a kind of personality laboratory.' Some laboratory.

The Social Context

Thus, since we can conclude that since clinical experience and tools can be shown to be worse than useless when tested for consistency, efficacy, agreement, and reliability, we can safely conclude that theories of a clinical nature advanced about women are also worse than useless. I want to turn now to the second major point in my paper, which is that, even when psychological theory is constructed so that it may be tested, and rigorous standards of evidence are used, it has become increasingly clear that in order to understand why people do what they do, and certainly in order to change what people do, psychologists must turn away from the theory of the causal nature of the inner dynamic and look to the social context within which individuals live.

Before examining the relevance of this approach for the question of women, let me first sketch the groundwork for this assertion.

In the first place, it is clear (Block, 1968) that personality tests never yield consistent predictions; a rigid authoritarian on one measure will be an unauthoritarian on the next. But the reason for this inconsistency is only now becoming clear, and it seems overwhelmingly to have much more to do with the social situation in which the subject finds himself than with the subject himself.

In a series of brilliant experiments, Rosenthal and his co-workers (Rosenthal and Jacobson, 1968; Rosenthal, 1966) have shown that if one group of experimenters has one hypothesis about what they expect to find, and another group of experimenters has the opposite hypothesis, both groups will obtain results in accord with their hypotheses. The results obtained are not due to mishandling of data by biased experimenters; rather, somehow, the bias of the experimenter creates a changed environment in which subjects actually act differently. For instance, in one experiment, subjects were to assign numbers to pictures of men's faces, with high numbers representing the subject's judgment that the man in the picture was a successful person, and low numbers representing the subject's judgment that the man in the picture was an unsuccessful person. Prior to running the subjects, one group of experimenters was told that the subjects tended to rate the faces high; another group of experimenters was told that the subjects tended to rate the faces low. Each group of experimenters was instructed to follow precisely the same procedure: they were required to read to subjects a set of instructions, and to *say nothing else*. For the 375 subjects run, the results showed clearly that those subjects who performed the task with experimenters who expected high ratings gave high ratings, and those subjects who performed the task with experimenters who expected low ratings gave low ratings. How did this happen? The experimenters all used the same words; it was something in their conduct which made one group of subjects do one thing, and another group of subjects do another thing.[2]

The concreteness of the changed conditions produced by expectation is a fact, a reality: even with animal subjects, in two separate studies (Rosenthal & Pode, 1960;

Rosenthal & Lawson, 1961), those experimenters who were told that rats learning mazes had been especially bred for brightness obtained better learning from their rats than did experimenters believing their rats to have been bred for dullness. In a very recent study, Rosenthal & Jacobson (1968) extended their analysis to the natural classroom situation. Here, they tested a group of students and reported to the teachers that some among the students tested 'showed great promise'. Actually, the students so named had been selected on a random basis. Some time later, the experimenters retested the group of students: those students whose teachers had been told that they were 'promising' showed real and dramatic increments in their IQs as compared to the rest of the students. Something in the conduct of the teachers towards those who the teachers believed to be the 'bright' students, made those students brighter.

Thus, even in carefully controlled experiments, and with no outward or conscious difference in behavior, the hypotheses we start with will influence enormously the behavior of another organism. These studies are extremely important when assessing the validity of psychological studies of women. Since it is beyond doubt that most of us start with notions as to the nature of men and women, the validity of a number of observations of sex differences is questionable, even when these observations have been made under carefully controlled conditions. Second, and more important, the Rosenthal experiments point quite clearly to the influence of social expectation. In some extremely important ways, people are what you expect them to be, or at least they behave as you expect them to behave. Thus, if women, according to Bettelheim, want first and foremost to be good wives and mothers, it is extremely likely that this is what Bruno Bettelheim, and the rest of society, want them to be.

There is another series of brilliant social psychological experiments which point to the overwhelming effect of social context. These are the obedience experiments of Stanley Milgram (1965a, 1965b) in which subjects are asked to obey the orders of unknown experimenters, orders which carry with them the distinct possibility that the subject is killing somebody.

In Milgram's experiments, a subject is told that he is administering a learning experiment, and that he is to deal out shocks each time the other 'subject' (in reality, a confederate of the experimenter) answers incorrectly. The equipment appears to provide graduated shocks ranging upwards from 15 volts through 450 volts; for each of four consecutive voltages there are verbal descriptions such as 'mild shock,' 'danger, severe shock,' and, finally, for the 435 and 450 volt switches, a red XXX marked over the switches. Each time the stooge answers incorrectly, the subject is supposed to increase the voltage. As the voltage increases, the stooge begins to cry in pain; he demands that the experiment stop; finally, he refuses to answer at all. When he stops responding, the experimenter instructs the subject to continue increasing the voltage; for each shock administered the stooge shrieks in agony. Under these conditions, about 62 ½% of the subjects administered shock that they believed to be possibly lethal.

No tested individual differences between subjects predicted how many would continue to obey, and which would break off the experiment. When forty psychiatrists predicted how many of a group of 100 subjects would go on to give the lethal shock, their predictions were orders of magnitude below the actual percentages; most expected only one-tenth of one per cent of the subjects to obey to the end.

But even though *psychiatrists* have no idea how people will behave in this situation, and even though individual differences do not predict which subjects will obey and which will not, it is easy to predict when subjects will be obedient and when they will be defiant. All the experimenter has to do is change the social situation. In a variant of Milgram's experiment, two stooges were present in addition to the 'victim'; these worked along with the subject in administering electric shocks. When these two stooges refused to go on with the experiment, only ten per cent of the subjects continued to the maximum voltage. This is critical for personality theory. It says that behavior is predicted from the social situation, not from the individual history.

Finally, an ingenious experiment by Schachter and Singer (1962) showed that subjects injected with adrenalin, which produces a state of physiological arousal in all but minor respects identical to that which occurs when subjects are extremely afraid, became euphoric when they were in a room with a stooge who was acting euphoric, and became extremely angry when they were placed in a room with a stooge who was acting extremely angry.

To summarize: If subjects under quite innocuous and non-coercive social conditions can be made to kill other subjects and under other types of social conditions will positively refuse to do so; if subjects can react to a state of physiological fear by becoming euphoric because there is somebody else around who is euphoric or angry because there is somebody else around who is angry; if students become intelligent because teachers expect them to be intelligent, and rats run mazes better because experimenters are told the rats are bright, then it is obvious that a study of human behavior requires, first and foremost, a study of the social contexts within which people move, the expectations as to how they will behave, and the authority which tells them who they are and what they are supposed to do.

Biologically Based Theories

Biologists also have at times assumed they could describe the limits of human potential from their observations not of human, but of animal behavior. Here, as in psychology, there has been no end of theorizing about sexes, again with a sense of absolute certainty surprising in 'science.' These theories fall into two major categories.

One category of theory argues that since females and males differ in their sex hormones, and sex hormones enter the brain (Hamburg & Lunde in Maccoby, 1966), there must be innate behavioral differences. But the only thing this argument tells us is that there are differences in physiological state. The problem is whether these differences are at all relevant to behavior.

Consider, for example, differences in levels of the sex hormone testosterone. A man who calls himself Tiger[3] has recently argued (1970) that the greater quantities of testosterone found in human males as compared with human females (of a certain age group) determines innate differences in aggressiveness, competitiveness, dominance, ability to hunt, ability to hold public office, and so forth. But Tiger demonstrates in this argument the same manly and courageous refusal to be intimidated by evidence which we have already seen in our consideration of the clinical and psychiatric tradition. The evidence does not support his argument, and in most cases, directly contradicts it. Testosterone level does not seem to be related to hunting ability, or dominance, or aggression, or competitiveness. As Storch has pointed out (1970), all normal *male mammals* in the reproductive age group produce much greater quantities of testosterone than females; yet many of these males are neither hunters nor are they aggressive (e.g., rabbits). And among some hunting mammals, such as the larger cats, it turns out that more hunting is done by the female than the male. And there exist primate species where the female is clearly more aggressive, competitive, and dominant than the male (Mitchell, 1969; and see below). Thus, for some species, being female and therefore having less testosterone than the male of that species means hunting more, or being more aggressive, or being more dominant. Nor does having *more* testosterone preclude behavior commonly thought of as "female": there exist primate species where females do not touch infants except to feed them; the males care for the infants at all times (Mitchell, 1969; see fuller discussion below). So it is not clear what testosterone or any other sex-hormonal difference means for differences in nature, or sex-role behavior.

In other words, one can observe identical types of behavior which have been associated with sex (e.g., "mothering") in males and females, despite known differences in physiological state, i.e., sex hormones, genitalia, etc. What about the converse to this? That is, can one obtain differences in behavior given a single physiological state? The answer is overwhelmingly yes, not only as regards nonsex-specific hormones (as in the Schachter and Singer 1962 experiment cited above), but also as regards gender itself. Studies of hermaphrodites with the same diagnosis (the genetic, gonadal, hormonal sex, the internal reproductive organs, and the ambiguous appearances of the external genitalia were identical) have shown that one will consider oneself male or female depending simply on whether one was defined and raised as male or female (Money, 1970; Hampton & Hampton, 1961):

"There is no more convincing evidence of the power of social interaction on gender-identity differentiation than in the case of congenital hermaphrodites who are of the same diagnosis and similar degree of hermaphroditism but are differently assigned and with a different postnatal medical and life history." (Money, 1970, p. 432).

Thus, for example, if out of two individuals diagnosed as having the adrenogenital syndrome of female hermaphroditism, one is raised as a girl and one as a boy, each will act and identify her/himself accordingly. The one raised as a girl will consider herself a girl; the one raised as a boy will consider himself a boy; and each will conduct her/himself successfully in accord with that self-definition.

So, identical behavior occurs given different physiological states; and different behavior occurs given an identical physiological starting point. So it is not clear that differences in sex hormones are at all relevant to behavior.

The other category of theory based on biology, a reductionist theory, goes like this. Sex-role behavior in some primate species is described, and it is concluded that this is the 'natural' behavior for humans. Putting aside the not insignificant problem of observer bias (for instance, Harlow, 1962, of the University of Wisconsin, after observing differences between male and female rhesus monkeys, quotes Lawrence Sterne to the effect that women are silly and trivial, and concludes that 'men and women have differed in the past and they will differ in the future'), there are a number of problems with this approach.

The most general and serious problem is that there are no grounds to assume that anything primates do is necessary, natural or desirable in humans, for the simple reason that humans are not nonhumans. For instance, it is found that male chimpanzees placed alone with infants will not 'mother' them. Jumping from hard data to ideological speculation, researchers conclude from this information that *human* females are necessary for the safe growth of human infants. It would be as reasonable to conclude, following this logic, that it is quite useless to teach human infants to speak, since it has been tried with chimpanzees and it does not work.

One strategy that has been used is to extrapolate from primate behavior to 'innate' human preference by noticing certain trends in primate behavior as one moves phylogenetically closer to humans. But there are great difficulties with this approach. When behaviors from lower primates are directly opposite to those of higher primates, or to those one expects of humans, they can be dismissed on evolutionary grounds—higher primates and/or humans grew out of that kid stuff. On the other hand, if the behavior of higher primates is counter to the behavior considered natural for humans, while the behavior of some lower primate is considered the natural one for humans, the higher primate behavior can be dismissed also, on the grounds that it has diverged from an older, prototypical pattern. So either way, one can select those behaviors one wants to prove as innate for humans. In addition, one does not know whether the sex-role behavior exhibited is dependent on the phylogenetic rank, or on the environmental conditions (both physical and social) under which different species live.

Is there then any value at all in primate observations as they relate to human females and males? There is a value but it is limited: its function can be no more than to show some extant examples of diverse sex-role behavior. It must be stressed, however, that this is an extremely limited function. The extant behavior does not begin to suggest all the possibilities, either for non-human primates or for humans. Bearing these caveats in mind, it is nonetheless interesting that if one inspects the limited set of observations of existing non-human primate sex-role behaviors, one finds, in fact, a much larger range of sex-role behavior than is commonly believed to exist. 'Biology' appears to limit very little; the fact that a female gives birth does not mean, even in non-humans, that she necessarily cares for the infant (in marmosets, for instance, the male carries the infant at all times except when the infant is feeding [Mitchell, 1969]); 'natural' female and male behavior varies all the way from females who are much more aggressive and competitive than males (e.g., Tamarins, see Mitchell, 1969) and male 'mothers' (e.g., Titi monkeys, night monkeys, and marmosets; see Mitchell, 1969) to submissive and passive females and male antagonists (e.g., rhesus monkeys).

But even for the limited function that primate arguments serve, the evidence has been misused. Invariably, only those primates have been cited which exhibit exactly the kind of behavior that the proponents of the biological fixedness of human female behavior wish were true for humans. Thus, baboons and rhesus monkeys are generally cited: males in these groups exhibit some of the most irritable and aggressive behavior found in primates, and if one wishes to argue that females are naturally passive and submissive, these groups provide vivid examples. There are abundant counter examples, such as those mentioned above (Mitchell, 1969); in fact, in general, a counter example can be found for every sex-role behavior cited, including, as mentioned in the case of marmosets, male 'mothers.'

But the presence of counter examples has not stopped florid and overarching theories of the natural or biological basis of male privilege from proliferating. For instance, there have been a number of theories dealing with the innate incapacity in human males for monogamy. Here, as in most of this type of theorizing, baboons are a favorite example, probably because of their fantasy value: the family unit of the hamadryas baboon, for instance, consists of a highly constant pattern of one male and a number of females and their young. And again, the counter examples, such as the invariably monogamous gibbon, are ignored.

An extreme example of this maiming and selective truncation of the evidence in the service of a plea for the maintenance of male privilege is a recent book. *Men in Groups* (1969) by Tiger. (See above and note 3.) The central claim of this book is that females are incapable of 'bonding' as in 'male bonding'. What is 'male bonding'? Its surface definition is simple:' . . . a particular relationship between two or more males such that they react differently to members of their bonding units as compared to individuals outside of it' (pp. 19–20). If one deletes the word male, the definition, on its face, would seem to include all organisms that have any kind of social organization. But this is not what Tiger means. For instance, Tiger asserts that females are incapable of bonding; and this alleged incapacity indicates to Tiger that females should be restricted from public life. Why is bonding an exclusively male behavior? Because, says Tiger, it is seen in male primates. All male primates? No, very few male primates. Tiger cites two examples where male bonding is seen: rhesus monkeys and baboons. Surprise, surprise. But not even all baboons: as mentioned above, the hamadryas social organization consists of one-male units; so does that of the Gelada baboon (Mitchell, 1969). And the great apes do not go in for male bonding much either. The 'male bond' is hardly a serious contribution to scholarship; one reviewer for *Science* has observed that the book ' . . . shows basically more resemblance to a partisan political tract than to a work of objective social science', with male bonding being ' . . . some kind of behavioral phlogiston' (Fried, 1969, p. 884).

In short, primate arguments have generally misused the evidence; primate studies themselves have, in any case, only the very limited function of describing some possible sex-role behavior; and at present, primate observations have been sufficiently limited so that even the range of possible sex-role behavior for non-human primates is not known. This range is not known since there is only minimal observation of what happens to behavior if the physical or social environment is changed. In one study (Itani, 1963), different troops of Japanese macaques were observed. Here, there appeared to be cultural differences: males in 3 out of the 18 troops observed differed in their amount of aggressiveness and infant-caring behavior. There could be no possibility of differential evolution here; the differences seemed largely transmitted by infant socialization. Thus, the very limited evidence points to some plasticity in the sex-role behavior of non-human primates; if we can figure out experiments which massively change the social organization of primate groups, it is possible that we might observe great changes in behavior. At present, however, we must conclude that, given a constant physical environment, non-human primates do not change their social conditions by themselves very much, and thus the 'innateness' and fixedness of their behavior is simply not known. Thus, even if there were some way, which there isn't, to settle on the behavior of a particular primate species as being the 'natural' way for humans, we would not know whether or not this were simply some function of the present social organization of that species. And finally, once again it must be stressed that even if non-human primate behavior turned out to be relatively fixed, this would say little about our behavior. More immediate and relevant evidence, i.e., the evidence from social psychology, points to the enormous plasticity in human behavior, not only from one culture to the next, but from one experimental group to the next. One of the most salient features of human social organization is its variety; there are a number of cultures where there is at least a rough equality between men and women (Mead, 1949). In summary, primate arguments can tell us very little about our 'innate' sex-role behavior; if they tell us anything at all, they tell us that there is no one biologically 'natural' female or male behavior, and that sex-role behavior in non-human primates is much more varied than has previously been thought.

Conclusion

In brief, the uselessness of present psychology (and biology) with regard to women is simply a special case of the general conclusion: one must understand the social conditions under which humans live if one is going to attempt to explain their behavior. And, to understand the social conditions under which women live, one must understand the social expectations about women.

How are women characterized in our culture, and in psychology? They are inconsistent, emotionally unstable, lacking in a strong conscience or superego, weaker, 'nurturant' rather than productive, 'intuitive' rather than intelligent, and, if they are at all 'normal,' suited to the home and the family. In short, the list adds up to a typical minority group stereotype of inferiority (Hacker, 1951): if they know their place, which is in the home, they are really quite lovable, happy, childlike, loving creatures. In a review of the intellectual differences between little boys and little girls, Eleanor Maccoby (1966) has shown that there are no intellectual differences until about high school, or, if there are, girls are slightly ahead of boys. At high school, girls begin to do worse on a few intellectual tasks, such as arithmetic reasoning, and beyond high school, the achievement of women now measured in terms of productivity and accomplishment drops off even more rapidly. There are a number of other, non-intellectual tests which show sex differences; I choose the intellectual differences since it is seen clearly that women start becoming inferior. It is no use to talk about women being different but equal; all of the tests I can think of have a 'good' outcome and a 'bad' outcome. Women usually end up at the 'bad' outcome. In light of social expectations about women, what is surprising is not that women end up where society expects they will; what is surprising is that little girls don't get the message that they are supposed to be stupid until high school; and what is even more remarkable is that some women resist this message even after high school, college, and graduate school.

My paper began with remarks on the task of the discovery of the limits of human potential. Psychologists must realize that it is they who are limiting discovery of human potential. They refuse to accept evidence, if they are clinical psychologists, or, if they are rigorous, they assume that people move in a context-free ether, with only their innate dispositions and their individual traits determining what they will do. Until psychologists begin to respect evidence, and until they begin looking at the social context within which people move, psychology will have nothing of substance to offer in this task of discovery. I don't know what immutable differences exist between men and women apart from differences in their genitals; perhaps there are some other unchangeable differences; probably there are a number of irrelevant differences. But it is clear that until social expectations for men and women are equal, until we provide equal respect for both men and women, our answers to this question will simply reflect our prejudices.

NOTES

1. It should be noted that psychologists have been as quick to assert absolute truths about the nature of homosexuality as they have about the nature of women. The arguments presented in this paper apply equally to the nature of homosexuality; psychologists know nothing about it; there is no more evidence for the 'naturalness' of heterosexuality than for the 'naturalness' of homosexuality. Psychology has functioned as a pseudo-scientific buttress for patriarchal ideology and patriarchal social organization: women's liberation and gay liberation fight against a common victimization.

2. I am indebted to Jesse Lemisch for his valuable suggestions in the interpretations of these studies.

3. Schwarz-Belkin (1914) claims that the name was originally Mouse, but this may be a reference to an earlier L. Tiger (putative).

REFERENCES

Astin, A. W., "The functional autonomy of psychotherapy." *American Psychologist*, 1961, *16*, 75–78.

Barron, F. & Leary, T., "Changes in psychoneurotic patients with and without psychotherapy." *Journal of Consulting Psychology*, 1955, *19*, 239–245.

Bergin, A. E., "The effects of psychotherapy: negative results revisisted." *Journal of Consulting Psychology*, 1963, *10*, 244–250.

Bettelheim, B., "The Commitment required of a woman entering a scientific profession in present day American society." *Woman and the Scientific Professions*, The MIT symposium on American Women in Science and Engineering, 1965.

Block, J., "Some reasons for the apparent inconsistency of personality." *Psychological Bulletin*, 1968, *70*, 210–212.

Cartwright, R. D. & Vogel, J. L., "A comparison of changes in psychoneurotic patients during matched periods of therapy and no-therapy."*Journal of Consulting Psychology*, 1960, *24*, 121–127.

Erikson, E., "Inner and outer space: reflections on womanhood." *Daedalus*, 1964, *93*, 582–606.

Eysenck, H. J., "The effects of psychotherapy: an evaluation." *Journal of Consulting Psychology*, 1952, *16*, 319–324.

Fieldcrest—Advertisement in the *New Yorker*, 1965.

Fried, M. H., "Mankind excluding woman," review of Tiger's *Men in Groups. Science*, 1969, *165*, 883–884.

Freud, S., *The Sexual Enlightenment of Children*. New York: Collier Books, 1963.

Goldstein, A. P. & Dean, S. J., *The Investigation of Psychotherapy: Commentaries and Readings*. 1966. New York: John Wiley & Sons.

Hacker, H. M., "Women as a minority group." *Social Forces*, 1951, *30*, 60–69.

Hamburg, D. A. & Lunde, D. T., "Sex hormones in the development of sex differences in human behavior." In Eleanor E. Maccoby (ed.), *The Development of Sex Differences*, pp. 1–24. Stanford, CA: Stanford University Press, 1966.

Hampton, J. L. & Hampton, J. C., "The ontogenesis of sexual behavior in man." In W. C. Young, (ed.), *Sex and Internal Secretions* 1401–1432. Baltimore: Williams & Wilkins, 1961.

Harlow, H. F., "The heterosexual affectional system in monkeys." *The American Psychologist*, 1962, *17*, 1–9.

Hooker, E., "Male homosexuality in the Rorschach." *Journal of Projective Techniques*, 1957, *21*, 18–31.

Itani, J., "Paternal care in the wild Japanese monkeys, *Macaca juscata*." In C. H. Southwick (ed.), *Primate Social Behavior*. Princeton, NJ: Van Nostrand, 1963.

Little, K. B. & Schneidman, E. S., "Congruences among interpretations of psychological and anamestic data." *Psychological Monographs*, 1959, *73*, 1–42.

Maccoby, Eleanor E., "Sex differences in intellectual functioning." In Eleanor E. Maccoby (ed.), *The Development of Sex Differences*, 25–55. Stanford, CA: Stanford U Press, 1966.

Masters, W. H. & Johnson, V. E., *Human Sexual Response*. Boston: Little Brown, 1966.

Mead, M., *Male and Female: A Study of the Sexes in a Changing World*. New York: William Morrow, 1949.

Milgram, S., "Some conditions of obedience and disobedience to authority." *Human Relations*, 1965a, *18*, 57–76.

Milgram, S., "Liberating effects of group pressures." *Journal of Personality and Social Psychology*, 1965b, *1*, 127–134.

Mitchell, G. D., "Paternalistic behavior in primates." *Psychological Bulletin*, 1969, *71*, 399–417.

Money, J., "Sexual dimorphism and homosexual gender identity," *Psychological Bulletin*, 1970, *6*, 425–440.

Powers, E. & Witmer, H., *An Experiment in the Prevention of Delinquency*. New York: Columbia University Press, 1951.

Rheingold, J., *The Fear of Being a Woman*. New York: Grune & Stratton, 1964.

Rosenthal, R., "On the social psychology of the psychological experiment: the experimenter's hypothesis as unintended determinant of experimental results." *American Scientist*, 1963, 51, 268–283.

Rosenthal, R., *Experimenter Effects in Behavioral Research*. New York: Appleton-Century Crofts, 1966.

Rosenthal, R. & Jacobson, L., *Pygmalion in the Classroom: Teacher Expectation and Pupil's Intellectual Development*. New York: Holt Rinehart & Winston, 1968.

Rosenthal, R. & Lawson, R., "A longitudinal study of the effects of experimenter bias on the operant learning of laboratory rats." Unpublished manuscript, Harvard University, 1961.

Rosenthal, R. & Pode, K. L., "The effect of experimenter bias on the performance of the albino rat." Unpublished manuscript, Harvard University, 1960.

Rotter, J. B., "Psychotherapy." *Annual Review of Psychology*, 1960, 11, 381–414.

Schachter, S. & Singer, J. E., "Cognitive, social and physiological determinants of emotional state." *Psychological Review*, 1962, 63, 379–399.

Schwarz-Belkin, M., "Les Fleurs de Mal." In *Festschrift for Gordon Piltdown*. New York: Ponzi Press, 1914.

Storch, M., "Reply to Tiger." Unpublished Manuscript, 1970.

Tiger, L., "Male dominance? Yes. A Sexist Plot? No." *New York Times Magazine*, October 25, 1970.

Tiger, L., *Men in Groups*. New York: Random House, 1969.

Truax, C. B., "Effective ingredients in psychotherapy: an approach to unraveling the patient-therapist interaction." *Journal of Counseling Psychology*, 1963, 10, 256–263.

B. Manifestos

Chapter Seventeen

SCUM
(Society for Cutting Up Men)
Manifesto

Valerie Solanas

Life in this society being, at best, an utter bore and no aspect of society being at all relevant to women, there remains to civic-minded, responsible, thrill-seeking females only to overthrow the government, eliminate the money system, institute complete automation and destroy the male sex.

It is now technically possible to reproduce without the aid of males (or, for that matter, females) and to produce only females. We must begin immediately to do so. The male is a biological accident: the y (male) gene is an incomplete x (female) gene, that is, has an incomplete set of chromosomes. In other words, the male is an incomplete female, a walking abortion, aborted at the gene stage. To be male is to be deficient, emotionally limited; maleness is a deficiency disease and males are emotional cripples.

The male is completely egocentric, trapped inside himself, incapable of empathizing or identifying with others, of love, friendship, affection or tenderness. He is a completely isolated unit, incapable of rapport with anyone. His responses are entirely visceral, not cerebral; his intelligence is a mere tool in the service of his drives and needs; he is incapable of mental passion, mental interaction; he can't relate to anything other than his own physical sensations. He is a half dead, unresponsive lump, incapable of giving or receiving pleasure or happiness; consequently, he is at best an utter bore, an inoffensive blob, since only those capable of absorption in others can be charming. He is trapped in a twilight zone halfway between humans and apes, and is far worse off than the apes because, unlike the apes, he is capable of a large array of negative feelings—hate, jealousy, contempt, disgust, guilt, shame, doubt—and moreover he is *aware* of what he is or isn't.

Although completely physical, the male is unfit even for stud service. Even assuming mechanical proficiency, which few men have, he is, first of all, incapable of zestfully, lustfully, tearing off a piece, but is instead eaten up with guilt, shame, fear and insecurity, feelings rooted in male nature, which the most enlightened training can only minimize; second, the physical feeling he attains is next to nothing; and, third, he is not empathizing with his partner, but is obsessed with how he's doing, turning in an A performance, doing a good plumbing job. To call a man an animal is to flatter him; he's a machine, a walking dildo. It's often said that men use women. Use them for what? Surely not pleasure.

Eaten up with guilt, shame, fears and insecurities and obtaining, if he's lucky, a barely perceptible physical feeling, the male is, nonetheless, obsessed with screwing; he'll swim a river of snot, wade nostril-deep through a mile of vomit, if he thinks there'll be a friendly pussy awaiting him. He'll screw a woman he despises, any snaggle-toothed hag, and, furthermore, pay for the opportunity. Why? Relieving physical tension isn't the answer, as masturbation suffices for that. It's not ego satisfaction; that doesn't explain screwing corpses and babies.

Completely egocentric, unable to relate, empathize or identify, and filled with a vast, pervasive, diffuse sexuality, the male is psychically passive. He hates his passivity, so he projects it onto women, defines the male as active, then sets out to prove that he is ("prove he's a Man"). His main means of attempting to prove it is screwing (Big Man with a Big Dick tearing off a Big Piece). Since he's attempting to prove an error, he must "prove" it again and again. Screwing, then, is a desperate, compulsive attempt to prove error, he must "prove" it again and again. Screwing, then, is a desperate, compulsive attempt to prove he's not passive, not a woman, but he *is* passive and *does* want to be a woman.

Being an incomplete female, the male spends his life attempting to complete himself, to become female. He attempts to do this by constantly seeking out, fraternizing with and trying to live through and fuse with the female, and by claiming as his own all female characteristics—emotional strength and independence, forcefulness, dynamism, decisiveness, coolness, objectivity, assertiveness, courage, integrity, vitality, intensity, depth of character, grooviness, etc.—and projecting onto women all male traits—vanity, frivolity, triviality, weakness, etc. It should be said, though, that the male has one glaring area of superiority over the female—public relations. (He has done a brilliant job of convincing millions of women that men are women and women are men.) The male claim that females find fulfillment through motherhood and sexuality reflects what males think they'd find fulfilling if they were female.

Women, in other words, don't have penis envy; men have pussy envy. When the male accepts his passivity, defines himself as a woman (males as well as females think men are women and women are men), and becomes a transvestite he loses his desire to screw (or to do anything else, for that matter; he fulfills himself as a drag queen) and gets his cock chopped off. He then achieves a continuous diffuse sexual feeling from "being a woman." Screwing is, for a man, a defense against his desire to be female. Sex is itself a sublimation.

The male, because of his obsession to compensate for not being female combined with his inability to relate and to feel compassion, has made of the world a shitpile. He is responsible for:

War

The male's normal method of compensation for not being female, namely, getting his Big Gun off, is grossly inadequate, as he can get it off only a very limited number of times; so he gets it off on a really massive scale, and proves to the entire world that he's a "Man." Since he has no compassion or ability to empathize or identify, proving his manhood is worth an endless number of lives, including his own—his own life being worthless, he would rather go out in a blaze of glory than plod grimly on for fifty more years.

Niceness, Politeness, and "Dignity"

Every man, deep down, knows he's a worthless piece of shit. Overwhelmed by a sense of animalism and deeply ashamed of it; wanting, not to express himself, but to hide from others his total physicality, total egocentricity, the hate and contempt he feels for other men, and to hide from himself the hate and contempt he suspects other men feel for him; having a crudely constructed nervous system that is easily upset by the least display of emotion or feeling, the male tries to enforce a "social" code that ensures a perfect blandness, unsullied by the slightest trace of feeling or upsetting opinion. He uses terms like "copulate," "sexual congress," "have relations with, (to men, "sexual relations" is a redundancy)" overlaid with stilted manners; the suit on the chimp.

Money, Marriage and Prostitution, Work, and Prevention of an Automated Society

There is no human reason for money or for anyone to work more than two or three hours a week at the very most. All non-creative jobs (practically all jobs now being done) could have been automated long ago, and in a moneyless society everyone can have as much of the best of everything as she wants. But there are non-human, male reasons for maintaining the money-work system:

1. Pussy. Despising his highly inadequate self, overcome with intense anxiety and a deep, profound loneliness when by his empty self, desperate to attach himself to any female in dim hopes of completing himself, in the mystical belief that by touching gold he'll turn to gold, the male craves the continuous companionship of women. The company of the lowest female is preferable to his own or that of other men, who serve only to remind him of his repulsiveness. But females, unless very young or very sick, must be coerced or bribed into male company.

2. Supply the non-relating male with the delusion of usefulness, and enable him to try to justify his existence by digging holes and filling them up. Leisure time horrifies the male, who will have nothing to do but contemplate his grotesque self. Unable to relate or to love, the male must work. Females crave absorbing, emotionally satisfying, meaningful activity, but lacking the opportunity or ability for this,

they prefer to idle and waste away their time in ways of their own choosing—sleeping, shopping, bowling, shooting pool, playing cards and other games, breeding, reading, walking around, daydreaming, eating, playing with themselves, popping pills, going to the movies, getting analyzed, traveling, raising dogs and cats, lolling on the beach, swimming, watching T.V., listening to music, decorating their houses, gardening, sewing, nightclubbing, dancing, visiting, "improving their minds" (taking courses), and absorbing "culture" (lectures, plays, concerts, "arty" movies). Therefore, many females would, even assuming complete economic equality between the sexes, prefer living with males or peddling their asses on the street, thus having most of their time for themselves, to spending many hours of their days doing boring, stultifying, non-creative work for somebody else, functioning as less than animals, as machines, or, at best if able to get a "good" job—co-managing the shitpile. What will liberate women, therefore, from male control is the total elimination of the money-work system, not the attainment of economic equality with men within it.

3. Power and control. Unmasterful in his personal relations with women, the male attains to general masterfulness by the manipulation of money and of everything and everybody controlled by money, in other words, of everything and everybody.

4. Love substitute. Unable to give love or affection, the male gives money. It makes him feel motherly. The mother gives milk; he gives bread. He is the Breadwinner.

5. Provides the male with a goal. Incapable of enjoying the moment, the male needs something to look forward to, and money provides him with an eternal, never-ending goal: Just think what you could do with 80 trillion dollars—Invest it! And in three years time you'd have 300 trillion dollars!!!

6. Provides the basis for the male's major opportunity to control and manipulate—fatherhood.

Fatherhood and Mental Illness (Fear, Cowardice, Timidity, Humility, Insecurity, Passivity)

Mother wants what's best for her kids; Daddy only wants what's best for Daddy, that is, peace and quiet, pandering to his delusion of dignity ("respect"), a good reflection on himself (status) and the opportunity to control and manipulate, or, if he's an "enlightened" father, to "give guidance." His daughter, in addition, he wants sexually—he gives her hand in marriage; the other part is for him. Daddy, unlike Mother, can never give in to his kids, as he must, at all costs, preserve his delusion of decisiveness, forcefulness, always-rightness and strength. Never getting one's way leads to lack of self-confidence in one's ability to cope with the world and to a passive acceptance of the status quo. Mother loves her kids, although she sometimes gets angry, but anger blows over quickly and even while it exists, doesn't preclude love and basic acceptance. Emotionally diseased Daddy doesn't love his kids; he approves of them—if they're "good," that is, if they're nice, "respectful," obedient, subservient to his will, quiet and not given to unseemly displays of temper that would be most upsetting to Daddy's easily disturbed male nervous system—in other words, if they're passive vegetables. If they're not "good," he doesn't get angry—not if he's a modern, "civilized" father (the old-fashioned ranting, raving brute is preferable, as he is so ridiculous he can be easily despised)—but rather expresses disapproval, a state that, unlike anger, endures and precludes a basic acceptance, leaving the kid with a feeling of worthlessness and a lifelong obsession with being approved of; the result is fear of independent thought, as this leads to unconventional, disapproved of opinions and way of life.

For the kid to want Daddy's approval it must respect Daddy, and, being garbage, Daddy can make sure that he is respected only by remaining aloof, by distantness, by acting on the precept "familiarity breeds contempt," which is, of course, true, if one is contemptible. By being distant and aloof, he is able to remain unknown, mysterious, and, thereby, to inspire fear ("respect").

Disapproval of emotional "scenes" leads to fear of strong emotion, fear of one's own anger and hatred, and to a fear of facing reality, as facing it leads at first to anger and hatred. Fear of anger and hatred combined with a lack of self-confidence in one's ability to cope with and change the world, or even to affect in the slightest way one's own destiny, leads to a mindless belief that the world and most people in it are nice and that the most banal, trivial amusements are great fun and deeply pleasurable.

The effect of fatherhood on males, specifically, is to make them "Men," that is, highly defensive of all impulses to passivity, faggotry, and of desires to be female. Every boy wants to imitate his mother, be her, fuse with her, but Daddy forbids this; he is the mother; he gets to fuse with her. So he tells the boy, sometimes directly, sometimes indirectly, to not be a sissy, to act like a "Man." The boy, scared shitless of and "respecting" his father, complies, and becomes just like Daddy, that model of "Man"-hood, the all-American ideal—the well-behaved heterosexual dullard.

The effect of fatherhood on females is to make them male—dependent, passive, domestic, animalistic, nice, insecure, approval and security seekers, cowardly, humble, "respectful" of authorities and men, closed, not fully responsive, half dead, trivial, dull, conventional, flattened out and thoroughly contemptible. Daddy's Girl, always tense and fearful, uncool, unanalytical, lacking objectivity, appraises Daddy, and thereafter, other men, against a background of fear ("respect") and is not only unable to see the empty shell behind the aloof facade, but accepts the male definition of himself as superior, as a female, and of herself, as inferior, as a male, which, thanks to Daddy, she really is.

It is the increase of fatherhood, resulting from the increased and widespread affluence that fatherhood needs in order to thrive, that has caused the general increase of mindlessness and the decline of women in the United States since the 1920s. The close association of affluence with fatherhood has led, for the most part, to only the wrong girls, namely, the "privileged" middle-class girls, getting "educated."

The effect of fathers, in sum, has been to corrode the world with maleness. The male has a negative Midas touch—everything he touches turns to shit.

Suppression of Individuality, Animalism (Domesticity and Motherhood), and Functionalism

The male is just a bundle of conditioned reflexes, incapable of a mentally free response; he is tied to his early conditioning, determined completely by his past experiences. His earliest experiences are with his mother, and he is throughout his life tied to her. It never becomes completely clear to the male that he is not part of his mother, that he is he and she is she.

His greatest need is to be guided, sheltered, protected and admired by Mama (men expect women to adore what men shrink from in horror—themselves) and, being completely physical, he yearns to spend his time (that's not spent "out in the world" grimly defending against his passivity) wallowing in basic animal activities—eating, sleeping, shitting, relaxing and being soothed by Mama. Passive, rattle-headed Daddy's Girl, ever eager for approval, for a pat on the head, for the "respect" of any passing piece of garbage, is easily reduced to Mama, mindless ministrator to physical needs, soother of the weary, apey brow, booster of the puny ego, appreciator of the contemptible, a hot water bottle with tits.

The reduction to animals of the women of the most backward segment of society—the "privileged, educated" middle-class, the backwash of humanity—where Daddy reigns supreme, has been so thorough that they try to groove on labor pains and lie around in the most advanced nation in the world in the middle of the twentieth century with babies chomping away on their tits. It's not for the kids' sake, though, that the "experts" tell women that Mama should stay home and grovel in animalism, but for Daddy's; the tit's for Daddy to hang onto; the labor pains for Daddy to vicariously groove on (half dead, he needs awfully strong stimuli to make him respond).

Reducing the female to an animal, to Mama, to a male, is necessary for psychological as well as practical reasons: the male is a mere member of the species, interchangeable with every other male. He has no deep-seated individuality, which stems from what intrigues you, what outside yourself absorbs you, what you're in relation to. Completely self-absorbed, capable of being in relation only to their bodies and physical sensations, males differ from each other only to the degree and in the ways they attempt to defend against their passivity and against their desire to be female.

The female's individuality, which he is acutely aware of, but which he doesn't comprehend and isn't capable of relating to or grasping emotionally, frightens and upsets him and fills him with envy. So he denies it in her and proceeds to define everyone in terms of his or her function or use, assigning to himself, of course, the most important functions—doctor, president, scientist—thereby providing himself with an identity, if not individuality, and tries to convince himself and women (he's succeeded best at convincing women) that the female function is to bear and raise children and to relax, comfort and boost the ego of the male; that her function is such as to make her interchangeable with every other female. In actual fact, the female function is to relate, groove, love and be herself, irreplaceable by anyone else; the male function is to produce sperm. We now have sperm banks.

Prevention of Privacy

Although the male, being ashamed of what he is and of almost everything he does, insists on privacy and secrecy in all aspects of his life, he has no real *regard* for privacy. Being empty, not being a complete, separate being, having no self to groove on and needing to be constantly in female company, he sees nothing at all wrong in intruding himself on any woman's thoughts, even a total stranger's anywhere at any time, but rather feels indignant and insulted when put down for doing so, as well as confused—he can't, for the life of him, understand why anyone would prefer so much as one minute of solitude to the company of any creep around. Wanting to become a woman, he strives to be constantly around females, which is the closest he can get to becoming one, so he created a "society" based on the family—a male-female couple and their kids (the excuse for the family's existence), who live virtually on top of one another, unscrupulously violating the females' rights, privacy and sanity.

Isolation, Suburbs, and Prevention of Community

Our society is not a community, but merely a collection of isolated family units. Desperately insecure, fearing his woman will leave him if she is exposed to other men or to anything remotely resembling life, the male seeks to isolate her from other men and from what little civilization there is, so he moves her out to the suburbs, a collection of self-absorbed couples and their kids. Isolation enables him to try to maintain his pretense of being an individual by becoming a "rugged individualist," a loner, equating non-co-operation and solitariness with individuality.

There is yet another reason for the male to isolate himself: every man is an island. Trapped inside himself, emotionally isolated, unable to relate, the male has a horror of civilization, people, cities, situations requiring an ability to understand and relate to people. So, like a scared rabbit, he scurries off, dragging Daddy's little asshole along with him to the wilderness, the suburbs, or, in the case of the "hippie"—he's way out, Man!—all the way out to the cow pasture where he can fuck and breed undisturbed and mess around with his beads and flute.

The "hippie," whose desire to be a "Man," a "rugged individualist," isn't quite as strong as the average man's, and who, in addition, is excited by the thought of having lots of women accessible to him, rebels against the harshness of a Breadwinner's life and the monotony of the one woman. In the name of sharing and co-operation, he forms the commune or tribe, which, for all its togetherness and partly because of it (the commune, being an extended family, is an extended violation of the females' rights, privacy and sanity) is no more a community than normal "society."

A true community consists of individuals—not mere species members, not couples—respecting each other's individuality and privacy, at the same time inter-acting with each other mentally and emotionally—free spirits in free relation to each other—and co-operating with each other to achieve common ends. Traditionalists say the basic unit of "society" is the family; "hippies" say the tribe; no one says the individual.

The "hippie" babbles on about individuality, but has no more conception of it than any other man. He desires to get back to Nature, back to the wilderness, back to the home of the furry animals that he's one of, away from the city, where there is at least a trace, a bare beginning of civilization, to live at the species level, his time taken up with simple, non-intellectual activities—farming, fucking, bead stringing. The most important activity of the commune, the one on which it is based, is gangbanging. The "hippie" is enticed to the commune mainly by the prospect of all the free pussy—the main commodity to be shared, to be had just for the asking but, blinded by greed, he fails to anticipate all the other men he has to share with, or the jealousies and possessiveness of the pussies themselves.

Men cannot co-operate to achieve a common end, because each man's end is all the pussy for himself. The commune, therefore, is doomed to failure: each "hippie" will, in panic, grab the first simpleton who digs him and whisk her off to the suburbs as fast as he can. The male cannot progress socially, but merely swings back and forth from isolation to gangbanging.

Conformity

Although he wants to be an individual, the male is scared of anything in himself that is the slightest bit different from other men; it causes him to suspect that he's not really a "Man," that he's passive and totally sexual, a highly upsetting suspicion. If other men are A and he's not, he must not be a man; he must be a fag. So he tries to affirm his "Manhood" by being like all the other men. Differentness in other men, as well as in himself, threatens him; it means they're fags whom he must at all costs avoid, so he tries to make sure that all other men conform.

The male dares to be different to the degree that he accepts his passivity and his desire to be female, his fagginess. The farthest out male is the drag queen, but he, although different from most men, is exactly like all other drag queens; like the functionalist, he has an identity—he is a female. He tries to define all his troubles away—but still no individuality. Not completely convinced that he's a woman, highly insecure about being sufficiently female, he conforms compulsively to the man-made feminine stereotype, ending up as nothing but a bundle of stilted mannerisms.

To be sure he's a "Man," the male must see to it that the female be clearly a "Woman," the opposite of a "Man," that is, the female must act like a faggot. And Daddy's Girl, all of whose female instincts were wrenched out of her when little, easily and obligingly adapts herself to the role.

Authority and Government

Having no sense of right or wrong, no conscience, which can only stem from an ability to empathize with others . . . having no faith in his non-existent self, being necessarily competitive and, by nature, unable to co-operate, the male feels a need for external guidance and control. So he created authorities—priests, experts, bosses, leaders, etc.—and government. Wanting the female (Mama) to guide him, but unable to accept this fact (he is, after all, a MAN), wanting to play Woman, to usurp her function as Guider and Protector, he sees to it that all authorities are male.

There's no reason why a society consisting of rational beings capable of empathizing with each other, complete and having no natural reason to compete, should have a government, laws or leaders.

Philosophy, Religion, and Morality Based on Sex

The male's inability to relate to anybody or anything makes his life pointless and meaningless (the ultimate male insight is that life is absurd), so he invented philosophy and religion. Being empty, he looks outward, not only for guidance and control, but for salvation and for the meaning of life. Happiness being for him impossible on this earth, he invented Heaven.

For a man, having no ability to empathize with others and being totally sexual, "wrong" is sexual "license" and engaging in "deviant" ("unmanly") sexual practices, that is, not defending against his passivity and total sexuality which, if indulged, would destroy "civilization," since "civilization" is based entirely on the male need to defend himself against these characteristics. For a woman (according to men), "wrong" is any behavior that would entice men into sexual "license"—that is, not placing male needs above her own and not being a faggot.

Religion not only provides the male with a goal (Heaven) and helps keep women tied to men, but offers rituals through which he can try to expiate the guilt and shame he feels at not defending himself enough against his sexual impulses; in essence, that guilt and shame he feels at being a male.

Most men, utterly cowardly, project their inherent weaknesses onto women, label them female weaknesses and believe themselves to have female strengths; most philosophers, not quite so cowardly, face the fact that male lacks exist in men, but still can't face the fact that they exist in men only. So they label the male condition the Human Condition, pose their nothingness problem, which horrifies them, as a philosophical dilemma, thereby giving stature to their animalism, grandiloquently label their nothingness their "Identity Problem," and proceed to prattle on pompously about the "Crisis of the Individual," the "Essence of Being," "Existence preceding Essence," "Existential Modes of Being," etc., etc.

A woman not only takes her identity and individuality for granted, but knows instinctively that the only wrong is to hurt others, and that the meaning of life is love.

Prejudice (Racial, Ethnic, Religious, Etc.)

The male needs scapegoats onto whom he can project his failings and inadequacies and upon whom he can vent his frustration at not being female.

Competition, Prestige, Status, Formal Education, Ignorance, and Social and Economic Classes

Having an obsessive desire to be admired by women, but no intrinsic worth, the male constructs a highly artificial society enabling him to appropriate the appearance of worth through money, prestige, "high" social class, degrees, professional position and knowledge and, by pushing as many other men as possible down professionally, socially, economically, and educationally.

The purpose of "higher" education is not to educate but to exclude as many as possible from the various professions.

The male, totally physical, incapable of mental rapport, although able to understand and use knowledge and ideas, is unable to relate to them, to grasp them emotionally; he does not value knowledge and ideas for their own sake (they're just means to ends) and, consequently, feels no need for mental companions, no need to cultivate the intellectual potentialities of others. On the contrary, the male has a vested interest in ignorance; he knows that an enlightened, aware female population will mean the end of him. The healthy, conceited female wants the company of equals whom she can respect and groove on; the male and the sick, insecure, unselfconfident male female crave the company of worms.

No genuine social revolution can be accomplished by the male, as the male on top wants the status quo, and all the male on the bottom wants is to be the male on top. The male "rebel" is a farce; this is the male's "society," made by him to satisfy his needs. He's never satisfied, because he's not capable of being satisfied. Ultimately, what the male "rebel" is rebelling against is being male. The male changes only when forced to do so by technology, when he has no choice, when "society" reaches the stage where he must change or die. We're at that stage now; if women don't get their asses in gear fast, we may very well all die.

Prevention of Conversation

Being completely self-centered and unable to relate to anything outside himself, the male's "conversation," when not about himself, is an impersonal droning on, removed from anything of human value. Male "intellectual conversation" is a strained, compulsive attempt to impress the female.

Daddy's Girl, passive, adaptable, respectful of and in awe of the male, allows him to impose his hideously dull chatter on her. This is not too difficult for her, as the tension and anxiety, the lack of cool, the insecurity and self-doubt, the unsureness of her own feelings and sensations that Daddy instilled in her make her perceptions superficial and render her unable to see that the male's babble is a babble; like the aesthete "appreciating" the blob that's labeled "Great Art," she believes she's grooving on what bores the shit out of her. Not only does she permit his babble to dominate, she adapts her own "conversation" accordingly.

Trained from early childhood in niceness, politeness and "dignity," in pandering to the male need to disguise his animalism, she obligingly reduces her "conversation" to small talk, a bland insipid avoidance of any topic beyond the utterly trivial—or, if "educated," to "intellectual" discussion, that is, impersonal discoursing on irrelevant abstractions—the Gross National Product, the Common Market, the influence of Rimbaud on symbolist painting. So adept is she at pandering that it eventually becomes second nature and she continues to pander to men even when in the company of other females only.

Apart from pandering, her "conversation" is further limited by her insecurity about expressing deviant, original opinions and the self-absorption based on insecurity and that prevents her conversation from being charming. Niceness, politeness, "dignity," insecurity and self-absorption are hardly conducive to intensity and wit, qualities a conversation must have to be worthy of the name. Such conversation is hardly rampant, as only completely self-confident, arrogant, outgoing, proud, tough-minded females are capable of intense, bitchy, witty conversation.

Prevention of Friendship (Love)

Men have contempt for themselves, for all other men, and for all women who respect and pander to them; the insecure, approval-seeking, pandering male females have contempt for themselves and for all women like them; the self-confident, swinging, thrill-seeking female females have contempt for men and for the pandering male females. In short, contempt is the order of the day.

Love is not dependency or sex, but friendship, and, therefore, love can't exist between two males, between a male and a female or between two females, one or both of whom is a mindless, insecure, pandering male; like conversation, love can exist only between two secure, free-wheeling, independent, groovy female females, since friendship is based on respect, not contempt.

Even among groovy females deep friendships seldom occur in adulthood, as almost all of them are either tied up with men in order to survive economically, or bogged down in hacking their way through the jungle and in trying to keep their heads above the amorphous mass. Love can't flourish in a society based on money and meaningless work; it requires complete economic as well as personal freedom, leisure time and the opportunity to engage in intensely absorbing, emotionally satisfying activities which, when shared with those you respect, lead to deep friendship. Our "society" provides practically no opportunity to engage in such activities.

Having stripped the world of conversation, friendship and love, the male offers us these paltry substitutes:

"Great Art" and "Culture"

The male "artist" attempts to solve his dilemma of not being able to live, of not being female, by constructing a highly artificial world in which the male is heroized, that is, displays female traits, and the female is reduced to highly limited, insipid subordinate roles, that is, to being male.

The male "artistic" aim being, not to communicate (having nothing inside him, he has nothing to say), but to disguise his animalism, he resorts to symbolism and obscurity ("deep" stuff). The vast majority of people, particularly the "educated" ones, lacking faith in their own judgment, humble, respectful of authority ("Daddy knows best" is translated into adult language as "Critic knows best," "Writer knows best," "Ph.D knows best"), are easily conned into believing that obscurity, evasiveness, incomprehensibility, indirectness, ambiguity and boredom are marks of depth and brilliance.

"Great Art" proves that men are superior to women, that men are women, being labeled "Great Art," almost all of which, as the anti-feminists are fond of reminding us, was created by men. We know that "Great Art" is great because male authorities have told us so, and we can't claim otherwise, as only those with exquisite sensitivities far superior to ours can perceive and appreciate the greatness, the proof of their superior sensitivity being that they appreciate the slop that they appreciate.

Appreciating is the sole diversion of the "cultivated"; passive and incompetent, lacking imagination and wit, they must try to make do with that; unable to create their own diversions, to create a little world of their own, to affect in the smallest way their environments, they must accept what's given; unable to create or relate, they spectate. Absorbing "culture" is a desperate, frantic attempt to groove in an ungroovy world, to escape the horror of a sterile, mindless existence. "Culture" provides a sop to the egos of the incompetent, a means of rationalizing passive spectating; they can pride themselves on their ability to appreciate the "finer" things, to see a jewel where there is only a turd (they want to be admired for admiring). Lacking faith in their ability to change anything, resigned to the status quo, they have to see beauty in turds because, so far as they can see, turds are all they'll ever have.

The veneration of "Art" and "Culture"—besides leading many women into boring, passive activity that distracts from more important and rewarding activities, from cultivating active abilities—allows the "artist" to be set up as one possessing superior feelings, perceptions, insights and judgments, thereby undermining the faith of insecure women in the value and validity of their own feelings, perceptions, insights and judgments.

The male, having a very limited range of feelings and, consequently, very limited perceptions, insights and judgments, needs the "artist" to guide him, to tell him what life is all about. But the male "artist," being totally sexual, unable to relate to anything beyond his own physical sensations, having nothing to express beyond the insight that for the male life is meaningless and absurd, cannot be an artist. How can he who is not capable of life tell us what life is all about? A "male artist" is a contradiction in terms. A degenerate can only produce degenerate "art." The true artist is every self-confident, healthy female, and in a female society the only Art, the only Culture, will be conceited, kookie, funky females grooving on each other and on everything else in the universe.

Sexuality

Sex is not part of a relationship; on the contrary, it is a solitary experience, non-creative, a gross waste of time. The female can easily—far more easily than she may think—condition away her sex drive, leaving her completely cool and cerebral and free to pursue truly worthy relationships and activities; but the male, who seems to dig women sexually and who seeks constantly to arouse them, stimulates the highly-sexed female to frenzies of lust, throwing her into a sex bag from which few women ever escape. The lecherous male excited the lustful female; he has to—when the female transcends her body, rises above animalism, the male, whose ego consists of his cock, will disappear.

Sex is the refuge of the mindless. And the more mindless the woman, the more deeply embedded in the male "culture," in short, the nicer she is, the more sexual she is. The nicest women in our "society" are raving sex maniacs. But, being just awfully, awfully nice they don't, of course, descend to fucking—that's uncouth—rather they make love, commune by means of their bodies and establish sensual rapport; the literary ones are attuned to the throb of Eros and attain a clutch upon the Universe; the religious have spiritual communion with the Divine Sensualism; the mystics merge with the Erotic Principle and blend with the Cosmos, and the acid heads contact their erotic cells.

On the other hand, those females least embedded in the male "Culture," the least nice, those crass and simple souls who reduce fucking to fucking, who are too childish for the grown-up world of suburbs, mortgages, mops and baby shit, too selfish to raise kids and husbands, too uncivilized to give a shit for anyone's opinion of them, too arrogant to respect Daddy, the "Greats" or the deep wisdom of the Ancients, who trust only their own animal, gutter instincts, who equate Culture with chicks, whose sole diversion is prowling for emotional thrills and excitement, who are given to disgusting, nasty, upsetting "scenes," hateful, violent bitches given to slamming those who unduly irritate them in the teeth, who'd sink a shiv into a man's chest or ram an icepick up his asshole as soon as look at him, if they knew they could get away with it, in short, those who, by the standards of our "culture" are SCUM ... these females are cool and relatively cerebral and skirting asexuality.

Unhampered by propriety, niceness, discretion, public opinion, "morals," the "respect" of assholes, always funky, dirty, low-down SCUM gets around ... and around and around ... they've seen the whole show—every bit of it—the fucking scene, the sucking scene, the dyke scene—they've covered the whole waterfront, been under every dock and pier—the peter pier, the pussy pier ... you've got to go through a lot of sex to get to anti-sex, and SCUM's been through it all, and they're now ready for a new show; they want to crawl out from under the dock, move, take off, sink out. But SCUM doesn't yet prevail; SCUM's still in the gutter of our "society," which, if it's not deflected from its present course and if the Bomb doesn't drop on it, will hump itself to death.

Boredom

Life in a "society" made by and for creatures who, when they are not grim and depressing are utter bores, can only be, when not grim and depressing, an utter bore.

Secrecy, Censorship, Suppression of Knowledge and Ideas, and Exposés

Every male's deep-seated, secret, most hideous fear is the fear of being discovered to be not a female, but a male, a subhuman animal. Although niceness, politeness and "dignity" suffice to prevent his exposure on a personal level, in order to prevent the general exposure of the male sex as a whole and to maintain his unnatural dominant position in "society," the male must resort to:

1. Censorship. Responding reflexively to isolated words and phrases rather than cerebrally to overall meanings, the male attempts to prevent the arousal and discovery of his animalism by censoring not only "pornography," but any work containing "dirty" words, no matter in what context they are used.

2. Suppression of all ideas and knowledge that might expose him or threaten his dominant position in "society." Much biological and psychological data is suppressed, because it is proof of the male's gross inferiority to the female. Also, the problem of mental illness will never be solved while the male maintains control, because first, men have a vested interest in it—only females who have very few of their marbles will allow males the slightest bit of control over anything, and second, the male cannot admit to the role that fatherhood plays in causing mental illness.

3. Exposés. The male's chief delight in life—insofar as the dense, grim male can ever be said to delight in anything—is in exposing others. It doesn't much matter what they're exposed as, so long as they're exposed; it distracts attention from himself. Exposing others as enemy agents (Communists and Socialists) is one of his favorite pastimes, as it removes the source of the threat to him not only from himself, but from the country and the Western world. The bugs up his ass aren't in him; they're in Russia.

Distrust

Unable to empathize or feel affection or loyalty, being exclusively out for himself, the male has no sense of fair play; cowardly, needing constantly to pander to the female to win her approval, that he is helpless without, always on edge lest his animalism, his maleness be discovered, always needing to cover up, he must lie constantly; being empty, he has no honor or integrity—he doesn't know what those words mean. The male, in short, is treacherous, and the only appropriate attitude in a male "society" is cynicism and distrust.

Ugliness

Being totally sexual, incapable of cerebral or aesthetic responses, totally materialistic and greedy, the male, besides inflicting on the world "Great Art," has decorated his unlandscaped cities with ugly buildings (both inside and out), ugly decors, billboards, highways, cars, garbage trucks and, most notably, his own putrid self.

Hate and Violence

The male is eaten up with tension, with frustration at not being female, at not being capable of ever achieving satisfaction or pleasure of any kind; eaten up with hate—not rational hate that is directed against those who abuse or insult you—but irrational, indiscriminate hate . . . hatred, at bottom, of his own worthless self.

Violence serves as an outlet for his hate and, in addition—the male being capable only of sexual responses and needing very strong stimuli his half-dead self—provides him with a little sexual thrill.

Disease and Death

All diseases are curable, and the aging process and death are due to disease; it is possible, therefore, never to age and to live forever. In fact, the problems of aging and death could be solved within a few years, if an all-out, massive scientific assault were made on the problem. This, however, will not occur within the male establishment, because:

1. The many male scientists who shy away from biological research, terrified of the discovery that males are females, and show marked preference for virile, "manly" war and death programs.
2. The discouragement of many potential scientists from scientific careers by the rigidity, boringness, expensiveness, time-consumingness and unfair exclusivity of our "higher" educational system.
3. Propaganda disseminated by insecure male professionals, who jealously guard their positions, so that only a highly select few can comprehend abstract scientific concepts.
4. Widespread lack of self-confidence brought about by the father system that discourages many talented girls from becoming scientists.
5. Lack of automation. There now exists a wealth of data which, if sorted out and correlated, would reveal the cure for cancer and several other diseases and possibly the key to life itself. But the data is so massive it requires high speed computers to correlate it all. The institution of computers will be delayed interminably under the male control system, since the male has a horror of being replaced by machines.

6. The money system. Most of the few scientists around who aren't working on death programs are tied up doing research for corporations.
7. The male likes death—it excites him sexually and, already dead inside, he wants to die.

Incapable of a positive state of happiness, which is the only thing that can justify one's existence, the male is, at best, relaxed, comfortable, neutral, and this condition is extremely short-lived, as boredom, a negative state, soon sets in; he is, therefore, doomed to an existence of suffering relieved only by occasional, fleeting stretches of restfulness, which state he can achieve only at the expense of some female. The male is, by his very nature, a leech, an emotional parasite and, therefore, not ethically entitled to live, as no one has the right to live at someone else's expense.

Just as humans have a prior right to existence over dogs by virtue of being more highly evolved and having a superior consciousness, so women have a prior right to existence over men. The elimination of any male is, therefore, a righteous and good act, an act highly beneficial to women as well as an act of mercy.

However, this moral issue will eventually be rendered academic by the fact that the male is gradually eliminating himself. In addition to engaging in the time-honored and classical wars and race riots, men are more and more either becoming fags or are obliterating themselves through drugs. The female, whether she likes it or not, will eventually take complete charge, if for no other reason than that she will have to—the male, for practical purposes, won't exist.

Accelerating this trend is the fact that more and more males are acquiring enlightened self-interest; they're realizing more and more that the female interest is *their* interest, that they can live only through the female and that the more the female is encouraged to live, to fulfill herself, to be a female and not a male, the more nearly *he* lives; he's coming to see that it's easier and more satisfactory to live *through* her than to try to *become* her and usurp her qualities, claim them as his own, push the female down and claim she's a male. The fag, who accepts his maleness, that is, his passivity and total sexuality, his femininity, is also best served by women being truly female, as it would then be easier for him to be male, feminine. If men were wise they would seek to become really female, would do intensive biological research that would lead to men, by means of operations on the brain and nervous system, being able to be transformed in psyche, as well as body, into women.

Whether to continue to use females for reproduction or to reproduce in the laboratory will also become academic: what will happen when every female, twelve and over, is routinely taking the Pill and there are no longer any accidents? How many women will deliberately get or (if an accident) remain pregnant? No, Virginia, women don't just adore being brood mares, despite what the mass of robot, brainwashed women will say. When society consists of only the fully conscious the answer will be none. Should a certain percentage of women be set aside by force to serve as brood mares for the species? Obviously this will not do. The answer is laboratory reproduction of babies.

As for the issue of whether or not to continue to reproduce males, it doesn't follow that because the male, like disease, has always existed among us that he should continue to exist. When genetic control is possible—and it soon will be—it goes without saying that we should produce only whole, complete beings, not physical defects or deficiencies, including emotional deficiencies, such as maleness. Just as the deliberate production of blind people would be highly immoral, so would be the deliberate production of emotional cripples.

Why produce even females? Why should there be future generations? What is their purpose? When aging and death are eliminated, why continue to reproduce? Why should we care what happens when we're dead? Why should we care that there is no younger generation to succeed us?

Eventually the natural course of events, of social evolution, will lead to total female control of the world and, subsequently, to the cessation of the production of males and, ultimately, to the cessation of the production of females.

But SCUM is impatient; SCUM is not consoled by the thought that future generations will thrive; SCUM wants to grab some swinging living for itself. And, if a large majority of women were SCUM, they could acquire complete control of this country within a few weeks simply by withdrawing from the labor force, thereby paralyzing the entire nation. Additional measures, any one of which would be sufficient to completely disrupt the economy and everything else, would be for women to declare themselves off the money system, stop buying, just loot and simply refuse to obey all laws they don't care to obey. The police force, National Guard, Army, Navy and Marines combined couldn't squelch a rebellion of over half the population, particularly when it's made up of people they are utterly helpless without.

If all women simply left men, refused to have anything to do with any of them—ever, all men, the government, and the national economy would collapse completely. Even without leaving men, women who are aware of the extent of their superiority to and power over men, could acquire complete control over everything within a few weeks, could effect a total submission of males to females. In a sane society the male would trot along obediently after the female. The male is docile and easily led, easily subjected to the domination of any female who cares to dominate him. The male, in fact, wants desperately to be led by females, wants Mama in charge, wants to abandon himself to her care. But this is not a sane society, and most women are not even dimly aware of where they're at in relation to men.

The conflict, therefore, is not between females and males, but between SCUM—dominant, secure, self-confident, nasty, violent, selfish, independent, proud, thrill-seeking, free-wheeling, arrogant females, who consider themselves fit to rule the universe, who have free-wheeled to the limits of this "society" and are ready to wheel on to something far beyond what it has to offer—and nice, passive, accepting, "cultivated," polite, dignified, subdued, dependent, scared, mindless, insecure, approval-seeking Daddy's Girls, who can't cope with the unknown, who want to continue to wallow in the sewer that is, at least, familiar, who want to hang back with the apes, who feel secure only with Big Daddy standing by, with a big, strong man to lean on and with a fat, hairy face in the White House, who are too cowardly to face up to the hideous reality of what a man is, what Daddy is, who have cast their lot with the swine, who have adapted themselves to animalism, feel superficially comfortable with it and know no other way of "life," who have reduced their minds, thoughts and sights to the male level, who, lacking sense, imagination and wit can have value only in a male "society," who can have a place in the sun, or, rather, in the slime, only as soothers, ego boosters, relaxers and breeders, who are dismissed as inconsequents by other females, who project their deficiencies, their maleness, onto all females and see the female as a worm.

But SCUM is too impatient to hope and wait for the de-brainwashing of millions of assholes. Why should the swinging females continue to plod dismally along with the dull male ones? Why should the fates of the groovy and the creepy be inter-twined? Why should the active and imaginative consult the passive and dull on social policy? Why should the independent be confined to the sewer along with the depend-ent who need Daddy to cling to?

A small handful of SCUM can take over the country within a year by systematically fucking up the system, selectively destroying property, and murder:

SCUM will become members of the unwork force, the fuck-up force; they will get jobs of various kinds and unwork. For example, SCUM salesgirls will not charge for merchandise; SCUM telephone operators will not charge for calls; SCUM office and factory workers, in addition to fucking up their work, will secretly destroy equipment. SCUM will unwork at a job until fired, then get a new job to unwork at.

SCUM will forcibly relieve bus drivers, cab drivers and subway token sellers of their jobs and run buses and cabs and dispense free tokens to the public.

SCUM will destroy all useless and harmful objects—cars, store windows, "Great Art," etc.

Eventually SCUM will take over the airwaves—radio and TV networks—by forcibly relieving of their jobs all radio and TV employees who would impede SCUM's entry into the broadcasting studios.

SCUM will couple-bust—barge into mixed (male-female) couples, wherever they are, and bust them up.

SCUM will kill all men who are not in the Men's Auxiliary of SCUM. Men in the Men's Auxiliary are those men who are working diligently to eliminate themselves, men who, regardless of their motives, do good, men who are playing ball with SCUM. A few examples of the men in the Men's Auxiliary are: men who kill men; biological scientists who are working on constructive programs, as opposed to bio-logical warfare; journalists, writers, editors, publishers and producers who dissemi-nate and promote ideas that will lead to the achievement of SCUM's goals; faggots who, by their shimmering, flaming example, encourage other men to de-man them-selves and thereby make themselves relatively inoffensive; men who consistently give things away—money, things, services; men who tell it like it is (so far not one ever has), who put women straight, who reveal the truth about themselves, who give the mindless male females correct sentences to parrot, who tell them a woman's primary goal in life should be to squash the male sex (to aid men in this endeavor SCUM will conduct Turd Sessions, at which every male present will give a speech beginning with the sentence: "I am a turd, a lowly, abject turd," then proceed to list all the ways in which he is. His reward for so doing will be the opportunity to fraternize after the session for a whole, solid hour with the SCUM who will be present. Nice, clean-living male women will be invited to the sessions to help clarify any doubts and misunderstandings they may have about the male sex); makers and promoters of sex books and movies, etc., who are hastening the day when all that will be shown on the screen will be Suck and Fuck (males, like the rats following the Pied Piper, will be lured by Pussy to their doom, will be overcome and submerged by and will eventually drown in the passive flesh that they are); drug pushers and advocates, who are hastening the dropping out of men.

Being in the Men's Auxiliary is a necessary but not a sufficient condition for making SCUM's escape list; it's not enough to do good; to save their worthless asses men must also avoid evil. A few examples of the most obnoxious or harmful types are: rapists, politicians and all who are in their service (campaigners, members of political parties, etc.); lousy singers and musicians; Chairmen of Boards; Breadwinners; landlords; owners of greasy spoons and restaurants that play Musak; "Great Artists"; cheap pikers; cops; tycoons; scientists working on death and destruction programs or for private industry (practically all scientists); liars and phonies; disc jockeys; men who intrude themselves in the slightest way on any strange female; real estate men; stock brokers; men who speak when they have nothing to say; men who loiter idly on the street and the mar the landscape with their presence; double dealers; film-flam artists; litterbugs; plagiarizers; men who in the slightest way harm any female; all men in the advertising industry; psychiatrists and clinical psychologists; dishonest writers, journalists, editors, publishers, etc.; censors on both the public and private levels; all members of the armed forces, including draftees (LBJ and McNamara give orders, but servicemen carry them out) and particularly pilots (if the bomb drops, LBJ won't drop it; a pilot will). In the case of a man whose behavior falls into both the good and bad categories, an overall subjective evaluation of him will be made to determine if his behavior is, in the balance, good or bad.

It is most tempting to pick off the female "Great Artists," double dealers, etc. along with the men, but that would be impractical, as there would be no one left; all women have a fink streak in them, to a great or lesser degree, but it stems from a lifetime of living among men. Eliminate men and women will shape up. Women are improvable; men are not, although their behavior is. When SCUM gets hot on their asses it'll shape up fast.

Simultaneously with the fucking-up, looting, couple-busting, destroying and killing, SCUM will recruit. SCUM, then, will consist of recruiters; the elite corps—the hard core activists (the fuck-ups, looters and destroyers) and the elite of the elite—the killers.

Dropping out is not the answer; fucking-up is. Most women are already dropped out; they were never in. Dropping out gives control to those few who don't drop out; dropping out is exactly what the establishment leaders want; it plays into the hands of the enemy; it strengthens the system instead of undermining it, since it is based entirely on the non-participation, passivity, apathy and non-involvement of the mass of women. Dropping out, however, is an excellent policy for men and SCUM will enthusiastically encourage it.

Looking inside yourself for salvation, contemplating your navel, is not, as the Dropping Out people would have you believe, the answer. Happiness lies outside yourself, is achieved through interacting with others. Self-forgetfulness should be one's goal, not self-absorption. The male, capable of only the latter, makes a virtue of an irremediable fault and sets up self-absorption, not only as a good but as a Philosophical Good, and thus gets credit for being deep.

SCUM will not picket, demonstrate, march or strike to attempt to achieve its ends. Such tactics are for nice, genteel ladies who scrupulously take only such action as is guaranteed to be ineffective. In addition, only decent, clean-living, male women, highly trained in submerging themselves in the species, act on a mob basis. SCUM consists of individuals; SCUM is not a mob, a blob. Only as many SCUM will do a job as are needed for the job. Also, SCUM, being cool and selfish, will not subject itself to getting rapped on the head with billy clubs; that's for the nice, "privileged, educated," middle-class ladies with a high regard for the touching faith in the essential goodness of Daddy and policemen. If SCUM ever marches, it will be over the President's stupid, sickening face; if SCUM ever strikes, it will be in the dark with a six-inch blade.

SCUM will always operate on a criminal as opposed to a civil disobedience basis, that is, as opposed to openly violating the law and going to jail in order to draw attention to an injustice. Such tactics acknowledge the rightness of the overall system and are used only to modify it slightly, change specific laws. SCUM is against the entire system, the very idea of law and government. SCUM is out to destroy the system, not attain certain rights within it. Also, SCUM—always selfish, always cool—will always aim to avoid detection and punishment. SCUM will always be furtive, sneaky, underhanded (although SCUM murders will always be known to be such).

Both destruction and killing will be selective and discriminate. SCUM is against half-crazed, indiscriminate riots, with no clear objective in mind, and in which many of your own kind are picked off. SCUM will never instigate, encourage or participate in riots of any kind or any other form of indiscriminate destruction. SCUM will coolly, furtively, stalk its prey and quietly move in for the kill. Destruction will never be such as to block off routes needed for the transportation of food and other essential supplies, contaminate or cut off the water supply, block streets and traffic to the extent that ambulances can't get through or impede the functioning of hospitals.

SCUM will keep on destroying, looting, fucking-up and killing until the money-work system no longer exists and automation is completely instituted or until enough women co-operate with SCUM to make violence unnecessary to achieve these goals, that is, until enough women either unwork or quit work, start looting, leave men and refuse to obey all laws inappropriate to a truly civilized society. Many women will fall into line, but many others, who surrendered long ago to the enemy, who are so adapted to animalism, to maleness, that they like restrictions and restraints, don't know what to do with freedom, will continue to be toadies, and doormats, just as peasants in rice paddies remain peasants in rice paddies as one regime topples another. A few of the more volatile will whimper and sulk and throw their toys and dishrags on the floor, but SCUM will continue to steamroller over them.

A completely automated society can be accomplished very simply and quickly once there is a public demand for it. The blueprints for it are already in existence, and its construction will only take a few weeks with millions of people working at it. Even though off the money system, everyone will be most happy to pitch in and get the automated society built; it will mark the beginning of a fantastic new era, and there will be a celebration atmosphere accompanying the construction.

The elimination of money and the complete institution of automation are basic to all other SCUM reforms; without these two the others can't take place; with them the others will take place very rapidly. The government will automatically collapse. With complete automation it will be possible for every woman to vote directly on every issue by means of an electronic voting machine in her house. Since the government is occupied almost entirely with regulating economic affairs and legislating against purely private matters, the elimination of money and with it the elimination of males who wish to legislate "morality" will mean that there will be practically no issues to vote on.

After the elimination of money there will be no further need to kill men; they will be stripped of the only power they have over psychologically independent females. They will be able to impose themselves only on the doormats, who like to be imposed on. The rest of the women will be busy solving the few remaining unsolved problems before planning their agenda for eternity and Utopia—completely revamping educational programs so that millions of women can be trained within a few months for high level intellectual work that now requires years of training (this can be done very easily once our educational goal is to educate and not to perpetuate an academic and intellectual elite); solving the problems of disease and old age and death and completely redesigning our cities and living quarters. Many women will for a while continue to think they dig men, but as they become accustomed to female society and as they become absorbed in their projects, they will eventually come to see the utter uselessness and banality of the male.

The few remaining men can exist out their puny days dropped out on drugs or strutting around in drag or passively watching the high-powered female in action, fulfilling themselves as spectators, vicarious livers* or breeding in the cow pasture with the toadies, or they can go off to the nearest friendly suicide center where they will be quietly, quickly and painlessly gassed to death.

Prior to the institution of automation, to the replacement of males by machines, the male should be of use to the female, wait for her, cater to her slightest whim, obey her every command, be totally subservient to her, exist in perfect obedience to her will, as opposed to the completely warped, degenerate situation we have now of men, not only existing at all, cluttering up the world with their ignominious presence, but being pandered to and groveled before by the mass of females, millions of women piously worshipping before the Golden Calf, the dog leading the master on the leash, when in fact the male, short of being a drag queen, is least miserable when abjectly

*It will be electronically possible for him to tune in to any specific female he wants to and follow in detail her every movement. The females will kindly, obligingly consent to this, as it won't hurt them in the slightest and it is a marvelously kind and humane way to treat their unfortunate, handicapped fellow beings.

prostrate before the female, a complete slave. Rational men want to be squashed, stepped on, crushed and crunched, treated as the curs, the filth that they are, have their repulsiveness confirmed.

The sick, irrational men, those who attempt to defend themselves against their disgustingness, when they see SCUM barreling down on them, will cling in terror to Big Mama with her Big Bouncy Boobies, but Boobies won't protect them against SCUM; Big Mama will be clinging to Big Daddy, who will be in the corner shitting in his forceful, dynamic pants. Men who are rational, however, won't kick or struggle or raise a distressing fuss, but will just sit back, relax, enjoy the show and ride the waves to their demise.

Chapter Eighteen

Redstockings Manifesto

I

After centuries of individual and preliminary political struggle, women are uniting to achieve their final liberation from male supremacy. Redstockings is dedicated to building this unity and winning our freedom.

II

Women are an oppressed class. Our oppression is total, affecting every facet of our lives. We are exploited as sex objects, breeders, domestic servants, and cheap labor. We are considered inferior beings, whose only purpose is to enhance men's lives. Our humanity is denied. Our prescribed behavior is enforced by the threat of physical violence.

Because we have lived so intimately with our oppressors, in isolation from each other, we have been kept from seeing our personal suffering as a political condition. This creates the illusion that a woman's relationship with her man is a matter of interplay between two unique personalities, and can be worked out individually. In reality, every such relationship is a *class* relationship, and the conflicts between individual men and women are *political* conflicts that can only be solved collectively.

III

We identify the agents of our oppression as men. Male supremacy is the oldest, most basic form of domination. All other forms of exploitation and oppression (racism, capitalism, imperialism, etc.) are extensions of male supremacy: men dominate women, a few men dominate the rest. All power structures throughout history have been male-dominated and male-oriented. Men have controlled all political, economic and cultural institutions and backed up this control with physical force. They have used their power to keep women in an inferior position. *All men* receive economic, sexual, and psychological benefits from male supremacy. *All men* have oppressed women.

IV

Attempts have been made to shift the burden of responsibility from men to institutions or to women themselves. We condemn these arguments as evasions. Institutions alone do not oppress; they are merely tools of the oppressor. To blame institutions implies that men and women are equally victimized, obscures the fact that men benefit from the subordination of women, and gives men the excuse that they are forced to be oppressors. On the contrary, any man is free to renounce his superior position provided that he is willing to be treated like a woman by other men.

We also reject the idea that women consent to or are to blame for their own oppression. Women's submission is not the result of brainwashing, stupidity, or mental illness but of continual, daily pressure from men. We do not need to change ourselves, but to change men.

The most slanderous evasion of all is that women can oppress men. The basis for this illusion is the isolation of individual relationships from their political context and the tendency of men to see any legitimate challenge to their privileges as persecution.

V

We regard our personal experience, and our feelings about that experience, as the basis for an analysis of our common situation. We cannot rely on existing ideologies as they are all products of male supremacist culture. We question every generalization and accept none that are not confirmed by our experience.

Our chief task at present is to develop female class consciousness through sharing experience and publicly exposing the sexist foundation of all our institutions. Consciousness-raising is not "therapy," which implies the existence of individual solutions and falsely assumes that the male-female relationship is purely personal, but the only method by which we can ensure that our program for liberation is based on the concrete realities of our lives.

The first requirement for raising class consciousness is honesty, in private and in public, with ourselves and other women.

VI

We identify with all women. We define our best interest as that of the poorest, most brutally exploited women.

We repudiate all economic, racial, educational or status privileges that divide us from other women. We are determined to recognize and eliminate any prejudices we may hold against other women.

We are committed to achieving internal democracy. We will do whatever is necessary to ensure that every woman in our movement has an equal chance to participate, assume responsibility, and develop her political potential.

VII

We call on all our sisters to unite with us in struggle.

We call on all men to give up their male privileges and support women's liberation in the interest of our humanity and their own.

In fighting for our liberation we will always take the side of women against their oppressors. We will not ask what is "revolutionary" or "reformist," only what is good for women.

The time for individual skirmishes has passed. This time we are going all the way.

Chapter Nineteen

The Bitch Manifesto

Joreen Freeman

> . . . man is defined as a human being and woman is defined
> as a female. Whenever she tries to behave as a human being
> she is accused of trying to emulate the male. . . .
> —Simone de Beauvoir

BITCH is an organization which does not yet exist. The name is not an acronym.

BITCH is composed of Bitches. There are many definitions of a bitch. The most complimentary definition is a female dog. Those definitions of bitches who are also *homo sapiens* are rarely as objective. They vary from person to person and depend strongly on how much of a bitch the definer considers herself. However, everyone agrees that a bitch is always female, dog or otherwise.

It is also generally agreed that a Bitch is aggressive, and therefore unfeminine (ahem). She may be sexy, in which case she becomes a Bitch Goddess, a special case which will not concern us here. But she is never a "true woman."

Bitches have some or all of the following characteristics:

1) Personality. Bitches are aggressive, assertive, domineering, overbearing, strong-minded, spiteful, hostile, direct, blunt, candid, obnoxious, thick-skinned, hard-headed, vicious, dogmatic, competent, competitive, pushy, loud-mouthed, independent, stubborn, demanding, manipulative, egoistic, driven, achieving, overwhelming, threatening, scary, ambitious, tough, brassy, masculine, boisterous, and turbulent. Among other things. A Bitch occupies a lot of psychological space. You always know she is around. A Bitch takes shit from no one. You may not like her, but you cannot ignore her.

2) Physical. Bitches are big, tall, strong, large, loud, brash, harsh, awkward, clumsy, sprawling, strident, ugly. Bitches move their bodies freely rather than restrain, refine and confine their motions in the proper feminine manner. They clomp up stairs, stride when they walk and don't worry about where they put their legs when they sit. They have loud voices and often use them. Bitches are not pretty.

3) Orientation. Bitches seek their identity strictly through themselves and what they do. They are subjects, not objects. They may have a relationship with a person or organization, but they never *marry* anyone or anything; man, mansion, or movement. Thus Bitches prefer to plan their own lives rather than live from day to day, action to action, or person to person. They are independent cusses and believe they are capable of doing anything they damn well want to. If something gets in their way, well, that's why they become Bitches. If they are professionally inclined, they will seek careers and have no fear of competing with anyone. If not professionally inclined, they still seek self-expression and self-actualization. Whatever they do, they want an active role and are frequently perceived as domineering. Often they do dominate other people when roles are not available to them which more creatively sublimate their energies and utilize their capabilities. More often they are accused of domineering when doing what would be considered natural by a man.

A true Bitch is self-determined, but the term "bitch" is usually applied with less discrimination. It is a popular derogation to put down uppity women that was created by man and adopted by women. Like the term "nigger," "bitch" serves the social function of isolating and discrediting a class of people who do not conform to the socially accepted patterns of behavior.

BITCH does not use this word in the negative sense. A woman should be proud to declare she is a Bitch, because Bitch is Beautiful. It should be an act of affirmation by self and not negation by others. Not everyone can qualify as a Bitch. One does not have to have all of the above three qualities, but should be well possessed of at least two of them to be considered a Bitch. If a woman qualifies in all three, at least partially, she is a Bitch's Bitch. Only Superbitches qualify totally in all three categories and there are very few of those. Most don't last long in this society.

The most prominent characteristic of all Bitches is that they rudely violate conceptions of proper sex role behavior. They violate them in different ways, but they all violate them. Their attitudes towards themselves and other people, their goal orientations, their personal style, their appearance and way of handling their bodies, all jar people and make them feel uneasy. Sometimes it's conscious and sometimes it's not but people generally feel uncomfortable around Bitches. They consider them aberrations. They find their style disturbing. So they create a dumping ground for all whom they deplore as bitchy and call them frustrated women. Frustrated they may be, but the cause is social, not sexual.

What is disturbing about a Bitch is that she is androgynous. She incorporates within herself qualities traditionally defined as "masculine" as well as "feminine." A Bitch is blunt, direct, arrogant, at times egoistic. She has no liking for the indirect, subtle, mysterious ways of the "eternal feminine." She disdains the vicarious life deemed natural to women because she wants to live a life of her own.

Our society has defined humanity as male, and female as something other than male. In this way, females could be human only by living vicariously through a male. To be able to live, a woman has to agree to serve, honor and obey a man and what she gets in exchange is at best a shadow life. Bitches refuse to serve, honor or obey anyone. They demand to be fully functioning human beings, not just shadows. They want to be both female and human. This makes them social contradictions. The mere existence of Bitches negates the idea that a woman's reality must come through her relationship to a man and defies the belief that women are perpetual children who must always be under the guidance of another.

Therefore, if taken seriously, a Bitch is a threat to the social structures which enslave women and the social values which justify keeping them in their place. She is living testimony that women's oppression does not have to be, and as such raises doubts about the validity of the whole social system. Because she is a threat she is not taken seriously. Instead, she is dismissed as a deviant. Men create a special category for her in which she is accounted at least partially human, but not really a woman. To the extent to which they relate to her as a human being, they refuse to relate to her as a sexual being. Women are even more threatened by her because they cannot forget she is a woman. They are afraid they will identify with her too closely. She has a freedom and an independence which they envy; she challenges them to forsake the security of their chains. Neither men nor women can face the reality of a Bitch because to do so would force them to face the corrupt reality of themselves. She is dangerous. So they dismiss her as a freak.

This is the root of her own oppression as a woman. Bitches are not only oppressed as women, they are oppressed for not being like women. Because she has insisted on being human before being feminine, on being true to herself before kowtowing to social pressures, a Bitch grows up an outsider. Even as girls, Bitches violated the limits of accepted sex role behavior. They did not identify with other women and few were lucky enough to have an adult Bitch serve as a role model. They had to make their own way and the pitfalls this uncharted course posed contributed to both their uncertainty and their independence.

Bitches are good examples of how women can be strong enough to survive even the rigid, punitive socialization of our society. As young girls it never quite penetrated their consciousness that women were supposed to be inferior to men in any but the mother/helpmate role. They asserted themselves as children and never really internalized the slave style of wheedling and cajolery which is called feminine. Some Bitches were oblivious to the usual social pressures and some stubbornly resisted them. Some developed a superficial feminine style and some remained tomboys long past the time when such behavior is tolerated. All Bitches refused, in mind and spirit, to conform to the idea that there were limits on what they could be and do. They placed no bounds on their aspirations or their conduct.

For this resistance they were roundly condemned. They were put down, snubbed, sneered at, talked about, laughed at and ostracised. Our society made women into slaves and then condemned them for acting like slaves. Those who refused to act like slaves they disparaged for not being true women.

It was all done very subtly. Few people were so direct as to say that they did not like Bitches because they did not play the sex role game. In fact, few were sure why they did not like Bitches. They did not realize that their violation of the reality structure endangered the structure. Somehow, from early childhood on, some girls didn't fit in and were good objects to make fun of. But few people consciously recognized the root of their dislike. The issue was never confronted. If it was talked about at all, it was done with snide remarks behind the young girl's back. Bitches were made to feel that there was something wrong with them; something personally wrong.

Teenage girls are particularly vicious in the scapegoat game. This is the time of life when women are told they must compete the hardest for the spoils (i.e., men) which society allows. They must assert their femininity or see it denied. They are very unsure of themselves and adopt the rigidity that goes with uncertainty. They are hard on their competitors and even harder on those who decline to compete. Those of their peers who do not share their concerns and practice the arts of charming men are excluded from most social groupings. If she didn't know it before, a Bitch learns during these years that she is different.

As she gets older she learns more about why she is different. As Bitches begin to take jobs, or participate in organizations, they are rarely content to sit quietly and do what they are told. A Bitch has a mind of her own and wants to use it. She wants to rise high, be creative, assume responsibility. She knows she is capable and wants to use her capabilities. This, not pleasing the men she works for, is her primary goal.

When she meets the hard brick wall of sex prejudice she is not compliant. She will knock herself out batting her head against the wall because she will not accept her defined role as an auxiliary. Occasionally she crashes her way through. Or she uses her ingenuity to find a loophole, or creates one. Or she is ten times better than anyone else competing with her. She also accepts less than her due. Like other women her ambitions have often been dulled for she has not totally escaped the badge of inferiority placed upon the "weaker sex." She will often espouse contentment with being the power behind the throne—provided that she does have real power—while rationalizing that she really does not want the recognition that comes with also having the throne. Because she has been put down most of her life, both for being a woman and for not being a true woman, a Bitch will not always recognize that what she has achieved is not attainable by the typical woman. A highly competent Bitch often deprecates herself by refusing to recognize her own superiority. She is wont to say that she is average or less; if she can do it, anyone can.

As adults, Bitches may have learned the feminine role, at least the outward style, but they are rarely comfortable in it. This is particularly true of those women who are physical Bitches. They want to free their bodies as well as their minds and deplore the effort they must waste confining their physical motions or dressing the role in order not to turn people off. Too, because they violate sex role expectations physically, they are not as free to violate them psychologically or intellectually. A few deviations from the norm can be tolerated but too many are too threatening. It's bad enough not to think like a woman, sound like a woman or do the kinds of things women are supposed to do. To also not look like a woman, move like a woman, or act like a woman is to go way beyond the pale. Ours is a rigid society with narrow limits placed on the extent of human diversity. Women in particular are defined by their physical characteristics. Bitches who do not violate these limits are freer to violate others. Bitches who do violate them in style or size can be somewhat envious of those who do not have to so severely restrain the expansiveness of their personalities and behavior. Often these Bitches are tortured more because their deviancy is always evident. But they do have a compensation in that large Bitches have a good deal less difficulty being taken seriously than small women. One of the sources of their suffering as women is also a source of their strength.

This trial by fire which most Bitches go through while growing up either makes them or breaks them. They are strung taughtly between the two poles of being true to their own nature or being accepted as a social being. This makes them very sensitive people, but it is a sensitivity the rest of the world is unaware of. For on the outside they have frequently grown a thick defensive callous which can make them seem hard and bitter at times. This is particularly true of those Bitches who have been forced to become isolates in order to avoid being remade and destroyed by their peers. Those who are fortunate enough to have grown up with some similar companions, understanding parents, a good role model or two and a very strong will, can avoid some of the worse aspects of being a Bitch. Having endured less psychological punishment for being what they were they can accept their different-ness with the ease that comes from self-confidence.

Those who had to make their way entirely on their own have an uncertain path. Some finally realize that their pain comes not just because they do not conform but because they do not want to conform. With this comes the recognition that there is nothing particularly wrong with *them*—they just don't fit into this kind of society. Many eventually learn to insulate themselves from the harsh social environment. However, this too has its price. Unless they are cautious and conscious, the confi-dence gained in this painful manner—with no support from their sisters—is more often a kind of arrogance. Bitches can become so hard and calloused that the last vestiges of humanity become buried deep within and almost destroyed.

Not all Bitches make it. Instead of callouses, they develop open sores. Instead of confidence they develop an unhealthy sensitivity to rejection. Seemingly tough on the outside, on the inside they are a bloody pulp, raw from the lifelong verbal whipping they have had to endure. These are Bitches who have gone Bad. They often go around with a chip on their shoulders and use their strength for unproductive retaliation when someone accepts their dare to knock it off. These Bitches can be very obnoxious because they never really trust people. They have not learned to use their strength constructively.

Bitches who have been mutilated as human beings often turn their fury on other people—particularly other women. This is one example of how women are trained to keep themselves and other women in their place. Bitches are no less guilty than non-Bitches of self-hatred and group-hatred and those who have gone Bad suffer the worst of both these afflictions. All Bitches are scapegoats and those who have not survived the psychological gauntlet are the butt of everyone's disdain. As a group, Bitches are treated by other women much as women in general are treated by society—all right in their place, good to exploit and gossip about, but otherwise to be ignored or put down. They are threats to the traditional woman's position and they are also an outgroup to which she can feel superior. Most women feel both better than and jealous of Bitches. While comforting themselves that they are not like these aggressive, masculine freaks, they have a sneaking suspicion that perhaps men, the most important thing in their lives, do find the freer, more assertive, independent Bitch preferable as a woman.

Bitches, likewise, don't care too much for other women. They grow up disliking other women. They can't relate to them, they don't identify with them, they have nothing in common with them. Other women have been the norm into which they have not fit. They reject those who have rejected them. This is one of the reasons Bitches who are successful in hurdling the obstacles society places before women scorn these women who are not. They tend to feel those who can take it will make it. Most women have been the direct agents of much of the shit Bitches have had to endure and few of either group has had the political consciousness to realize why this is. Bitches have been oppressed by other women as much if not more than by men and their hatred for them is usually greater.

Bitches are also uncomfortable around other women because frequently women are less their psychological peers than are men. Bitches don't particularly like passive people. They are always slightly afraid they will crush the fragile things. Women are trained to be passive and have learned to act that way even when they are not. A Bitch is not very passive and is not comfortable acting that role. But she usually does not like to be domineering either—whether this is from natural distaste at dominating others or fear of seeming too masculine. Thus a Bitch can relax and be her natural nonpassive self without worrying about mascerating someone only in the company of those who are as strong as she. This is more frequently in the company of men than of women but those Bitches who have not succumbed totally to self-hatred are most comfortable of all only in the company of fellow Bitches. These are her true peers and the only ones with whom she does not have to play some sort of role. Only with other Bitches can a Bitch be truly free.

These moments come rarely. Most of the time Bitches must remain psychologically isolated. Women and men are so threatened by them and react so adversely that Bitches guard their true selves carefully. They are suspicious of those few whom they think they might be able to trust because so often it turns out to be a sham. But in this loneliness there is a strength and from their isolation and their bitterness come contributions that other women do not make. Bitches are among the most unsung of the unsung heroes of this society. They are the pioneers, the vanguard, the spearhead. Whether they want to be or not this is the role they serve just by their very being. Many would not choose to be the groundbreakers for the mass of women for whom they have no sisterly feelings but they cannot avoid it. Those who violate the limits, extend them; or cause the system to break.

Bitches were the first women to go to college, the first to break through the Invisible Bar of the professions, the first social revolutionaries, the first labor leaders, the first to organize other women. Because they were not passive beings and acted on their resentment at being kept down, they dared to do what other women would not. They took the flak and the shit that society dishes out to those who would change it and opened up portions of the world to women that they would otherwise not have known. They have lived on the fringes. And alone or with the support of their sisters they have changed the world we live in.

By definition Bitches are marginal beings in this society. They have no proper place and wouldn't stay in it if they did. They are women but not true women. They are human but they are not male. Some don't even know they are women because they cannot relate to other women. They may play the feminine game at times, but they know it is a game they are playing. Their major psychological oppression is not a belief that they are inferior but a belief that they are not. Thus, all their lives they have been told they were freaks. More polite terms were used, of course, but the message got through. Like most women they were taught to hate themselves as well as all women. In different ways and for different reasons perhaps, but the effect was similar. Internalization of a derogatory self-concept always results in a good deal of bitterness and resentment. This anger is usually either turned in on the self-making one an unpleasant person—or on other women—reinforcing the social clichés about them. Only with political consciousness is it directed at the source—the social system.

The bulk of this Manifesto has been about Bitches. The remainder will be about BITCH. The organization does not yet exist and perhaps it never can. Bitches are so damned independent and they have learned so well not to trust other women that it will be difficult for them to learn to even trust each other. This is what BITCH must teach them to do. Bitches have to learn to accept themselves as Bitches and to give their sisters the support they need to be creative Bitches. Bitches must learn to be proud of their strength and proud of themselves. They must move away from the isolation which has been their protection and help their younger sisters avoid its perils. They must recognize that women are often less tolerant of other women than are men because they have been taught to view all women as their enemies. And Bitches must form together in a movement to deal with their problems in a political manner. They must organize for their own liberation as all women must organize for theirs. We must be strong, we must be militant, we must be dangerous. We must realize that Bitch is Beautiful and that we have nothing to lose. Nothing whatsoever. This Manifesto was written and revised with the help of several of my sisters, to whom it is dedicated.

Chapter Twenty

The Woman-Identified-Woman

Radicalesbians

What is a lesbian? A lesbian is the rage of all women condensed to the point of explosion. She is the woman who, often beginning at an extremely early age, acts in accordance with her inner compulsion to be a more complete and freer human being than her society—perhaps then, but certainly later—cares to allow her. These needs and actions, over a period of years, bring her into painful conflict with people, situations, the accepted ways of thinking, feeling and behaving, until she is in a state of continual war with everything around her, and usually with her self. She may not be fully conscious of the political implications of what for her began as personal necessity, but on some level she has not been able to accept the limitations and oppression laid on her by the most basic role of her society—the female role. The turmoil she experiences tends to induce guilt proportional to the degree to which she feels she is not meeting social expectations, and/or eventually drives her to question and analyze what the rest of her society more or less accepts. She is forced to evolve her own life pattern, often living much of her life alone, learning usually much earlier than her "straight" (heterosexual) sisters about the essential aloneness of life (which the myth of marriage obscures) and about the reality of illusions. To the extent that she cannot expel the heavy socialization that goes with being female, she can never truly find peace with herself. For she is caught somewhere between accepting society's view of her—in which case she cannot accept herself, and coming to understand what this sexist society has done to her and why it is functional and necessary for it to do so. Those of us who work that through find ourselves on the other side of a tortuous journey through a night that may have been decades long. The perspective gained from that journey, the liberation of self, the inner peace, the real love of self and of all women, is something to be shared with all women— because we are all women.

It should first be understood that lesbianism, like male homosexuality, is a category of behavior possible only in a sexist society characterized by rigid sex roles and dominated by male supremacy. Those sex roles dehumanize women by defining us as a supportive/serving caste *in relation to* the master caste of men, and emotionally cripple men by demanding that they be alienated from their own bodies and emotions in order to perform their economic/political/military functions effectively. Homosexuality is a by-product of a particular way of setting up roles (or approved patterns of behavior) on the basis of sex; as such it is an inauthentic (not consonant with "reality") category. In a society in which men do not oppress women, and sexual expression is allowed to follow feelings, the categories of homosexuality and heterosexuality would disappear.

But lesbianism is also different from male homosexuality, and serves a different function in the society. "Dyke" is a different kind of put-down from "faggot," although both imply you are not playing your socially assigned sex role . . . are not therefore a "real woman" or a "real man." The grudging admiration felt for the tomboy and the queasiness felt around a sissy boy point to the same thing: the contempt in which women—or those who play a female role—are held. And the investment in keeping women in that contemptuous role is very great. Lesbian is the word, the label, the condition that holds women in line. When a woman hears this word tossed her way, she knows she is stepping out of line. She knows that she has crossed the terrible boundary of her sex role. She recoils, she protests, she reshapes her actions to gain approval. Lesbian is a label invested by the Man to throw at any woman who dares to be his equal, who dares to challenge his prerogatives (including that of all women as part of the exchange medium among men), who dares to assert the primacy of her own needs. To have the label applied to people active in women's liberation is just the most recent instance of a long history; older women will recall that not so long ago, any woman who was successful, independent, not orienting her whole life about a man, would hear this word. For in this sexist society, for a woman to be independent means she *can't* be a *woman*—she *must* be a *dyke*. That in itself should tell us where women are at. It says as clearly as can be said: Women and person are contradictory terms. For a lesbian is not considered a "real woman." And yet, in popular thinking, there is really only one essential difference between a lesbian and other women: that of sexual orientation—which is to say, when you strip off all the packaging, you must finally realize that the essence of being a "woman" is to get fucked by men.

"Lesbian" is one of the sexual categories by which men have divided up humanity. While all women are dehumanized as sex objects, as the objects of men they are given certain compensations: identification with his power, his ego, his status, his protection (from other males), feeling like a "real woman," finding social acceptance by adhering to her role, etc. Should a woman confront herself by confronting another woman, there are fewer rationalizations, fewer buffers by which to avoid the stark horror of her dehumanized condition. Herein we find the overriding fear of many women towards exploring intimate relationships with other women: the fear of being used as a sexual object by a woman, which not only will bring her no male-connected compensations, but also will reveal the void which is woman's real situation. This dehumanization is expressed when a straight woman learns that a sister is a lesbian; she begins to relate to her lesbian sister as her potential sex object, laying a surrogate male role on the lesbian. This reveals her heterosexual conditioning to make herself into an object when sex is potentially involved in a relationship, and it denies the lesbian her full humanity. For women, especially those in the movement, to perceive their lesbian sisters through this male grid of role definitions is to accept this male cultural conditioning and to oppress their sisters much as they themselves have been oppressed by men. Are we going to continue the male classification system of defining all females in *sexual relation* to some *other* category of people? Affixing the label lesbian not only to a woman who aspires to be a person, but also to any situation of real love, real solidarity, real primacy among women is a primary form of divisiveness among women: it is the condition which keeps women within the confines of the feminine role, and it is the debunking/scare term that keeps women from forming any primary attachments, groups, or associations among ourselves.

Women in the movement have in most cases gone to great lengths to avoid discussion and confrontation with the issue of lesbianism. It puts people up-tight. They are hostile, evasive, or try to incorporate it into some "broader issue." They would rather not talk about it. If they have to, they try to dismiss it as a "lavender herring." But it is no side issue. It is absolutely essential to the success and fulfillment of the women's liberation movement that this issue be dealt with. As long as the label "dyke" can be used to frighten women into a less militant stand, keep her separate from her sisters, keep her from giving primacy to anything other than men and family—then to that extent she is controlled by the male culture. Until women see in each other the possibility of a primal commitment which includes sexual love, they will be denying themselves the love and value they readily accord to men, thus affirming their second-class status. As long as male acceptability is primary—both to individual women and to the movement as a whole—the term lesbian will be used effectively against women. Insofar as women want only more privileges within the system, they do not want to antagonize male power. They instead seek acceptability for women's liberation, and the most crucial aspect of the acceptability is to deny lesbianism—i.e., any fundamental challenge to the basis of the female role.

It should also be said that some younger, more radical women have honestly begun to discuss lesbianism, but so far it has been primarily as a sexual "alternative" to men. This, however, is still giving primacy to men, both because the idea of relating more completely to women occurs as a *negative reaction to men*, and because the lesbian relationship is being characterized simply by sex which is divisive and sexist. On one level, which is both personal and political, women may withdraw emotional and sexual energies from men, and work out various alternatives for those energies in their own lives. On a different political/psychological level, it must be understood that what is crucial is that women begin disengaging from male-defined response patterns. In the privacy of our own psyches, we must cut those cords to the core. For irrespective of where our love and sexual energies flow, if we are male-identified in our heads, we cannot realize our autonomy as human beings.

But why is it that women have related to and through men? By virtue of having been brought up in a male society, we have internalized the male culture's definition of ourselves. That definition views us as relative beings who exist not for ourselves, but for the servicing, maintenance and comfort of men. That definition consigns us to sexual and family functions, and excludes us from defining and shaping the terms of our lives. In exchange for our psychic servicing and for performing society's non-profit making functions, the man confers on us just one thing: the slave status which makes us legitimate in the eyes of the society in which we live. This is called "femininity" or "being a real woman" in our cultural lingo. We are authentic, legitimate, real to the extent that we are the property of some man whose name we bear. To be a woman who belongs to no man is to be invisible, pathetic, inauthentic, unreal. He confirms his image of us—of what we have to be in order to be acceptable by him—but not our real selves; he confirms our womanhood—as he defines it, in relation to him—but cannot confirm our personhood, our own selves as absolutes. As long as we are dependent on the male culture for this definition, for this approval, we cannot be free.

The consequence of internalizing this role is an enormous reservoir of self-hate. This is not to say the self-hate is recognized or accepted as such; indeed, most women would deny it. It may be experienced as discomfort with her role, as feeling empty, as numbness, as restlessness, a paralyzing anxiety at the center. Alternatively, it may be expressed in shrill defensiveness of the glory and destiny of her role. But it does exist, often beneath the edge of her consciousness, poisoning her existence, keeping her alienated from herself, her own needs, and rendering her a stranger to other women. Women hate both themselves and other women. They try to escape by identifying with the oppressor, living through him, gaining status and identity from his ego, his power, his accomplishments. And by not identifying with other "empty vessels" like themselves. Women resist relating on all levels to other women who will reflect their own oppression, their own secondary status, their own self-hate. For to confront another woman is finally to confront one's self—the self we have gone to such lengths to avoid. And in that mirror we know we cannot really respect and love that which we have been made to be.

As the source of self-hate and the lack of real self are rooted in our male-given identity, we must create a new sense of self. As long as we cling to the idea of "being a woman," we will sense some conflict with that incipient self, that sense of I, that sense of a whole person. It is very difficult to realize and accept that being "feminine" and being a whole person are irreconcilable. Only women can give each other a new sense of self. That identity we have to develop with reference to ourselves, and not in relation to men. This consciousness is the revolutionary force from which all else will follow, for ours is an organic revolution. For this we must be available and supportive to one another, give our commitment and our love, give the emotional support necessary to sustain this movement. Our energies must flow toward our sisters, not backwards towards our oppressors. As long as women's liberation tries to free women without facing the basic heterosexual structure that binds us in one-to-one relationships with our oppressors, tremendous energies will continue to flow into trying to straighten up each particular relationship with a man, how to get better sex, how to turn his head around—into trying to make the "new man" out of him, in the delusion that this will allow us to be the "new woman." This obviously splits our energies and commitments, leaving us unable to be committed to the construction of the new patterns which will liberate us.

It is the primacy of women relating to women, of women creating a new consciousness of and with each other which is at the heart of women's liberation, and the basis for the cultural revolution. Together we must find, reinforce and validate our authentic selves. As we do this, we confirm in each other that struggling incipient sense of pride and strength, the divisive barriers begin to melt, we feel this growing solidarity with our sisters. We see ourselves as prime, find our centers inside of ourselves. We find receding the sense of alienation, of being cut off, of being behind a locked window, of being unable to get out what we know is inside. We feel a realness, feel at last we are coinciding with ourselves. With that real self, with that consciousness, we begin a revolution to end the imposition of all coercive identifications, and to achieve maximum autonomy in human expression.

Chapter Twenty-One

The Fourth World Manifesto

Barbara Burris in agreement with Kathy Barry, Terry Moore, Joann DeLor, Joann Parent, and Cate Stadelman

Background

The "Fourth World Manifesto" was originally written partly as a reply to the way in which a "women's liberation" conference was planned. We were upset at the dishonesty of the call for a "women's liberation" conference with Indochinese women in the spring of 1971.

The women who planned and worked on the conference defined themselves as anti-imperialist women. Some of them have also been active in the women's movement. While stating in one of their planning leaflets that it was necessary to be "upfront about our politics," they discussed, sometimes subtly and sometimes very blatantly, the use of the women's liberation movement to further their own political ends.

As we stated in the original "Manifesto," we do not concede to the women who planned the conference the title of "anti-imperialists." We feel they used a very narrow definition of imperialism taken without question from the male-dominated Left. We find it self-evident that women are a colonized group who have never—anywhere—been allowed self-determination. Therefore, all women who fight against their own oppression (colonized status) as females under male domination are anti-imperialist by definition. In the second part of this "Manifesto" is a detailed discussion of women as a colonized group.

It should go without saying that those of us connected with the "Fourth World Manifesto" are deeply opposed to the war in Indochina. As individuals all of us have strong commitments against this war. There are plenty of anti-war groups (however male-dominated) that women, as individuals, can relate to if they wish. But it would be disastrous to turn the independent feminist movement into simply another adjunct to the anti-war and anti-imperialist movements—with the same male-dominated perspective which those movements have.

The anti-imperialist women, like the rest of the anti-war and anti-imperialist Left movement, never question war and national imperialism as male-supremacist institutions. They ignore the roots of domination, aggression, imperialism, and war in male-supremacist society. Because they do not see imperialism and war in their deepest aspects as male-supremacist institutions in *all* societies, the anti-imperialist women are anxiously concerned that an "anti-imperialist consciousness" be injected into the women's movement. They make a strong effort to change the direction of the women's movement from independent feminist issues to anti-imperialist activities as these have been narrowly defined by the male Left.

The anti-imperialist women were less than honest in calling their conference a women's liberation conference with the Indochinese women. We would have had no objections to their conference if they had stated honestly that they were calling an anti-imperialist conference for women interested in anti-war work. It was the dishonesty of the anti-imperialist women's attempt to use and convert the women's liberation movement to their brand of anti-imperialist politics that roused our anger. We have experienced too much of this kind of manipulation of the women's movement by Left groups.

Most of our criticism of the conference was developed in the original "Manifesto." We do not want to go over the details of it here. However, we do feel that it is crucial to open up a discussion of the emotional and ideological reasons underlying attempts to co-opt the women's movement into other "more important" struggles.

In an expanded edition of the "Manifesto" we have worked out a deeper analysis of the emotional, psychological, and social assumptions underlying the attitude that women's liberation is less important than black liberation, anti-imperialism, anti-capitalism, etc. In the expanded "Manifesto" we criticize the male definition of oppression which does not recognize the unique position of females as a subjugated group.

But we feel it is necessary in this limited space to focus strongly on the male-dominated Left. The anti-imperialist women are criticized here only as they are one of the most recent examples in a series of attempts to re-direct the women's movement into male Left-dominated priorities.

Now that the women's movement (thanks to independent women) has become a force to be reckoned with in society, there are many Left groups trying to get a finger in the women's movement pie. Over the last year and a half the SWP-YSA (Socialist Workers Party-Young Socialist Alliance) has made a nationally coordinated attempt to infiltrate and take over women's centers and organize women's liberation groups (which they hope to mold to their "single issue" approach and subordinate to their organizational aims). This "Manifesto" is not simply directed at the "anti-imperialist" women. What is said of the anti-imperialist women's manipulation of the women's movement applies equally well to every other Left group—the Communist Party, Socialist Workers Party, Young Socialist Alliance, International Socialist, Students for a Democratic Society, Progressive Labor, Youth Against War and Fascism, etc. The criticisms we make of the anti-imperialist women apply equally to all of the male Left and the women in the male-dominated Left.

The Invisible Audience

In an honest article in the February issue of *Radical America*, Marlene Dixon described the pressures on women radicals to conform to a male-dominated movement.

In discussing the First National Conference of Women's Liberation near Chicago in 1968, she says:

> The Invisible Audience at the Chicago Conference were the very "male heavies" who had done so much to bring about the existence of a radical Women's Female Liberation Movement. (p. 27)
>
> The radical women were decimated by the invisible male audience. Thus the real split among the women hinged upon the significant audience that women addressed: other women, or Movement men. (p. 28)

But why were these women so super-conscious of a "male presence" at an all-women conference of women's liberationists at a camp near Chicago—with no Left males for miles around?

> Because women had learned from 1964 to 1968 that to fight for or even sympathize with Women's Liberation was to pay a terrible price: what little credit a woman might have earned in one of the Left organizations was wiped out in a storm of contempt and abuse. (p. 27)

But perhaps becoming a "success" in the male Left is not the highest of all possible goals for a woman—or for anyone.

> Women must face facts. Men will never, until forced by circumstances, place first, or even urgent, priority upon a struggle against the oppression of women. Witness the fact that there is not one male dominated organization, from the Left-liberal New University Conference to the radical Youth Movement, that has been willing to place top priority upon the women's struggle. Indeed the idea is so repugnant to many men that they cannot tolerate a woman who refuses male leadership in order to address her energies primarily to the liberation of her sisters. (p. 33)

Women who still are acting for the Left male invisible audience but who now form women's collectives to organize women in relation to the priorities set up by a male Left are little more independent than they were working with the males. They are somewhere between fear and open rebellion. They fear to work on their own definition of women and women's issues and so still relate primarily to the invisible audience of "male heavies."

What a difference it would make—in terms of male approval—if the women working in "anti-imperialist" collectives or on "anti-imperialist" issues were working on their own women's issues.—If they themselves developed a perspective on how women are a colonized group in relation to men all over the world, in all classes and races, including the Third World. With that perspective they would no longer be a part of the male Left. But it doesn't even seem to occur to the "anti-imperialist" women that the male definition of imperialism may be extended and perhaps truly was originally applicable to women.

The "anti-imperialist" women are trying to get women to work on "anti-imperialist" issues in a certain way in which they are defined by the male Left. We quote an article describing the last planning meeting that was held in Baltimore (October 24–25). "In order to spread the word about the Conferences [planning] more widely and to get women involved in anti-war activities, a series of actions are being planned as part of a whole anti-imperialist offensive of women." (From "Battle Acts," published by Women of Youth Against War and Fascism.)

It is one thing to be against the Vietnam War and all wars and quite another for a group of women to try to draw women working in their own Movement away from it into the male-dominated, very narrowly defined anti-war and anti-imperialist movements. The same mistake happened at one point (there's always something more "important" than female liberation) when a large segment of the earlier Feminist Movement went into the Women's International League for Peace and Freedom and fizzled out as a threatening force in the society.

The demand for an end to sex roles and male imperialist domination is a real attack on the masculine citadel of war. After all, women don't declare or fight in offensive wars. War is a male institution—as are all other institutions in the society—and war is simply an extension of the colonial policy of the subjection of the female culture and "weaker" male cultures, i.e., "weaker" national cultures. Women, who have nothing to say about running the country or fighting in the war, will never end war except by attacking and ending male domination and the sex roles where men learn their war mentality. The women who went into WILPF took the safest and therefore totally ineffective and reactionary (for women) way out. They opted to reinforce the split between male and female and to use their "feminine myths" to act as adjuncts to the male peace movement and claim that women's voice was needed (in the same old role, of course) to save men from themselves—their own self-imposed slaughter. The oppressed are going to "save" with their oppressed "virtues" (defined by males and unsifted and unquestioned) their own oppressors.

The anti-imperialist women, in a new refrain to an old song, are in essence asking that women in the independent Women's Movement focus their energies on "anti-imperialism" as the male Left defines it. This is like asking the Women's Movement to move from a position of independence to a position of subservience to the male-dominated Left.

But the Women's Liberation Movement started out from the Civil Rights Freedom Movement, Student Movement, and Anti-War Movement. Women got the notion working in these movements that the idea of freedom should apply to women too. But the males in these movements never intended the freedom struggle to extend to women. It is still too subversive an idea for any of these movements to tolerate on any real level. So many women who got the freedom bug too bad left to relate to women in a Female Movement.

And just as the freedom and anti-war struggle never applied to women, so neither does the present Left anti-imperialist movement. Is there *any* analysis about imperialism against women? Is there any recognition in writing or action that women are a colonized group, brutally exploited by their colonizers—men—and that this is a primary fact of women's existence? No. And this kind of analysis will never happen in the male-dominated Left or its periphery because males are the colonizers. And the colonizer has never yet defined his privileges out of existence—only the colonized will.

The male Left has absolutely no interest in a female revolution. Rather, the male Left has a direct interest in perpetuating the status quo, i.e., male privileges, and preventing any real threats to male supremacy from both within the Left and without it.

A Specter Is Haunting the Left—The Specter of Feminism

The only real threat to male supremacy is the independent Women's Movement. Therefore the male Left has done a great deal to impede the development of independent Women's Liberation and tried in numerous ways to co-opt the energies of women away from working independently with other women on women's issues. There have been numerous devices used by the Left to this end depending on the situation and the consciousness of the women involved.

The first tactic in reaction to Women's Liberation was laughter. But that didn't stop some women—in fact it made some of them so furious they left and began "organizing" other women. The next tactic was anger. "You castrating bitches." "What do you women want anyway?" And that didn't work either—even more women left to join the newly emerging independent Women's Movement.

Then the men began to get really nervous—after all women were leaving the Left in increasing numbers—and the men began to play guilt games. "So what makes *you* think *you're* oppressed, you white middle-class chick?" (Notice the order of the defining words the male Left uses—"chick" is last.) That tactic made some women even madder but it began to cut deep into many women. And this tactic began to work on some of the less strong women—those who were still full of white male-imposed guilt and self-hatred. The Left males realized that they had struck a tender nerve. And they began to manipulate women's guilt and started becoming very liberal toward the Women's Liberation Movement—that is, when they weren't chuckling about those "frustrated bitches" in male-only company. And they had to be liberal anyway because that Goddamned Women's Liberation Movement composed only of females was putting the heat on them and they might lose "their" women to it if they didn't play it cool. So they put up with the discomfort of women's caucuses rather than lose all "their" women to the independent Women's Movement. At first it was pretty rough and more than one male Left organization folded under the pressures of the women's caucuses.

But then the Left males began to see that the women's caucuses could have some real value for their organizations. They could be used as important organizing tools for recruiting new members and for working with women associated with the males whose problems the Left organization was concerned with. Such as having the women work with GI wives while the men worked at "organizing" the GI's in the army. Women in the caucuses express best the male attitudes of the organization toward "women's issues" and women's struggle for liberation. We give only two examples out of many. One is a leaflet passed out by PAR (People Against Racism) women at a women's liberation conference in Detroit in 1968. They list as one of their concerns something which reveals the manipulative way in which the Women's Movement is viewed: They wish to use Women's Liberation "as an organizing tactic for broader political movement."

Bernadine Dohrn's equally blatant statement in the *New Left Notes* special issue on women is every bit as revealing. She says, "Everywhere around us there are concentrations of women: dorms, women's schools, education and home economics departments, high schools, jobs—women can be mobilized to fight against imperialism and racism." Maybe women's caucuses were really a boon to the male Left and not the threat they had expected them to be and which they were at first.

So a pattern was generally established throughout the male Left that women could stay in the caucuses and organize other women into the Left male-dominated Movement as long as they concentrated on:

(1) Raising women's issues mainly as they related to the structure of the male-dominated organization which the women remained working for;

(2) Raising women's issues on the periphery of the male-defined "important" issues of the organization;

(3) Relating to the Women's Liberation Movement as caucus members only of the primary male organization to "raise" the issues of the male organization in the Women's Movement, and, if possible, get its focus off independent women's struggle and onto how women can relate to male-defined Left issues.

Women's collectives, unless they are truly autonomous women's collectives working from their own analysis on women's issues, can be and are used in much the same manner as the Left women's caucuses. Because they too relate primarily to the male Left Movement and only secondarily as females to female liberation issues. They are one step ahead of the women's caucuses if only because they know they can no longer work with the males in the organization—but they still remain working *for* them even though now working in women's collectives. Also, "women's collectives" is now being used by a number of women as synonymous with caucus group—but a more "hip" term than caucus.

The Myth of the White Middle-Class Woman

The male Left tries to intimidate Left women into not taking a strong and independent stand on the female liberation struggle with the "abusive" statement, "They're only a bunch of white, middle-class women." It would take another long article to refute this statement, but we will do it in a very cursory manner here.

White is the first defining word of "white middle-class women." This implies that the primary position of women in the society is due to white privileges. *If* this is so, then *all* whites must have the same privileges, i.e., *all* whites must control the institutions, make the laws, control the army and police, control the government, the religion, education, and business, and have the very best positions in jobs, etc. But it is white males only who are in positions of power and control in all of the institutions of the society. Women are excluded from control and decision-making, are discriminated against in jobs more than any other group, get the lowest pay, are defined as inferiors and as a sexual caste, etc. Also, women were the first group to be subjected as a caste all over the world, thousands of years ago—long before blacks were subjected to whites in America or anywhere else. Obviously whiteness does not overcome the caste position of being a woman in this society. There are some incidental advantages to being white for a woman who is white, but there are also advantages for black males in being males in this society. But the incidental advantages—which are meaningless in terms of woman's true caste position as a sex—come to her mainly in her affiliation with a dominant white male.

The Left very shallowly sees women associating and living with white males and therefore assumes that women share white male privileges. This is false. Being integrated *as subordinates* does not mean that women share the privileges of the ruling caste—white males. Women get the crumbs. In fact, as the black liberation struggle found out, there are distinct disadvantages to being "integrated" with your oppressor, especially when he still has all the power. The control over the oppressed is just that much more complete.

The second defining word in the series, "white middle-class women," is middle-class. If class defines women before her sex does, then she should be able to compete with any male for any job on an equal level. But this is not the case. Women are almost in a different labor market than men because of the extremely rigid female caste labor role. The discrimination against females in the economy is the most intense of any group. Female labor is the lowest paid. Doesn't everyone know the statistics by now? In 1966, the median income for a white man was $7,164; for a nonwhite man, $4,528; a white woman, $4,152; a nonwhite woman, $2,949 (full-time year-round labor). In 1955, the median wage of women working full time was 64 percent of that of men; in 1967, it was down to 60 percent. Things are getting worse and we could go on and on quoting statistics you have probably already heard. But it is clear that the white male and the black male get paid more and the white female and the black female get paid less. The black female is doubly disadvantaged as a female and black, and has the lowest pay level of all. That "female" work is the lowest and the caste lines of labor are most rigid in terms of sex can be proved by the fact that black males—while demanding integration in jobs in male fields, i.e., better paying jobs—have never demanded to integrate (sexually, that is) as secretaries, waitresses, salesgirls, etc. When black males integrate into a female job (which is rare) such as nursing, they are paid more than the females doing the same job.

A woman's class is almost always determined by the man she is living with. From her father's house to her husband's house, his income determines her class. Her income and job are only "extra." In fact, if all women were to be put out of all their men's houses and had to depend on their own earning power, almost all of them would be lower or working class—no matter what their class positions were when living with the man. They would be lower or working class because of women's sexual caste position in the economy. Class is therefore basically a distinction between males, while the female is defined by her sexual caste status.

So we have only the last word left in the "taunt" of "white middle-class women." And women—a sexual caste subordinated to the dominant ruling sex, man—is defined primarily by that relationship.

But it is true that women—through self-hatred and manipulation by male culture (as evidenced by the male Left example above)—do not necessarily identify with their true caste position as women. She often identifies with her oppressor's privileges as white or middle or upper class or even as male. But the Left, which is so upset about her identification with whiteness, and class, does not have a comparable critique of black and Third World male identification with male supremacy and privileges (humorously referred to as "foreskin privileges"). This is because the identification with male privileges by black and Third World males—even in their movements—fits in with white male movement domination.

But as women, we are upset about any inequality—any identification with privileges—between women or within the Women's Movement. We have tremendous barriers to overcome. As the Female Liberation Movement must cut across all (male-imposed) class, race, and national lines, any false identification of women with privileges that are really male (such as whiteness or class, etc.) will be fatal to our Movement. Any identification with privileges will destroy the basis of communication which we females share as a suppressed caste and will divide us up as enemies where we should be friends and equals. And the male Right and the male Left movements will manipulate these differences among women to prevent women from overcoming the barriers that keep us apart and therefore unable to effectively change our sexual caste position as females.

Many women do identify with white and class privileges. Our task as women is not, as the male Left does, to write them off as white bourgeois but to patiently discuss and communicate with women, as sisters, what our true caste position in society is. Once we really understand our suppressed caste status and begin to move to free ourselves from it, we women can then understand other groups' oppression—but not before. But it is not an automatic result. People can see their own oppression clearly and be blind to others' oppression. So the understanding of the oppression of other groups needs to be a very conscious and important part of the Women's Liberation Movement, but only from the basis of an understanding and struggle for our own freedom as females—not as an imposed lecture by some "movement organizers" who will "raise our consciousness" about oppression, and try to impose their white male guilt on us.

The male Left tries, through guilt, to play one oppressed group off against another oppressed group in much the same way the Establishment plays one against the other. They are always going in circles with the "who's most oppressed" musical chairs. How does one decide who is "most oppressed"? Surely the male white Left—as oppressors—cannot decide this. But they do and try to impose their decision on everyone, especially women. And women are—of course—defined as "least oppressed" by the male-dominated Left.

Let us suppose, for a moment, that we are in a male Left meeting and they are trying to decide who is "most oppressed," therefore who most deserves their solicitous attentions and rhetoric. First of all they decide that blacks are most oppressed.

But then someone says that black females are more oppressed than black males. Someone else counters that black females in Third World countries are even more oppressed than are black females in the U.S. Then another person realizes that a black female in the Third World who is in the working class is more oppressed. But someone else says that a black female in the Third World country who is in the working class and under eighteen years of age is even *more* oppressed. But the *most* oppressed, and therefore logically and morally the only people they should try to "organize" and work with, are black females in Third World countries, in the working class, under eighteen years of age, pregnant, and culturally defined as ugly.

Such is the "logic" of the "most oppressed." But we can take one last look at it from another angle.

A Dramatic Meeting of Two Oppressed/Oppressors, or "Who Is More Guilty?"

A black man meets a white woman on the street. He is oppressed because he's black and so need feel no guilt toward her. She feels guilty because she's white. But then the balance shifts as she realizes she's a woman and therefore oppressed and needn't feel guilt. But then he feels guilty because he's a male. Then she begins to feel guilty because she's middle class. Then he feels free of guilt because he's working class. But he begins to feel guilty because he's older and she's very young and oppressed. She feels oppressed as a youth and therefore doesn't feel guilty . . . *ad infinitum.*

The fact that has to be faced by the male Left at some point is that *everyone* in the society—including the white male—is both oppressor and oppressed. Psychologically this could be a revolutionary concept for the Left. If we can only identify with our oppression and not see how we also oppress others we are fooling ourselves. If we feel only guilty about being oppressors we are also fooling ourselves.

The male Left is in a vicious circle of guilt and righteousness, because people in the male Left refuse to go deep enough into their own personal processes of guilt and anger at their own oppression, which becomes a confused mixture of violence and revenge. The male Left has become so hung-up on guilt and "who's most oppressed" that they have lost an elemental sense of justice for *all* human beings.

We, as women, do not want males to feel guilty. We don't care about guilt; what we want is change. All we demand is justice for our sisters, and that cannot come from a guilt-ridden movement which has defined half of humanity's freedom as a "side effect" of the "real" revolution which will be made by other "vanguard," "more oppressed" groups.

The males in the Left continue, through control of leadership, control of the Left organizations, control of writing and publishing, to define the issues which Left workers will concentrate on. This often goes in fads. The latest one is anti-imperialism. (Which is not to negate the importance of imperialism but to say it has been taken up in a shallow and faddish manner and as an escape from the realities of American society.) The definition of imperialism is carefully male-controlled and does not include women's colonial status.

The women who are organizing this "women's" Conference have accepted the male Left priorities and their definition of "anti-imperialism," which excludes women's movements for self-determination.

The women who call themselves anti-imperialists made this statement in their planning leaflet:

> Discussions followed concerning the level of anti-imperialist consciousness within the Women's Liberation Movement in the various cities represented. It was evident that although there was both a high degree of women's consciousness and of anti-imperialist consciousness in various parts of the Movement, the relation between the two has not been made clear to most women in the Movement. (p. 3).

Let us explain to the "anti-imperialist" women what imperialism and anti-imperialism really are to women.

There are two definitions of imperialism. The Webster dictionary states that imperialism is:

> ... the policy and practices of forming and maintaining an empire, in modern times, it is characterized by a struggle for the control of raw materials and world markets, the subjugation and control of territories, the establishment of colonies, etc.

The imperialist is defined by Webster's as a person favoring imperialism.

Fanon and the whole black liberation struggle have recently extended the dictionary definition of imperialism or colonialism to mean a group which is prevented from self-determination by another group—whether it has a national territory or not. The psychological and cultural mutilation is particularly intense and the colonialism more brutal when the group that colonizes and the group colonized have different defining physical characteristics that set them clearly apart.

All of the above definitions apply to the subjection of women, as a sex.

The dictionary definition of imperialism included "the subjection and control of territories. ..." Women, set apart by physical differences between them and men, were the first colonized group. And the territory colonized was and remains our women's bodies.

Our bodies were first turned into property of the males. Men considered female bodies as territory over which they fought for absolute ownership and control. Consider the imperialist implications of the language: He related his sexual "conquests," she "surrendered" to him, he "took her," etc. Marriage (exclusive of property rights) and the patriarchal family system are colonial institutions created and controlled by males for the subjugation of females.

Our bodies are free territory to other male colonizers when not "protected" by an individual male colonist. What is rape but an imperialist act upon the territory of our bodies?

There are two forms of the colonization of our bodies (territories) by males. Most males have an individual colonial relationship to an individual female and most males identify with and act on the group colonization of women. For instance, rape is an individual male imperialist act against an individual woman while the abortion laws are male group control over their collective female territories. (We realize that we are generalizing here about males and that some of them do not perceive women simply as open territory for conquest. But unfortunately, there are too few males who perceive females as equal human beings to change the generalization much at this point.)

Another example of group colonization of women is the way our bodies are defined as open territory for exploitation (compare the exploitation for sexual satisfaction of the male colonizer to exploitation for raw materials—female bodies are the raw materials). In all forms of the dominant male culture—advertising, pornography, the underground press, literature, art, etc.—female bodies are exploited as territory to demean, subject, control, and mock.

The fact that each male petty colonialist has an individual interest in perpetuating the subjection of his individual territory, i.e., woman, makes the colonization of women more complete than that of any other group. The colonial rule is more intense for females as we have no escape into a ghetto and at all times are under the watchful eye of the male colonizers, from father to lover to husband. Therefore our suppression as a group (culture) and as individuals has been more complete as has been our identification with our masters' interests (much like the proverbial house nigger).

Fanon shows that it is not enough for the colonizer to control the territory and subject the inhabitants of it to his rule. The colonizer must destroy the culture and self-respect of the colonized. And colonialism's condemnation of the colonized's culture transcends any national boundaries, for it is the essence of the colonized physical and cultural differences that threaten the colonizer.

Fanon says in *The Wretched of the Earth* that "Colonialism . . . turns to the past of the oppressed people, and distorts, disfigures and destroys it." (p. 210) He says that the colonized (in his book, speaking of blacks) "must demonstrate that a Negro culture exists."

The great mass of women have been totally ignored in history except where they appear as adjuncts to men. And the history of Female Liberation Movements has been distorted and almost completely censored. Through the almost complete censorship of the realities of women's condition throughout history, women have been robbed of the means to knowledge about the origins and extent of their subjugation. History (of art, politics, literature, etc.) as related by males has engraved upon women's minds a male image of the world.

Women Are Now in the Process of Having to Prove that a Female Culture Exists.

Culture is defined by Webster's as the "concepts, habits, skills, art, instruments, institutions, etc. of a given people in a given period." We will show that the concepts, habits, skills, art, and instruments of women in any period have been different from men's and have been ridiculed and/or suppressed by them. We will show that in all the major institutions of society women receive unequal treatment and the appearance that these institutions are the same for men and women is false.

A female culture exists.

We also hold that female and male culture began with the definition of females as embodying all those human attributes which males as dominators could not reconcile with their own self-image and therefore projected onto females, thus causing a schizophrenic split of personality into masculine and feminine.—That women, defined by these attributes (such as emotional, intuitive, etc.) by males and further limited by their physical position in society as to work and tools, developed a female or "feminine" culture, and a culture of resistance to male domination. Although the concept of the "feminine" was imposed upon women, we have, through the centuries, developed and created within the confines of the feminine, a female culture.

Female and Male Culture

What do most people imagine when they think of differences in culture? They most often think of strange customs and a different language. The traveler to a foreign culture will notice women carrying pails of water on their heads or men riding donkeys, different and strange costumes and white-washed houses. In another culture she will notice people riding bicycles, small towns, sidewalk cafés, small shops, more chic dress, different foods, etc. Especially will the traveler notice the difference in language if there is one.

Although these are just a few of the differences of national culture that distinguish the lives that both women and men lead, and we respect these differences, they are the superficialities that cover up the fundamental similarity of all national cultures the world over. This fundamental similarity is the split between male culture and female culture.

Let us go back to some of those superficial differences that the traveler noticed. In the first culture, the women were carrying pails of water on their heads and the men riding donkeys to market. What was seen as one whole is now divided up by sexual work role. The different costumes which were seen as a whole unit are now divided up into male costumes and female costumes. The small shops noticed are owned by men and sometimes staffed by women. A split is now seen between male ownership and female workers. The cafes are served by women, if cheap, and staffed by male waiters if more expensive. A difference in value of work and pay between male and female is perceived. The food production in agriculture is done primarily by males but prepared in each home by females. What was seen as culinary differences now reminds the traveler of the role of women in the home and woman's caste work roles all over the world. The traveler in this second look at the culture begins to notice the basic sameness of the male-female cultural split under the superficial differences that were so striking to her at first.

The problem is that the split is so obvious and taken for granted that practically nobody can see it. Things which are conceived of as "natural" cannot ordinarily be perceived. But the emperor had no clothes in spite of what everybody "saw," and a female culture exists whether or not most people will acknowledge the facts of its existence.

Let us again take up those things (habits, skills, art, concepts, and institutions) which distinguish one culture from another according to Webster's definition. Part of the customs of a culture are its habits. Habits here means what people do in their daily lives. It can also include how they go about doing these things. It is clear that women and men have very different daily habits. Women in practically all parts of the world, whether they are working outside the home or not, have responsibility for the cooking, cleaning, and child "raising" chores of the society. This means that most women spend their time with children. This in itself is a cultural split, as men go out and mix mainly with other males in the male world outside the home. Generally males do not do any of the work designated as "female work." Women, mainly in the company of other women and children, organize their time and routines and socializing on an entirely different basis than males. Female work, being so completely caste labor, is organized and done by women in ways peculiar to the female view of things (which is very much determined by woman's secluded work place, i.e., the home and its environs). The whole daily routine of a man and a woman is totally different.

The woman develops skills associated with her work role. Her skills are usually entirely different than the male's. She usually knows a lot about cooking, child care, washing, sewing, colors, decorating, and cleaning, while he knows mechanical or carpentry skills and anything he may learn as a skill at his job. The instruments or tools a woman uses are defined by the work and skills she is allowed.

If the woman goes out to "work" she will have all the home chores in addition to her outside "job." But women's skills outside the home are limited by what the male-run economy will train her for or let her do. She usually fills "service" roles which utilize the "skills" she has learned in her role as wife and mother. She is allowed limited acquisition of physical skills in such things as typing and small tedious work. She fills completely different job roles than males in the male-dominated economy and is segregated into "female jobs" almost completely. Males do almost all the specialized skillful work—for higher pay.

At one time in the process of the cultures, women did almost everything and men did nothing but hunt and make weapons and war. As men had free time due to women's performing all the drudge work for them (as slave labor, really), they began to develop skills in certain things. As a skill developed, women were no longer allowed to perform the task and it was passed on from father to son. As specialization increased women had more of the skills and trades taken away from them and were left only with the drudge chores of cleaning, washing, cooking, "raising" children, etc. This culminated in Europe in the all-male guilds of feudal times.

When the feudal guild system broke down with the onset of industrialism, cheap unskilled labor was needed and women were used again—sewing, weaving, mining, working metal in factories, etc. It was on the backs of cheap "unskilled" female labor (and child labor) that the grotesque edifice of Western industrialism was built. Female slave labor in the cotton mills and black slave labor in the cotton fields produced industrialism for the white male Western world.

And when industrialism was achieved, hordes of women were sent back home and men replaced them in the factories. So that now we have a small body of lowest-paid female labor in the factories but almost totally female personnel in sales and service roles (typing, nursing) which were once male "skills" but are now just very low-paying drudge work.

The final three parts of Webster's definition of culture are the art, concepts, and institutions of a people.

Women have been excluded from contributing to the art, philosophy, and science of all national cultures. These things are in tight male control. The male culture, which is the dominant culture in every nation, i.e., is synonymous with the national culture, cannot accept a female view of things as expressed by female writers, artists, and philosophers. When some women break through male prejudice to create truly great art—which is often very sensitive to the female culture and values—they are not given the recognition they deserve, because males, looking through their own culturally distorted view of the world, cannot give any credence to an art that expresses the female view. In fact, most males cannot understand what is going on in female culture and art. The worth of female art is thoroughly suppressed in a male-dominated society.

The female soul, suppressed and most often stereotyped in male art, is defined by negative comparisons to the male. The eternal feminine is seen as a passive, earthy, malleable, mysterious, unthinking, emotional, subjective, intuitive, practical, unimaginative, unspiritual, worldly, evil, lustful, super-sexual, virginal, forever waiting, pain-enduring, self-sacrificing, calculating, narcissistic, contradictory, helpless, quivering mass of flesh.

The fact that women live under the power of belief in these characterizations causes a certain outlook which molds the female culture. Woman's position in society, her economic and psychological dependence, reinforce the female stereotypes. Because of the belief in these attributes and woman's position in society—not because of our inherent "female nature"—women's concepts of the world are much different than men's.

Almost everything that has been defined as a male view of the world has its opposite in a female view. Because of the child raising role and the emphasis on personal relationships, women have a more personal, subjective view of things. Because of our subjection, women have a more fatalistic, passive view of the world. We are more in touch with our emotions and often find it necessary to use emotions in manipulating men. Through the imposition of a servant status on women, the female culture has elaborated a whole servile ethic of "self-sacrifice." As the major ethic of the female culture, self-sacrifice has been one of the most effective psychological blocks to women's open rebellion and demand for self-determination. It has also been a major tool of male manipulation of females.

The institutions of a people are an essential part of their culture. The major institutions of every culture are the same: the family, religion, government, army, and economy. Men and women have a completely different relationship to the institutions of "their" culture. In fact there are two cultures hidden by the appearance of one culture under one set of institutions.

Women are excluded, except sometimes in token numbers and in the lowest working ranks, from participation in government, the army, and religion. There are basically two economic institutions of a society: the substructure or family and the superstructure or outside world of work. Women are limited to an economic dependence in "their" caste work in the family. In work outside the family, women are caste laborers in the lowest-paid drudge work. Women are kept from management or decision-making in work outside the home.

Though it appears that both men and women live together within the institutions of a society, men really define and control the institutions while women live under their rule. The government, army, religion, economy, and family are institutions of the male culture's colonial rule over the female.

A FEMALE CULTURE EXISTS. IT IS A CULTURE THAT IS SUBORDINATED AND UNDER MALE CULTURE'S COLONIAL, IMPERIALIST RULE ALL OVER THE WORLD. UNDERNEATH THE SURFACE OF EVERY NATIONAL, ETHNIC, OR RACIAL CULTURE IS THE SPLIT BETWEEN THE TWO PRIMARY CULTURES OF THE WORLD—THE FEMALE CULTURE AND THE MALE CULTURE.

National cultures vary greatly according to the degree of the suppression of the female culture. The veil and seclusion of women and their almost total segregation in Arab culture make for differences between them and, for example, Swedish women. A Swedish woman may not be able to tolerate the suppressed life of Arab women but she also, if she is sensitive, may not be able to tolerate her suppression as a female in Sweden. Crossing national boundaries often awakens a woman's understanding of her position in society. We cannot, like James Baldwin, even temporarily escape from our caste role to Paris or another country. It is everywhere; there is no place to escape.

The repression of female culture is only a question of degree all over the world; the underlying reality is basically the same: the denial of self-determination for women. Women traveling to a foreign country can readily communicate and understand other women in that country because female work and roles (culture) are basically the same all over the world. But it too often happens that women falsely identify with "their" country's dominant male culture and so cannot communicate with their sisters in subjection in other lands or in other races. This female identification with male cultural supremacy must be overcome if the Women's Movement is to be a truly liberating force.

Most males all over the world perceive and compare females as a caste group. A male of any culture perceives a woman as a woman first and only secondly as "representing" a national or ethnic culture. And he treats every woman as females as a caste are treated. The "Miss World" and "Miss Universe" etc. female flesh auctions, comparing various nationalities of female flesh, are only one example of many. The best way for any woman to find out the truth of this statement is to do some traveling to different countries.

"National" Culture Is the Dominant Male Culture

Whoever defines and controls the institutions of a society controls that society. Males define and control all the institutions of all "national" cultures—including every purportedly socialist nation that has ever existed.

Because the male culture is dominant and in control in every nation, the "national" culture becomes synonymous with, and in fact is, the male culture. The female culture exists "invisibly," in subjection to the male-defined "national" culture.

What appears as one national culture, due to male propaganda, is in reality the male culture setting itself up as *the* national culture through subordination of the female. The male army, the male government, the male religion, the male-run economy, the male-defined institution of the family, along with the male culture in the "narrower" sense—i.e., the male arts, sciences, philosophy, and technology—are defined as *the* national culture when in fact they represent nothing but the male view and male interests.

One national culture vs. another national culture is simply one male-dominated society vs. another male-dominated society, with women carried along or used outside their subservient role temporarily if this is necessary for victory of the male national culture. Women are obviously hurt doubly by the imposition on them of two male-dominated cultures—one "their" own males', the other the foreign males'. But the confusion comes when "our" own males, who dominate and define the female culture, refuse to recognize that for women it is simply two dominant male cultures that have to be resisted. "Our" own male dominators always want us *only* to resist the *other* males' domination in the guise of fending off the destruction of "our common culture"—which they have always excluded us from and subordinated us to.

Because of this identification of the male culture with the national, ethnic, racial, or revolutionary culture, some very oppressive male-supremacist attitudes are widespread in national and racial liberation movements. For this reason it is extremely important to make a clear distinction between national or racial liberation and female liberation, although the basis is the same: self-determination. Fanon, for example, in the chapter called "Algeria Unveiled" in *A Dying Colonialism*, makes the mistake of confusing the two and exposes his own identification with male cultural supremacy. Fanon takes the veil as the symbol of Arab and Algerian culture:

> The veil worn by the women appears with such constancy that it generally suffices to characterize Arab society. . . . The way people clothe themselves, together with the tradition of dress and finery that custom implies, constitutes the most distinctive form of a society's uniqueness. . . . (p. 35)

Now the veil can be seen as a distinctly Arabian cultural trait or a national cultural trait. We have shown that the national culture is synonomous with the male culture. In this case the male Arab culture has a unified way of defining and limiting the female through the veil. The female cultural suppression is symbolically represented by the veil, which must be worn by females from the age of puberty on.

Fanon is correct in saying that the French tried to destroy Algerian (male) culture and that this is a typical colonial tactic of one male culture vs. another colonized male culture. But Fanon shows a typical male inability to see the brutal colonization of females by males. In his use of the veil as a symbol of Algerian culture that the French were trying to destroy, he oversimplifies in order to avoid a recognition of his own male guilt and the Algerian males' culpability toward the Algerian females' repressed and demeaned culture.

If Fanon were more honest he would recognize that the French, as a male culture, had no more interest in the Algerian woman's freedom than the Algerian male had. But Fanon, who has such passionate anger against the French colonizers, does not extend his vision to demand justice for the Algerian female. In fact he pooh-poohs the idea that Algerian women are oppressed at all. Nowhere, except in what he reveals unknowingly, does he admit the fact of female oppression by the male in Algeria. (We will later quote an Algerian woman who, for obvious reasons, does not share his bigoted blindness on the colonized status of women in Algeria.) Fanon says:

> To begin with there is the much-discussed status of the Algerian woman—her alleged confinement, her lack of importance, her humility, her silent existence bordering on quasi-absence. And "Moslem society" had made no place for her, amputating her personality, allowing her neither development nor maturity, maintaining her in a perpetual infantilism. . . . Such affirmations, illuminated by "scientific works," are today receiving the only valid challenge: the experience of revolution. (pp. 65, 66)

For one who is so concerned with the psychological mutilation of the colonized group, this statement shows a callousness equaled only by colonial French statements about the "non-oppression" of French rule. Compare this to a statement Fanon made about the mutilation of the Algerian personality by the French:

> French colonialism has settled itself in the very center of the Algerian individual and has undertaken a sustained work of cleanup, of expulsion of self, of rationally pursued mutilation. (p. 65)

But not only does Fanon deny the existence of female oppression in Algeria, like any other colonizer he must justify it as chosen by the colonized:

> The Algerian woman's ardent love of the home is not a limitation imposed by the universe [no, it was imposed by males]. It is not flight from the world. The Algerian woman, in *imposing such a restriction on herself* [in not taking off the veil, and staying home], in *choosing* a form of existence limited in scope, was deepening her consciousness of struggle and preparing for combat. (p. 66)

In this a typical male-supremacist attitude emerges. Women who give up their own struggle for freedom are the most "conscious" women if they are then prepared to fight alongside their male oppressors. Fanon says: "What was most essential was that the occupier should come up against a united front." (p. 66) And a united front means women must give up their "silly, trivial" ideas of a female anti-colonial movement and fight in the male-dominated "anti-" colonial revolution.

Fanon shows that the Algerian national liberation struggle was a male struggle and that when, out of necessity, women were included, they were under male leadership and control.

> Until 1955, the combat was waged exclusively by the men. The revolutionary characteristics of this combat, the necessity for absolute secrecy, obliged the militant to keep his woman in absolute ignorance. (p. 48)

Fanon never questions what made possible the male's position of fighting and the female's of being kept in ignorance. He never questions male control of the revolution. He states: "As the enemy gradually adapted himself to the forms of combat, new difficulties appeared which required original solutions." (p. 48) Among the "original solutions" was the possibility of including women in the fighting—but not really in the revolution, because women were not to be freed by it. The excuse given before was male chivalry: after all, women might get tortured and killed. But when it was necessary to use women the chivalry arguments were conveniently forgotten.

The decision to involve women was made wholly by males. "The decision to involve women as active elements of the Algerian Revolution was not reached lightly." (p. 48) But before it was decided to include women in the revolution, the male revolutionists came up against the effects of their own colonization of women. They pondered how the Algerian woman's colonized status in relation to Algerian males might interfere with her "use" in the revolution. Fanon never says it occurred to the Algerian males that Algerian women needed to engage in an anti-colonial resistance to Algerian male domination. Women's colonized status was seen simply as an obstacle to her "use."

> Having been accustomed to confinement, her body did not have the normal mobility before a limitless horizon of avenues, of unfolded sidewalks, of houses, of people dodged or bumped into. This relatively cloistered [i.e. slave] life, with its known, categorized, regulated [by males] comings and goings, made an immediate revolution seem a dubious proposition. The political leaders were perfectly familiar with these problems [i.e., with the suppressed status of Algerian females], and their hesitations expressed their consciousness of their responsibilities. They were entitled to doubt the success of this measure. Would not such a decision [to involve Algerian women] have catastrophic consequences for the progress of the Revolution? (p. 49)

Here the revolution is defined as male and women are to be used; but female liberation is never considered. In fact, the idea is how to use women without too much upsetting their colonial status.

In the final decision to "admit" them to the revolution, women, naturally, were not consulted:

> After a final series of meetings among leaders, *and especially in view of the urgency of the daily problems that the Revolution faced*, the decision to concretely involve women in the national struggle was reached. (p. 51; emphasis added)

Fanon waxes euphoric in discussing Algerian womanhood's role in the revolution. Even though woman's position in Algerian society did not change during or after the revolution, he continues to state that women fought as sisters alongside the Algerian brothers and this proves that the Algerian women are not slaves of the Algerian men. In fact it only shows that the Algerian men needed them and were able to tolerate them outside of their traditional role in order to win the revolutionary battle. There are many quotes from Fanon to show that women within the revolution had a subservient role. He makes some incredibly paternalistic remarks about "accepting" women's "support" in the revolution. This seems to show a subconscious understanding on his part that it was a revolution made by and for the Algerian males. He says:

> The married women whose husbands were militants were the first to be chosen. Later, widows or divorced women were designated. In any case, there were never any unmarried girls—first of all, because a girl of even twenty or twenty-three hardly ever has occasion to leave the family domicile unaccompanied. But the woman's duties as mother and spouse, the desire to limit to the minimum the possible consequences of her arrest and her death, and also the more and more numerous volunteering of unmarried girls, led the political leaders [male] to make another leap, to remove all restrictions, to accept indiscriminately the support of all Algerian women. (p. 51)

Notice that he said "support" instead of "equal participation."

The Algerian woman's role was limited and defined by the males in spite of Fanon's glowing rhetoric about her equality in the revolution and how this gave the lie to accusations of Algerian male unfairness to her.

> ... the Algerian woman assumes all the tasks entrusted to her. Among the tasks entrusted to the Algerian woman is the bearing of messages or complicated verbal orders learned by heart, sometimes despite complete absence of schooling. But she is also called upon to stand watch for an hour and often more, before a house where district leaders are conferring. (p. 53)

That the district and revolutionary leaders are all male and do not include women in the decision-making is evident from a number of statements (emphasis is added):

> During those interminable minutes when she must avoid standing still, so as not to attract attention, and avoid venturing too far since she is responsible for the safety of the *brothers* within, incidents that are at once funny and pathetic are not infrequent. (p. 53)
>
> Meanwhile the woman who might be acting as a liaison agent, as a bearer of tracts, as she walked some hundred or two hundred meters ahead of the *man under whose orders she was working*, still wore a veil ... (p. 51)

Fanon reveals the hypocrisy of the male Third World when he mocks the "allegations" that the Algerian female is oppressed. His defense of Algerian male culture is every bit as smooth as the French justification of colonial rule. And he denies female oppression under the guise of defending the Algerian national culture from vulture-like attacks by the French. No one will doubt that the French were brutal colonizers of the Algerians, but that does not either deny or excuse the equally brutal colonization of Algerian females by Algerian males. Fanon says:

> ... the dominant administration solemnly undertook to defend this woman, pictured as humiliated, sequestered, cloistered. ... It described the immense possibilities of woman, unfortunately transformed by the Algerian man into an inert, demonetized, indeed dehumanized object. The behavior of the Algerian was very firmly denounced and described as medieval and barbaric.
>
> Lamentations were organized. "We want to make the Algerian ashamed of the fate that he metes out to women." Algerian women were invited to play a "functional,

capital role" in the transformation of their lot. They were pressed to say no to a centuries-old subjection.

> After it had been posited that the woman constituted the pivot of Algerian society, all efforts were made to obtain control over her. (p. 38)

Never once does Fanon see the Algerian woman simply as a pawn of both the French male-supremacist culture and the Algerian males, neither of whom were interested in her humanity. What he does instead is to deny her oppression and then to sympathize with Algerian male colonists who used her oppression as a symbol of their manhood and Algerian culture. In fact he is terribly moved by the plight of the Algerian male in his fight to retain control over "his woman." The Algerian male has his manhood (synonymous with male culture and control) destroyed by any attempts to "free" the Algerian woman. So he clings more tenaciously to his dominance which he equates with his culture.

> Converting the woman . . . wrenching her free from her status, was at the same time achieving a real power over the man and attaining a practical effective means of destructuring Algerian culture.
>
> The Algerian men, for their part, are a target of criticism for their European comrades, or more officially for their bosses. "Does your wife wear the veil? Why don't you take your wife to the movies, to the fights, or to the cafe? . . . The boss will invite the Algerian employee and his wife. Before this formal summons, the Algerian sometimes experiences moments of difficulty. If he comes with his wife, it means admitting defeat, it means prostituting his wife, exhibiting her, abandoning a mode of resistance. . . . [There are] traps set by the European in order to bring the Algerian to expose himself, to declare: "My wife wears a veil, she shall not go out," or else to betray: "Since you want to see her, here she is," would bring out the sadistic and perverse character of these contacts and relationships and would show in microcosm the tragedy of the colonial situation on the psychological level, the way the two systems directly confront each other, the epic of the colonized society, with its specific ways of existing, in the face of the colonialist hydra. (pp. 39, 40)

It seems never to occur to Fanon that the "sadistic and perverse character of these contacts and relationships" between the male and female in Algerian culture shows also the "tragedy of the colonial situation" of females "on the psychological level." Fanon, for all his justified bitterness and hatred of the French and European colonizer, does not have a corresponding sense of justice for the plight of the colonized Algerian female.

Perhaps it would be too difficult, psychologically, to admit that the Algerian males have been doing to the Algerian females for many centuries what has been done to Algeria for 130 years by the French. Perhaps it would not be so easy to appear the "innocent" oppressed if the Algerian males had also to admit their own colonial rule of Algerian females. Because the Algerian male then might have to identify consciously with his own French oppressor to see his own role in relation to "his" women. This is why Fanon reacts so vehemently against the idea—the actual facts— of female domination by the Algerian male. And this is probably why the French male colonizers knew they could cut so deep on this issue.

But there is such a thing as justice, whether our own personal guilt is touched or not. And if, as Fanon so passionately argued, anything necessary to win freedom for the oppressed colonial culture is to be done, then he should honestly accept that principle for the colonial oppression of women. Otherwise he should reconsider whether he himself as a male does not have a strong interest in and identification with being a colonial oppressor. Perhaps he should then consider what this means in terms of his philosophy of violence and terrorism for the "unredeemable" oppressor. Perhaps women too can achieve catharsis through terrorism against the colonial male culture. But does Fanon want that? Does any male "revolutionary" want that?

The Betrayal of Female Culture in the Anti-Imperialist Revolution

All of Fanon's emotional sympathy is wrapped up with the male Algerian wherever it is a question of two male cultures—European and Algerian—clashing over who will control the colonized status of the female Algerian. But a female has a different view of things—that is, a female who can see through both the European and Algerian colonial male cultures.

A few years after Algeria won its independence, Fadela M'Rabet, an Algerian woman, wrote a book entitled *La Femme Algérienne* (published by Maspero). In it she charged that the women who fought in the Resistance were used in the Algerian nationalist revolution only to be returned to their former subservience after "independence" was gained. She said that not very many women participated in the struggle and their lives were never affected in any way. She compared the position of women in Algeria before and after the "revolution" to the position of black Africans in South Africa, and cites case after case of the oppression of women in "liberated" Algeria. She says:

> In order to understand the situation of the woman (and her reactions) it is necessary to start with the man; if she submits or revolts, if she accepts her condition or does not, the Algerian woman has evolved in a world which is made by men, for men, and at his advantage only. The Constitution, without doubt, and the resolutions of the Congress proclaim the equality of all citizens; but the gap is such between the texts and the facts that all is as if the texts did not exist.
>
> Socially the most honorable, the state of the married woman is, *in fact*, as degrading as that of the concubine. . . . The mother, the wife; there is for the Algerian man a third category of women—the sister. And if it is not very comfortable to be the mistress or the wife of an Algerian man, it is nearly a calamity to be his sister . . . it is allowed to him to completely dominate her.

Let us listen to another Algerian woman concerning the "cultural symbol" of the Arab culture, the veil. Claudine, in an interview in a *New York Times Magazine* article (October, 1967) after Algerian independence was won, said that she was lucky that her father allowed her to go to school and not wear the veil. Most Algerian girls get no schooling—even after the revolution—because, as Fadela M'Rabet has said, too much schooling for a girl is considered very dangerous by the male society. But the local Mufti intervened when Claudine was sixteen. By that time there were only two other girls in her class at the lycée, and twenty-five boys. The other girls went veiled. The Mufti insisted that Claudine do the same or quit school; her father would be banned from the Mosque if she refused. She says:

> ... so I had to agree. The Mufti still complained though. When I rode to school, he always stood watching for me, and I had to get down off my bicycle and kiss his hand on my way to and from school. It wasn't easy because in Constantine they don't use the nose veil. There is just a great big square you wrap all around you, covering everything except one eye. You have to hold it closed with your teeth and your hands....

It is also interesting to note that Ben Bella in 1964—two years after independence—did not share Fanon's opinion that women's oppression was a fabrication of the French colonialists. Ben Bella said at this time:

> There are in our country five million women who submit to a servitude unworthy of Socialist and Moslem Algeria. The liberation of the woman is not a secondary aspect which is to be put under our other objectives: it is a problem, the solution of which is a preliminary to the whole nature of socialism. [quoted in *La Femme Algérienne*]

But Fadela M'Rabet lays the blame for women's oppression on the Moslem tradition of male privilege in the home, separation of the sexes in school, and perpetuation of a racist notion that women are objects worthy only of disdain. She says, "If we really want to end our underdeveloped status, then let's not wait. Let's ban apartheid." She argues eloquently for a female revolution now.

> Must we wait several generations under the pretext that our society is not "ready"? We [Algeria] are the product of 130 years of colonialism. *But how many centuries of exploitation have women lived under: Their colonizers have been the men.* (Emphasis added)

We use the example of Algeria only to show that a nationalist, anti-imperialist revolution does not free women because the dominant male culture is identified as the national culture and male supremacy is never attacked.

Women have always been used and abused in male revolutions because the male revolutionists are colonialist imperialists in relation to females. It is as if the Algerians fighting with the French in World War II expected the French to liberate Algeria. The French didn't want to be dominated by another country but they wanted to continue their own domination of Algeria. Males don't want to be dominated by other males or another male culture, but they have no intention of discontinuing their domination of the female culture.

No anti-capitalist, working-class, Third World, anti-imperialist etc. movement will ever free women. There is too much at stake for the male colonialists to ever give up their privileges without a struggle. And they control all of those movements as they control all the national cultures.

The female culture will continue to be betrayed by the ruling male culture and by male revolutionaries whose primary identification is with male culture.

The anti-imperialist movement as it is defined by males is a dead end for women. Males, as members of the dominant male culture in the Third World as well as in the imperialist countries, are equally concerned with maintaining male dominance though they may be in a death struggle between themselves.

Oppressed Groups and the Feminine

There have been a great deal of comparisons of woman's position with the position of minority groups in feminist literature. Particularly, there have been comparisons between stereotypes of black people and women. Women are described as fitting the typical Negro stereotype and comparisons are made between black oppression and female oppression to prove that females are in fact an oppressed group.

But really the analogy should go the other way around. One should compare the stereotypes of blacks and other minority groups and suppressed cultures to the female stereotypes.

Woman was the first group to be oppressed and subordinated as a caste to another group—men. Without going into all the reasons for this subordination, we can still discuss the psychological and cultural results. A schizophrenic split developed when the dominating males projected onto women all of their emotions which they could not reconcile with their self-image and role as dominators, and which they were afraid of and would not allow themselves to be "weakened" by.

This schizophrenic split made female and male definitions into opposites. Generally, since males are defined as the human norm, females are defined as their subhuman negatives. Yin and Yang define the male and female stereotypes as opposites, with females getting the negative characteristics. Men are seen as "day," positive, forceful, aggressive, dominant, objective, strong, intellective, etc. Women have been defined for thousands of years as weak, "night," passive, emotional, intuitive, mysterious, unresponsible, quarrelsome, childish, dependent, evil, submissive, etc.

(A study was done at Worcester State Hospital in Massachusetts using a sex-role questionnaire with over a hundred polar items, one pole being stereotypically male and the other stereotypically female. The subjects, a group of clinical professionals, assigned a mentally healthy adult and a mentally healthy male the same characteristics. But a mentally healthy female was seen as passive, emotional, dependent, less competitive, non-objective, submissive, and more easily influenced.—*Psychology Today*, September, 1970, p. 53.)

As females were the first colonized group and the first to be stereotyped as a caste, male culture, when it extended its boundaries and subjected other males or male cultures to its rule, defined them as inferior by assigning them female characteristics. Female characteristics were the only negative characteristics the male culture knew.

A male as a male in relation to females is defined by all the masculine stereotypes, but that same male in subjection to another male is defined as inferior through having female qualities. He is then "effeminate" or passive, or weak—all of which are female stereotypes. This idea can be extended to a culture. One male culture which dominates and controls another male culture defines the subservient males and their culture as feminine, i.e., all the female stereotypes become the minority stereotypes for the subjected males. They are defined, by being subservient, as mysterious, emotional, intuitive, personal, childlike, evil, irresponsible, quarrelsome, passive, dependent, etc. This holds for all subjected male national cultures and racial cultures.

But the female within the subjected male national or racial culture is defined twice as female. In other words, her definition as a female is her primary definition. For example a black woman is defined as a woman by all the female stereotypes—as passive, emotional, intuitive, personal, mysterious, quarrelsome, irresponsible, dependent, etc. The imposition of these stereotypes on her again in the form of racial stereotypes is unnecessary as they are basically the imposition of female stereotypes on the males of the race. And when the racial battle is won and her race is free, she will realize that the stereotypes—though they no longer oppress her man—are still her defining stereotypes as a woman. He now has his manhood back (defined as opposites of female stereotypes), but she continues to be defined by her womanhood as inferior.

The problem of male supremacy comes in again when national (male) and racial (male) cultures repudiate the female characterizations and stereotypes assigned to them in revolting against their male dominators. What happens is that they assert their manhood, i.e., male dominance stereotypes, against the female stereotypes which they have come to loathe as depriving them of virility and their "natural" "birthright" as dominators, i.e. males. They make a super-identification with the male culture in reaction to the female. They try to become tough super-males in reaction to the imposition of female stereotypes upon them. Then we have the "don't deprive me of my manhood, i.e. balls" and "stand behind me, woman, where you belong" syndrome. Often there is such a strong open reaction against the female culture that the females of the suppressed national or racial group are threatened and defined as castrating females if they don't become invisible and get where they belong—in the subservient female culture, into silence, and "prone" as Stokely Carmichael once said.

The males of the suppressed national or racial group never question the values of the male culture which impinges upon them and which they impose upon "their" women. They accept the right of a male to dominate but feel it should be limited to females and revolt to overthrow the dominant male culture's rule over them.

The problem is that the original split between the stereotypes of male and female which started this whole mess will never be resolved by the suppressed male national or racial culture, as the suppressed males are too busy trying to prove they are super-males and that they don't have female characteristics in any way. They loathe the female principle as having defined them as inferiors—with its symbolic castration.

Up with the Female Principle

Only the suppressed female culture in all races, in all lands, can be proud of the female principle. For females need not prove their "manhood," as they can never be males or a part of the dominant male world culture. Therefore women will be forced, by the very fact of being female, to defend and raise the banner of the female principle.

All of the female culture traits are defined as negatives by the dominant world culture. We do not believe them to be so (except all those that keep us subservient, such as passivity, self-sacrifice, etc.).

We are proud of the female culture of emotion, intuition, love, personal relationships, etc., as the most essential human characteristics. It is our male colonizers—it is the male culture—who have defined essential humanity out of their identity and who are "culturally deprived."

We are also proud as females of our heritage of known and unknown resisters to male colonial domination and values.

We are proud of the female principle and will not deny it to gain our freedom.

It is only by asserting the long suppressed and ridiculed female principle that a truly human society will come about. For the split between the male and the female will only be bridged and a fully human identity developed—encompassing in each person all human characteristics which were previously split up into male and female—when the female principle and culture is no longer suppressed and male domination is ended forever.

We identify with all women of all races, classes, and countries all over the world. The female culture is the Fourth World.

Author's Postscript

The female culture and the male culture are not natural; they are artificial creations of a male-dominated world. The artificial split between what has been defined as female and what has been defined as male has nothing to do with the inherent nature or potential of females or males. The definitions of the male principle and female principle and the female and male cultures are social definitions only. They are abstractions of a primal abstraction—the splitting up of the whole human personality into the caricatures known as male and female, masculine and feminine.

This "Manifesto" was never intended to be a glorification of the female principle and culture. It was never intended to imply that women have more "soul" than men or that women are inherently more human than men. It is simply a truth that there is a split between the female and male and that the female half of life has been suppressed by the male half of life. Those things which have been socially defined as female have been suppressed in males and suppressed in society through the oppression of females.

If one is born a male one is taught to repress one's "female" self and to develop only those things which will make one a true "man" and a part of the male culture. If one is born a female one is taught to repress that part of oneself which is "male" and to develop only those parts of the self which will make one a "true woman" and able to fit into the submissive female culture.

The extreme of the male culture has become a grotesque caricature of part of the potential inherent in every human being, whether female or male. Why are so many blind to the grotesqueness of the tough, hard, super-balls, insensitive, unemotional male image in John Wayne, James Bond, the Marines, etc.? Or so blind to the grotesqueness of the super-mind, intellect, reasoning, and abstraction removed from any connection with life in the "think tanks" of the Rand Corporation, the academy, the corporations, the Army Corps of Engineers, most scientific research, war games strategies, etc.?

The extreme of the female culture has also become a grotesque caricature of the potential inherent in every human being. Why are so many blind to the grotesqueness of the super-sex goddesses, the sex-object removed from mind and emotion, the motherhood myth, the pettily personal existence which is not allowed to transcend itself into the individual autonomous existence, the enforced delicacy without full feeling and intensity, the sentiment turned into bathos because removed from direct sexual or creative expression, etc.?

The abstractions of male and female are extreme and many people are not molded wholly into either category—there is a great deal of overlap. But no one in the society is allowed to be a whole human being as long as the tyranny of the male and female culture or sex role split exists.

Recently there has been an unfortunate reaction among some women's liberationists and feminists. Some women have begun to call anything which they do not like "male." They seem to think that anything that has been defined as a "male quality" is inherently bad. A woman who is strong or takes initiative is told that she is "acting like a man" or "talking like a man." The crushing of initiative and strength and self-expression in women is now being done by other women in the movement under the guise of "anti-elitism," "anti-male-identification," and "collective self-suppression." It would be a tragedy if women were to make our oppressed state into a virtue and a model of humanity and the new society. We need to sift out what is good in our imposed definition as females and to honestly examine what is stupid and self-destructive. We need also to sift out what is good in what has been defined as male and therefore denied expression in us. We need no more glorification of the oppressed and their "super-soul" and "superior" culture, for that will blind us to our weaknesses and only lead us back into the same mire from which we have been trying to free ourselves.

Neither the male culture nor the female culture is a model for a human society.

It is true that women have no recourse other than to rise up in a strong feminist movement to end male domination. We must have our own independent women's movement free from male interference and domination. But we should not lose sight of our ultimate goals. There is a danger that the women's movement will help destroy its own ends if the split between the female and male is made into a new feminist orthodoxy. The women's movement has to be free enough to explore and change the entire range of human relationships and it must be open enough to heal the split between the female and male and draw out the total human potential of every person. If we want to be free as female human beings, we must really be willing to end the split of the human personality that has cut men off from a part of themselves and which has caused untold suffering to women.

Chapter Twenty-Two

The Comingest Womanifesto

Jill Johnston

first or second off i'm into thinking weird all in these difference places in fact in as many places as we are women and so i ask myself when i meet this one or that one i ask where is them politically sexually & where is one in relation to this one or me or where am i now sexually politically since i'm not the me i was yesterday or last year and where are we going or am i already ahead of myself or behind and is somebody else slightly behind or ahead of that and if not then what or what anything i mean how should we behave and where should we think or what are we permitted to assume much less concerning anybody else their total life their total past who are they who am i who am i to them to become if anything & so on like is the one i'm talking to about to sleep with a woman for the first time in which case would i cause her not to if i accused her of oppressing me by being the kind of woman who sleeps with the man and if she does anyway will she then be terrified to think she might be thought a lesbian and if so should we condemn her for thinking what we were all brought up all these centuries to actually think altho we now think we're so smart just because a few of us now know that it not only isn't bad it's great in fact it's the best and that that when you ponder it makes us the Ultimate Feminists etc. i mean we think we're really hot shit and we are and so what is that gonna do for us when so many women are still so scared the question is do we want more of us or do we want to just go around saying what hot shit we are and how you straight women are lousing us up just to make sure they'll go on doing it and if so how long would it take before the women called lesbians reemerge as a special interest group and how long after that before you can't say the word lesbian at all any more as if there *is* such a thing as a lesbian the boggler being the more i say it the more i feel it doesn't exist since so many women now actually are lesbians and you wouldn't hear anybody anymore say well huff huff this woman must be a lesbian because she hated her father and her mother was a bitch or whatever they say along those lines or she got to be a lesbian harumph because she had a terrible first sexual experience with a man and all that you wouldn't hear that except in these clinical psychiatric journals anyway even tho from this new point of view there may be no such thing as a lesbian any more and besides which we know now that all lesbians are women i have to go on saying it to make sure anybody knows i'm defining myself politically as a woman committed woman and the word feminist to me doesn't totally convey that idea since so many feminists advocate a change in our situation in relation to the man rather than the devotion of our energies to our own kind to women i have to ask does this make us enemies when we are all potentially dedicated to ourselves and when we believe in feminist issues per se i.e., abortion reform and when we are in a sense each of us all the women we ever were including straight possibly just yesterday or last year or the last time i slept with a man two years ago or four years before that in a tenement on houston street with two kids still thinking i was straight and i was even tho i was in love with a woman i still am that woman i am all the women i ever was which is all the women of the world in transition i become more completely a lesbian or woman commited woman as the centuries pass and more of me becomes me or the me i think it's such hot shit to be which it is by which i mean a woman the more i sleep with myself and eat myself and write myself and breathe myself the more woman i become i become the woman myself i am who i sleep with it doesn't mean you're not a lesbian if you never slept with a woman before if you consider the person you sleep with the most is yourself and that's you a woman from this point of view we all are lesbians right from the start altho what we are and what we think or say we are can be altogether different things it doesn't matter even by the sights of advanced ideology you can't demand that people be where they're not yet ready to be even if you say all persuasive and important listen a woman committed to herself meaning a woman as combined image of mother daughter and sister was is absolutely at odds with society which has been in the modern western world organized around the principle of heterosexuality which in effect means the prime commitment of woman to man who is committed to himself or saying it another way if you say what i really mean when i say you're oppressing me when you sleep with the man is that you're giving something so vital to the man is the same as withholding it from me your daughter your sister or how in effect you go to bed with my brother by paying him more attention you deprive me in proportion as you do so is all very good logic possibly especially when we can say furthermore look you who have for centuries given your best services to your sons what in the end have the sons done for us if not to persuade us or coerce us to serve more sons okay and go on and say and look around you do you see any lesbians becoming straight and so on no matter what we say however i'm convinced we can't very well demand what anybody isn't ready to give who may in fact be ready to change tomorrow or next year who may know a lot more in advance of her current opportunities or her present practical situation or emotional readiness or who may be putting her life in order to make big changes we don't know about anyway who probably won't be significantly impressed by anything so much as the example of our own togetherness all of which doesn't alter it's true the social fact that the very women we wait for continue to hurt us by damning us or ignoring us or hating us or tolerating us or condescending us for loving ourselves or oppressing us by objectifying us as potential Lesbian Experiences or projecting onto us the sexism and puritanism and chauvinism of their own expectations of all they've known in relation to the man we won't stop them from doing this by accusing them of it or by objectifying them in turn by say making any woman a princess or an all purpose mommie or even necessarily by carrying on about how when you saw me at that party and said so you have breasts what you meant was so you're a woman after all like a guy saying to a faggot in a locker room you really do have balls as though a lesbian or woman committed women is less than a woman or somehow a male for liking other women the way males do supposedly and thus being less a woman not being a woman in the sisterhood of man pandering females or when you say oh i happen to love a woman now but i could as well have a relationship with a man if he were the right sort of person as tho we were not all *persons* before the *feminists* taught us we were women in the sense of being a political class in which case what you're really saying is if the right sort of *man* came along or when you say if all else fails we'll try loving our sisters as if your sister was a last resort and even if you do think you mean just sex i translate it to mean loving your sisters which means sex and *every*thing i still know the truth is demonstrable only by example and the only way to proceed historically is to respect personal places places even we feel are detaining us or delaying us or detering us we respect them nevertheless for being the places any woman is capable of being the way we respect a wasp for being a wasp we don't condemn a wasp for being the type of animal who would sting us if she could i don't want to pursue the example the example that concerns me here is the assertion of our own logic and model in this way enough women by a few centuries time will become the hot shit we think we are to make a viable amazon nation or tribe or tribes of women capable of sustaining themselves independently of the male specious we have to remind ourselves that in 1972 in amerika we are a fugitive band who can't afford to isolate ourselves from the woman in the middle who in any case remains a potentially total ally or the woman we are gradually becoming as we become more of ourselves as we leave more of our straight selves of ourselves behind ourselves we gradually become ourselves all the women we ever were we are ourselves still the woman in the middle it doesn't make any sense to be our own enemy and if we don't see common cause with feminists feminists are not likely to see it with us either especially when it's so easy to find reason by offense to say we'll have nothing to do with you when it's still so scary to proclaim the legitimacy of an identity so recently criminal or sick or sinful we must therefore as i see it take all the chances and risk being the ones to continue being hurt and insulted by exposing our thought as the logic of the feminist/ lesbian position and exposing our selves as the models of the revolution by realizing we are each and all all the women of the world in transition and not placing ourselves thus above and beyond or ahead but directly in the center as the moving force of our collective conscience.

RESOLUTION OF LESBIANS INTERNATIONAL*

Resolution of Lesbians International in its western hemispherical conference of an estimated 70,000 lesbians at the Lavender Whale Inn, Round Grove, Missouri:

*This piece is a very slight modification—a turn-about—of a resolution of the National Organization for Women (N.O.W.) which "recognized lesbianism as a feminist issue."

Lesbians International came out in favor of feminist rights.

Whereas, because she defines herself in relation to men, the straight feminist is considered unnatural, incomplete, not quite a woman—as though the essence of womanhood were to be identified with women; and

Whereas, feminists were never excluded from Lesbians International, but we have been evasive or apologetic about their presence within the organization. Afraid of encouraging public (i.e. male) support, we have often treated feminists as the step-sisters of the movement, allowed them to work with us, but then expected them to hide in the upstairs closet when the company comes. Asking women to disguise their identities so that they will not "embarrass" the group is an intolerable form of oppression, like asking white women to join us in black face. Lesbians International must reassess the priorities that sacrifice principles to "image."

Whereas, we are affected by society's prejudices against the heterosexual woman whether we acknowledge it or not: as lesbians we are all subject to straight-baiting by opponents who use the tactic of labeling us the worst thing they can think of, "heterosexual," in order to divide and discredit the movement and bring women to heel. Even within Lesbians International this tactic has been employed by some members who insist that feminists are a special interest group whose primary concern is men. Lesbians International is inevitably weakened by these attempts to undermine the spirit and efforts of its members; we can no longer afford to ignore the problem.

Therefore, be it resolved: That Lesbians International recognizes feminism as a lesbian issue.

Chapter Twenty-Three

Radical Women Manifesto, Seattle

As RADICAL WOMEN we understand and promulgate the concept that THE WOMAN QUESTION IS A DECISIVE ISSUE IN THE UNFOLDING OF THE AMERICAN REVOLUTION, because the special and peculiar exploitation of women in the United States has created specially oppressed sex whose potential for revolt and capacity of leadership are second to none.

The current leadership of the women's movement is largely student, professional, middle-class, and white. But its future leadership will emerge from the vast ranks of militant women from the working class and from ethnic and sexual minorities. These women come into direct and daily conflict with bosses on the job, and with racists and sexists on every level of life. They develop a keener awareness and consciousness of the triple nature of oppression—class, race, and sex—than is possible for most white, non-working, middle-class women.

The raw battle for sheer survival in the everyday world of imperialist America has equipped minority women, women workers, and lesbians with a talent for discipline and respect for theory because the life of the ghetto woman, the working mother, and the independent woman depends upon clear-headedness, self-control, and organization. They accordingly demand these qualities in any movement that claims to be mature and realistic. They have the least to lose and the most to gain in changing capitalism. They are radicalized and tempered by their actual victimization in life, rather than through intellectual choice.

It is precisely such women who are still studying and watching "women's lib" with mingled interest and suspicion—those women who join nothing lightly but are ready to devote their lives completely when they do commit—who are destined for eventual leadership of the entire movement.

Feminism: Class Struggle or Sex Struggle

The "radical feminists" have decreed that, contrary to Engels, women's oppression was an inevitable result of what they describe as our physical inferiority—our smaller size and lesser physical prowess. Women, they say, were historically oppressed by men because men were bigger and stronger and could push women around, and because, women, by virtue of their child-bearing function, were slaves of their own biology. Shulamith Firestone, in *The Dialectics of Sex*, describes in detail the supposed agonies of women in primitive child-bearing, and women's constant death and disease due to our inferior biology. This historical variation of Freud's spurious "biology is destiny" holds that the conflicts between men and women are innate, and that male supremacy is and always has been the fundamental problem of human society, surpassing class and race in depth and historical importance. The quest for power is seen by radical feminists as an inevitable male trait, rather than a relatively recent social phenomenon developing out of the economic needs of private property relations.

Equality for women, they contend, is only now possible due to birth control and cybernetics. Only by abolishing our child-bearing function can we be free, they say, thus implying that our child-bearing functions do, in fact, make us inferior to men.

What is needed, they say, is a pitched battle with men, *all* men, for control of society. The real revolution, to them is the sex revolution, in which women will simply overthrow male control of the system—regardless of what the character of the system might be.

In their confusion of biology for history and psychology for culture, "radical feminists" ignore the economic foundations of women's historic exploitation and oppression, claiming that *no* economic system can guarantee equality for women, because no economic system can guarantee changes in the attitudes and culture of male chauvinism.

Fortunately, the "radical feminists" are wrong—wrong in their historical analysis, and wrong in their conclusions. The facts are that women are and always have been more adaptable and more capable of survival than men, and that the relationship between child-bearing, physical strength, and oppression is a development that is an effect of private property and the evils of an economic system. The key to emancipation for women is given to us by the very history of women in primitive communes where modern value judgements on childbirth and physical size were unheard of, and where equality was determined by women's equal status in the productive labor force of the society. THIS IS STILL THE CASE, AND THAT IS WHY FOR MODERN WOMEN, SOCIALISM, NOT CYBERNETICS, IS THE ROAD TO EQUALITY, BECAUSE ONLY SOCIALISM CAN ONCE AGAIN BRING WOMEN BACK INTO EQUALITY IN SOCIAL PRODUCTION, AND THUS, TO FULL SOCIAL, ECONOMIC, AND PERSONAL EQUALITY.

Women are the majority of this country, and the majority of the world's population. And we constitute not only an absolute majority, but at least half of every ethnic grouping and every class. We are potentially the greatest social and political force in the world, because we have the least economic, political, and social stake in the status quo, and the most pressing need for revolutionary social change. THE NEED AND STRENGTH OF WOMEN IS THE REALITY THAT MUST DICTATE OUR TACTICS.

C. Methods:
Consciousness-Raising

Chapter Twenty-Four

A Program For Feminist Consciousness-Raising

Kathie Sarachild

Our feelings (emotions) revolve around our perceptions of our self-interest.

We assume that our feelings are telling us something from which we can learn . . . that our feelings mean something worth analyzing . . . that our feelings are saying something *political*, something reflecting fear that something bad will happen to us or hope, desire, knowledge that something good will happen to us.

Feelings aren't something we assume ahead of time that we should be on top of or underneath. Feelings are something that, at first anyway, we are with, that is we examine and try to understand before we decide it's the kind of feeling to stay on top of (that is, control, stifle, stop), or the kind of feeling to be underneath (that is, let ourselves go with, let it lead us into something new and better . . . at first to a new and better *idea* of where we want to go and then to action which might help us get there).

Now male culture assumes that feelings are something that people should stay on top of and puts women down for being led by their feelings (being underneath them).

We're saying that women have all along been generally in touch with their feelings (rather than underneath them) and that their being in touch with their feelings has been their greatest strength, historically and for the future. We have also been so in touch with our feelings, as a matter of fact, that we have used our feelings as our best available weapon—hysterics, whining, bitching, etc.—given that our best form of defense against those with power to control our lives was their feelings toward us, sexual and otherwise, feelings which they always tried to fight themselves.

We're saying that for most of history sex was, in fact, both our undoing and our only possible weapon of self-defense and self-assertion (aggression).

We're saying that when we had hysterical fits, when we took things "too" personally, that we weren't underneath our feelings, but responding with our feelings correctly to a given situation of injustice. I say correctly because at that time in history (and maybe even still), by first feeling and then revealing our emotions we were acting in the best strategical manner. And this may be the reason we learned how to be so in touch with our feelings to begin with.

In our groups, let's share our feelings and pool them. Let's let ourselves go and see where our feelings lead us. Our feelings will lead us to ideas and then to actions.

Our feelings will lead us to our theory, our theory to our action, our feelings about that action to new theory and then to new action.

November, 1968

This is a consciousness-raising program for those of us who are feeling more and more that women are about the most exciting people around, at this stage of time, anyway, and that the seeds of a new and beautiful world society lie buried in the consciousness of this very class which has been abused and oppressed since the beginning of human history. It is a program planned on the assumption that a mass liberation movement will develop as more and more women begin to perceive their situation correctly and that, therefore, our primary task right now is to awaken "class" consciousness in ourselves and others on a mass scale. The following outline is just one hunch of what a theory of mass consciousness-raising would look like in skeleton form.

I. The "bitch session" cell group
    A. Ongoing consciousness expansion
        1. Personal recognition and testimony
            a. Recalling and sharing our bitter experiences
            b. Expressing our feelings about our experiences both at the time they occurred and at present
            c. Expressing our feelings about ourselves, men, other women
            d. Evaluating our feelings
        2. Personal testimony—methods of group practice
            a. Going around the room with key questions on key topics
            b. Speaking our experience—at random
            c. Cross examination
        3. Relating and generalizing individual testimony
            a. Finding the common root when different women have opposite feelings and experiences
            b. Examining the negative and positive aspects of each woman's feelings and her way of dealing with her situation as a woman
    B. Classic forms of resisting consciousness, or: How to avoid facing the awful truth
        1. Anti-womanism
        2. Glorification of the oppressor
        3. Excusing the oppressor (and feeling sorry for him)
        4. False identification with the oppressor and other socially privileged groups
        5. Shunning identification with one's own oppressed group and other oppressed groups
        6. Romantic fantasies, utopian thinking and other forms of confusing present reality with what one wishes reality to be
        7. Thinking one has power in the traditional role—can "get what one wants," has power behind the throne, etc.
        8. Belief that one has found an adequate personal solution or will be able to find one without large social changes.
        9. Self-cultivation, rugged individualism, seclusion, and other forms of go-it-alonism
        10. Self-blame!
        11. Ultra-militancy; and others??
    C. Recognizing the survival reasons for resisting consciousness
    D. "Starting to Stop"—overcoming repressions and delusions
        1. Daring to see, or: Taking off the rose-colored glasses

      a. Reasons for repressing one's own consciousness

        1) Fear of feeling the full weight of one's painful situation

        2) Fear of feeling one's past wasted and meaningless (plus wanting others to go through the same obstacles)

        3) Fear of despair for the future

      b. Analyzing which fears are valid and which invalid

        1) Examining the objective conditions in one's own past and in the lives of most women throughout history

        2) Examining objective conditions for the present

      c. Discussing possible methods of struggle

        1) History of women's struggle and resistance to oppression

        2) Possibilities for individual struggle at present

        3) Group struggle

    2. Daring to share one's experience with the group

      a. Sources of hesitancy

        1) Fear of personal exposure (fear of being thought stupid, immoral, weak, self-destructive, etc. by the group)

        2) Feeling of loyalty to one's man, boss, parents, children, friends, "the Movement"

        3) Fear of reprisal if the word gets out (losing one's man, job, reputation)

        4) Fear of hurting the feelings of someone in the group

        5) Not seeing how one's own experience is relevant to others, or vice versa

      b. Deciding which fears are valid and which invalid

      c. Structuring the group so that it is relatively safe for people to participate in it

D. Understanding and developing radical feminist theory

    1. Using above techniques to arrive at an understanding of oppression wherever it exists in our lives—our oppression as black people, workers, tenants, consumers, children, or whatever as well as our oppression as women

    2. Analyzing whatever privileges we may have—the white skin privilege, the education and citizenship of a big-power (imperialist) nation privilege, and seeing how these help to perpetuate our oppression as women, workers

E. Consciousness-raiser (organizer) training—so that every woman in a given bitch session cell group herself becomes an "organizer" of other groups

    1. The role of the consciousness-raiser ("organizer")

      a. Dares to participate; dares to expose herself, bitch

      b. Dares to struggle

    2. Learning how to bring theory down to earth

      a. Speaking in terms of personal experience

    3. Learning to "relate"

      a. To sisters in the group

      b. To other women

      c. Friends and allies

      d. Enemies

    4. Particular problems of starting a new group

II. Consciousness-raising Actions

  A. Zap actions

    1. Movie benefits, attacks on cultural phenomena and events, stickers, buttons, posters, film

   B. Consciousness programs
      1. Newspapers, broadsides, storefronts, women's liberation communes, literature, answering mail, others . . . ??
   C. Utilizing the mass media
III. Organizing
   A. Helping new people start groups
   B. Intra-group communication and actions
      1. Monthly meetings
      2. Conferences

Chapter Twenty-Five

The Small Group Process

Pamela Allen

The group processes described in this chapter were discussed and identified by Sudsofloppen after we had been meeting for over a year. This was one of the first times that we turned our growing ability to analyze onto ourselves and our own activity. The experience of working out these concepts collectively was very exciting for us all. The processes may seem a little arbitrary and too structured for some of you but we are a group which believes that there is always a structure, the issue is to consciously choose one that will encourage our growth rather than just hope that it will happen. We think this way because our early activity was consciously unstructured—we thought—and we found that letting things just happen meant that the strongest personalities controlled the meetings and that it was very easy to avoid areas of discussion that were difficult. The group processes as described here are impersonal and they ensure that those of us who find it hard to open up about feelings will be challenged to do so. The same is true for women who fear analysis and would rather stay only on the subjective level. The total process is not easy but we feel that *each* process is necessary to understanding the human experience. We believe that theory and analysis which are not rooted in concrete experience (practice) are useless, but we also maintain that for the concrete, everyday experiences to be understood, they must be subjected to the processes of analysis and abstraction.

Opening Up

This is a very individual need: the need for a woman to open up and talk about her feelings about herself and her life. In the beginning of a group experience opening up is a reaching out to find human contact with other women. Later it becomes a way to communicate to others about one's subjective feelings—about the group, about the women's movement, about one's life.

Our society alienates us from our feelings. However, this is less true for women than for men. It is imperative for our understanding of ourselves and for our mental health that we maintain and deepen our contact with our feelings. Our first concern must not be with whether these feelings are good or bad but what they are. Feelings are a reality. To deny their existence does not get rid of them. Rather it is through admitting them that one can begin to deal with her feelings.

Opening up is an essential but difficult process for a group. In its early stages a group usually fosters a feeling of intimacy and trust which frees women to discuss their fears and problems. This is because most women have been isolated and alone and the group experience is the first time they have found others who like themselves are frustrated with their lot as women in this society. Every woman who has tried to articulate her loss of a sense of identity to her husband knows the despair of not being understood. Any woman who has tried to explain her driving need to have a life of her own and sees her words falling on the incomprehending ears of family and friends knows the horror of being alone, being seen by others as some kind of freak. Any woman who has admitted that she is unhappy and depressed but can't explain why, knows the pain of not being taken seriously. Isolated, always getting negative responses to her attempts to communicate her feelings about her condition, it is very easy to begin to question herself, to see her problems in personal terms.

The group offers women a place where the response will be positive. "Yes, we know." "Yes, we understand." It is not so much the words that are said in response that are important; rather it is the fact that someone listens and does not ridicule; someone listens and acknowledges validity of another's view of her life. It is the beginning of sisterhood, the feeling of unity with others, of no longer being alone.

The early group experience of closeness—the honeymoon period as some call it— fosters opening up about one's feelings towards oneself and one's life. But as the group begins to function on a long term basis and the members participate in activities in a women's movement, it becomes harder to be honest about one's feelings for sometimes they are negative and may involve another woman. Yet such disclosures are necessary if trust and sisterhood are to become long term realities. Neither a group nor a movement can function if there is latent distrust and hostility or overt back biting going on. In addition an individual cannot be free to trust in herself and in others if she is suppressing feelings and allowing them to cloud her thinking and activity.

Opening up is a personal need to admit to and express one's emotions—her joys as well as her sorrows. In addition it is a group need in that no group can continue to function over a long period of time which does not deal with the feelings of its members. Unless women are given a *non-judgmental* space in which to express themselves, we will never have the strength or the perception to deal with the ambivalences which are a part of us all. It is essential that the group guarantee confidentiality; that we know that our feelings will not be told elsewhere or used against us. This is a group commitment without which there can be no trust.

Sharing

The opening up process is centered on the individual's expressive needs, and carried to an extreme it can become self indulgence. However, there is another experience that can take place in the group which is similar to the first yet different, for the emphasis is on teaching one another through sharing experiences. Not only do we respond with recognition to someone's account, but we add from our own histories as well, building a collage of similar experiences from all women present. The intention here is to arrive at an understanding of the social conditions of women by pooling description of the forms oppression has taken in each individual's life. Revealing these particulars may be very painful, but the reason for dredging up these problems is not only for the therapeutic value of opening up hidden areas. Through experiencing the common discussion comes the understanding that many of the situations described are not personal at all, and are not based on individual inadequacies, but rather have a root in the social order. What we have found is that painful "personal" problems can be common to many of the women present. Thus attention can turn to finding the real causes of these problems rather than merely emphasizing one's own inadequacies.

Almost any topic can be used for the sharing process. All that is necessary is that women have experience in that area. Some of the topics we have used for discussion have been communal living, job experiences, movement experiences in civil rights, SDS and the peace movement, relationships with men focusing on examples of male chauvinism, relationships with women with emphasis on our adolescent experiences and how these affect our present feelings toward women, and our self images—how we perceive ourselves and how we think others perceive us. Agreeing on a topic, and preparing for the discussion for a week or so, seems to ensure the most productive sharing discussion.

The sharing occasions have shown us that the solutions to our problems will be found in joining with other women, because the basis of many of our problems is our status as women. It was not only sharing the stories of our childhood, school, marriage and job experiences which led us to this realization. It was as much the positive feelings, the warmth and comradeship of the small group which reinforced the conviction that it is with other women both now and in the future that solutions will be found. The old, stereotypes that women can't work together and don't like one another are shown to be false in practice.

After sharing we *know* that women suffer at the hands of a male supremacist society and that this male supremacy intrudes into every sphere of our existence, controlling the ways in which we are allowed to make our living and the ways in which we find fulfillment in personal relationships. We know that our most secret, our most private problems are grounded in the way women are treated, in the way women are allowed to live. Isolation turns frustration into self doubt; but joining together gives women perspective that can lead to action. Through sharing they can see that they have been lied to, and begin to look critically at a society which so narrowly defines the roles they may play. But before they can take their destinies into their own hands, they must understand the objective condition of women and the many forms that oppression takes in the lives of women.

Analyzing

A third stage now takes place in the group: the experience of analyzing the reasons for and the causes of the oppression of women. This analysis rises out of the questions which are posed by the basic raw data of the opening up and sharing periods. It is a new way of looking at women's condition: the development of concepts which attempt to define not only the why's and how's of our oppression but possible ways of fighting that oppression. Because the analysis takes place *after* the sharing of individual examples of oppression, it is based on a female understanding of the reality of women's condition.

This period is important because it is the beginning of going beyond our personal experiences. Having gained a perspective on our lives through the sharing process, we now begin to look at women's predicament with some objectivity. This new approach is difficult for many of us as our lives as women exist predominantly in the realm of subjectivity; we perform functions but seldom get on top of a situation to understand how something works and why. This is a new and difficult procedure to learn.

In analyzing the role the group has played in our lives, for example, we have come to understand the ways in which women are kept from feeling they are worthwhile. We have discussed the need to have a social identity and how women are prevented from acquiring one. Women's roles as wife and mother have been analyzed. We have come to see that women are relegated to a private sphere, dependent both psychologically and financially on their husbands. The group is a first step in transcending the isolation. Here sometimes for the first time in her life a woman is allowed an identity independent of a man's. She is allowed to function intellectually as a thinker rather than as a sex object, servant, wife or mother. In short, the group establishes the social worth of the women present, a necessity if women are to take themselves seriously.

We have had to face realistically the inability of many of us to think conceptually. This inability comes from being encouraged to stay in the private sphere and to relate to people on personal levels even when working. We are training ourselves to get out from under our subjective responses and look at our reality in new ways. Although this is not easy for us, we see the absolute necessity of analysis, for our oppression takes both obvious and subtle forms which vary depending on our class and educational status. The complexity of women's situations necessitates that we bring information outside of our individual experiences to bear on our analysis of women's oppression. This is the period when questions can be asked about how the entire society functions. This is the period when books and other documentation become crucial.

It is our contention, however, that this period of analysis belongs *after* the opening up and sharing experiences, for concepts we find must answer the questions which come from our problems as women. It is not in our interest to fit experiences into preconceived theory, especially one devised by men. This is not only because we must suspect all male thinking as being male supremacist, but also because we must teach ourselves to think independently. Our thinking must grow out of our questions if it is to be internalized and if we are to have the tools to look objectively at new experience and analyze that correctly. Thus a period of analysis will come after each new experience and will add new thinking to an ever growing ideology.

Abstracting

A synthesis of the analyses is necessary before decisions can be made as to priorities in problems and approach. For this to happen a certain distance must exist between us and our concerns. When we remove ourselves from immediate necessity, we are able to take the concepts and analysis we have developed and discuss abstract theory. We are able to look at the totality of the nature of our condition, utilizing the concepts we have formulated from discussions of the many forms our oppression takes. Further we begin to build (and to some extent, experience) a vision of our human potential. This does not mean we become more like men. Rather we come to understand what we could be if freed of social oppression. We see this abstracting experience as the purest form of Free Space.

We are only beginning to experience this Free Space, abstracting, now that we have a year of opening up, sharing, and analyzing behind us. We are beginning to see how different institutions fulfill or prevent the fulfillment of human needs, how they work together and how they must be changed. We are beginning to gain an overview of what type of women's movement will be necessary to change the institutions that oppress women. Specifically we have begun to have a clear understanding of what role the small group can and cannot play in this social revolution. It is clear to us that the small group is neither an action-oriented political group in and of itself nor is it an alternative family unit. Rather this is where ideology can develop. And out of this emerging ideology will come a program grounded in a solid understanding of women's condition which will have its roots, but not its totality, in our own experience. Intellectually this is the most exciting stage. It is a joy to learn to think, to begin to comprehend what is happening to us. Ideas are experiences in themselves, freeing, joyous experiences which give us the framework for formulating our actions.

It is important to stress that opening up, sharing, analyzing and abstracting are not limited to certain periods of time. One never completes any of the processes. Opening up is not limited to the past and one does not graduate through the various processes until one is only abstracting to the exclusion of all else. Analyzing and abstracting are only valid processes if they continue to be rooted in the present feelings and experiences of participants. The order may be fixed but the processes themselves are ongoing.

The total group process is not therapy because we try to find the social causes for our experiences and the possible programs for changing these. But the therapeutic experience of momentarily relieving the individual of all responsibility for her situation does occur and is necessary if women are to be free to act. This takes place in both the opening up and sharing phases of the group activity and gives us the courage to look objectively at our predicament, accepting what are realistically our responsibilities to change and understanding what must be confronted societally.

Chapter Twenty-Six

Consciousness-Raising

June Arnold

When I joined a consciousness-raising group last fall, I believed that I was in women's liberation for my daughters' sakes—to make a better world for them. At our first meeting one woman said, "The exciting thing about this movement to me is that finally women are doing something for themselves. That's how change really comes about. I mean, for the first time in my life I am my own cause."

My consciousness jumped up a foot. Later I realized that this is where the energy of the movement is coming from: we are working to liberate ourselves.

Our group, culled spontaneously from a larger meeting and a few telephone calls around the neighborhood, consisted of ten women, all over thirty-five, and all mothers. Some of us were artists, tucking our work in around the edges of the children's schedules; others supported ourselves in the business world at jobs which would have paid a man of the same age and background at least double what we made. Most of us were politically cynical.

We had all been in psychoanalytic and/or encounter therapy; we tacitly agreed that our consciousness-raising sessions were to be something else: as a group, we would refuse to consider the charge that we were personally inadequate, neurotic, or not pretty or smart enough. For me the charge was exposed as ridiculous when I saw the other nine women—however inept, sick, ugly or dumb *I* might feel, *they* were obviously here for no such reason; they probably thought the same of me, where then did the charge originate? Where did the definitions of what women are come from?

We asked the question everywhere during the week and discovered that once you have changed the question you have changed the world. There was no way to un-see what we had begun seeing. How? Why? Where did the idea get started? Every scrap of our lives was infected with the fact that we were women and someone else had decided for us what being a woman was.

The next week we sat in the circle that has become the motto of women's liberation—no one in the position of leader—and prepared to accept chaos. We would examine everything we had been believing as if we were suddenly reborn. We all came from different backgrounds: some of us needed to sum up to protect the mind from a too-sudden liberation, others were freer and jumped about in chaotic hops; some of us wanted to define where we were going before we started, others were able to let go and see what happened, see what defined itself as it happened, if anything.

We chose to listen to each sister whatever point she was at because we understood that women have had no voice in the culture, have been denied a voice in every area of our society, even in those that are conventionally female: child rearing, fashion, housekeeping. In the beginning it was hard for anyone to speak at all; our voices trembled and we felt we succeeded if we just got out the gist of what we wanted to say. I remember that at first when I talked my ears rang and I did not hear anything I said; my hands sweated when the woman before me talked because I knew my turn was next; I spent the evening or afternoon before each session making notes on the subject and then found myself actually saying something entirely different, a trivial detail which I thought of in the sweat of the moment. Such details were far from trivial, in fact: they pointed up both the pervasiveness of woman's conditioning to her role and also the fact that our lives, however divergent on the surface, were all composed of identical "trivial" details. "Trivial" we had picked up from men as a word to put ourselves down with and we agreed to consign the word to the past and listen.

"The counterman where I get a sandwich for lunch always tells me that I don't mind waiting while he serves the men first, do I? because they have to get back to work. He's been saying that for years and today I knew I did mind. [If I'd been a male novelist my writing would have been considered *work* too.]"

"My husband asked if he could wash the dishes for me and I suddenly exploded: what do you mean for *me?* They're not *my* dishes."

"Coming out of the subway, I saw a cop coming in an exit door just as a woman was going out. She was almost as big as he was and she pushed back. He pushed and she pushed back again. Of course he succeeded but I felt that she had won. I said, 'Good work, sister.' I couldn't have said anything a week ago."

"When I told Joe that I was going to come to these meetings once a week, he said, 'Boy, this takes up more and more in your life! Are you going to become one of those women who're always flitting around?' "

Reinforced by the group, knowing the same sisters would be there again next week with more support, we took our new self-assertiveness back into our separate lives. I no longer excused my son from housework which I expected from my daughters, and stopped seeing myself as Mother Cupboard. Carol, another woman in the group, began to *demand equality* from her husband—the right to join women's liberation, in fact. Florence refused to do "a little extra typing" (she was a copywriter) for a male co-worker and was threatened with being fired. Louise found herself the target of a Saturday night attack, ridiculed and sneered at by a roomful of men and women for believing women were *oppressed.*

During that week our anger came out; as if we had each been simmering for years like a back-stage volcano, we erupted all over the place—at home, at work, in the streets, in restaurants, subways, at parties, in bed . . . from Madison Avenue to Brooklyn it spurted out all over everything, redhot. We were too new to know what to do with our anger; for the present we were exhilarated just to let it out. We came together the next week high on our own energy.

We discussed sex—a huge and crucial subject—three times. The first time the startling reality was that ten women who were strangers to each other were making public statements about what has been considered sacredly private. One by one, we testified that we had always seen our sexuality in terms of the male, that we learned our roles from male psychologists, novelists, social scientists, philosophers—that even the jokes we had cut our *vagina dentata* on were totally and oppressively male. We agreed that we had spent most of our lives pleasing men sexually, so eager were we to be considered a good lay, and had only incidentally and sometimes disastrously demanded our own pleasure. The men we had known who claimed they wanted to give their women pleasure, in a surprising number of cases, tended to stop when they were obviously on the point of doing just that. We had been able to satisfy ourselves by fitting our sexuality into his, but no man had ever really grooved on *our* sexuality. How could he? We didn't know really what it was, yet.

One of the group dropped out. A visitor (who might have joined us had we discussed politics or economic change) never came back.

A month later we discussed sex again. We trusted each other more and brought to the group our most devasting experiences; for example: one woman told of her former husband who got drunk often and was insistently jealous. His most common swear-word was "mother fucker" which he usually shortened to "mother" and shouted obscenely at everyone who angered him. She was eight months pregnant with their fourth child when he flew into a rage and denied that the child was his; he stripped away a dressing gown he had given her, tearing it, ripping it off, shouting, "You mother! you goddamned *mother!*" until she was naked, protruding pregnant, standing in the middle of the kitchen. He slapped her to the floor and left. "After he left," she said now, "I thought how to handle his explosion—if I were truly Christ-like I would understand how terrible he would feel tomorrow for doing that and I would do something to relieve him of his guilt. I did a lot of that kind of thinking then. So I picked up the scraps of material and carefully sewed them back together and made the robe over again—it didn't look bad; I had it on when he came home the next night. I also had on a sweet smile, naturally." She laughed. "When I told that story to my psychiatrist he picked up on my wanting to be Christ-like and said, 'Do you see how you always try to identify with the man?' "

We were stunned by the multiple political content of what used to be called hard luck:

1. A wife is a uterus and it is the husband's possession.
2. The insane glorification of motherhood barely covers the fact that men think it is an obscenity.
3. Women are responsible for men's vileness of temper and also for patching things up afterwards.
4. Men use their superior strength to dominate and oppress anyone weaker, especially those they are supposed to protect.
5. Whatever a woman does in this culture will be interpreted to suit the male-chauvinist system that *is up*.

Generalizations? No, by now we knew that what happened to one woman could happen to any woman; politically we had learned that women were oppressed by what *could* happen and were effectively kept in their place by what might actually happen only to a few.

The third time we talked about sex we had been together for five months; we had gotten rid of the past and were eager to act on our new energy. We abandoned going around the room by turns; we each talked as we felt like it but no one interrupted anyone else. We had found our voices and with them the confidence that we *had* voices and could wait, if someone else was talking, without feeling anxious.

We talked about masturbation: "It is a startlingly liberated feeling to be able to give yourself an orgasm, whenever you want to, without guilt."

About homosexuality: "I used to feel I had to keep it a secret when I made love to women even though I knew that if we had free choices that would be one of them. The only one who gains from the taboo on lesbianism is the man—it's his way of protecting his possession."

About marriage: "I can't enjoy intercourse unless I have a relationship, am really in love, you know. So when I'm not in love, like for the last three years, I have nothing. How did I limit myself so?"

"I can only have sex when I don't have a relationship . . . I have marvelous sex with practically anybody but I'm a failure when it comes to a relationship. I just saw something: maybe that's why I can have marvelous sex."

"Does anybody else have to have fantasies?"

"Sure. I can't have sex with Joe at all unless I close my eyes and imagine that I'm a slave girl being stolen as a prize and dragged off to the pirate's den."

"Well, I guess I'm the only one who still enjoys sex with the same man after ten years. It gets better every year."

"I guess we're not going to get any conclusions from this session—we're all saying completely different things."

"Beautiful! Maybe that's what liberation really is."

A month later the group split up. Each of us had grown, none of us was even tempted to blame our past inaction on personal faults or private circumstances. Mr. Kingpin was out there and he was real. In fact we had learned indelibly that the accusation—you are not pretty or smart enough—was a way of dividing women by setting them in competition with each other, a way of sustaining the Horatio Alger myth of America which benefits only the ruling males. Women's place under Horatio was as rungs to his feet, to support him each step of his climb; women were at best the soles of his shoes, to be dragged up the ladder with him but always on the bottom. We had been glued to our men and separated from each other all our lives, even to the extent that we used male language-dichotomies and thought in opposites. Male equals aggressive, female equals passive. Really? We found that our ability to cooperate was astonishing, whether innate or learned. Male equals aggressive, female equals cooperative.

We saw the state as a macrocosm of the family: Papa at the head of the table (having come from Business), Mama at the foot (out of the kitchen), children learning their manners along the sides. We saw that children were raised to uphold Papa and that we, as Papa's paramours, had played his cop to our kids. His money, his physical strength, his Biblically-upheld pre-eminence had structured our minds and led us to see as natural Papa-President, Uncle Congress, First-Lady Charming— and the kids squabbling among themselves out of sight. The family is the essential teacher of inequality.

What had begun in a small group, what had in fact depended upon the small group where trust and confidence could open up and become solid, was the recognition of our common sisterhood. If it were really communal, it could not be contained within any group. Sisterhood—not the same thing as friendship: a sister can be someone you don't especially like personally or agree with politically—is the common bond you feel with another woman because you understand that she has been oppressed and because you know you can work with her as a woman for all women.

We left our mother-group to join other, action groups and saw that we could work with and trust other women as easily as we could our "real" sisters. When we were engaged in projects with other women, it was immediately clear which ones had been through a consciousness-raising group and which had not; those who had not were still behaving according to male patterns. We saw it because we were doing it ourselves a short six months before—ordering people around, trying to control, arguing, interrupting, criticizing, giving advice, manipulating, putting people down. Consciousness-raising is essential to the movement for that reason: to avoid cooperation being infiltrated by aggression.

Consciousness-raising as a dynamic probably never stops because there is no doubt that Mr. Kingpin is really there and we haven't even budged him yet. As the movement grows in members and strength, he will feel himself being pushed and fight back. He is capable of starting World War III to protect his cock-right (and glorify it). But first he'll throw crumbs to the floor and hope we'll fight each other for them, because that's what we've been doing all our lives. And every crumb will be addressed: "To a Very Special Sweetheart."

Chapter Twenty-Seven

Consciousness

Vivian Gornick

In a lower Manhattan office a legal secretary returns from her lunch hour, sinks into her seat and says miserably to a secretary at the next desk: "I don't know what's happening to me. A perfectly nice construction worker whistled and said, 'My, isn't that nice,' as I passed him and suddenly I felt this terrific anger pushing up in me. . . . I swear I wanted to *hit* him!"

At the same time, a thoughtful 40-year-old mother in a Maryland suburb is saying to a visiting relative over early afternoon coffee: "You know, I've been thinking lately, I'm every bit as smart as Harry, and yet he got the Ph.D. and I raised the girls. Mind you, I *wanted* to stay home. And yet, the thought of my two girls growing up and doing the same thing doesn't sit well with me at all. Not at all."

And in Toledo, Ohio, a factory worker turns to the next woman on the inspection belt and confides: "Last night I told Jim: 'I been working in the same factory as you 10 years now. We go in at the same time, come out the same time. But I do all the shopping, get the dinner, wash the dishes and on Sunday break my back down on the kitchen floor. I'm real tired of doin' all that. I want some help from you.' Well, he just laughed at me, see? Like he done every time I mentioned this before. But last night I wouldn't let up. I mean, I really *meant* it this time. And you know? I thought he was gonna let me have it. Looked mighty like he was gettin' ready to belt me one. But you know? I just didn't care! I wasn't gonna back down, come hell or high water. You'll just never believe it, he'd kill me if he knew I was tellin' you, he washed the dishes. First time in his entire life."

None of these women are feminists. None of them are members of the Women's Liberation Movement. None of them ever heard of consciousness-raising. And yet, each of them exhibits the symptomatic influence of this, the movement's most esoteric practice. Each of them, without specific awareness, is beginning to feel the effects of the consideration of woman's personal experience in a new light—a political light. Each of them is undergoing the mysterious behavioral twitches that indicate psychological alteration. Each of them is drawing on a linking network of feminist analysis and emotional up-chucking that is beginning to suffuse the political-social air of American life today. Each of them, without ever having attended a consciousness-raising session, has had her consciousness raised.

Consciousness-raising is the name given to the feminist practice of examining one's personal experience in the light of sexism; i.e., that theory which explains woman's subordinate position in society as a result of a cultural decision to confer direct power on men and only indirect power on women. The term of description and the practice to which it alludes are derived from a number of sources—psychoanalysis, Marxist theory and American revivalism, mainly—and was born out of the earliest stages of feminist formulation begun about three years ago in such predictable liberationist nesting places as Cambridge, New York, Chicago and Berkeley. (The organization most prominently associated with the growth of consciousness-raising is the New York Redstockings.)

Perceiving that woman's position in our society does indeed constitute that of a political class, and, secondly, that woman's "natural" domain is her feelings, and, thirdly, that testifying in a friendly and supportive atmosphere enables people to see that their experiences are often duplicated (thereby reducing their sense of isolation and increasing the desire to theorize as well as to confess), the radical feminists sensed quickly that a group of women sitting in a circle discussing their emotional experiences as though they were material for cultural analysis was political dynamite. Hence, through personal testimony and emotional analysis could the class consciousness of *women* be raised. And thus the idea of the small "woman's group"—or consciousness-raising group—was delivered into a cruel but exciting world.

Consciousness-raising is, at one and the same time, both the most celebrated and accessible introduction to the woman's movement as well as the most powerful technique for feminist conversion known to the liberationists. Women are *drawn*, out of a variety of discontents, by the idea of talking about themselves, but under the spell of a wholly new interpretation of their experience, they *remain*.

Coming together, as they do, week after week for many months, the women who are "in a group" begin to exchange an extraordinary sense of multiple identification that is encouraged by the technique's instruction to look for explanations for each part of one's history in terms of the social or cultural dynamic created by sexism—rather than in terms of the personal dynamic, as one would do in a psychotherapist's group session. (Although there are many differences between consciousness-raising and group therapy—e.g., the former involves no professional leader, no exchange of money—the fundamental difference lies in this fact: in consciousness-raising one looks not to one's personal emotional history for an explanation of behavioral problems but rather to the cultural fact of the patriarchy.)

Thus looking at one's history and experience in consciousness-raising sessions is rather like shaking a kaleidoscope and watching all the same pieces rearrange themselves into an altogether *other* picture, one that suddenly makes the color and shape of each piece appear startlingly new and alive, and full of unexpected meaning. (This is mainly why feminists often say that women are the most interesting people around these days, because they are experiencing a psychic invigoration of rediscovery.)

What *does* take place in a consciousness-raising group? How do the women see themselves? What is the thrust of the conversation at a typical session? Is it simply the manhating; spleen-venting that is caricatured by the unsympathetic press? Or the unfocused and wrong-headed abstracting insisted upon by the insulated intellectuals?

Or yet again, the self-indulgent contemplation of the navel that many tightlipped radical activists see it as?

"In this room," says Roberta H., a Long Island housewife speaking euphemistically of her group's meetings, "we do not generalize. We do not speak of any experience except that of the women here. We follow the rules for consciousness-raising as set out by the New York Radical Feminists and we do not apply them to 'woman's experience'—whatever on earth that is—we apply them to ourselves. But, oh God! The samenesses we have found, and the way in which these meetings have changed our lives!"

The rules that Roberta H. is referring to are to be found in a mimeographed pamphlet, an introduction to the New York Radical Feminists organization, which explains the purpose and procedures of consciousness-raising. The sessions consist mainly of women gathering once a week, sitting in a circle and speaking in turn, addressing themselves—almost entirely out of personal experience—to a topic that has been preselected. The pamphlet sets forth the natural limitations of a group (10 to 15 women), advises women to start a group from among their friends and on a word-of-mouth basis, and suggests a list of useful topics for discussion. These topics include Love, Marriage, Sex, Work, Femininity. How I Came to Women's Liberation, Motherhood, Aging and Competition With Other Women. Additional subjects are developed as a particular group's specific interests and circumstances begin to surface.

When a group's discussions start to revolve more and more about apparently very individual circumstances, they often lead to startling similarities. For instance, a Westchester County group composed solely of housewives, who felt that each marriage represented a unique meaning in each of their lives, used the question, "Why did you marry the man you married?" as the subject for discussion one night. "We went around the room," says Joan S., one of the women present, "and while some of us seemed unable to answer that question without going back practically to the cradle, do you know?, the word love was never mentioned *once*."

On the Upper West Side of Manhattan, in the vicinity of Columbia University, a group of women between the ages of 35 and 45 have been meeting regularly for six months. Emily R., an attractive 40-year-old divorcée in this group, says: "When I walked into the first meeting, and saw the *types* there, I said to myself: 'None of these broads have been through what I've been through. They couldn't possibly feel the way I feel.' Well, I'll tell you. None of them have been through what I've been through if you look at our experience superficially. But when you look a little *deeper*—the way we've been doing at these meetings—you see they've *all* been through what I've been through, and they all feel pretty much the way I feel. God, when I saw *that!* When I saw that what I always felt was my own personal hangup was as true for every other woman in that room as it was for me! Well, that's when my consciousness was raised."

What Emily R. speaks of is the phenomenon most often referred to in the movement, the flash of insight most directly responsible for the feminist leap in faith being made by hundreds of women everywhere—i.e., the intensely felt realization that what had always been taken for symptoms of personal unhappiness or dissatisfaction or frustration was so powerfully and so consistently duplicated among women that perhaps these symptoms could just as well be ascribed to *cultural* causes as to psychological ones.

In the feminist movement this kind of "breakthrough" can occur no place else than in a consciousness-raising group. It is only here, during many months of meetings, that a woman is able finally—if ever—to bring to the surface those tangled feelings of anger, bafflement and frustrated justice that have drawn her to the movement in the first place. It is only here that the dynamic of sexism will finally strike home, finally make itself felt in the living detail of her own life.

Claire K., a feminist activist in Cambridge, says of women's groups: "I've been working with women's groups for over two years now. The average life of a group is a year to 18 months, and believe me, I've watched a lot of them fold before they ever got off the ground. But, when they *work!* There is a rhythm to some of them that's like life itself. You watch a group expand and contract, and each time it does one or the other it never comes back together quite the same as when the action started. Something happens to each woman, and to the group itself . . . But each time, if they survive, they have *grown.* You can see it, almost smell it and taste it."

I am one of those feminists who are always mourning after the coherent and highminded leadership of the 19th century. Often, when I observe the fragmented, intellectually uneven, politically separated components of the woman's movement I experience dismay, and I find myself enviously imagining Elizabeth Cady Stanton and Lucretia Mott and Susan B. Anthony sitting and holding hands for 40 years, sustaining and offering succor to one another in religious and literary accents that make of their feminism a heroic act, an act that gave interwoven shape to their lives and their cause. And I think in a panic: "Where would we all be without them? Where would we be? They thought it all out for us, and we've got not one inch beyond them." Lately, however, I have changed my mind about all that . . .

I was on my way to a meeting one night not too long ago, a meeting meant to fashion a coalition group out of the movement's many organizations. I knew exactly what was ahead of me. I knew that a woman from NOW would rise and speak about our "image"; that a Third Worlder would announce loudly she didn't give a good goddamn about anybody's orgasms, her women were starving, for chrissake; that a Radicalesbian would insist that the woman's movement must face the problem of sexism from within right now; and 10 women from the Socialist party would walk out in protest against middle-class "élitist" control in the movement. I knew there would be a great deal of emotional opinion delivered, a comparatively small amount of valuable observation made, and some action taken. Suddenly, as the bus I was on swung westward through Central Park, I realized that it didn't matter, that none of it mattered. I realized it was stupid and self-pitying to be wishing that the meeting was going to be chaired by Elizabeth Cady Stanton; what she had done and said had been profoundly in the idiom of her time, and in the idiom of *my* time no woman in the movement was her equal, but something else was: the consciousness-raising group.

I saw then that small, anonymous consciousness-raising group was the heart and soul of the woman's movement, that it is not what happens at movement meetings in New York or Boston or Berkeley that counts, but the fact that hundreds of these groups are springing up daily—at universities in Kansas, in small towns in Oregon, in the suburbs of Detroit—out of a responsive need that has indeed been urged to the surface by modern radical feminism. It was here that the soul of a woman is genuinely searched and a new psychology of the self is forged. I saw then that the consciousness-raising group of today is the true Second Front of feminism; and as I thought all this I felt the ghost of Susan B. Anthony hovering over me, nodding vigorously, patting me on the shoulder and saying: "Well done, my dear, well done."

That ghost has accompanied me to every movement meeting I have attended since that night, but when I am at a consciousness-raising session that ghost disappears and I am on my own. Then, for better or worse, I am the full occupant of my feminist skin, engaged in the true business of modern feminism, reaching hard for self-possession.

And now let's go to a consciousness-raising session.

Early in the evening, on a crisp autumn night, a young woman in an apartment in the Gramercy Park section of Manhattan signed a letter, put it in an envelope, turned out the light over her desk, got her coat out of the hall closet, ran down two flights of stairs hailed a taxi and headed west directly across the city. At the same time, on the Upper West Side, another woman, slightly older than the first, bent over a sleeping child, kissed his forehead, said goodnight to the babysitter, rode down 12 flights in an elevator, walked up to Broadway and disappeared into the downtown subway. Across town, on the Upper East Side, another woman tossed back a head of stylishly fixed hair, pulled on a beautiful pair of suede boots and left her tiny apartment, also heading down and across town. On the Lower East Side, in a fourth-floor tenement apartment, a woman five or six years younger than all the others combed out a tangled mop of black hair, clomped down the stairs in her Swedish clogs and started trudging west on St. Marks Place. In a number of other places all over Manhattan other women were also leaving their houses. When the last one finally walked into the Greenwich Village living room they were all headed for, there were 10 women in the room.

These women ranged in age from the late 20's to the middle 30's; in appearance, from attractive to very beautiful; in education, from bachelor's degrees to master's degrees; in martial status, from single to married to divorced to imminently separated; two were mothers. Their names were Veronica, Lucie, Diana, Marie, Laura, Jen, Sheila, Dolores, Marilyn and Claire. Their occupations, respectively, were assistant television producer, graduate student, housewife, copywriter, journalist, unemployed actress, legal secretary, unemployed college dropout, school-teacher and computer programmer.

They were not movement women; neither were they committed feminists; nor were they marked by an especial sense of social development or by personal neurosis. They were simply a rather ordinary group of women who were drawn out of some unresolved, barely articulated need to form a "woman's group." They were in their third month of meetings; they were now at Marie's house (next week they would meet at Laura's, and after that at Jen's, and so on down the line); the subject for discussion tonight was "Work."

The room was large, softly lit, comfortably furnished. After 10 or 15 minutes of laughing, chatting, note and book exchanging, the women arranged themselves in a circle, some on chairs, others on the floor. In the center of the circle was a low coffee table covered with a coffeepot, cups, sugar, milk, plates of cheese and bread, cookies and fruit. Marie suggested they begin, and turning to the woman on her right, who happened to be Dolores, asked if she would be the first.

> **Dolores** (*the unemployed college dropout*): I guess that's okay . . . I'd just as soon be the first . . . mainly because I hate to be the last. When I'm last, all I think about is, soon it will be *my* turn. (She looked up nervously.) You've no idea how I *hate* talking in public. (*There was a long pause; silence in the circle.*) . . . Work! God, what can I say? The whole question has always been absolute hell for me . . . A lot of you have said your fathers ignored you when you were growing up and paid attention only to your brothers. Well, in my house it was just the opposite. I have two sisters, and my father always told me I was the smartest of all, that I was smarter than he was, and that I could do anything I wanted to do . . . but somehow, I don't really know *why*, everything I turned to came to nothing. After six years in analysis I still don't know *why*. (*She looked off into space for a moment and her eyes seemed to lose the train of her thought. Then she shook herself and went on.*) I've always drifted . . . just drifted. My parents never forced me to work. I needn't work even now. I had every opportunity to find out what I really wanted to do. But . . . nothing I did satisfied me, and I would just stop. . . . Or turn away. . . . Or go on a trip. I worked for a big company for a while. . . . Then my parents went to Paris and I just went with them. . . . I came back . . . went to school . . . was a researcher at Time-Life . . . drifted . . . got married . . . divorced . . . drifted. (*Her voice grew more halting.*) I feel my life is such a *waste*. I'd like to write, I really would; I feel I'd be a good writer, but I don't know. I just can't get going. . . . My father is so disappointed in me. He keeps hoping I'll really do something. Soon. (*She shrugged her shoulders but her face was very quiet and pale, and her pain expressive. She happened to be one of the most beautiful woman in the room.*)
>
> **Diana** (*the housewife*): What do you think you will do?
>
> **Dolores** (*in a defiant burst*): Try to get married!
>
> **Jen** (*the unemployed actress*) **and Marie** (*the copy writer*): Oh, no!
>
> **Claire** (*the computer programmer*): After all that! Haven't you learned yet? What on earth is marriage going to do for you? Who on earth could you marry? Feeling about yourself as you do? Who could save you from yourself? Because that's what you want.
>
> **Marilyn** (*the school teacher*): That's right. It sounds like "It's just all too much to think out so I might as well get married."
>
> **Lucie** (*the graduate student*): Getting married like that is bound to be a disaster.
>
> **Jen:** And when you get married like that it's always to some creep you've convinced

yourself is wonderful. So understanding. (*Dolores grew very red and very quiet through all this.*)

Sheila (*the legal secretary*): Stop jumping on her like that! I know *just* how she feels. . . . I was *really* raised to be a wife and a mother, and yet my father wanted me to do something with my education after he sent me to one of the best girls' schools in the East. Well, I didn't get married when I got out of school like half the girls. I graduated with, and now seven years later I'm *still* not married. (*She stopped talking abruptly and looked off into the space in the center of the circle, her attention wandering as though she'd suddenly lost her way.*) I don't know how to describe it exactly, but I know just how Dolores feels about drifting. I've always worked, and yet something was always sort of confused inside me. I never really knew which way I wanted to go on a job: up, down, sideways . . . I always thought it would be the most marvelous thing in the world to work for a really brilliant and important man. I never have. But I've worked for some good men and I've learned a lot from them. But (*her dark head came up two or three inches and she looked hesitantly around*) I don't know about the rest of you, but I've always wound up being propositioned by my bosses. It's a funny thing. As soon as I'd being doing really well, learning fast and taking on some genuine responsibility, like it would begin to excite them, and they'd make their move. When I refused, almost invariably they'd begin to *browbeat* me. I mean, they'd make my life miserable! And, of course, I'd retreat. . . . I'd get small and scared and take everything they were dishing out . . . and then I'd move on. I don't know, maybe something in my behavior was really asking for it, I honestly don't know anymore. . . .

Marie: There's a good chance you *were* asking for it. I work with a lot of men and I don't get propositioned every other day. I am so absolutely straight no one *dares*. . . . They all think I am a dike.

Sheila (*plaintively*): Why is it like that, though? Why are: men like that? Is it something they have more of, this sexual need for ego gratification? Are they made differently from us?

Jen (*placing her coffee cup on the floor beside her*): No! You've just never learned to stand up for yourself! And goddammit, they know it, and they play on it. Look, you all know I've been an actress for years. Well, once, when I was pretty new in the business, I was playing opposite this guy. He used to feel me up on the stage. All the *time*. I was scared. I didn't know what to do. I'd say to the stage manager: That guy is feeling me up. The stage manager would look at me like I was crazy, and shrug his shoulders. Like: What can *I* do? Well, once I finally thought: I can't stand this. And I bit him. Yes, I bit the bastard, I bit his, tongue while he was kissing me.

A Chorus of Voices: You *bit* him????

Jen (with great dignity): Yes, dammit, I bit him. And afterward he said to me, "Why the hell did you do that?" And I said, "You know goddam well why I did that." And do you know? He respected me after that. (*She laughed.*) Didn't *like* me very much. But he respected me. (*She looked distracted for a moment.*) . . . I guess that *is* pretty funny. I mean, biting someone's tongue during a love scene.

Veronica (*the assistant TV producer*): Yeah. Very funny.

Laura (*the journalist*): Listen, I've been thinking about something Sheila said. That as soon as she began to get really good at her job her boss would make a pass—and that would pretty much signal the end, right? She'd refuse, he'd become an S.O.B., and she'd eventually leave. It's almost as if sex were being used to cut her down, or back, or in some way stop her from rising. An *instinct* he, the boss, has—to sleep with her when he feels her becoming really independent.

Lucie (*excitedly*): I'll buy that! Look, it's like Samson and Delilah in reverse. *She* knew that sex would give her the opportunity to destroy his strength. Women are famous for wanting to sleep with men in order to enslave them, right? That's the great myth, right? He's all spirit and mind, she's all emotion and biological instinct. She uses this instinct with *cunning* to even out the score, to get some power, to bring him down—through sex. But, look at it another way. What are these guys always saying to us? What are they always saying about women's liberation?—"All she needs is a good——." They say that *hopefully. Prayerfully.* They know. We all know what all that "All she needs is a good——" stuff is all about.

Claire: This is ridiculous. Use your heads. Isn't a guy kind of super if he wants to sleep with a woman who's becoming independent?

Marie: Yes, but not in business. There's something wrong every time, whenever sex is operating in business. It's always like a secret weapon, something you hit your opponent below the belt with.

Diana: God, you're all crazy! Sex is *fun.* Wherever it exists. It's warm and nice and it makes people feel good.

Dolores: That's a favorite pipe dream of yours, isn't it?

Sheila: It certainly doesn't seem like very much fun to me when I watch some secretary coming on to one of the lawyers when she wants a raise, then I see the expression on her face as she turns away.

Marie: God, that sounds like my mother when she wants something from my father!

Veronica (*feebly*): You people are beginning to make me feel *awful!* (*Everyone's head snapped in her direction.*)

Marie: Why?

Veronica: The way you're talking about using sex at work. As if it were so horrible. Well, I've *always* used a kind of sexy funniness to get what I want at work. What's wrong with that?

Lucie: What do you do?

Veronica: Well, if someone is being very stuffy and serious about business, I'll say something funny—I guess in a sexy way—to break up the atmosphere which sometimes gets so heavy. You know what I mean? Men can be so pretentious in business! And then, usually, I get what I want—while I'm being funny and cute, and they're laughing.

Diana (*heatedly*): Look, don't you see what you're doing?

Veronica (*testily*): No, I don't. What am I doing?

Diana (*her hands moving agitatedly through the air before her*): If there's some serious business going on you come in and say: Nothing to be afraid of, folks. Just frivolous, feminine little me. I'll tell a joke, wink my eye, do a little dance, and we'll all pretend nothing's really happening here.

Veronica: My God, I never thought of it like that.

Laura: It's like those apes. They did a study of apes in which they discovered that apes chatter and laugh and smile a lot to ward off aggression.

Marilyn: Just like women! Christ, aren't they always saying to us: *Smile!* Who tells a man to smile? And how often do you smile for no damned reason, right? It's so *natural* to start smiling as soon as you start talking to a man, isn't it?

Lucie: That's right! You're right! You know—God, it's amazing!—I began to think about this just the other day. I was walking down Fifth Avenue and a man in the doorway of a store said to me, "Whatsamatta, honey? Things can't be *that* bad." And I was startled because I wasn't feeling depressed or anything, and I couldn't figure out why he was saying that. So I looked, real fast, in the glass to see what my face looked like. And it didn't look like anything. It was just a face at rest. I had just an ordinary, sort of thoughtful expression on my face. And he thought I was *depressed*. And, I couldn't help it, I said to myself: "Would he have said that to you if you were a man?" And I answered myself immediately: "No!"

Diana: That's it. That's really what they want. To keep us barefoot, pregnant, and *smiling*. Always sort of begging, you know? Just a little supplicating—at all times. And they get anxious if you stop smiling. Not because you're depressed. Because you're *thinking!*

Dolores: Oh, come on now. Surely, there are lots of men who have very similar kinds of manners? What about all the life-of-the-party types? All those clowns and regular guys?

Claire: Yes, what about them? You *never* take those guys seriously. You never think of the men of real power, the guys with serious intentions and real strength, acting that way, do you? And those are the ones with real responsibility. The others are the ones women laugh about in private, the ones who become our confidantes, not our lovers, the ones who are *just like ourselves.*

Sheila (*quietly*): You're right.

Lucie: And it's true, it really does undercut your seriousness, all that smiling.

Sheila (*looking suddenly sad and very intent*): And underscore your weakness.

Dolores: Yes, exactly. We smile because we feel at a loss, because we feel vulnerable. We don't quite know how to accomplish what we want to accomplish or how to navigate through life, so we act *feminine*. That's really what this is all about, isn't it? To be masculine is to take action, to be feminine is to smile. Be coy and cute and sexy— and maybe you'll become the big man's assistant. God, it's all so sad . . .

Veronica (*looking a bit dazed*): I never thought of any of it like this. But it's true, I guess, all of it. You know (*and now her words came in a rush and her voice grew stronger*), I've always been afraid of my job, I've always felt I was there by *accident*, and that any minute they were gonna find me out. Any minute, they'd know I was a fraud. I had the chance to become a producer recently, and I fudged it. I didn't realize for two weeks afterward that I'd done it deliberately, that I don't *want* to move up, that I'm afraid of the responsibility, that I'd rather stay where I am, making my little jokes and not drawing attention to myself . . . (*Veronica's voice faded away, but her face seemed full of struggle, and for a long moment no one spoke.*)

Marilyn (*her legs pulled up under her on the couch, running her hand distractedly through her short blond hair*): Lord, does *that* sound familiar. Do I know that feeling of being there by accident, any minute here comes the ax. I've never felt that anything I got— any honor, any prize, any decent job—was really legitimately mine. I always felt it was luck, that I happened to be in the right place at the right time and that I was able to put up a good front and people just didn't *know* . . . but if I stuck around long enough they would . . . So, I guess I've drifted a lot, too. Being married, I took advantage of it. I remember when my husband was urging me to work, telling me I was a talented girl and that I shouldn't just be sitting around the house taking care of the baby. I wanted so to be persuaded by him, but I just couldn't do it. Every night I'd say: Tomorrow's the day and every morning I'd get up feeling like my head was full of molasses, so sluggish I couldn't *move*. By the time I'd finally get out of that damn bed it was too late to get a baby-sitter or too late to get a job interview or too late to do anything, really. (*She turned toward Diana.*) You're a housewife, Diana. You must know what I mean. (*Diana nodded ruefully.*) I began concentrating on my sex life with my husband, which had never been any too good, and was now getting really bad. It's hard to explain. We'd always been very affectionate with one another, and we still were. But I began to *crave* . . . passion. (*She smiled, almost apologetically.*) What else can I call it? There was no passion between us, practically no intercourse. I began to *demand* it. My husband reacted very badly, accused me of—oh God, the most awful things! Then I had an affair. The sex was great, the man was very tender with me for a long while. I felt *revived*. But then, a funny thing happened. I became almost hypnotized by the sex. I couldn't get enough, I couldn't stop thinking about it, it seemed to consume me; and yet, I became as sluggish now with sexual desire as I had been when I couldn't get up to go look for a job. Sometimes, I felt so sluggish I could hardly prepare myself to go meet my lover. And then . . . (*She stopped talking and looked down at the floor. Her forehead creased, her brows drew together, she seemed pierced suddenly by memory. Everyone remained quiet for a long moment.*)

Diana (*very gently*): And then?

Marilyn (*almost shaking herself awake*): And then the man told my husband of our affair.

Jen: Oh, Christ!

Marilyn: My husband went wild . . . (*her voice trailed off and again everyone remained silent, this time until she spoke again.*) He left me. We've been separated a year and a half now. So then I *had* to go to work. And I have, I have. But it remains a difficult, difficult thing. I do the most ordinary kind of work, afraid to strike out, afraid to try anything that involves real risk. It's almost as if there's some *training* necessary for taking risks, and I just don't have it . . . and my husband leaving me, and forcing me out to work, somehow didn't magically give me whatever it takes to get that training.

Laura (*harshly*): Maybe it's too late.

Diana: Well, that's a helluva thought. (*She crossed her legs and stared at the floor. Everyone looked toward her, but she said no more. Jen stretched, Claire bit into a cookie, Lucie poured coffee and everyone rearranged themselves in their seats.*)

Marie (*after a long pause*): It's your turn, Diana.

Diana (*turning in her chair and running thin hands nervously through her curly red hair*): It's been hard for me to concentrate on the subject. I went to see my mother in the hospital this afternoon, and I haven't been able to stop thinking about her all day long.

Jen: Is she very sick?

Diana: Well, yes, I think so. She underwent a serious operation yesterday—three hours on the operating table. For a while there it was touch and go. But today she seemed much better and I spoke to her. I stood by her bed and she took my hand and she said to me: "You need an enormous strength of will to live through this. Most people need only one reason to do it. I have three: you, your father and your grandmother. And suddenly I felt furious. I felt *furious* with her. God, she's always been so strong, the strongest person I know, and I've loved her for it. All of a sudden

I felt tricked. I felt like saying to her: "Why don't you live for yourself?" I felt like saying: "I can't take this burden on me! What are you doing to me?" And now suddenly, I'm here, being asked to talk about work, and I have nothing to say. I haven't a goddamn thing to say! What do I do? After all, what do I *do*? Half my life is passed in a fantasy of desire that's focused on leaving my husband and finding some marvelous job ... At least, my mother worked *hard* all her life. She raised me when my real father walked out on her, she put me through school, she staked me to my first apartment, she never said no to me for anything. And when I got married she felt she'd accomplished *everything*. That was the end of the rainbow....

Dolores (*timidly*): What's so terrible, really, your mother saying she lived for all of you? God, that used to be considered a moral virtue. I'm sure lots of men feel the same way, that they live for their families. Most men *hate* their work ...

Marilyn: My husband used to say that all the time, that he lived only for me and the baby, that that was everything to him.

Lucie: How did you feel about that? What did you think of him when he said it?

Marilyn (*flushing*): It used to make me feel peculiar. As though something wasn't quite right with him.

Lucie (*to Diana*): Did you think something wasn't *quite right*, when your mother said what she said?

Diana (*thinking back*): No. It wasn't that something wasn't quite right. It seemed "right," if you know what I mean, for her to be saying that, but terribly wrong suddenly.

Lucie: That's odd, isn't it? When a man says he lives for his family it sounds positively unnatural to me. When a woman says it, it sounds so "right." So expected.

Laura: Exactly. What's pathology in a man seems normal in a woman.

Claire: It comes back, in a sense, to a woman always looking for her identity in her family and a man never, or rarely, really doing that.

Marie: God, this business of identity! Of wanting it from my work, and not looking for it in what my husband does ...

Jen: Tell me, do men ever look for their identities in their wives' work?

Veronica: Yes, and then we call them Mr. Streisand. (*Everybody breaks up, and suddenly cookies and fruit are—being devoured. Everyone stretches and one or two women walk around the room. After 15 minutes ... *)

Marie (*peeling an orange, sitting yogi-fashion on the floor*): I first went to work for a small publicity firm. They taught me to be a copywriter, and I loved it from the start. I never had any trouble with the people in that firm. It was like one big happy family there. We all worked well with each other and everyone knew a bit about everybody else's work. When the place folded and they let me go I was so depressed, and so lost. For the longest time I couldn't even go out looking for a job. I had no sense of how to go about it. I had no real sense of myself as having a transferable skill, somehow. I didn't seem to know how to deal with Madison Avenue. I realized then that I'd somehow never taken that job as a period of preparation for independence in the world. It was like a continuation of my family. As long as I was being taken care of I functioned, but when I was really on my own I folded up. I just didn't know how to operate ... And I still don't, really. It's never been the same. I've never had a job in which I felt I was really operating responsibly since that time.

Sheila: Do you think maybe you're just waiting around to get married?

Maire: No, I don't. I know I really want to work, no matter what. I know that I want some sense of myself that's not related to a husband, or to anyone but myself, for that matter . . . But I feel so lost, I just don't know where it's all at, really. (*Five or six heads nodded sympathetically.*)

Claire: I don't feel like any of you. Not a single one.

Dolores: What do you mean?

Claire: Let me tell you something. I have two sisters and a brother. My father was a passionately competitive man. He loved sports and he taught us all how to play, and he treated us all exactly as though we were his equals at it. I mean, he competed with us exactly as though we were 25 when we were 8. Everything: sailing, checkers, baseball, there was nothing he wouldn't compete in. When I was a kid I saw him send a line drive ball right into my sister's stomach, for God's sake. Sounds terrible, right? We loved it. All of us. And we thrive on it. For me, work is like everything else. *Competitive.* I get in there, do the best I can, compete ferociously against man, woman or machine. And I use whatever I have in the way of equipment: sex, brains, endurance. You name it, I use it. And if I lose I lose, and if I win I win. It's just doing it as well as I can that counts. And if I come up against discrimination as a woman, I just reinforce my attack. But the name of the game is competition.

(*Everyone stared at her, openmouthed, and suddenly everyone was talking at once; over each other's voices; at each other; to themselves; laughing; interrupting; generally exploding.*)

Laura (*dryly*): The American dream. Right before our eyes.

Diana (*tearfully*): Good God, Claire, that sounds awful!

Lucie (*amazed*): That's the kind of thing that's killing our men. In a sense, it's really why we're here.

Sheila (*mad*): Oh, that love of competition!

Marie (*astonished*): The whole idea of just being is completely lost in all this.

Jen (*outraged*): And to act *sexy* in order to compete! You degrade every woman alive!

Veronica (*interested*): In other words, Claire, you imply that if they give you what you want they get you?

Diana (*wistfully*): That notion of competition is everything we hate most in men, isn't it? It's responsible for the most brutalizing version of masculinity. We're in here trying to be men, right? Do we want to be men at their worst?

Lucie (*angrily*): For God's sake! We're in here trying to be ourselves. Whatever that turns out to be.

Marilyn (*with sudden authority*): I think you're wrong, all of you. You don't understand what Claire's really saying. (*Everyone stopped talking and looked at Marilyn.*) What Claire is really telling you is that her father taught her not how to win but how to lose. He didn't teach her to ride roughshod over other people. He taught her how to get up and walk away intact when other people rode roughshod over her. And he so loved the idea of teaching *that* to his children that he ignored the fact that she and her sisters were girls, and he taught it to them, anyway. (*Everyone took a moment to digest this.*)

Laura: I think Marilyn has a very good point there. That's exactly what Claire has inside her. She's the strongest person in this room, and we've all known it for a long time. She has the most integrated and most *separate* sense of herself of anyone I know. And I can see now that that probably has developed from her competitiveness. It's almost as though it provided the proper relation to other people, rather than no relation.

Sheila: Well, if that's true then her father performed a minor miracle.

Jen: You're not kidding. Knowing where you stand in relation to other people, what you're supposed to be doing, not because of what other people want of you but because of what you want for yourself . . . *knowing* what you want for yourself . . . that's everything, isn't it?

Laura: I think so. When I think of work, that's really what I think of most. And when I think of *me* and work, I swear I feel like Ulysses after 10 years at sea. I, unlike the rest of you, do not feel I am where I am because of luck or accident or through the natural striving caused by a healthy competitiveness. I feel I am like a half-maddened bull who keeps turning and turning and turning, trying to get the hell out of this maze he finds himself in . . . I spent 10 years not knowing what the hell I wanted to do with myself. So I kept getting married and having children. I've had three children and as many husbands. All nice men, all good to me, all meaningless to me. (*She stopped short, and seemed to be groping for words . . .*) I wanted to do something. Something that was real, and serious, and would involve me in a struggle with myself. Every time I got married it was like applying Mercurochrome to a festering wound. I swear sometimes I think the thing I resent most is that women have always gotten married as a way out of the struggle. It's the thing we're encouraged to do, it's the thing we rush into with such *relief*, it's the thing we come absolutely to *hate*. Because marriage itself, for most women, is so full of self-hatred. A continual unconscious reminder of all our weakness, of the heavy price to be paid for taking the easy way out. Men talk about the power of a woman in the home . . . That power has come to seem such a lopsided and malevolent thing to me. What kind of nonsense is that, anyway, to divide up the *influences* on children's lives in that bizarre way? The mother takes care of the *emotional* life of a child? The vital requirement for nourishment? Out of what special resources does *she* do that? What the hell principle of growth is operating in *her*? What gives a woman who never tests herself against structured work the wisdom or the self-discipline to oversee a child's emotional development? The whole thing is crazy. Just crazy. And it nearly drove me crazy . . . What can I say? For 10 years I felt as though I were continually vomiting up my life. . . . And now I work. I work hard and I work with great relish. I want to have a family, *too*. Love. Home. Husband. Father for the children. Of course, I do. God, the loneliness! The longing for connection! But work first. And family second. (*Her face split wide open in a big grin*). Just like a man.

Lucie: I guess I sort of feel like Laura. Only I'm not sure. I'm not sure of anything. I'm in school now. Or rather "again." Thirty years old and I'm a graduate student again, starting out almost from scratch . . . The thing is I could never take what I was doing seriously. That is, not as seriously as my brother, or any of the boys I went to school with, did. Everything seemed too long, or too hard, or too something. Underneath it all, I felt sort of *embarrassed* to study seriously. It was as if I was really feeling: "That's something the *grownups* do. It's not something for *me* to do." I asked my brother about this feeling once, and he said most men felt the same way about themselves, only they fake it better than women do. I thought about that one a long time, and I kept trying to say myself: What the hell, it's the same for them as it is for us. But . . . (*she looked swiftly around the circle*) it's not! Dammit, it's *not*. After all, style is content, right? And ours are worlds away . . .

Veronica: Literally.

Lucie: I don't know . . . I still don't know. It's a problem that nags and nags and nags at me. So often I wish some guy would just come along and I'd disappear into marriage. It's like this secret wish that I can just withdraw from it all, and then from my safe position look on and comment and laugh and say yes and no and encourage and generally play at being the judging mother, the "wise" lady of the household . . . But then I know within six months I'd be miserable! I'd be climbing the walls and feeling guilty . . .

Marilyn: Guilty! Guilty, guilty. Will we ever have a session in which the word guilty is not mentioned once? (*Outside, the bells in a nearby church tower struck midnight.*)

Diana: Let's wrap it up okay?

Veronica (*reaching for her bag*): Where shall we meet next week?

Marie: Wait a minute. Aren't we going to sum up? (*Everyone stopped in mid-leaving, and sank wearily back into her seat.*)

Lucie: Well, one thing became very clear to me. Everyone of us in some way have struggled with the idea of getting married in order to be relieved of the battle of finding and staying with good work.

Diana: And every one of us who's actually done it has made a mess of it!

Jen: And everyone who *hasn't* has made a mess of it.

Veronica: But, look. The only one of us who's really worked well—with direction and purpose—is Claire. And we all jumped on her! (*Every one was startled by this observation and no one spoke for a long moment.*)

Marilyn (*bitterly*): We can't do it, we can't admire anyone who *does* do it, and we can't let it alone . . .

Jen (*softly*): That's not quite true. After all, we were able to see finally that there was virtue in Claire's position. And we are here, aren't we?

Marie: That's right. Don't be so down. We're not 10 years old, are we? We're caught in a mess, damned if we do and damned if we don't. All right. That's exactly why we're here. To break the bind. (*On this note everyone took heart, brightened up and trooped out into the darkened Manhattan streets. Proud enough of being ready to battle.*)

Sites of Contestation
An Introduction

Though it was difficult to isolate some of the writings under these specific headings, I have organized this work around themes that radical feminism explored and disputed: lesbianism, heterosexuality, children, race, and class. Radical feminists and their activist work in the women's liberation movement focused on a range of issues and kinds of oppressions. While many of the pieces could be located in other sections of *Radical Feminism*, I have brought these together to focus and reveal the ways in which radical feminism articulated and engaged with particular key issues. Moreover, I have highlighted these areas because subsequent writings and revisions of the women's liberation movement and radical feminism have been accused of examining only issues of sex (Jaggar 1983, Tong 1994). Reading the quality and the breadth of the writing in "Sites of Contestation" should render this idea obsolete.

Many radical feminists struggled not only with why women were oppressed, but tried to reveal how various practices based on race, class position, sexual orientation, and parental status affected women. Radical feminists raised a number of issues and questions that continue to shape the thought and direction of contemporary feminist theories and women's everyday lives.

D. Lesbianism

Chapter Twenty-Eight

Lesbianism and the Women's Liberation Movement

Martha Shelley

The worst epithets used against women in the Women's Liberation Movement have been (and still are) "lesbian" and "manhater." I shall attempt here to examine what these names mean—why most women fear these labels, and why they have been so effectively used against women.

Men don't like uppity women. They don't like independent women—women who make as much money as they do, women who are as well-educated, as mobile, as free in their actions. They don't like women who aren't dependent on them—who aren't sitting at home waiting for the phone to ring, waiting for "him" to come home, women who don't feel totally crushed at the thought that some man doesn't love them anymore, women who are not terrified at the idea that a man might leave them.

So we must have two definitions for the lesbian—one in terms of her sexual relations, the other in terms of her independence of men. There are many lesbians who enjoy the company of men and who are lesbian in sexual practice only. There are many women who are celibate, but who would be perfectly happy if all men were exiled to Outer Mongolia and reproduction were carried on by means of artificial insemination.

The physical and economic oppression of women could not be carried on so effectively without a corresponding psychological oppression, the indoctrination of women which results in their desperate need for men's approval. Men are not so dependent on women—it is considered shameful for a man to refrain from a course of action simply because his wife wouldn't approve. He may keep some actions secret (such as sexual affairs) in order to keep peace in the household—but his psychological well-being does not depend on his wife's frame of mind. He is not really upset if she forgets his birthday—although he may be annoyed if he feels that she is not giving him the respect due to her lord and master. Her lack of consideration may provoke him into finding another slave.

His lack of consideration is something she blames herself for, something she feels she must bear, in spite of her feeling of utter desolation.

A woman who doesn't care what men think of her—ah, this is dangerous. This is the worst conceivable insult to the male ego. Some men find true lesbianism impossible to imagine. I once knew a fellow who believed that when two women made love, they imagined that a man was watching them. He simply could not conceive that women could function at all without a male presence. I suspect that most men who enjoy watching pornographic films about "lesbians" have his turn of mind. Most heterosexual men cannot endure watching films about male homosexuals—they find it "disgusting," "unexciting," "repulsive;" in other words, too threatening.

This attitude on the part of men has actually protected the lesbian to some degree. The male homosexual has endured much more in the way of physical persecution than the female—because straight men must at all costs eradicate the homosexual in themselves. But they don't take women seriously enough to consider lesbianism a real threat—or didn't until the Women's Liberation Movement came along. As women become more independent, I suspect that violence against us will increase.

Most lesbians have always attempted to live secretly. The few who are obvious in appearance are despised by gay and straight communities alike. Yet this schizophrenic existence takes its toll psychologically. It may be true that a higher percentage of homosexuals end up in mental institutions—driven there not by homosexuality, but by the knowledge that one slip could cost them their jobs, their education, their family and friends. Those few who are recognizable are despised under the rationale, "You shouldn't advertise what you do in bed." Those people who collapsed under the strain were simply unable to take the deception that most of us have had to live with. It isn't what you do in bed that matters so much—but the fact that you can't walk down the street holding the hand of someone you love, you can't announce to your family, your friends, your world, "This is my beloved."

The lesbian has needed more strength than most in order to survive. Besides having to develop a sense of self-esteem that can withstand intense disapproval, besides having to retain her sanity, she also has had to survive economically without the aid of men. As a result, there have been a disproportionate number of lesbians among successful women. Many of us have fought against tremendous odds to get a decent education and decent jobs. Women who need male approval have an even harder time making it in the face of men's anger at their successes.

We pay heavily for our successes, as well as for our failures. A successful woman is considered a lesbian, whatever her sexual preferences. The only way she can combat this stigma is by putting other women down and playing up to men, thus reassuring them that whatever her income, whatever her position, she still needs male approval. As for failures, if a lesbian drinks heavily or takes pills, this is ascribed to her homosexuality. No one but the most unreconstructed racist would say that black people who take drugs or commit violent acts are violent because they are black; yet men consider the self-destructiveness of homosexuals to be a result of their homosexuality, not a result of their oppression.

And men love nothing better than to hear the story of a lesbian who committed suicide.

The Psychoanalytic Myths

We all know how psychoanalysis is used against women to pressure them into conforming to their roles. This is particularly true in the case of the lesbian. The psychoanalyst, in this case, considers it his duty to "cure" her, i.e., to make her go straight. All her woes are ascribed to her homosexuality. Translated into street language, his sophisticated terminology boils down to "All she needs is a good fuck." Any changes which take place in the course of therapy, which result in her living a happier life as a lesbian, are considered as making an adjustment to a regrettable but untreatable condition. If the psychoanalyst gets the patient to state that she enjoys intercourse with men, hallelujah, he's a success!—she has been turned into a woman who needs male approval. If he fails, she was probably too far gone, and anyway, he did the best he could.

Another interesting psychoanalytic myth is that of "stages of development." It is held by some neo-Freudians that everyone passes through a homosexual period in early adolescence, and that some people become "arrested" at the homosexual stage. The heterosexual has apparently passed through that stage of development and has "put away childish things." Now let us take this theory as it is explained by its more sophisticated exponents. A homosexual period is not defined merely in terms of genital behavior, but in terms of those whom one loves. Therefore, a young person who deeply loves her best friend is considered to be passing through such a period. Someone who has genital relationships with the opposite sex but can only form enduring friendships with the same sex could not be considered a "mature" heterosexual.

I used to subscribe to this theory until it became apparent to me that there is very little love between men and women, and that most heterosexual relationships are based on a master-slave psychology which can hardly be said to characterize mature adulthood. Most relationships called "mature" by psychoanalysts are also relationships which would be acceptable to the most orthodox church-monogamous marriages, with the male as the head of the household. So this psychoanalytic construct ends up meaning that you can fool around in your youth, but you must end up "saved."

Since most heterosexuals are so frightened of homosexuality, it is hard to believe that they have successfully passed through a homosexual stage—indeed, it seems more likely that they have totally avoided the possibility of love for their own sex. And if it is true that you cannot love others until you love yourself, and that you cannot love people who are different from you (different sex, different race, different culture) until you love those who are like yourself, then it seems to me that there is very little love in the world indeed. A glance at this morning's paper confirms my impression.

I suppose I must go into the myth of the naturalness of heterosexual intercourse, although that argument has begun to bore me. Taken to its extreme, it means that sex is meant for reproduction, and that therefore any sexual act which cannot lead to reproduction (anal or oral intercourse, masturbation, intercourse with contraception) is perverted. The leading exponents of this extreme position are the hierarchy of the Roman Catholic Church. The more sophisticated position of the psychoanalyst is that all methods are permissible, but that a normal person must clearly prefer "straight" sex. This totally ignores any objective surveys in the area, which show, for example, that most people masturbate more often than they perform any other sexual acts in their lives. Or that straight sex may be most satisfactory to men, but that most women have difficulty having orgasms by this method, and that there is no such "animal" as a vaginal orgasm.

A more disturbing finding by Masters and Johnson is that frigidity is extremely rare among lesbians. This could be interpreted to mean that women simply know more about women's bodies than men do; or that women who don't care much for sex generally marry men for social convenience, since a relationship with a woman would give them the status of outcasts without any compensatory benefits.

Lesbianism and Manhating

To me, lesbianism is not an oddity of a few women to be hidden in the background of the Movement. In a way, it is the heart of the Women's Liberation Movement. In order to throw off the oppression of the male caste, women must unite—we must learn to love ourselves and each other, we must grow strong and independent of men so that we can deal with them from a position of strength. The idea that women must teach men how to love, that we must not become manhaters is, at this point in history, like preaching pacifism to the Vietcong. Women are constantly being assaulted, raped and killed if they dare to violate the unwritten curfew that says they do not belong on the streets after certain hours, but in the homes. They are told to be weak, dependent and loving. That kind of love is masochism. Love can only exist between equals, not between the oppressed and the oppressor.

Men do not love women. They perhaps become entranced at the image of the seductress, or challenged by the woman who plays "hard to get." They do not want women as people, they want only those who fit properly into the roles of sexual and domestic slaves. Any time a woman aspires to independent personhood, the reaction of men is rage.

You don't believe it. Your man lets you go on to graduate school, is encouraging you to develop a career of your own. He wants you to work. But supposing you told him that your company wanted you to move to another city—how would he like to relocate? Wives are always supposed to relocate, not husbands.

Pick up the daily newspaper in any large city and every day you will read the story of another woman brutally raped and murdered by men. When this is done to black men by white men, it is called lynching. People no longer apologize for lynching by calling it the work, of a few sick men—they recognize that lynching is the product of racism, that it is fostered by attitudes of white supremacy. The daily lynchings of women are equally the product of supremacy. They are not merely the work of a few sick individuals, but the natural outcome of a disease which affects the whole human race.

Men hate women. Some are more open about it; others are merely quietly thankful that they were not born women. And yet our whole function in life is, we are told, to love men.

The strength of an oppressed class is the love between its members, its solidarity, and its hatred of the oppressor. We are the oldest oppressed class in history—why are we afraid to hate?

Let us learn, then, to hate men, instead of hiding our rage behind a screen of placidity and niceness and pacifism. Let us not use pacifism as a screen for cowardice—even Ghandi said that it is better to have the courage of a soldier than no courage at all.

We are told that it is our job to teach men how to love, since we are so much better at it. It is not our job—not at this time—to teach men how to love. Men are not babies. Shall we continue to behave as did Uncle Tom, dying under the lash, whispering, "I love you, master—God save you?" You cannot teach while you are on your knees.

Every time a woman betrays another woman, acts bitchy for the sake of a man, she weakens the Women's Liberation Movement. Every woman whose primary loyalty is to a man draws strength away from the Movement. The lesbian is not someone for the Movement to be ashamed of, not someone to be denied, apologized for, hidden, explained away. We must stop assuring men that lesbians are in the minority, that we are mostly nice girls who really love men.

I find it very odd that I am expected to love, or at least like, men who rape my sisters. Shall I work to bring the boys home from Vietnam, our poor dear boys, so that they can turn their violence against us instead of the poor women of Mylai? I want to bring the boys home simply to end the slaughter of the Vietnamese people—but I shudder at the thought of having to deal with those whoremongers and ear-collectors when they return.

Our ultimate aim must be a loving society—one in which people can love each other regardless of sex. But we cannot confuse the future with the present. We cannot preach love to murderers and victims. We cannot pretend that it is possible to love those who torture us with their contempt, their arrogance and their violence, saying that the poor overgrown boys only act out of ignorance.

The most common reaction of "straight" women in the Movement towards their lesbian sisters has been irrational fear—the fear that we will physically attack them. Frankly, I've never heard of a homosexual attacking a heterosexual (prison rapes are usually conducted by brutalized straight men against weak or effeminate inmates). The other reaction has been that we will give the Movement a bad name—to me, this is grasping at the last straw of male approval. But more and more women in the Movement are discovering and dealing with homosexual feelings in themselves, and many are entering lesbian relationships.

I can only hope that, as the Movement grows, more and more women will come to depend on other women for emotional support, for love and comradeship. For it is only when women have ceased to fear lesbianism, have ceased to fear the consequences of their hatred for men, that we will have our liberation.

Chapter Twenty-Nine

Is Women's Liberation a Lesbian Plot?

Sidney Abbott and Barbara Love

Those threatened by or irritated with women's liberation often dismiss the movement by saying, "Oh, they're just a bunch of dykes." The response of the women's liberation movement to this charge is vital to the feminists, the lesbians, the many who accept both identities, as well as to the life and the meaning of the movement itself.

The words "dyke" and "lesbian," especially when used by men, are charged words calculated to send shivers of horror up the spines of women who want a more independent life style. Men who pride themselves on their capacity for rational responses cannot keep a cool head on this subject. They are upset and confused by women who do not fit into categories they can handle: unmarried and seeking domination, married and dominated, frustrated career woman, or incomplete old maid or spinster. But a lesbian? "Let's face the truth," says one feminist, "the greatest threat to men is solidarity among women and 'lesbianism' epitomizes that solidarity." Few words carry as much emotional meaning, independent of context, as "dyke." The word brings a heavy load of prejudice with it and blocks any discriminating thought, preventing everyone—including the feminists—from discussing the real questions involved. When the word is used women usually respond with an uneasy silence.

Women need to think through the lesbian issue so that such name calling cannot be used to divide women who should be united in a common struggle. In their paper, "The Woman-Identified Woman," members of a new Women's Liberation group, the Radicalesbians, make it very clear: "As long as the word 'dyke' can be used to frighten women into a less militant stand, keep women separate from their sisters, and keep them from giving primacy to anything other than men and family— then to that extent they are dominated by the male culture."

Lesbians have always been linked with women's liberation. Articles on the movement by the mass media alluded to them long before feminists were even willing to acknowledge their existence. But the feminists were deluding themselves. The signs were clear. They had only to examine the life style of other women in the movement or listen to their friends to see there had to be a connection somewhere. Feminists who thought the lesbians were not there for legitimate reasons and would soon leave are disillusioned by now. Conservative elements in the movement are still trying to keep the lesbians in the closet by saying lesbianism is not important and at the same time, too dangerous to deal with. From motives of safety, not honest feeling, feminists dealing with the mass media still deny there are lesbians in women's liberation. The radical feminists, however, most of whom do not cooperate with the media, have never been afraid to discuss common objectives with lesbians, and now that the lesbian's sense of self has begun to flower through the women's movement and the Gay Liberation Front, to march with them, support them in public, even aspire to a genuine exploration of the lesbian way of life.

Who are lesbians? What kind of women are they? How does their experience, both in and out of the movement, shed light on women's liberation? What do they add to the movement? To the exploration of sexism? To the idea of cultural revolution as conceived by the feminists? To the idea of self-possession?

Lesbians are women who survive without men financially and emotionally, representing the ultimate in an independent life style. Lesbians are the women who battle day by day to show that women are valid human beings, not just appendages of men. Lesbians are the women whose relationships attempt a true break with the old sexual-emotional divisions. Lesbians are the women who are penalized for their sexuality more than any other women on earth. Thus, it is no wonder that lesbians are attracted to the women's liberation movement, are active in it, and feel that they are in the vanguard of it. If women's liberation does mean liberation from the dominance of men, lesbians' opinions should be actively sought out, for in many ways the lesbian *has* freed herself from male domination.

Lesbians are women who have chosen to love other women. They have a positive attitude toward women and do not think of their lives as an alternative, or as an aggressive rejection of men. Because they have little interest in pleasing men, lesbians are not usually man-haters, as the stereotype so often has it. They do not see men as a threat to them personally, as feminists often do.

Any kind of woman may be a lesbian, even concurrently with marriage and children. Lesbians may be rich, poor, good-looking, or homely. In short, they are like anybody else, except for their sexual preference. Research since Kinsey's day indicates that there are more women who are lesbians than men who are homosexuals. In one study 50 percent of the women queried had had intense emotional relationships with other women as adults, which is defined by some as homosexuality—while 27 percent admitted overt lesbian experience.[1] Other experts estimate that there are a large number of hidden lesbians among married women. There are probably more lesbians than male homosexuals.

Some feminists have reservations about supporting the militant lesbian feminists, and their reasons should be discussed. Some insist that lesbianism is merely a practice, not a political issue. However, Cellestine Ware points out in her book *Woman Power* that "radical feminists believe that radical feminism is the only truly political cause now in existence . . . To achieve the elimination of dominance in human relationships, sex roles, i.e. stereotyped male and female identities, would have to be eradicated."[2] Peter Cohen comments that: "to live an alternative *that is totally outside the alternative of the culture* is a profoundly political act."[3]

One must look to the lesbians' oppression as part of women's oppression. One must look to the lesbians' desire to escape from the male power structure and achieve independent being. The penalties the feminist will face for openly denying her sex role will resemble those the lesbian now faces for showing an open preference for her own sex. To be a lesbian is unnatural—in men's eyes. To be a feminist is unnatural—in men's eyes. The price of rebellion against men's authority is living as an outcast without the approval and support of men.

The common enemy of feminists and lesbians is sexism. Sexism is not merely the preference of society for one sex, and the attribution to that sex of various preferred qualities and attitudes at the expense of the other sex. Sexism emerges from making reproduction rather than personal pleasure or personal development the goal of sexual intercourse. That society sanctions sex only for reproduction is clearly shown in various sex laws which make sex acts that do not lead to reproduction illegal, whether performed by two men, two women, or a man and a woman—married or unmarried. Clearly, these laws speak to our deepest fears of our own sexuality. Clearly too, these laws are obsolete, especially in light of our overpopulation problems and the growing popular belief that sex is acceptable for pleasure alone (evidenced by the widespread use of the pill and demand for repeal of abortion laws). This new acceptance of sexual liberation primarily benefits the most traditional male-female kind of sex. The homosexual is still considered perverted, although homosexual couples have not invented anything that heterosexuals cannot and do not do. Yet only the homosexual still bears the full burden of sexist fears.

Although women's liberation has insisted on the right of all women to control their own bodies, the subject has only been discussed in terms of abortion. In liberationist thinking the concept of the right to one's own body does not include freedom of sexual activities or freedom of sexual preference, which would logically seem to be a part of the kind of self-ownership and self-determination at the heart of feminist demands. This is probably because such a viewpoint would seem to come frighteningly close to actually endorsing lesbianism. Clearly, sexual freedom of all kinds would liberate women from guilt about sexual activities (heterosexual or homosexual), from performing on demand, and from the kind of sexual disappointment that comes from being held largely responsible for fulfilling sexual pleasure, as well as for conception, child-bearing, and childrearing.

People outside the movement are questioning sexist customs and attitudes within the scope of women's liberation, particularly in regard to same-sex marriages. The blessings of God for homosexual unions are now given in some churches, and various individuals have urged that same-sex marriages be more acceptable and common in the future. Rita Hauser, the United States representative to the United Nations Human Rights Commission, speaking to the American Bar Association, on "Women's Liberation and the Law," argued that laws banning marriages between persons of the same sex were unconstitutional and were based on the outmoded notion that sex was for reproduction. Margaret Mead, the well-known author and anthropologist, has advocated for a long time two-career marriages, childless marriages, same-sex marriages, and communes of adults where sex is not the central organizing factor. Only one acknowledged feminist has made this case: Caroline Bird, author of *Born Female*, speaking to the Daughters of Bilitis, a lesbian group, predicted that "in the future we will see the stranglehold of reproduction on human relations broken, and numerous life styles will be possible."

Women's liberation's great importance is that it provides an opportunity for reexamination of modes of human behavior; this should include the idea that heterosexual relationships are the only acceptable life style. If, as some interpreters of the new Equal Rights Amendment point out, the new legislation would make homosexual marriages legal, this fact should be analyzed and accepted, even promoted, but not hidden.

The fight of all women against sexism is not the only common battleground of feminists and lesbians. Both groups are part of the larger struggle against oppression waged by all groups that refuse to be dominated by a hierarchical system in which certain groups are considered naturally superior, and others naturally inferior. In this battle, assimilation is the characteristic trademark. Lesbians who conceal their sexual preference are not persecuted; feminists who remain housewives and mothers are not rejected; prostitutes who conceal their occupations are not admonished; blacks who can pass for white are not discriminated against. It is only when oppressed people stand up and openly announce who and what they are that they are either pressured into assuming their correct roles and levels in society, or they are crucified.

Feminists who continue to live off their husband's incomes and perform the traditional duties of wife and mother *at the expense of their own development* are hiding and only paying lip service to their cause, much as lesbians who flirt with men in the office. They are trying to escape discrimination by appearing to perpetuate the system. But when a feminist truly joins the movement and steps off the pedestal, temporarily leaving men or defying them, she is moving from a recognized and valued position with certain kinds of privileges into a new, lonely place, one that may involve open hostility.

Today's cultural revolution consists of group after group saying, "We won't take it anymore. We want to be human." Lesbians are now emulating some of the tactics and the practices of women's liberation, even as that movement took its cues from black liberation. What is afoot here is a general rebellion of the dispossessed of the earth; as such, feminists and lesbians are deeply tied, one to the other. It was no accident that a 1970 meeting of revolutionary groups included the Black Panthers, homosexuals, and feminists.

Out of her activism in the feminist movement, more often than not, a new kind of lesbian has emerged, a lesbian who calls herself a lesbian activist or a radical lesbian and has learned most recently the enormous power and freedom of the open assertion of who and what one is. Not only is the radical lesbian no longer ashamed of her commitment to the lesbian way of life, but after some self-searching and self-analysis, she has come to realize that most of her problems are due not to any necessarily unhealthy traits in her personality, but rather to her social oppression.

The emotional development that enables the lesbian to throw off the sex roles and sex restrictions universally accepted in our society has been commonly described as a psychopathology: a mental sickness. It is assumed that something in the individual's family environment has caused the child's development to take a wrong turn. However, some progressive psychiatrists and social workers have begun to talk about a concept called sociopathology: a sickness in society. They have found that the individuals they have treated for so-called personal problems have real problems which they are in no position to control. The environment threatens them, even physically. This continual state of threat leads to tension, which leads to various emotional problems, which cannot be solved by treatment because they are perpetuated by real pressures from a hostile society. The concept of sociopathology fosters a need for systematic analysis of all women's behavior and sheds particular light on the society's rigidity and unwillingness to tolerate many life styles for women. It points to external reasons for lesbians' distress and emotional problems. The problems of lesbians—guilt, fear, self-hatred—can therefore be regarded as part of a sociopathology, part of what is wrong with our society, preventing whole categories of people from being happy and productive.

If women are generally dominated by men in all phases of their lives, from birth until death—and if this domination is unnatural—then all of women's modes of behavior are forms of evasive action or adjustment to survive the domination. They are all ways to live in a basically threatening environment. Thus, the clinging vine, the caretaker-housewife, and the child-woman are women who have succumbed to male dominance; the driving career woman, the feminist, and the lesbian are women who have struggled to reject male dominance. Lesbianism is one reaction on the part of the growing female to the emotional understanding, shared by all females, of what it means to become a woman in our society.

According to the Radicalesbians,

> The lesbian is the rage of all women, condensed to the point of explosion. She is a woman who, often at an early age, acts in accordance with an inner compulsion to be a more complete human being than her society will allow her [to be]. These needs and conflicts, over a period of years, bring her into painful conflict with people, situations, and the accepted way of thinking, until she is in a continual state of war with everything around her, and usually with herself. She may not be fully conscious of the political implications of what for her began as personal necessity, but, on some level, she has not been able to accept the limitations and oppression laid upon her by the most basic role in society, the female role.

The lesbian often refused to play the game by rejecting dolls, kitchen playthings, sexual cunning, and instead showed an interest in the mental and physical pursuits reserved for boys—and later men. She knew that when boys said sneeringly that they didn't want to play girls' games and she mimicked them, saying she didn't want to play boys' games, she was lying. She *did* want to play boys' games. This was difficult to comprehend. As a child she was natural; at the time of puberty, when she refused to change, suddenly she was considered unnatural. When her interests and feelings did not coincide with the demands of society, the pain, bitterness, and rejection began. The pressure was on and would stay on until some force greater than the individual—liberation or death—would change it.

Women who have tried to adopt any of those human qualities and attitudes not considered natural to a female have always been labeled male-identified or lesbian. This seems unfair since the man is allowed the status of a male at the same time that he seeks all those very same human qualities. To associate the woman or the lesbian with male qualities, when she is simply trying to develop in a positively human way, is to consider both the feminist and the lesbian inauthentic. That is to say, if a woman can never be considered anything but less courageous, less intelligent, less creative, and less independent, we will only have acceptable women who are less than males. Any woman who is equal to or better than a man will be considered an aberration—a non-woman.

It is generally recognized that career role playing is unforgivable for feminists as well as for lesbians. And yet some feminists say that they once wanted to be generals, pilots, lawyers, or senators. The women who were forced by social pressure to give up these dreams are enraged.

Learning what careers or duties a woman could choose was only one lesson in the psycho-social education of a woman. She was also taught how to love men. During the preteen years a crush on another girl was considered natural, much the same as "immature" aspirations to "men's" careers were considered natural. The girls would grow out of both. But today, more and more, it appears that women are socialized into sex roles as well as career roles; there is nothing to prove that heterosexuality is any more normal than homosexuality. Women's liberation has not yet dealt with role playing in terms of sexual orientation.

Certainly by role playing, both in career aspirations and in love relationships, the woman is not truly living. She is living life much as an actress who assumes or is assigned a part. She is not living a fully conscious life, making her own choices. Role playing must be seen as an escape from reality, much like the use of alcohol, drugs, or hypnosis. These are forms of half-death or semiconsciousness. Implicit in the act of jettisoning the role is the need to live a fully conscious life.

In *The Second Sex* Simone de Beauvoir expresses her conception of the natural response of women: "If nature is to be invoked, one can say that all women are naturally homosexual. The lesbian, in fact, is distinguished by her refusal of the male and her liking for feminine flesh; but every adolescent female fears penetration and masculine domination, and she feels a certain repulsion for the male body; on the other hand, the female body is for her, as for the male, an object of desire."[4]

People must come to realize and admit openly that there are varieties of sexuality, of which heterosexuality happens to be the most popular but not necessarily the most valid. Women's liberation must promote the issue as a nonissue of no more importance than a person's preference for Swiss or American cheese.

The return of those natural feelings for other women is a phenomenon that has certainly been released for investigation by the women's movement. It is expressed by two women from the Class Workshop who attended an all-women's dance held by the Gay Liberation Front. These feminists—not lesbians—published their reactions in the underground newspaper *Rat:* "I saw the possibility of having an experience that would counter the limited dance definition . . . there would be present only women, in a social context of wanting to relate to women. What I experienced was a sense of emotional feeling without restriction, for women. When I danced close to another woman I was aware of how much feeling for one another we do have, yet are told not to express—and how this must stultify our personal relationships." The second reaction: "I was moved but experienced no great upheaval. It was not anything like a religious conversion. The idea of women loving other women just became more palpable and natural to me."

Because both feminists and lesbians lead independent lives, feminists are more likely to understand the lesbian point of view and accept their own homosexual feelings without the hysteria often seen in other women. It is also interesting to note that one of the few women recognized as a poet and a teacher in early Greek culture when women were confined to their homes was the "original" lesbian, Sappho, from the island of Lesbos.

The lesbian has taken the ultimate liberty heterosexual women are not permitted: to live and love exactly as she pleases. She does not make emotional tradeoffs for the privileges of being a lady. For this she is violently hated and tormented. Lesbianism is the one response to male domination that is unforgivable. The lesbian is labeled unnatural and forced to live unnaturally. As expressed blatantly by Simone de Beauvoir in *The Second Sex*, "If there is a great deal of aggressiveness and affection in the attitude of Lesbians, there is no way they can live naturally in their situations; being natural implies being unselfconscious, not picturing one's acts to oneself. She can go her own way in calm indifference only when she is old enough or backed by considerable social prestige."[5]

Lesbians are doubly outcast, both as women and as homosexuals. Lesbians, like all women, are not encouraged to be independent or to educate themselves; as women they are always treated as inferior. On the other hand, they are denied the benefits of the sexist system: financial security, recognition in the home, maternal power. They suffer the oppression of all women but are not eligible for any of the rewards. Whereas heterosexual women are moving from a position in society that is privileged—wife and mother—to a freer position, lesbians are a minority fighting for the right to exist. The lesbian suffers the oppression of all women—only more so. Women get lower pay than men on the job, while lesbians are fired when their sexual preference is discovered. (Lesbians have not yet reached the level of tokenism.) A woman in college is fighting for grades equal to men's, but a lesbian is coping with fears and anxieties about being expelled. A divorced woman has a nearly unchallenged right to her children but a lesbian's children are forcibly taken from her. Men are satisfied if a woman remains silent, but a lesbian triggers anger and hostility. A gigantic law suit should be instituted against schools, industry, and the psychiatric profession for severe psychic damage done to homosexuals, as well as to women.

Allies are difficult to find. Lesbians do not have the benefit of reliable support from straight sisters or gay brothers. Women—even those in women's liberation—are often sexist, in that they do not accept the lesbian's sexual preference; male homosexuals are often sexist, in that they often dismiss women or overlook them.

Male homosexuals who want unity with lesbians are being confronted with their sexism, but they do have other differences that keep them from identifying completely with lesbians. Male homosexuals are persecuted by police harassment and by legal sanctions. They suffer a fairly direct oppression, designed to limit their numbers or even eliminate them. Lesbians are spared much of this harassment, but they are ridiculed instead. Seen as imitation men, they are a laughingstock for both sexes.

Although not considered important enough to harass and persecute very often, they live under an extreme form of psychological censure. Women who feel little or no threat from male homosexuals dread and are repulsed by lesbians, men who are not threatened by male homosexuals are curiously afraid of lesbians.

More than male homosexuals, lesbians are seen as a threat to the entire system based on sexual relationships. A male homosexual retains his male life style. In fact, he often views himself as a supermale, freed from the need for women and active in an all-male world not altogether different from that of a select men's club or sports team. He is promiscuous, and his promiscuity is a male privilege. He sometimes feels superior to the domesticated, suburban male. Lesbians try to live a stable life, more often they try to build a home life without men. Clearly, this is not permissible within the male sexist system. It is acceptable for a man to do without women, as in men's clubs, sports, or the army, but it is never acceptable for a woman to be without a man. A woman is defined in relationship to men and family. A female without a man and a family is not considered a complete woman, but rather a failed woman. The single man is a bachelor; the single woman is an old maid—or a lesbian.

Many women conceal parts of themselves from men, but as a homosexual, the lesbian suffers the pain of living entirely underground. In an article entitled "Gay Is Good," Martha Shelley explains:

> Understand this—that the worst part of being homosexual is having to keep it a secret. Not the occasional murders by police or teenage queer-beaters, not the loss of jobs or expulsion from school, nor dishonorable discharges—but the daily knowledge that what you are is so awful that it cannot be revealed. The violence against us is sporadic. Most of us are not affected. But the internal violence of being made to carry—or choosing to carry—the load of your straight society's unconscious guilt—this is what tears us apart, what makes us want to stand up in the office, in the factories, and in the schools and shout our true identity.

Some of the effects of living the lie are shown in the following excerpts taken from "Journals of Two Lovers," the story of a lesbian relationship. The first entry talks about the effects of trying to live without hiding: "The only way we can imagine living as lesbians together is to have a fast car and lots of money—to set up a temporary life for a few weeks before moving on—living an interim existence between discovery and discovery. Running, like fugitives. No way to settle down and live a productive life, no matter how great the desire, knowing that whatever we built would be ruined the instant our love was revealed." Another entry reveals the price of remaining silent: "I was sitting at the dinner table with my family ready to enjoy a beautiful meal—a virtual feast. We were celebrating a family reunion. My parents had just come back from Europe. Our hearts warmed as Pop stood up to give his traditional toast: 'When your mother and I were in Europe we had two boys at the next dinner table who were living together. It was very sad. The parents must suffer terribly. We thought how lucky we are that all of our kids are healthy. Skol.' My throat closed off and my whole body was racing. This meal was clearly not for me— a lesbian. It was for someone in my family who did not exist."

Any well-intentioned individual, including a lesbian, needs self-respect for a positive outlook on the world. Self-respect demands honesty. For a lesbian to have to deny who she is—outright or by default—is dishonest and destructive. The guilt associated with lying is tremendous especially when that lying is for life. The lesbian has lived the lie because honesty means confronting society's hate alone. To declare oneself a lesbian is still tantamount to a Jew declaring himself in Nazi Germany. Maybe the lesbian will not be killed, but she risks losing everything and everybody important to her and putting a burden of suspicion or guilt on anyone who accepts her.

The lesbian is bombarded daily by society's thousands of little messages that insist her very life is a crime, just as heterosexual women absorb thousands of messages that insist they are not equal to men. The lesbian may carry guilt like a criminal; during the period called "coming out," when she begins to accept her lesbianism, she may feel very like Raskolnikov in *Crime and Punishment:* she wants to cry out to the world, but she dares not. As explained by Theodor Reik, "Something of the need for punishment finds partial gratification in the compulsion to confess." Fear of punishment creates tremendous anxiety, even though punishment may not occur. Lesbians have committed suicide rather than confess what should be a joyous and celebrated love. They still do. It is evidence of the individual courage of lesbians that they are not jumping out of buildings every day.

The one protection offered many lesbians is the possibility of hiding. It is relatively easy for perhaps 90 percent to "pass for white." The obvious lesbians, the ones who look boyish and are usually identified as lesbians, are a minority within a minority. The homosexual movement is different from other movements because of the *ease* of concealment. As a social movement fighting for acceptance, lesbians and male homosexuals will have to find a way to mobilize the many homosexuals who still feel they cannot afford to "come out" into the open.

Lesbians early saw women's liberation as a salvation—a movement that recognized women in a new way and seemed to advocate an independent life style similar to the lesbian life style. Lesbians not only needed better jobs, education, and pay, and the benefit of public accommodations laws, but also felt an affinity with the angry, struggling feminists who want their own identities. In fact, lesbians had a sense of déjà vu: they knew the frustration, the torn state of mind of the feminists very well. Their present life styles and outlook seemed to have a great deal in common. For lesbians who were still very alone and divided, it was intoxicating to be suddenly a part of a broad societal movement for human rights that could bring about lasting social change and a recognition of women's equality and independence. That was the strong pull. The push was that the Daughters of Bilitis, a fifteen-year-old lesbian organization, was not an activist group at a time when action became imperative. The DOB has always billed itself as "a home away from home"; it urges adjustment of the individual to society. When women's liberation opened the door to an activist role in the outside world, lesbians did not hesitate to step across that threshold, immediately joining NOW and other groups.

But there was one catch. Although active in a movement that touched on everything they lived and fought for, lesbians still had to remain silent. Early on, this silence stemmed from habit, tradition, and a sense of survival, as well as courtesy to the straight feminists, who were tense enough about the "dyke" accusations anyway. Later, lesbians hid because they were openly put down and fear was expressed that a large number of lesbians would join the movement. They were called the Achilles' heel of the movement and referred to by a star-studded NOW official as the Lavender Menace, a tag first given to Oscar Wilde. But the final blow was an open act of discrimination. A NOW official took the liberty of editing the one official press release from the first Congress to Unite Women, held in the fall of 1969. From the total of approximately fifteen organizations, she deleted the names of two lesbian groups. Then, in the report on the congress, she and another NOW woman described as "tabled" a workshop motion that was pro-lesbian. Other women recalled that the workshop motion had passed.

Discrimination was recognized in other feminist groups as well. A lesbian in Redstockings, for example, reported at the time that there was no interest in dealing with lesbian problems, no matter how often or how vehemently lesbians fought for abortion repeal and child-care centers. The lesbians became aware that only certain kinds of life styles were acceptable to the movement, and only the problems of those life styles would be considered.

Three volatile young women dropped out of NOW early in 1970. They made clear to everyone in the organization why they were leaving and published an addendum to the organization's newsletter at their own expense, damning NOW on several charges, including sexism. The notice stated in part: "We protest New York NOW's sexist viewpoint. The leadership constantly oppresses other women on the question of sexual preference—or, in plain words, enormous prejudice is directed against the lesbian. 'Lesbian' is the one word that causes the executive committee to have a collective heart attack ... the prevailing attitude is 'Suppose they flock to us in droves, how horrible.' May we remind you that this is a male-oriented image of lesbianism."

One of the three then called a meeting at her apartment to discuss the discrimination against lesbians in women's liberation. The meeting was attended by some thirty women who were active in women's liberation and the Gay Liberation Front. Three consciousness-raising groups were formed. The GLF women proposed preparing a position paper on lesbianism for the women's liberation movement.

As work on the paper proceeded, the writers and others began to plan its presentation. Nothing seemed more natural than to bring it to the second Congress to Unite Women (this time the congress was not being run by NOW, but by a coalition of more radical feminists). The planning and writing group called themselves the Radicalesbians. As they grew and transformed themselves into an action group, they began to call themselves the Lavender Menace in memory of the NOW official's indictment.

At the opening Friday evening session of the congress, the lights in the public auditorium suddenly went out. When they flashed on again there were thirty Menaces in lavender T-shirts boldly lettered with the derisive name they had taken for their own. Much as the blacks had taken "Black is Beautiful" as a slogan to reverse their image, lesbians now said "Gay is Good" and used the words "lesbian" and "dyke" in a positive, fun-loving manner. Signs they carried read "Take a lesbian to lunch" and "Super-dyke loves you." The Menace liberated the microphone for the evening and led an open forum on sexism within the movement. One of the first to speak was a gray-haired feminist, Ruth Gage Colby. She said slowly: This is an historic moment. For the first time in thousands of years, since the days of Sappho, these women, many of whom are intelligent and talented, and who have much to offer, have come out of hiding." Even the Menace had not expected this reaction. The next day lesbians held workshops on sexism in the movement, and they also invited the feminists to a dance after the congress.

Predictably, reactions to the weekend's activities were varied, but many women felt in their guts (and some verbalized it) that the lesbians' openness was a kind of bravery that provided an opportunity to reevaluate their own opinions of lesbianism and the genuine issues of sexism within feminism. The feminists' acceptance of the lesbians' action was the first *revolutionary* step toward bidding themselves of the sexist, male-identified, and over-powering sex-role system. The massive conscious-ness-raising among lesbians marked the beginning of a joint struggle, with women— both heterosexual and homosexual—fighting together openly for a social revolution that seeks to dissolve traditional sex roles and to bring about a new world of self-possession, one which must admit the emotional life of the homosexual and allow all women to live their lives as they themselves define them.

The new lesbian attitudes and actions are a kind of paradigm of the women's liberation movement: the lesbians decided to get up from the human garbage pile and walk away. As blacks had done and women had done they took to the streets and marched for their rights. On June 28, 1970, 5,000 to 10,000 homosexuals (mass media estimates) marched up Sixth Avenue to Central Park in New York, proclaim-ing their new pride and solidarity and protesting laws that make homosexual acts between consenting adults illegal and social conditions that make is impossible for homosexuals to display affection in public maintain jobs, or rent apartments. There were also marches in Los Angeles and Chicago and a Gay-in on the Boston Com-mons. The Reverend Troy Perry, pastor of the Metropolitan Community Church in Los Angeles, and two lesbians began a fast.

Lesbians in New York marched behind the banner "Lesbians Unite." One tall blonde girl, who marched with her shoulders back and a ready smile, wore a gigantic sign, "I am a lesbian and I am beautiful"; her picture was carried by hundreds of papers across the country. Although the call was not put out to women's liberation groups, a few feminists—even members of NOW—did join the lesbians without the benefit of distinguishing banners or signs. One woman from WITCH was confronted in her apartment building about her participation. She refused to justify her actions by saying she was not a lesbian, but rather a feminist realizing that such a distinction would be a put down of her lesbian sisters.

Women's liberation should consider lesbianism a total life style that is valid in itself, not simply a matter of sexual union. In terms of their experience, lesbians have a great deal to offer the women's liberation movement since they live independently of men and form bonds based on much more equitable relations. Also, a number of lesbians have been married or have children and so don't understand the position of the lone woman.

The lesbian who unlearns or never learns what society tries to teach her about how to lead her life, and who lives as she wants and needs to live, indicates that sex roles and attributes are learned or arbitrary, not natural. The lesbian foreshadows a time when individuals will create themselves from the total range of human qualities and not limit themselves to those ascribed by culture's reading of their biology.

When faced with actually developing those male identified traits necessary for independent survival, many women are ambivalent; they feel threatened; they have no idea of how to go about acquiring independence. The lesbian has learned the hard way. Now the feminist must start learning. Lesbians develop an awareness of the reality of independence at an early age. When you are in conflict with society, you need all the assets you can get. Independence from men means total responsibility for self, for a love relationship, and even for children.

Women who oppose the basic social notion that a woman should have a man must realize that what this actually means is: if you do not have a man around, you must be prepared to take total responsibility for your life. Women must set their own goals because they will no longer be merely supporters of men's goals. Therefore, a middle-class woman, for example, must consider higher education, study opportunities for promotions and pensions, and learn about real estate, insurance, politics, banking, and stocks. She will also have to respond to the smaller challenges like caring for a car, understanding simple mechanical and electrical appliances, painting, carpentry, and doing the budget. And naturally she will have to open her own doors and light her own cigarettes. Life becomes greatly expanded. Responsibilities both small and large multiply. Because the lesbian was not trying to interest men and probably rejected much limiting and damaging advice, she has an advantage over the feminist. She knows how to survive as a loner.

Equality in emotional-sexual relationships is another feminist ideal that makes an investigation of lesbian relationships important for women's liberation. Men find it difficult really to accept women as equals. Behind every man is a woman, men say, and that is the way it has always been. It will be a long time, it seems, before men will be willing to give up their positions of power, prestige, knowledge, and privilege. A few are trying and may be into men's liberation, but they are often ridiculed by other men who consider them less than men. Men want to be accepted in the male society of club-rooms; it is important for a man to be a man's man. That means being in control of one's family, not being equal partners. Thus, in the average heterosexual relationship the woman is still forced to give up many career and educational possibilities to support her husband and be a good wife. She is also expected to give up her friends and associate with the wives of her husband's friends, robbing herself of much stimulation in areas that might have interested her.

Feminists who have men in their lives and are free to demonstrate and fight for equality complain that the wonderful feelings of independence, self-possession, and self-determination they have around other women are shot down when they come home and are dominated by men in bed. No matter what the feminist does, the physical act throws both woman and man back into role playing: the male as conqueror asserts his masculinity and the female is expected to be a passive receiver. All of her politics are instantly shattered.

Love has only recently been analyzed in terms of power, a type of mass domination of women through personal domination in heterosexual love relationships. As long as women wait, accept, and succumb to domination physically, there is no hope that they will be free emotionally. Because there are very few men at this time willing to work at truly equal relationships, certain radical women's groups have turned with an almost religious dedication to celibacy or masturbation. Some have made a conscious or political decision to be lesbians.

Freedom from sexual domination by men has left lesbians free to pursue other areas or interest, albeit guilt and fear have in many ways kept them from achieving. Thus, when men call all women who succeed *lesbians*, there is an unconscious recognition that these women are not devoting 100 percent of their efforts to their duty of serving men. Man goes without love, puts it second, or treats it casually because his life is so much greater than the home. It extends to the community, the nation, the world, the universe. He not only brings the bacon home, he brings the outside world home for his woman to experience vicariously. He has a much greater love than that for his wife. The wife, on the other hand, may have no other love.

Love between equals provides the most fulfilling relationship. Anything short of equality in a love relationship is destructive, as one person usually gives always and lacks fulfillment. That one is almost invariably the woman. Total love is total vulnerability and unselfishness and should allow both parties to receive maximum pleasure. A mutual giving and taking provides a mutual renewal. If a woman always gives emotionally, which is her accepted role—in and out of love-making—her emotions are not replenished, certainly not through material goods, as the system would indicate. An equal experience is an enrichment shared by two lovers; this can be two women who instinctively know each other's needs and honor them.

The lesbian both expands and curtails her activities to work things out so that both partners have maximum opportunities. She sees very clearly that there are no specific roles, that the song-and-dance about men's jobs often merely keeps women from performing tasks that are stimulating and interesting. Lesbians have found that equality requires a great deal of honesty and understanding. In the absence of roles there is no prescribed way of thinking or acting. Everything is open for new consideration, from who will wash the dishes, to who will aggress in love, to who will relocate for whom. There are no traditional, social, legal, or moral statutes to base decisions on. Like all freedoms, freedom from role playing requires work. Each couple has to find its own way and there is no "how to do it" book available.

Unquestionably decisions made with the understanding of two people are more difficult than those made by a single person—the man. Decisions between equals are always difficult and can bring on a new kind of stress. But usually it is the kind of stress that results in healthy decisions and not in practiced reactions. The equality can lead to flexibility, change, and growth.

What happens when big decisions come along, such as one woman accepting a job promotion that requires moving? Because of the simplicity of the heterosexual role as it is currently structured, the woman would simply follow the man. However, in a homosexual relationship, where both women usually have careers, the second woman is not necessarily obligated to follow; with no marriage, no children, no common property, no legal binds, and no social pressures or supports to keep them together, lesbians can and often do split. What happens here is something for feminists to observe carefully, an object lesson for the future difficulties that will come with working out the most challenging relationship of all.

With equality in relationships with men so difficult, many woman are now considering separatism—in whole or in part—as a temporary way of life. This would mean that during the struggle men and women remain apart to discover who they are and what they are capable of. A frightening idea, perhaps, but separatism for a time may be healthy. In active relationships with men, women often spend more time and energy fighting old ways of relating and defining themselves, rather than creating new ones.

A vital relationship between lesbians and women's liberation is in their mutual interest in a time of changing relationships. Lesbians are the women who potentially can demonstrate life outside the male power structure that dominates marriage as well as every other aspect of our culture. Thus, the lesbian movement is not only related to women's liberation, it is at the very heart of it. The attitude toward lesbians is an indicator by which to measure the extent of women's actual liberation. On the other hand, women's liberation undoubtedly addresses the deepest interests of lesbians, who have the greatest stake in women's social, economic, and cultural progress, as they will never benefit from the rewards and privileges that normally come only with male relationships.

Del Martin, a founder of the Daughters of Bilitis, defines the interests lesbians have in common with women's liberation:

> By her very nature, the lesbian is cast in the role of breadwinner and will be a member of society's working force for the rest of her life. Because of [women's] traditionally low-paying work, the lesbian is very much concerned with equal job opportunities and equal pay. Because of her anticipated longevity in the working force, she is concerned with equal opportunities and for professional careers for women. Because she is taxed as a single person at the highest rate, regardless of commitments, the lesbian is also concerned with tax deductions for head of household. Because she may be a working mother and alone, she has a definite stake in proposals for child-care centers. Because of social pressures against manifestations of lesbianism, she may even have need for birth control information, and/or abortion. Economically and family-wise, the lesbian is very much tied to the Women's Movement.

With so many strong common grievances, women's liberation should expect lesbians to enter the movement in greater numbers than in other organizations and in greater proportion than in the general population. And they will be vocal, even on those relatively establishment-type demands that concern them. If the relationship between women's liberation and lesbianism can be dealt with intellectually and without emotional fear and prejudice, lesbians could become the bulwark of the movement instead of its Achilles' heel.

Recognition of the validity of the lesbian life style and acceptance of lesbian activism in women's liberation is crucial to the women's movement's ultimate goal— a new, harmonious, cooperative, nonauthoritarian society in which men and women are free to be themselves. To end the oppression of the lesbian is to admit of a wider range of being and acting under the generic name "woman." It is a cause that must be undertaken by women's liberation if women are truly to free themselves.

NOTES

1. The 2,200 women study quoted in *Female Homosexuality*, Frank S. Caprio (New York: Citadel Press, 1954), p. 56.

2. Cellestine Ware, *Woman Power* (New York: Tower Public Affairs Book, 1970), p. 107.

3. Peter Cohen in *ibid.*, p. 18. Our italics.

4. Simone de Beauvoir, *The Second Sex* (New York: Bantam Books, 1961), p. 382.

5. Beauvoir, *op. cit.*, p. 396.

Chapter Thirty

The Black Lesbian

Elandria V. Henderson

We are oppressed triply by society: (1) Black-Racism (2) Women-Sexism (3) Homosexual-Heterosexual bias. We naively entered the gay movement hoping to fight for common goals. In our gay movement we find ourselves subjected to racism and sexism. We find ourselves unable to relate with our gay white sisters and brothers. We cannot deal with this type of oppression. We must have a chance to work on our own oppression as black gay women. After meeting this in our gay movement, we turn to black liberation, but then find we are oppressed as gay women. We are asked to make a choice. We are Black, we are gay, we are women, we are Black Gay Women. We cannot split ourselves. We cannot fight against heterosexual bias and be subjected to racism. We cannot fight racism and be subjected to sexism. We cannot battle sexism and be subjected to heterosexual bias. It is inconceivable for us to win our battle against heterosexual bias and be placed in a role of an abnormal perverted alternative to straight society, that is Aunt Jemima. It is inconceivable for us to win equality for black people and be placed in the role of a push-button man-made woman, i.e. sick Lesbian. It is inconceivable for us to win our war against sexism and be put in the role of Uncle Tom, nigger, happy slave, i.e., Playboy-bunny. We must work on all three oppressions or not at all. I don't want to go for a job, be hired, receive lower pay because I am a woman, forced to do subordinate work because I am black and be fired because I am a Lesbian. After my clash with society because of my three-fold oppression I don't want to come to a gay meeting and have to put up with racism because whitey's problems come first. I don't want to be told to be a lady, or asked to speak softly, because I am a woman. We should be sheltered from our oppression by our own people. By our own people I mean Gay people, Black people and Women. By our own people I don't mean white, straight middle-class men. We have to fight women's liberation, because we are gay and we have to fight whitey because we are black. We have to fight men because we are women. Do we have to become completely separate in our revolution? Do we have to break off from our gay white sisters and brothers? Is there no place for us in Gay Liberation, in Black Liberation, in society? Don't think I am begging you, Mr. Oppressor, to give us a place to work on our common oppression. Don't think I am straight, Uncle-Tom pricking it. By no means. We will continue to demand our right to exist as productive, free, equal, black, gay beautiful women. We are not for a second about to forget that we are against racism, sexism and heterosexual bias. There is a place for us in this society, and we will proudly take it at all costs. Even if it means breaking off from our so-called liberal white sisters and brothers, so-called liberal gay sisters and brothers, so-called liberal black sisters and brothers. Get-it-together, because we are.

Chapter Thirty-One

Black and Blacklesbian

Margaret Sloan

What have you got to offer us? You wonder where we are and we say right in front of you. You offer us psychological rhetoric and we give you feelings and emotions which you charge are loud and violent. You cry dry tears while we bleed. You like to watch us dance for you but you never ask us to dance with you. You imagine/think/fantasize we fuck better which either keeps you on our backs or miles away. You assume we are mostly all dykes and the fem in us you try to butch. You use our blackness as an excuse more than we do and you never try to see the pain behind all our laughter. When you are around us you talk black and we find ourselves talking white and you even come to our parties bringing a 1969 Aretha Franklin record and when we confront you, you say we're too powerful to deal with and you don't come to our neighborhood after dark except in groups when *your* men have raped us (you too) for over 300 years. I can't call you my sister until you stop participating in my oppression. You can't have a struggle without all oppressed people—and black women, particularly black lesbians, have struggled harder than anyone. You need us and we can work and will work with you if only you accept us where we've been. Where we are, where we come from.

Chapter Thirty-Two

The Soul Selects
A New Separate Way

Frances

Some decisions are easy. I knew quickly that I did not want to be part of a Marxist discussion group which was going to read and discuss what Marx, Lenin and Stalin had to say about the "woman question." I knew when I was being treated as a "reliable" woman, who would support the positions of the now defunct central women's liberation group in Washington. In retreat into the male culture, I realized that my life had become dominated by three males: my husband, a political co-worker and a male friend. I came to *oob* [off our backs] to be with women again. The most basic morality is that we ought to care about ourselves, look out for what is clearly ourself-interest. But it is also important to implement our beliefs with respect to ourselves as part of the women's movement. Radicalesbianism speaks to the question of the liberation of all women and challenges us to take action. The conflict between my own interest as a self and my interest as a woman gives rise to a dilemma in my life. This article is an attempt to resolve this dilemma.

Radicalesbianism

The essence of the radicalesbian challenge to the rest of the women's movement is that men fuck women over, yet women continue to live with them, screw them and pick up after them. Women, tell men to fuck off and be with women. Further radicalesbian demands are: leave men, including your male children, become a lesbian, live with women, preferably in a women's commune, understand that sexism is the root cause of all the world's ills and that the hope of the planet is a woman's revolution, and devote all your energies to women, in an extreme form, to lesbians alone. Radicalesbians hope to persuade "straight" women to become lesbians and lesbians to a radical political position.

Radicalesbianism is strategically a super-Lysistrata action to bring men to terms, an extreme form of feminism which gives women's interests exclusive attention. "A crock of shit," says a friend. "I counter, But a challenging crock of shit." It is daring, reckless to say, "We will not depend on men. We will be strong human beings and build our own culture and collectivity outside the culture which says it's human but which is in reality white, heterosexual, male." Okay radicalesbianism is fanaticism and theology, but sometimes it is more conducive to self-respect to be an extremist, to take "the leap of faith," whether as anarchists, radicals, radicalesbians, whatever, and risk making fools of ourselves and being wrong than to sit back and finger and count the prune pits of our oppression. At some point, some, if not all of us, are going to have to turn our lives inside out.

To be in Women's Liberation even before radicalesbianism was to be somewhat of a separatist. Men were not allowed to participate, except when it came to day care and then on female terms, for female convenience, however tokenistic this male support was. The difference now is that separatism is not meetings two or three nights a week but a commitment of an ever-widening area of one's life to women, and at a deeper level.

Feminism

But feminism, even as simply an espousal of women's rights offers postponed gratification. Terms some women can't or won't accept. I am reminded of a woman just out of college who went with me to a course on women's liberation and refused to go back. She said: "I know I'll have to cope with all of that someday, but it will ruin all my relationships and change my life, and I'm having a good time." She was right. If we say we are feminists, we must be prepared to take responsibility for ourselves in our own right and give up the "protections" granted by males to our sex. Perhaps that the women's movement depends on women who are able to deny the gratification of tokenism, individual solutions, and upward mobility for the greater gratification of liberation is one reason for its being so middle class. And the immediate gratifications seem real and attainable.

The temptation to buy time is great, to retreat into domesticity, another baby, a career, graduate school, to do labor union organizing, to start a literary magazine with a male friend, or to patch it up with a rejected husband. I fantasize sometimes that my inherant abilities and talents will propel me over-all the sexual barriers into success in the male culture. But this is only a fantasy, for the reality is that we must finally come face to face with ourselves, with taking control of that portion of our lives we have control over. While we are in the male culture we are not going to be great artists, or anything, because while we are in it we are going to either identify with men and ultimately be sneered at by them and know in our hearts we are living a lie, trading off our womanhood for a sham personhood, or accept ourselves solely in our relation to men without even the pretence of being persons in our own right.

And does radicalesbianism work, or is it merely an impractical moral challenge? It doesn't work in the sense that every woman will eventually become a lesbian separatist and bring men to their knees under benevolent female despotism. It does in the respect that radicalesbians exhibit vitality and commitment. "They flagellate themselves to frenzy," says a friend. Another friend, trying to fight her way out of her own dependencies thinks that radicalesbians work with impressive energy and seriousness "because they are more dependent on one another." This is only partly true. Those of us on *oob* who do not have secure readily available social structures outside the collective put more emotional demands on the group and resent the others who would make the collective a work group alone. But another factor is the congruence of the radicalesbian social structure with the radicalesbian work group, which tends to be stronger with radicalesbians than with non radicalesbians. Social structures outside the work group use up a lot of energy in their maintenance. When the need for secure emotional relationships; shifts from outside to within the work group, energy is freed for other conscious women and their struggles and we push harder and longer towards liberation.

A second is that our husbands, quasi-husbands, male friends, etc., no matter how well meaning and supportive they are, and most are not, will lag behind us in confronting sexism and raising their own human consciousness, because they can only indirectly know the conflict we feel in trying to be whole persons in a male world. It will always be women who will initiate breaking out of sexist structures.

A third reason separatism works is that being separated from men frees us from heterosexual privilege. One is the ego reinforcement of being accepted for filling a socially admirable role.

For about six months, my husband and I have been living apart. Caught up in the general regression of the holidays and the precocious manipulation of our son, "I want both my parents," we went on Christmas Eve to the big department store downtown to see Santa Claus. For the first time I noticed the smiles of approval and understanding and the good-natured comments about our son. If I had been alone or with women friends the same people would have rejected me at once. I used to never question this unearned acceptance.

But giving up of privilege forces us into the sink-or-swim situation of learning to live without the props of male approval and support.

Lesbianism

Yet there is a strength that comes not from the freedom due to separation, but from what we are open and give ourselves to. Being able to and wanting to love another woman, however flawed that love may be, seem generally to be accompanied by a greater seriousness about oneself and all women, including those we experience sexual desire for. The empowering love described in Rita Mae Brown's "Dancing the Shout to the True Gospel, Or the Song My Movement Sisters Won't Let Me Sing" (awful title), which causes the poet to feel as if she could "rip great holes in the night / so the sun blasts through" is an undeniably precious elixir.

Although lesbianism frees women from heterosexual dependence on men, the false glamour with which the women's movement has endowed lesbianism cannot help but cause a replay of disillusionment with the sisterhood myth. Most of us have learned the limits of the sisterhood myth, and no longer can be guilted by the expectations of sisterly solidarity into uncritical acceptance of all women, whitewashing it with sisterhood rhetoric. That we are women isn't going to prevent us from being liberal about other women. That we are lesbians isn't automatically going to free us from our own sexism or solve our interpersonal problems. I fear for the women who tell me "If this (heterosexual) relationship fails, I'll become a lesbian. Sometimes I think the feminists who advocated celibacy and sublimation of sexual impulses were right when they argued that all sexual relationships are painful, self-destructive and ought to be avoided. A friend reminds me that "anything requiring effort is potentially self-destructive."

The question of whether radicalesbianism works or not is really beside the point of my dilemma. Even if the strategy were clearly the most effective way toward female liberation, I would not espouse it as the package deal in which it is usually presented.

Ultimately it is an abuse of human eros to channel its power for political purposes, to lend solidarity to a collective or to effect a strategy. I would mistrust sexual feeling which were motivated by a political consideration, however worthy the political objective was. I'm selfish enough to want to be loved for me, or mostly so.

A radicalesbian said when I asked her whether she thought all women had sexual feelings for other women: "If they don't they ought to." Ought to! Ought to is as bad as the ought not to have. Granted lesbianism is not a "personal choice" in a heterosexual society. But lesbianism should not be a "political choice." If it is true, and I suspect it may be, that lesbianism generates energy, assertiveness and strength, to demand that women "become" lesbians so that they may be more useful to the women's movement seems only slightly less inhuman than demanding that "mentally ill" people submit to behaviorist manipulation so they can more quickly become useful members of society.

For myself at present the resolution of this moral dilemma is to sort out the separatist elements of radicalesbianism and advocate this separatism on grounds that offer women a chance for personhood, a place to get free of male definitions and identifications and decide what kind of revolutionary person she wants to be: Of course, it is easier to be a separatist if you are gay and know it than if you are in a close emotional relationship with a man and have never been aware of a sexual feeling for another woman. Nevertheless, separatism can be a political decision.

From this perspective women's movement activity will no longer be a counter-irritant to our oppression, a "radical night out," and an escape from making hard decisions about our personal lives.

Arguing in meetings, making political decisions, and enjoying female comradeship are great fun. It is liberating, but not fun to learn difficult skills and end destructive marriages. But ultimately to feel right about ourselves we must get out of situations which distort us and sap our strength.

Chapter Thirty-Three

Lesbians in Revolt

Charlotte Bunch

The development of lesbian-feminist politics as the basis for the liberation of women is our top priority; this article outlines our present ideas. In our society, which defines all people and institutions for the benefit of the rich, white male, the lesbian is in revolt. In revolt because she defines herself in terms of women and rejects the male definitions of how she should feel, act, look, and live. To be a lesbian is to love oneself, woman, in a culture that denigrates and despises women. The lesbian rejects male sexual/political domination; she defies his world, his social organization, his ideology, and his definition of her as inferior. Lesbianism puts women first while the society declares the male supreme. Lesbianism threatens male supremacy at its core. When politically conscious and organized, it is central to destroying our sexist, racist, capitalist, imperialist system.

Lesbianism Is a Political Choice

Male society defines lesbianism as a sexual act, which reflects men's limited view of women: they think of us only in terms of sex. They also say lesbians are not real women, so a real woman is one who gets fucked by men. We say that a lesbian is a woman whose sense of self and energies, including sexual energies, center around women—she is woman-identified. The woman-identified-woman commits herself to other women for political, emotional, physical, and economic support. Women are important to her. She is important to herself. Our society demands that commitment from women be reserved for men.

The lesbian, woman-identified-woman, commits herself to women not only as an alternative to oppressive male/female relationships but primarily because she loves women. Whether consciously or not, by her actions, the lesbian has recognized that giving support and love to men over women perpetuates the system that oppresses her. If women do not make a commitment to each other, which includes sexual love, we deny ourselves the love and value traditionally given to men. We accept our second-class status. When women do give primary energies to other women, then it is possible to concentrate fully on building a movement for our liberation.

Woman-identified lesbianism is, then, more than a sexual preference; it is a political choice. It is political because relationships between men and women are essentially political: they involve power and dominance. Since the lesbian actively rejects that relationship and chooses women, she defies the established political system.

Lesbianism, by Itself, Is Not Enough

Of course, not all lesbians are consciously woman-identified, nor are all committed to finding common solutions to the oppression they suffer as women and lesbians. Being a lesbian is part of challenging male supremacy, but not the end. For the lesbian or heterosexual woman, there is no individual solution to oppression.

The lesbian may think that she is free since she escapes the personal oppression of the individual male/female relationship. But to the society she is still a woman, or worse, a visible lesbian. On the street, at the job, in the schools, she is treated as an inferior and is at the mercy of men's power and whims. (I've never heard of a rapist who stopped because his victim was a lesbian.) This society hates women who love women, and so, the lesbian, who escapes male dominance in her private home, receives it doubly at the hands of male society; she is harassed, outcast, and shuttled to the bottom. Lesbians must become feminists and fight against woman oppression, just as feminists must become lesbians if they hope to end male supremacy.

U.S. society encourages individual solutions, apolitical attitudes, and reformism to keep us from political revolt and out of power. Men who rule, and male leftists who seek to rule, try to depoliticize sex and the relations between men and women in order to prevent us from acting to end our oppression and challenging their power. As the question of homosexuality has become public, reformists define it as a private question of whom you sleep with in order to sidetrack our understanding of the politics of sex. For the lesbian-feminist, it is not private; it is a political matter of oppression, domination, and power. Reformists offer solutions that make no basic changes in the system that oppresses us, solutions that keep power in the hands of the oppressor. The only way oppressed people end their oppression is by seizing power: people whose rule depends on the subordination of others do not voluntarily stop oppressing others. Our subordination is the basis of male power.

Sexism Is the Root of All Oppression

The first division of labor, in prehistory, was based on sex: men hunted, women built the villages, took care of children, and farmed. Women collectively controlled the land, language, culture, and the communities. Men were able to conquer women with the weapons that they developed for hunting when it became clear that women were leading a more stable, peaceful, and desirable existence. We do not know exactly how this conquest took place, but it is clear that the original imperialism was male over female: the male claiming the female body and her service as his territory (or property).

Having secured the domination of women, men continued this pattern of suppressing people, now on the basis of tribe, race, and class. Although there have been numerous battles over class, race, and nation during the past three thousand years, none has brought the liberation of women. While these other forms of oppression must be ended, there is no reason to believe that our liberation will come with the smashing of capitalism, racism, or imperialism today. Women will be free only when we concentrate on fighting male supremacy.

Our war against male supremacy does, however, involve attacking the latter-day dominations based on class, race, and nation. As lesbians who are outcasts from every group, it would be suicidal to perpetuate these man-made divisions among ourselves. We have no heterosexual privileges, and when we publicly assert out Lesbianism, those of us who had them lose many of our class and race privileges. Most of our privileges as women are granted to us by our relationships to men (fathers, husbands, boyfriends) whom we now reject. This does not mean that there is no racism or class chauvinism within us, but we must destroy these divisive remnants of privileged behavior among ourselves as the first step toward their destruction in the society. Race, class, and national oppressions come from men, serve ruling-class white male interests, and have no place in a woman-identified revolution.

Lesbianism Is the Basic Threat to Male Supremacy

Lesbianism is a threat to the ideological, political, personal, and economic basis of male supremacy. The lesbian threatens the ideology of male supremacy by destroying the lie about female inferiority, weakness, passivity, and by denying women's "innate" need for men. Lesbians literally do not need men, even for procreation.

The lesbian's independence and refusal to support one man undermines the personal power that men exercise over women. Our rejection of heterosexual sex challenges male domination in its most individual and common form. We offer all women something better than submission to personal oppression. We offer the beginning of the end of collective and individual male supremacy. Since men of all races and classes depend on female support and submission for practical tasks and feeling superior, our refusal to submit will force some to examine their sexist behavior, to break down their own destructive privileges over other humans, and to fight against those privileges in other men. They will have to build new selves that do not depend on oppressing women and learn to live in social structures that do not give them power over anyone.

Heterosexuality separates women from each other; it makes women define themselves through men; it forces women to compete against each other for men and the privilege that comes through men and their social standing. Heterosexual society offers women a few privileges as compensation if they give up their freedom: for example, mothers are "honored," wives or lovers are socially accepted and given some economic and emotional security, a woman gets physical protection on the street when she stays with her man, etc. The privileges give heterosexual women a personal and political stake in maintaining the status quo.

The lesbian receives none of these heterosexual privileges or compensations since she does not accept the male demands on her. She has little vested interest in maintaining the present political system since all of its institutions—church, state, media, health, schools—work to keep her down. If she understands her oppression, she has nothing to gain by supporting white rich male America and much to gain from fighting to change it. She is less prone to accept reformist solutions to women's oppression.

Economics is a crucial part of woman oppression, but our analysis of the relationship between capitalism and sexism is not complete. We know that Marxist economic theory does not sufficiently consider the role of women or lesbians, and we are presently working on this area.

However, as a beginning, some of the ways that lesbians threaten the economic system are clear: in this country, women work for men in order to survive, on the job and in the home. The lesbian rejects this division of labor at its roots; she refuses to be a man's property, to submit to the unpaid labor system of housework and child care. She rejects the nuclear family as the basic unit of production and consumption in capitalist society.

The lesbian is also a threat on the job because she is not the passive/part-time woman worker that capitalism counts on to do boring work and be part of a surplus labor pool. Her identity and economic support do not come through men, so her job is crucial and she cares about job conditions, wages, promotion, and status. Capitalism cannot absorb large numbers of women demanding stable employment, decent salaries, and refusing to accept their traditional job exploitation. We do not understand yet the total effect that this increased job dissatisfaction will have. It is, however, clear that as women become more intent upon taking control of their lives, they will seek more control over their jobs, thus increasing the strains on capitalism and enhancing the power of women to change the economic system.

Lesbians Must Form Our Own Movement to Fight Male Supremacy

Feminist-lesbianism, as the most basic threat to male supremacy, picks up part of the women's liberation analysis of sexism and gives it force and direction. Women's liberation lacks direction now because it has failed to understand the importance of heterosexuality in maintaining male supremacy, and because it has failed to face class and race as real differences in women's behavior and political needs. As long as straight women see lesbianism as a bedroom issue, they hold back the development of politics and strategies that would put an end to male supremacy and they give men an excuse for not dealing with their sexism.

Being a lesbian means ending identification with, allegiance to, dependence on, and support of heterosexuality. It means ending your personal stake in the male world so that you join women, individually and collectively, in the struggle to end your oppression. Lesbianism is the key to liberation and only women who cut their ties to male privilege can be trusted to remain serious in the struggle against male dominance. Those who remain tied to men, individually or in political theory, cannot always put women first. It is not that heterosexual women are evil or do not care about women. It is because the very essence, definition, and nature of heterosexuality is men first. Every woman has experienced that desolation when her sister puts her man first in the final crunch: heterosexuality demands that she do so. As long as women still benefit from heterosexuality, receive its privileges and security, they will at some point have to betray their sisters, especially lesbian sisters who do not receive those benefits.

Women in women's liberation have understood the importance of having meetings and other events for women only. It has been clear that dealing with men divides us and saps our energies, and that it is not the job of the oppressed to explain our oppression to the oppressor. Women also have seen that collectively, men will not deal with their sexism until they are forced to do so. Yet, many of these same women continue to have primary relationships with men individually and do not understand why lesbians find this oppressive. Lesbians cannot grow politically or personally in a situation which denies the basis of our politics: that lesbianism is political, that heterosexuality is crucial to maintaining male supremacy.

Lesbians must form our own political movement in order to grow. Changes that will have more than token effects on our lives will be led by woman-identified lesbians who understand the nature of our oppression and are therefore in a position to end it.

Chapter Thirty-Four

Selections from *Lesbian Nation*

Jill Johnston

The Making of a Lesbian Chauvinist

At a time when many feminists are considering the alternative or possibility of another woman as a lover the struggles of those who came to the feminist movement as lesbians and call themselves Gay or Lesbian/Feminists are more often than not conceived and projected by the feminists per se as the female equivalent of the male chauvinist whose behavior defined by that term indicates the oppression of sex roles the feminist movement is dedicated to eliminating. Lesbian chauvinism was the new phrase by spring 1971 if not earlier. I think the phrase naturally emerged out of the old stereotyped ideas of gay women being either butch or femme in imitation of the heterosexual role dichotomies. Although my own lesbian relationships never conformed to these role playing types, I too had some preconceived notions about lesbianism along these lines. And often tried to explain myself in passive and/or aggressive terms. As though I had to be either one or the other. Mainly the phrase was an easy invention by association to further discredit the lesbian as the upsetting gadfly of the feminist movement. Possibly a few feminists had the experience of being pressured to "come out" on ideological grounds by a political lesbian. Certainly the pressure from lesbians in general as a tacit force naturally accompanying their personal persuasion projected into a political framework could not have been overlooked. "Woman Identified Woman" is a powerful document. The new political feminist lesbian who was especially clamorous coming from the angry aggressive positioning of the Gay Liberation Front—an unprecedented uprising of both gay women and gay men to assert pride in homosexual identity. The conjunction of the Gay Liberation Front with the Feminist Movement produced this amazing phenomenon of the sexually straight woman confronted with the challenge of their straight identification at the embarrassing bullseye center of their problem with the man—the sexual foundation of the social institutions. Many feminists could see the instant logic of sex with another woman as the basic affirmation of a powerful sisterhood. Most however were committed at the outset to "reform" of the institutions of oppression—leaving intact the staple nuclear unit of oppression: heterosexual sex. Most were terrified of the implications of their own radical politics and remained firmly entrenched behind barricades of conditioned attitudes toward homosexuality.

Knowing perhaps full well that an illness is created by an attitude and not by the intrinsic nature of the sexuality. Suspecting perhaps that in that very taboo against their own homosexuality lay the key to their oppression. It was a jubilant historical moment for the confirmed lesbian. The militant gays had moved very fast from the conservative 60's homophile organizations seeking civil libertarian reform and other appeals for integration into society as an "oppressed minority group." The militant Gay now was conceived that Gay Liberation was the axis for revolutionary change. This was a momentous series of steps from self hatred in guilt and secrecy to apologetic pleas for greater acceptance and legal sanctions to affirmation of identity to aggressive redefinition in the context of revolution. Thus the ideological pressure from the politically advanced articulate lesbians on their straight sisters constituted a state of continuous psychic siege to which the feminists have responded or retaliated according to their various capacities or limitations for change and sexual liberation. The lesbian denounced as chauvinist was a neat way of delaying the issue. I picked the phrase out of the air spring of '71 just when a certain amplified notoriety resulting from the town hall affair and the exposure of Lois Lane as lesbian made me suddenly the object of attentions that could be said to qualify me as a score for a certain type of groupie. Hero to lesbian groupies, far out! Or put another way: token lesbian to the curious and succumbing straights. Sex was available! Lesbian chauvinism was a reality! It isn't easy to convey the great import of the availability of sex to a woman, who was a secret unacknowledged lesbian for any amount of time before the gay revolution. The significance of such a fugitive life is integral to the tone and message of my travel and despair piece "Love at First Sex" in the still dark ages of my unawakened political consciousness. The significance of that life as I reiterated over and over was its hopeless apposition to the codes of the heterosexual institution. The sexual deprivation of the woman in relation to man has been well established, but the double deprivation of the woman whose orientation was toward her own sex in relation to whom she was much more severely circumscribed by compulsive secrecy is an intolerable de profundis and derangement of destiny that few women were lucky enough to transcend. Looking back from the precarious standpoint of 1968 I could say I was fortunate to have had three consummated relationships with women. Within his oppression the male homosexual has always moved more freely in the extensive underground urban network of bars and baths and highly developed cruising techniques and designated places to cruise. By comparison the lesbian meeting grounds have been nonexistent to singular. Woman has *always* been defined sexually in relation to man and many people even now never *heard* of a lesbian. During my life in New York consistently I knew male homosexual couples and observed male homosexual flirtations and seductions and phallocentric groupings at parties conveying ineluctably the impression of an exclusive male sexual fraternity which we know very well to be inherited from at least the Greek tradition of acceptable male pleasure apart from their secluded and sequestered women. From this perspective the claim of the militant male gay activist to greater persecution than the lesbian from straight society is a truth which continues to obscure the unrecognized sexuality of the woman who is naturally not persecuted for a condition she is barely exhibiting and following which she is not even imputed to possess. The male gay activist pursues the enlargement of his already recognized sexuality by protesting the loudest against his own persecution which is the social affirmation however negative of that acknowledged sexuality. During my life in New York I never knew a lesbian couple other than my own arrangement except by hearsay and I never observed in any social situations whatever the phenomenon of women paying prime attention to each other the way the men did. The woman was invariably hanging on the privilege of the man. The lesbianism of all these women was inaccessible to them in direct proportion to the social definition of themselves exclusively in relation to the sexual needs of the man, whose pre-emption of the woman as sexual functionary has never deterred him from the enjoyment of his own sex as well. Not only has the sexuality of the woman been thus circumscribed but we know too that the woman has been profoundly conditioned to orient herself toward accepting a single partner around whom her life would center in a "marriage for life" and for whom she waits in suspended animation as for the storybook prince who will arouse her love and sexuality simultaneously. Love and sex. Sex without love was the condition of prostitution. For the woman there was no inbetween. The historical origins of that organ of the psychic life called romantic love are highly conjectural but a number of educated suppositions place the evolution of the emotion in direct relation to the evolution of the family. This is the way I comprehend it. The cultivation of such an emotion would naturally be encouraged as a coercive tool in the development of the family. The family organically perpetuates the emotional apparatus for its own duplication or continuation in the prolonged dependency of the children in the exclusive oedipally focused two-parent ménage. In primitive societies in which child-rearing is communally diffused the bonds between parents and children are more casual and the children grow up realizing there exist many alternative suppliers of love. Philip Slater deftly and briefly deals with the oedipal backward looking fantasy image of romantic love so characteristic of the isolated nuclear western family in his *Pursuit of Loneliness*. Slater analyzes the "scarcity mechanism" upon which romantic love is based. He says the intensification of the parent-child relationship creates scarcity by inculcating a pattern of concentrating one's search for love onto a single object and by focusing one's erotic interest on an object with whom consummation is forbidden. "The magnification of the emotionality and exclusiveness of the parent-child bond, combined with the incest taboo, is the prototypical scarcity mechanism." He doesn't indicate the far greater effects of the process on females, but everywhere in civilized societies the adult male moves with a relatively much more extensive mobility and success in the variety and quantity of sexual encounter. The political rhetoric of the feminist movement directed toward economic and representative equality I think obscures perhaps even to the feminists themselves the fundamental drive of feminism which is sexual liberation. I don't think the feminists, generally, envision their liberation in this form. I think their orientation basically is toward the material male superstructure within which they want parity. All the feminist issues—abortion, child care, prostitution, political representation, equal pay—are in relation to the man. In other words in relation to reproductive sexuality. Within which the woman remains trapped as a sexual nonentity. The function of the woman as reproductive agent and her isolated situation in the family and her oedipal orientation toward the single sex-love partner are inseparable components comprising her sexual deprivation. The so-called liberation of the male-oriented woman in the "sexual revolution" has been exposed for what it is and I've made my own remarks here and there in this book, including key quotes on hippiedom by Valerie Solanas. Here's Juliet Mitchell on the subject. "Women are enjoying a new sexual freedom (changing moral attitudes and availability of reliable contraception) but this is often only for their greater exploitation as 'sexual objects' within it." Women will have little or nothing to gain from these up-dated forms of tribal "group marriages" until their matrilineal honor is reestablished and the male privilege has disappeared. That eventuality is something the Gay/Feminist perceives as a possibility only through instant revolutionary withdrawal of women from the man or the system (Man and system being synonymous) whose privilege remains impregnable while the woman persists in accommodating herself to it either of course by convention and tradition or even by the new standard of feminists in revolt for all the items I mentioned by which women will remain in definitive conjunction to the system after the minor and major concessions have been made. The lesbian/feminist is the woman who defines herself independently of the man. "The lesbian's refusal to be an inferior to man is absolute, while with 'normal' woman the rejection of man's superiority remains relative" (Charlotte Wolff). The woman in sexual and social relation to herself who retains the tragic oedipal and monogamous and role playing solutions of the straight heterosexual institution (defined by the domination of one sex over another, modelled after the original authoritative parent-child relationship) is not necessarily any more liberated into her sexual autonomy than the straight feminist, as the feminists keep pointing out in their objections to the lesbian alternative. Many lesbians like myself can testify to the terrible oppression we experienced waiting in long draughts for a "true beloved" in the form of a woman instead of a man. Although as I said my own lesbian relationships never conformed to the role playing models of heterosexuality I was just as hopelessly addicted to the ultimate oedipal for life romantic fantasy stuff as any straight girl. Moreover, conditioned to be a "passive female"—to wait and die politely—made the prospects of the appearance of your savior grimly unlikely in the scheme of things whereby *all* women are more or less similarly passive. A woman could thus easily wait forever for another without suspecting that the other was also waiting for her and this is the tale of many unrequited and unconsummated "friendships" between women. The question being which passive woman is going to make the first verboten aggressive gesture. Passivity is *the* accommodation of the woman to her oppression at every level of the straight male defined society. Passivity is *the* index to a woman's proper behavior as a role playing feminine counterpart to the aggressor. Passivity is *the* dragon that every woman has to murder in her quest for independence. Independence means autonomy means aggressive control of one's own destiny. Lesbian chauvinism defined very simplistically as the aggressive assertion of your sexual and sensual needs and interests is a good phrase. If all women were lesbian chauvinists we would all be aggressive equals and the phrase would be meaningless in its negative aspect as associated with the male whose chauvinism as aggressor implies his entire privilege in which his biological function is united with his social authority. Chauvinism as a pejorative is only meaningful in reference to the role dichotomies which the feminists oppose and out of which the word was revived to describe the superior half of the dichotomy. Considering the social position of the lesbian—the woman who refuses any participation in the male privilege except to rip it off if possible (I mean the man is paying me to write this book)—the allegation of lesbian chauvinism as the female equivalent of the male of that description seems to me quite grandly ironic. There is however a sense in which lesbian chauvinism as pejorative is appreciable and that is when applied to indicate a lesbian still held up in her male identification—a lesbian not yet turned feminist. The woman in this extraordinarily oppressed place of herself naturally tends to oppress other women in the male determination of property and possessiveness, persuading and coercing by involving all the emotions of greed envy fear guilt anger jealousy and so on all the defensive aggressive equipment attending the onset of romantic love. Playing the aggressive or passive roles at their extremes. The butch and femme. Aggressive as I always was in the pursuit of my accomplishments I was a lesbian femme par excellence and was ready to oppress any potential lover with the most excessive monogamous demands. Any potential lover always being of course a remote possibility. The remoteness and the oedipal need being features of each other. It may seem contradictory to say I was a lesbian femme and at the same time that my relationships never conformed to the role playing types of the heterosexual model. But that is true. There was never any conventional division of labor in or out of bed or command and submission program; yet I would characterize myself as femme (conventionally socialized female) in my inability to make a move to satisfy my needs either by regarding a woman as a potential lover or by doing anything about it once a potentiality was established. And further, once a contact had actually been made, strict monogamous expectations and a terrifying dependency were common to both butch and femme. The elimination of butch and femme as we realize our true androgynous nature must inevitably mean the collapse of the heterosexual institution with its role playing dualities which are defined as the domination of one sex over another and with it all enclaves of sexuality such as love between women which have aped the normative institution. My personal liberation began with a rebellion against passivity. Dennis Altman has said, "most male homosexuals . . . pass through a period during which we seek to protect ourselves by refusing any contact other than the purely physical one." This was a phase I had never experienced and I'd venture to say *most* gay women had never experienced. As Altman also emphatically noted: "gay women are after all doubly oppressed and suffer particularly from the social norms that expect women to repress not only their homosexual but even to a considerable extent their heterosexual urges." In similar words, if the oppression of homosexuals is part of the general repression of sexuality and women especially suffer from this repression then the repression of the lesbian woman or the "woman identified woman" will be doubly severe. I said I was fortunate to have had three consummated lesbian relationships—within such a suffocating system—but they were plagued by guilt and secrecy and the great fear of loss or abandonment, and it was necessary for me to plunge through the fires at the gates of the forbidden *twice*—to come out *twice*—with an intervening period of a decade!—in order to establish my sexual identity. My indictment of society rests on the revelation of the degree to which I obliterated my true sexual nature or identity by internalizing the social hatred of women as woman and as gay/woman (which means the same thing to me) and conforming to the heterosexual ideal. During that intervening decade I even sacrificed myself totally in the feudal agonies of marriage and two infants for four years. An aberration of nature! A perversion of narcissus! A lapse of moral instinct. A serious deviation of destiny! For if the phrase biology is destiny has any meaning for a woman right now it has to be the urgent project of woman reclaiming her self, her own biology in her own image, and this is why the lesbian is *the* revolutionary feminist and every other feminist is a woman who wants a better deal from her old man. At a time when many feminists are considering the alternative or possibility of another woman as a lover the struggles of those who came to feminism as lesbians and call themselves Gay or Lesbian/Feminists are more often than not conceived and projected by the feminists per se as the female equivalent of the male chauvinist whose behavior defined by that term indicates the oppression of sex roles the feminist movement is dedicated to eliminating. No woman is in a better position to comprehend a state of existence in which these roles have actually been eliminated than the lesbian. For all her posturing and stylistic imitations of the heterosexual models and her longing for monogamous security or stability the lesbian is the woman who has experienced real equality in relationships in which no party has the biological or social advantage which characterizes heterosexual coupling. It's the liberation of the lesbian from this very projected idea from her prefeminist past into her natural polymorphic state of identification with other women at multiple levels of the physical intellectual and spiritual which should constitute the new ideal for any feminist aspiring to equality and self realization or reintegration with her own female principle. The light-handed use of the phrase lesbian chauvinism as pejorative by feminists shows little understanding of the incredible wasteland most of us have come from. The use of the phrase by lesbians themselves is something else. It isn't easy to convey the great import of the availability of sex and affection to a woman who was a secret (unacknowledged) lesbian before the gay revolution. You were either of three things: an embittered angry bar dyke; a eunuch by default; or a partner in a fearfully tenacious dependent isolated remote déclassé illegal and paranoid marriage. Or any sequential or simultaneous combination of these impossibilities. In so much as to many feminists chauvinism has meant the aggressive attention of any male in relation to which she felt like a sex object the term would naturally apply to any woman who behaved the same. Yet it was this very aggressive behavior that has been a key expression in the initial liberation of many lesbians. Speaking for myself certainly. And whether the new assertion was undertaken before or after the dawning of a feminist consciousness could account for the type of chauvinism involved. For myself some of my behavior before acquiring a Gay/Feminist head may have been deplorable from any standard of sisterhood. But there was no other way. Just before my last fierce monogamy the summer of '68 the door opened to my sexual liberation. In Lois Lane I mentioned that my momentous visit to London that summer prompted my return to America as "a roaring lesbian." I meant that I discovered I could sleep with a woman and not feel like it was the beginning or the end of the world. Meaning it was possible to just go to bed and have a good time and get up and share a cup of coffee or not and say goodbye and thank you quite amicably like any self respecting male chauvinist for whom the pleasures of the body are not necessarily complicated and constrained by the emotions of greed envy fear guilt anger jealousy etcetera all the defensive aggressive equipment attending the onset of romantic love. The British taught me this lesson. They were very hard on me. I arrived a gaping tourist and left a hardened sexist. Not really. I cried all the way home. I don't remember why. But I remained as mushy as ever which was pretty mushy. Possibly I hadn't grasped yet that it wasn't a crime to fall in love with every British princess who seemed as interested as I was in the mere pleasures of the body. Actually, there were only three, I think. That was enough. For a three week visit the average was outstanding. For a pure innocent virginal american it was lurid and licentious. For a victim of lesbian monogamy it was a revelation. Having dutifully tramped through Westminster and St. Paul's and Charing Cross and the National Museum and Trafalgar Square and Piccadilly Circus and the Tube System and Soho and the Tower and around the Palace and so forth one day I decided impulsively I had to visit a Gay Bar. I had never done this in my life before. Except once as a very young lesbian naturally not connecting my thinking into my activities or fantasies, therefore imagining I was a nice normal person, I went slumming with a friend to a Village place to be a tourist and watch the freaks and get excitedly aghast at *members of the same sex dancing together!* By this summer of '68 I was still disconnected in such a way my thinking or my attitudes or prejudices and my true nature were distinctly and neurotically separate from each other. I was a walking contradiction in turns. I just couldn't see myself as a freak. It was bad enough I was too tall for my age and wore my freckles when the sun came out. I was even strolling around in those fashionable gabardine culottes or leather miniskirts. I must've looked ridiculous. A lesbian still pretending to be available for invasion. Anyway, I went all out there in London and learned about a place called the Gates or Gateways Club. George Brecht located it for me. Very reluctantly. He said he was disappointed in me. I guess he thought he had an exclusive patent on chauvinism, not that I knew at the time that's what he was. I assumed all men had the right to drink a lot and insult womankind and drag as many as possible off by the hair to their caves. So naturally he was not enthusiastic about being an accomplice to my initiation as a rival chauvinist of the lesbian variety. Not that either of us realized the ultimate significance of his innocent investigation. The Gates, by the way, was the bar that figured as the freak joint in "The Killing of Sister George" which I saw a few months later in New York. The entrance had a speakeasy feeling about it. You'd never see it if you didn't know where it was exactly. The door opened directly on a flight of stairs leading down to I imagined a dark den of sin. It was just a smallish well lit rather cheery basement room with comfortable round booths, a bar, a jukebox. The woman at a cash register at the bottom of the stairs was a hardened something or other. Dressed high femme lipstick earrings stockings heels etc. with an incongruously low dark voice and garish features. The bartenders were handsome heavy set butch, a type that always repelled bewildered and frightened me. I sat down and waited. Eventually the only other customer addressed me sort of like over her shoulder from her position turned three quarters away from me. I could appreciate her bleached blond straight short hair and middling cockney accent. Hearing my own american she warmed up and even not too much later turned round to face me. She introduced herself as Maureen. She got so warm in fact she was inviting me to her place to meet her roommate who "likes american girls" and her own lover who was an ex-patriot american. I said I'd like to do that but later on if possible after I found out what this bar was all about. Soon I found out. It seemed the entire gay woman population of London must have decided this was the place to be that night. I had no idea there were so many gay people in the world, never mind London. I was very embarrassed. I didn't know what to do. I didn't do anything. I think I just sat there transfixed with horrified curiosity. I had a very snobbish attitude. I'm sure I didn't think I was a lesbian too. Yet I was rigged out to conform to one of the two stereotyped roles obtaining in conventional old line gay society. Excepting my long hair. But they overlooked the hair because of my tie. The tie seemed to guarantee my role as a female who would play the part of a male. In my three lesbian marriages I had never played any part whatsoever unless it was all parts, so I regarded the attitude with amused toleration, thankful to be attractive to one half of the jam-packed room for inadvertently wearing the right thing. I became friendly and adventurous. I asked someone the time and was threatened with murder by her girlfriend. I supposed she was desperate. It was a good thing I just asked the time. I realized right then I'd better not make a move to talk or dance or anything or they'd be flying me home as a corpse. So I waited. I didn't wait too long. I was pretty popular as I said. Thus there were a succession of sidewise or bizarre approaches. All femmes. I was a butch! The most exciting proposition was a note pressed into my hand by the femme I thought to be the most beautiful in the place; she was so expert in her treachery, passing the message on the run as it were and no doubt while her "steady" was collecting their coats and momentarily out of sight. It was very dramatic. A sequence in a spy movie. I repaired to the ladies right away to read it and find her name and a telephone no. scrawled in pencil. I took the names and numbers of two others who weren't as spectacular in their looks or approach and left to go to Maureen's flat to see about her roommate who "likes american girls." I felt saturated by London lesbiana. I felt I had learned something. I didn't know what exactly. Probably my unconscious was fast at work transforming me overnight into a raging chauvinist. One thing was certain. It no longer seemed bizarre for two members of the same sex to be dancing together. One other thing was certain. There were lots of lesbians in the world. Maybe half the world were lesbians. And I suppose I left with the faint suspicion that I too might be one of them.

At Maureen's house I met her ex-patriot american lover and her roommate Sammy who had me on the floor within minutes. I had sex with Sammy all night and left in the morning thinking I was supposed to see her again immediately and possibly get married for life. Sammy was an Experienced young bar dyke and she didn't care to see me again. She thought I was an american tourist and I was. The second one thought so too and I had to give her up right away as well. She was the "beautiful femme" and I didn't understand her anyway. She came on very butch once you got inside the door. The third had a name out of Ivanhoe—Roxanne or Rowena or something—and I had to give her up immediately too. She was 20 and beautiful and voluptuous and she appeared at a pub one late evening out by the Tower where I was drinking with George Brecht and some English friends of his. One of the friends was a raunchy lowdown art student kid from up north who was coming on to the Ivanhoe princess. All pissed somehow the three of us became involved necking at the bar and we closed the place down tottering out on the deserted street looking for a taxi to go to my flat which was big and empty or so I thought. There was no taxi at that hour out around the Tower so we piled up like a totem in a phone booth still groping each other and called for one. The princess was all over me inside my pants exclaiming she'd never done it with a woman before. We fell into the taxi and she turned into a herd of cows in heat. Sprawling agape and wet and panting in between me and the art student, whose attitude leering at me suggested what was supposed to happen was that both of us do the princess somehow. It was a new kind of scene and a half for me. I don't think I was properly piggish at all. I was still ready to "fall in love" as soon as I put my hands on her. Anyway we staggered into my flat and concluded the orgy to the best of my imagination, taking advantage of Roxanne or Rowena, who probably wanted to be tied up and beaten, whose appetite at any rate for assault and ravishment seemed enormous and unappeasable.

Back in New York I looked round at the world with new interested eyes. As though I was noticing for the first time a certain kind of bird or tree that had always been in the neighborhood and I had until then overlooked. One evening outside Max's I caught a glimpse of two women necking in a VW bug and I went right up and rapped on the window. They jumped apart and looked out at me frightened. I said I'd just returned from London and things were very good over there. They invited me in and drove me up to 47th St. and a mafia bar on floor thirty something of the ——— Hotel. They wanted to know why I'd never been to a bar before. I didn't know what to say. And I didn't begin going to them either. But I *was* giving off a new air of poised bait for the sex I wanted. One night at Max's a Nancy sat down cross from me in a booth and transfixed herself into my eyes and followed me out and home and into my bed and some excellent sex until she realized a week or two later we were both women. I was still a fall dyke for a romance. So such encounters the end of that summer of '68 or the beginning of the fall were just preliminary skirmishes for the real awful thing again. The real awful thing I've described in "Love at First Sex." I met Polly that October. The following spring I made my true leap into chauvinism. "Most male homosexuals . . . pass through a period during which we seek to protect ourselves by refusing any contact other than the purely physical one." The way I explained it to myself and with great anger aforethought was what the hell was I supposed to do now wait around for another couple of years pining after an old princess while waiting for a new one and rotting in my skin from sexual death and my mind from the sentimental malaise over yer lost love and all that and I rebelled in earnest at last against my own ancient passivity. I took command of my sexual destiny. The results could be brutally or balefully bizarre. I have to remind anyone my feminist consciousness was so underground as to be close to the center of the earth on the other side of China. One afternoon shortly after P. flew off to

Spain a British woman called me to interview me for a British magazine. We talked for two hours. Then she called back and wanted to fall by. After ten minutes and a drink her questions shifted gear into the provocatively personal and within another few minutes I got the message and said brusquely if she wanted an "experience" I had fifteen minutes before an appointment and we could try to do something in that time and I went and lay down on the bed and waited for her to wrestle out of her dress and a cumbersome difficult bra and made some halfhearted love to the poor woman whom I then briskly bundled into a taxi as I went on my way to the aforementioned appointment. Not much later I found myself upstairs in the bedroom of a huge rambling house in Pittsburgh coming on the stomach of a skinny pretty girl and casually saying goodbye as I turned over to sleep and she left the party to go home. Back in New York I was on stage at the finish of a panel I'd arranged about myself called "The Disintegration of a Critic" at Loeb Student Center of NYU telling the panel and the auditorium in answer to the moderator's question about where I'd just come from and what I'd been doing that I'd just seduced a woman at my place and as soon as the panel was over I left with another woman collecting on my way out my wallet from the first woman who had come with me and was sitting in the audience I went back home to seduce the second woman. Also around that time I remember a movie type hustler set me up with his "beautiful mistress" who met me on a sort of blind date basis at Penn Station and went with me to the Chelsea Hotel to register for a room for the night on the hustler's donated bread. The desk man recognized me and referred to me as a "famous writer" which seemed to fit the general design. But the "mistress" was so "beautiful" in some dead or deadpan dumb movie queen sense that we lay in bed like corpses and I couldn't do much on a very dry mouth and a shaky hand and her apathetic posture and anticlimactic question "don't you like men" to which I think I gave up completely and wasn't sorry. What could I say then that was not the story of so many others. Such were the chances and corruptions and concupiscent precipitations of my new life as a liberated lesbian chauvinist. I was delighted and startled. I hoped I would never perish over another woman again. The only thing wrong with it was that I was still a male identified lesbian. Later on, that fall of '69, returning from Europe I met the women of Gay Liberation Front and I've documented my alterations and growth of consciousness in this book. At least I found out that some one night stands can be rewarding just as some lasting relations can be disastrous. But whatever a lesbian does if she does it out loud she'll be condemned by some new twist of the language. More than anything else the phrase lesbian chauvinism as pejorative is another way of negating the sexuality of woman by impugning any move by the woman to take charge of her own sexual destiny.

The Myth of the Myth of the Vaginal Orgasm

Should the hypothesis be true that one of the requisite cornerstones upon which all modern civilizations were founded was coercive suppression of women's inordinate

sexuality, one looks back over the long history of women and their relationships to
men, children and society since the Neolithic revolution with a deeper, almost awesome,
sense of the ironic tragedy in the triumph of the human condition.

Mary Jane Sherfey, M.D.

The process of physical and psychic self-affirmation requires full relation with those like
oneself, namely women.

Ecstasy, a paper written by
a gay revolutionary party

Many of the new theories and descriptions of woman's basic equipment and orgasm
may sound right to a lot of women. They don't sound bad to me, but they're almost
exclusively written in relation to the man with the implicit instruction that the man
had better shape up and recognize this "inordinate" sexuality of women and learn
the more effective means of stimulating and satisfying his partner. Although many
women can satisfy themselves in relation to the man it's not well known at all that
the woman can satisfy herself just as well if not better in relation to herself or to
other women. The sexual satisfaction of the woman independently of the man is the
sine qua non of the feminist revolution. This is why Gay/Feminism expresses the
proper sexual-political stance for the revolutionary woman. Sexual dependence on
the man is inextricably entangled in the interdependence of man and woman at all
levels of the social structures by which the woman is oppressed. It is in any case
difficult to conceive of an "equal" sexual relationship between two people in which
one member is the "biological aggressor." Although a hole also moves forward to
enclose a sword it is the sword in all known personal-political forms of life thruout
history which has assumed initiative to invade and conquer. The man retains the
prime organ of invasion. Sexual congress between man and woman is an invasion of
the woman, the woman doesn't get anything up to participate in this congress, and
although a woman may be conditioned to believe that she enjoys this invasion and
may in fact grow to like it if her male partner makes rare sacrifices of consideration
in technical know-how, she remains the passive receptive hopeful half of a situation
that was unequal from the start. The fate that woman has to resign herself to is the
knowledge of this biological inequity. A fate that was not originally the occasion for
the *social* inequities elaborated out of the biological situation. From this knowledge
the woman can now alter her destiny or at least reclaim certain ancient historical
solutions, namely the self sufficient tribes of amazons, to a physical problem in
relation to men. Some Marxist-Socialist thinkers envision the solution in our technological advancement whereby the test-tube baby will relieve the woman of her
reproductive function and release her to the wideranging sexual pleasures traditionally arrogated by the man. But *no* technological solution will be the answer to the
spiritual needs of the woman deprived of herself in relation to the man. Feminism at
heart is a massive complaint. Lesbianism is the solution. Which is another way of
putting what Ti-Grace Atkinson once described as Feminism being a theory and
lesbianism the practice. When theory and practice come together we'll have the
revolution. Until all women are lesbians there will be no true political revolution. No
feminist per se has advanced a solution outside of accommodation to the man. The

complaints are substantial and articulate and historically sound and they contain by implication their own answers but the feminists refuse to acknowledge what's implicit in their own complaint or analysis. To wit: that the object of their attack is not going to make anything better than a *material* adjustment to the demands of their enslaved sex. There's no conceivable equality between two species in a relation in which one of the two has been considerably weakened in all aspects of her being over so long a period of historical time. The blacks in America were the first to understand that an oppressed group must withdraw into itself to establish its own identity and rebuild its strength through mutual support and recognition. The first unpublicized action of many feminists *was* in fact to withdraw from the man sexually. Feminists who still sleep with the man are delivering their most vital energies to the oppressor. Most feminists understood this immediately but were confounded in their realization by the taboo against the obvious solution of sex with another woman. Not only is the psychic-emotional potential for satisfaction with another woman far greater than that with a man, insomuch as every woman like every man was originally most profoundly attached to herself as her mother, but there is more likelihood of sexual fulfillment with another woman as well since all organisms best understand the basic equipment of another organism which most closely resembles themselves. The erotic potential between like organisms consists in the enhancement of self through narcissistic identification. Narcissism is the ideal appreciation of self. Women who love their own sex love the sameness in the other. They become both subject and object to each other. That makes two subjects and two objects. Narcissism is the totality of subject-object unity within the self extended to another. "When a heterosexual woman loves a man she is confronted with otherness, and so is a man who loves a woman. Otherness implies something completely different from oneself, something one has to learn to understand and live with . . . At one time or another, the 'normal' (heterosexual) woman will always be put back into the place of being an object." (Charlotte Wolff) Normalcy for women is the adaptation to their own oppression. Or to the male standard for perpetuating his privilege in unequal relationships. Normalcy is the fucked up condition of woman. Normalcy is the unsuccessful attempt to overcome the obstacle of otherness by resigning oneself to one's own deprivation of self. Normalcy is an appeal to numbers in the form of majorities to justify coercion in plans to cooperate for the benefit of "mankind." Normalcy is the disease of maladjusted coupling by different or hetero or otherness species. Normalcy is achieved by puritan ethical appeals to the moral correctness of doing things that are worthwhile by their difficulty and hard labor through delayed gratification of real instincts, or uniting with self. True normalcy would mean the return of all women to themselves. Majority behavior, which defines civilized schizophrenia, is pseudo-normalcy. The first order of business for a woman is the redefinition, of herself through assertion of her sexuality in relation to herself or her own equal, in other words, independently of the man. Early feminist writings project the suggestion of lesbianism as an alternative to the widespread sexual dissatisfaction of women in relation to men. There was, in these early manifestos, both fortunately and not so fortunately, a concentration on that aspect of the basic equipment in which orgastic satisfaction originates. I thought everybody knew the clitoris was the doorway to orgasm, the way a certain type of jill-in-the-box might pop open after sufficient rhythmic friction against its trap door. Apparently this glorification of the clitoris was a revelation to women who remained frigid in intercourse through neglect of prior stimulation of the external or clitoral part of the organ. Or who remained frigid in intercourse regardless of said prior stimulation, this actually being the true situation, according to early pronouncement, based on the total absence of feeling or orgastic potential within the vagina itself. I have a record entry June 18, 1970: "find out what they mean by the myth of the vaginal orgasm." Subsequently I asked a few "feminists." They informed me, in effect, that I don't experience what I say I feel or feel what I say I experience or any combined way of being a liar. And their chief authority was Masters & Johnson. Studying the feminist literature I decided that the feminists had found the perfect rationale for their frustration and excuse for not being required to fuck with the man any more. They didn't actually say this. They were mainly contesting the "myth of the liberated woman and her vaginal orgasm." The refutation of Freud's thesis of sexual maturity in the woman consisting of her transference to the father as proper love object developing parallel to the shifting of orgasmic location in the clitoris to the "mature" vagina. Wherever these feminists obtained their "evidence" for an insensitive vagina, if not in themselves, it seemed not to matter either about the source or the (in)sensitivity if the issue constituted a rebellion against being defined sexually in terms of what pleases the man. It seems actually amazing that what they were asserting was a stubborn refusal to submit to conventional intercourse on grounds of an insensitive vagina. *Equating* intercourse with vaginal orgasm as it were. (No mention of hands or bananas or dildoes.) Really as though one was unthinkable without the other. As though the case for an insensitive vagina provided women with their first legal brief for the indictment of phallic imperialism. This rather misguided attempt of women to dissociate themselves from the suppression of their pleasure in "reproductive sexuality" was nonetheless a crucial rudimentary step in establishing sexual independence from the man and leading to the fuller dimension of womanhood in Gay/Feminism. In fact within two years or so after the appearance of these papers the feminist line includes more overt accommodation to and recognition of lesbians, as well as lesbianism itself within the ranks. I said "misguided" because the feminist equation along the old standard of "reproductive sexuality" or penis-in-vagina as proper model or primal scene, and their "discovering" of the insensitive female half of the bargain, important as it was, left them with only one operable part of the basic equipment—the clitoris—and the ignorance of a solution involving all the equipment with their sisters. I always agreed with one half of Freud's equation. That a woman moves from clitoral to vaginal orgasm. And that the latter *is* more mature in the sense that the activation of the inner walls brings about a more profound intensification of orgasm. I would add that this shift occurs in two kinds of time—over a period of month or years as a "discovery" of the orgastic potential of the internal walls, and as a transition in every sexual encounter, moving from initial stimulation of clitoris (as the seat of sensation, the *origin* of satisfaction) to full orgasm experienced in the total organ which includes the "deep" vaginal wall. I take issue like the feminists with Freud's postulation of "heterosexual maturity." Since a woman can achieve vaginal orgasm herself or with another woman clearly his case for maturity was in the interests of the continuation of phallic imperialism. The rights of the father to the mother. The Gay/Feminist revolution involves the rights of the mother to the mother. Woman's thighs are the gateways to infinity for women as well as for men. For women give birth to themselves as well as to boys. I was struck particularly by these remarks in the Masters & Johnson book on female orgasm: "During the first stage of subjective progression in orgasm, the sensation of intense clitoral-pelvic awareness has been described by a number of women as occurring concomitantly with a sense of bearing down or expelling. This last sensation was reported only by parous study subjects, a small number of whom expressed some concept of having an actual fluid emission or of expending in some concrete fashion." And: "Twelve women, all of whom have delivered babies on at least one occasion without anesthesia or analgesia, reported that during the second stage of labor they experienced a grossly intensified version of the sensations identified with this first stage of subjective progression through orgasm." These reports seemed to confirm my long suspicion that orgasm itself originated in the parthenogenetic birth of our unicellular beginnings. The daughter cells. The immaculate conception is the female fantasy of her own birth without the aid of the male. I can personally testify to the aboriginal reality of this state of being through having experienced a "psychic parthenogenesis" in certain hallucinatory symptoms of childbirth—psychosomatic labor pains—attending the birth of myself during a critical period of cosmic consciousness more commonly called insanity. Women of course do the same for each other in any intense relationship. I should also remark that my "rebirth" was accompanied by a great expansion of sexuality in the realms of both sensual awareness and orgastic potential. During this time for instance I began to experience the intensification or deepening of orgasm that I could only describe as "inner" or "internal." The feminists claimed Masters & Johnson as an authority in their case for an insensitive vagina. Yet Masters & Johnson say "The physiologic onset of orgasm is signaled by contractions of the target organs, starting with the *orgasmic platform in the outer third of the vagina*. This platform, created involuntarily by localized vasocongestion and myotonia, contracts with recordable rhythmicity as the tension increment is released" (italics mine). And "Vaginal spasm and penile grasping reactions have been described many times in the clinical and non-professional literature." And "Regularly recurring orgasmic-platform contractions were appreciated subjectively as pulsating or throbbing sensations of the vagina." And "Finally, as the third stage of subjective progression, a feeling of involuntary contraction with a specific focus in the vagina or lower pelvis was mentioned consistently." The Masters & Johnson team remain loyal to the standard of heterosexual coupling but they've presented the most impressive physiological findings to date of the extensive orgasmic response of the woman. I really think the feminists basically were making a common complaint in the new terminological context of feminism. That the man was no good in bed. That he was insensitive to the essential clitoris. That he just didn't know how to do it. And as an added fillip the new challenge that a woman or feminist anyway would henceforth refuse to accept responsibility for a frigidity that wasn't her own fault. The solution has still not been posed within feminist theory. It can't be because feminism is not a solution.

It's the complaint that got the movement going. When the feminists have a solution they'll be Gay/Feminists. Until then, they've got the best problem around and that's the man. Feminism is a struggle terminology. Concerning women at odds with the man. Since women have always been at odds with the man feminism is the collectivized articulated expression of women's demeaned status. Feminism will no longer need itself when women cease to think of themselves as the "other" in relation to the "other" and unite with their own kind or species. Being male and female is, above all, defined in terms of the other. Feminists could begin by realizing that not only do they not need a penis to achieve their supreme satisfaction but they could easily do better without one since the timing involving the essential stimulation of the outer tissues prior to and/or concomitant with penetration requires a penis that can be erect for entry at a more or less precise moment in the progress toward climax. Some women and men work this thing out, or in, but most women, as the feminists observed, consistently receive a penis into a dead or dying chamber from which the penis eventually emerges as the savior in the form of a child. In any case the question many peoples are asking now is if "reproductive sexuality" is no longer the standard for sexual approach—for men it never was completely—what is keeping women from their total pleasure with other women. We know why. "Women far more than men are trapped in a social view that suggests that their ultimate worth is derived from a suitable heterosexual attachment and the result of this is that they come to despise both themselves and other women." (Altman) In order for a girl to achieve an adequate motherhood, she must to some degree relinquish her libidinal attachment to her own mother. The acculturation of women to believe most exclusively in "reproductive sexuality" remains pervasive and powerful. Altman again: "As a consequence of the utilitarian view of sex there is an extremely strong negative attitude toward all sexual urges other than those that are genital and heterosexual." Or: "Sex has been firmly linked, and nowhere more clearly than in Christian theology, with the institution of the family and with child bearing. Sex is thus legitimized for its utilitarian principles, rather than as an end in itself . . . even where sexual pleasure is accepted as a complementary goal, the connection between marriage and sex still remains." As a complementary goal women have no need to stay in relation to the aggravation caused by the "biological aggressor." If the male fears absorption and the female penetration, and both fears represent the disturbance of a static equilibrium—in which nothing is either gained or lost—(Slater) it seems clear that the various global disturbances now accelerated by technological expansion are material visible extensions of the primal antagonism between men and women in some evolutionary distortion of destiny. (Not that there is such a thing as an evolutionary distortion.) Marcuse commented on Norman O. Brown: "If I understand his mysticism correctly it includes abolition of the distinction between male and female and creation of an androgynous person. He seems to see the distinction between male and female as the product of repression. I do not. It is the last difference I want to see abolished." Speaking of sexism in high places! If I understand Marcuse correctly. Since I too would not like to see the distinction abolished, but not I think for the same reasons. Agreeing with Brown, I'm not sure that he would envision the solution in the withdrawal of women from participation in that repression by which the distinction was created and sustained. Or even that he would define it that way. The fall was from some primeval division into two sexes. I think any bio-analytically oriented person knows we were originally one sex. The fall is a constant reoccurrence through birth or separation. "The sin is not between the lover and the beloved, but in parentage." The project in our cycle toward species extinction should be clear enough. The present revolution of women is a clamorous reminder of that destiny and the proper organic means of achieving it. Many male intellects hope to see the abortion of this destiny. Not necessarily specifically identifying the agent of that abortion in the potential technological disasters of the male power problem. The key to survival in the interests of a natural death is the gradual extinction of the repro-ductive function as it is now still known and practiced. For it is by this function that the woman is so desperately deprived of herself. Lesbian or woman prime is *the* factor in advance of every projected solution for our embattled world. In her reali-zation of herself both sensually polymorphously and genitally orgasmically she expe-riences her original self reproductive or parthenogenetic recreation of herself apart from the intruding and disturbing and subjugating male. Genitalorgasmic sex be-tween women is absolutely consistent with our total sensual and emotional mutually reflecting relations with each other. The lesbian woman is not properly equipped to oppress her own kind. But she *is* equipped to give herself pleasure, and she doesn't need any artificial substitute for the instrument of oppression to give herself that pleasure.

The Second Sucks and the Feminine Mystake

A lesbian's best friend is an upside down cake. The feminist issue is an instruction sheet for getting on better in the system. There is no feminist issue. After there are proper child care centers and free abortions and easy contraception and equal pay and representation and job opportunities—then what? There'll still be a man. And biology is definitely destiny. The woman in relation to man historically has always been defeated. Every woman who remains in sexual relation to man is defeated every time she does it with the man because each single experience for every woman is a reenactment of the primal one in which she was invaded and separated and fashioned into a receptacle for the passage of the invader and that's why every woman is a reluctant and a fearful bride throughout all time the woman has capitulated by custom and custom alone to an invasion that was originally the outcome of a biological warfare and is now sanctioned by those very social structures that the feminists somehow keep insisting are merely learned behaviors as though the social structures were a diabolical invention of no consequence in relation to a difference of clear disadvantage in mobility to the female. Role playing is the elaboration of that (dis) advantage into the various passive-aggressive or sado-masochistic dualities. The role-behavior of the man which entitles him to power and prestige is the expression of an original biological advantage accrued in some primeval victory and defined as brute strength in surviving a hazardous environment. The female was the original test of that strength. The female became a separate species subdued and subsumed like the other animals in the competition for survival. The female is a separate species. The female in relation to herself is not *naturally* a role playing animal. The female in relation to the man is only half a woman and a disadvantaged one at that. The man in relation to woman is an advantaged half of a man. The message of learned behavior is that a woman fulfills herself by uniting with her opposite but in reality she becomes lost to herself in service to a foreign species. You are who you sleep with. Thus the lesbian rightfully says she is the woman par excellence. "I *know* I'm a woman, I'm the most woman that can *be* a woman." The only radical feminists around here worthy of the name that I know of are Ti-Grace Atkinson and Valerie Solanas and they don't have to use the word lesbian to define the man as the enemy we can take instruction from the pathological purity of their fury. The lesbian has no quarrel with them unless it be personal. One could suppose them to be beyond the necessities of erotic gratification. The woman in relation to herself is beset with the inherited bull of the heterosexual institution in its hype of ownership and romantic love and role playing or the guilt resentment syndrome reassurance tenacity confluence principle fear anxiety loss cancellation escape mechanism all equaling marriage for life. The woman in relation to herself is at the beginning of a prolonged struggle to purge herself of all that manmade shit. The projected accusation of sexism and chauvinism and oppression by many feminists onto the lesbian is their own expectation based on all they know in relation to the man. The lesbian herself is emerging from these expectations in a new identification of her own womanhood. The butch or diesel dyke is fast disappearing. The butch or diesel dyke is a stylistic imitation of the male whose structures she thought she had to transpose in relation to herself to obtain gratification. Likewise the femme. The woman in relation to herself is not a butch or a femme but a woman. She is not *naturally* a role playing animal. Role playing occurs through differences in which one different animal can't tolerate the difference of another in some restless sense of insecurity and incompletion. Identity achieved by superiority and submission. If radical feminism is addressing itself to the "total elimination of sex roles" while still talking sex in relation to the man who defines these roles in the sex act by a certain historical biological-cultural imperative they are going in circles of unadulterated contradictory bullshit. Seeking a "better" place beside the man in his own system moreover is to perpetuate the same authoritative hierarchical oppressive ordering of things by which the woman would remain subjugated by class, if not caste. Attaining a better place beside the man the woman would remain still half a woman while resting secure in the *apparent* privilege of some greater material advantage. A spiritually dead woman beside the spiritually dead man. The feminists are now asserting the possibility or alternative of sex with another woman under conditions learned from the very male power structure they claim to be oppressed by. The straight woman can't yet *think* of relating to another person sexually as an equal. Her sexual situation has always been defined as passive and invisible. The puritanism of the feminists is rooted in sexism—sexism being synonymous with the repression of her sexuality as the passive invisible partner. Thus she projects her experience of the straight world onto the lesbian with a preconceived opinion of role playing or sexism. She thinks for sample that any woman who expresses an interest in her sexually is being oppressive (oppressive equals aggressive equals male equals sexist) and so she converts this interest into the sex-seductive game maneuvering of the straight world in which the lesbian is objectified as desirable for an "Experience" or for a "Relationship" if the lesbian plays the game correctly by pretending that the straight woman is a special prize difficult to obtain or to be treated as a delicate passive instrument of exceptional concern. The lesbian is thus oppressed by being considered an aggressor in the manner of the man. In mutual aggression where equals all express their sexual needs and interests there is no aggression in the sense of mastery and control. The most effective means of control and mastery in the straight world is the cultivation of attachment by love and romance. The love object is a special instance. And as such a private one. Nobody else's business. A personal matter. The lesbian relationship has been a personal matter for so long that many lesbians are practicing lesbians without thinking they are lesbians. Women actually live together without acknowledging they are doing so. The woman they are with is a "special case." The more unusual overt looking lesbian who is now a militant one in the context of the feminist revolution was very often a woman who endured a major disappointment or two or more in relation to another "special" woman and was thus forced to consider her sexuality in broader social terms and define herself as a woman who loved women or not—a hard choice in a world in which the personal is not yet a political issue. Now you can hear many experienced lesbians saying of these reform type feminists gingerly considering another woman as a lover "well maybe they need to fall in love to make it happen" and that's precisely the way many feminists hope it will happen and we hope so too that they bring each other out that way if it has to be that way because no self respecting lesbian can tolerate the oppression of even pretending to be the total end of the world oedipal answer to another woman's straight fantasy. It's quite true that such lesbian relationships are little threat to the male in his structure since they remain "isolated lesbian examples" and as in the movie "The Fox" the first guy who steps into a limbo of consciousness gets one or both of the girls. Otherwise known as arrested development by the straights (O'Wyatt). The lesbians many feminists consider oppressive—the self-confident, swinging thrill-seeking female females (who) have contempt for men and for the pandering male females as Solanas said— are oppressed by the reactionary puritan attempt of these feminists to bait them and solicit them or condemn them according to the very sexist definitions the lesbians are struggling in their peer relalationships with each other to transcend and leave behind in the heap of personal isolated solutions to a vast political problem. Dig this exchange in an *anonymous* interview with a woman: Q: What made you fall in love with a woman? A: I didn't fall in love with "a woman"—I fell in love with Jen (or Jan)—which is not exactly the same thing. A better way to ask the question is: How were you able to *overcome* the fact that it was a woman?—(Italics mine)—Dig she didn't fall in love with a *woman*. I think the way you translate that is that she fell in love with a *person*. A special person. Who just *happens* to be a woman. Meaning love is indiscriminate and it could as well be a woman as a man or vice versa. It's great that this woman is getting it on with another woman. I'm not disparaging the relationship. Which may be her primer step in gay-feminist consciousness. But for such an approach to be put forth as an official definition of acceptable lesbianism *within* feminism is a whole bunch of backward reactionary crap that seriously retards the revolution. It belongs to the baggage of bisexual excuse and delay formation that characterizes the best part of adjustment and compromise or don't worry to the wondering male who won't mind a lesbian turn-on if it doesn't interfere with his own prerogative. Bisexuality is an intermediary solution for women on the way to relating completely with their sisters. Bisexuality is not so much a cop-out as a fearful compromise. Many women pride themselves on their bisexuality, claiming they happily have it both ways. But one half of those both ways is a continued service to the oppressor, whose energies are thus reinforced to perpetuate the oppression of that part of the woman who would make it with another woman. For as Wendy Wonderful said at a Columbia panel in 1970 "I'm bisexual, and when I say I'm having an affair with a man it's groovy, but when I'm having an affair with a woman not only is it not so groovy but it's not acceptable, thus the oppressed part of me is the lesbian and therefore I say I'm a lesbian!" Bisexuality is staying safe by claiming allegiance to heterosexuality. Everybody assumes you are heterosexual so bisexuality is a cop-out because if I say to you I'm a bisexual you would assume I was a heterosexual who sometimes has sex with a woman rather than I am a lesbian who occasionally indulges in sex with a man. She's still on the right side of the fence but occasionally strays to the wrong side. Bisexuality is still heterosexuality. In the gay revolution the lesbian most jealously guards her exclusive relations to women, for the male privilege is rampant and ubiquitous. The gay male can talk and behave bisexually without relinquishing his privilege. The gay woman has nothing to gain in sexual relations to the man except the illusion of a momentary status by association with male privilege and the illusion perhaps of a "total" sexual life. Bisexuality is a condition *within*, and not a condition to achieve *outside* oneself by running from one sex to another with the idea of uniting the two sexes in oneself in this fashion. In fact in that half of the transaction with the opposing sex the woman upsets the bisexual balance within herself by surrendering some part of that "internal" totality to the totality of the other who doesn't *feel* so total, who feels historically and so notoriously incomplete without mother or woman. Bisexuality for women in the revolution in any case is collaboration with the enemy. Bisexuality is a state of political oblivion and unconsciousness. "The claim to bisexuality is commonly heard within the movement, and while bisexuality is not physiologically impossible, the term cannot be used to characterize a stable socio-sexual orientation. Because no heterosexual relationship is free of power politics and other masculine mystifications, women who assert that they are bisexual retain their definition by men and the social advantages accruing from this. Bisexuality is a transitional stage, a middle ground, through which women pass from oppressive relationships to those of equality and mutuality. It is a struggle with privilege and fear, and not all women come through it to their sisters on the other side." (*Ecstasy, a Paper of a Gay Revolution* party.) The new hysteria of feminism is a second wave of accommodation to the lesbian element that was originally considered a side or nonexistent issue or an annoying embarrassment. The hysteria obscures their advanced analysis to which many lesbians are indebted and which the feminists are still refusing to make explicit by obvious inference in their own lives. And denying their social analysis by reverting to individual solutions. If you're not part of the solution you're part of the problem. Many women are dedicated to working for the "reconstructed man"—or any translation into movement rhetoric of the old saw of a woman with clout in the home who gently prods her provider and protector into being a more thoughtful oppressor. The energy expended in convincing or persuading or working on the man and at length at its most exhausting in the creative strategies employed to defend new positions against the aroused opposition is energy best directed toward the building and refining of new interactive structures among the very people, namely women, who form the subject of this new offensive revolution. Feminists who still sleep with the man are delivering their most vital energies to the oppressor. To work out a suitable compromise or *apparent* equality, at any private level, is an exceptional solution between exceptional people, and although not a solution to disregard or denounce in a disjunctive culture, it remains an effort in isolation from the ground thrust of the most fundamental social revolution in the world. Out of the interactive energies of women at all levels of physical mental emotional chemical spiritual will arise the new autonomous identities or aristocracy of women whose mutual energies and identities will define the new social structures. If you're not part of the solution you're part of the problem. A personal solution or exceptional adjustment to a political problem is a collusion with the enemy. The solution is getting it together with women. Or separatism. The non-separatist woman who is not included in the common conception of the feminist solution may be viewed as a co-opted part of the problem. At this time all women are a co-opted part of the problem insomuch as every sphere of government and influence is controlled at the top by the man; thus the essential separatist solution is operative at present in theory and in consciousness and at the local manifest levels of communal fugitive enterprises. The lesbian feminist's withdrawal as far as possible from the source of her oppression can in no way be construed as a political cop-out. On the contrary it is at this point that the confluence of the personal/political (articulated but not significantly explored by feminists as a whole) attains the dimension of imperative reality to the lesbian. With her consciousness that she alone has no vested interest in prevailing cultural forms she finds that she must struggle within her sexual peer group to create wholly new nonhierarchical modes of interactive behavior. She *must* face her acculturated alienation from herself and other women and for her very survival she must learn to tap the source of her erotic energy, i.e., reclaim her sexuality. Radical lesbians know that men will not soon "get better" through the efforts of women to reeducate them. They envision the process of gay feminist revolution as an extended struggle. Tribal groupings of such women, the fugitive Lesbian Nation, have begun and will continue to serve as sustaining support and psychic power bases within the movement. The woman in relation to herself is not *naturally* a role playing animal.

REFERENCES

Altman, Dennis. *Homosexual Oppression and Liberation.* New York: Outerbridge and Dienst-frey, 1971.

Ecstasy, a Paper of a Gay Revolution. N.p.: n.d.

Johnson, Virginia, and Masters, William, H. *Human Sexual Response.* Boston: Little, Brown, 1966.

Slater, Philip. *The Pursuit of Loneliness.* Boston: Beacon Press, 1971.

Wolff, Charlotte. *Love between Women.* New York: St. Martin's Press, 1971.

Chapter Thirty-Five

Radical Feminism? Dyke Separatism?

Jeanne Cordova

One set of crucial topics raised and lost, raised and lost again in the emotionalism and choas of the Lesbian Conference was that of Independence, Separatism, and Alliances/Coalitions within the Lesbian Feminist Movement. This article will take up the four primary political perspectives (Radical Feminism, Socialist Feminism, Amazon Nationism and Dyke Separatism) which surfaced at the Conference with regard to these issues.

For initial clarity, the political definition of *INDEPENDENCE*, according to Webster, is: "self governing, not subject to control by others. Not affiliated with a larger controlling unit. Not requiring or relying on something else, not contingent." When applied to lesbian feminism this issue takes the form of questions like, "Is there, or should there be, a distinct, independent movement of, by, and for lesbian feminists?"

SEPARATISM: "Advocating for independence or autonomy for a part of a nation or political unit. A belief in, movement for, or state of separatism (i.e., one of a group of 16th Century English Protestants *preferring to separate from rather than to reform* the Church of England)." I have quoted two similar but distinct definitions of separatism in order to focus on the fact that the term was applied at the Conference to two different groups of lesbians with similar, but distinct orientations. The first definition refers to those who advocate a separate, independent Lesbian Feminist Movement (see Lesbian Feminist Perspective). The second refers to those who call upon that independent movement to take a separatist direction (see Lesbian/Amazon Nation Perspective). Examples of separatism as a proposed direction for a movement are the Black Nationalists of the Black Movement who call for "back to Africa," or a secession to a separate all-black state, country, etc. Again, when applied to the Feminist Movement, separatism as a political direction calls for the economic, psychological, cultural, emotional separation from men and all they have created (specifically, everything). Ultimately, feminist separatism calls for a return to a gynocratic state (one governed by women).

COALITION: "A temporary alliance of distinct parties, persons, or states for joint action." In their ongoing discussions of alliances in the Lesbian Feminist Movement, the *Furies* (March/April, 73) defines coalitions as occurring "when two or more groups come together by mutual agreement for a specific reason." Examples of coalitions involving lesbian feminists are: a coalition between gay women (as members of an all-lesbian organization/group) and gay men, to work together around the issue of gay civil rights; and hypothetically, a coalition between lesbians and straight feminists around issues such as rape, abortion, or childcare. I say hypothetically because lesbian groups have rarely separated themselves from the Feminist Movement and therefore lesbians have rarely worked on feminist issues as *lesbians*. Exceptions to this rule are: a) the 1971 Los Angeles coalition efforts of the Daughters of Bilitis, the Lesbian Feminists, and the National Organization of Women to work toward the adoption of a Lesbian Resolution by NOW's National Convention. Another example is NOW's (Portland, Oregon, and New York City Chapters) recent coalition efforts with gay organizations (Portland Gay People's Alliance and N.Y. Gay Activists Alliance) to work on behalf of gay civil rights legislation. These latter coalitions however must properly be termed coalitions between feminist and male-dominated gay organizations. *The Furies* makes a further point regarding coalitions by postulating that "in order to form a coalition to work to the best advantage of both groups, each group must come from a place of mutual strength and bargaining power. In this way two groups can perhaps work together without danger of one group being swamped by the politics of another." (I.e. When lesbians work with gay men on gay civil rights, issues of sodomy and lewd conduct often receive more emphasis than those of child custody or employment discrimination.)

At the Conference

In the context of the Lesbian Feminist Movement and specifically, the West Coast Lesbian Conference, the above topics were both controversial and unclear. Usually a group of people define themselves first and then begin to sort out who is or is not a part of the group/movement. They then proceed to decide what direction the group should go in, why, and with whom. Unfortunately, but naturally, "unequal, but combined development" was very much the case at the Conference. Discussion was hodgepodge as numerous speakers and participants from different consciousness, backgrounds, and parts of the country, took up these questions simultaneously. No one ever began at anyone else's beginning. Nevertheless, a number of distinct, though overlapping, perspectives did emerge.

Radical Feminist Perspective—Robin Morgan

Independence, separatism, and alliances/coalitions were very much the theme of Robin Morgan's passionately delivered, volatile keynote address in which she described lesbian feminist withdrawal from the Feminist Movement as a "difficult and dangerous theme" and called upon her audience to continue as a "united woman's movement."

Morgan, herself a bisexual and married to an effeminist [sic] gay man, opposed "dyke separatism" and the formation of an independent lesbian movement, saying, "The rapist doesn't stop to ask whether his victim is straight or lesbian."

1. On Men and Man-Hating

Asserting that "man-hating is an honorable and viable political act," Morgan called upon lesbians as women to refute and separate themselves from "male (gay and straight) attempts to destroy the united women's movement." Referring to the word "gay" as a "trivializing male-invented and male-defined term," Morgan questioned, "Why do any of us (lesbians) use the word 'gay' to describe ourselves at all?" Suggesting that "gay men capitalized on the split between straight feminists and lesbians by suggesting and insisting that we lesbians were better, basically different from straight women," she concluded that gay women "are choosing false allies when we align politically with gay men." Terming male transvestism (the practice of men wearing female clothes) as "obscenity" because transvestites "deliberately re-emphasize gender roles," Morgan analogized both transvestites and transsexuals to "whites who wear black faces."

2. On the Left

Morgan also called for "further polarization" from "the straight men, the rulers, the rapists, and the right-on radicals" of the 'New' and 'Old' (male) Left. Morgan explained her view that there is a new wave of male oppression and exploitation of women's power, this time taking the form of leftist groups' use of their women members as "their standard bearers" in the Women's Movement. Morgan wrote off the women of the Socialist Worker's Party and other "male-dominated Left" groups as "feminist collaborators." In a later workshop Morgan was more specific, saying, "I have a non-struggle attitude" toward these women and their political affiliation. She recommended "quick elimination" of these and all women who "do not have a feminist analysis and place women first."

3. Against a Counterculture

Further defining her perspective on the correct political role for lesbians, Morgan also spoke against tendencies popular among lesbian feminists, such as the concept of Lesbian/Amazon Nation, which "cannot be the feminist solution, much less the vanguard." She called advocates of Lesbian/Amazon Nation "elite isolationists" who "fall into the personal solution error" of "the life style cop-out" and think that "the revolution has already been won." Morgan also spoke against "killer dyke separatists" who think of straight women as the enemy and "trash lesbian feminists who work with them as 'anathema,'" as well as lesbians who work with the system "to elect male legislators or lobby to pass bills which will in practice primarily profit men."

Morgan concluded by blaming gay and straight men, women's "collective false consciousness," and "the intercine [sic] hostility of any oppressed people" for the "so-called" lesbian-feminist split. Herself a radical feminist, poet, and activist, Morgan called upon lesbians to ally themselves with: "the hundreds of thousands of housewives who created . . . the meat boycott, the asexual and celibate woman, . . . genuine functioning bisexuals (women bisexuals only, presumably), . . . heterosexual women who jet-set from one desperate heterosexual affair to another, . . . the butch bar dyke who cruises for a cute piece of ass." Saying that "when the crunch (the revolution) comes, I for one won't give a damn whether she's at home in bed with a man or a woman," Morgan negated the political relevance of sexual orientation.

This perspective on independence, separatism, and coalitions/alliances culminates in and springs from Morgan's vision of "a real feminist revolution, a proud dynocratic world that runs on the power of women."

Race and Class—A Socialist Feminist Perspective

A second, though less vocal, perspective on the topic of 'friends, enemies, and where to from here' was heard several times from the socialist feminist Seattle-based Radical Women, as well as nationally famous lesbian poet, Rita Mae Brown. This view is similar to "the feminist analysis" in that it does not advocate a separate Lesbian Feminist Movement, but differs distinctly in that its perception of lesbians' political role heavily emphasizes the issues of class and race. Cindy Gipple (Radical Women) spoke during several of the Emergence and Directions workshops and called for unification around "our identity as women." She cautioned against "isolating our movement to talk just about sexism" and called upon lesbians to place the questions of race and class as "top priorities" and therefore "organize around the needs and priorities of minority women."

Dyke Separatism

I would like to return to the concept of "dyke separatism" because this direction was also significantly represented at the Conference. The phrase "dyke separatist" is new to our movement and is not yet clearly defined. However, there seem to be two basic interpretations of this perspective.

Lesbian/Amazon Nations Perspective

The concept and call for an Amazon Nation has been propounded by Betty Peters of Chicago's Amazon Nation Collective (via *Lavendar Woman*) and by Jill Johnston's writings (summarized in her recent book, *Lesbian Nation*). Taking issue with Morgan's perspective that lesbians should work alongside straight women, Johnston asserts that "the continued economic dependence of women upon men, both individually and through the social institutions, is perhaps the central factor holding back the liberation of women." Dyke Separatism calls for the building of an Amazon Nation as well as a separation from straight women and ALL men. However, the nature of the separation from straight women is not the same as that envisioned from men. This ideology sees that a feminist analysis alone falls short because "no feminist per se has advanced a solution outside accommodation to the man" (Johnston). They assert that "lesbianism IS the feminist solution" and therefore, "until all women are lesbians there will be no true political revolution." Where Robin Morgan stops short of the question of how straight women of the "gynocratic world" will relate to men, or whether in fact there are to be any men in that world, Amazon Nationalists state clearly that neither straight men, gay men, nor straight women will be a problem because 'the plan is an amazon nation world wide . . . all physically together in one place taking over an area for the first lesbian city ever built" (*Lavendar Women*, Peters). Many who attended the turbulent Lesbian Conference would suggest the fallacy of this plan on the grounds that the lesbian city would have too many demolition crews and not enough construction crews. Ideologically this perspective emphasizes the building of a counter culture as the avenue to freedom from lesbian oppression.

Lesbian Feminist

Another interpretation of "dyke separatism" is similar to the Lesbian/Amazon Nation perspective in that it also advocates a separate Lesbian Feminist Movement. However, this group does not necessarily call for a separatist withdrawal of that Movement. The following conversation (taped at Lesbian Conference) speaks to the dissatisfaction this perspective has with the Feminist Movement (taped immediately after Morgan's Saturday address):

> Woman A: "What do you think of her [Morgan's] speech?"
> Women B: "I thought it was fucked. I agree with not working with men, but she didn't say anything about working with straight women."
> Woman A: "Yes she did, she said lesbians should work with all feminists because . . ."
> Woman B: "That's where I think she's wrong. The Feminist Movements co-opts lesbian energy too. They get us to work with them on childcare and abortion and when we bring up lesbian issues, or even lesbianism itself, they say, 'Oh my! The lavender menaces are at it again!" They say 'ALL women can't relate to that, what about the housewives . . . the Women's Movement isn't ready for that yet.' I got tired of them not being ready for us and split."

Lesbian Activist Women, the Conference sponsoring organization, had a similar orientation, which was put forth by Jeanne Cordova, at the Saturday Press Conference. Cordova said, "Our perspective in sponsoring this Conference was that we as lesbians have felt for a long time that we have been batted between the Gay Movement and the Women's Movement, between the Old Left and the New Left. . . . I mean we've been everywhere fighting under everyone else's banner for five or six years now, for centuries. We wanted to build this Conference as the founding convention of the Lesbian Feminist Movement. Many of us, probably most of us have been heavily involved in the Women's Movement, some of us have gone into and out of the Gay Movement, as long as we could stand the sexism! Now it's time for us to come home. 'Amazon Nation' is our base."

Even within the perspective of dyke separatism, however, there are wide differences of opinion on the subject of alliances and coalition. One opinion is that it is a mistake to consider coalitions with men at this time. There are very few men close to the point of taking up the fight against male supremacy ... and we do not at this time have a strong enough power base. It is more likely that we would work within the broad-based Women's Movement with women such as celibate and radical feminists ... but ... now is not the time to search for coalitions" (*The Furies*, March/April).

A differing point of view is, "This Conference shows that it is time for lesbians to draw together as lesbians ... but ... if and when there is a need and a time a consciousness with groups outside our movement, that is the time to draw together in coalition. Especially in terms of our political aims, be they civil rights or the development of an alternative institution like a Center, we seek uniting with our sisters and brothers in the Women's and Gay Movements" (Cordova, for Lesbian Activist Women).

Do We Agree on Anything?

Sorting through, writing through, and living through the confusion of the preceding perspectives is, to say the least, very taxing on one's emotions and intellect. If there was any point of unity that weekend at UCLA, it was that almost all lesbians are conscious of and hopeful for the development and existence of a Lesbian Feminist culture/movement. Anyone who attended the West Coast Conference would have difficulty in denying the existence of lesbian feminism as a distinct and unique force.

Second, there was little disagreement that men had no place in the Lesbian Feminist movement. The presence and performance of San Francisco pre-operative transsexual Beth Elliott exploded in a mismanaged, miscalculated setting surrounded by general ignorance, in that the great majority of women had no prior concept or knowledge of the issue. Laying aside the issue of whether the person in question or any transsexual is "man" or "woman," there was little doubt that the very topic of "men" was an issue of rage. This rage again surfaced and partially vented itself when a "Jesus Freak" appeared at the opening keynote address with a sign saying "Lesbian Dykes Repent." Several dozen women raced toward him, screaming "Get him!" He was knocked to the ground and struck by one woman, while conference monitors tried to form a line in front of him to prevent a full-scale riot. Again, in the Lesbian Activism Workshop, a woman from Berkeley stated, "I would personally not like to have to deal with men at all. Some of us are working to make that happen ... we are getting together with a woman chemist to find something perhaps to put in water to make men impotent ... prevent male babies from being born, or in some way eliminate men for existence." A less extreme, but definite example of feelings toward men was that the Conference was publicized as an exclusive, all-women event and that even male press were not allowed except at a scheduled press conference.

The 2nd West Coast Lesbian Conference will long be remembered for its turbulent magnitude. We have attempted to objectively present the major directions, hands, and thoughts of the present stage of our newly developing movement, rather than to editorialize on the merits and fallacies of any particular perspective. Such a presentation seems important because at the Conference these issues were never set forth in a clear or focused context for the hundreds who came to learn, discuss, and share.

The West Coast Lesbian Conference did not decide the nature or composition of our movement, much less its directions or allies (if there be any). In our future, many sisters will be working to form the Amazon Nation. Others will be working to directly confront and change existing institutions. Many sisters will remain purist separatists, others will work with straight women and/or gay men. But most of the issues have at least been uncovered. Our movement is young and we have a lot of growing and learning to do. Our movement will have to deal with our anger as we have had to deal with our loving. Our movement will have to deal with our differences while we explore and guard the basis of our unity. Most importantly, our movement challenges us to understand, in the personal and political way that is the unique contribution of feminist women, the real issues which must be uncovered and dealt with. The life of our community, our lives and our eventual freedom depend on this understanding. Our eventual freedom depends on the clarity of thought, the necessary political sophistication, and the love we have for each other in the long and difficult struggle to create a new world. It is important that we find the correct ways to build, but equally important that we not kill each other on the way. There is little point in that kind of struggle. We live in a society that has expertly taught us the ways of KILL and HATE. We must separate and divorce ourselves from this socialization, and perhaps spend some time separate from each other to sort out our differences.

Pat Lecher (Lansing, Michigan) was one of 400 lesbians who sat through the long and chaotic Closing Session of the Conference. Pat Lecher was the woman, quite accidentally so, who unofficially but quite thoroughly ended the 2nd West Coast Lesbian Conference by standing up in the middle of the hall and shouting, "This Conference is adjourned." Later asked by a *Lesbian Tide* reporter to describe her feelings about this move, Pat echoed the thoughts of over a thousand as they left that weekend: "This Conference is never going to be adjourned. It's going to go on for years."

Chapter Thirty-Six

Women Divided?

Judy White

Despite factionalism which continually threatened to blow up the *Congress* to Unite Women held in *New York City, May 1–3* over 600 women registered for the gathering and participated in workshops and discussions. One very significant thing was a show of hands taken at the opening plenary which revealed that over half the women attending were new to the women's liberation movement.

Workshops on a whole range of topics of concern to the women's movement were marked by fruitful, serious discussion and many came up with proposals for continuing action around issues such as childcare, secondary education and an end to abortion restrictions.

As compared with the first Congress to Unite Women held in the Northeast last November, the level of discussion on the issues was higher, reflecting the development of the movement and a deeper consciousness of the oppression of women. It was also clear that some women in the movement have developed more defined positions over the past months, so the differences among us were clearer and sharper.

This fact became obvious on the very first night of the Congress when the gay women's caucus took the floor and led a discussion on their special problems as gay women in the women's liberation movement.

The gay women, along with some women from a group called the Class Workshop, set a tone of attacking the other women present at the Congress of being racist, sexist and unconcerned about the problems of working class women. And while some of the issues these women raised were valid the way they presented them was not conducive to a discussion on how to deal with these issues within the framework of our common concerns as women.

This same lack of respect for the other women present at the Congress carried over into the second day when the workshop on "How Women are Divided" came into the evening plenary with an ultimatum that we discuss only the subject matter of their group—that all issues other than class and race were irrelevant.

The situation was not improved at all by the moderate women (Democratic Party supporters) present at the plenary, one of whom had been arbitrarily appointed chairwoman for the session and started it off in a very heavy-handed way.

The result was that most workshops never could be reported out to the plenary, action proposals could not be adequately discussed, and no continuing structure for Congress participants was set up.

Under the pretext that the Congress was using male forms of organization (Roberts' Rules of Order), the groups that disrupted virtually prevented any fruitful discussion from taking place among the women as a whole—even on the issues they felt should be the focus of discussion for the group: Such strong arm tactics were hardly a departure from male *or* female form of disruption at many radical conferences in recent months. Furthermore, there was no chance for the many new women attending the Congress to even express opinions on what they wanted to discuss.

These problems clearly resulted from the fact that there was no clear focus for the Congress and a lack of leadership.

One thing which was shown clearly by the Congress was the fact that, given the disagreements within the movement, if we are to continue to have broad conferences which are representative of women of many different points of view—the only way to settle the inevitable disagreements which come up is democratically, that is, by majority rule.

Despite the differences that exist within the women's movement, there are questions which can and *must* unite us—demands for free twenty-four hour childcare centers controlled by those who use them, free abortion on demand, an end to tracking and sexist education in public schools and a whole number of other things. We have to be organized so that programs of action to fight for the things that unite us can be hammered out.

Only in a setting where the right of all to be heard and the right of all ideas to be discussed are established by majority rule can we build the women's liberation movement and reach out to all the millions of women of all beliefs whom we all need to involve in order for us to be successful in our fight to end our oppression as women.

Chapter Thirty-Seven

Have You Ever Asked a Black Lesbian to Dance?

Julie Jenkins

I do not want to go into rhetorical analysis coupled with philosophical bullshit, and I do not speak for all black lesbians, but I am sure that most of us have wondered at some time or another—what the motivation is behind the psyche of white lesbians. Exactly, what is your deal?

Frequently we are asked by those of you who are dangerously entangled in the ideas of lesbian politics and lesbian centers and lesbian nations, "Why don't black lesbians become members of our groups?" or "Why don't you want to participate?" To this I say, radical lesbianism can go nowhere. There is no economic, social, or political power within the lesbian movement. When the world as a whole looks upon black lesbians, they don't see lesbians, they see black aggressive women. Thusly, our goals are best served by other societal processes. I mean, really, why should we further burden ourselves with other oppressive yokes—we're already black and are women. And too, the dues we pay to be members of the 'talented tenth' are high.

Historically the 'talented tenth' were those black people who became college educated and somehow slipped into middle class America. Here, I am referring to that special one tenth of the lesbian population that by birth were born into blackness and by social stratification have been ascribed various talents. To continue, physically I am a large woman, but why must my size dictate how I am to relate to other gay women? I am not afforded the opportunity to pick and choose amongst an array of black lesbians because our numbers are few, and by the same token, I am not able to pick and choose amongst white lesbians because of a subtle system of stereotyping that exists in most lesbian communities. It seems to follow that if you are black, you have to be nice looking, five feet six and no more than 110 pounds, quiet and smile a lot—otherwise you are labeled a stud/dyke/butch. White women expect us to party harder, be more promiscuous, have no valid white Anglo/Saxon feelings or emotions; and when they do enter into an intimate relationship with a black woman, eight times out of ten, the white woman expects to be economically pampered and supported. After you have been forced into the role for so long you become part of it and can no longer function as an individual, especially the individual you fantasize yourself being. White women have made black women afraid of each other because black women have been emasculated by the lesbian community for so long.

There are so many times when I'd like to just meet someone on an equal basis without having this image consciousness subtly or actually thrown at me. Someday I'd like to be able to freely ask a black woman to dance with me or have coffee with me or sleep with me without having her go through a serious mind hassle as to her role in our relationship or question my motivations and objectives. Someday I'm going to trip out of this life . . . someday you're going to free me.

E. Heterosexuality

Chapter Thirty-Eight

The Myth of the Vaginal Orgasm

Anne Koedt

Whenever female orgasm and frigidity are discussed, a false distinction is made between the vaginal and the clitoral orgasm. Frigidity has generally been defined by men as the failure of women to have vaginal orgasms. Actually the vagina is not a highly sensitive area and is not constructed to achieve orgasm. It is the clitoris which is the center of sexual sensitivity and which is the female equivalent of the penis.

I think this explains a great many things: First of all, the fact that the so-called frigidity rate among women is phenomenally high. Rather than tracing female frigidity to the false assumptions about female anatomy, our "experts" have declared frigidity a psychological problem of women. Those women who complained about it were recommended psychiatrists, so that they might discover their "problem"—diagnosed generally as a failure to adjust to their role as women.

The facts of female anatomy and sexual response tell a different story. Although there are many areas for sexual arousal, there is only one area for sexual climax; that area is the clitoris. All orgasms are extensions of sensation from this area. Since the clitoris is not necessarily stimulated sufficiently in the conventional sexual positions, we are left "frigid."

Aside from physical stimulation, which is the common cause of orgasm for most people, there is also stimulation through primarily mental processes. Some women, for example, may achieve orgasm through sexual fantasies, or through fetishes. However, while the stimulation may be psychological, the orgasm manifests itself physically. Thus, while the cause is psychological, the *effect* is still physical, and the orgasm necessarily takes place in the sexual organ equipped for sexual climax—the clitoris. The orgasm experience may also differ in degree of intensity—some more localized, and some more diffuse and sensitive. But they are all clitoral orgasms.

All this leads to some interesting questions about conventional sex and our role in it. Men have orgasms essentially by friction with the vagina, not the clitoral area, which is external and not able to cause friction the way penetration does. Women have thus been defined sexually in terms of what pleases men; our own biology has not been properly analyzed. Instead, we are fed the myth of the liberated woman and her vaginal orgasm—an orgasm which in fact does not exist.

What we must do is redefine our sexuality. We must discard the "normal" concepts of sex and create new guidelines which take into account mutual sexual enjoyment. While the idea of mutual enjoyment is liberally applauded in marriage manuals, it is not followed to its logical conclusion. We must begin to demand that if certain sexual positions now defined as "standard" are not mutually conducive to orgasm, they no longer be defined as standard. New techniques must be used or devised which transform this particular aspect of our current sexual exploitation.

Freud—A Father of the Vaginal Orgasm

Freud contended that the clitoral orgasm was adolescent, and that upon puberty, when women began having intercourse with men, women should transfer the center of orgasm to the vagina. The vagina, it was assumed, was able to produce a parallel, but more mature, orgasm than the clitoris. Much work was done to elaborate on this theory, but little was done to challenge the basic assumptions.

To fully appreciate this incredible invention, perhaps Freud's general attitude about women should first be recalled. Mary Ellman, in *Thinking about Women*, summed it up this way:

> Everything in Freud's patronizing and fearful attitude toward women follows from their lack of a penis, but it is only in his essay *The Psychology of Women* that Freud makes explicit . . . the deprecations of women which are implicit in his work. He then prescribes for them the abandonment of the life of the mind, which will interfere with their sexual function. When the psychoanalyzed patient is male, the analyst sets himself the task of developing the man's capacities; but with women patients, the job is to resign them to the limits of their sexuality. As Mr. Rieff puts it: For Freud, "Analysis cannot encourage in women new energies for success and achievement, but only teach them the lesson of rational resignation."

It was Freud's feelings about women's secondary and inferior relationship to men that formed the basis for his theories on female sexuality.

Once having laid down the law about the nature of our sexuality, Freud not so strangely discovered a tremendous problem of frigidity in women. His recommended cure for a woman who was frigid was psychiatric care. She was suffering from failure to mentally adjust to her "natural" role as a woman. Frank S. Caprio, a contemporary follower of these ideas, states:

> . . . whenever a woman is incapable of achieving an orgasm via coitus, provided the husband is an adequate partner, and prefers clitoral stimulation to any other form of sexual activity, she can be regarded as suffering from frigidity and requires psychiatric assistance. (*The Sexually Adequate Female*, p. 64.)

The explanation given was that women were envious of men—"renunciation of womanhood." Thus it was diagnosed as an anti-male phenomenon.

It is important to emphasize that Freud did not base his theory upon a study of woman's anatomy, but rather upon his assumptions of woman as an inferior appendage to man, and her consequent social and psychological role. In their attempts to deal with the ensuing problem of mass frigidity, Freudians created elaborate mental gymnastics. Marie Bonaparte, in *Female Sexuality*, goes so far as to suggest surgery to help women back on their rightful path. Having discovered a strange connection between the non-frigid woman and the location of the clitoris near the vagina,

> it then occurred to me that where, in certain women, this gap was excessive, and clitoridal fixation obdurate, a clitoridal-vaginal reconciliation might be effected by surgical means, which would then benefit the normal erotic function. Professor Halban, of Vienna, as much a biologist as surgeon, became interested in the problem and worked out a simple operative technique. In this, the suspensory ligament of the clitoris was severed and the clitoris secured to the underlying structures, thus fixing it in a lower position, with eventual reduction of the labia minora. (p. 148)

But the severest damage was not in the area of surgery, where Freudians ran around absurdly trying to change female anatomy to fit their basic assumptions. The worst damage was done to the mental health of women, who either suffered silently with self-blame, or flocked to psychiatrists looking desperately for the hidden and terrible repression that had kept from them their vaginal destiny.

Lack of Evidence

One may perhaps at first claim that these are unknown and unexplored areas, but upon closer examination this is certainly not true today, nor was it true even in the past. For example, men have known that women suffered from frigidity often during intercourse. So the problem was there. Also, there is much specific evidence. Men knew that the clitoris was and is the essential organ for masturbation, whether in children or adult women. So obviously women made it clear where *they* thought their sexuality was located. Men also seem suspiciously aware of the clitoral powers during "foreplay," when they want to arouse women and produce the necessary lubrication for penetration. Foreplay is a concept created for male purposes, but works to the disadvantage of many women, since as soon as the woman is aroused the man changes to vaginal stimulation, leaving her both aroused and unsatisfied.

It has also been known that women need no anesthesia inside the vagina during surgery, thus pointing to the fact that the vagina is in fact not a highly sensitive area.

Today, with extensive knowledge of anatomy, with Kelly, Kinsey, and Masters and Johnson, to mention just a few sources, there is no ignorance on the subject. There are, however, social reasons why this knowledge has not been popularized. We are living in a male society which has not sought change in women's role.

Anatomical Evidence

Rather than starting with what women *ought* to feel, it would seem logical to start out with the anatomical facts regarding the clitoris and vagina.

The Clitoris is a small equivalent of the penis, except for the fact that the urethra does not go through it as in the man's penis. Its erection is similar to the male erection, and the head of the clitoris has the same type of structure and function as the head of the penis. G. Lombard Kelly, in *Sexual Feelings in Married Men and Women*, says:

> The head of the clitoris is also composed of erectile tissue, and it possesses a very sensitive epithelium or surface covering, supplied with special nerve endings called genital corpuscles, which are peculiarly adapted for sensory stimulation that under proper mental conditions terminates in the sexual orgasm. No other part of the female generative tract has such corpuscles. (Pocketbooks; p. 35)

The clitoris has no other function than that of sexual pleasure.

The Vagina. Its functions are related to the reproductive function. Principally, 1) menstruation, 2) receive penis, 3) hold semen, and 4) birth passage. The interior of the vagina, which according to the defenders of the vaginally caused orgasm is the center and producer of the orgasm, is:

> like nearly all other internal body structures, poorly supplied with end organs of touch. The internal entodermal origin of the lining of the vagina makes it similar in this respect to the rectum and other parts of the digestive tract. (Kinsey, *Sexual Behavior in the Human Female*, p. 580)

The degree of insensitivity inside the vagina is so high that "Among the women who were tested in our gynecologic sample, less than 14% were at all conscious that they had been touched." (Kinsey, p. 580)

Even the importance of the vagina as an *erotic* center (as opposed to an orgasmic center) has been found to be minor.

Other Areas. Labia minora and the vestibule of the vagina. These two sensitive areas may trigger off a clitoral orgasm. Because they can be effectively stimulated during "normal" coitus, though infrequently, this kind of stimulation is incorrectly thought to be vaginal orgasm. However, it is important to distinguish between areas which can stimulate the clitoris, incapable of producing the orgasm themselves, and the clitoris:

> Regardless of what means of excitation is used to bring the individual to the state of sexual climax, the sensation is perceived by the genital corpuscles and is localized where they are situated: in the head of the clitoris or penis. (Kelly, p. 49)

Psychologically Stimulated Orgasm. Aside from the above mentioned direct and indirect stimulations of the clitoris, there is a third way an orgasm may be triggered. This is through mental (cortical) stimulation, where the imagination stimulates the brain, which in turn stimulates the genital corpuscles of the glans to set off an orgasm.

Women Who Say They Have Vaginal Orgasms

Confusion. Because of the lack of knowledge of their own anatomy, some women accept the idea that an orgasm felt during "normal" intercourse was vaginally caused.

This confusion is caused by a combination of two factors. One, failing to locate the center of the orgasm, and two, by a desire to fit her experience to the male-defined idea of sexual normalcy. Considering that women know little about their anatomy, it is easy to be confused.

Deception. The vast majority of women who pretend vaginal orgasm to their men are faking it to "get the job." In a new bestselling Danish book, *I Accuse*, Mette Ejlersen specifically deals with this common problem, which she calls the "sex comedy." This comedy has many causes. First of all, the man brings a great deal of pressure to bear on the woman, because he considers his ability as a lover at stake. So as not to offend his ego, the woman will comply with the prescribed role and go through simulated ecstasy. In some of the other Danish women mentioned, women who were left frigid were turned off to sex, and pretended vaginal orgasm to hurry up the sex act. Others admitted that they had faked vaginal orgasm to catch a man. In one case, the woman pretended vaginal orgasm to get him to leave his first wife, who admitted being vaginally frigid. Later she was forced to continue the deception, since obviously she couldn't tell him to stimulate her clitorally.

Many more women were simply afraid to establish their right to equal enjoyment, seeing the sexual act as being primarily for the man's benefit, and any pleasure that the woman got as an added extra.

Other women, with just enough ego to reject the man's idea that they needed psychiatric care, refused to admit their frigidity. They wouldn't accept self-blame, but they didn't know how to solve the problem, not knowing the physiological facts about themselves. So they were left in a peculiar limbo.

Again, perhaps one of the most infuriating and damaging results of this whole charade has been that women who were perfectly healthy sexually were taught that they were not. So in addition to being sexually deprived, these women were told to blame themselves when they deserved no blame. Looking for a cure to a problem that has none can lead a woman on an endless path of self-hatred and insecurity. For she is told by her analyst that not even in her one role allowed in a male society—the role of a woman—is she successful. She is put on the defensive, with phony data as evidence that she'd better try to be even more feminine, think more feminine, and reject her envy of men. That is, shuffle even harder, baby.

Why Men Maintain the Myth

1. Sexual Penetration is Preferred. The best stimulant for the penis is the woman's vagina. It supplies the necessary friction and lubrication. From a strictly technical point of view this position offers the best physical conditions, even though the man may try other positions for variation.

2. The Invisible Woman. One of the elements of male chauvinism is the refusal or inability to see women as total, separate human beings. Rather, men have chosen to define women only in terms of how they benefited men's lives. Sexually, a woman was not seen as an individual wanting to share equally in the sexual act, any more than she was seen as a person with independent desires when she did anything else in society. Thus, it was easy to make up what was convenient about women; for on top of that, society has been a function of male interests, and women were not organized to form even a vocal opposition to the male experts.

3. The Penis as Epitome of Masculinity. Men define their lives primarily in terms of masculinity. It is a universal form of ego-boosting. That is, in every society, however homogeneous (i.e., with the absence of racial, ethnic, or major economic differences) there is always a group, women, to oppress.

The essence of male chauvinism is in the psychological superiority men exercise over women. This kind of superior-inferior definition of self, rather than positive definition based upon one's own achievements and development, has of course chained victim and oppressor both. But by far the most brutalized of the two is the victim.

An analogy is racism, where the white racist compensates for his feelings of unworthiness by creating an image of the black man (it is primarily a male struggle) as biologically inferior to him. Because of his power in a white male power structure, the white man can socially enforce this mythical division.

To the extent that men try to rationalize and justify male superiority through physical differentiation, masculinity may be symbolized by being the *most* muscular, the most hairy; having the deepest voice, and the biggest penis. Women, on the other hand, are approved of (i.e., called feminine) if they are weak, petite; shave their legs; have high soft voices, and no penis.

Since the clitoris is almost identical to the penis, one finds a great deal of evidence of men in various societies trying to either ignore the clitoris and emphasize the vagina (as did Freud), or, as in some places in the Mideast, actually performing clitoridectomy. Freud saw this ancient and still practiced custom as a way of further "feminizing" the female by removing this cardinal vestige of her masculinity. It should be noted also that a big clitoris is considered ugly and masculine. Some cultures engage in the practice of pouring a chemical on the clitoris to make it shrivel up into "proper" size.

It seems clear to me that men in fact fear the clitoris as a threat to masculinity.

4. Sexually Expendable Male. Men fear that they will become sexually expendable if the clitoris is substituted for the vagina as the center of pleasure for women. Actually this has a great deal of validity if one considers *only* the anatomy. The position of the penis inside the vagina, while perfect for reproduction, does not necessarily stimulate an orgasm in women because the clitoris is located externally and higher up. Women must rely upon indirect stimulation in the "normal" position.

Lesbian sexuality could make an excellent case, based upon anatomical data, for the extinction of the male organ. Albert Ellis says something to the effect that a man without a penis can make a woman an excellent lover.

Considering that the vagina is very desirable from a man's point of view, purely on physical grounds, one begins to see the dilemma for men. And it forces us as well to discard many "physical" arguments explaining why women go to bed with men. What is left, it seems to me, are primarily psychological reasons why women select men at the exclusion of women as sexual partners.

5. Control of Women. One reason given to explain the Mideastern practice of clitoridectomy is that it will keep the women from straying. By removing the sexual organ capable of orgasm, it must be assumed that her sexual drive will diminish. Considering how men look upon their women as property, particularly in very backward nations, we should begin to consider a great deal more why it is not in men's interest to have women totally free sexually. The double standard, as practiced for example in Latin America, is set up to keep the woman as total property of the husband, while he is free to have affairs as he wishes.

6. Lesbianism and Bisexuality. Aside from the strictly anatomical reasons why women might equally seek other women as lovers, there is a fear on men's part that women will seek the company of other women on a full, human basis. The establishment of clitoral orgasm as fact would threaten the heterosexual *institution*. For it would indicate that sexual pleasure was obtainable from either men *or* women, thus making heterosexuality not an absolute, but an option. It would thus open up the whole question of *human* sexual relationships beyond the confines of the present male-female role system.

REFERENCES

Sexual Behavior in the Human Female, Alfred C. Kinsey, Pocketbooks, 1953.

Female Sexuality, Marie Bonaparte, Grove Press, 1953.

Sex without Guilt, Albert Ellis, Grove Press, 1958 and 1965.

Sexual Feelings in Married Men and Women, G. Lombard Kelly, Pocketbooks, 1951 and 1965.

I Accuse (Jeg Anklager), Mette Ejlersen, Chr. Erichsens Furlag (Danish), 1968.

The Sexually Adequate Female, Frank S. Caprio, Fawcett Gold Medal Books, 1953 and 1966.

Thinking about Women, Mary Ellman, Harcourt, Broce & World, 1968.

Human Sexual Response, Masters and Johnson, Little, Brown, 1966.

Chapter Thirty-Nine

A Critique of the Miss America Protest

Carol Hanisch

The protest of the Miss America Pageant in Atlantic City in September told the nation that a new feminist movement is afoot in the land. Due to the tremendous coverage in the mass media, millions of Americans now know there is a Women's Liberation Movement. Media coverage ranged from the front pages of several newspapers in the United States to many articles in the foreign press.

The action brought many new members into our group and many requests from women outside the city for literature and information. A recurrent theme was, "I've been waiting so long for something like this." So have we all, and the Miss America protest put us well on our way.

But no action taken in the Women's Liberation Struggle will be all good or all bad. It is necessary that we analyze each step to see what we did that was effective, what was not, and what was down-right destructive.

At this point in our struggle, our actions should be aimed primarily at doing two inter-related things: 1) awakening the latent consciousness of women about their own oppression, and 2) building sisterhood. With these as our primary immediate goals, let us examine the Miss America protest.

The idea came out of our group method of analyzing women's oppression by recalling our own experiences. We were watching *Schmearguntz*, a feminist movie, one night at our meeting. The movie had flashes of the Miss America contest in it. I found myself sitting there remembering how I had felt at home with my family watching the pageant as a child, an adolescent, and a college student. I knew it had evoked powerful feelings.

When I proposed the idea to our group, we decided to go around the room with each woman telling how she felt about the pageant. We discovered that many of us who had always put down the contest still watched it. Others, like myself, had consciously identified with it, and had cried with the winner.

From our communal thinking came the concrete plans for the action. We all agreed that our main point in the demonstration would be that all women were hurt by beauty competition—Miss America as well as ourselves. We opposed the pageant in our own self-interest, e.g., the self-interest of all women.

Yet one of the biggest mistakes of the whole pageant was our anti-womanism. A spirit of every woman "doing her own thing" began to emerge. Sometimes it was because there was an open conflict about an issue. Other times, women didn't say anything at all about disagreeing with a group decision; they just went ahead and did what they wanted to do, even though it was something the group had definitely decided against. Because of this egotistic individualism, a definite strain of anti-womanism was presented to the public to the detriment of the action.

Posters which read "Up Against the Wall, Miss America," "Miss America Sells It," and "Miss America is a Big Falsie" hardly raised any woman's consciousness and really harmed the cause of sisterhood. Miss America and all beautiful women came off as our enemy instead of as our sisters who suffer with us. A group decision had been made rejecting these anti-woman signs. A few women made them anyway. Some women who had opposed the slogans were in the room when the signs were being made and didn't confront those who were making the anti-woman signs.

A more complex situation developed around the decision of a few women to use an "underground" disruptive tactic. The action was approved by the group only after its adherents said they would do it anyway as an individual action. As it turned out, we came to the realization that there is no such thing as "individual action" in a movement. We were linked to and were committed to support our sisters whether they called their action "individual" or not. It also came to many of us that there is at this time no real need to do "underground" actions. We need to reach as many women as possible as quickly as possible with a clear message that has the power of our person behind it. At this point women have to see other women standing up and saying these things. That's why draping a, women's liberation banner over the balcony that night and yelling our message was much clearer. We should have known, however, that the television network, because it was not competing with other networks for coverage, would not put the action on camera. It did get on the radio and in newspapers, however.

The problem of how to enforce group decisions is one we haven't solved. It came up in a lot of ways throughout the whole action. The group rule of not talking to male reporters was another example.

One of the reasons we came off anti-woman, besides the posters, was our lack of clarity. We didn't say clearly enough that we women are all *forced* to play the Miss America role—not by beautiful women but by men who we have to act that way for, and by a system that has so well institutionalized male supremacy for its own ends.

This was none too clear in our guerrilla theater either. Women chained to a replica, red, white and blue bathing-suited Miss America could have been misinter-preted as against beautiful women. Also, crowning a live sheep Miss America sort of said that beautiful women *are* sheep. However, the action did say to some women that women are *viewed* as auction-block, docile animals. The grandmother of one of the participants really began to understand the action when she was told about the sheep, and she ended up joining the protest.

There is as great a need for clarity in our language as there is in our actions. The leaflet that was distributed as a press release and as a flyer at the action was too long, too wordy, too complex, too hippy-yippee-campy. Instead of an "in" phrase like "Racism with Roses" (I still don't know exactly what that means), we could have just called the pageant RACIST and everybody would have understood our opposition on that point. If we are going to reach masses of women, we must give up all the "in-talk" of the New Left/Hippie movements—at least when we're talking in public. (Yes, even the word FUCK!) We can use simple language (*real* language) that everyone from Queens to Iowa will understand and not misunderstand.

We should try to avoid the temptation to say everything there is to say about what is wrong with the world and thereby say nothing that a new person can really dig into and understand. Women's liberation itself is revolutionary dynamite. When other issues are interjected, we should clearly relate them to our oppression *as women*.

We tried to carry the democratic means we used in planning the action into the actual *doing* of it. We didn't want leaders or spokesmen. It makes the movement not only *seem* stronger and larger if everyone is a leader, but it actually is stronger if not dependent on a few. It also guards against the time when such leaders could be isolated and picked off one way or another. And of course many voices are more powerful than one.

Our first attempt at this was not entirely successful. We must learn how to fight against the media's desire to make leaders and some women's desire to be spokesmen. Everybody talks to the press or nobody talks to the press. The same problem came up in regard to appearances on radio and television shows after the action. We theoretically decided no one should appear more than once, but it didn't work out that way.

The Miss America protest was a zap action, as opposed to person-to-person group action. Zap actions are using our presence as a group and/or the media to make women's oppression into social issues. In such actions we speak to men as a group as well as to women. It is a rare opportunity to talk to men in a situation where they can't talk back. (Men must begin to learn to listen.) Our power of solidarity, not our individual intellectual exchanges will change men.

We tried to speak to individual women in the crowd and now some of us feel that it may not have been a good tactic. It put women on the spot in front of their men. We were putting them in a position which we choose to avoid ourselves when we don't allow men in our discussion groups.

It is interesting that many of the non-movement women we talked to about the protest had the same reaction as many radical women. "But I'm not oppressed" was a shared response. "I don't care about Miss America" was another. If more than half the television viewers in the country watch the pageant, somebody cares! And many of us admitted watching it too, even while putting it down.

It's interesting, too, that while much of the Left was putting us down for attacking something so "silly and unimportant" or "reformist," the Right saw us as a threat and yelled such things as "Go back to Russia" and "Mothers of Mao" at the picket line. Ironically enough, what the Left/underground press seemed to like best about our action was what was really our worst mistake—our anti-woman signs.

Surprisingly and fortunately, some of the mass media ignored our mistakes and concentrated on our best points. To quote from the *Daily News*, ". . . some women who think the whole idea of such contests is degrading to femininity, took their case to the people . . . During boardwalk protest, gals say they're not anti-beauty, just anti-beauty contest." Shana Alexander wrote in a *Life* magazine editorial that she "wished they'd gone father." Together, *Life* and the *Daily News* reach millions of Americans.

We need to take ourselves seriously. The powers that be do. Carol Giardino of Gainesville, Florida, was fired from her job because of her activities in women's liberation and her participation in the protest. Police cars were parked outside the planning meeting one night. The next day we got a call from the Mayor of Atlantic City questioning us about just what we planned to do. Pepsi-Cola is withdrawing as a sponsor of the pageant. They produce a diet cola and maybe see themselves as next year's special target.

Unfortunately the best slogan for the action came up about a month after, when Roz Baxandall came out on the David Susskind show with "Every day in a woman's life is a walking Miss America Contest." We shouldn't wait for the best slogan; we should go ahead to the best of our understanding. We hope all our sisters can learn something as we did from our first foray.

Chapter Forty

The Pill
Genocide or Liberation

Toni Cade

After a while meetings tend to fade, merge, blur. But one remains distinct, at least pieces do, mainly because of the man-woman pill hassle. I don't recall who called the meeting or what organizations were present. But I do remember that one speaker, in mapping out what should be done to make the Summer of Support G.I. coffee-house venture effective—it was a mere idea then—said that we should stock the coffee shops with items guaranteed to attract our Brothers in Khaki so that re-education could begin. He began the list of *things* to be sent to the off-base radical projects: "Packages containing homecooked soul food, blues and jazz records, Black journals, foxy Sisters who can rap, revolutionary pamphlets, films that . . ." My gut cramped on the "Sisters." Talk about being regarded as objects, commodities. Not one to sit on my hands, I raised a few questions about the insensitivity of that cataloguing and about the agenda in general, which nicely managed to skirt any issue of the woman's struggle or man-woman relationships. These remarks triggered off all around me very righteous remarks from equally "overly sensitive, salty bitches trying to disrupt our meeting with that feminist horseshit."

During the break before the workshops began, the chairman invited us all to the refreshment table and urged the Sisters to help out in the kitchen. This would not have been so bad except that during the formation of work committees, the Sisters were arbitrarily assigned to man the phones and the typewriters and the coffeepots. And when a few toughminded, no-messin'-around politico Sisters began pushing for the right to participate in policymaking, the right to help compose position papers for the emerging organization, the group leader would drop his voice into that mellow register specially reserved for the retarded, the incontinent, the lunatic, and say something about the need to be feminine and supportive and blah, blah, blah. Unfortunately quite a few of the ladies have been so browbeaten in the past with the Black Matriarch stick that they tend to run, leap, fly to the pots and pans, the back rows, the shadows, eager to justify themselves in terms of ass, breasts, collard greens just to prove that they are not the evil, ugly, domineering monsters of tradition.

When we got back into a large group again, we were offered a medley of speakers dipping out of a variety of bags, each advocating his thing as the thing. One woman, the only female speaker out of twelve speakers, six group leaders, two chairmen, and three moderators, spoke very passionately about the education of our children. She was introduced as so-and-so's wife. Others were for blowing up the Empire State, the Statue of Liberty, the Pentagon. A few more immediate-oriented types were for blowing the locks off the schools if the strike ever came to pass. Finally, one tall, lean dude went into deep knee bends as he castigated the Sisters to throw away the pill and hop to the mattresses and breed revolutionaries and mess up the man's genocidal program. A slightly drunk and very hot lady from the back row kept interrupting with, for the most part, incoherent and undecipherable remarks. But she was encouraged finally to just step into the aisle and speak her speech, which she did, shouting the Brother down in gusts and sweeps of historical, hysterical documentation of mistrust and mess-up, waxing lyric over the hardships, the oatmeal, the food stamps, the diapers, the scuffling, the bloody abortions, the bungled births. She was mad as hell and getting more and more sober. She was righteous and beautiful and accusatory, and when she pointed a stiff finger at the Brother and shouted, "And when's the last time you fed one of them brats you been breeding all over the city, you jive-ass so-and-so?" she tore the place up.

Since then I've been made aware of the national call to the Sisters to abandon birth controls, to not cooperate with an enemy all too determined to solve his problem with the bomb, the gun, the pill; to instruct the welfare mammas to resist the sterilization plan that has become ruthless policy for a great many state agencies; to picket family-planning centers and abortion-referral groups, and to raise revolutionaries. And it seems to me that once again the woman has demonstrated the utmost in patience and reasonableness when she counters, "What plans do you have for the care of me and the child? Am I to persist in the role of Amazon workhorse and house slave? How do we break the cycle of child-abandonment-ADC-child?"

It is a noble thing, the rearing of warriors for the revolution. I can find no fault with the idea. I do, however, find fault with the notion that dumping the pill is the way to do it. You don't prepare yourself for the raising of super-people by making yourself vulnerable—chance fertilization, chance support, chance tomorrow—nor by being celibate until you stumble across the right stock to breed with. You prepare yourself by being healthy and confident, by having options that give you confidence, by getting yourself together, by being together enough to attract a together cat whose notion of fatherhood rise above the Disney caliber of man-in-the-world-and-woman-in-the-home, by being committed to the new consciousness, by being intellectually and spiritually and financially self-sufficient to do the thing right. You prepare yourself by being in control of yourself. The pill gives the woman, as well as the man, some control. Simple as that.

So while I agree to the need to produce, I don't agree to the irresponsible, poorly thought-out call to young girls, on-the-margin scufflers, every Sister at large to abandon the pill that gives her certain decision power, a power that for a great many of us is all we know, given the setup in this country and in our culture. I'm told, though, by women in the movement that movement women shouldn't use the pill because it encourages whorishness. That shocked me at first. The first group I'd thought would rally around the yes-pill position were the Sisters actively involved with revolutionary work. But given the inbred, cult-like culture that can develop in any group with messianic impulses, given the usual ratio of men to women in the organizations, given the "it's unfeminine to be ideological" undercurrent that makes the Sisters defeated and defensive, given the male-female division chumpbait we've eaten up of late via a distortion of our African heritage—given all this, perhaps these women should stop using the pill because they are, I've been told, reducing themselves to pieces of ass. Perhaps the abandonment of birth controls will produce less cruising, less make-out, less mutually exploitive sexual hookups, and more warmth in the man-woman relationship. That's playing a long shot, it seems to me. But I can see the point. And after all, it's through the fashioning of new relationships that we will obliterate the corrosive system of dominance, manipulation, exploitation.

Fortunately, while we Black women have often been held in contempt, we have never been irrelevant—as irrelevant, say, as the middle-class woman in the Latin culture. We've contributed too much to the household, to the social fabric, to the movement, been too indispensable and productive and creative to be invisible, overlooked, laid aside, laid aside as, say, the upper-caste women in feudal Asian society. We've been too mobile, too involved with the larger world outside of the immediate home, to be duped into some false romantic position of *the liberated woman*, as romanticized, say, as our Vietnamese and Guatemalan Sisters who were told to stay home and did; told to pick up the gun and did; and after the fight is over, they will be told to return to the mattress or to the factory or to wherever the Brother needs them. So while we've hassled and become divided from time to time (often with the help of the parochial social scientists who keep telling us we're in-fighting), while the Big Put-Down has had to suffice as the love link, our relationship has never been thoroughly fragmented, mutilated. Together under fire. So there's hope in dialogue. Hope in the idea of establishing a viable hookup. There's hope that we can shed yesterday's evil Black bitch and shiftless jive nigger and pursue a new vision of man and woman. She as something more than Amazon, breadwinner, domestic, mammy, as an intellectual, political vanguard being who has a voice in calling the shots about pregnancy because she's prepared. He as something more than sucker, trick, buffoon, slickster, abandoner, as an intellectual, political vanguard being who has a voice in calling the shots about pregnancy because he's there and is responsible.

It is revolutionary, radical, and righteous to want for your mate what you want for yourself. And we can't be rhapsodizing about liberation, breeding warriors, revolution unless we are willing to address ourselves to the woman's liberation. So what about the pill? Does it liberate or does it not? Will it help us forge new relationships or not? Does it make us accomplices in the genocidal plot engineered by the man or does it not? Does dumping the pill necessarily guarantee the production of warriors? Should all the Sisters dump the pill or some? What's the Brother's responsibility in all this? Who says the pill means you're never going to have children? Do we need to talk about communes, day-care centers, pregnancy stipends?

Personally, Freud's "anatomy is destiny" has always horrified me. *Kirche, Kusse, Kuche, Kinde* made me sick. Career woman vs. wife-mother has always struck me as a false dichotomy. The-pill'll-make-you-gals-run-wild a lot of male-chauvinist anxiety. Dump-the-pill a truncated statement. I think most women have pondered, those who have the heart to ponder at all, the oppressive nature of pregnancy, the tyranny of the child burden, the stupidity of male-female divisions, the obscene nature of employment discrimination. And day-care and nurseries being what they are, paid maternity leaves being rare, the whole memory of wham bam thank you ma'am and the Big Getaway a horrible nightmare, poverty so ugly, the family unit being the last word in socializing institutions to prepare us all for the ultimate rip-off and perpetuate the status quo, and abortion fatalities being what they are—of course the pill.

On the other hand, I would never agree that the pill really liberates women. It only helps. It may liberate her sexually (assuming that we don't mean mutually exploitive when we yell "sexual equality"), but what good is that if in other respects her social role remains the same? And it is especially doubtful that the pill can liberate her in these other areas—note how easily the sexual freedom has been absorbed into the commodity framework, used to push miniskirts, peekaboo blouses, and so forth so we can go on being enslaved to consumerism. But the pill gives her choice, gives her control over at least some of the major events in her life. And it gives her time to fight for liberation in those other areas. But surely there would be no need to shout into her ear about dumping the pill if the Brother was taking care of business on a personal plane and analyzing the whole issue of liberation on a political plane. Men are invariably trying to create a woman who will answer their needs, assuage their fears, boost their morale, confirm their romantic fantasies, lull them into the comforting notion that they are ten steps ahead simply because she is ten paces behind. And this invariably makes her not very true to herself. Women who've thought about this whole question have my support. The Brothers who merely rant and rave set my teeth on edge.

It's a sad thing that we haven't really looked at the education of our women. That they grow up knowing that our men were not the dragon slayers and the giant stalkers and that the only men who did do those gloriously grim storybook things are the greedy corporate kings and the bloody beef emperors and the six-gun generals and the chairmen of the boards of overkill cartels—none of whom they could ever love. And so they read instead those other storybooks, those sepia-tan love confessionals of summer boatrides and blue bulbs and belly rub and big belly and cutout and heartbreak. And shorting out on the celluloid Prince Charming and the minuet, they wallowed in those lost-my-man-loosin-my-mind and no-matter-how-you-mess-with-me-ain't-goin'-to-give-you-up-doo-ahh songs we've been hammering out for years. And they fashion a very defeated, strung-out, hung-up, lousy sense of worth/notion guaranteed to land them always on their asses, wigs askew, mind awry, clothes every which way, at the bottom of the heap, weeping about how some slick dude took them off while he in turn is crying about how the man done him in and it ain't his fault. As drama—hardly enough to keep the mind alive. As a life style—not likely to produce tomorrow's super-people.

I bring it up, this grotesque training, this type of girl eager to cut a tragic figure simply because she is the only type of woman at these meetings who cheers on the Brother burning the little packet of pills, telling me in breathless ecstasy that it's very revolutionary having babies and raising warriors, conjuring up this Hollywood image of guerrilla fighter in the wilds of Bear Mountain with rifle in hand and baby strapped on back under the Pancho Villa bullet belt. And given her suicidal glamorizing, that was enough to make me: one, worry about those kids she was dreaming of having; two, think unwholesome thoughts about those Brothers standing on the stage addressing themselves to an anonymous house of Sisters; three, want to write the whole thing off as another dumb comic book.

I agree it is a sinister thing for the state to tell anyone not to have a child. And I know it's not for nothing, certainly not for love, that b.c. clinics have been mushrooming in our communities. It's very much tied up with the man's clinging to that long since refuted "10 percent" when so many census agencies agree that we more than likely comprise 30 percent of the population. But. Let's talk about murder and about these Sisters who rise to the occasion. Seems to me the Brother does us all a great dis-service by telling her to fight the man with the womb. Better to fight with the gun and the mind. Better to suggest that she use all that time, energy, money for things other than wigs, nails, and clothes to ensnare the Aqua Velva Prince of her dreams who always turns out to be the ugly ogre who rips her off and rots her life anyway. That time, money, energy could be invested in taking care of her health so that the champion she plans to raise isn't faced from the jump with the possibility of brain damage because of her poor nutrition; could be invested in a safe home, so the baby isn't hazarded by lead poison in the falling plaster and by rats; in the acquiring of skills and knowledge and a groovy sense of the self so the child isn't menaced by stupidity and other child-abuse practices so common among people grown ugly and dangerous from being nobody for so long. The all too breezy no pill/have-kids/mess-up-the-man's-plan notion these comic-book-loving Sisters find so exciting is very seductive because it's a clear-cut and easy thing for her to do for the cause since it nourishes her sense of martyrdom. If the thing is numbers merely, what the hell. But if we are talking about revolution, creating an army for today and tomorrow, I think the Brothers who've been screaming these past years had better go do their homework.

"Raise super-people" should be the message. And that takes some pulling together. The pill is a way for the woman to be in position to be pulled together. And I find it criminal of people on the podium or in print or wherever to tell young girls not to go to clinics, or advise welfare ladies to go on producing, or to suggest to women with flabby skills and uncertain options but who are trying to get up off their knees that the pill is counter-revolutionary. It would be a greater service to us all to introduce them to the pill first, to focus on preparation of the self rather than on the abandonment of controls. Nobody ever told that poor woman across the street or down the block, old and shaggy but going on, long-suffering and no time off, trying to stretch that loaf of bread, her kitchen tumbled down with dirty laundry and broken toys, her pride eroded by investigators and intruders from this agency or that, smiling and trying to hold the whole circus together—nobody ever told her she didn't have to have all those kids, didn't have to scuffle all her life growing mean and stupid for being so long on the receiving end and never in position even to make decisions about her belly until finally she's been so messed with from outside and inside ambush and sabotage that all the Brothers' horses couldn't keep her from coming thoroughly undone, this very sorry Sister, this very dead Sister they drop into a hole no bigger, no deeper than would hold a dupe. And what was all that about? Tell her first that she doesn't have to. She has choices. Then, Brother, after you've been supportive and loving and selfless in the liberation of your Sisters from this particular shit—this particular death—then talk about this other kind of geno-cide and help her prepare herself to loosen the grip on the pill and get a hold of our tomorrow. She'll make the righteous choice.

Chapter Forty-One

On the Temptation to Be a Beautiful Object

Dana Densmore

We are constantly bombarded in this society by the images of feminine beauty. There is almost an obsession with it.

It is used extensively in advertising, particularly in advertising directed at women: be like this, they are saying, use our product.

The image sells everything, not just beauty products, but the beauty products reap the benefits of the image having sunk so well into everyone's consciousness.

And oh! those beauty products. Shimmering, magical, just waiting to turn the plainest girl into a heartbreakingly beautiful, transfixing graven image.

Or so they claim and imply, over and over, with extravagant hypnotizing advertising copy and photograph after photograph of dewy-fresh perfect faces.

Inevitably it penetrates the subconscious in an insidious and permanent way.

We may be sophisticated enough (or bitter enough) to reject specific advertising claims, but we cannot purge the image from us: if only we *could* get that look with a few sweeps of a lambsdown buffer dusting on translucent powder making our faces glow like satin, accented with shimmery slicked-on lip glow, a brush of glittery transparent blusher, eyes soft-fringed and luminous, lash-shaded and mysteriously shadowed ... suppose we *could* get the look they promise from their products and the look they all sell in their advertising? Ah, how few could resist!

Many of us are scarred by attempts as teenagers to win the promised glamor from cosmetics. Somehow it always just looked painted, harsh, worse than ever, and yet real life fell so far short of the ideals already burned into our consciousness that the defeat was bitter too and neither the plain nor the painted solution was satisfactory.

How often the date sits impatiently below while the girl in anguish and despair tinged with self-loathing applies and wipes away the magical products that, despite their magic, are helpless against her horrifying plainness. She will never be a woman, mysteriously beautiful.

Then, as we grow older and better looking, our faces more mature and our handling of cosmetics more expert, there are times when nature and artifice combine to make us unquestionably beautiful, for a moment, an hour, or an evening.

The incredible elation of looking in a mirror (the lighting just right ...) and seeing, not the familiar, plain, troublesome self, but a beautiful object, not ourselves, but a thing outside, a beautiful thing, worthy of worship . . . no one could resist falling in love with such a face.

The lighting changes, or the evening wears on, and the face slips imperceptibly back into plainness, harshness. Happy gaiety becomes forced gaiety, we laugh louder because we must make up for the ugliness we suddenly found, must distract attention from it.

Or we crawl back into ourselves in an agony of humiliated self-consciousness. We had thought ourselves beautiful, and carried on, attracting attention to what we thought was irresistible beauty but had somehow shifted into plainness again. How they must be laughing at us.

We do succeed when we make ourselves objects, outside ourselves, something we expect others to admire because we admire, and which we admire through others' admiration.

But it's not us really. Narcissism is not really love of the self, because self is the soul, the personality, and that is alway something quite different, something complex and complicated, something strange and human and very familiar and of this earth.

That beautiful object we stand in awe before has nothing to do with the person we know so well; it is altogether outside, separate, object, a beautiful image, not a person at all. A feast for the eyes.

A feast for the eyes, and not for the mind. That beautiful object is just an object, a work of art, to look at, not to know, total appearance, bearing no personality or will. To the extent that one is caught up in the beauty of it, one perceives object and not person.

This goes for others as well as for ourselves. The more beautiful we are, the more admired our appearance, the closer we approach the dream of the incredible beauty, the less reality our personality or intellect or will have.

It is unthinkable that this work of art has a will, especially one which is not as totally soft and agreeable as the face it presents. You cannot be taken seriously, people will not even hear what you say. (If they did they would be shocked and displeased—but since they do not take it seriously they say "You are too pretty to be so smart"—by which they mean, you are an object, do not presume to complicate the image with intellect, for intellect is complex and not always pleasing and beautiful. Do not dare to spoil my pleasure in your beauty by showing it to be only the facade of a real person; I will not believe that, you will only succeed in marring your beauty.)

How can anyone take a mannequin seriously? How, even, can one take a heartbreakingly beautiful face seriously? One is far too caught up in admiration of the object presented. It is merely beautiful, but it becomes an object when it is presented to the world.

This only goes for women, of course; men's character and personality and will always shine through their appearance, both men and women look at them that way. But one is taught in society by the emphasis on the images of feminine beauty to view women differently. The important thing is not the mind, the will, but the appearance. You ARE your appearance.

And if your appearance is pleasing, you are sunk, for no one will ever look beyond.

You have fulfilled all that is expected of you and you may rest (this all assumes you have the feminine womanly virtues of noncharacter such as kindness, gentleness, and the "pleasing personality").

In fact, if you are beautiful, or if you have made yourself beautiful, you had BETTER leave it at that, because you have no chance of compelling people to look beyond. They are so enchanted with what they see.

They adore you for your appearance. If you are "brainy" it will be taken as quaint, a charming affectation. If you are disagreeable it is offensive, a particularly stinging affront, disrespect for your beauty, the sacrilege of a work of art. (This does not detract from the mystique of the beautiful bitch. That is just another form of flirtation, tantalizing the man by simultaneously alluring with the beauty and by playing hard to get by putting up a verbal fence—a fence, by the way, which the man sees himself ultimately surmounting in triumph.)

Chapter Forty-Two

A Marriage Agreement

Alix Shulman

When my husband and I were first married a decade ago, "keeping house" was less of a burden than a game. We both worked at full-time jobs and we each pretty much took care of ourselves. We had a small apartment which stayed empty most of each day so that taking care of it was very little trouble. Every couple of weeks we'd spend a Saturday morning cleaning it and take our laundry to the laundromat. Though I usually did the cooking, our meals were casual and simple. We shopped for food together after work; sometimes we ate out; we had our breakfast at a diner near work; sometimes my husband cooked; there were few dishes. In the evenings we went for long walks and weekends we spent in Central Park. Our domestic life was beautifully uncomplicated.

Then our first child was born. I quit my job to stay home with him. Our domestic life was suddenly very complicated. When our second child was born, domestic life, the only life I had any longer, became a tremendous burden.

Once we had children, we totally accepted the sex-roles society assigns. My husband worked all day at an office and I was at home, so the domestic burden fell almost entirely on me. We had to move to a larger apartment to accommodate the children. Keeping it minimally livable was no longer a matter of an hour or two a week but took hours of every day: children make unbelievable messes. Our one meal a day for two people turned into a half dozen meals a day for anywhere from one to four people at a time, and everyone ate different food. To shop for this brood—or even just to run out for a quart of milk—became a major project. It meant putting on snowsuits, boots, and mittens, getting strollers or carriages up and down stairs, and scheduling the trip so it not interfere with someone's feeding or nap or illness or some other domestic job. Laundry turned from a weekly to a daily chore. And all this tumult started for me at six in the morning and didn't let up until nine at night, and *still* there wasn't time enough to do everything.

But even more burdensome than the physical work of child-rearing was the relentless responsibility I had for the children. There was literally nothing I could do or even contemplate without having to consider first how the children would be affected. Answering their questions alone ruled out for me such a minimum of privacy as a private *mental* life. They were always *there*. I couldn't read or think. If there ever was a moment to read, I read to them.

My husband's job began keeping him at work later and later, and sometimes took him out of town. If I suffered from too much domesticity, he suffered from too little. The children were usually asleep when he got home and I was too exhausted to talk. He became a stranger. Though he had sometimes, when we were first married, cooked for the two of us, it was no longer possible. A meal had become a major complicated production, in which timing counted heavily and someone might be crying in the background. No longer could we decide at the last moment what we felt like having for supper. And there were always dishes in the sink.

As the children grew up our domestic arrangement seemed increasingly odious to me. I took free-lance work to do at home in order to keep some contact with the world, but I had to squeeze it into my "free" time. My husband, I felt, could always change his job if the pressure was too great, but I could never change mine. When I finally began to see my situation from a women's liberation point of view, I realized that the only way we could possibly survive as a family (which we wanted to do) was to throw out the old sex-roles we had been living by and start again. Wishing to be once more equal and independent as we had been when we met, we decided to make an agreement in which we could define our roles our own way. We wanted to share completely the responsibility for caring for our household and for raising our children, by then five and seven. We recognized that after a decade of following the traditional sex-roles we would have to be extremely vigilant and wary of backsliding into our old domestic habits. If it was my husband's night to take care of the children, I would have to be careful not to check up on how he was managing; if the baby-sitter didn't show up for him, it would have to be *his* problem.

When our agreement was merely verbal, it didn't work; our old habits were too firmly established. So we made a formal agreement instead, based on a detailed schedule of family duties and assignments. Eventually, as the old roles and habits are replaced, we may be able to abandon the formality of our arrangement, but now the formality is imperative. Good intentions are simply not enough.

Our agreement is designed for our particular situation only, in which my husband works all day at a job of his choice, and I work at home on a free-lance basis during the hours the children are in school (from 8:30 till 3:00). If my husband or I should change jobs, income, or working hours, we would probably have to adjust our agreement to the altered circumstances. Now, as my husband makes much more money than I, he pays for most of our expenses.

Marriage Agreement

I. Principles

We reject the notion that the work which brings in more money is the more valuable. The ability to earn more money is already a privilege which must not be compounded by enabling the larger earner to buy out of his-her duties and put the burden on the one who earns less, or on someone hired from outside.

We believe that each member of the family has an equal right to his/her own time, work, value, choices. As long as all duties are performed, each person may use his/her extra time any way he/she chooses. If he/she wants to use it making money, fine. If he/she wants to spend it with spouse, fine. If not, fine.

As parents, we believe we must share all responsibility for taking care of our children and home—not only the work, but the responsibility. At least during the first year of this agreement, *sharing responsibility* shall mean:

A) Dividing the *jobs* (see Job Breakdown below), and
B) Dividing the *time* (see Schedule below) for which each parent is responsible.

In principle, jobs should be shared equally, 50-50, but deals may be made by mutual agreement. If jobs and schedule are divided on any other than a 50-50 basis, then either party may call for a re-examination and redistribution of jobs or a revision of the schedule at any time. Any deviation from 50-50 must be for the convenience of both parties. If one party works overtime in any domestic job, she/he must be compensated by equal extra work by the other. For convenience, the schedule may be flexible, but changes must be formally agreed upon. The terms of this agreement are rights and duties, not privileges and favors.

II. Job Breakdown

A) *Children.*

1. *Mornings*: Waking children; getting their clothes out, making their lunches; seeing that they have notes, homework, money, passes, books, etc.; brushing their hair; giving them breakfast; making coffee for us.
2. *Transportation*: Getting children to and from lessons, doctors, dentists, friends' houses, park, parties, movies, library, etc. Making appointments.
3. *Help*: Helping with homework, personal problems, projects like cooking, making gifts, experiments, planting, etc.; answering questions, explaining things.
4. *Nighttime*: Getting children to take baths, brush their teeth, go to bed, put away their toys and clothes; reading with them; tucking them in and having night-talks; handling if they wake and call in the night.
5. *Baby-sitters*: Getting baby-sitters, which sometimes takes an hour of phoning.
6. *Sick care*: Calling doctors, checking out symptoms, getting prescriptions filled, remembering to give medicine, taking days off to stay home with sick child; providing special activities.
7. *Weekends*: All above, plus special activities (beach, park, zoo, etc.)

B) *Housework.*

8. *Cooking*: Breakfasts; dinners (children, parents, guests).
9. *Shopping*: Food for all meals; housewares; clothing and supplies for children.
10. *Cleaning*: Dishes daily; apartment weekly, bi-weekly, or monthly.
11. *Laundry*: Home laundry; making beds; drycleaning (take and pickup).

III. Schedule

(The numbers on the following Schedule refer to Job Breakdown list.)

1. *Mornings*: Every other week each parent does all.
2. and 3. *Transportation* and *Help*: Parts occurring between 3:00 and 6:30 P.M. fall to wife. She must be compensated (see 10 below). Husband does all weekend transportation and pickups after 6:00. The rest is split.
4. *Nighttime* (and all *Help* after 6:30): Husband does Tues., Thurs., and Sun. Wife does Mon., Wed., and Sat. Friday is split according to who has done extra work during the week.
5. *Baby-sitters* must be called by whomever the sitter is to replace. If no sitter turns up, the parent whose night it is to take responsibility must stay home.
6. *Sick care*: This must still be worked out equally, since now wife seems to do it all. (The same goes for the now frequently-declared school closings for so-called political protest, whereby the mayor gets credit at the expense of the mothers of young children. The mayor only closes the schools; not the places of business or the government offices.)
7. *Weekends*: Split equally: husband is free all of Saturday, wife is free all of Sunday, except that husband does all weekend transportation, breakfasts, and special shopping.
8. *Cooking*: Wife does all dinners except Sunday night; husband does all weekend breakfast (including shopping for them and dishes), Sunday dinner, and any other dinners on his nights or responsibility if wife isn't home. Breakfast are divided week by week. Whoever invites the guests does shopping, cooking, and dishes; if both invite them, split work.
9. *Shopping*: Divide by convenience: generally, wife does local daily food shopping, husband does special shopping for supplies and children's things.
10. *Cleaning*: Husband does all the house-cleaning, in exchange for wife's extra childcare (3:00 to 6:30 daily) and sick care. *Dishes*: same as 4.
11. *Laundry*: Wife does most home laundry. Husband does all dry cleaning delivery and pickup. Wife strips beds, husband remakes them.

After only four months of strictly following our agreement, our daughter said one day to my husband, "You know, Daddy, I used to love Mommy more than you, but now I love you both the same."

Chapter Forty-Three

Roxanne Dunbar

How a Female Heterosexual Serves the Interests of Male Supremacy

Rita Mae Brown

The following article is a comment on Roxanne Dunbar's latest work, "The Movement and the Working Class."

I hesitate to write this response to Roxanne Dunbar's latest article because it is so critical. There are women and men who will lick their lips at the prospect of one woman raised in the working class criticizing another. Therefore, let me state that this article is a political criticism, not a personal attack. Criticism is a form of respect because you take the individual seriously enough to reply to her ideas.

"The Movement and the Working Class" is both helpful and harmful. It takes a sharp look at the various groups existent in the U.S. The article does us all a service by analyzing how the different movements ignore class or sell working class people down the river. It is unfair to summarize the article, you owe it to yourself to read it. The address is: Roxanne Dunbar, Box 3983, Lafayette, Louisiana 70501. Send in and ask for the article by name. The point here is to single out areas where Roxanne Dunbar has overlooked something or made a disastrous mistake.

The most glaring disastrous factual error in the article is where the author includes the Lesbian movement under the banner of the New Left and then goes on to vilify that struggle as being totally removed from the class struggle. She represents Lesbians as promoting bourgeois ideology. Nothing could be farther from fact.

"The young people who make up the base of the New Left are organized by 'constituencies.' There is 'Gay Liberation' and 'Women's Liberation' which have merged at points into a more virulent, all-female form called 'Radical Lesbians'." In this quote from her article, Roxanne simply puts us all in the same pot and throws it out the window. There is no explanation, just a slam in the word "virulent." The fact is that the Lesbian struggle has been operating in this country since the '50's when a group of Lesbians formed Daughters of Bilitis. The majority of those women were not working class but they did pull themselves together at a dangerous time— in the middle of the McCarthy era when homosexuality was as great a sin as communism. The Lesbian movement is older than the New Left and has little to do with fashionable radicalism among white, middle class youth.

A second push toward Lesbian organizing came through oppression suffered by young Lesbians from all classes in the Women's Liberation Movement and the Gay Liberation Movement—the push was to get out of the boat. Some of these women, particularly the ones of middle class origin, are more tainted with youth culture rhetoric than the older DOB women or the Lesbians who came out on their own, independent of political movements.

Roxanne is one of the women who turned Lesbians away from the Women's Liberation Movement by her insistence that Lesbianism was a bedroom issue. This is a variation of the same argument that men use against women when women fight for their own liberation. It's the old "your oppression isn't all that important" line. As men deal with women only as sexual beings so Roxanne locks Lesbians in the bedroom.

Roxanne goes on to put us down by saying, "—nothing could be further removed from the class struggle than the question of homosexuality as a freedom, even among homosexuals in the working class. Nothing could be further removed from the consciousness of a working woman with children than the 'freedom' to be a Lesbian." As a woman born and raised in the working class who is a Lesbian living with other working class Lesbians (and some from the middle class) I know this is not true. Except for two of us, all the working class women are new Lesbians and since becoming Lesbians have doubled their work output; they are also happier. They are free from having their energies drained by struggles with individual men or with white men in groups. Now they pool their energies with other women and have that much more time for political work. Materially we have pooled our resources and don't have to spend as much time working outside at straight jobs. When is it counter to class struggle to free people more to work in the fight to end class oppression, race oppression, sex oppression?

Roxanne attempts to smash Lesbianism by treating it as a personal luxury rather than dealing with it as a political ideology. This sweeping us under the rug as some great apolitical, individualistic freedom is classic heterosexual blindness. Her thesis that Lesbianism is a simple personal choice is a cover to avoid recognizing the political implication of Lesbianism: Lesbianism is the greatest threat to male supremacy that exists. As for this simple choice, this unimportant freedom—which, frees women's bodies, heads, time and energies—it is also the freedom to get fired from jobs, betrayed by straight women in the movement and spit at by one's own race and class. Why? Because if all women were Lesbians male supremacy would have the impossible task of maintaining itself in a vacuum. Men know what a threat we are to their power so they heap the worst abuse upon the Lesbian in order to keep women from becoming Lesbians. They also know that when their male supremacist order topples so will race and class differences since it is not in our self interest to foster divisions based on race and class. Male supremacists foster those divisions, especially the white, rich variety, because it keeps people fragmented and preserves their power. If people are divided from one another they will not unite against the common oppressor, the white, rich capitalist male. This ruling class male encourages working class men of all races to participate in his system by giving those men the power of sexism. Depending on their usefulness to his plans he can also bestow race and class privilege on men. In this way he can turn those men against other men below them who see the truth and organize to end the white, rich man's rule. He can also turn all men, not just segments of the male population, against all women who would organize to end sexist oppression—the privilege all men share: they control the women in their sub-group. The big man preys on the other men's fears of losing control over their women to keep them from seeing that any attack on him, The Big Man, weakens his power. So by oppressing women, particularly Lesbians since they fight sexism the hardest, working class males are cutting their own throats. The Big Man controls their jobs, housing and worse, the inside of their heads for he has shaped their concept of masculinity, he has forced them to identify with him both emotionally and economically. Even the man farthest away from The Big Man, the working class Black male, identifies with The Man's phallic imperialism. Roxanne Dunbar's smothering of the politics of working class Lesbians keeps all men, especially working class men, from understanding how sexism most benefits the ruling class male. It keeps the working class man from changing those parts of his behavior that oppress Lesbians and women. No solid alliance can be built between working class women and men until he changes his oppressive actions toward women. The only people who effectively challenge those oppressive actions are Lesbians, and Roxanne, a woman, legitimizes male power by writing off Lesbians. So once again we have political struggle in the hands of men. This time it is the class struggle with a few token women to mask male oppressiveness.

Does this mean that working class Lesbians are intent upon destroying working class men and weakening the class struggle? No, it does not. It means that working class Lesbians are not going to work for an ideology, practical plan or people who oppress us. Men have not purged themselves of supremacist behavior regardless of class/race background. To encourage women to ally with them now perpetuates our oppression. How will men, especially working class men, learn to shed sexism? If we leave them flat, that's how. As long as there is a woman to wipe their noses, cushion reality for them, serve them, men aren't going to change. When women remove themselves from the dominion of men the men will have a hard time hanging onto sexist behavior and ideas. The male concept of self depends on the subservience and debasement of women. Male power depends on female acceptance of it. If you don't accept their power then they don't have any. Only the rich, white capitalist will have power and that will be economic—and that too, can be crushed.

Also, when we are gone who will be men's escape valves, shit-workers, peacemakers? Without our necks to stand on for a better view the men will be forced to look at themselves and change. The serious ones will join women in the struggle against this society/state/international store.

This same process holds for straight women. As long as they do male supremacy's dirty work and keep Lesbians down, Lesbians must leave the straight women to wallow in a cesspool of their own making. Sexism is not limited to men and must be fought wherever it is found.

By keeping straight women from seeing that Lesbianism is political, that their individual lives and the relationships in it are political, Roxanne allows straight women to continue to support individual men as well as collective male supremacy.

The political Lesbian is committed to the destruction of male supremacy, therefore the Lesbian is serious about a women's movement.

Roxanne gives straight women an excuse for not building a strong women's movement to destroy male supremacy. You can't build a women's movement if women are tied to their oppressors—individually and ideologically. Holding onto male values and privileges granted to women for heterosexuality (which insures that each man will have his slave) subverts the women's movement. You cannot build a women's movement if you don't commit yourselves to women, totally. Heterosexual women are still committed to men. Roxanne guarantees that they will stay that way.

Lesbians contain the only hope for women to realize their own strength, their political power. This explains why working-class Lesbians prefer to work with Lesbians in the Lesbian movement (a mixed-class movement to smash male supremacy) rather than work with heterosexual working-class women in a movement devoted solely to class oppression. Why work with someone who ties you to your oppressor when you have just freed yourself from him on a one-to-one level? Why work in a movement that drains your energies fighting the supremacist attitudes of your supposed working-class brothers—who will also try to screw you? Why work with someone who derides your oppression or who actively suppresses you with another brand of Marxist intellectualism?

We'll be damned if we'll work with people who oppress us, no matter what class they come from. Roxanne herself says, "for the working class and the poor, the loss of one of its number from the struggle is a great loss—." Yet she insists on insuring that working class Lesbians defect from her appointed class struggle.

By cutting down Lesbians without ever dealing with our politics, by lumping us with the New Left and middle class concerns, Roxanne safely avoids the real crises that would be caused by a meeting of working class women and men. The crisis being that the men would be forced to stop oppressing the women and both would be forced to stop oppressing the Lesbian.

Like many women faced with the choice of renouncing their heterosexual privilege and fighting sexism/racism/classism, Roxanne has chosen to retreat into class struggle, heterosexual to the core. This pattern is repeated wherever Lesbians have asserted themselves. To become a Lesbian is to renounce all sexist privileges, privileges which keep you apart from other women. Men refuse to give privileges to women who reject their control. Lesbians reject male control and lose heterosexual securities. But they gain through that loss—women.

By turning your back on sexist struggle and embracing class as the only road to liberation, straight women allow men to retain their power over women. They also have the added advantage of being taken seriously as class struggle has a respectable history, after all, it includes men. The battle against sexism is, to date, exclusively a women's fight.

You get points from men for joining a heterosexual class struggle and you get bonus points for attacking Lesbians who are the people attacking sexism. Once again, men have gotten women to do their dirty work for them. Having the straight women attack the Lesbians, their hands remain clean.

Another debilitating feature of the class struggle as it now exists is that it allows middle-class people to "join" it. These people reared in middle class homes do not have to give up their privileges or their behavioral patterns cemented in childhood, patterns that are destructive to people reared in working class homes. Often these middle class joiners do not even have to share their material resources with the working class people. All too often all they have to do is accept the intellectual premises of class struggle and go on to organize others for the fight. How revolutionary.

The world has witnessed a number of class revolutions led by Marxist intellectuals who originated in the middle class. In all those countries women still do not share political power commensurate with their number. Their economic situation is improved but that hardly alters the realities of political power: Women have none. In Cuba for all its miracles, sexism is so fierce that homosexuals are "rehabilitated." To tell a woman, especially a working-class Lesbian, to repeat the class struggle as defined by men in this country, is to tell her to forget her own oppression, tow the class line, to once more, like a good woman, give herself over to politics as constructed by men.

Sexism is rampant under socialism. Having seen what happens repeatedly in class revolutions to women it is clear that we must try another way.

Does this mean we junk class struggle? As a person who grew up in the working classes I can hardly endorse that. I believe the class and race struggle is and must be part of the fight against sexism. This is an absolute truth for Lesbians. It is not in our self-interest to promote oppression based on class and race. We are despised by all sects, to continue among ourselves destructive divisions of class/race invented by rich, white capitalist men is to commit political suicide. A Lesbian who comes out loses many of her class/race privileges although she doesn't necessarily lose her behavioral patterns that reek of those disgusting privileges. No one wants their Lesbians—not the rich, not the poor, not the Black, not the White not Roxanne Dunbar. We need each other. We cannot weaken ourselves by hurting each other with left over daggers from white, rich, capitalist male America. Lesbians of all people, have the greatest stake in destroying class and racial oppression.

You can't destroy class without destroying capitalism. A Lesbian movement is necessarily socialist. A socialist movement is not necessarily non-sexist. Therein lies the great gap between Roxanne Dunbar and myself.

Roxanne misses this precisely because she is not a Lesbian. No straight woman knows what a Lesbian's life is like and she never will as long as she remains straight. She has not suffered the ultimate sexist oppression. The Lesbian has. She has not experienced Lesbian strength/love. The Lesbian has. Roxanne thinks that Lesbian communities are a New Left hoax. We know they are the tiny space of freedom we have created in the male world. We know they are the beginning of the end for male supremacy and its hideous younger brothers, racial oppression and class oppression.

A word of common sense. When I speak of Lesbians and Lesbian communities, I am not speaking about all Lesbians everywhere. I am speaking about those women who have developed a political ideology, who have committed themselves to the destruction of male supremacy et al., who have committed themselves to women, who want to build a new world. I know full well there are women who physically love other women who could sell us out as quickly as any man or straight woman. Some of them are racist, class snobs and outright reactionaries. By the same token, all working class people are not committed to the destruction of capitalism. There are plenty of racists and facists among the workers. The essential point is that workers carry the greatest threat to capitalism if organized just as Lesbians carry the greatest threat to male supremacy if organized.

Roxanne envisions organizing by breaking through the brainwash of ruling-class ideology in the workers. She is absolutely right. But she had better break through the brainwash of male supremacist ideology in her own head or she and other women like her will find themselves deeply betrayed by their own analysis.

F. Children

Chapter Forty-Four

Cooperative Nurseries

Rosalyn Baxandall

Nearly two years ago when my child was 17 months, I heard of a storefront with a backyard which some mothers had rented to establish a playgroup, called the Children's Workshop. The rent was $90 a month. Most young children need naps and so there being no place for cots and sleeping bags in the nursery, we established two groups: a morning group for children under three years of age and an afternoon group for children over three. Indoor toys and equipment were obtained free from a local poverty program nursery that was closing, and from contributions. Outdoor equipment was built by a boyfriend of one of the women, who was an architect. Unfortunately this paraphernalia, though interesting and colorful, was not designed for children. It was too complex, and it fell apart quickly. We found that in general toys that weren't sturdily made were broken when used daily by twenty children. Expensive wooden toys or wooden boxes and spools found in the street and then painted were best. Paper was obtained from a local paper factory, and shelves for toys were built of milk crates. Other supplies were purchased after rent, telephone, gas and light had been paid.

Dues were paid in accordance with the number of days worked by a mother. Those who couldn't work at all paid $20 a month, those who worked once a week paid $12.50, and those who worked twice weekly paid $5. When someone new entered the group that person generally began enthusiastically to work twice weekly, but usually as a woman found more to do with her free time she began to work less in the nursery. Several fathers worked as well.

Most of the group were white middle-class hippy or radical type women, a third of whom had black children. There were no black mothers, and most efforts to recruit black or Puerto Rican mothers failed. The objection seemed to be that our nursery was non-institutional: dirty and sloppy, and emphasis was placed on free play rather than structured learning. One black mother did join the group but left because she didn't feel at ease with the other mothers who seemed like hippies to her. Also, there were fewer girl children in the nursery. The ratio at best was seven boys to four girls. It seems that mothers of girls don't find them a hassle and they therefore keep them at home helping and rehearsing with mom the cleaning, washing, ironing and shopping. Some people believe it is because more boys are born.

Soon we had a large waiting list and a couple of mothers decided to try to obtain another storefront nursery because in the afternoon (older) group at Children's Workshop there were ideological differences which a new group could be expected to alleviate. Some women wanted to seek a grant to run the nursery and thus to work toward professional standards and legally recognized status. Others were more Summerhillian; we wanted no grants and preferred that the children be permitted to do anything: smear food on themselves, dance naked, paint the toys, and the walls, etc. Those who sought the more free atmosphere entered the new group.

Another problem we had in the original nursery was with mothers who found it hard to cooperate to the extent required: arriving on time in the morning, picking up children on time at the session's conclusion, notifying the others when one couldn't appear as planned. The majority felt that all should equally contribute, although I feel that ideally, a cooperative could work if everyone puts in what they are able to and takes out what is needed. Women who have more time should put in more time, those with more money should contribute more, and those who have neither money nor time contribute in another way. As these nurseries operated, we discriminated against the most needy, those who were so disorganized generally as to have trouble in participating in this project. Another example of this discrimination appeared when the group decided that a mother of an extremely disruptive child, who would have tantrums throughout a session, would have to withdraw. Certainly this mother and child had greater need of the nursery than the average woman.

Our new nursery, called the Liberation Nursery, was formed slowly as we had to accumulate enough money to pay rent and security on a storefront with backyard. Most of the money was lent by parents but some was secured by donations from relatives or friends. Major efforts were required to put the storefront in repair: putting down a new floor, painting and plastering, installing shelves, purchasing toys, and clearing away the accrued garbage heaped about the backyard. Mothers and fathers did the majority of the work.

Locating in a dilapidated storefront has several drawbacks. In cold weather we have insufficient heat and the electric heaters we bought ourselves were stolen. A fire on the floor above resulted in a flooded nursery and a collapsed ceiling. Our toilet and refrigerator are constantly broken, and the threat of robbery is constant. The backyard is inundated with garbage as fast as we can clean it up. The recent death of a rat in the wall of the nursery has added an odor which can hardly be countered by the use of heavy incense.

Some of us in the new nursery were in Women's Liberation and wanted to fuse the operation of the nursery with Women's Liberation: we have avoided segregating girl's games from boy's; both girls and boys play with trucks and dolls, all dressed in pants, and we invested $22 in a petit frere boy doll with genitals because we didn't want to give the impression that all dolls were female. Parents seemed to be the only ones to take note of the stressedly male doll. Recently we obtained some small figures that balance one upon another and look like football players. Some children started to call them football men, and my son chimed in saying, *and* football women. But so far as I know there are not any football women. It was decided that they were football people. It is hard to give children a realistic, honest picture of life and not be sexist, as our society reflects the sexist values. On the whole the girls in the group might be termed more passive and more interested in so-called "female" activity such as cooking, or dressing the dolls, than were the boys who proved more aggressive and interested in active games. I think the pre-nursery school is already too late. Sex typing begins in the hospital with the pink or the blue blanket. Another reason for falling short of success is that the group's members are not fully involved in Women's Liberation.

In the Liberation Nursery we try to build a community by sharing our children and encouraging them to relate to adults other than their parents. A parent will take an added child or two for the afternoon in exchange for the other parent taking her child at another time. Rarely do children eat dinner together and sleep at one another's house, as we had originally discussed in planning. This has happened mostly in individual cases, not as a group phenomenon. The group has, however, responded as a group when a family has been in crisis. When two mothers were ill, different people in the group looked after their children on a rotating basis and without expecting repayment of any kind.

It has been a slow process, nearly two years, but we have come to know each other better. We have monthly meetings to discuss problems at the nursery and they broaden often into daycare and Women's Liberation issues. It's hard to get to know each other well as we see each other only for a few minutes when dropping off or picking up the children; in the morning there is the desire to hurry to work or other activity, while at noon the kids are hungry and sleepy and the rush is to get home.

There are differences of opinion on how to group the children. The majority of women feel the children should be with a similar age group, because this makes it easier for the mothers to engage the children in activity. My personal opinion is that various ages should be combined in a group; the younger children can learn from the older and it is good for the kids to relate to all different ages.

Every day two people take care of ten children. Most women at the nursery began by wanting a purely cooperative arrangement, but as winter colds and childhood illness arose, it grew difficult to make schedule readjustments. The group decided that so long as at least one parent was on duty, anyone else who wished to help was welcome. When the nursery first started most women had much free time and their schedules were flexible. As people began to count on the free time and found work or activities to be involved in, it became harder for them to adapt their schedules in cases of sickness or other crises, and a continual shortage of people to work has developed. Much time is spent, on the phone, changing and hassling with the schedule: who can work on which day in replacement of somebody else, who had been scheduled to work, etc. Volunteers have helped but the arrangement hassle remains. We would like fathers to work but in some cases fathers are not in the home, and in others they have full-time nine to five jobs. Others are hesitant. We have recently had volunteers from Men's Liberation and everyone has been pleased with them.

Very few children have had trouble adjusting to the nursery. The few who had some difficulty at the beginning were not accustomed to other children and not used to being left in custody of other adults. All of the children do not yet seem completely engaged or happy throughout the sessions.

Activities vary daily, usually in accord with the skills of the parents present. Some of us are musical, others are good at arts and crafts, dance, story-telling or gymnastics. We have juice and cookies daily followed by a quiet time, which the adults need as well as the children. We encourage the children to do their own thing most of the time, but have found that some need more direction than others, and when unsupervised too long, get bored and start fighting. We have had several wild scenes of biting, spitting, pushing and hitting, but decided, as a group, not to interfere in a fight unless it appeared as though someone had been hurt since often the kids are just wrestling or playing physically with one another. If someone is hurt they and the person who did the hitting or biting *both* get individual love and care. We found that the child who does the hurting is also upset and scolding just makes her or him feel worse. The older children seemed to be fighting a great deal from boredom and we recently decided to make more effort at planned activity. The persons who work at session now talk to each other before and they work out at least one activity, and talk about the morning's general plan. This planning plus our concerted effort seems to work better.

Every day unless it is frightfully cold or pouring rain, the kids go out to the backyard, to the park, or for a walk somewhere. The children who are less adept at walking go in large strollers or a large wagon which seems to be more fun than the strollers are. Often the children go on trips to a zoo, a pony farm, a museum, the carousel or a special park. This requires one additional adult.

We have never had a problem with legal authorities, thought we are illegal; because we do not comply with the Board of Health code restriction that children be over three years old and that we hire professionals. However, we don't advertise and we have a curtain over the storefront window. Several lawyers have said they would be interested in taking the case if we are threatened as some illegal nurseries have been. If it ever came to a legal showdown we would, I think, be able to mobilize the community to support us.

We have deliberately not hired a teacher or parent to run the group. We want to further cooperative spirit and want the nursery to reflect our values. We also don't like the expert idea, and want everyone working to solve problems. Everyone finds working at the nursery exhausting and difficult; some like it more than others.

Money has always been a tremendous hassle. Many women can't afford anything, and others can't afford very much. We are always behind in our rent gas and electricity and our telephone was shut off because we were behind in paying the bill. This has led some of us to think about making efforts to get the nursery supported by the community. We were against getting government support for the nursery as this would only mean higher taxes for the poor. One local health food store was asked to contribute juice and cookies and they seemed amenable. There is some talk of asking, and then threatening, some large Lower East Side slumlord to give us free space. Other suggestions have been trying to get the people who really exploit women to support the nurseries—Revlon, Pampers (which is Colgate Palmolive), Beechnut,

Squibb, and Johnson & Johnson. We've talked about sitting in with our children at the local Chase Manhattan Bank or Pioneer and A&P supermarkets. Unfortunately this type of effort requires more time and energy than those in our nursery are willing to invest.

In order to keep the nursery going two or three people who are really interested in its development are needed. Otherwise people tend to let things slide and it doesn't function.

A few of the mothers at our nursery opened up a mother's coop exchange. Mothers bring in their old clothes and toys and get others in exchange. This storefront coop hopes to expand and start buying staples like Pampers and baby-food at wholesale cost and selling them. Already the back of the quarters is used for mothers who want to read or write and have no quiet space at home to do so. The coop has posted Women's Liberation literature and magazines, welfare, abortion and neighborhood activities. A washing machine and dryer might also be bought so women could do their laundry there. This coop attracts many black and Puerto Rican women. Mothers in the nursery have also grown more interested in Women's Liberation and radical politics as a result of participating in our cooperative effort. However radicalization has occurred slowly and the process has, after two years, only really begun.

Chapter Forty-Five

Action Committee for Decent Childcare
Organizing for Power

Day Creamer and Heather Booth

In Chicago, the Action Committee for Decent Childcare (ACDC) was organized a year ago as a coalition of women who work in child care centers, need childcare or are interested in the problem. As a result of experience in attempting to develop client-controlled childcare centers, women realized the need for building a movement which could challenge existing policies and win reforms. ACDC was formed as a direct action, mass organization which supports but does not become directly involved in setting up centers. ACDC's goal is to change the existing political situation (and the codes and financing which reflect it) which ultimately will mean that groups will be able to develop centers in Chicago.

Before discussing in more detail the specific strategies and tactics of ACDC, our underlying concepts should be made clear to put our work in context with respect to our perspective on the women's movement.

In the past few years our movement has expanded rapidly, involving thousands of women across the country in the search for understanding women's oppression. At this point we feel it important to move on this understanding, with organization that can unite us in order to actively fight for ways to immediately improve our lives and build a base of power for women.

We have learned women are oppressed in a variety of ways; but we are just beginning to learn the meaning of our own self-interest and how to act on it. For our movement to continue to expand, we must develop the ability to challenge existing power relations and win power for ourselves. This can only be accomplished if we can relate to all women's needs, beyond identifying the sources of our oppression and understanding them (as in consciousness raising alone). Our task must be to organize for power.

Organizing for power means that we must create those structures which will enable us to move forward in developing our abilities and skills and bring about change.

Organizing for power also means that we must have a conception of the kinds of reforms we are fighting for. In many places the word reform is associated with cooptation—if you win, you must be doing something wrong, or what you are fighting for must be "counterrevolutionary." A few people in our society have power.

Our task is to build a movement which can change that fact. This means organizing around specific demands which can be won, and which in the process will alter power relations, thus building our power base as women. Winning in one situation will give us the ability to move beyond that victory to greater challenges and the accumulation of more power. We feel one of our movement's worst enemies is its lack of visible successes—to give us faith that we can win. Such small, tangible successes also help to make our vision concrete.

At the same time, in the struggle for concrete victories women will gain both a sense of our power and the meaning of power in society. As women, one of the major obstacles we must confront is the belief that we have no power and there is nothing we can do about it. Most of us have never had any influence over policies which affect our lives; and we have never experienced a situation where that might be different. Our challenge is to prove that wrong by building organizations which, in fact, win.

The basic question is determining what issues are in our self-interest as women and then determining what kinds of reforms are possible. On the basis of self-interest, alliances can be built between groups of women.

With these underlying assumptions the Action Committee for Decent Childcare was begun.

When we first began to organize, it was clear that most women in Chicago did not realize that there is a crisis in childcare services in the City. Thus our initial work involved publicizing the crisis. We organized a demonstration of women and children at the City Council when the 1971 budget was passed to publicize the fact that no allocation for childcare services was being made. We then held a series of community meetings in various areas of the City, both as an educational program and as a way to find women who might be interested in working with us.

In July, a delegation of 60 women and children and the press met with Mr. Wade Parker of the City's Department of Human Resources. Visibly shaken by the angry group, he agreed to three of our five demands—to undertake a review of licensing codes and procedures, to end closed door meetings of the department and to attend a public hearing on problems with licensing in the City.

Following up on the demands, ACDC prepared for the public hearing scheduled for August 30th. The plan was that day care center operators would present their grievances to the City and demand action. Women who had attempted to open centers would also discuss their problems of harassment from the City due to its arbitrary licensing policies.

On August 6th, Mayor Daley appointed Mrs. Murrell Syler as Director of Child Care Services and shifted control of day care operations (but not really since she didn't have any power). Syler then agreed to attend the meeting. By the next week, both Parker and Syler tried to back out on their commitment. Additional pressure from women (calls from center operators all over the city—both black and white and a delegation going to see Mrs. Syler) and from the press convinced them to attend.

Through a carefully developed citywide network, over 200 people attended the public hearing. The testimony about the City's codes and procedures and the specific questions raised about the City's plans, broke the wall of silence on the issue. Press coverage was extensive and for the next several weeks, day care was in the news with charges and countercharges by City departments. At the public hearing, ACDC presented its analysis of the licensing code and procedures with specific recommendations for change.

As a result of the meeting a complete review of licensing codes is underway. A City committee was created of which ACDC is a part. As in the case with most such committees, work is progressing, but very slowly. An action is being planned at the next meeting to demand a timetable for implementing the recommendations of the committee.

In September, ACDC conducted a citizen's investigation of a center which the City was threatening to close down because it did not have a fire alarm (even though it was a modern, brick building with steel structures)! The press coverage proved significant enough pressure to force the City to back down. In another case, we accompanied a center in their court hearing and the case has been given a continuance based on the City changing the code.

Currently a series of three community meetings is being planned in preparation for the City's budget bearings and a State Summit on Day Care called by Governor Ogilvie. Demands will be made to local politicians that they support legislation to provide funds for childcare facilities. In addition, ACDC will organize demonstrations at both of these meetings to provide pressure for our demands.

ACDC is a citywide organization with representatives to a steering committee from six local communities and one representing women at-large. We have a chairwoman and one staff person. Our goal is to organize local chapters in various Chicago communities but this depends on our ability to raise funds for the organization. We meet weekly to discuss strategy and evaluate our work.

What has ACDC won? At this point, we have succeeded in forcing the City to review its arbitrary licensing codes and many changes are highly likely (assuming our continued pressure). Two centers have not been closed down due to our efforts. The day care issue is now a public one and the City has been affected by our pressure (calling us and demanding that we get off their backs, and telling us, "you don't bite the hand that feeds you"). And, perhaps most importantly, ACDC is established as an organization committed to fighting for free, client-controlled, 24 hour childcare in Chicago.

The struggle has just begun and we feel the pressure of developing quickly enough so that we will have enough power to prevent the City from taking control of day care as part of its patronage system. We also anticipate the development of forced childcare for women on welfare (already a reality in Nixon's and Gov. Ogilvie's proposals) and we must be strong enough to prevent that from happening. Further, as money becomes available, we must be in a position to ensure that community groups can establish the kind of services they need and under their control.

Significantly, as women, we are developing skills to be able to confront the City and to be able to use the press to our advantage. All of us have developed skills and confidence during the past year. As a women's organization, we feel that ACDC is a viable model for organizing for power. With all of the frustration, disappointments, difficulties, and hard work, we are slowly learning and helping each other to learn the meaning of power and how to fight for it.

Chapter Forty-Six

The Liberation of Children

Deborah Babcox

A friend of mine called me recently, disturbed about her sister-in-law. The woman had given birth to a baby several weeks before, and when she got home from the hospital, she had slipped into a state of utter depression. She cried all the time and was very irritable, insisting that she was too weak to take care of the baby and certainly couldn't manage the housework. Her mother and mother-in-law had been going over every day to help, but they were beginning to feel she should snap out of it. Would I go over with her and try to talk to the woman?

I went reluctantly—I had never known the woman well—and it was worse than I could have imagined. She was listless, uninterested in the baby, and generally distracted. She kept getting up to walk idly about the room, forgetting what she'd been saying. Twice while we were there she burst into tears when her mother-in-law asked her to do something—hold the baby for a minute, or get some coffee cups from the cupboard. "How can you stand it!" she wailed to me. "A baby takes over your life. . . . I can't even take a shower with it in the house!"

I had remembered the woman as being a reasonable person, not unusually self-centered or unstable, and while many women are afflicted with similar feelings after having a baby, she was obviously suffering from this depression more than most. I left the house feeling very depressed myself . . . for both the mother and the baby. The mother's condition seemed to border on real mental illness, but her family was treating her as if she were a spoiled child who would snap out of it at any time. I didn't know if they would ever seek treatment for her, and if they didn't, what would happen to the child? He already seemed strangely subdued, not a very responsive baby. I hated to think of him growing up bewildered and hurt, an unwitting victim of his mother's situation. So many people—most of my friends, in fact—complain all the time about the horrible things their mothers did (or do) to them, and few of them have been able to come to terms with their feelings about it even as supposedly mature adults.

And for perhaps the first time, I really began to connect that with my difficulties with my children. Heaven knows I understood the emotions of the woman whose house I had just left all too well. I remember vividly standing in my doorway, tears streaming down my cheeks, as I watched my mother leave for her home 1,000 miles away, leaving me alone for the first time with my newborn son. I was twenty-six, quite well aware of the responsibilities involved in having a child and of the limitations that would be placed on my freedom. I had wanted—longed—to have that baby, but somehow all the education and thinking in the world can't prepare you for the gut-level realization of how a baby imprisons you with its dependence.

The difference between us was really only one of degree. I had, in the end, learned to cope, and even accept the idea that I had to do housework, and I didn't have much confidence that she would. Even now, I don't always find life easy with my two wild little boys, but I am charmed by them anyway. We enjoy each other, and I would rather stay home and take care of them than do most other jobs I can think of.

Even so, there are days when their sheer energy makes for inevitable conflict. Once, when he was about two years old, my older son came in early to our bedroom to lie down beside me and drink his bottle. After a few minutes of lying there, humming to himself, he sat up and looked at me with a surprised expression. "You *are* a nice Mommy!" he said. Evidently he had gone to bed feeling about me exactly as I had felt about him—that I was a monster! And we both had recovered our good nature during the night, because by the morning I thought him delightful, too. But there are still more days than I care to think about when everything in the household falls apart and I feel like taking to my bed and pulling the covers over my head, grieving in my heart for the injury I have that day done my children. Why me? Why should I feel so deeply this all-encompassing responsibility for them that is sometimes so corrosive?

I do know that it is very much a part of our tradition. When the first child-raising literature began to appear in America at the beginning of the nineteenth century great emphasis was placed on the exclusive role of the mother in the forming of her child's character. Industrialization and urbanization were accelerating, and the role of the father and of men in general in the upbringing of children was declining markedly. Women were taking over most of the teaching of young children in the newly established public school system, and more and more fathers worked out and away from their homes.

In the nineteenth century, of course, the moral character of the developing child was the mother's crucial responsibility. (The essential depravity of the child had to be overcome by her loving guidance and the purity of her example.) These days we are more modern: mothers are only responsible for the child's adjustment to society and its intelligence. Thus, Dr. Spock warns in his new book that women had best forget about "liberation" and stay home with the children, or society will suffer. And Burton White at Harvard finds that superior ability in school is the result of a child's having been nurtured by a "super-mother" who lavishes love and attention and conversation on her small baby.

All of this may be quite true, but at what price do we place such exclusive responsibility on the mother for the child's well-being? Almost everyone I grew up with resented their mothers terribly; almost every young mother I know resents in some degree her children's dependence on her. It seems to me that it places intolerable burdens on both mothers and children to bind them so closely together, and both are hurt by it. Dr. Spock is wrong, though the problem he speaks to is a real one. He sees that children are growing up in this society without the emotional support they need to be healthy adults. But the source of that difficulty is not that women are too free: it lies in the fact that they are still too restricted by the exclusive bonds of child-care to be good mothers. To raise a child to be self-confident, loving, curious, and capable of autonomous behavior is extremely difficult. It requires a great deal of self-control, understanding, and love, and one mother in this kind of family (a nuclear family) with the father gone most of the time, is most likely to lack just those qualities.

There is no reason that men and women should not share the care of their children to the benefit of all concerned; neither men or women are more biologically suited for doing dishes or deciding whether a child should wear its boots, and it's unfair to make these things the exclusive responsibility of the mother. It is unfair to women, who are then forced to live through other people's lives and devote themselves to the day-to-day well-being of the other members of the family. It is also unfair, and probably destructive, to the children. Since it is the mother who is alone with the children most in the circumstances in which most of us now live, and since it is she whose life is most restricted by them, she is naturally the one most likely to injure them.

And how can a girl growing up in this society fail to be ambivalent about motherhood? She is ceaselessly exhorted to be attractive, tend to her makeup and hair color, be smart but not too smart, get a good job, but only so as to be able to meet eligible men—all for what? Why, to get married, to stay home and take care of baby, in soap-powder bliss. Even those of us who scoff at these images are affected by them; they subtly contribute to our expectations of ourselves and our future lives. We imagine ourselves the impeccable housewives in all the TV ads, perhaps with part-time jobs, contented, sweet-smelling babies and self-cleaning ovens to make our lives manageable—or even that hackneyed favorite, the lovely wife greeting her husband at the door every evening with his slippers and a drink. Most women find out very quickly that babies don't permit that kind of nonsense, and that working with children is no picnic. It's difficult to provide for them during the day, and then there's all that housework to do in the evenings—which all of our "modern conveniences" have done little to make more convenient. And the realization that your life is no longer your own is often quite a startling one, trite as that may sound to unmarried nonmothers (who always think, "Oh, that won't happen to me. . . .").

But I think that life in our small families is often quite difficult for men, too, and when a woman who finds that her life is hard turns to her husband for sympathy and help, she may find herself rebuffed. A young man may find the financial responsibility of his family burdensome. Perhaps he hadn't realized, either, how his freedom would be restricted. He will probably often come in from a demanding job, expecting to relax, watch TV, and be comforted by his loving family, only to find that his wife has been waiting all day for him to come home so *she* could relax. Chances are that each feels he or she has the harder life, and that the other should understand and be sympathetic. Both parents will probably have expectations of each other and of the children that they are hardly aware of, and both may feel disgruntled and resentful when these are not fulfilled.

It can't be said to be anybody's fault. It is the way in which we live together that makes the life of each member of the family difficult. Most popular psychologists and the women's magazines recognize these problems, but their advice is geared toward helping people adjust to them. Perhaps we should begin to consider, instead, that we may have reached a point in the development of our society in which the nuclear families we have come to accept as the norm no longer serve to provide their members with the solace and support they need to deal with the society. Instead, the tensions within the family are likely to undermine the individual's confidence and stability. We are encouraged to find our only emotional support within our small families; usually we are not prepared or able to go elsewhere for sympathy or affection, especially from members of the opposite sex. But the tensions we encounter in our families make it rather unlikely that each of us *can* get support, understanding, and affection we need there—everybody is demanding too much of too few people.

I suppose it can be said that the nuclear family still serves another important function and that is the function of the socialization of children, of training them in the behavior and values most acceptable to society. As a basically capitalist society, this one values competitiveness and individual achievement. But a constantly striving person, interested in consumption for himself and his family, may not be especially concerned about other people's welfare, and great social and personal conflict will be the result.

The development of the nuclear family has paralleled, everywhere in the world and in history, the development of industrialization, urbanization, and the rise of ideas about individual liberty and individual achievement. But individualism carried to extremes can only lead to an alienation and loneliness that is both socially and psychologically destructive.

I think small families do indeed tend to produce children who are competitive and insecure, who are taught to seek self-fulfillment but lack self-confidence. They are "oppressed" children, who need to be liberated. Freedom, for children, does not mean lack of authority, which is something they need. It entails having both adults and teachers who are willing to let the children grow, discover, and learn according to his inner necessities and not according to some arbitrary adult standard. But when mothers and fathers and children are so oppressively dependent upon one another and only upon one another, that freedom can't be offered to the children easily. So they are told to use initiative, but follow the rules; value freedom but "don't talk back to your father" and "clean your room before you go out"; they are encouraged to value money and respect their possessions, but forced to share things and not be too possessive.

If a child is dependent on only two adults—and really mostly on one, the mother—for so much of his emotional well-being and psychic health he is terribly at their mercy. If the parents happen to be sick or warped, the child will be injured. If they are too busy or worn down by hard work and lack of money to show much affection or support, he will no doubt feel unloved and unworthy. The child in a small family may find it difficult to see himself and the adults in any sort of perspective; he will find it difficult as he grows not to blame people very personally for whatever they do, himself included.

Of course there are reasonably happy families and reasonably well-adjusted children, but I think even many fairly happy people bear a residue of guilt, anger, and lack of confidence deep within them, and it contributes to the general loneliness, alienation, and lack of social concern so pervasive in our society.

The damage done to children is not always merely emotional. Dr. Ray Helfer, of the University of Colorado School of Medicine, says that more children under five die each year from injuries inflicted by their parents or guardians than from TB, whooping cough, diabetes, rheumatic fever and appendicitis combined. In his book *The Battered Child*, Dr. Helfer estimates that 60,000 children in the United States are willfully burned, smothered, or starved every year. These are from educated as well as uneducated families, rich and poor. In addition, the incidence of serious mental disturbance in American children is higher than in almost any other country in the world. Suicide among children has been increasing, as has drug addiction. All of us need to find more cooperative ways of living. But I think in seeking to liberate women and children, especially, from the conflicts and tensions within the family it is necessary to consider alternatives very carefully.

Certainly there should be child-care centers on a much larger scale than we now have them, to give women options in their lives they do not now have. But if women were to drop their children off at day-care centers in the morning, work at dreadful jobs all day, and pick the children up so they could go home, do all the housework, and cook their husbands' suppers—the tensions in the family wouldn't be much eased. Parents would have two salaries to spend instead of one, but they need be no less competitive with other families.

Unless men and women can come to share the responsibilities—and the joys—of child care and household work neither women nor children will be much freer. Perhaps that means enlarging our families somehow, possibly to include several couples and several children. Some people have already begun to move toward new kinds of cooperative living, and it may be that communal "families" will be the rule in future societies. There are obvious advantages, some economic, but not least psychological. Several adults and several children of different ages living together may provide opportunities for the children to be intimate with several adults and not so dependent on one or two, and because the children's dependence is not felt so keenly by any one person, everyone can be more loving, less impatient. Children seem to be happier and learn better in groups of mixed ages. Everyone can get the perspective on growth processes in human beings that help them see themselves as participating in growth instead of regarding their problems at each age as unique and insoluble.

It is important that men and women establish control over their own lives and become accustomed to helping themselves, each other, and sharing the concern of their children. If women, whether they work or not, can think of ways to alleviate their immediate problems, good! Baby-sitting pools, play groups for the children—many things can foster cooperation among women and help mothers learn to be concerned about all the children and not just their own. Perhaps efforts could be made to get the state or city to put attendants in every playground, as is done in Denmark, so that mothers could leave their children to play safely while they do errands (or take a shower!). Maybe landlords in large buildings could be obliged to put aside an apartment or a large room for an indoor playroom. The important thing is the sharing, the gaining of options, of control over your life.

If we want to change society, we can begin by changing the kind of people we are and the kind of children we raise. People who are more loving, more concerned about each other, more secure and less competitive will have attitudes that are contrary to the ones on which our society is based, and while the creation of new attitudes is not in itself a revolution, perhaps it helps create the preconditions. The nuclear family was a product of specific social forces, and the fact that it has assumed the proportions of an ideology should not blind us to the possibility that new family forms would be more appropriate to our age. We needn't be afraid to try new ways of living or discard modes that have outlived their usefulness. History and anthropology tell us that human behavior is infinitely variable—and suggest that the possibilities for human perfection and human happiness have barely been explored.

Chapter Forty-Seven

Day Care

Furies Action

We want the daycare center to express revolutionary lesbian politics so that our children can love themselves and each other. We are not just another special interest group asking for tolerance and a little part of the daycare center's program. As lesbians we are challenging the basic structure and value of the daycare center. We want you to question them too, struggle with us over its present politics and become part of the new vision.

We are trying to provide an environment in which children have a chance to become new people. That means that we have to be in the process of becoming revolutionary ourselves. Revolutionary lesbians are not only fighting against the institutions of male heterosexual power and privilege but are attacking the very foundations of the male world view—a view which is based on competition, aggression, and acquisitiveness. Lesbians choose to reject that world view and to live apart from men who have perpetuated those values for thousands of years. We have broken our last dependence on male dependence on male privilege which kept us from being revolutionary. As long as women cannot love each other they still see themselves as second class persons. We are building a new vision. We are creating a new identity, a new politic. Since we have begun to experience what it is to become new women—new persons—we have a vision of what children can become.

Our criticisms of the daycare center are in the context of that vision. Because we are becoming women identified women, we can see how the daycare center is failing in helping the children become new persons. We must start to change the daycare center now.

Criticisms

1) The primary content of the meetings is how to keep the daycare center running, not how we relate to children and to each other and what environment we want them to be in.

2) The basic sexism of the daycare center has not been challenged. The main challenge to sexism has been that of requiring men to take equal responsibility for children (at the daycare center!). with some subsequent changing of home housework

roles. The daycare center is still oriented towards heterosexuality and the nuclear family. No sustained effort has been made to encourage girls to become more active and boys less macho. The rampant sexism is evident in the fact that people still believe that "a fucked-up man is better than no man at all."

3) Homosexuality has been ignored. There has been no effort to encourage children to love themselves and those of their own sex.

4) The daycare center is not a collective. How much time people work is based not on need and ability but on a mechanical rule. People's relationships to each other and to the children are not open to challenge and pushing within the group.

5) There has been little attempt to deal with adult chauvinism—beyond the liberal dictum of permissiveness. The parent/child relationship of exclusivity, dependency, and monogamy has not been called in question.

The daycare center must change now if it is to begin to express the politics of what we want the world to become. It is destructive to our children for them to continue to be in this environment. The expression of our politics in terms of the daycare center means the following changes:

1) The heterosexual bias of the center has to go. There must be a continual gay presence so children can see women loving women and men loving men. Books and games that only express the heterosexual world view should be thrown out. We must develop new ones that show positively homosexuality and alternatives life styles.

2) The daycare center must be run on communist principles. Scheduling in terms of needs and abilities must be worked out collectively in group meetings. The primacy of the parent/child relationship can no longer be assumed. Those who belong to the daycare center must be moving towards collective living themselves.

3) The primary subject of meetings must be the content of our relationships and and the goals towards which we are moving—not the mechanics of running the daycare center. Adult chauvinism must be struggled with, along with class and race.

4) The nuclear family prejudice must end. Single women and lesbians with children must be the top recruiting priority.

5) Men who are not struggling with their sexism *must* leave. The women will decide who can stay. The men who stay must be in men's consciousness raising groups that help them express their homosexuality.

6) The kids should be encouraged to explore their own bodies and the bodies of each other and to masturbate.

Those Women
Coletta,
Helaine,
Sue,
Ginny,
Sharon,
Joan,

Susan,
Rita,
Tasha,
Betty,
Charlette, and
Marlene

G. Race

Chapter Forty-Eight

Introduction to *The Blackwoman: An Anthology*

Toni Cade

We are involved in a struggle for liberation: liberation from the exploitive and dehumanizing system of racism, from the manipulative control of a corporate society; liberation from the constrictive norms of "mainstream" culture, from the synthetic myths that encourage us to fashion ourselves rashly from without (reaction) rather than from within (creation). What characterizes the current movement of the 60's is a turning away from the larger society and a turning toward each other. Our art, protest, dialogue no longer spring from the impulse to entertain, or to indulge or enlighten the conscience of the enemy; white people, whiteness, or racism; men, maleness, or chauvinism: America or imperialism . . . depending on your viewpoint and your terror. Our energies now seem to be invested in and are in turn derived from a determination to touch and to unify. What typifies the current spirit is an embrace, an embrace of the community and a hardheaded attempt to get basic with each other.

If we women are to get basic, then surely the first job is to find out what liberation for ourselves means, what work it entails, what benefits it will yield. To do that, we might turn to various fields of studies to extract material, data necessary to define that term in respect to ourselves. We note, however, all too quickly the lack of relevant material.

Psychiatrists and the like, while compiling data on personality traits and behavioral patterns, tend to reinforce rather than challenge social expectations on the subject of woman; they tell us in paper after paper that first and foremost the woman wishes to be the attractive, cared-for companion of a man, that she desires above all else motherhood, that her sense of self is nourished by her ability to create a comfortable home. Hollywood and other dream factories delight in this notion and reinforce it, and it becomes the social expectation. The woman who would demand more is "immature," "anti-social," or "masculine."

And on the subject of her liberation, when it is considered at all, the experts (white, male) tell us that ohh yes she must be free to enjoy orgasm. And that is that.

When the experts (white or Black, male) turn their attention to the Black woman, the reports get murky, for they usually clump the men and women together and focus so heavily on what white people have done to the psyches of Blacks, that what

Blacks have done to and for themselves is overlooked, and what distinguishes the men from the women forgotten.

Commercial psychologists, market researchers, applied psychologists (by any other name are still white, male) further say, on the subject of women and their liberation, that she must feel free to buy new products, to explore the new commodities, to change brands. So thousands of dollars are spent each year to offer her a wide range of clothes, cosmetics, home furnishings, baby products so that she can realize herself and nourish her sense of identity.

The biologists are no help either. Either they are busily assisting the psychologist in his paper on the Sex Life of the Swan or they are busily observing some primate group or other and concluding, on the basis of two or three weeks, acting as voyeurs to captive monkeys, that the female of the species is "basically" submissive, dependent, frivolous; all she wants to do is be cared for and be played with. It seems not to occur to these scientists (white, male) that the behavioral traits they label "basic" and upon which the psychologists breezily build their theories of masculine/feminine are not so "basic" at all; they do not exist, after all, in a context-free ether. They may very well be not inherent traits but merely at-the-moment traits. What would happen to the neat rows of notes if alterations were made in the cage, if the situation were modified, if the laboratory were rearranged. Add another monkey or two; introduce a water wheel or a water buffalo. Would other traits then be in evidence? Would the "basic" traits change or disappear? People, after all, are not only not rhesus monkeys, they also do not live in a static environment.

The biochemists have been having their day on the podium too. They, too, have much to say on the subject of woman. Chemical agents, sex hormones or enzymes, are the base of it all. They do make an excellent case for sex hormones' influencing physiological differences. But when it comes to explaining the role of either the hormones or the physiological differences in the building of personality, the fashioning of the personality that will or will not adapt to social expectations—all the objective, step-by-step training is out the window. As for woman and the whole question of her role, they seem to agree with Freud: anatomy is destiny.

History, of course, offers us much more data . . . and much more difficulty. For the very movements not traditionally taught in the schools or made available without glamorized distortions by show business: the movement against the slave trade, the abolitionist movement, the feminist movement, the labor movement. But even our skimpy knowledge of these phenomena show us something: the need for unified effort and the value of a vision of a society substantially better than the existing one.

I don't know that literature enlightens us too much. The "experts" are still men, Black or white. And the images of the woman are still derived from their needs, their fantasies, their second-hand knowledge, their agreement with the other "experts." But of course there have been women who have been able to think better than they've been trained and have produced the canon of literature fondly referred to as "feminist literature": Anais Nin, Simone de Beauvoir, Doris Lessing, Betty Friedan, etc. And the question for us arises: how relevant are the truths, the experiences, the findings of white women to Black women? Are women after all simply women? I don't know that our priorities are the same, that our concerns and methods are the same, or even similar enough so that we can afford to depend on this new field of experts (white, female).

It is rather obvious that we do not. It is obvious that we are turning to each other.

Throughout the country in recent years, Black women have been forming work-study groups, discussion clubs, cooperative nurseries, cooperative businesses, consumer education groups, women's workshops on the campuses, women's caucuses within existing organizations, Afro-American women's magazines. From time to time they have organized seminars on the Role of the Black Woman, conferences on the Crisis Facing the Black Woman, have provided tapes on the Attitude of European Men toward Black Women, working papers on the Position of the Black Women in America; they have begun correspondence with sisters in Vietnam, Guatemala, Algeria, Ghana on the Liberation Struggle and the Woman, formed alliances on a Third World Women plank. They are women who have not, it would seem, been duped by the prevailing notions of "woman," but who have maintained a critical stance.

Unlike the traditional sororities and business clubs, they seem to use the Black Liberation struggle rather than the American Dream as their yardstick, their gauge, their vantage point. And while few have produced, or are interested in producing at this time, papers for publication, many do use working papers as part of their discipline, part of their effort to be clear, analytical, personal, basic; part of their efforts to piece together an "overview," an overview of ourselves too long lost among the bills of sale and letters of transit; part of their effort to deal with the reality of being Black and living in twentieth-century America—a country that has more respect for the value of property than the quality of life, a country that has never valued Black life as dear, a country that regards its women as its monsters, celebrating wherever possible the predatory coquette and the carnivorous mother.

Some of the papers representing groups and individuals are presented here along with poems, stories, and essays by writers of various viewpoints. What is immediately noticeable are the distinct placements of stress, for some women are not so much concerned with demanding rights as they are in clarifying issues; some demand rights as Blacks first, women second. Oddly enough, it is necessary to point out what should be obvious—Black women are individuals too.

For the most part, the work grew out of impatience: an impatience with the all too few and too soon defunct Afro-American women's magazines that were rarely seen outside of the immediate circle of the staff's and contributors' friends. It grew out of an impatience with the half-hearted go-along attempts of Black women caught up in the white women's liberation groups around the country. Especially out of an impatience with all the "experts" zealously hustling us folks for their doctoral theses or government appointments. And out of an impatience with the fact that in the whole bibliography of feminist literature, literature immediately and directly relevant to us wouldn't fill a page. And perhaps that impatience has not allowed me to do all that needs to be done in this volume.

I had thought, in the overly ambitious beginnings, that what we had to do straightaway was (1) set up a comparative study of the woman's role as she saw it in all the Third World Nations; (2) examine the public school system and blueprint some viable alternatives; (3) explore ourselves and set the record straight on the matriarch and the evil Black bitch; (4) delve into history and pay tribute to all our warriors from the ancient times to the slave trade to Harriet Tubman to Fannie Lou Hamer to the woman of this morning; (5) present the working papers of the various groups around the country; (6) interview the migrant workers, the quilting-bee mothers, the grandmothers of the UNIA; (7) analyze the Freedom Budget and design ways to implement it; (8) outline the work that has been done and remains to be done in the area of consumer education and cooperative economics; (9) thoroughly discuss the whole push for Black studies programs and a Black university; (10) provide a forum of opinion from the YWCA to the Black Women Enraged; (11) get into the whole area of sensuality, sex; (12) chart the steps necessary for forming a working alliance with all nonwhite women of the world for the formation of, among other things, a clearing house for the exchange of information . . .

And the list grew and grew. A lifetime's work, to be sure. But I am comforted by the fact that several of the contributors here have begun books; several women contacted have begun books; several magazines are in the making; several groups are talking about doing documentary films. So in the next few months, there will be appearing books dealing exclusively with the relationships between Black men and women, with the revolutionary Black women of the current period, with the Black abolitionists, with the whole question of Black schools.

This then is a beginning—a collection of poems, stories, essays, formal, informal, reminiscent, that seem best to reflect the preoccupations of the contemporary Black woman in this country. Some items were written especially for the collection. Some were discovered tucked away in notebooks. Many of the contributors are professional writers. Some have never before put pen to paper with publication in mind. Some are mothers. Others are students. Some are both. All are alive, are Black, are women. And that, I should think, is credentials enough to address themselves to issues that seem to be relevant to the sisterhood.

I should like to thank Marvin Gettleman; my agent, Cyrilly Abels; my editor, Nina Finkelstein; my typists, Jean Powell of City College and Nat White of the Lower East Side. And especial thanks to my man Gene.

The book is dedicated to the uptown mammas who nudged me to "just set it down in print so it gets to be a habit to write letters to each other, so maybe that way we don't keep treadmilling the same ole ground."

Chapter Forty-Nine

Women's Liberation and the Black Panther Party

YAWF Women's Caucus

Many women in Women's Liberation are deeply concerned about the savage persecution to which the Black Panther Party is being subjected by the government. And
many Women's Collectives and groupings are trying to show solidarity and support
for the Panther men and women in a variety of ways. Of particular interest to many
women are the Breakfast Programs, Child-Care and Health Care programs initiated
by the Panthers.

As a matter of fact, many attribute the rapid growth of Women's Liberation itself,
at least in part to the inspiration derived from the Black Liberation struggle.

However, at all too many Women's Liberation meetings where the question of
support to the Black Panther Party is raised, a disagreeable trend is developing. No
matter how enthusiastically support for the Panthers is first raised, it often degener-
ates into an attack on Panther men for alleged male chauvinism. And the issue of
support to them in their life and death struggle against government attack becomes
blurred.

Why is this so?

Are All Women in the Same Boat?

There is a current of thought in Women's Liberation that starts with the premise
that ALL women—Black and white—are in the same boat. That they are, to one
degree or another, oppressed—and that all men are oppressors.

It is true we are told, that there are differing degrees of oppression. But that is
supposedly of secondary importance. What is of primary significance, it is alleged, is
the common oppression we are all subjected to regardless of degree of oppression.
And that is the bond which ought to unite ALL the women, Black and white, in one
common struggle against male supremacy.

In formulating this particular view of the general emancipation of women,
Women's Liberation obviously DID NOT CONSULT THE BLACK WOMAN. What
the above view of Women's Liberation does is to totally ignore the significance of
the tremendous exploitation to which the Black woman is subjected. The white

woman is not in the same boat with the Black woman and should not be appropriating the right to speak for her as the formulation "ALL WOMEN" implies.

Same Sex—Different Worlds

Evidence of the fact that Black women view the question quite differently than Women's Liberation (white women) can easily be seen by examining a newly published book entitled "The Black Woman," which is described in the preface by Toni Cade as "a collection of poems, stories, essays—that seem best to reflect the preoccupations of the contemporary Black woman in this country."

"They," (the Black women) says the editor of this extremely revealing anthology, "seem to use the Black Liberation struggle—as their yardstick, their gauge, their vantage point." (Our emphasis.)

In other words, the primary struggle as voiced by this writer, is not, as she says "the experiences, the findings of the white woman." And she adds, "I don't know that our priorities are the same, that our concerns and methods are the same or even similar—."

Toni Cade by no means dismisses Black Women's Liberation, but she sees the context of the Black woman's relations to the Black man within the broader context of the struggle for Black Liberation.

To show how little relevance the Black woman finds in white feminism, the author notes, "In the whole bibliography of feminist literature, literature immediately and directly relevant to us wouldn't fill a page."

The Aim: A Working Alliance with Black Women

Many women in Women's Liberation are distressed by the lack of numbers of Black women in the ranks, and they even castigate themselves for failure to attract Black Women.

But it is precisely because Women's Liberation represents white women that it is unable to attract Black women. The aim should be for a working alliance with Black women.

But the basis for that alliance with Black women is not a common struggle against male supremacy, but support to the struggle for Black Liberation against racist imperialism.

To clarify this further—in our relations for example, with Vietnamese women, we can surely agree that when our women's representatives meet with Vietnamese women, our primary concern should be to forge an alliance to combat U.S. imperialist war against the Vietnamese people. Surely that is what our Vietnamese sisters want of us.

The U.S. is conducting a ruthless, predatory war against the Black people in this country that's fundamentally no different than the war being conducted against the

Vietnamese. In any working alliance with Black women for Black Liberation, why should we raise the question of male chauvinism?

Black Women Will Win Their Own Liberation

The relations between the Black woman and the Black man is something for the Black woman to deal with in the context of the struggle for Black Liberation. It is interesting to note that in the preface of "The Black Woman" there are indications that that is exactly what the Black woman intends to do.

Chapter Fifty

Racism
The Sexism of the Family of Man

Shulamith Firestone

The slave may be freed and woman be where she is, but women cannot be freed and the slave remain where he is.
—Angelina Grimké, in *a letter to* Theodore Weld

What must be done, I believe, is that all these problems, particularly the sickness between the white woman and the black man, must be brought out into the open, dealt with, and resolved . . . I think all of us, the entire nation, will be better off if we bring it all out front.
—Eldridge Cleaver, *On Becoming*

The first American book to deal specifically with the connection of sex and racism was Calvin Hernton's *Sex and Racism in America*. The immediate popularity of the book in both black and white communities confirmed what everyone had known all along: that sex and racism are intricately interwoven. However, Hernton, not sufficiently grasping the depth of the relationship, merely described the obvious: that white men have a thing for black women, that black men have a thing for white women, that black men can't respect black women and white men can't get turned on by white women, that white women have a secret sympathy and curiosity about black men, that black women hate and are jealous of white women, and so on. Even so, the book, as have the many such books and articles since, made instant waves. Why is this?

The early civil rights movement had hushed up the truth too long: Suited and tied, it had tiptoed about speaking in low tones on the "Negro Problem"; black people were "colored people," they wanted only the same simple things white (uncolored) people wanted ("we're just folks"). Whereupon whites obligingly filtered their vision to screen out the obvious physical, cultural, and psychological differences. Words like "nigger" were dropped. Statements like, "Would you want your sister to marry one?" became unforgivable bad taste, a sign of poor breeding. "You're prejudiced!" was the accusation of the year. And Martin Luther King masterfully utilized this guilt, turning liberal Christian rhetoric back on itself.

But then came Black Power. A rumble of I-told-you-sos issued from the nation, especially from the working class, who were closest to the blacks: What they really want is our power—they're after our women. Eldridge Cleaver's honesty in *Soul on Ice* clinched it. The heavily sexual nature of the racial issue spilled out. Internally as well, the Black Power movement was increasingly involved in a special kind of *machismo*, as busy proclaiming manhood as protesting race and class injustice.

But it was not the *machismo* element of Black Power that shook up its enemies. This part of it was rarely questioned by the Establishment proper, by the liberal Establishment (in fact, Moynihan's paper on "black matriarchy" can be said to have *created* that massive castration complex within the black community which he describes), or even by the New Left. It was eminently understandable, after all, that black men would eventually want what all men want: to be on top of their women. In fact this part of it was reassuring: black men might become interested in black beauty instead of white (the wave of recent articles bemoaning the black woman's "double burden" and her lack of an appreciative mate are suspicious), a "purity" of home and family would lead eventually, perhaps, to conservatism and predictability. No, it was not black manhood itself that got whites up-tight—it was what manhood means in action: power. Black men were now out in the open in the male power struggle: we want what you've got, no more tap dances. White men breathed with relief and began arming: they knew how to cope with *this*. For once again, it was men vs. men, one (rigged) power force against the other. They drew the battle lines with glee.

What is this truth that was censored in order to make the civil rights movement acceptable to white America? What is the connection between sex and racism that makes any book on it sell so well? Why are the fears of the common man so sexual in nature when it comes to the Negro? Why does just the sight of a Negro so often evoke strong sexual feelings in a white man? Why do black men lust after white women? Why is racial prejudice so often phrased in sexual terms? Why does lynching (often accompanied by castration) occur as the most extreme manifestation of racism?

The connection between sex and racism is obviously much deeper than anyone has cared to go. But though the connection has never been more than superficially explored, already in the one decade of the new movement we have a new set of platitudes concerning sex and race, a new dogma for the "hip." For example, in the Who's Who of Oppression, a ranking of white man-white woman-black woman-black man is still in circulation, despite recent statistics of the Department of Labor.[1] Then there is the Brains vs. Brawn Antagonism, as developed by Mailer, Podhoretz, et al., and continued by Cleaver, basically the mystique of the black man's greater virility. And the Black Womb of Africa, Big Black Mammy in African garb. But this superficial exposure of sex-racism was meant only to seal up the issue a different way, this time in the interests of the male Anti-Establishment.

In this chapter I shall attempt to show that *racism is a sexual phenomenon*. Like sexism in the individual psyche, we can fully understand racism only in terms of the power hierarchies of the family: In the Biblical sense, the races are no more than the various parents and siblings of the Family of Man; and as in the development of sexual classes, the physiological distinction of race became important culturally only due to the unequal distribution of power. Thus, *racism is sexism extended.*

I
The Racial Family: Oedipus/Electra, the Eternal Triangle,
the Brothel-Behind-the-Scenes

Let us look at race relations in America,[2] a macrocosm of the hierarchical relations within the nuclear family: The white man is father, the white woman wife-and-mother, her status dependent on his; the blacks, like children, are his property, their physical differentiation branding them the subservient class, in the same way that children form so easily distinguishable a servile class vis-à-vis adults. This power hierarchy creates the psychology of racism, just as, in the nuclear family, it creates the psychology of sexism.

Previously we have described the Oedipus Complex in the male as that neurosis resulting from enforced subservience to the power of the father. Let us apply this interpretation to the psychology of the black male. The black male at first makes a sympathetic identification with the white female, who is also visibly oppressed by the white man. Because both have been "castrated" (i.e., made impotent, powerless) in the same way by the Father, there is much similarity in the types of psychological oppressions they each must endure, in the sex-repressive nature of these oppressions—and thus in their resulting character formations. They have a special bond in oppression in the same way that the mother and child are united against the father.

This accounts for the white woman's frequent identification with the black man personally, and in a more political form, from the abolitionist movement (cf. Harriet Beecher Stowe) to our present black movement. The vicarious nature of this struggle against the white man's dominion is akin to the mother's vicarious identification with the son against the father. The woman has no real hope of her own self-determined struggle, for her it's all lost from the beginning: she is defined *in toto* as the appendage of the white man, she lives under his day-to-day surveillance isolated from her sisters; she has less aggressive strength. But the mother (white female) knows that if not herself, then at least her son (black male) is potentially "male," that is, powerful.

But while some women may still attempt to achieve their freedom vicariously through the struggle of the black man or other racially oppressed (also biologically distinct) groups, many other women have resigned from this struggle altogether. Instead they choose to embrace their oppression, identifying their own interests with those of their men in the vain hope that power may rub off; *their* solution has been to obliterate their own poor egos—often by love—in order to merge completely into the powerful egos of their men.

This hopeless identification is the racism of white women—which perhaps produces an even greater bitterness in black men than the more immediately understandable racism of these women's husbands; for it betokens a betrayal by the Mother. Yet it is an inauthentic form of racism, for it arises from a false class consciousness, from the threat to what is, after all, only an illusion of power. If and when it is as strong as or stronger than the white man's racism, it is still different in kind: It is characterized by a peculiar hysteria, which, like the conservatism of the black bourgeoisie—or like the wife screaming at her husband that he treats the children better than he treats her—is, in itself, directly the product of the precariousness of her own class(less) situation. Thus the black man may become a scapegoat for the venom the woman feels for her husband, but is incapable of admitting directly.

So the white woman tends to oscillate between either a vicarious identification with the black man or a hysterical (but inauthentic) racism. Radical women, who, like most women, suffer from benefit-of-the-doubtism toward men in general, especially tend to trust and sympathize with black men—and then are often bitterly disillusioned when black men take personal advantage of them, or when the black movement does not move quickly enough to support the woman's cause.

For it is seldom all love and sympathy on the part of the black male either. To return to our analogy: Just as the child begins with a bond of sympathy with the mother, and is soon required to transfer his identification from the mother to the father, thus to eradicate the female in himself, so too the black male, in order to "be a man," must untie himself from his bond with the white female, relating to her if at all only in a degrading way. In addition, due to his virulent hatred and jealousy of her Possessor, the white man, he may lust after her as a thing to be conquered in order to revenge himself on white man. Thus, unlike the more clear-cut polarization of feelings in white women, the black man's feelings about the white woman are characterized by their ambivalence—their intense *mixture* of love and hate; but however he may choose to express this ambivalence, he is unable to control its intensity.

LeRoi Jones's early play *Dutchman* illustrates some of these psychological tensions and ambivalences in the relationship of the black man to the white woman. In a subway encounter. Clay, a young bourgeois black, and Lula, a blonde vampire, personify them: Clay's contempt for Lula as the white man's plaything mixed with a grudging erotic attraction, her deep and immediate understanding of him, and finally her betrayal, ending with a literal backstab (after which she cries "rape," getting off scot free—one must presume to destroy more young black men who were only minding their own business). This is a black man's inner view of the white woman. Lula never comes across as a real woman, so much is she a product of the racial Oedipus Complex I have described.

The relationship of the black man with the white man, similarly, duplicates the relationship of the male child to the father. We have seen how at a certain point, in order to assert his ego, the child must transfer his identification from the female (powerless) to the male (powerful). He hates the powerful father. But he is offered the alternative: If he does make that transition (on the father's terms, of course), he is rewarded; if he denies it, his "manhood" (humanity) is called into question. A black man in America can do only one of the following:

1) He can give in to the white man on the white man's terms, and be paid off by the white man (Uncle Tomism).

2) He can refuse such an identification altogether, at which he often surrenders to homosexuality. Or he may continue desperately to try to prove that if not a "man" in the eyes of white society, at least he is not a woman (the Pimp Complex): By treating "the bitches" with open contempt, he demonstrates to all the world that he is in the superior sex class.

3) He may attempt to overthrow the Father's power. Such an attempt may, but will not necessarily, encompass a wish to *become* the Father, through subsuming his position of power.

Unless the black man makes the first choice, identification with the Father on the Father's own terms, he is subject to castration (destruction of his maleness, his *illegitimate* "male" power), particularly if he tampers with the Father's treasure, the cushion for and embodiment of the Father's power—his woman. This racial castration occurs not only metaphorically, but literally, in the form of lynching.

Let us now apply our political interpretation of the Electra Complex to the psychology of the black woman. If the black man is Son to the American family, then the black woman is Daughter. Her initial sympathy with the white woman (mother), her bond of oppression with her (mother) against the white man (father) is complicated by her later relationship with the white male (father). When she discovers that the white male *owns* that "world of travel and adventure," she, in the subservient position of child, attempts to identify with him, to reject the female in herself. (This may be the cause of the greater aggressiveness of the black woman compared with the docility of her white sisters.) In the effort to reject the womanly (powerless) element in herself, she develops contempt for the Mother (white woman). Like the young girl, she may react to her powerlessness in one of two ways: She may attempt to gain power directly by imitating white men, thus becoming a "big achiever," a woman of strong character who rises high ("especially for a black woman"), or she may attempt to gain power indirectly by seducing the Father (voilà the black sexpot), thus putting herself in sexual competition with the white woman for the Father's favor—causing her to hate and be jealous of the white woman, whom she now must attempt to imitate.

Meanwhile the relationship of the Brother (black man) and Sister (black woman) is one of rivalry and mutual contempt. Each sees the other as powerless, a lackey desperately trying to get in good with the Parents (white man and woman). Each is onto the other's sexual games. It is difficult for them to direct their erotic energies toward each other: they see through each other too well.

We can use the family in another way to illuminate the psychology of racism. Let us look at racism as a form of the Eternal Triangle. In this situation the white man is Husband, the white woman is Wife, and the black woman is the Other Woman. We have seen how this kind of dichotomy between the "good" and the "bad" woman is in itself a product of the Oedipus Complex. A man is unable to feel both sex and affection for the same object, so he must divide up his feelings: for his wife and mother of his children he feels respect and affection; for the "other" woman, his sexual receptacle, he feels passion. The further exaggeration of this division through biological differentiation, e.g., color,[3] or economic class distinctions, makes the acting out of the sexual schizophrenia itself very convenient: One does not have to bother actually degrading one's sex object to avoid the guilt of breaking the incest taboo; her attributes, by social definition, already render her degraded. (Perhaps the measure of corruption of the individual male psyche can be judged by the degree to which it lusts after black flesh as something exotic, erotic, because forbidden.) The black woman, while made to pay the sexploitation price of this schism, is at least freed of the enslavement of the family structure. The white woman, though revered in her role as Mother, is permanently chained to her own private tyrant.

How do the women of this racial Triangle feel about each other? Divide and Conquer: Both women have grown hostile to each other, white women feeling contempt for the "sluts" with no morals, black women feeling envy for the pampered "powder puffs." The black woman is jealous of the white woman's legitimacy, privilege, and comfort, but she also feels deep contempt: white women are "frigid bitches" who have it too easy, leaving black women to do all their white woman's work—from supplying their husbands' sex/passion needs and taking care of their children to doing their literal dirty work ("help"). Similarly, the white woman's contempt for the black woman is mixed with envy: for the black woman's greater sexual license, for her gutsiness, for her freedom from the marriage bind. For after all, the black woman is not under the thumb of a man, but is pretty much her own boss to come and go, to leave the house, to work (much as it is degrading work) or to be "shiftless." What the white woman doesn't know is that the black woman, not under the thumb of *one* man, can now be squashed by all. There is no alternative for either of them than the choice between being public or private property, but because each still believes that the other is getting away with something, both can be fooled into mischanneling their frustration onto each other, rather than onto the real enemy, "The Man."

If, in the white man's sex drama, the white woman plays Wife (his private property), and the black woman plays Whore (his public property), what role does the black man play? The black man plays Pimp. The black man is a pawn in the game of the white man's sexuality. For as we have seen, the black man is not a complete man, nor yet a homosexual (who has given up the struggle for male identity altogether), but a *degraded* male. (That pimp signifies "degraded male" is borne out by the fact that in the male code to call someone a pimp is tantamount to setting up a duel. I have pointed out that degrading animal terms for the male as well as the female occur regularly only in ghetto slang—stud, cat, dude, spade, jack, etc.) The black man's malehood is so insecure in relation to The Man that it registers only in terms of his power and control over—i.e., ill-treatment of—women, who are at least more powerless than himself. Because women are his major weapon in the war of masculinity with the white man, his relation to them becomes corrupted—not like that of man over woman, husband over wife, but like that of pimp over whore. His patronage of the black woman is a false one: though he may even, at times protect her from the evils of the marketplace, he does so for his own interests. But even when the black man most appears to be her primary exploiter, he is in reality only the indirect agent of her exploitation. For though he may play the mares of his "stable" against each other, drink and gamble away their money (the hard-won fruits of their direct exploitation by the white man), beat them and call them names, it will never qualify him as a real man. The *real* man, as they both know, is The Man. He alone can confer legitimacy on either the black male or the black female. And again, as in his Wife-Whore triangle, he keeps both the Pimp and the Whore dangling, fighting with him *through each other*. Most of the tensions of these overlapping triangles appear in the following short quote by a black woman addressed to her man:

> Of course you will say, "How can I love you and want to be with you when I come home and you're looking like a slob? Why, white women never open the door for their husbands the way you black bitches do."
>
> I should guess not, you ignorant man. Why should they be in such a state when they've got maids like me to do everything for them? There is no screaming at the kids for her, no standing over the hot stove; everything is done for her and whether her man loves her or not, he provides . . . *provides* . . . do you hear that, nigger? PROVIDES!
>
> —Gail A. Stokes in "Black Woman to Black Man,"
> *Liberator*, December, 1968.

But it is not only the black man's relation to black women that is corrupted by his preoccupation with the white man. For though the black woman may give her last dollar to buy the black man a drink, *her* real involvement, too, is with the white man. Here is The Infidel speaking, from Cleaver's "Allegory of the Black Eunuchs":

> Ever since then I always believed that marrying a white man, to a black woman, is like adding the final star to her crown. It's the apex of achievement in her eyes and in the eyes of her sisters. Look at how many family black celebrities marry white men. All of the Negro women who are not celebrities wish they were so that they too, could marry white men. Whitey is their dream boy. When they kiss you, it ain't really you they're kissing. They close their eyes and picture their white dream boy. Listen to the grapevine. . . . Jesus Christ the pure is the black woman's psychic bridegroom. You will learn before you die that during coition and at the moment of her orgasm, the black woman, in the first throes of her spasm, shouts out the name of Jesus. "Oh Jesus, I'm coming!" she shouts to him. And to you it will hurt. It will be like a knife in your heart. It will be the same as if your woman, during orgasm, calls out the name of some sneaky cat who lives down the block.

Thus the black woman has as much contempt for the black man as he has for her—a *real* man could elevate her through marriage, by virtue of his superior class. She can't respect the black man, because she knows he has no power. The white man at least "provides" for his women, and doesn't beat them. The white man is civil, kind, and polite at all times. She doesn't see that it is in his interests to be: that way neither the Pimp nor the Whore will suspect that their Polite White Customer is responsible for both their destructions.

Thus, the All-American Family is predicated on the existence of the black ghetto Whorehouse. The rape of the black community in America makes possible the existence of the family structure of the larger white community, just as sexual prostitution in general maintains the respectable middle-class family. The black community is the outgroup that supplies the sexual needs of the white human family, keeping it functioning. And *that's* why there is no family solidity in the ghetto.

The way this sex/race system is so often recreated in miniature in private life reveals the depth of the problem. The individual white household is sustained by the life-long domestic, as well as sexual, exploitation of individual black women. Or, the average ghetto youth does some pimping or even whoring as a matter of course, his value as a "man" measured by the way he is able to command his bitches—and how many he can command at once. He becomes a master of the smooth line, of doubletalk. If he is able to string along a white "chick," this is an added notch on his belt—for it's a direct blow to the white man (Father). This explains the frequent pairing of the white whore with the black pimp: the white woman (Mother) is degraded to whore along with the black woman, a direct slap at the white man. She is the Father's most precious property, now sold back to him as damaged merchandise. As for the white whore herself—in those few cases where it was a matter of choice—she has expressed the ultimate in masochism. She becomes totally the prey of the white man, rubbing his nose in her acquiescence to the extreme humiliation: A black pimp.

II
"Black Manhood"

What is the attitude of the militant black community to this psychosexual degradation that is racism? I have stated that the black male has three choices in reacting to the white male's power over him.

1) He can submit on the terms set up by the white male (at best to become a black celebrity—comedian, athlete, or musician—or a member of the black bourgeoisie).

2) He can refuse the identification altogether, with all the consequences of being defined as less than "a man" (the ravaged ghetto youth I have described).

3) He can try to revolt and overthrow the Father, which *may* include stealing that power position for himself (political organization for revolution, especially the recent militance).

The black movement has chosen the third alternative, by far the healthiest. But how does it plan to accomplish this? One way is to unite with the white forces that are also attempting the same thing.[4] The Family once again: the white male left is the weakling Legitimate Son. The black male is the tough guy Bastard Brother, the illegitimate son wanting a chance at that power. The Half Brothers have made a deal: the disinherited Brother's street "smarts" and raw strength of discontent to aid the pampered neurotic Legitimate Son, in exchange for tactics, rhetoric, and, above all, for a promise of a portion of that son's birthright when he attains the throne. What the two brothers are really talking about is not justice and equality but (male) power.

And who is Little Sister? White women on the Left are allowed to tag along, occasionally, if they do the dirty work; but more often they get put down, and left out ("pests," with their constant demands for inclusion, throwing tantrums at any little "male chauvinist" remark). The Sister fools herself, identifying so strongly with Big Brother that she actually at times begins to believe herself just like him. She finds it harder and harder to identify with that dimming mass of ordinary women out there (Mother) whom she must kill in herself in order to win Big Brother's approval. He encourages her in this. He knows illusions of her coming power will make her more docile in the long run. She can be useful, especially in getting at the Father.

Moreover, the Brothers have made a blood pact: you give me your chicks (the Bastard Brother fulfills his fantasies on Little Sister while the white boy pretends not to notice), and I'll give you mine (the white boy gets his first real screw while the Bastard Brother snickers).

And the black sister? Black male militants, going for the "legit" this time, are reordering their sexuality to conform with the going model. Attempts are now being made to institute the family in the black community, to transform the black community from Whorehouse for the white family to Black Family. The black woman is being converted from her previous role, Whore, to Revered-Black-Queen-Mother-of-My-Children. Thus, the Bastard Son has assumed the role of Father within his own community in anticipation of his coming power. Here is a much-circulated poster, tacked up in an East Village store window:

BLACK GOLD

[a large, formidable profile of a black woman in an Afro]

I AM THE BLACK WOMAN, MOTHER OF CIVILIZATION, QUEEN OF THE UNIVERSE.
THROUGH ME THE BLACK MAN PRODUCES HIS NATION.

If he does not protect his woman he will not produce a good nation.
It is my duty to teach and train the young, who are the future of the nation.
I teach my children the language, history, and culture when they are very young.
I teach them to love and respect their father, who works hard so that they may have adequate food, clothing, and shelter.
I care and make our home comfortable for my husband.
I reflect his love to the children as the moon reflects the light from the sun to the earth.
I sit and talk with my husband to work out the daily problems and necessities of running a stable and peaceful household.
The best that I can give my nation is strong, healthy, intelligent children who will grow to be the leaders of tomorrow.
I'm always aware that the true worth of a nation is reflected through the respect and protection of the woman, so I carry myself in a civilized manner at all times, and teach my children to do the same.
I am the Black Woman.

But such a transformation, when it succeeds, is based on fantasy, for as long as the white man is still in power, he has the privilege to define the black community as he chooses—they are dependent on him for their very survival—and the psychosexual consequences of this interior definition must continue to operate. Thus the concept of the Dignified Black Family rarely penetrated beyond the circles of the Copycat Bourgeoisie or the True Believer Revolutionaries. Indeed, one would have to believe fanatically in The Revolution to fight off the mind sets resulting from the present sex/race system; one could embrace such a foreign structure only through steadfast visionary anticipation of a different world. That hard-core ghetto youth aren't eager to put such a family structure into practice is understandable: Daily they are at the mercy of the real sexual needs of the White Family; they can't afford not to jive with their unpleasant reality or to forget for a moment who has the power. In this respect black revolutionaries are as dangerous as a small band of Nat Turners trying to institute marriage in the slave quarters in anticipation of the coming rebellion. And, all exhortations to the contrary, even the revolutionaries have a hard time purging themselves of the sex/race psychology, finding themselves still irresistibly drawn to the "white she-devils." For it lies too deep in their psyches, backed up by the day-to-day realities of power. Here is Cleaver battling with himself:

> One day I saw in a magazine a picture of the white woman who had flirted with [and thus caused the death of] Emmett Till. While looking at the picture, I felt a little tension in the center of my chest I experience when a woman appeals to me. I looked at the picture again and again and in spite of everything and against my will and my hate for the woman and everything she represented, she appealed to me. I flew into a rage at myself, at America, at white women, at the history that had placed those tensions of lust and desire in my chest. Two days later I had a "nervous breakdown."

Cleaver's greatest virtue as a writer is his honesty. In *Soul on Ice* we have the psychology of the black man, particularly the consuming love/hate for the "Ogre" (white woman). In fact Cleaver's development contains most of the ambivalences we have described. We are given some idea of what his previous attitude toward (black) women was before he here falls in love with a (white) woman:

> I even respect you behind your back. I have a bad habit, when speaking of women while only men are present, of referring to women as bitches. This bitch this and that bitch that, you know. A while back I was speaking of you to a couple of cutthroats and I said, "this bitch . . ." And I felt very ashamed of myself about that. I passed judgment upon myself and suffered spiritually for days afterward. This may seem insignificant, but I attach great importance to it because of the chain of thought kicked off by it. I care about you, am concerned about you, which is all very new for, and a sharp departure from, Eldridge X.
>
> "Prelude to Love—Three Letters"

In general, in these letters, originally written to San Francisco lawyer Beverly Axelrod, Cleaver attempts to rid himself of all the smooth talk, the clever come-on that is the trademark of the black man. He is not always successful. One senses that he has to fight with himself; he catches himself just in time (almost too cleverly) by admitting what he is doing:

NOW TURN THE RECORD OVER AND PLAY THE OTHER SIDE: I have tried to mislead you. I am not humble at all.

But when Beverly expresses cynicism about his love, he assures her elaborately that she must "open up" to him, trust him.

Beverly was right. Her female cynicism, as usual, was more than justified—she wasn't cynical *enough*. (Cleaver, to set an example, married just-black-enough Kathleen, leaving Beverly stranded. Latest pictures include an infant son.) His letters to Beverly, about as personalized and honest as probably he will ever get toward any woman, are followed by a florid letter (testimonial? doctrine?) To All Black Women From All Black Men. Its balls-and-womb imagery includes such gems as:

Across the naked abyss of my negated masculinity, of four hundred years [!] minus my balls, we face each other today, my queen.

He reminds her that:

Torrents of blood flow today from my crotch . . .

And finally, triumphantly:

I have entered the den and seized my balls from the teeth of a roaring lion . . .

His pages-long incantations to the Black Womb of Africa are, to say the least, hardly the best way to go about flattering a woman.

For despite his address to Black Womanhood ("Queen-Mother-Daughter of Africa, Sister of My Soul, Black Bride of My Passion, My Eternal Love") Cleaver, in this supposed love letter, is hung up on himself, and on his "masculinity." There is no conception of the black woman as a human being in her own right; she is merely a buttress for his own (masculine) self-image. The same old trick in revolutionary guise: the male defining himself negatively as man-strong by distinguishing himself from woman-weak, through his control of her—like the pimp who rejects the female in himself, achieving a false sense of manhood (power) through domination of all females in his vicinity. The sexual nature of Cleaver's racial agonies is revealed in his attack on Baldwin, which is no more than the vicious attack of the Black Pimp on the Black Queen. The Queen has chosen to give up the male (power) identification altogether rather than accept the degrading sexual definition handed down by the white man, thus threatening the Pimp, who is fighting a losing battle. And if this attack weren't enough, Cleaver gives away his sexual insecurity through his superstud self-image—Norman Mailer in black. Some promotion, judging by the hysterics of his chestpounding.

The transformation of the black woman into the traditional passive female creates a useful negative backdrop against which the black male's own definition of himself as masculine (aggressive) can emerge. And in her capacity as springboard, or practice bouting-dummy, the black woman is valuable and must be "humbly" wooed; her cooperation is important, for the black man can only be the "man" if someone becomes the "woman."

Black women, so hip to "lines," seem to have fallen for this one. Here is a rebuke written by another black woman in reply to the accusation of black men by Gail A. Stokes that I have quoted above. It is noted for its female antiwomanism:

> Sure [black men] blunder and make mistakes, but don't we? This is normal for someone trying something new, i.e. leadership. . . . So how could you, Gail Stokes, scrounge up the audacity to prick the Black man's balloon! How could you dare to attempt to break his winning streak? Did it ever occur to you that it is you, in fact, who is inadequate? Check yourself, sister; a woman reflects her man.

She turns to the black man:

> Black men: I too have heard your cry, ringing from within your new-found pride, and African garb. And to that cry I reply: Take your rightful place ahead of me, my love. . . . Yes, my Black man, you're a real man, a rare man. And in all your struggles I want you to know that I struggle only a few steps behind you, for that is my place in your life. . . . You are all I am here for.

She then assuages his pricked ego by assuring him of her undying loyalty to his Balls:

> Having your balls torn from you and still trying to be a man! Oh, those anguished moments of puberty . . . those growing pains. . . . *Tell me how many men have been castrated only to defy that emasculation and grow new balls!* . . . You need to be held and loved and told how wonderful you really are.
> —Edith R. Hambrick, "Black Woman to Black woman,"
> *Liberator*, December, 1968.
> (Italics hers. And notice the capitalization of the title: a warning to the sister to start toeing the line?)

But when she does toe the line, her reward will not be a personalized kind of love (as in the letters to Beverly Axelrod) but an impersonal one addressed through her to all Black Womanhood. Here is Bobby Seale from his much-published *Letter To My Wife* (like the budding poet's inscription on his girlfriend's Christmas gifts, inevitably appearing in the spring issue of the college poetry journal):

> Artie Honey . . .
> Now if I ain't in love with you because I saw something on your face the other morning that said you were a revolutionary, then something is wrong. . . . What's Malik [their three-year-old son] doing? Teach him how to serve the people by your examples, Artie. . . . Artie, I hope you are not being selfish and keeping this letter to yourself. Aw, I know you are reading it to the other party members. . . .

Why do black women, so shrewd about their men in general, settle for this patronizing, impersonal, and uninspired kind of love? Because of The Triangle: as we have seen, the black woman has played Whore, used and abused by white men (her "tricks") and black men (her "pimps") for centuries. All this time she has looked with envy at the white woman's legitimacy and security. Now, offered that legitimacy, under whatever crude guise, she is tempted to set it up for herself, not knowing the horrors in store. The Wife is the only one who could tell her, but they are not on speaking terms. For, as we have seen, each has learned to focus her frustrations on the other. Their long antagonism makes it hard for them to trade the valuable (and painful) lessons they have learned about The Man. If they could, they might soon discover that neither Wife nor Whore grants freedom, for neither of these roles is self-determined. They might alert to Eldridge Cleaver's warning, as he anticipates his future male power, in one of his rare moments of honesty with women:

> NOW TURN THE RECORD OVER AND PLAY THE OTHER SIDE:
> I have tried to mislead you. I am not humble at all. I have no humility and I do not fear you in the least. If I pretend to be shy, if I appear to hesitate, it is only a sham to deceive. By playing the humble part, I sucker my fellow men and seduce them of their trust. And then if it suits my advantage, I lower the boom mercilessly. I lied when I stated that I had no sense of myself. I am very well aware of my style. My vanity is as vast as the scope of a dream, my heart is that of a tyrant, my arm is the arm of the executioner. It is only the failure of my plots I fear.

NOTES

1. In 1969, white men who worked full-time the year around earned a median income of $6,497; black men, $4,285; white women, $3,859; and black women, $2,674.
But in only a few radical circles affected by the Women's Liberation Movement has even the black woman been acknowledged to be at the bottom economically.

2. I shall deal here only with the domestic race relations with which I am most familiar, though I have no doubt that the same metaphor could be applied equally well to international and Third World politics.

3. An interesting illustration of their common and interchangeable political function is the psychological substitution of the racial caste distinction for the sexual caste distinction, e.g., a black lesbian often automatically assumes the male role in a black-white lesbian relationship.

4. Here, and throughout the chapter, I am assuming the position of the Black Panther Party as representative of Black Power, through I am well aware that the BPP has violent disputes with other Black Power groups over many things.

Chapter Fifty-One

Selections from *Black Lesbian in White America*

Anita Cornwell

THE BLACK LESBIAN IN A MALEVOLENT SOCIETY

I

At a Radical Therapist's Conference several years ago, a middle-aged womin in the Lesbian/Feminist workshop complained that it was extremely difficult to find companions her own age. "Where are all the forty-year-old Lesbians?" she asked in a plaintive tone.

Then I called out, "Here we are, back here in the rear of the bus!" The entire room seemed to think that was humorous, but one of the other middle-aged womyn in the place laughed so hard she nearly fell out of her chair.

Not only was I one of the few persons in the room over forty, but I was, at that moment, the only Black person present. Now, I cannot recall most of the details concerning what went on in that workshop, but I do remember that as time wore on, I became more and more alienated, so much so that by the end of the session, I had a tremendous headache.

I am fairly certain, however, that one of the things contributing to my headache was that all of those therapists, and most of the other participants, kept referring to everyone as *he*. It was *he* this and *he* that until I finally felt like screaming, "Dammit, don't you know half the world population is *She*?" But I suppose I was too filled with rage, and despair, to speak out.

Another startling contrast, within my own mind at least, was the situation facing those young people and the realities that confronted me when I was about their age. They had conferences they could attend, to at least discuss their problems, while we of the fifties (and the forties and on back to when) not only had to operate from the closet but, worse yet, most of us seemed to exist in a vacuum.

During that time, about the only visible Gays were the swaggering butch and the swishing faggot, who were about as welcome in that "genteel" climate of the fifties as a grizzly bear. In fact, I do believe the bear would have had a decided advantage.

The major consequence of being born an outcast in this land of bitter honey is that unless you are gifted with the luck of fortune's child and the wisdom of an ancient matriarch, you're likely to find that you are forever wanting to be someone other than yourself, or you are always wishing to be any place rather than where you are.

Fortunately, though, my Mother was a Feminist, although she probably has never used the word. But the concept, ah! That is the thing! For anyone born poor Black and female in this white, middle-class, male-oriented society had damn sure better quickly learn the concepts of Feminism if she wants to survive.

I was born in the Deep South at a time when Black people were lynched on a routine basis, when we worked for slave's wages—if we found work at all—and when *integration* was a term seen only in the dictionary. Consequently, my first intense desire was to leave the South and "Go Up North," where so many Black people had migrated.

Yet, once I was eventually settled in the North, I still felt rootless and insecure. I often had the feeling that any moment the ground I trod upon was going to give way, plunging me into some ancient abyss from which I could never escape. I rarely enjoyed the present for worrying about the future while unsuccessfully trying to blot out the past that I carried around like a second skin.

Oddly enough, I believe the beginning of the Womyn's Movement raised my morale far more than the Black Movement had. Nevertheless, I did take great pride in seeing my people finally asserting themselves. I suppose the main reason I could never get carried away over the Civil Rights Movement was that most of the leaders were men who seemed to possess the traditional attitudes toward womyn.

In spite of this, however, I was extremely reluctant to make any effort to join the Womyn's Movement, largely because I was Gay. Or at least that is what I told myself, and that thought was uppermost in my mind.

I had never really come to terms with my ambivalences toward white people, and since I was no longer gainfully employed, I seldom came into close personal contact with them. So I had simply left that aspect of my life in the background while I continued to pursue my slippery writing career. Slippery because during those years "Girl Meets Boy" stories reigned supreme, and she who was not interested in that subject was simply out of it.

II

Practically speaking, I find it difficult to imagine anyone more oppressed than the Black Lesbian in America. Perhaps that is why so many still cling so desperately to their niche in the closet even during these times of the so-called sexual revolution.

One of the main problems facing Black womyn, it seems to me, is that most of them simply refuse to even admit that such a phenomenon as sexism exists. Admittedly, all straight womyn seem to have difficulty acknowledging that fact.

And Black womyn, locked as they are in the airtight prison that America's racist-sexist attitude erects about them, seem to feel that whitey is their sole enemy, and that anyone who dares to suggest otherwise is trying to disrupt *The Black Family*, et cetera, et cetera, et cetera.

The thing I find most disturbing regarding womyn in general is the seeming impossibility of their thinking clearly when it comes time to deal with men. Womyn with advanced university degrees often seem utterly unable to dot an *i* when they are confronted with the realities of man's barbaric treatment of womin. To put it bluntly, I find it absolutely terrifying to see just how effective men have been in eradicating womyn's sense of self, a condition that seems to prevail in at least 90 percent of all womyn all over this male-infected globe.

One morning, on a nationally televised program, I watched a studio full of Black womyn, who supposedly were there to talk about themselves, waste the whole damn hour talking about Black men (not about Black male oppression, that is). And when one of the three panel members tried to point out that she thought the program was to be about Black womyn, she was quickly put in her place.

Another of the factors that help keep so many Black womyn locked in their isolation ward is their seemingly innate distrust of white womyn. (I realize this feeling is mutual, but that is not my subject at the moment.) And this distrust often causes them to either ignore or put down the Womyn's Liberation Movement, which we so desperately need.

A friend of mine once said she used to come home from work and complain to her husband—sitting out in the living room reading the paper—"My feet are so tired." And he would calmly suggest, "Why don't you prop your feet up on something while you fix the dinner?"

Then at a party one night, a young Black Lesbian said to me, "I don't see why you're wearing that Womyn's Lib button. The Bible says men should lead."

Although I really got pissed off, I managed to keep my cool and asked her, "Then why aren't you somewhere letting some man lead you instead of living with a womin?"

"Well, my case is slightly different," she replied.

At first, I thought she was trying to put me on, but when I realized she was serious, I asked, "If you're going to make allowances for yourself, why can't other womyn do the same for themselves?"

She didn't seem to have an answer to that, but then as if to explain her position once and for all, she said, "I believe in equal pay for equal work, though."

"Well, who the hell is going to give you equal pay for equal work if they know you think you are not capable of leading yourself?" I asked. "And furthermore, who is going to give you a decent-paying job in the first place if they think you should be home scrubbing floors and doing other shitwork for some man for free? Well, I will tell you who, no damn body, that's who!"

"I guess you've got a point there," she conceded after staring at me for a long moment, but the troubled expression remained on her face.

III

For a long time I tried to figure out why most womyn continue to practice all manner of atrocities on our minds, our spirits, and our bodies. To assert that such womyn are brainwashed is quite true, but that alone, it seemed to me, was only a tip of the iceberg.

If this were an earlier age when most womyn were largely uneducated, I would have simply concluded that these womyn were just too ignorant to understand how much men really hated them. But look at all the college degrees that abound in the female sector these days.

Well, perhaps it's a matter of sexual attraction, I thought. But then why didn't sexual attraction cause men to love and cherish womyn instead of engaging in the terroristic warfare they've waged against us lo these many centuries?

Then one day I happened to take a good look at the words *male* and *malevolent* in my old abridged Merriam-Webster, which indicated that *malevolent* meant [male (fr.) *ill* plus *volens* wishing]—wishing evil; arising from, or indicative of, ill will.

But what of the term *female*? Did it have the same evil root? I thought not, and was relieved to find, in the same dictionary, *female* [OF. femelle, fr. L. femella, dim. of femina woman].

That gave me one answer, the why of man's vicious treatment of womin. But how account for womin's slavish adoration of this evil being? The answer came one afternoon while I was reading the comments of some straight womyn who were enthralled over a certain cockrock group well known for their contemptuous attitude toward womyn.

One of these deluded females declared, in a manner that said, this explains it all, and oh, how happy we are, "They are *evil*, girls. *Evil*."

Indeed they are, and so are the entire brotherhood. Thus, I finally had the other half of the equation. Men are evil, and most womyn are fatally attracted to that evil.

Now, anybody in doubt about any of this, *just look at the record!* The crimes that men have perpetrated against womyn throughout the ages are simply too numerous and too gruesome to contemplate.

Finally, giving weight to my theory, I recalled reading that one Buddhist sect (or some such group) believe that men should spend all of their lives trying to purify their souls. And what about womyn? Well, they believe womyn are automatically in that state of grace or worthiness from the moment they are born.

When I first read that, I thought, "Oh, oh, here we go again, purified." But after coming up with my thesis, I have changed my mind, as it seems the Buddhists have come up with the same theory. Or rather, they came up with it eons ago. And they should know, *for they are it!*

Someone once wrote, "Men are the missing link." I believe they are too, the link between evil and good. Which is not to say that womyn are not capable of doing bad things. But if womyn were as evil as men, the species would have come to an end long ago, for no one with that malevolent strain in them would have continued to breed the seeds of its own destruction.

So where does that leave womyn in general and the Black Lesbian in particular? It leaves us all in one hell of a fix. A fix we will never even remotely begin to cope with so long as we continue to deny the very existence of the evil that surrounds us.

THE LESSER OF THE WORST

Since joining the Womyn's Movement, I find myself associating mainly with white womyn. Most of the time I forget there is a racial gap between us, but I sometimes feel that such may not be the case with many of them.

That is not a sneaky way of saying racism exists within the Movement—which it does, of course, yet not nearly as much as one would expect considering the nature of our society—but rather that I do miss my Black Sisters and yearn for the day when they will embrace the Movement more wholeheartedly.

Still, I know why they have not, the main reason being that age-old sickness, racism and sexism, and the damage it has done to all of us.

What really got me onto this train of thought, though, was neither sexism nor racism, per se, but Lesbianism. I was somewhat shocked recently when I realized that most of the white Lesbians I know seem to feel more oppressed as *Lesbians* than I do.

At first I thought it was because I am older than most of them, that since I had been oppressed longer, I noticed it less. Normally, I guess I would have assumed it was because I am Black. But, really, one does grow weary of making *that* assumption.

One of the absolute certainties of life in this country is the almost endless parade of dilemmas you find crossing your path daily. Not that you take such a rational, detached attitude while trying to grapple with one, however.

As a case in point, when George Jackson, the Soledad Brother, was killed, I happened to be in Kent, Connecticut, at a Conference for Gay Womyn. I had gone there in a caravan of three cars consisting of ten womyn, two of us Black. About 125 Sisters attended the conference, and at most I can recall only about twelve Black womyn being present.

Which means that at any given time, one could look in all directions and see only white faces.

Then, as I lay in our tent on Sunday morning, I heard one white Sister saying to another, "There's a story on the front page of the *Sunday Times* that says George Jackson was killed in prison. . . ."

I lay there, not unmindful of the fact that I was a fairly great distance from home, from any public transportation apparently as we were out on a large farm, that I had come in a white womin's car, and was at that moment lying in another white womin's tent. *And their white Brothers had killed my Black Brother!*

Their Brothers were pigs, I thought then, and I think so now. But what of my Brother? A pig too, in all probability, as most Black men are no different from white men as far as sexism is concerned.

But they didn't shoot him because he was a pig. They got him because he was Black. I am Black, too, and as James Baldwin is reputed to have said to Angela Davis, "If they get you in the morning, they will certainly come for me in the night."

So what does one do at such a time? Do you get drunk at eight o'clock in the morning, although you're already on the verge of ulcers and you don't want a drink anyway? Do you go on a rampage, ripping white Sisters apart merely because they are white like your oppressors who are coming for you also? Or do you shove the problem into the vast, overstuffed room located somewhere in the deep recesses of the mind and slam the door?

I lay there a while longer; then, finally realizing that divine inspiration was not forthcoming, I turned to stare at the canvas wall of the tent and told myself I would deal with the situation after breakfast.

Yet many hours later, when I saw the black headline regarding Jackson's death, I quickly averted my eyes, unable to even look at the newspaper, let alone cope with the dilemma it had dropped in my lap. I still haven't for that matter.

Then, several months afterwards, I heard a bleating voice on the radio describing how Angela Davis's health had deteriorated in prison (because of poor medical care and other environmental stresses) before they let her out on bail. And again I had to swallow my impotent rage because I knew she would not have been treated in such fashion had her skin not been the color of mine.

But why travel far across the country? Why not consider the Black Sisters in my own front yard who are raped, beaten, or/and murdered with monotonous regularity and whose violators are almost never apprehended because our white law insists that Black womyn do not exist, nor poor white womyn either for that matter?

Thus year after year, the hidden chamber is crammed with repressed fury, but you dare not stop to wonder what would happen if the walls should suddenly give way. You simply keep on hoping that with a little luck, the reckoning will not come today. Yet there is always tomorrow, which haunts the mind like a half-forgotten nightmare.

I suppose that is why I was so surprised when I first heard some of my Gay white Sisters complaining about Castro's oppression of homosexuals in Cuba. Not that I don't think they should complain. Indeed, I am just as pissed off as they are!

But why didn't I or the other Black Lesbians I know get more uptight over the oppression of Gay people? Don't we feel just as threatened by a Castro as we do by the cop on the corner? Weren't we just as concerned as our white Lesbians that "society" forbids us to hold hands or kiss in public?

Inevitably, one comes up with the indisputable truth that oppression no matter what the ideology behind it. And just as there is no such thing as a little bit of pregnancy, ditto with oppression. So why should one be concerned about which label is attached to one's oppression? Does it make any difference?

Then a tiny door of the vast room opened just a crack, and a few of the outrages I have faced on a daily basis because of my color floated through my mind. I had to admit, yes, there is a difference. It matters like hell! Because as someone has said, "When things go wrong, all Blacks are black, and all whites are whitey."

That things stay wrong in this nation, can be readily seen by even a casual reading of the morning paper. And the moment I or any other Black forget we *are* black, it may be our last moment. For when the shooting starts, *any* Black is fair game. The bullets don't give a damn whether I sleep with a womin or man, their only aim is to put me to sleep forever.

Chapter Fifty-Two

An Argument for Black Women's Liberation as a Revolutionary Force

Maryanne Weathers

"Nobody can fight your battles for you; you have to do it yourself." This will be the premise used for the time being for stating the case for black women's liberation, although certainly it is the least significant. Black women, at least the black women we have come in contact with in the movement have been expounding all their energies in "liberating" black men (if you yourself are not free, how can you "liberate" someone else?). Consequently, the movement has practically come to a standstill—not entirely due, however, to wasted energies but, adhering to basic false concepts rather than revolutionary principles—and at this stage of the game we should understand that if it is not revolutionary it is false.

We have found that Women's Liberation is an extremely emotional issue, as well as an explosive one. Black men are still parroting The Man's prattle about male superiority. This now brings us to a very pertinent question: How can we seriously discuss reclaiming our African heritage—cultural living modes which clearly refute not only patriarchy and matriarchy, but our entire family structure as we know it. African tribes live communally where households, let alone heads of households, are nonexistent.

It is disgusting to hear black women talk about giving black men their manhood—or allowing them to get it. This is degrading to other black women and thoroughly insulting to black men (or at least it should be). How can someone "give" one something as personal as one's adulthood? That's precisely like asking the beast for your freedom. We also rap about standing behind our men. This forces me to the question: Are we women or leaning posts and props? It sounds as if we are saying if we come out from behind him, he'll fall down. To me, these are clearly maternal statements and should be closely examined.

Women's Liberation should be considered as a strategy for an eventual tie-up with the entire revolutionary movement consisting of women, men, and children. We are now speaking of real revolution. If you can not accept this fact purely and without problems examine your reactions closely. We are playing to win and so are they. Vietnam is simply a matter of time and geography.

Another matter to be discussed is the liberation of children from a sick slave culture. Although we don't like to see it, we are still operating within the confines of the slave culture. Black women use our children for our own selfish needs of worth and love. We try to live our lives which are overbearingly oppressing through our children and thereby destroy them in the process. Obviously the plaudits of the love of the black mother has some discrepancies. If we allow ourselves to run from the truth we run the risk of spending another 400 years in self-destruction. Assuming of course the beast would tolerate us that long, and we know he wouldn't.

Women have fought with men and have *died with men* in every revolution, more recently in Cuba, Algeria, China, and now in Vietnam. (If you notice, it is a woman heading the "Peace Talks" in Paris for the NLF.) What is wrong with black women? We are clearly the most oppressed and degraded minority in the world, let alone the country. Why can't we rightfully claim our place in the world?

Realizing fully what is being said, you should be warned that the opposition for liberation will come from everyplace, particularly from other women and from black men. Don't allow yourselves to be intimidated any longer with this nonsense about the "Matriarchy" of black women. Black women are not matriarchs but we have been forced to live in abandonment and have been used and abused. The myth of the matriarchy must stop and we must not allow ourselves to be sledgehammered by it any longer—not if we are serious about change and ridding ourselves of the wickedness of this alien culture. Let it be clearly understood that black women's liberation is not anti-male; any such sentiment or interpretation as such can not be tolerated. It must be taken clearly for what it is—pro-human for all peoples.

The potential for such a movement is boundless. Whereas in the past only certain type black people have been attracted to the movement—younger people, radicals, and militants—the very poor, the middle class, older people and women have not become aware or have not been able to translate their awareness into action. Women's liberation offers such a channel for these energies.

Even though middle-class black women may not have suffered the brutal supression of poor black people, they most certainly have felt the scourge of the male superiority oriented society as women, and would be more prone to help in alleviating some of the conditions of our more oppressed sisters by teaching, raising awareness and consciousness, verbalizing the ills of women and this society, helping to establish communes.

Older women have a wealth of information and experience to offer and would be instrumental in closing the communications gap between the generations. To be black and to tolerate this jive about discounting people over thirty is madness.

Poor women have knowledge to teach us all. Who else in this society can be more realistic about themselves, about this society and faults that lie within us than our poor women? Who else could profit and benefit from a communal setting than these sisters? We women must begin to unabashedly learn to use the word "love" for one another. We must stop the petty jealousies, the violence that we black women have so long perpetrated on one another about fighting over this man or the other. (Black men should have better sense than to encourage this kind of destructive behavior.) We must turn to ourselves and one another for strength and solace. Just think for a moment what it would be like if we got together and internalized our own 24-hour-a-day communal centers knowing our children would be safe and loved constantly. Not to mention what it would do to everyone's egos, especially the children. Women should not have to be enslaved by this society's concept of motherhood through their children. Children merely suffer a mother's resentment of discipline. All one has to do is look at the institutions to know that the time for innovation and change and creative thinking is here. We cannot sit on our behinds waiting for someone else to do it for us. We must save ourselves.

We do not have to look at ourselves as someone's personal sex objects, maids, baby sitters, domestics and the like in exchange for a man's attention. Men hold this power, along with that of the breadwinner, over our heads for these services and that's all it is—servitude. In return we torture him, and fill him with insecurities about his manhood, and literally force him to "cat" and "mess around" bringing in all sorts of conflicts. This is not the way really human people live. This is whitey's thing. And we play the game with as much proficiency as he does.

If we are going to bring about a better world, where better to begin than with ourselves? We must rid ourselves of our own hang-ups, before we can begin to talk about the rest of the world and we mean the world and nothing short of just that (let's not kid ourselves). We will be in a position soon of having to hook up with the rest of the oppressed peoples of the world who are involved in liberation just as we are, and we had better be ready to act.

All women suffer oppression, even white women, particularly poor white women, and especially Indian, Mexican, Puerto Rican, Oriental and black American women whose oppression is tripled by any of the above mentioned. This means that we can begin to talk to other women with this common factor and start building links with them and thereby strengthen and transform the revolutionary force we are now beginning to amass. This is what Dr. King was doing. We can no longer allow ourselves to be duped by the guise of racism. We are all being exploited, even the white middle class, by the few people in control of this entire world. And to keep the real issue clouded, he keeps us at one another's throats with this racism jive. Although, whites are most certainly racist, we must understand that they have been programmed to think in these patterns to divert their attention. If they are busy fighting us, then they have no time to question the policies of the war being run by this government. With the way the elections went down it is clear that whites are as powerless as the rest of us. Make no question about it, folks, this fool knows what he is doing. This man is playing the death game for money and power, not because he doesn't like us. He couldn't care less one way or the other. But think for a moment if we all got together and just walked on out. Who would fight his wars, who would run his police state, who would work his factories, who would buy his products?

We women must start this thing rolling.

Chapter Fifty-Three

What the Black Woman Thinks about Women's Lib

Toni Morrison

They were always there. Whenever you wanted to do something simple, natural and inoffensive. Like drink some water, sit down, go to the bathroom or buy a bus ticket to Charlotte, N.C. Those classifying signs that told you who you were, what to do. More than those abrupt and discourteous signs one gets used to in this country—the door that says "Push," the towel dispenser that says "Press," the traffic light that says "No"—these signs were not just arrogant, they were malevolent: "White Only," "Colored Only," or perhaps just "Colored," permanently carved into the granite over a drinking fountain. But there was one set of signs that was not malevolent; it was, in fact, rather reassuring in its accuracy and fine distinctions: the pair that said "White Ladies" and "Colored Women."

The difference between white and black females seemed to me an eminently satisfactory one. White females were *ladies*, said the sign maker, worthy of respect. And the quality that made ladyhood worthy? Softness, helplessness and modesty—which I interpreted as a willingness to let others do their labor and their thinking. Colored females, on the other hand, were *women*—unworthy of respect because they were tough, capable, independent and immodest. Now, it appears, there is a consensus that those anonymous sign makers were right all along, for there is no such thing as Ladies' Liberation. Even the word "lady" is anathema to feminists. They insist upon the "woman" label as a declaration of their rejection of all that softness, helplessness and modesty, for they see them as characteristics which served only to secure their bondage to men.

Significant as that shift in semantics is, obvious as its relationship to the black-woman concept is, it has not been followed by any immediate comradery between black and white women, nor has it precipitated any rush of black women into the various chapters of NOW. It is the *Weltanschauung* of black women that is responsible for their apparent indifference to Women's Lib, and in order to discover the nature of this view of oneself in the world, one must look very closely at the black woman herself—a difficult, inevitably doomed proposition, for if anything is true of black women, it is how consistently they have (deliberately, I suspect) defied classification.

It may not even be possible to look at those militant young girls with lids lowered in dreams of guns, those middle-class socialites with 150 pairs of shoes, those wispy girl junkies who have always been older than water, those beautiful Muslim women with their bound hair and flawless skin, those television personalities who think chic is virtue and happiness a good coiffure, those sly old women in the country with their ancient love of Jesus—and still talk about The Black Woman. It is a dangerous misconception, for it encourages lump thinking. And we are so accustomed to that in our laboratories that it seems only natural to confront all human situations, direct all human discourse, in the same way. Those who adhere to the scientific method and draw general conclusions from "representative" sampling are chagrined by the suggestion that there is any other way to arrive at truth, for they like their truth in tidy sentences that begin with "all."

In the initial confrontation with a stranger, it is never "Who are you?" but "Take me to your leader." And it is this mode of thought which has made black-white relationships in this country so hopeless. There is a horror of dealing with people one by one, each as he appears. There is safety and manageability in dealing with the leader—no matter how large or diverse the leader's constituency may be. Such generalizing may be all right for plant analysis, superb for locating carcinogens in mice, and it used to be all right as a method for dealing with schools and politics. But no one would deny that it is rapidly losing effectiveness in both those areas— precisely because it involves classifying human beings and anticipating their behavior. So it is with some trepidation that anyone should undertake to generalize about still another group. Yet something in that order is legitimate, not only because unity among minorities is a political necessity, but because, at some point, one wants to get on with the differences.

What do black women feel about Women's Lib? Distrust. It is white, therefore suspect. In spite of the fact that liberating movements in the black world have been catalysts for white feminism, too many movements and organizations have made deliberate overtures to enroll blacks and have ended up by rolling them. They don't want to be used again to help somebody gain power—a power that is carefully kept out of their hands. They look at white women and see them as the enemy—for they know that racism is not confined to white men, and that there are more white women than men in this country, and that 53 per cent of the population sustained an eloquent silence during times of greatest stress. The faces of those white women hovering behind that black girl at the Little Rock school in 1957 do not soon leave the retina of the mind.

When she was interviewed by Nikki Giovanni last May in *Essence* magazine, Ida Lewis, the former editor-in-chief of *Essence*, was asked why black women were not more involved in Women's Lib, and she replied: "The Women's Liberation Movement is basically a family quarrel between white women and white men. And on general principles, it's not good to get involved in family disputes. Outsiders always get shafted when the dust settles. On the other hand, I must support some of the goals [equal pay, child-care centers, etc.]. . . . But if we speak of a liberation movement, as a black woman I view my role from a black perspective—the role of black women is to continue the struggle in concert with black men for the liberation and self-determination of blacks. White power was not created to protect and preserve us as women. Nor can we view ourselves as simply American women. We are black women, and as such we must deal effectively in the black community."

To which Miss Giovanni sighed: "Well, I'm glad you, didn't come out of that Women's Lib or black-man bag as if they were the alternatives. . . ."

Miss Lewis: "Suppose the Lib movement succeeds. It will follow, since white power is the order of the day, that white women will be the first hired, which will still leave black men and women outside. . . ."

It is an interesting exchange, Miss Lewis expressing suspicion and identifying closely with black men, Miss Giovanni suggesting that the two are not necessarily mutually exclusive.

But there is not only the question of color, there is the question of the color of experience. Black women are not convinced that Women's Lib serves their best interest or that it can cope with the uniqueness of their experience, which is itself an alienating factor. The early image of Women's Lib was of an élitist organization made up of upper-middle-class women with the concerns of that class (the percentage of women in professional fields, etc.) and not paying much attention to the problems of most black women, which are not in getting into the labor force but in being upgraded in it, not in getting into medical school but in getting adult education, not in how to exercise freedom from the "head of the house" but in how to be head of the household.

Black women are different from white women because they view themselves differently, are viewed differently and lead a different kind of life. Describing this difference is the objective of several black women writers and scholars. But even without this newly surfacing analysis, we can gain some understanding of the black women's world by examining archetypes. The archetypes. The archetypes created by women about themselves are rare, and even those few that do exist may be the result of a female mind completely controlled by male-type thinking. No matter. The most unflattering stereotypes that male minds have concocted about black women contain, under the stupidity and the hostility, the sweet smell of truth.

Look, for example, at Geraldine and Sapphire—Geraldine, that campy character in Flip Wilson's comic repertory, and Sapphire, the wife of Kingfish in the Amos and Andy radio and TV series. Unlike Nefertiti, an archetype that black women have appropriated for themselves, Geraldine and Sapphire are the comic creations of men. Nefertiti, the romantic black queen with the enviable neck, is particularly appealing to young black women, mainly because she existed (and there are few admirable heroines in our culture), was a great beauty and is remote enough to be worshiped. There is a lot of talk about Sojourner Truth, the freed slave who preached emancipation and women's rights, but there is a desperate love for Nefertiti, simply because she was so pretty.

I suppose at bottom we are all beautiful queens, but for the moment it is perhaps just as well to remain useful women. One wonders if Nefertiti could have lasted 10 minutes in a welfare office, in a Mississippi gas station, at a Parent Association meeting or on the church congregation's Stewardess Board No. 2. And since black women have to endure, that romanticism seems a needless *cul de sac*, an opiate that appears to make life livable if not serene but eventually must separate us from reality. I maintain that black women are already O.K. O.K. with our short necks. O.K. with our callused hands O.K. with our tired feet and paper bags on the Long Island Rail Road O.K. O.K. O.K.

As for Geraldine, her particular horror lies in her essential accuracy. Like any stereotype she is a gross distortion of reality and as such highly offensive to many black women and endearing to many whites. A single set of characteristics provokes both hatred and affection. Geraldine is defensive, cunning, sexy, egocentric and transvestite. But that's not all she is. A shift in semantics and we find the accuracy: for defensive read survivalist; for cunning read clever; for sexy read a natural unembarrassed acceptance of her sexuality; for egocentric read keen awareness of individuality; for transvestite (man in woman's dress) read a masculine strength beneath the accouterments of glamour.

Geraldine is offensive to many blacks precisely because the virtues of black women are constructed in her portrait as vices. The strengths are portrayed as weaknesses— hilarious weaknesses. Yet one senses even in the laughter some awe and respect. Interestingly enough, Geraldine is absolutely faithful to one man, Killer, whom one day we may also see as caricature.

Sapphire, a name of opprobrium black men use for the nagging black wife, is also important, for in that marriage, disastrous as it was, Sapphire worked, fussed, worked and fussed, but (and this is crucial) Kingfish did whatever he pleased. Whatever. Whether he was free or irresponsible, anarchist or victim depends on your point of view. Contrary to the black-woman-as-emasculator theory, we see, even in these unflattering caricatures, the very opposite of a henpecked husband and emasculating wife—a wife who never did, and never could, manipulate her man. Which brings us to the third reason for the suspicion black women have of Women's Lib: the serious one of the relationship between black women and black men.

There are strong similarities in the way black and white men treat women, and strong similarities in the way women of both races react. But the relationship is different in a very special way.

For years in this country there was no one for black men to vent their rage on except black women. And for years black women accepted that rage—even regarded that acceptance as their unpleasant duty. But in doing so, they frequently kicked back, and they seem never to have become the "true slave" that white women see in their own history. True, the black woman did the housework, the drudgery; true, she reared the children, often alone, but she did all of that while occupying a place on the job market, a place her mate could not get or which his pride would not let him accept. And she had nothing to fall back on: not maleness, not whiteness, not ladyhood, not anything. And out of the profound desolation of her reality she may very well have invented herself.

If she was a sexual object in the eyes of men, that was their doing. Sex was one of her dimensions. It had to be just one, for life required many other things of her, and it is difficult to be regarded solely as a sex object when the burden of field and fire is on your shoulders. She could cultivate her sexuality but dared not be obsessed by it. Other people may have been obsessed by it, but the circumstances of her life did not permit her to dwell on it or survive by means of its exploitation.

So she combined being a responsible person with being a female—and as a person she felt free to confront not only the world at large (the rent man, the doctor and the rest of the marketplace) but her man as well. She fought him and nagged him—but knew that you don't fight what you don't respect. (If you don't respect your man, you manipulate him, the way some parents treat children and the way white women treat their men—if they can get away with it or if they do not acquiesce entirely). And even so, the black man was calling most of the shots—in the home or out of it. The black woman's "bad" relationships with him were often the result of his inability to deal with a competent and complete personality and her refusal to be anything less than that. The saving of the relationship lay in her unwillingness to feel free when her man was not free.

In a way black women have known something of the freedom white women are now beginning to crave. But oddly, freedom is only sweet when it is won. When it is forced, it is called responsibility. The black woman's needs shrank to the level of her responsibility; her man's expanded in proportion to the obstacles that prevented him from assuming his. White women, on the other hand, have had too little responsibility, white men too much. It's a wonder the sexes of either race even speak to each other.

As if that were not enough, there is also the growing rage, of black women over unions of black men and white women. At one time, such unions were rare enough to be amusing or tolerated. The white woman moved with the black man into a black neighborhood, and everybody tried to deal with it. Chances are the white woman who married a black man liked it that way, for she had already made some statement about her relationship with her own race by marrying him. So there were no frictions. If a white woman had a child out of wedlock by a black man, the child was deposited with the black community, or grouped with the black orphans, which is certainly one of the reasons why lists of black foundling children are so long. (Another reason is the willingness of black women to have their children instead of aborting—and to keep them, whatever the inconvenience.)

But now, with all the declarations of independence, one of the black man's ways of defining it is to broaden his spectrum of female choices, and one consequence of his new pride is the increased attraction white women feel for him. Clearly there are more and more of these unions, for there is clearly more anger about it (talking black and sleeping white is a cliché) among black women. The explanations for this anger are frequently the easy ones: there are too few eligible men, for wars continue to shoot them up; the black woman who complains is one who would be eliminated from a contest with any good-looking woman—the complaint simply reveals her inadequacy to get a man; it is a simple case of tribal sour grapes with a dash of politics thrown in.

But no one seems to have examined this anger in the light of what black women understand about themselves. These easy explanations are obviously male. They overlook the fact that the hostility comes from both popular beauties and happily married black women. There is something else in this anger, and I think it lies in the fact that black women have always considered themselves superior to white women. Not racially superior, just superior in terms of their ability to function healthily in the world.

Black women have been able to envy white women (their looks, their easy life, the attention they seem to get from their men); they could fear them (for the economic control they have had over black women's lives) and even love them (as mammies and domestic workers can); but black women have found it impossible to respect white women. I mean they never had what black men have had for white men—a feeling of awe at their accomplishments. Black women have no abiding admiration of white women as competent, complete people. Whether vying with them for the few professional slots available to women in general, or moving their dirt from one place to another, they regarded them as willful children, pretty children, mean children, ugly children, but never as real adults capable of handling the real problems of the world.

White women were ignorant of the facts of life—perhaps by choice, perhaps with the assistance of men, but ignorant anyway. They were totally dependent on marriage or male support (emotionally or economically). They confronted their sexuality with furtiveness, complete abandon or repression. Those who could afford it, gave over the management of the house and the rearing of children to others. (It is a source of amusement even now to black women to listen to feminists talk of liberation while somebody's nice black grandmother shoulders the daily responsibility of child rearing and floor mopping and the liberated one comes home to examine the housekeeping, correct it, and be entertained by the children. If Women's Lib needs those grand-mothers to thrive, it has a serious flaw.) The one great disservice black women are guilty of (albeit not by choice) is that they are the means by which white women can escape the responsibilities of womanhood and remain children all the way to the grave.

It is this view of themselves and of white women that makes the preference of a black man for a white woman quite a crawful. The black women regard his choice as an inferior one. Over and over again one hears one question from them: "But why, when they marry white women, do they pick the raggletail ones, the silly, the giddy, the stupid, the flat nobodies of the race? Why no real women?" The answer, of course, is obvious. What would such a man who preferred white women do with a real woman? And would a white woman who is looking for black exotica ever be a complete woman?

Obviously there are black and white couples who love each other as people, and marry each other that way. (I can think of two such.) But there is so often a note of apology (if the woman is black) or bravado (if the man is) in such unions, which would hardly be necessary if the union was something other than a political effort to integrate one's emotions and therefore, symbolically the world. And if all the black partner has to be is black and exotic, why not?

This feeling of superiority contributes to the reluctance of black women to embrace Women's Lib. That and the very important fact that black men are formidably oppose to their involvement in it—and for the most part the women understand their fears In the *Amsterdam News*, an editor, while deploring the conditions of black political organizations, warns his readers of the consequences "White politicians have already organized. And their organizers are even attempting to co-opt Black women into their organizations structure, which may well place Black women against Black men, that is, if the struggle for women's liberation is viewed by Black women as being above the struggle for Black liberation.

The consensus among black is that their first liberation has not been realized; unspoken is the conviction of black men that any more aggressiveness and "freedom for black women would be intolerable, not to say counter evolutionary.

There is also a contention among some black women that Women's Lib is nothing more than an attempt on the part of whites to become black without the responsibilities of being black. Certainly some of the demands of liberationist seem to rack up as our thing common-law marriage (shacking); children out of wedlock which is even fashionable not if you are a member of the Jet Set (if you are poor and black it is still a crime); families without men; right to work; sexual freedom, and an assumption that a woman is equal to a man.

Now we have come full circle: the morality of the welfare mother has become the avant-garde morality of the land. There is a good deal of irony in all of this. About a year ago in the *Village Voice* there was a very interesting exchange of letters Cecil Brown was explaining to a young black woman the "reasons" for the black man's interest in white girls a good deal about image, psychical needs and what not. The young girl answered in a rather poignant way to this effect. Yes, she said, I suppose, again, we black women have to wait, wait for the brother to get himself together—be enduring, understanding, and yes, she thought they could do it again . . . but, in the meantime, what do we tell the children?

This woman who spoke so gently in those letters of the fate of the children may soon discover that the waiting period is over. The softness, the "she knows how to treat me" (meaning she knows how to be a cooperative slave) that black men may be looking for in white women is fading from view. If Women's Lib is about breaking the habit of genuflection, if it is about controlling one's own destiny, is about female independence in economic, personal and political ways, if it is indeed about working hard to become a person, knowing that one has to work hard at becoming anything, *Man or Woman*—and if it succeeds, then we may have a nation of white Geraldines and white Sapphires, and what on earth is Kingfish gonna do then?

The winds are changing, and when they blow, new things move. The liberation movement has moved from shrieks to shape. It is focusing itself, becoming a hard-headed power base, as the National Women's Political Caucus in Washington attested last month. Representative Shirley Chisholm was radiant: "Collectively we've come together, not as a Women's Lib group, but as a women's political movement." Fannie Lou Hamer, the Mississippi civil-rights leader, was there. Beulah Sanders, chairman of New York's Citywide Coordinating Committee of Welfare Groups, was there. They see, perhaps, something real: women talking about human rights rather than sexual rights—something other than a family quarrel, and the air is shivery with possibilities.

Chapter Fifty-Four

Women in the Struggle

Third World Women's Alliance

History of the Organization

The foundation of our present organization was laid in December, 1968. Within SNCC, a black women's caucus was formed to begin to address itself to the problems that the women of SNCC encountered within the organization. Women were generally confined to secretarial and/or supportive roles and no matter what a woman's capabilities were, never seemed to be able to rise above this situation. The women in SNCC who had been meeting over a period of several months decided that the organization should be expanded beyond the confines of SNCC and that we should be drawing in women from other organizations, welfare mothers, community workers and campus radicals. An attempt was made to reach out to these women and the name of the organization was changed to the Black Women's Alliance. As of now, the organization is independent of SNCC and at the same time, SNCC has decided to retain its women's caucus.

We decided to form a black women's organization for many reasons. One was and still is the widespread myth and concept in the black community of the matriarchy. We stated that the concept of the matriarchy was myth and that it has never existed in the United States. A matriarchy denotes a society where the economic power of a group rests in the hands of the women and we all know where the economic power of this nation rests. Our position would be to expose this myth.

There was also the widespread concept that by some miracle, the oppression of slavery for the black woman was not as degrading, not as horrifying, not as barbaric as it had been for the black man. However, we state that in any society where men are not yet free, women are less free because we are further enslaved by our sex.

Now we noticed another interesting thing. And that is, that with the rise of black nationalism and the rejection of white middle class norms and values, that this rejection of whiteness—white culture, white norms and values took a different turn when it came to the black woman. That is, black men began defining the role of black women in the movement. They stated that our role was a supportive one, others stated that we must become breeders and provide an army; still others stated that we had kotex or pussy power. We opposed these concepts stating that a true revolutionary movement must enhance the status of women.

Further discussion and study began to point out to us the intimate connection between the oppression of women and the form of government which was in control. We began to see the economic basis of our oppression and we became convinced that capitalism and imperialism were our main enemies. It is economically, profitable to exploit and oppress third world women. We represent a surplus labor supply, a cheap labor supply, a free labor supply (in our homes.)

The development of an anti-imperialist ideology led us to recognize the need for Third World solidarity. Although Asian, Black, Chicana, Native American and Puerto Rican sisters have certain differences, we began to see that we were all affected by the same general oppressions. Industries employing mainly third world women are among the most exploitive in the country. Domestic workers, hospital workers, factory workers and farm laborers are prime objects of this exploitation as are the garment workers.

Stereotypes which are forced upon our peoples and which try to mold them with the acceptable white values, large use of drugs and alcoholism in our respective communities used as escapes from the daily oppression suffered by our peoples and other problems mentioned above gave us the realization that our similarities transcended our differences. We realized that we would be much more effective and unified by becoming a third world women's organization. So our group was expanded to include all third world sisters since our oppression is basically caused by the same factors and our enemy is the same. The name of the organization was changed to reflect this new awareness and composition of the group—THIRD WORLD WOMEN'S ALLIANCE.

Is a Third World Women's Group Divisive to the Liberation Struggle?

The third world woman must always be fighting against and exposing her triple exploitation in this society. A third world women's group can potentially be one of the most revolutionary forces confronting the U.S. ruling class. The third world woman consciously aware of the depth of her oppression and willingness to fight against it will never give up until all forms of racist, sexist, and economic exploitation is eliminated.

An independent third world women's organization, rather than divide the national liberation struggle would actually enhance that struggle. The rulers of this society would like to keep us thinking that the problem is only one of racism or that men are inherently the enemy, thus diverting our attention from the economic basis of our oppression. Thus our brothers who tell us not to get involved in women's liberation fail to realize that this idea, if carried out, would tend to contain rather than expand the revolutionary fervor of third world women and would harm the liberation struggle as a whole.

An independent third world women's organization gives us the opportunity to reach women who might not ordinarily be reached by male-female organizations and thus heighten the political consciousness of third world women. An independent third world women's group creates an atmosphere whereby women who are overly shy about speaking in a mixed group about "women's problems" would not have that same hesitation in an all women's group. We can train third world women for leadership roles and help them gain confidence in her own abilities and help to eliminate the concept of what is "feminine" and "masculine."

It must be understood that we are not just for civil rights for women or civil rights for third world people, but for the elimination of all forms of sexist and racist oppression-liberation for women and the third world. We understand that national liberation can come about under an atmosphere of economic equality and economic equality cannot be achieved under this system. We understand that the elimination of our oppression as women can only be achieved from a revolutionary government who understands with the help of women the need for women to be liberated.

It is the position of the Third World Women's Alliance that the struggle against racism and imperialism must be waged simultaneously with the struggle for women's liberation, and only a strong independent socialist women's group can ensure that this will come about.

Goals and Objectives

"Our purpose is to make a meaningful and lasting contribution to the Third World community by working for the elimination of the oppression and exploitation from which we suffer. We further intend to take an active part in creating a socialist society where we can live as decent human beings, free from the pressures of racism, economic exploitation, and sexual oppression."

(1) To create a sisterhood of women devoted to the task of developing solidarity among the peoples of the Third World, based on a socialist ideology of struggling for the complete elimination of any and all forms of oppression and exploitation based upon race, economic status, or sex and to use whatever means are necessary to accomplish this task.

(2) To promote unity among Third World people within the United States in matters affecting the educational, economic, social and political life of our peoples.

(3) To collect, interpret, and distribute information about the Third World, both at home and abroad, and particularly information affecting its women.

(4) To establish an education fund to be used to promote educational projects, to publish articles, and to employ such other media as is necessary to carry out such educational projects.

(5) To recreate and build solid relationships with our men, destroying myths that have been created by our oppressor to divide us from each other, and to work together to appreciate human love and respect.

Ideological Platform

We recognize the right of all people to be free. As women, we recognize that our struggle is against an imperialist sexist system that oppresses all minority peoples as well as exploiting the majority. The United States is ruled by a small ruling class clique who use the concepts of racism and chauvinism to divide, control and oppress the masses of people for economic gain and profit.

We want equal status in a society that does not exploit and murder other people and smaller nations. We will fight for a socialist system that guarantees fuil, creative, nonexploitive lives for all human beings, fully aware that we will never be free until all oppressed people are free.

Family

WHEREAS in a capitalist culture, the institution of the family has been used as an economic and psychological tool, not serving the needs of people, we declare that we will not relate to the private ownership of any person by another. We encourage and support the continued growth of communal households and the idea of the extended family. We encourage alternative forms to the patriarchal family and call for the sharing of all work (including housework and child care) by men and women.

Women must have the right to decide if and when they want to have children. There is no such thing as an illegitimate child. There should be free and SAFE family planning methods available to all women, including abortions if necessary.

There should be no forced sterilization or mandatory birth control programs which are presently used as genocide against third world woman and against other poor people.

Employment

WHEREAS third world women in a class society have been continuously exploited through their work, both in the home and on the job, we call for:

(1) Guaranteed full, equal and nonexplosive employment, controlled collectively by the workers who produce the wealth of this society.
(2) Guaranteed adequate income for all. This would entail the sharing of non-creative tasks and the maximum utilization of revolutionary technology to eliminate these tasks.
(3) An end to the racism and sexism which forces, third world women into the lowest paying service jobs and which ensures that we will be the lowest paid of all.
(4) The establishment of free day care centers available to all including facilities for pre-school and older children.

Sex Roles

WHEREAS behavior patterns based on rigid sex roles are oppressive to both men and women, role integration should be attempted. The true revolutionary should be concerned with human beings and not limit themselves to people as sex objects.

Furthermore, whether homosexuality is societal or genetic in origin, it exists in the third world community. The oppression and dehumanizing ostracism that homosexuals face must be rejected and their right to exist as dignified human beings must be defended.

Education

WHEREAS women historically have been deprived of education, or only partially educated and miseducated in those areas deemed appropriate for them by those ruling powers who benefit from this ignorance, we call for:

(1) The right to determine our own goals and ambitions.
(2) An end of sex roles regarding training and skills.
(3) Self-Knowledge—the history of third world women and their contributions to the liberation struggle, their relation to society and the knowledge of their bodies:

Services

WHEREAS the services provided for the masses of third world people have been inadequate, unavailable, or too expensive, administered in a racist, sexist manner, we demand that all services necessary to human survival—health care, housing food, clothing, transportation and education—should be free and controlled and administered by the people who use them.

Women in Our Own Right

WHEREAS we do not believe that any person is the property of any other and whereas all people must share equally in the decisions which affect them, we hereby demand:

(1) That third world women have the right to determine their own lives, not lives determined by their fathers, brothers, or husbands.
(2) That all organizations and institutions (including all so-called radical, militant and/or so-called revolutionary groups) deal with third world women in their own right as human beings and individuals, that as property of men and only valued in relationship to their association or connection with some man.

(3) That third world women be full participants on all levels of the struggle for national liberation, i.e. administrative, political and military.

Self-Defense

WHEREAS the struggle for liberation must be borne equally by all members of an oppressed people, we declare that third world women have the right and responsibility to bear arms.

Women should be fully trained and educated in the martial arts as well as in the political arena. Furthermore, we recognize that it is our duty to defend all oppressed peoples.

Chapter Fifty-Five

Notes Prompted by the National Black Feminist Organization

Rita Laporte

When I first heard about the NBFO I considered it a milestone for the feminist movement. The words of Margaret Sloan pleased me almost to the point of euphoria. Today, January 11, 1974, after reading in *oob* about the NBFO conference last November, I was less euphoric and considerably more realistic. And a welter of thoughts sped through my mind which I feel I must put on paper.

1. Analogy: White Lesbian—Black Heterosexual Woman

I believe feminists should always speak from their own experience. I leave speaking from someone else's experience to men. And I have the idealistic notion that somehow, despite the immense diversity of women's experience, a feminist sisterhood will emerge that no power on earth can destroy. My own experiential starting point is that of a 62 year old white lesbian feminist. I should add that I am an American by birth: this is important when viewing feminism as a worldwide movement, which it must be if it is to prevail. If I were an Italian feminist, say, I would spend little if any time wondering when black feminists would emerge and help to put an end to black/white racism within the women's movement.

Racism is not peculiar to white Americans. Where conditions are "right" any race or people succumbs to racism in this patriarchal world. Examples are the racism of the South Vietnamese toward their fellow countrypeople, the Neo tribesmen, and toward the offspring of Vietnamese women and black GI's. Another worldwide "ism" of particular concern to me is what I call "heterosexism," the oppression of lesbians and homosexuals by heterosexuals. I have seen the phrase "radical feminist" refer to women who, like me, know that the prototype of all oppressions—racism, classism, heterosexism, etc.—is sexism, or the oppression of women by patriarchy, i.e., men. But I am not surprised that this fundamental oppression we call sexism is not grasped by many women who are nevertheless aware that all is not well in our society. For it is the deepest and most all pervasive oppression that is the last to be sensed. Patriarchy is so complete and of such long standing—at least as long as written history—that it is easily taken for granted by its victims, women, as the way of things. By contrast, the oppression of blacks, or racism, in the US is only about 300 years old.

I tend to analogize from my oppression as a lesbian to the oppression of a heterosexual black woman as black. It is not a good analogy as a black woman cannot hide her blackness while a lesbian, with the help of lipstick and earrings, can easily pass for heterosexual. (The lipstick/earring bit often fails for us experienced old lesbians, but it works wonders in fooling heterosexuals.) I use the analogy nevertheless for want of anything better. I can know only *about* the experience of being black in this country, but never know the experience directly, while I *do* know directly the experience of being lesbian.

Before the woman's movement really took off I was a slightly active member of what was then called the homosexual movement, now Gay Liberation. It seemed to me better than nothing to work with men to combat heterosexism. But as soon as I heard of a women's movement, back in 1967, I could not sever my connections with those sexist gay males soon enough. I think I was enabled so quickly to see my true "place" to be with women's liberation and not gay liberation because I was a feminist long before I realized I was a lesbian. My earliest recollections include taking it for granted that everything boys had and did was good and everything girls were meant to be and do was rotten and sissy. (My feminism today has changed greatly from my childhood feminism, of course.) This was my particular experiences: I felt the oppression of sexism at age four and only at sixteen did I become conscious of the terrible weight of heterosexism.

The experience of most other women cannot be expected to follow mine. A heterosexual white woman can experience neither racism nor heterosexism, though she may well experience classism, economic oppression and poverty long before she becomes aware of sexism. By the same token, it seems most likely that black women would experience racism before realizing they too are victims of sexism. In like manner, many white lesbians felt heterosexism first and only later did some come to see sexism as the prior and more ruinous oppression. I remember how infuriated I was with lesbians who insisted upon serving their male counterparts in a manner exactly paralleling heterosexual women in their little women's auxiliary groups. I kept my fury to myself, that being my way, and walked as far from such lesbians as I could. To cope with this uncomfortable fury of mine I told myself that many of these lesbians would come to see the light and, anyway, who was I to question the wellsprings of their experience?

The white lesbian and the black heterosexual woman have something in common, namely, a vicious oppression that in a sense competes in the soul with the oppression of sexism. These two oppressions, heterosexism and racism, come together in the black lesbian. While she is faced with an almost impossible combination of oppressions, if she can climb out of them into realization of her humanhood, she will have the strength of tan. I look, perhaps a bit naively, to the black lesbian to bring about an end to the division between black and white heterosexual feminists. I find this division, this black/white hostility in the women's movement, infinitely depressing.

I see a damaging racism on the part of black women. While white feminists may seem too little concerned with racism in the eyes of black women, they are not anti-black in the way many black women are anti-white. Black women must realize that white women are forever barred from direct experience of being black, just as I must realize that the heterosexual woman will never directly experience the alienation felt by the lesbian. Nor will any black heterosexual woman know what it means to live one's entire life in "the closet" nor know the constant background of fear the closet lesbian must live with day in and day out in order to survive. The women's movement will never do away with all the differences with which we each begin and live out our lives, nor should it wish to. Our strength ultimately rests upon our diversity, our intimate knowledge, taken all together, of every facet of patriarchy. Our unity in sisterhood comes only from our shared oppression *as women* and only as this oppression becomes consciously realized.

2. A Man's a Man

I was immensely interested in *oob*'s report of the NBFO conference and sorry that there was no report on the workshops. I got the feeling from the report taken as a whole that the conference was made up primarily of black radical feminists plus a few vocal women wishing to coopt the organization to the issue of racism and the black man. This reminded me of the loud, not to say vicious, socialist women who, a few years back, tried to take over feminist groups for the purposes of male socialism.

I cannot resist commenting on two of the more outlandish statements by this minority group at the NBFO conference. To say that it is racist for white feminists to put all women first aroused in me not fury but amusement. I am, according to those black woman, a staunch "racist" and proud of it. It is true that I have no more interest in furthering the power and prestige of the black man than I do of the white man. In fact, I withdrew my membership in NOW because NOW seemed to spend as much time helping the black man as furthering the interests of women. I am simply unable to see any difference in a man's skin color. This is racism? I find men's oppression of man totally unjust, but that, after all, is brotherhood and for me the future of humankind lies in sisterhood. The charge that white feminists use black women as a cover for a devious lust for black men is most interesting, but not properly developed by those making the charge. It is, first of all, a reverse sexist remark and I am all for reverse sexism. There is no hint that perhaps black men are stealing away white women because, of course, the male is merely the helpless sex object of the all-powerful female—in this case the all-powerful *white* female. But I am sure this was not what was meant. It is also a heterosexist remark, or do these black women also fear that we white lesbians will steal their black sisters? There are a number of black/white lesbian couples, but who steals whom I cannot say. So I dismiss this foolishness with the comment that heterosexuals of all colors do get into some "queer" hang ups.

Before I get too angry with black women for their anti-white stance, I must remind myself that I tend to fall into what for me is the same kind of trap. That is, often unbidden and contrary to my intellectual pretensions, there rises up in me emotions clearly labelled anti-heterosexual, or what I call "anti-het dame." In our household (two women) "het-dame" is a pejorative expression. So there is no denying that emotionally I have a large reservoir of hostility directed toward heterosexual "feminists." I know there are many of these so-called feminists and they are black as well as white. But it would not be fair for me to castigate the whole women's movement because it includes the Betty Friedan anti-lesbian faction. I assume, too, that there are racist "feminists" in the women's movement, though I have not met any. This is again no reason for black women to deny the whole women's movement. A real feminist is neither racist nor heterosexist and there are many real feminists.

I decided a long time ago that Shirley Chisholm courted black votes rather than women's votes and simply wrote her off. Just as there are millions of white women locked into their roles in patriarchy and unable through fear and habit to comprehend feminism, so most black women are still locked into the same patriarchy, seeing their role as helping black men achieve what white men already have. But whatever happened to Florynce Kennedy? I had thought she was a true feminist, an inspiration to us less outspoken, because more cowardly, feminists.

3. *"Het Dames" and Fighting Close to Home*

There is a real problem lying behind my anti-het damism" and black feminists' suspicion of or hatred for the white feminist movement. I have read, in even the best of feminist writings (e.g., Jane Alpert and Mary Daly), that the stigma of lesbianism will automatically disappear in sisterhood. I do not for one minute believe this. How many times (thousands?) have I read the words "women" or "all women" seen what is clearly meant is "heterosexual women"? Is this any different from reading, in books by male authors, the words "men" and "mankind" that mean "males" and "malekind"? Women are invisible to and ignored by men; lesbians are invisible to and ignored by "het dames." It is so deeply rooted in the minds of heterosexual women that all real women have a basic, ineradicable need for one or more men. If they think of us lesbians at all, it is as a tiny minority of warped creatures of no basic significance. On the contrary, we are not only a large minority but a growing one as more and more women discover as part of consciousness raising that they are, after all, lesbians "sisterhood" based upon the a priori assumption that all women need men to be made whole will be a "sisterhood" doomed to go the way of the first women's movement. It is a "sisterhood" mired in the notions of femininity and anxious to disown those of us who find men unnecessary to any deep emotional and sexual relationship. Were it not for the threat men bore to the existence of humanity, I for one is inclined to look upon them merely as sperm plants. I have no faith in a "sisterhood" fluid to men.

By analogy, I question whether racism will automatically disappear in sisterhood. Black feminists must feel this way too. A feminism whites only would, as a feminism of heterosexuals only, lead at best to a slight amelioration of our present slave status, with eventual collapse of the women's movement.

What it comes down to, in my view, is that true feminists must see sexism, or patriarchy, as the fundamental evil of human society. Our ultimate goal is its replacement with a new and higher *human* consciousness. But tactics is another matter altogether. The fight must be carried on at every level and in every segment of society. Black women are hardly able or qualified to carry feminism into Oriental societies, academic women are not able or qualified to fight the battles of union women, domestic workers cannot remove sexism from the financial and banking world, etc., etc. I am angered by the futility of one group of women, say working women, maligning, say, academic women for not paying attention to the needs of working women. Sexism is rampant on our campuses and what women are better qualified to combat it than those who work there? And are not working women those best qualified to tackle the sexism of their union and/or their employers? This is not to say that one group cannot help another, but the expertise of the many specific groups of women will be lost if each feminist feels she must fight furthest from home, so to speak. I wonder why, on the contrary, women do not see this matter of special interest groups in the women's movement the other way around. What is unique to women's liberation as opposed to other liberation movements is that women are totally infiltrated into patriarchy, if only by marriage. And here, however reluctantly, I must admit that the "het dame" is indispensable to the women's movement. Similarly, black feminism is tied to white feminism. Keeping our favorite prejudices at bay may not be easy, especially for us over-50 women, but it is entirely possible. The birth of the NBFO *is* a milestone for all feminists and I shall enjoy my realistic euphoria.

Chapter Fifty-Six

On Women as a Colonized People

Robin Morgan

As a radical feminist, I make an analogy between women and colonized peoples, a parallel which works well—inevitably, even—if one dares to examine it carefully, overcoming a sense of shock or our women's curse of guilt.

Frantz Fanon and Albert Memmi, as sexist as other men but considerable authorities on the process of colonization and its effects, wrote of certain basic characteristics by which that process could always be identified. Primary among these were the following: The oppressed are robbed of their culture, history, pride, and roots—all most concretely expressed in the conquest of their *land* itself. They are forced (by a system of punishment and reward) to adopt the oppressor's standards, values, and identification. In due course, they become alienated from their own values, their own land—which is of course being mined by the oppressor for its natural resources. They are euphemistically permitted (forced) to work the land, but since they do not benefit from or have power over what it produces, they come to feel oppressed by *it*. Thus, the alienation from their own territory serves to mystify that territory, and the enforced identification with their colonizing masters provokes eventual contempt both for themselves and their land. It follows, of course, that the first goal of a colonized people is to *reclaim their own land*.

Women are a colonized people. Our history, values, and *cross-cultural culture* have been taken from us—a gynocidal attempt manifest most arrestingly in the patriarchy's seizure of our basic and precious "land": our own bodies.

Our bodies have been taken from us, mined for their natural resources (sex and children), and deliberately mystified. Five thousand years of Judeo-Christian tradition, virulent in its misogyny, have helped enforce the attitude that women are "unclean." Androcentric medical science, like other professional industries in the service of the patriarchal colonizer, has researched better and more efficient means of *mining* our natural resources, with (literally) bloody little concern for the true health, comfort, nurturance, or even survival of those resources.[1] This should hardly surprise us; our ignorance about our own primary terrain—our bodies—is in the self-interest of the patriarchy.

We must begin, as women, to reclaim our land, and the most concrete place to begin is with our own flesh. Self-and-sister-education is a first step, since all that fostered ignorance and self-contempt dissolve before the intellectual and emotional knowledge that our women's bodies are constructed with great beauty, craft, cleanliness, yes, holiness. Identification with the colonizer's standards melts before the revelations dawning on a woman who clasps a speculum in one hand and a mirror in the other. She is demystifying her own body for herself, and she will never again be quite so alienated from it.

From education we gain higher expectations, and from there we move through anger and into the will for self-determination, to seizing power over our own lives, to reclaiming the products of our labor (our own sexual definition, and our own children), and, ultimately, to transforming the quality of life itself in society, as a whole—into something new, compassionate, and truly sane.

This is why, as radical feminists, we believe that the Women's Revolution is potentially the most sensible hope for change in history. And this is why the speculum may well be mightier than the sword.

NOTE

1. Adrienne Rich has assembled chilling documentation about this subject, with particular emphasis on medical industrialization of childbirth, in her important work *Of Woman Born, Motherhood as Experience and Institution,* Norton, New York, 1976.

Chapter Fifty-Seven

International Feminism
A Call for Support of the Three Marias

Robin Morgan

I want to welcome you to this evening of dramatic readings from the forbidden texts of the Three Marias of Portugal. As part of the international feminist protest action attendant on the case—which I will explain more fully in a moment—this one-time performance has been put together by women, including, of course, the three actresses who will read from the texts and the feminist musicians who will accompany that reading.

Some background on why we are here seems in order, for although the whole world appears to know about the censoring of Solzhenitsyn, shockingly but not surprisingly few people are aware of, or concerned about, the repression of the work of three *women*.

In April of 1972, a book entitled *New Portuguese Letters* was published in Portugal. Its authors were: Maria Isabel Barreño (who previously had written two novels about the problems of being female in a patriarchal world), Maria Teresa Horta (who has written nine books of poetry and one novel—and who has been persecuted by censorship before, regarding one of her books of poetry), and Maria Velho Da Costa (who also has written a book of short stories and a novel). All three women work. All three women have children. All three women are feminists. All three women are published writers. And all three women are therefore regarded as dangerous to the patriarchal state of Portugal.

Their collectively written book explores themes such as the loneliness and isolation of women, the exploitation of our sexuality and the denial of our own fulfillment as whole human beings. It speaks of the suffering caused by rape, prison, sadistic abortions; it explores our political and economic condition; it talks of religion and the cloister, of adultery and madness and suicide. It is not a timid work—it is a strong and womanly book.[1]

Two-thirds of all copies in the first printing sold out within a few days of the publication. By May 1 of that same year the remaining one-third had been seized by the Portuguese political police. One month later to the day, the Portuguese Committee of Censorship requested that the authors be sued. This was quite a departure, since the seizure of books is frequent in Portugal but suits are rare. Seven or eight years ago there were two government suits over literary works, but the defendants were not required to pay bail. The Three Marias, however, were arrested, and bail was subsequently set at approximately six hundred dollars for each women. The actual charge accuses the authors of having committed "an outrage to public morals and good customs."

Meanwhile the book is being sold—but only in a clandestine manner. The publisher himself, using the seizure as a reason for his action, paid the authors only one-third of what had been promised them in their contracts—thus each of the three has received only a little more than one hundred dollars for her work.

In May of 1973, a copy of *New Portuguese Letters* reached some feminists in Paris, almost by accident. These sisters took the issue to the world feminist community, with the result that there have been protest demonstrations before Portuguese embassies and consulates in major cities all over the world, including large and militant demonstrations in London, Paris, and New York. Feminists have readied a statement presenting the case to the Human Rights Commission of the United Nations. Portuguese intellectuals have signed petitions demanding that the charge be lifted. These and other activities germinated by the international feminist community have functioned so far as what could be called "holding actions"—the Portuguese government has responded to the pressure by delaying sentencing of the Three Marias, hoping, no doubt, that we would all go away and the case would become yesterday's news, in which circumstance the three women could be sent to prison for a minimum of six months to two years on the charge of "outrage to the public morality" alone. One of the three, Maria Teresa Horta, is tubercular. We do not know if she has medical care. But we do know that it is vital to continue pressure on the government, by demonstrations, by information about and press coverage of the case, and by events such as this one tonight. This Thursday, January 31, 1974, is the date set for the final sentencing of the Three Marias in Lisbon.

Those are the simple facts of the case, the superficial facts, one might say. Because the issues at stake here go much deeper than a mere recitation of those facts may imply.

It would be possible, for example, to see the case merely as another in a deplorable series of repressive acts against artists by governments all over the world, each in their turn. It might be especially tempting for some to come away with an analysis that pointed an accusing finger at the reactionary politics of the Portuguese government, that same government which has on its hands the blood of Angola. Yet both such interpretations, while valid in part, stop short of the issue itself—the heart of the matter.

Because the Three Marias are not solely artists—they are *women* artists. And they are not solely free-speaking persons living under a reactionary political regime—they are free-speaking *women* living under a reactionary political regime. They are feminist artists writing passionately on the condition of women. And their persecutors, coincidentally, are all men.

So we must look at these three women in their and our historical context—which is larger and older than Portugal and 1974. Radical feminists have said for some time now that until the issue of the oppression of women is dealt with, all

revolutions will continue to be coups d'état by men, that feminism with all its re-
verberations is, in fact, the central issue facing the human species today. One could
use the metaphor of a tree—the Tree of Ignorance, if you will—and note that for
a long time progressive peoples have been hacking away at various evils represented
by its branches: one branch, war; one branch, racism; one, ecological disaster; one,
greed; one, competition; one, repression of the young and callousness toward the
old, etc. Well, the word radical does imply "going to the root" after all, and if one
wishes to do that and not merely hack away at branches that continually grow back
then one must eventually deal with the oldest oppression on the face of the earth,
the primary contradiction which entails the subjugation of half the species by the
other half. One must deal with the largest oppressed group on the planet—the
majority of humans not only in the United States but in the world. One must deal
with women—and with sexism, male supremacy, and what de Beauvoir called the
initial "alienizing act"—for once *women* could be viewed as "the Other" then it
was a simple, inevitable, and tragic process to see more "Others"—people of a
different height or weight or skin color or language or age. So the Tree of Ignorance
has grown.

We as feminists have begun to un-recognize those male-defined and patriarchally
imposed false barriers. National boundaries, for one. Women didn't create them; it
has been a big boys' game to carve out the earth and claim "this country is mine,
that yours"—and it is absurd. Which is why there is a growing international feminist
community, from Melbourne to Montana, from Senegal to Switzerland, from main-
land China to Cherbourg. And which is why we are here tonight, one part of that
whole.

The Three Marias stand in a long and honorable tradition of women—women
artists in this case—who have been repressed, persecuted, prosecuted, or killed,
overtly or covertly, for daring to speak our truths. This process is how the history of
women, like that of other oppressed peoples, has been hidden, and how we have
been robbed of our culture. It isn't new, but it *is* necessary—how else can the
oppressor continue to ask his tedious question "But then where are your great
women?" Fill in the blank. First the evidence must be destroyed or at least distorted;
only then may the inquiry be put.

So it was with Anne Hutchinson, who dared speak out against the theology of her
day in Puritan New England, who was silenced, ostracized, exiled. So it was with
George Sand, who was ridiculed and reviled, and her contemporary George Eliot—
both great writers forced to use male pen names to be published—both considered
female aberrants, and treated accordingly by the male literary establishments of their
time. Male pen names—the enforced masquerading as men in order to be taken
seriously as artists at all—were also used of necessity by the genius Brontë sisters,
one of whom, Emily, was in effect killed by the world's attitude toward her work.
The other, Charlotte, literally vomited to death during pregnancy. So it was with
Elizabeth Barrett (let's begin using the name she wrote under, shall we, even if it was
her father's; we needn't compound the indignity and any more by adding her
husband's for identification): Elizabeth Barrett, who was an articulate feminist and
radical writer and a poet whose effect on Emily Dickinson was the one influence that

later writer acknowledged; Elizabeth Barrett, who read Mary Wollstonecraft when she was fourteen—and whose work has been so trivialized by male literary historians that her image is now one of the stereotyped "poetess" reclining in lavender and lace on her sofa, writing love poems to her more famous husband. Made more famous by whom, we might ask.

So it has been all along. So it was with Akhmatova, who saw the suffering of Russian women, wrote of it, and then saw the grim prison-wall reply of Russian men. So it was with Anna Wickham, dead of despair by her own hand, a hand that had written about the female condition. So it was with Virginia Woolf, for whom the writing of these truths became too much to endure—another suicide. Or with Charlotte Mew, driven by patriarchal literary indifference to suicide. *Another* suicide. I call it murder, you see. As I call the deaths of great women artists such as Bessie Smith and Billie Holiday—poets both—murder. As I call the death of Sylvia Plath, revered and reviled and analyzed over and over in the desperate attempt to defuse that electric voice—I call it murder.

And these are only a few such examples. Most of the above wrote in English. And most even squeaked through to the extent that we know they existed. There have been other such women, singing their genius onto the page (when they were allowed to learn how to read and write, that is) or singing it onto the empty air, in every language humans are capable of. What of the lost ones—the creators who died never having been permitted to solidify their art in something lasting at all? Is that censorship? What of those who did create art but were refused publication or gallery showings or performance of their work—because they were women and to give them such credence even if (or especially if) they deserved it would be to "outrage public morals"? What of those who scribbled their insights and visions on diary leaves, letters, recipe books, in between housework and child care and husband-nurturing? What are the names of these silenced ones? Who can compute the loss to human society of their voices, their knowledge, their creative passion?

The censor has used differing means. He has quite a repertoire. The repression has ranged from blatant (death, exile, imprisonment) to subtle (male pen names, ridicule, distortion). But such categorization and comparison seem obscene when suffering is the end result. What *are* "public morals and good customs"? Does patriarchally defined public morality include the rationalization of everything from Vietnam to Watergate, from pollution of life-sustaining natural resources to the colonization and murder of the Angolans? And what are "good customs"? Rape? Enforced sterilization or enforced child-bearing? "Proper" sexual conduct for women—as defined by men? Economic deprivation, educational discrimination, emotional repression, psychological channeling, artistic censorship, political invisibility, spiritual suffocation? "Good customs" all—for women. Honored traditions all—originated by men.

Today, such morality and such customs are being challenged, not only by individual women of courage and genius forced to fight alone, without support, accompanied only by their despair. Today we speak in all languages. We see past the patriarchal barriers of age, race, class, economic distinction, and national boundaries. We will not be ignored. We will not be patronized. We will not accept the institutions which have tried to destroy us, whether the institution be one of a certain type of sexuality, or a certain mode of motherhood, or a certain standard of literary excellence which either corrupts us or indulges us, when it notices us at all.

Today Maria Isabel Barreño, Maria Teresa Horta, and Maria Velho Da Costa are not alone. They are three specific voices singing in a great and varied chorus which is determined, whatever its differences, to speak the unspeakable, to create our song even out of our singing, to approach the universe within and without us on terms which have never been conceived, let alone allowed.

Join us. You have fingers—write or wire or telephone the Portuguese Embassy, the Portuguese Consulate, the Portuguese Mission to the United Nations, the Portuguese Airlines and other businesses in this city. You have feet—visit these places, picket them, pressure them. You have tongues—speak of these three women, tell their/our story. Tell of their bravery, their risk. Tell of the extra punishment inherent in long prison sentences for women who must think about their children on the outside. You have minds—act.

Most of all, open yourselves to what you as women are feeling, to what you as men are being told—more clearly now than at any other time in history. The survival of sentient life on this planet depends upon it.

Nor will we be stopped this time. There are too many of us. Furthermore, if speaking out was made impossible for us before, silence is impossible now.

Listen, then, to the inexhaustible, uncontainable words of the Three Marias. Different voices speak them, but they sing for all of us.

NOTE

1. I regret to say that when the book was published in the United States, the English translation seemed to me somewhat less inspiring than the selections done by Gilda Grillo and Louise Bernikow for this evening's performance.

H. Class

Chapter Fifty-Eight

On Class Structure within the Women's Movement

Barbara Mehrhof

What has become known as the "equality issue" in the women's movement is viewed by many radical feminists as one of the most burning questions of our movement. That there is unequal participation among movement members is undeniable; in addition, a "star system" has developed whereby certain individuals have gained recognition as "leaders" or spokesmen for the movement. They have emerged both within the context of superficially structureless groups like Redstockings, as well as in organizations such as NOW whose hierarchical framework ensures that power will be concentrated in the hands of a few. Usually these are the women who talk the loudest, the longest, and the most often, but whatever their style the consequence is the same: they are in a position to unduly influence policy and to use the movement and other women for their own purposes. In the past this phenomenon has generally been ignored, denied, or put down. The result is that the problem is not discussed and the reasons for this situation go unexamined.

In the face of this kind of dismissal, some of us in the movement have nevertheless sought to understand the reasons for the inequities that exist and to further explore our feelings that we are being taken advantage of by other women. Our starting point in this examination has been the failure of the movement to broaden its class base with the result that it is still composed predominantly of middle and upper-middle-class women with only a sprinkling of those of us from a lower-middle-class or working-class background. We have come to the conclusion that the existing inequality has its basis, to a great extent, in class. Therefore, in order to provide a better understanding of this issue, I will first describe the two basic class systems operating in society as they affect women, and then offer the proposition that the women's movement is in the process of establishing a tertiary class system, a system under which the liberation of women becomes impossible.

The Primary Class System

Males originated class and have fostered terrible inequities in society through the oppression of one group by another; their justifications for these inequalities began when they first declassed women out of humanity. Thus, "humanity" or "society" in effect refers only to those individuals making up the male class—all men. Society consists of an opposition of a group or groups of men to another group or groups of men. The class of men is self-defining and well organized vis à vis its counterclass—the class of women.

The class of women is a class defined by the class of men. Both classes together constitute all those individuals called human beings; since, in addition, this political division is the basic one in all societies, it is the *primary class system*. Through it each individual receives a primary class identification and is a member of one class or the other.

These two classes do not face each other on an equal footing nor are women in fact organized into a unit which can stand face to face with the correlative unit. In this division the male class is the oppressor, powerful class; the female class is the oppressed, powerless class. The original declassment of women serves as a model for all other class systems and the construction of levels of power among the males themselves.

The Secondary Class System

The class of men is composed of a ranking of individuals within the class itself. That is, all men are not equal and a hierarchy exists. Having once thrown women out of humanity, males then went about setting up divisions within their own ranks. Though each male in the hierarchy is an embodiment of the masculine role, and thus in a position to oppress women, all males do not have the same opportunity to oppress each other. This hierarchy of males we shall call the *secondary class system*.

Money and power are the major determinants of a particular male's position in the hierarchy of his class. Unlike the primary class identification in which all men stand united against women, the hierarchy is a place where men are poised one against the other in competition, or allied in groups against other groups. In this stratification all males do not always display a "class-consciousness," so that frequently one group, such as those on the top of the heap, are united against those on the bottom, whereas the lower-ranking men might be disorganized and uncertain of their real class interests.

The economic structure of the society is the basic instrument for distributing the money and the power among those individuals who make up the class. The males at the top of this hierarchy have the resources and the power to oppress all the females, as well as most of the other males. The power of these upper-class men is derived from their position in the hierarchy, education, money, access to knowledge, and an awareness of the workings and operations of the society. They have an individualistic mentality and also display the psychological benefits of self-confidence and feelings of superiority. Like all members of their class, they assume that men are the masters of women because men are better (superior) than women; but they are also superior, they think, to most of the other males. Their attitudes are based on the most precious value of the male value system—the idea that some people are just naturally better than others. It is the underlying premise implicit in the male/female contradiction, and it is used to rationalize all other class systems.

The Female Hierarchy

As a class defined by men, women have little or no comprehension of themselves as a class and little "class-consciousness" within the primary class system. A hierarchy of females such as could be juxtaposed next to that described as existing among the males is hardly possible. Instead, their ranking within their class is entirely dependent upon where they are distributed among the males through marriage and the family in the economic rankings of the male class. In these arrangements women make up a part of the property these economic groups possess and which is a medium of exchange among them. Since women are dispersed among the entire male class, they will of necessity be attached to men along all the levels of the hierarchy. But as they are not men, they never enter into the secondary class structure; on the contrary, women form a part of the property to be distributed among the individuals who comprise the secondary system. What will happen is that women will reflect the position and power of the men, rather than becoming occupants of those positions or the possessors of that power. Thus, the female hierarchy is not a power source unto itself, although distribution among all levels of males will have its effect upon women too, so that there will also be divisions among the females, a ranking order which is the product of the construction of classes among the males themselves.

Lacking primary class consciousness, and more attached to particular males than they are to other women since their dispersal achieves their isolation from one another, women are in danger of losing sight of the real nature of their class interest, of recognizing the fact that their situation will always remain defined by their minor position in the primary class structure.

Class and the Women's Movement

The ranking of women in a hierarchy achieves significance *only* when women organize among themselves. When women separate off from men in a movement of their own and agitate specifically for "women's rights," the implication is clear that they consider their problems have something to do with the fact that they are women; but whereas in time they may become aware of themselves as a class vis à vis men, they tend to ignore the effects of their distribution in the secondary class structure— that is, what types of males they've been attached to, the ones on the top or the ones on the bottom of the male hierarchy. A situation arises in which all women are glad just to be getting together with other women. The idea emerges that we are all powerless and that the way in which men arrange themselves within their own class has nothing to do with the structure women are building among themselves.

In assuming this position, women in the movement are refusing to examine a basic contradiction in our situation: whereas in society *all* women are reduced to a subordinate, minor position in the male/female class system, they are at the same time dispersed among males representing very different levels of power within the male hierarchy. Once women get together on their own without men, this contradiction in their situation will appear for the first time when the women of the upper-class males will move from a minor position in relation to men to a major position in relation to other women. This puts them into a position to oppress other women since the very fact that women are getting together is generating power and the women of the upper classes have been there to grab it so far. Thus, the women's movement has become the occasion whereby these class antagonisms will make themselves known, class conflicts which have their origin in the secondary class system.

Who are these women who have risen to the top of the women's movement and how are they able to maintain a leadership position? In general, they come from either the middle or the upper classes. As women belonging to the men of these classes they are often equipped with many of the same advantages and attitudes as the males—educational privileges, self-confidence (if not toward men, at least toward other women), feelings of superiority toward the masses, etc.—which would be put to use in the exercise of leadership and power if they were men and belonged to the male class. Equally important is the fact that the women of these classes have had the opportunity to observe at close range the male wielding his power so that, given the opportunity, they are able to imitate him to a remarkable degree. Like him, they often accuse the grumblers at the bottom of suffering from personality or psychological disorders and have even alleged that restive women in the movement are trying to castrate them.

Women of the upper classes, in addition to being better educated than lower-class women, usually have greater verbal ability and the resulting capacity to be able to come into a group and take over. Unequal participation among members of the movement is either accepted or overlooked by them. Some have money, some have connections; unfortunately, many still retain the hope of making a good life for themselves even if there is never a feminist revolution. The danger exists in that many of them feel they have an escape hatch—they can still be great writers or painters—or even worse, they see the movement as a place to perfect their tools of expression (opportunism) and become more concerned about being famous than with making a revolution. They use the movement not to destroy the male class, but to "make it" in his world. But that world is really the distribution of power within the male hierarchy. Women cut themselves off from their class when they try to get a piece of the power that is reserved only for men, when they aim for an equalized pecking order. What they have failed to realize is that there is no place for them in the secondary class system—as token women they are constantly tested and the final test will be the betrayal of women.

Internalizing male values, since they so often deeply respect the male, they assume like him that some people are just naturally better and more talented than others. This idea is very prevalent in the women's movement and makes impossible any pretense at equality. To say in the women's movement that some people are better than others, to feel that some just naturally have leadership qualities, is to be thinking and acting on the basis of the male value system. It is to act toward other women—women with whom you supposedly identify your interests—as men do.

When we do not organize ourselves in the women's movement on the basis of equality, the female hierarchy which has its origins in the secondary class system is ossified in the movement itself, serving as it does the form along which women consciously structure themselves. In doing this, we not only reinforce the divisions within the female class, but take part in the creation of a viable female hierarchy of power. Once the female hierarchy becomes a source of power itself, it can be said to constitute a tertiary class system, and it puts some women in a position to oppress other women. This has in fact already happened in the women's movement. Here women are coming into the movement because they feel oppressed, and yet they're put down, only this time not by men but by other women. This will continue to happen unless the women's movement has the courage to examine the class issue.

The chances that this tertiary class system based on inequality among women will be capable of constituting a solid unit in opposition to the male class is extremely unlikely. The temptation for middle-class and upper-middle-class women not to move out will be too great. The reason for this is that middle and upper-class women are not really willing to throw in their lot with all women. For in not helping to root out the existing inequities among us, they sanction further exploitation of other women and give renewed vigor to the underlying assumptions of the primary class system.

What the women's movement has to do is to develop a self-defined class of women based on equality among all. If we keep within our class the hierarchical structure which results from our displacement among men, our struggles will be doomed to failure. It is within our power to change the nature of the female class itself and to destroy the premises on which our class was set up in the first place. For if we do not change it, we cannot be expected to attract the great masses of women. We cannot be unified. We will not move out. To confront men we must stand in relation to them as an independent and autonomous grouping of human beings. Organized on the basis of equality, we will offer the alternative for the future society.

Chapter Fifty-Nine

Female Liberation as the Basis for Social Revolution

Roxanne Dunbar

I

Women form the oldest and largest continually oppressed group in the family of humankind, their subjugation dating from the downfall of primitive communal society and the rise of private property.

This, the introduction to the SDS Resolution on Women's Liberation, was the theme of the policy question on women discussed at the National Conference in December 1968. The resolution covers several important areas of Female Liberation, particularly "male supremacy." Yet there is nothing in the resolution which would suggest what many of us mean by Female Liberation. The resolution calls for "free speech" within SDS. The masculine structure of SDS is built-in, and not much will change if a few specially selected women are allowed to speak pedantically enough to share some power with the big guys, and exert power in a new territory of their own—women.

Marriage or living arrangements, an overwhelmingly important and absorbing matter in the day to day lives of the majority of people, including SDS organizers, was simply not discussed. But the programmed subservience of women in the domestic situation assures continued masculine domination in public. Most SDS people come from 'privileged' families, and though they question many of the values of their heritage, they do not seem to question the economic and psychological basis of the middle class—the nuclear family and the private possession of children. In fact, by jazzing it up a bit with drugs, colors, music, approved affairs, even a few orgies (group "love"), intimate meetings, they have managed to make the coupling and breeding tradition of the bourgeoisie appear more attractive than ever before. But the frills do not diminish the oppressive nature of the institution for the female, and especially the children (male and female).

Upon what basis do New Left Americans and Europeans analyze (or refuse to analyze) the family? Surely not Marx and Engels. In 1846, they wrote: "The first division of labor is that between man and woman for the propagation of children." Later Engels wrote: "The first opposition that appears in history coincides with the development of the antagonism between man and women in monogamous marriage, and the first class oppression coincides with that of the female sex by the male' (p. 5).[1]

The materialist conception of history is an analysis of the production and reproduction of the immediate essentials of life—the production of the means of existence, and the production of human beings themselves—the propagation of the species. Contemporary radicals tend to totally ignore the latter, and emphasize the former. In strategy, Marx and Engels also downgraded the reproductive faculties, since they thought that the family had practically been demolished among the working class in the nineteenth century. One could, they thought, deal with the two functions separately, since they believed that socialism would finally annihilate the family (though not monogamy). It would seem that the rationale was in error then because the family has not been destroyed automatically through revolution, nor has capitalism destroyed the proletariat's sense of family. Certainly the rationale is in error now in America when the family (including its degeneration, divorce) has attained a whole new lease on life, even among the working class.

It is no accident, Engels said, that the enslavement of the woman coincides with the rise of private property; in fact, woman (her labor and her product) was (and still is psychologically) the most valuable property that a man could possess. (Today every pop song, every movie, every TV show, every personal statement from a man—including working class and radical men—attest to that fact.) If women were not so valued as property, or as a possession (psychological and possible in societies after a socialist revolution), they would not be so "happy" in their situations. Slaves are always "happy" (hopeless).

"The modern individual family is founded on the open or concealed domestic slavery of the wife, and modern society is a mass composed of these individual families as its molecules." (Engels, p. 65) This precise statement suggests that to attempt to reform or transform the institution would be analogous to the attempts made to reform the institution of Slavery in the United States (see southern almanacs and sociologists) or to transform the institution into peonage. Just like the African slaves, when a woman is declared legally free, her bondage is unbroken. Engels pointed out that 'in the majority of cases today, the husband is obliged to earn a living and support his family, and that in itself gives him a position of supremacy without any need for special legal titles and privileges. *Within the family, he is the bourgeois and the wife represents the proletariat*' (pp. 65–66).

This is still the case, since the working woman is considered a temporary worker, a surplus labor force within a structure which idealizes the little wife and mother in the home with her brood.

Engels did not suggest that women or anyone else can be free from oppression within the capitalist system, but he certainly did not say that battles should be postponed, or that only working class men's women should be "organized." Quite the contrary. Engels saw the middle class man's woman as a domestic slave, not a middle class person. It is unfortunate that radicals are so programmed by the system's propaganda that they believe there is such a person as a "middle class woman."

As with the strategy for building revolutionary consciousness among the proletariat, Marx and Engels saw the necessity for a democratic republic to provide a 'clear field' on which the ultimate battles could be fought. They saw that legal equality of rights had to exist before the peculiar character of the supremacy of the husband over the wife could be revealed. "Then it will be plain that the first condition for the liberation of the wife is to bring the whole female sex back into public industry and that this in turn demands the abolition of the monogamous family as the economic unit of the society." (p. 66)

Even the present liberal demands of NOW (National Organization of Women) are not contradictory to our communist thesis, since those women are advancing the legal equality of women so that we have a clear field for the battles we are fighting, and such rights give women breathing space. It is disheartening to hear radicals condemning such reform activity as counterrevolutionary. Not everyone has to involve herself in such activities, but we should be glad that someone is doing it, and not condemn them for their labors which are ultimately necessary for our own fight, into which we hope to bring the women of NOW, when they see the reality of the system.

We now operate within the democratic republic (capitalist government) which Marx and Engels rightly saw as necessary to the revolutionary process in an industrial economy. Women will soon have nominal equal rights, and perhaps will even gain rights to their own bodies through legalized abortion. These legal rights do not mean much in reality for women (or for anyone), and such rights are never really won, but given by the system to preserve itself, as it needs to absorb pressures. But equal rights give women confidence to fight, and they expose the nature of the vicious prejudice against women at every level, just as analogous demands on the part of Blacks have revealed the character of racism.

Engels pointed out that in his time working class men enjoyed only the psychological and not the economic advantages of the oppression of women, but apparently Engels underestimated the tenacity with which these little men tend to hold on to their need for the servility of others. The working class white man in America enjoys the psychological and economic aspects of two servile castes—women and Blacks—which makes the working class white man doubly arrogant and filled with a false sense of power. In both cases, the worker compensates for his own wretched condition by venting his resentment on his competitors for jobs and the lower echelons of power (the family mainly).

In Engels' time, industry was taking the proletariat wife out of the home, and putting her on the labor market, then making her the breadwinner. In this way, the proletariat escaped the monogamous family through the 'freedom' of the working class woman to support herself and her children. Today in the United States, this is the case among the very poor, mostly immigrant and Black people. Generally the system, because of cybernation, has put the woman back in the home, making that situation at any rate the ideal, in order to get her off the labor market.

The counterrevolutionary freedom of the working class man in America is that he, too, can own a wife, kids, and a house just like a good bourgeois. The psychological rewards are enormous, even if the economic and social status is illusory. As a compensation for lost bargaining power (leaving public industry), women ("the happy housewife") have been given "buying power." Of course, we are educated (brainwashed) to buy certain things—never our freedom. Women have also been given the right to engage in debilitating activities, formerly allowed only to men and

courtesans—drinking, smoking, drug-use, sexual promiscuity, all of which profits a
capitalist economy based on consumerism at home. The crass Virginia Slims slogan
capsulizes the new "freedom": "You've come along way, baby; now you have your
own cigarette."

There is much confusion about the "right" of a man to support, protect, and
defend (i.e., possess) a family. This notion has led the Black movement onto a path,
already tred by the White working class. That is, among the demands of Black
radicals is the right to "family." The system agrees. Every major magazine and
television special pronounces the virtues of family, and the tragedy of the Black
man's inability to get one in his economic situation. And though Black radicals
oppose Moynihan and his Report, they agree with his thesis: The Plight of the Negro
Man. Get your manhood; get a Black woman, put her in a house, breed her, then
you will be a man, just like the White man. And Kathleen Cleaver tells the San
Francisco Chronicle Society reporter that she wants nothing more than a private life
as mother and housewife: that she is only fighting to help her man out, so he can be
a good father and breadwinner. This nonsense will surely change as poor Black
women protest their falling from 0 to -10 on the scale of relative freedom to even
function in this sick society. Indeed poor Black women will have to emerge before
the movement will move toward real liberation. For truly the last shall be first, and
the first shall be last in the revolutionary effort.

II

Now we can begin to think the unthinkable, ask questions never before posed. For
instance: Why should the main organ for revolution be a masculine organ within
which women's liberation is a faction (caucus)? The existence of power is always the
rationale for continued power. When we insist on the primary importance of female
liberation, we do not mean that men are excluded (really wishful thinking on the
part of radical men), or that men are to become better domestic slaves. Nor do we
hold that our oppression is greater than others; we simply say it is basic to all other
struggles. The origin of caste (therefore class) was the subjugation of the female sex.
The struggle against the basis of oppression is at a higher stage of revolution than
the archaic strategy of the present radical analysis. In a time when nearly every
American male is economically capable of possessing a household slave or a pretty
toy, we consider women to be the proletariat.

Black people identify as a colony with colonized people all over the world. Spanish
Americans and Indians identify similarly. Unless the men of those groups insist on
sharing the privileges of the White man—possession of a woman and children—
they might be able to establish organs for national liberation as a united front (men
and women) with a conscious basis of female liberation.

The case is very different for the privileged white man. White male radicals are
the inheritors of power, the golden boys of the society, the cream of the crop. They
must prove their ability to lead to the fathers. They seem to think they are free of all

that. Yes, indeed, Black people, Chicanos, women, workers need to be liberated in the revolutionary struggle, which White men will lead. The White man's role is the White Man's Burden—updated. Protect little brown people and women. But by what perogative? What makes these men think they are equipped to deal with anyone's liberation when they have not even begun to analyze their own consciousness?

I do not find men all that oppressed by this society, though I hear men and women all the time argue that men are just as oppressed. I can not see it; they do not seem to find it unbearable. The compensations for men seem to leave them freer for creative activity than the compensations (humiliating at best) offered women in place of real power. Radical men want power, but they have a social conscience, so they must establish a new order of sorts. Yet they do not appear to be operating as leaders in a revolutionary effort (like Lenin, Mao, Fidel) or as theorists and cultural workers teaching the people (like Fanon, Sartre, Marcuse), but rather as politicians. They so accept their right to power that they do not even think it is a problem. No one of the master class has escaped the damage done to him in a caste society. Every White man in this country has been raised with a false sense of power.

Men run the Movement. There is not much possibility that the situation will change automatically. Masters do not relinquish power. It is wrested from them. Radical men show no inclination to change their attitudes toward women, the family, the use of the economy (what else is there except rhetoric—a politician's only tool?). These men transmit ideology for the radical movement. It is essential to know how they structure reality, if they are to retain positions of authority as teachers and leaders. If they consider themselves cultural workers in the service of the revolution (the people), would they not seek self-criticism, correct thinking? Would they not seek knowledge from the oppressed, rather than authoritatively directing their "liberation"?

Women are now formulating ideology for a female liberation movement, and we have our own ideas and tactics for building a revolutionary base which we think will be more effective than the present ideology of the movement. The SDS resolution assumes that the ideal model of humanity is the man (the radical man, of course), and that women must be allowed to participate on an equal basis, but on masculine terms. We do not agree. In Female Liberation meetings, much of the meeting is spent in reminding ourselves to stop "acting like men." All of us seem to be infected with the competitive-aggressive structure to some extent, but the point is that we do not like it—in ourselves or in men. We consider such behavior alien to what we are trying to do, and become. Nor do we like the identity men have given us—femininity. We see that we must begin creating the new person—in ourselves, and not by breeding heirs. We want men and women to reject their programmed roles, and question every single aspect of this society, their role in it, and their behavior.

The first question from a male radical to a woman threatening liberation is: "What about sex?" This seems strange. Apparently, women can "do their thing" as long as they don't cut off the sex supply which is the major use radical men have for women (like politicians). I answer such a question by saying that it is not an important question—as women should, of course, have control of their own bodies, and never feel they must submit to sexual relations simply because they fear they might appear frigid or lose a friendship with a man. The response from the man is almost always that my attitude is *repressive*. It seems clear that the "sex problem" is the man's problem, and he will have to work with it. Women have been accepting the responsibility for it for far too long. Females should be talking about political strategy, not sex. Men should be experiencing a little psychotherapy, group therapy and T-groups to straighten out their minds.

III

The female liberation movement will undoubtedly continue to develop at many levels to meet the varying situations and needs of women. Groups have formed spontaneously throughout the society. The direction so far in these groups has been educational and analytical. We all seem to feel a need for new analysis, ideology, because little of traditional analysis relates to the timeless situation of woman. Our most accurate ideologists have been Socialists and Communists, but Marx and Engels are consistently used against us by male radicals, to the point that many feminists have rejected Marxist analysis completely. Though no man has ever completely overcome his mystification of women, and his need for an alter-ego, Marx, Engels, Bakunin, J. S. Mill, Lenin, and Mao have analyzed the situation of the female in history accurately.

Though female liberation is the most advanced revolutionary thought available to us at this point in history, we should not fight on an exclusive, narrow front. Ultimately, we want to destroy the three pillars of class and caste society—the family, private property, and the state—and their attendant evils—corporate capitalism, imperialism, war, racism, sexism, annihilation of the balance of nature. By exposing attendant evils, as SDS does so well with racism, imperialism, war, and lately sexism, the nature of the system is revealed, but we do not begin to annihilate it. We must attack the pillars of the class system directly, as well as the attendant evils. They are so interrelated (private property, the family and the state) that an attack upon one should be an attack upon the other, but the family is often left free of attack because it is such a convenient unit for the very people who are attacking the system. But it is also basic to the continuance of the system. We should question whether we have truly attacked private property and the state, or are we still capitalists, trying to make a niche for ourselves?

The state and private property are being attacked from many sides. The struggle against American imperialism in process throughout the world is a battle against the State and private property (the claim of American corporations to the people's resources). Within each of these national liberation wars, a female liberation movement will emerge and radically reorient and radicalize the movement toward communism. It is vital that a Southern separatist movement (and other regional and cultural separatist movements) take form. The South, as a colony, can be mobilized against the State with a united front of women and poor Black and White men. The disintegration of the national structure is the key to the political revolutionary movement in North America, a fact that Northern radicals find hard to swallow since they identify with the nation and not with any colony. If they look they will find that they, too, are part of a colony, and must work from there (i.e. New England, Midwest, Jewish, Irish, Greek, etc.).

If men are to become truly revolutionary, though, they, too, must fight the institution of the family and not 'leave it to the women' as the family is now left. Everyone must fight for the end of caste, not just women.

There is only one way to overcome the enormous propaganda influence of the media and political liars which program the people: We must go directly to the people and teach them to think for themselves within a revolutionary framework. To do that we must enter communities, not use the political platform or the media. The people do not believe anything they hear through those organs; the programming is subtle and we can not hope to overcome it through the existing media or to replace the media. The key area of influence will be through the educational system, and through the cell organizations that are being formed by women. First organizers must be taught. It would seem that the American school teacher is a committed enough teacher to be convinced of the need for revolution. There is little tendency to Fascism among them; perhaps this is due in part to the fact that so many teachers are women, a unique historical situation. We should attempt to organize these women as organizers for female liberation.

We must avoid one major error of previous organizers. In an effort to 'win' people over to the movement (win a vote?), organizers often imitate the style of life of those they are organizing. This is patronizing and unliberating and cruel. People who are oppressed want new alternatives, and want to learn. They do not want to be further entrenched in their oppressive style of life. We must be generous with our knowledge, and not underestimate the desire for freedom on the part of the oppressed, and not mistake ignorance for desire. California is proof that people can radically alter their mores and style of life in a short time, and indeed want to do so. If we do not open doors to people, they will find 'liberation' through the oppressive structure—through the California illusions of liberation.

IV

Many radicals (male and female) seem to think that female liberation will be divisive, because women will be fighting the agents of their oppression—men. Such a thought reveals the prejudice against women. That is, men make revolutions; women help. And if men have pressures on them from women, their power as fighters is diminished. I fail to see how women fighting the authoritarian power-hunger in men can but greatly aid the revolution.

There is a strong fascist trend developing among American men and I can imagine that somewhere even there is a young man developing into a Hitler. Such a force of Fascism could spell doom to a revolutionary effort by recreating a situation of genocide similar to Nazi Germany. Most of us would quickly be put away. Fascism is a man's game, not very appealing to women (Hitler had to brainwash the women to be earth mothers and breed, offering them freedom from men—a budding woman power movement perverted to womb power). I do not think men can be trusted as long as they hold the kind of personal and social power they do, and they will hold it until it is taken from them, when women refuse to continue the game.

Finally, I want to explain the term 'female liberation' so that its full revolutionary meaning is grasped. I use the term 'female' rather than 'woman' to denote a principle. When I say female liberation, I mean the liberation of the female principle in all human beings—the worldview which is maternal, materialist, and peaceful (non-competitive). I do not suggest that all women exhibit these qualities, though many do; certainly some men do, but not many. Women are programmed for a role—motherhood—which does allow the female principle to take ascendance over the male principle. The position of the women in relation to the man in America is analogous to the position of the Black in relation to the White man or bossman. One must not romanticize that position, but it is clear that the excluded are less corrupt, therefore the potential leadership of the revolution.

NOTE

1. Page numbers cited from Frederick Engels, *The Origin of the Family, Private Property, and the State* (International Publishers, N.Y.).

Chapter Sixty

Woman and Her Mind
The Story of Daily Life

Meredith Tax

Production of the Self: The Most Alienated Work of All

So far this paper has examined the problem of women's alienation from herself, through the lenses of experience and of existential psychology. We can also view it through a Marxist analysis, by examining woman's work and her place in the modern capitalist economy. (Note: a similar analysis could be made of woman's place in earlier economic stages, or in a socialist society.) To begin with, let's take a look at the general terrain: what is work?

Work is a relationship that takes place between you and nature, involving some material interchange. You take a chunk of raw material and do something to it; both you and the raw material are changed as a result. You put some of your mental and physical energy into the material, thus losing this energy, and the material becomes a product, a thing to be consumed by others.

In capitalist society, the chunk of raw material belongs to the capitalist; so does your energy, which you rent out at some fixed rate. So the capitalist takes the product that you have made. You have been making whatever-it-is, not for yourself, but for someone else, as his agent or tool. This is alienated labor—when your work is done on material you don't own, towards ends that are mysterious to you, and from which you get nothing but money. You lose part of yourself and get nothing back but the ability to buy the products of other people's labor.

Labor takes place when the same interchange between you and nature (raw material) goes on, but without an intermediary between you (the producer) and the consumer. There is no very good example of this in capitalist society. Even work done for yourself becomes alienated before it reaches the consumer; the fine art market is an example of this alienation in its crassest form. The only comprehensible example in capitalist society would be selling something you've made to a friend. Say you carve a statue form from wood. The wood is changed in the process; it becomes a statue. You are changed as well; you are exhilarated and exhausted. You are not *made less* as you are under capitalist conditions of production; you have had an experience you can understand, it has given you pleasure, and you have something that you made out of yourself and wood. Unalienated labor is similar to play, but in play the producer and the consumer are one.

Leisure is the span of time that is free from alienated labor.

In your labor, you build up certain abilities. Take muscular ones as an example: by toting that barge and lifting that bale, you become physically strong. This strength, your productive power, is what the capitalist buys. When you go home, you must recoup this productive power that has been used up, by eating, sleeping, watching TV, etc. This is *recuperation*.

On the brute levels of existence, where survival is at stake, recuperation cannot be elevated to an art form as it is on higher economic levels. The important thing is for the worker to recoup himself physically and mentally; the quality of the means by which he does it (hamburger or filet mignon, comic books or Shakespeare) isn't important.

All work in this society is alienating. Jobs which prohibit friendly contact between workers, which are highly regimented, repetitive, physically exhausting, and degrading, are brutalising as well. The greater the degree of brutalization, the less possible it is for the worker to recover his humanity. He is likely to use his leisure time expressing his despair: getting drunk, or beating his wife and children, are such expressions. Where labor is less exhausting (professional jobs, for instance), artistic means of recuperation become possible; a man may use yoga, for example, to recover the use of a body which has been sacrificed to a sedentary form of labor.

Some jobs do not use up all a man's labor power (strength of various kinds); he has some left over, or can build up a little extra over the weekend. In such cases, he can use what energy he has left for himself. This is *play*, the consumption of one's labor power by oneself for one's own ends. It can mean exercise, sex, going to the movies or on an excursion. It can involve an interchange with nature, or the kind that characterizes unalienated work, but in this case the work will be for oneself alone. One will paint a picture or practise an instrument for the sake of doing it, not for the public utility or pleasure in the result, and not for money.

Many people cannot play; they never recoup themselves to that point. Others have developed labor skills, or powers, that are so specialised that they cannot use them off the job, and they are unable to ease the extreme character of their alienation. Computer programmers or skilled machinists are examples of this problem. They will attempt to play on the job—by making up joke programs or stamping out jewelry—but this is fake play, a reaction against the extremity of their alienation rather than a completed game, for the joke programmes are never carried out, and the programmers cannot make up real ones of their own (play as *invention*) under capitalist conditions.

If the categories describing man's use of his labor-power are work, labor, recuperation, and play, what categories describe woman's use of her labor-power? Women are not only exploited as workers in the same ways as men; women are also exploited as housewives and as sex-objects, both at the workplace and at home.

What men produce on the job are labor-products for someone else's consumption. What do women produce at home for other people's consumption?

Laundry. Cleaning. Taking care of children. Sewing and mending. Washing clothes and dishes. Shopping. Cooking.

In our stage of society, where most necessary production work has been taken out of the home (like baking bread, raising chickens, weaving cloth), the job of housewife is to produce the labor-power of others. The housewife feeds, clothes, cares for, and does psychological repair work on her husband and children, so that they can be resold in the capitalist marketplace each morning. She is not paid in any way that is defined as remuneration for this work, because it is not defined as a job. Her husband supports her as an appendage of himself, but no employer pays her for her labor. Apart from this central fact, the jobs of cooking, cleaning, and child-care are not intrinsically more alienating, or as alienating, as work in an office or a factory.

But there are two crucial differences between a housewife's work and work in the public sphere, and in these lie the peculiar alienation of the job.

The housewife does not produce anything tangible, anything that lasts, or that has market value. Her job is to maintain the *status quo*. Her labor never ends, because it is involved in maintaining a process, rather than making products.

The other difference is that unlike other lowgrade maintenance work, the work of the housewife is done in solitude. Its reality and value are not acknowledged either by payment, or by the presence of others engaged in the same work. The housewife's work is treated by society simply as though it did not exist as work! It takes place in some limbo of private time and space. Even its standards are subjective; there are certain obvious things the housewife must do (like cook dinner), but she does them according to standards set by her own or someone else's personal preferences, and not by some necessary standard inherent in the work. Mostly no one else even notices her work or considers it as such. It is as if the 60 to 80 hour work week she puts in (according to the chase Manhattan Bank) were imaginary and all she really did as far as others were concerned, was to sit on the sofa, munch chocolates, and read *True Romances,* as she does in cartoons.

There is one other thing that woman produces for the consumption of others: *herself.* This is obvious on the material level. She interacts with material objects (makeup, curlers, diet soda, pretty clothes) and both come out changed. She had made the *material* part of herself a more appealing article of consumption, but what has happened to the *producer* part of herself? What more severe alienation can there be than in this case? A split between mind and body is inevitable; the kind of fear, or disgust, or wonder, or ignorance, that most women feel about their bodies is a by-product.

But yet another kind of labor is involved, for women must be desirable objects of consumption not only in body, but also in behavior. This necessitates a kind of *immaterial production* difficult to define, which consists of one part of a woman's mind directing her behavior (to be appealing, sexy, comforting, etc.) to be attractive. Her behavior is an object of consumption not only as a sex-object, but also as a 'wife,' in which role she must be comforting, undemanding, restful, without needs of her own, a buffer zone between a man and his rage at being alienated from himself. The split in a woman's mind which this process necessitates is more severe and detrimental than the split between mind and body, and can be called *female schizophrenia.*

When producing your own mind and body is your work, there's no such thing as leisure—no time when you can really recuperate. The hour or two of privacy which are free from housework are insufficient to relieve the strain. And so the housewife's production process, nervous and physical, frequently breaks down.

In the ideal form of male-dominated society, sex is *labor* for *women* and *play* for *men.* For men, sex is the consumption of their labor-power for their own ends. For women, sex is the consumption of their labor-power by another (the consumer), and the use of their labor-product (which is their material and behavioral selves) by another. It is therefore alienated.

In this ideal pattern, sex appears to men as a means of transcending their everyday experience, that is, it is something special and extraordinary, the subject of fantasy. In sex, men make use of their labor-power, the productive ability they have built up at work and use on the job. They experience sex as play because it is 1) using this ability for themselves, not for others, and 2) using it in a qualitatively different way from labor. It is a transcendence of their role as worker.

In fact, in our society, many men cannot experience sex as transcendent. The patterns that they bring to relationships with women are those they have been taught are 'masculine' in other situations: the same anxiety about not measuring up; the same competitiveness; the same tendency to regard everything as a threat to their masculinity; and the same achievement-orientation, which concentrates on results rather than process, prevail. These attitudes which are socialized into men, are tremendously destructive of any possibility of meaningful personal relationships. But these patterns, while oppressive to the men involved, also cause these men to oppress women. Men may suffer from the fragmentation, the anxiety, the false consciousness, and the sense of undefined loss common to oppressors in other situations. But messed up as they may be, they still have the power in most sexual relationships.

For it is material power in society, not psychological givens, that determines the structure of sexual relationships in general. Men are consumers of women because they hold most of the power in our society. Some men have more power than other men. And a few women, like the Queen of the Netherlands, have more power than most men. But almost every man has power over some woman; and men as a sex control almost all social institutions, including those that only women use (like pregnancy wards), dictate public policy, earn most of the national income, and control almost all jobs. The marriage relation is a business deal; the man hires the woman, in both her aspects of producer and product, for an unspecified length of time. Either one of them can get out of the contract, these days, if they wish; but the woman will have to end up being 'hired' by someone else (unless she gets lots of 'severance pay') if they do. Getting doors opened for you isn't power.

Sex is not transcendent to women, because it is a continuation of their work role. Even in their housework, in their shopping, they are trained to relate to everything, to all the world, as a latent sexual object. Sex is no enrichment of their work experience, or change from it; it is no alternative mode of being; it is merely the fulfillment of an everyday expectation. It is a relief (they have been successful on their job) but not an escape. It is just another way of giving service. Women are taught to think that they are sexual failures if they don't take pleasure in even the most perfunctory or brutalized sex (cf. *Cosmopolitan*), and so they will act the part of mistress, even when they feel nothing but exhaustion or despair. They fake their own experience so that their man will not be denied the illusion that he has pleased them, so that they will not feel failures as women, so that they will not have to answer a string of questions beginning with 'Did you come?' This falsification of the emotional content of sex adds another dimension of alienation to the problem. But at least their product has been consumed. Most women's lives are so limited that their only outlet is fantasy. And even their fantasy life is all too often merely a glorification of the objectified sex roles they are cast in every day.

In the socialist society one imagines, all labor will be unalienated. The worker will understand the whole process, know what it is for, know how he fits in and feels so much a part of the community that consumes his product that it will be as if he were producing for his friends and himself. There will be time for play, on the job, with the same raw materials. Women will work alongside of men, at the same jobs. Power relationships between people will vanish, and institutions which are based on inequities in power, like the bourgeois family, will vanish or be transformed.

How does this projection relate to sex? What will sexual relationships be like in a truly socialist society? Will women free themselves from being both objects of consumption and the products of their own labor? Is it possible that they will cease to need to be 'attractive' or 'comforting' as these are now defined?—that men will cease to demand it of them, or that equal material opportunities will change the relation between men and women so drastically as this? If work were not so decimating, 'comfort' would be unnecessary. 'Attractiveness' would become a personal quality in each of us, rather than a market ideal. Will we live to see such changes in society as a whole?

One thing is certain: women will never be able to experience sex as play—for ourselves—until each of us has a self—that is, not three or four conflicting selves, but one integrated self. Out of the conflict between our pain and the way we were socialized has been born a new creation: the women's liberation movement. Out of the conflict between the women's liberation movement and society will be born a creature who does not yet exist: a liberated woman.

Chapter Sixty-One

Class Beginnings

Nancy Myron

A revolutionary women's movement must understand the subtle yet dynamic barriers of class that exist in this advanced consumer capitalist society because class is one of the main pillars that keeps the male power system standing sturdy. Class keeps women down and divided through middle class women's oppressive behaviour towards lower class women. Instead of recognizing class for what it is middle-class women refuse to see it in order to keep many of the privileges that they get from that same class system.

Movements to date have dealt with class only in its romantic and academic Marxist sense. The romantic view of the working class is some groovy simplistic way of living rather than an oppressive product of capitalism. There's nothing cool or gutsy about being working class . . . it's a brutalizing and dehumanizing way to grow up. In a society responsive to images it is hard to break that romantic vision of the working class. Witness the popularity of the downwardly mobile life style.

Before we begin to figure out class and how it specifically affects our movement, we have to understand the devastating psychological effects that poverty has on the working class in this country. The conditioning and behaviour that comes from financial security and the lack of financial security are radically different. In a society based on materialism, your worth is defined by where you are on the economic ladder. One of the reasons that [poverty] continues in the richest country in the world is because people are brainwashed with the protestant ethic. If you're successful, it's because you work hard and are a good, clean, ambitious American. If you are poor, you haven't tried hard enough, therefore you are lazy and useless and your poverty is your punishment. The sad truth is that most poor people believe that they're inferior and act in a way that confirms it. Everything in this society keeps them thinking it. Every ad and TV show confirms their economic inferiority. Every bureaucratic insult and humiliation makes their place in society more secure in its horror. Even the material goods you acquire work against you. One can buy a color TV and car "on time", but these are visual pacifications that keep people off the streets, in debt, and even more dependent on the system.

For example, if Marsha Marvelous has nice clothes, eats good food and has a little spending money then all of her social maintenance things are taken care of. Her place is now secure in the community. If Gracie O'Neil eats boiled potatoes, Hostess

Twinkies and drinks Kool Aid most of her childhood then chances are her teeth will rot out by age 15 and she will have a lousy disposition from lack of proper nutrition. And if her clothes are from the bargain table of St. Vincent De Pauls Goodwill Shop it doesn't exactly instill her with an air of graciousness and confidence as she walks down the halls of her high school. Her worth and potential in this society are questionable and at best shakey. Marsha thinks Gracies a real frump and is that way because that's just the way things are. Gracie will usually think Marsha's better because she has a nice disposition and pretty teeth and that's just the way things are.

America has set up a scale of worth that affects everyone. If you are not white, 25, male, middle class, and exude an aurora of virile sexuality then you are inferior (this includes about 98% of the population). At the top of this scale are the wealthy white males and at the bottom are the penniless powerless trash. This scale keeps everyone in line. Within it, everyone, including those near the bottom, cling to that part of their idenity that makes them superior to someone else, middle class over working class, white over black, male over female, etc. And it works especially well in keeping women divided. Sexism and classism reinforce each other sometimes in outrageous ways.

For example, I moved from Boston (where I was with my own kind) to a middle class village in upstate NY when I was 12. We were the trash of the community, and were treated accordingly. I'm filled with rage when I think of what happened to one of my sisters who had the misfortune, to not only be trash but to also be endowed with large breasts. She was called a whore and an easy lay. I spent much time defending her against these awful insinuations and the sad truth being that she was a shy sensitive virgin till the ripe old age of 18 when she got married. Any other woman in the village with a little financial status and the same physique as my sister was "dated" and had the respect of that foul little society. I'm not saying that the sweet magnolia blossoms of lawyers' daughters escaped sexual objectification but that they had a less traumatic time of it. Someone has to be on the bottom to hold up the top. And in this case part of the female citizenry was projected into the shadows of alleys while the rest went steady with basketball stars. It becomes clear who were the good and who were the bad. If women were stripped of these illusions of superiority they would begin to see the reality of the oppressed state of all women in this culture.

As a white lower class female, I still got one small compensation from this scale of value . . . racial superiority. I grew up in poverty but I had white skin privilege. Despite all my feelings of inferiority I could still "improve" my lot and even make it in the "middle-class." Not that I wouldn't pay for it with bits of my soul. My education as bad as it was wasn't as bad as a Black woman's. And as poor as we were, we still weren't as poor as the Blacks in Roxbury. I latched on to this one confirmation of my superiority with much enthusiasm.

It was only when I started to put my racism in a broader political context that I was really able to begin to deal with it. It didn't take political genius to see the similarity between the way my family was treated in the context of a middle class village and the way Blacks were treated in the context of the whole white system.

Women in our society have little control over the political system. Class privilege is one of the things given to a woman and that is given to her because she's attached to or has been attached to some male along the way (her father, boy friend, husband) and got it from him. Most people do not deal with their racism, classism, and sexism because they accept whatever tokens of power this privileged society gives them through these systems. It is true that middle class women gain certain privileges and identity from their classism but only at the expense of lower class women. Thus they carry around a miniscule version of a larger oppressive power system. Yet because women have so little control, when you tell middle-class women this, they think you're nuts. What the hell do they have to do with all that power? If you're wallowing in that shaky class security then you're not likely to admit that it exists.

There are many ways and reasons why middle-class women never confront their own classism. They can intellectualize, politicize, accuse, abuse, and contribute money to in order to not deal with it. Even if they admit that class exists, they are not likely to admit that their behaviour is a product of it. They will go through every painful detail of their lives to prove to me or another working class woman that they really didn't have any privilege, that their family was exceptional, that they actually did have an uncle who worked in a factory. To ease anyone's guilt is not the point of talking about class. Some women still think that because they have a working class friend they have licked the class problem. One of the most horrifying responses in the women's movement today is that of the "political" woman who actually goes out and works in a factory so she can look at the working class women and talk to them and maybe drop a little socialism now and then. You don't get rid of oppression just by merely recognizing it. This patronization is outrageous and every woman in the place is sure to smell the stench a mile off.

Refusal to deal with class behaviour in a lesbian/feminist movement is sheer self-indulgence and leads to the downfall of our own struggle. Middle class women should look first at that scale of worth that is the class system in America. They should examine where they fit on that scale, how it affected them, and what they thought of the people below and above them. But this examination does not get middle class women off the hook; they still have to change their behaviour. Seeing your class position points out that you are not necessarily the enemy but that you too have been taken by the system. Start thinking politically about the class system and all the power systems in this country. Stop being immersed in political idealism and abstractions that have little or nothing to do with your life or anyone else's.

You are an enemy of lower class women if you continue destructive behaviour, based on your sense of middle class superiority. But you will become an ally in the feminist revolution if you will examine that behaviour and change those patterns. If women start forcing confrontation with their own class, race and heterosexual privileges, then they will both oppress other women less and begin to confront a whole system based on power and privilege. As women and as lesbians we can only count on each other to bring male supremacy down and must deal with class chauvinism before we can build a movement to make that happen.

Women
Caste, Class, or Oppressed Sex?

Evelyn Reed

The new stage in the struggle for women's liberation already stands on a higher ideological level than did the feminist movement of the last century. Many of the participants today respect the Marxist analysis of capitalism and subscribe to Engels' classic explanation of the origins of women's oppression. It came about through the development of class society, founded upon the family, private property and the state.

But there still remain considerable misunderstandings and misinterpretations of Marxist positions which have led some women who consider themselves radicals or socialists to go off course and become theoretically disoriented. Influenced by the myth that women have always been handicapped by their child-bearing functions, they tend to attribute the roots of women's oppression, at least in part, to biological sexual differences. In actuality its causes are exclusively historical and social in character.

Some of these theorists maintain that women constitute a special class or caste. Such definitions are not only alien to the views of Marxism but lead to the false conclusion that it is not the capitalist system but men who are the prime enemy of women. I propose to challenge this contention.

The findings of the Marxist method, which have laid the groundwork for explaining the genesis of woman's degradation, can be summed up in the following propositions:

First, women were not always the oppressed or "second" sex. Anthropology, or the study of prehistory, tells us the contrary. Throughout primitive society, which was the epoch of tribal collectivism, women were the equals of men and recognized by man as such.

Second, the downfall of women coincided with the breakup of the matriarchal clan commune and its replacement by class-divided society with its institutions of the patriarchal family, private property and state power.

The key factors which brought about this reversal in woman's social status came out of the transition from a hunting and food-gathering economy to a far higher mode of production based upon agriculture, stock raising and urban crafts. The primitive division of labor between the sexes was replaced by a more complex social division of labor. The greater efficiency of labor gave rise to a sizable surplus product, which led first to differentiations and then to deepgoing divisions between the various segments of society.

By virtue of the directing roles played by men in largescale agriculture, irrigation and construction projects, as well as in stock raising, this surplus wealth was gradually appropriated by a hierarchy of men as their private property. This, in turn, required the institution of marriage and the family to fix the legal ownership and inheritance of a man's property. Through monogamous marriage the wife was brought under the complete control of her husband who was thereby assured of legitimate sons to inherit his wealth.

As men took over most of the activities of social production, and with the rise of the family institution, women became relegated to the home to serve their husbands and families. The state apparatus came into existence to fortify and legalize the institutions of private property, male dominion and the father-family, which later were sanctified by religion.

This, briefly, is the Marxist approach to the origins of woman's oppression. Her subordination did not come about through any biological deficiency as a sex. It was the result of the revolutionary social changes which destroyed the equalitarian society of the matriarchal gens or clan and replaced it with a patriarchal class society which, from its birth, was stamped with discriminations and inequalities of many kinds, including the inequality of the sexes. The growth of this inherently oppressive type of socio-economic organization was responsible for the historic downfall of women.

But the downfall of women cannot be fully understood, nor a correct social and political solution worked out for their liberation, without seeing what happened at the same time to men. It is too often overlooked that the patriarchal class system which crushed the matriarchy and its communal social relations also shattered its male counterpart, the fratriarchy—or tribal brotherhood of men. Woman's overthrow went hand in hand with the subjugation of the mass of toiling men to the master class of men.

The import of these developments can be more clearly seen if we examine the basic character of the tribal structure which Morgan, Engels and others described as a system of "primitive communism." The clan commune was both a sisterhood of women and a brotherhood of men. The sisterhood of women, which was the essence of the matriarchy, denoted its collectivist character. The women worked together as a community of sisters; their social labors largely sustained the whole community. They also raised their children in common. An individual mother did not draw distinctions between her own and her clan sisters' progeny, and the children in turn regarded all the older sisters as their mutual mothers. In other words, communal production and communal possessions were accompanied by communal child-raising.

The male counterpart of this sisterhood was the brotherhood, which was molded in the same communal pattern as the sisterhood. Each clan or phratry of clans comprising the tribe was regarded as a "brotherhood" from the male standpoint just as it was viewed as a "sisterhood" or "motherhood" from the female standpoint. In this matriarchal-brotherhood the adults of both sexes not only produced the necessities of life together but also provided for and protected the children of the community. These features made the sisterhood and brotherhood a system of "primitive communism."

Thus, before the family that had the individual father standing at its head came into existence, the functions of fatherhood were a *social*, and not a *family* function of men. More than this, the earliest men who performed the services of fatherhood were not the mates or "husbands" of the clan sisters but rather their clan brothers. This was not simply because the processes of physiological paternity were unknown in ancient society. More decisively, this fact was irrelevant in a society founded upon collectivist relations of production and communal child-raising.

However odd it may seem to people today, who are so accustomed to the family form of child-raising, it was perfectly natural in the primitive commune for the clan brothers, or "mothers' brothers," to perform the paternal functions for their sisters' children that were later taken over by the individual father for his wife's children.

The first change in this sister-brother clan system came with the growing tendency for pairing couples, or "pairing families" as Morgan and Engels called them, to live together in the same community and household. However, this simple cohabitation did not substantially alter the former collectivist relations or the productive role of the women in the community. The sexual division of labor which had formerly been allotted between clan sisters and brothers became gradually transformed into a sexual division of labor between husbands and wives.

But so long as collectivist relations prevailed and women continued to participate in social production, the original equality between the sexes more or less persisted. The whole community continued to sustain the pairing units, just as each individual member of these units made his and her contribution to the labor activities.

Consequently, the pairing family, which appeared at the dawn of the family system, differed radically from the nuclear family of our times. In our ruthless competitive capitalist system, every tiny family must sink or swim through its own efforts—it cannot count on assistance from outside sources. The wife is dependent upon the husband while the children must look to the parents for their subsistence, even if the wage-earners who support them are stricken by unemployment, sickness or death. In the period of the pairing family, however, there was no such system of dependency upon "family economics," since the whole community took care of each individual's basic needs from the cradle to the grave.

This was the material basis for the absence, in the primitive commune, of those social oppressions and family antagonisms with which we are so familiar.

It is sometimes said or implied that male domination has always existed and that women have always been brutally treated by men. Contrariwise, it is also widely believed that the relations between the sexes in matriarchal society were merely the reverse of our own—with women dominating men. Neither of these propositions is borne out by the anthropological evidence.

It is not my intention to glorify the epoch of savagery nor advocate a romantic return to some past "golden age." An economy founded upon hunting and food-gathering is the lowliest stage in human development and its living conditions were rude, crude and harsh. Nevertheless, we must recognize that male and female relations in that kind of society were fundamentally different from ours.

Under the clan system of the sisterhood of women and the brotherhood of men there was no more possibility for one sex to dominate the other than there was for one class to exploit another. Women occupied the most eminent position because they were the chief producers of the necessities of life as well as the procreators of new life. But this did not make them the oppressors of men. Their communal society excluded class, racial or sexual tyranny.

As Engels pointed out, with the rise of private property, monogamous marriage and the patriarchal family, new social forces came into play in both society at large and in the family setup which destroyed the rights exercised by earliest womankind. From simple cohabitation of pairing couples there arose the rigidly fixed, legal system of monogamous marriage. This brought the wife and children under the complete control of the husband and father who gave the family his name and determined their conditions of life and destiny.

Women, who had once lived and worked together as a community of sisters and raised their children in common, now became dispersed as wives of individual men serving their lords and masters in individual households. The former equalitarian sexual division of labor between the men and women of the commune gave way to a family division of labor in which the woman was more and more removed from social production to serve as a household drudge for husband, home and family. Thus women, once "governesses" of society, were degraded under the class formations to become the governess of a man's children and his chief housemaid.

This abasement of women has been a permanent feature of all three stages of class society, from slavery through feudalism to capitalism. So long as women led or participated in the productive work of the whole community, they commanded respect and esteem. But once they were dismembered into separate family units and occupied a servile position in home and family, they lost their prestige along with their influence and power.

Is it any wonder that such drastic social changes should bring about intense and long-enduring antagonism between the sexes? As Engels says:

> Monogamy then does by no means enter history as a reconciliation of man and wife, and still less as the highest form of marriage. On the contrary, it enters as the subjugation of one sex by the other, as the proclamation of an antagonism between the sexes unknown in all preceding history... The first class antagonism appearing in history coincides with the development of the antagonism of man and wife in monogamy, and the first class oppression with that of the female by the male sex. (*Origin of the Family, Private Property and the State*, Kerr edition, p. 79.)

Here it is necessary to note a distinction between two degrees of women's oppression in monogamous family life under the system of private property. In the productive farm family of the pre-industrial age, women held a higher status and were accorded more respect than they receive in the consumer family of our own city life, the nuclear family.

So long as agriculture and craft industry remained dominant in the economy, the farm family, which was a large or "extended" family, remained a viable productive unit. All its members had vital functions to perform according to sex and age. The women in the family helped cultivate the ground and engaged in home industries, as well as bearing children, while the children and older folks produce their share according to ability.

This changed with the rise of industrial and monopoly capitalism, and the nuclear family. Once masses of men were dispossessed from the land and small businesses to become wage earners in factories, they had nothing but their labor power to sell to the capitalist bosses for their means of subsistence. The wives of these wage earners, ousted from their former productive farm and home-craft labors, became utterly dependent upon their husbands for the support of themselves and their children. As men became dependent upon their bosses, their wives became more dependent upon their husbands.

By degrees, therefore, as women were stripped of their economic self-dependence, they fell ever lower in social esteem. At the beginning of class society they had been removed from *social* production and social leadership to become farm-family producers, working through their husbands for home and family. But with the displacement of the productive farm family by the nuclear family of industrial city life, they were driven from their last foothold on solid ground.

Women were then given two dismal alternatives. They could either seek a husband as provider and be penned up thereafter as housewives in city tenements or apartments to raise the next generation of wage slaves. Or the poorest and most unfortunate could go as marginal workers into the mills and factories (along with the children) and be sweated as the most downtrodden and underpaid section of the labor force.

Over the past generations women wageworkers have conducted their own labor struggles or fought along with men for improvements in their wages and working conditions. But women as dependent housewives have had no such means of social struggle. They could only resort to complaints or wrangles with husband and children over the miseries of their lives. The friction between the sexes became deeper and sharper with the abject dependency of women and their subservience to men.

Despite the hypocritical homage paid to womankind as the "sacred mother" and devoted homemaker, the *worth* of women sank to its lowest point under capitalism. Since housewives do not produce commodities for the market nor create any surplus value for the profiteers, they are not central to the operations of capitalism. Only three justifications for their existence remain under this system: as breeders, as household janitors, and as buyers of consumer goods for the family.

While wealthy women can hire servants to do the dull chores for them, poor women are riveted to an endless grind for their whole lives. Their condition of servitude is compounded when they are obliged to take an outside job to help sustain the family. Shouldering two responsibilities instead of one, they are the "doubly oppressed."

Even middle-class housewives in the Western world, despite their economic advantages, are victimized by capitalism. The isolated, monotonous, trivial circumstances of their lives lead them to "living through" their children—a relationship which fosters many of the neuroses that afflict family life today. Seeking to allay their boredom, they can be played upon and preyed upon by the profiteers in the consumer goods fields. This exploitation of women as consumers is part and parcel of a system that grew up in the first place for the exploitation of men as producers.

The capitalists have ample reason for glorifying the nuclear family. Its petty household is a gold mine for all sorts of hucksters from real estate agents to the manufacturers of detergents and cosmetics. Just as automobiles are produced for individual use instead of developing adequate mass transportation. So the big corporations can make more money by selling small homes on private lots to be equipped with individual washing machines, refrigerators, and other such items. They find this more profitable than building large-scale housing at low rentals or developing community services and child-care centers.

In the second place, the isolation of women, each enclosed in a private home and tied to the same kitchen and nursery chores, hinders them from banding together and becoming a strong social force or a serious political threat to the Establishment.

What is the most instructive lesson to be drawn from this highly condensed survey of the long imprisonment of womankind in the home and family of class society—which stands in such marked contrast to their stronger, more independent position in preclass society? It shows that the inferior status of the female sex is not the result of their biological makeup or the fact that they are the child-bearers. Child-bearing was no handicap in the primitive commune; it *became* a handicap, above all, in the nuclear family of our times. Poor women are torn apart by the conflicting obligations of taking care of their children at home while at the same time working outside to help sustain the family.

Women, then, have been condemned to their oppressed status by the same social forces and relations which have brought about the oppression of one class by another, one race by another, and one nation by another. It is the capitalist system—the ultimate stage in the development of class society—which is the fundamental source of the degradation and oppression of women.

Some women in the liberation movement dispute these fundamental theses of Marxism. They say that the female sex represents a separate caste or class. Ti-Grace Atkinson, for example, takes the position that women are a separate *class*; Roxanne Dunbar says that they comprise a separate *caste*. Let us examine these two theoretical positions and the conclusions that flow from them.

First, are women a caste? The caste hierarchy came first in history and was the prototype and predecessor of the class system. It arose after the breakup of the tribal commune with the emergence of the first marked differentiations of segments of society according to the new divisions of labor and social functions. Membership in a superior or inferior station was established by being born into that caste.

It is important to note, however, that the caste system was also inherently and at birth a class system. Furthermore, while the caste system reached its fullest development only in certain regions of the world, such as India, the class system evolved far beyond it to become a world system, which engulfed the caste system.

This can be clearly seen in India itself, where each of the four chief castes—the Brahmans or priests, the soldiers, the farmers and merchants, and the laborers, along with the "out-castes" or pariahs—had their appropriate places in an exploitative society. In India today, where the ancient caste system survives in decadent forms, capitalist relations and power prevail over all the inherited precapitalist institutions, including the caste relics.

However, those regions of the world which advanced fastest and farthest on the road to civilization bypassed or overleaped the caste system altogether. Western civilization, which started with ancient Greece and Rome, developed from slavery through feudalism to the maturest stage of class society, capitalism.

Neither in the caste system nor the class system—nor in their combinations—have women comprised a separate caste or class. Women themselves have been separated into the various castes and classes which made up these social formations.

The fact that women occupy an inferior status as a *sex* does not *ipso facto* make women either an inferior caste or class. Even in ancient India women belonged to different castes, just as they belong to different classes in contemporary capitalist society. In the one case their social status was determined by birth into a caste; in the other it is determined by their own or their husband's wealth. But the two can be fused—for women as for men. Both sexes can belong to a superior caste and possess superior wealth, power and status.

What, then, does Roxanne Dunbar want to convey when she refers to all women (regardless of class) as comprising a separate caste? And what consequences for action does she draw from this characterization? The exact content of both her premise and her conclusion are not clear to me, and perhaps to many others. They therefore deserve closer examination.

Speaking in a loose and popular way, it is possible to refer to women as an inferior "caste"—as is sometimes done when they are also called "slaves" or "serfs"—when the intent is merely to indicate that they occupy the subordinate position in male-dominated society. The use of the term "caste" would then only expose the impoverishment of our language, which has no special word to indicate womankind as the oppressed sex. But more than this seems to be involved, if we judge from the paper by Roxanne Dunbar dated February 1970 which supersedes her previous positions on this question.

In that document she says that her characterization of women as an exploited caste is nothing new; that Marx and Engels likewise "analyzed the position of the female sex in just such a way." This is simply not the case. Neither Marx in *Capital*, nor Engels in *The Origin of the Family, Private Property and the State*, nor in any writings by noted Marxists from Lenin to Luxemberg on this matter, has woman been defined by virtue of her sex as a "caste." Therefore this is not a mere verbal squabble over the misuse of a term. It is a distinct departure from Marxism, although presented in the name of Marxism.

I would like clarification from Roxanne Dunbar on the conclusions she draws from her theory. For, if all women belong to an inferior caste, and all men belong to the superior caste, it would consistently follow that the central axis of a struggle for liberation would be a "caste war" of all women against all men to bring about the liberation of women. This conclusion would seem to be confirmed by her statement that "we live under an international caste system . . ."

This assertion is equally non-Marxist. What Marxists say is that we live under an international *class* system. And they further state that it will require not a caste war, but a *class struggle*—of all the oppressed, male and female alike—to consummate women's liberation along with the liberation of all the oppressed masses. Does Roxanne Dunbar agree or disagree with this viewpoint on the paramount role of the class struggle?

Her confusion points up the necessity for using precise language in a scientific exposition. However downtrodden women are under capitalism, they are not chattel slaves any more than they are feudal serfs or members of an inferior caste. The social categories of slave, serf and caste refer to stages and features of past history and do not correctly define the position of women in our society.

If we are to be precise and scientific, women should be defined as an "oppressed *sex.*"

Turning to the other position, it is even more incorrect to characterize women as a special "class." In Marxist sociology a class is defined in two interrelated ways: by the role it plays in the processes of production and by the stake it has in the ownership of property. Thus the capitalists are the major power in our society because they own the means of production and thereby control the state and direct the economy. The wageworkers who create the wealth own nothing but their labor power which they have to sell to the bosses to stay alive.

Where do women stand in relation to these polar class forces? They belong to all strata of the social pyramid. The few at the top are part of the plutocratic class; more among us belong to the middle class; most of us belong to the proletarian layers of the population. There is an enormous spread from the few wealthy women of the Rockefeller, Morgan and Ford families to the millions of poor women who subsist on welfare dole. *In short, women, like men, are a multiclass sex.*

This is not an attempt to divide women from one anther but simply to recognize the actual divisions that exist. The notion that all women as a sex have more in common than do members of the same class with one another is false. Upper-class women are not simply bedmates of their wealthy husbands. As a rule they have more compelling ties which bind them together. They are economic, social and political bedmates, united in defense of private property, profiteering, militarism, racism— and the exploitation of other women.

To be sure, there can be individual exceptions to this rule, especially among young women today. We remember that Mrs. Frank Leslie, for example, left a $2 million bequest to further the cause of women's suffrage and other upper-class women have devoted their means to secure civil rights for our sex. But it is quite another matter to expect any large number of wealthy women to endorse or support a revolutionary struggle which threatens their capitalist interests and privileges. Most of them scorn the liberation movement, saying openly or implicitly, "What do we need to be liberated from?"

Is it really necessary to stress this point? Tens of thousands of women went to the

Washington antiwar demonstrations on November 1969 and again in May 1970. Did they have more in common with the militant men marching beside them on that life and death issue—or with Mrs. Nixon, her daughters, and the wife of the attorney general, Mrs. Mitchell, who peered uneasily out of her window and saw the specter of another Russian Revolution in those protesting masses? Will the wives of bankers, generals, corporation lawyers and big industrialists be firmer allies of women fighting for liberation than working-class men, Black and white, who are fighting for theirs? Won't there be both men and women on both sides of the class struggle? If not, is the struggle to be directed against men as a sex rather than against the capitalist system?

It is true that all forms of class society have been male-dominated and that men are trained from the cradle on to be chauvinistic. But it is not true that men as such represent the main enemy of women. This crosses out the multitudes of downtrodden, exploited men who are themselves oppressed by the main enemy of women, which is the capitalist system. These men likewise have a stake in the liberation struggle of the women; they can and will become our allies.

Although the struggle against male chauvinism is an essential part of the tasks that women must carry out through their liberation movement, it is incorrect to make that the central issue. This tends to conceal or overlook the role of the ruling powers who not only breed and benefit from all forms of discrimination and oppression but are also responsible for breeding and sustaining male chauvinism. Let us remember that male supremacy did not exist in the primitive commune, founded upon sisterhood and brotherhood. Sexism, like racism, has its roots in the private property system.

A false theoretical position easily leads to a false strategy in the struggle for women's liberation. Such is the case with a segment of the Redstockings who state in their *Manifesto* that "women are an oppressed *class*." If all women compose a class then all men must form a counterclass—the oppressor class. What conclusion flows from this premise? That there are no men in the oppressed class? Where does this leave the millions of oppressed white working men who, like the oppressed Blacks, Chicanos and other minorities, are exploited by the monopolists? Don't they have a central place in the struggle for social revolution? At what point and under what banner do these oppressed peoples of all races and both sexes join together for common action against their common enemy? To oppose women as a class against men as a class can only result in a diversion of the real class struggle.

Isn't there a suggestion of this same line in Roxanne Dunbar's assertion that female liberation is the basis for social revolution? This is far from Marxist strategy since it turns the real situation on its head. Marxists say that social revolution is the basis for full female liberation—just as it is the basis for the liberation of the whole working class. In the last analysis the real allies of women's liberation are all those forces which are impelled for their own reasons to struggle against and throw off the shackles of the imperialist masters.

The underlying source of women's oppression, which is capitalism, cannot be abolished by women alone, nor by a coalition of women drawn from all classes. It will require a worldwide struggle for socialism of the working masses, female and male alike, together with every other section of the oppressed, to overthrow the power of capitalism which is centered today in the United States.

In conclusion, we must ask, what are the connections between the struggle for women's liberation and the struggle for socialism?

First, even though the full goal of women's liberation cannot be achieved short of the socialist revolution, this does not mean that the struggle to secure reforms must be postponed until then. It is imperative for Marxist women to fight shoulder to shoulder with all our embattled sisters in organized actions for specific objectives from now on. This has been our policy ever since the new phase of the women's liberation movement surfaced a year or so ago, and even before.

The women's movement begins, like other movements for liberation, by putting forward elementary demands, such as equal opportunities with men in education, jobs and equal pay; for free abortions on demand; for childcare centers financed by the government but controlled by the community. Mobilizing women behind these issues not only gives us the possibility of securing some improvements but exposes, curbs and modifies the worst aspects of our subordination in this society.

Second, why do women have to lead their own struggles for liberation, even though in the end the combined anticapitalist offensive of the whole working class will be required for the victory of the socialist revolution? The reason is that no segment of society which has been subjected to oppression, whether it consists of Third World people or of women, can delegate the leadership and promotion of their fight for freedom to other forces—even though other forces can act as their allies. We reject the attitude of some political tendencies which say they are Marxists but refuse to acknowledge that women have to lead and organize their own independent struggle for emancipation, just as they cannot understand why Blacks must do the same.

The maxim of the Irish revolutionists—"who would be free themselves must strike the blow"—fully applies to the cause of women's liberation. Women must themselves strike the blows to gain their freedom. And this holds true after the anticapitalist revolution triumphs as well as before.

In the course of our struggle, and as part of it, we will reeducate men who have been brainwashed into believing that women are naturally the inferior sex due to some flaws in their biological makeup. Men will have to learn that, in the hierarchy of oppressions created by capitalism, their chauvinism and dominance is another weapon in the hands of the master class for maintaining its rule. The exploited worker, confronted by the even worse plight of his dependent housewife, cannot be complacent about it—he must be made to see the source of the oppressive power that has degraded them both.

Finally, to say that women form a separate caste or class must logically lead to extremely pessimistic conclusions with regard to the antagonism between the sexes in contrast with the revolutionary optimism of the Marxists. For unless the two sexes are to be totally separated, or the men liquidated, it would seem that they will have to remain forever at war with each other.

As Marxists we have a more realistic and hopeful message. We deny that women's inferiority was predestined by her biological makeup or has always existed. Far from being eternal, woman's subjugation and the bitter hostility between the sexes are no more than a few thousand years old. They were produced by the drastic social changes which brought the family, private property and the state into existence.

This view of history points up the necessity for a no less thoroughgoing revolution in socio-economic relations to uproot the causes of inequality and achieve full emancipation for our sex. This is the purpose and promise of the socialist program, and this is what we are fighting for.

Chapter Sixty-Three

Women and the Left

Ellen Willis

The women's liberation movement was created by women activists fed up with their subordinate position in radical organizations. Their first goal was to take an equal, active part in the radical movement instead of being relegated to secretarial and other service chores.

This circumstance has led to certain assumptions about the women's movement. In the standard radical view, women's liberation is a branch of the Left and women a constituency like students or GIs. Granted that we suffer our own forms of oppression and that radical men have oppressed us as women, the emphasis is on contributing our special insights to the Left as a whole and using feminist issues as an organizing tool. In return, male radicals are expected to endorse women's liberation and combat their male chauvinism.

Many of us now reject this view of our purpose as anti-woman. We have come to see women's liberation as an independent revolutionary movement, potentially representing half the population. We intend to make our own analysis of the system and put our interests first, whether or not it is convenient for the (male-dominated) Left. Although we may cooperate with radical men on matters of common concern, we are not simply part of the Left. We do not assume that radical men are our allies or that we want the same kind of revolution they want.

This divergence in outlook was apparent when several women's liberation groups met in Washington in January, 1968 to plan anti-Inaugural activities. The theme of the women's liberation was "Give back the vote." Since women's 80-year struggle for the vote had achieved a meaningless victory and vitiated the feminist movement, we planned to destroy our voter registration cards publicly as a symbol that suffragism was dead and a new fight for real emancipation beginning. Some women wanted to invite men to burn their voters' cards with us during or after our action. This idea was rejected on grounds that it would change the action from a repudiation of suffrage as a sop for women to a general protest against the electoral process.

There was also some wrangling over the speech we had scheduled. Some of us wanted to inform movement men that we were sick of participating in other people's revolutions and were working for ourselves. Others were horrified at the thought of criticizing the movement publicly. We decided on two short speeches—one a general statement of women's oppression, the other a militant declaration of independence from radical men.

Ensuing events bore out the separatist argument. The Mobilization Committee, supposedly sympathetic, neither included women's liberation among the issues listed in its *Guardian* ad, nor mentioned our action in its mimeographed program. Mobe spokesman Dave Dellinger announced at the Saturday rally that the Mobe had come to demonstrate against the war and for black liberation. When some women on the stage yelled at him, he mentioned women's liberation as an afterthought. During our presentation—which began with the moderate, pro-movement statement—men in the audience booed, laughed, catcalled and yelled enlightened remarks like "Take her off the stage and fuck her." Instead of reprimanding the hecklers (as he did during an unpopular speech by a black GI), Dellinger tried to hurry us off the stage.

It is a mistake to think that education alone will change this. Radical men have a power position that they will not give up until they have to. They will support our revolution only when we build an independent movement so strong that no revolution at all is possible without our cooperation.

To work within the movement is to perpetuate the idea that our struggle is secondary. We will continually be tempted to defer to "the larger good of the movement" just as we have always deferred to "the larger good of the family." We must remember that women are not just a special interest group with sectarian concerns. *We are half the human race.* Our oppression transcends occupations and class lines. Femaleness, like blackness, is a biological fact, a fundamental condition. Like racism, male supremacy permeates all strata of this society. And it is even more deeply entrenched. Whites are at least defensive about racism; men—including most radicals, black and white—are proud of their chauvinism. Male supremacy is the oldest form of domination and the most resistant to change.

The radical movement has been dominated by men. Its theory, priorities and strategies reflect male interests. Here are some of the more obvious points radical feminists must consider:

Theory: An anti-capitalist, anti-imperialist analysis is insufficient for our purposes. Women's oppression antedated capitalism by some 2000 years and has outlasted it in socialist countries.

Priorities: Women are the only oppressed people whose biological, emotional and social life is totally bound to that of the oppressors. The function of the ghetto, the army, the factory, the campus in reifying an oppressed group's separate existence must be assumed by women's liberation. We must provide a place for women to be friends, exchange personal griefs and give their sisters moral support—in short, develop group consciousness. Yet this function is often derogated by movement-oriented women—"How can we indulge in group therapy while *men* [my italics] are dying in Vietnam?"

Strategies: (1) In deciding what role, if any, confrontation and violence should play in our movement, we must consider that women are at a disadvantage physically and that our aggressiveness has been systematically inhibited. On the other hand, we must realize that one reason men don't take us seriously is that they are not physically afraid of us.

(2) We must admit that we will often have more in common with reformist women's organizations like NOW (National Organization for Women) than with radical men. Repeal of abortion laws, for example, is not a radical demand—the system can accommodate it. But it is of gut concern to radical as well as liberal women.

(3) We will never organize the mass of women by subordinating their concrete interests to a "higher" ideology. To believe that concentrating on women's issues is not really revolutionary is self-depreciation. Our demand for freedom involves not only the overthrow of capitalism but the destruction of the patriarchal family system.

It is not only possible but imperative for women to build a specifically feminist radical consciousness. As radicals we must do our best to foster this consciousness. But we should have the humility to realize that women who have never been committed to a male-oriented radical analysis may have clearer perspectives than we. Unless we shed our movement prejudices and help women's liberation go its own way, we will not be a revolutionary vanguard but reactionary obstructionists.

Chapter Sixty-Four

Domestics

Vivien Leone

The day I suddenly found out I was a lawful domestic servant I was flat on my back in a hospital bed with 47 stitches in my face and a broken arm in traction, as a result of an auto accident from which my then-husband, the driver, emerged unmarked. A lawyer was telling us that in addition to my own massive suit, hubby would be able to sue for *loss of services* during my hospitalization and convalescence, although these services, on which a monetary value was being placed, had been performed free of charge throughout a decade of marriage.

That was when it hit me: when you do it for free, you're a wife; when you do it for money, you're a maid.

A maid may be a nubile virgin according to the dictionary, but according to the latest figures from the U.S. Department of Labor, she is not single (72% are either married, divorced, separated or widowed). She (98% are female) represents a work force of almost two million, and more than a quarter of a million of her number are heads of families. She is overwhelmingly poor (median income below the annual $1,635 Federal poverty level), aging (46 is the median age, but 40 % are over 55) and black (64%).

That she is poorly educated (most never finished high school) is no surprise.

The shocker is that 4.2 % have had some college (even some graduate school) and it's not the way you're thinking, either, that it's the black woman with the degree who's necessarily forced into servitude of the college-trained, there were more than five whites for every black.

The work is long (more than one third of the full-timers exceed the 40-hour week), fragmented (only slightly over one third are full time) and unsteady (only four out of 10 have year-round employment).

Not that there hasn't been some improvement: thirty years ago, the typical wage was a quarter an hour, and for that domestics rendered a whole spectrum of services such as laundry, cooking, rug-beating and window-washing, that today have become specialties seldom included in the "plain maid" category that commands, at least in the Metropolitan area, an average rate of $1.75 an hour or $77 a week.

In the rarefied air of Eastside agencies run by the likes of a princess (she says) from Poland, the weekly wage ranges from $85 to $130. These are outlets for the steadily diminishing minority of those white immigrant domestics who still, at least up North, staff our patrician palaces without rubbing so much as a black shoulder. At the other end of the mop are the workers who, according to the National Council of Negro Women, average $1.50 an hour or $55 a week, and "the greatest tragedy," says Council President Dorothy Height, "is that there is absolutely no wage enforcement."

Upgrading is very much on the Federal mind these days. Two years ago, the Government allotted $1.5 million so that the National Committee on Household Employment (NCHE) could set up pilot projects to attack the problem. Director Mary Schlick says, "We must learn to distinguish between being a servant and giving service . . . somehow, because most women can do work around a house, they don't regard housework as the skill it actually is." Schlick feels "the old master-servant relationship still prevails, with the workers given used clothing and the leftovers I call "used food," rather than a living wage."

Of the seven experimental projects being coordinated by NCHE—in Alexandria, Va., at Kansas State University, in Boston, Chicago, Philadelphia, Pittsburgh and New York—Household Management, Inc. (HMI) in New York, is the only one geared to commercial operation as a training-and-employment agency. Its graduates go on the company payroll at a guaranteed $95 weekly minimum, and the company assigns jobs, supervises them, arranges for Social Security, paid vacations, unemployment, disability, compensation and hospitalization insurance. Training Director Louise Bopp, thinks the hardest thing to teach students, most of whom are black, is to care about themselves. "They must learn to want something," she said, "so we start with self-improvement courses, where experts in such fields as beauty and physical fitness let employees know we're interested in them, and try to get them interested in themselves." The old women's-magazine approach.

"I have lost some weight," reports one graduate, "I cut my hair. HMI gave me the confidence to enjoy life more." Men, too, want to be beautiful and fit, but imagine a professional training program for them that featured beauty and physical fitness.

The curriculum consists of courses in food purchasing, money management, decision making, food preparation and serving, table setting and decoration, laundering and cleaning, and care of infants and the elderly. "Another important area," says the brochure, "is the introduction to practical aesthetics: students learn that small, inexpensive touches can greatly enhance the home. One student took her whole family to Macy's to show them what she had learned about at school."

Director Edward M. Blackoff, may have fine intentions, but from a feminist point of view, the program's riddled with contradictions that show up most in the vocabulary of housework. HMI calls its graduates "household technicians" or "home-management specialists," (HMI charges customers $28 to $32 a day) but Blackoff's book is titled *How to Solve Your Servant Problems*, and HMI's only ad in the Yellow Pages appears under the heading of *Maid Service*.

There is nothing quite like the Yellow Pages, that great sociological index of the status quo. It tells you the way things really are. All the elegant agencies appear under *Maid Service*, and there's nothing at all under *Housekeeping*.

A champion eupheminist is Mildred Feldman, field manager of the N.Y. State

Employment Service Household Office (NYSES), who insists, "a domestic worker should be referred to as a housekeeper or by her name... *never* use "maid." Yet *Maids* are in the Yellow Pages, and *Housekeepers* are not. And one visit to NYSES headquarters suffices to convince one of the futility of attempts at upgrading.

A victim of urban renewal, NYSES recently moved from the dinginess of West 90th Street to new quarters among experimental theaters and dance studios across from a municipal garage on West 54th. The shape-up area is spacious and pleasant, but hints of social categorization abound. Adjacent to a pair of quite clean and neat rest rooms marked for Men and Women is one marked Staff, lest we forget whose behind is whose. Among the graffiti in the Women's room was one contributed by someone apparently experienced in the Other Oldest Female Profession. "If you sleep with dog," she wrote sadly-but-wisely, "you wake up with fees!"

At the public relations office a mile downtown, director Kay Weidlich explained that in order to take a photograph on State premises (forbidden), she could authorize our photographer only a shot from the rear—no faces. The message is clear. Like addicts and unwed mothers, domestics must remain faceless. The common denominator is shame—deep, mindless and abiding.

The Why of this shame is all wrapped up with guilt and the class distinctions that divide women. In my own family, we never did pick up the knack of *How To Treat The Maid*, a designation my mother, the kind of true-believer in American Democracy that only an immigrant can be, would never use. She early learned she lacked the knack, when her first maid caught her re-cleaning a difficult corner and quit, with the contemptuous comment, "You ain't no lady."

We were always losing help for want of knowing how to be served, for trying to make the servant feel like one of the family. It got out of hand. It simply did not work. Something inside tells us that, having the capacity to do these tasks—a capacity we have been taught to feel is inbred because we are women—we ought to be down there on our own hands and knees.

Housework and Femininity

They say even Marlene Dietrich scrubs her own floors, but you'd have to be a Dietrich to get away with it. By "get away with it" I mean emerge with your femininity intact, for as the feminine image is currently constructed, housework makes a woman less feminine, whereas the male equivalents of the lowest job women can do—the job of trucker, day laborer or longshoreman, only enhance masculinity in the eyes of the present-day world.

How could any government on earth ever manage to elevate women from such ingrained and complicated depths of degradation?

One of the most relentless exponents of the Government's upgrading efforts is Elizabeth Duncan Koontz of the Labor Department's Women's Bureau. At a conference in Virginia Director Koontz spoke of her hopes for what she calls "the quiet revolution in household employment." But the "revolution" she has in mind makes upgrading seem a hoax, designed to ensnare more workers into the field by making the job seem worthwhile, in order to liberate the housewife, who knows it is not.

"Compared with 50 years ago," says Koontz, "a lot is expected of today's housewife in the way of keeping the house looking neater and the family better pressed and dressed, and for some, doing fancier entertaining, and making it all look easy. And the more machines free her, the more society expects her to do in the community, in school, and in church."

A leaflet distributed by the Women's Bureau makes it even plainer: "If only I could get some household help!" reads the cover. Over a photo these touchy times cause me to notice is footnoted "Courtesy National Council of Jewish Women." The leaflet declares that "More trained, reliable household employees would allow women to: *Enjoy dual roles as homemakers and earners,* or *Spend more time with their children and husbands,* or *Serve as volunteers,* or *Continue their education,* or *Make clothes for themselves and their children,* or *Have time for other activities of their own choice.*"

Free women, in other words, for some futureless job they must combine with homemaking, for mothering, with maybe some wife-ing thrown in, for volunteerism in a society that honors only paid work, for taking courses, for self-decoration, and for those freely-chosen activities known in suburbia as excess leisure, the ones that daily lure more middle-aged matrons to the bar stools. Quiet revolution indeed, for when translated into these terms, the upgrading of the domestic worker only downgrades the housewife.

The Unpaid Domestics

The housewife without domestic help earns no wages at all, let alone a minimum. The housewife has a 24-hour job without sick leave or regulated vacations, without disability insurance and without Social Security. Her unemployment insurance is dispensed in the debasing form of alimony. The stoves, furs and roses that masquerade as her bonuses are merely the professional equipment needed to run her family's home and increase her husband's stature. With no earned cash of her own, she remains a dependent, powerless child.

"A housewife is a very valuable piece of property," says Joseph Kelner, a topknotch attorney who specializes in accident cases and admirably handled my own. "The list of individual servants needed to replace her is staggering, and the cost astronomical." The job the housewife does for society is an essential one. The wheels simply could not turn without it, yet it remains unpaid, undignified and unrewarding.

I am a member of Older Women's Liberation (OWL), the group that has been developing a program, for which I have until now expressed only lukewarm support, that would petition the Government to *pay* housewives for this essential job. The first time I heard about the OWL program, I laughed. I am not laughing any more.

When I began this investigation into the domestic worker's plight, I had no idea the research would lead me logically and irrevocably toward supporting this very program, for as long as housewives are the scabs who do this job for free, domestic work must remain degrading.

The rallying call of Women, Unite! never had a more urgent objective than to solve the Servant Problem, because the Servants are Us. All of us.

Chapter Sixty-Five

To My White Working-Class Sisters

Debby D'Amico

We are the invisible women, the faceless women, the nameless women . . . the female half of the silent majority, the female half of the ugly Americans, the smallest part of the "little people." No one photographs us, no one writes about us, no one puts us on TV. No one says we are beautiful, no one says we are important, very few like to recognize that we are *here*. We are the poor and working-class white women of America, and we are cruelly and systematically ignored. All of our lives we have been told, sometimes subtly, sometimes not so subtly, that we are not worth very much. This message has been put across to me, a white working-class woman, all my life. I think the time has come to speak out against these insults, and so I have decided to write about parts of my life and my ideas. I am doing this for all my sisters who have been made to feel that they are not worth writing about, and for all those people who have to be convinced of poor white existence, those same people who told us that because we are all white our lives are the same as those of the middle and upper class.

When I was in the second grade, we were given a sample aptitude test to accustom us to the test-taking rut that would ultimately determine whether we would be programmed toward college or a dead-end job. After we had answered several multiple-choice questions, the teacher had us check our answers against the "right" ones. One of the questions pictured a man in a tuxedo, a man in a suit, and a man in overalls. The question read: "Which man is going to work?" The "correct" answer was: the man in the suit. I can still feel the shame that came with the realization that what went on in my home was marked "incorrect." I responded the way oppressed people often respond—by secretly hating myself and my family. I remember constantly begging my father to put on a suit—my father who worked an average of 65 to 80 hours a week driving trucks, checking out groceries in a supermarket, and doing any of the other deadening jobs which came his way. My mother didn't escape my judgments either. The unreal Dick, Jane, and Sally world our school books presented as the "right" way of life, reinforced by TV and middle-class school-mates' homes, made me viciously attack her grammar whenever she spoke and ask her questions like: "How come *you* never wear dresses or get your hair done?" The world of my home gave me concrete answers: at the time my mother had three kids in diapers and another on the way, hardly a life-style that called for a well-dressed mannequin. But the middle-class world of America was bigger than my home and I was overcome by its judgments.

As I went on through school, I continued to be taught about an America that had little to do with me. The picture of American life drawn in history books was almost always a comfortable one, with exceptions like wars and the Depression (hardships which the middle class participated in and thus wanted to talk about). Working-class sisters, wake up! Black people were not the only ones left out of history books. George Washington is no relative of yours; neither is Henry Ford, or Nixon and Agnew. While George Washington was relaxing at his Mt. Vernon estate, *your* ancestors may have been among the two-thirds majority of white settlers who served as indentured servants for Master George and others like him. They may have been servants who were kidnapped from the slums of England and Ireland and brought here in chains to be sold to the highest bidder. Your grandmother might have been one of the "huddled masses yearning to breathe free," who came to America and wound up in a tenement where free air never blew, working from can see to can't see, made to feel alien and ashamed of an Old World culture infinitely more alive and colorful than the drab, Puritan, "Mr. Clean" ways of America. I have listened to the old folks in my family talk about how they "came over," and how they survived, the first Italians in an all-Irish neighborhood. That is *my* history. While Mr. Pullman was amassing his fortune, our people were fighting and dying for the rights of working men and women, our people were being shot and beaten for what they believed. I was not taught this in school but learned it later on my own. In high school I continued to learn middle-class ways. I spent years learning to talk like them, eat like them, look like them. I learned a language that had little to do with the concrete terms of my life or the lives of my family and fellow workers.

At the same time that books were deluging me with middle-class culture, I began to feel the pinch of unworthiness in other ways. I attended a parochial high school for one year which was upper-middle-class dominated. If your family had no influential friends to take out $50 ads in the yearbook, you were punished—shame on you! they said, for your failure to measure up in America, shame on you because you haven't made it in the land of the free and the home of the brave.

During my high school years I entered the great rat race of women who were dedicated to snagging any and all men considered desirable. I was again led by middle-class values, and so I rejected the knit-shirted, "greasy"-haired, dark-skinned Italians I grew up with and made a mad dash for the Brylcreem man. All the while, of course, feeling I could never get him, because I wasn't the *girl* in the Brylcreem commercial. I read all the middle-class fashion and glamour magazines and tried to look like people who were able to look that way because of a life-style that included a closet full of clothes I couldn't afford and a leisurely existence that allowed them to look cool and unruffled all the time. And there I was working in a luncheonette so shabby I never mentioned it to anyone for a lousy six dollars a Saturday that I immediately spent in vain efforts to make myself "acceptable"-looking. During the day I gossiped condescendingly about the way people dressed, playing at being the glorious magazine girl, and at night I sulked off to the phone company to be bitten by cord lice and told all night that I was either very slow or innately stupid.

And people, in social and job situations, have been saying that ever since. In social situations it is said as I sit quietly by and watch well-dressed, slick, confident women of the upper classes, America's idea of beauty, steal the eyes, applause, and the image of woman from me. It is said in many ways on the job: at my last job I was mimeographer at a school, a "liberal, progressive" school at that. I once spoke up at a staff meeting and the first remark to follow the stunned silence was, "Why doesn't someone put her on the faculty?" Yes, put me among the educated middle class because you absolutely can't deal with a worker who thinks and has ideas. After I mentioned this, I was told that it was a compliment and that I should be *grateful*. Grateful that they thought I was as good as them. At the same school I was once asked, "Are you the switchboard?" Naturally—since we are looked on as extensions of the machines we operate, not as human beings.

What all this has done to us is create a deep, deep sense of unworthiness, a sense so deep it dooms us. I have a thirteen-year-old friend who is well on the way to life either in prison or on heroin. We, *as a people*, have nothing that says to him, "You shouldn't ruin your life. You're a good, worthwhile person." If or when he does go to jail, there will be no Black Muslims to tell him he is a worth-while person just because of what he is. No one will be there to give him the respect and support of an alternate culture that respects what he is. That is what the judgment of middle-class America has done to us.

Why has this happened to us? It has happened because we believed in the American dream, in the dream that *anyone* can be *anything* if he only tries, works hard, and if he doesn't make it, it's only because something about *him* is rotten. Since we don't have much to begin with, we're made to feel we don't deserve much. And we believe it—even though the truth of our lives tells us that we have worked, and damned hard, but we still didn't have the kinds of lives we read about and saw on TV. And America has kept us out of magazines and off TV *because* our faces and voices are full of this truth. We have hated black people, but we have hated ourselves more. By believing black people are inferior, we have kept the truth about ourselves from each other—that the people who have the power and money in America never intend to raise our incomes or those of black people, not because we aren't worthy, but because it would cut into their profits to do so. We believed black people were so inferior that they weren't supposed to make it—we believed we were superior and could make it—but we never did and we blame ourselves. As white people who haven't made it, we are the living proof of the American lie and we hate ourselves for it.

What can we do about all this? As poor and working-class women, we can start asking what is wrong with America and *stop* asking what is wrong with ourselves. In a culture where women are often judged by beauty alone, the standard of beauty does not fit us. We, as *ourselves*, as we go to work or wash dishes, we, *in our daily lives*, are never called beautiful. Black women have told themselves that they are beautiful in their natural lives, and we need to do the same for ourselves. We must begin to see ourselves as beautiful in our ability to work, to endure, in our plain, honest lives, and we must stop aspiring to a false-eyelash existence that is not and never has been for us. We are not the women in *Vogue, Glamour,* or *As The World*

Turns, nor should we want to be. We are the women who have dealt all our lives with the truths and tragedies of real life, because we never had the option of the armchair-beautiful-people existence. We are the people who have no maids or therapists to dump our troubles on. We know what it is to work hard and we are not guilty of wearing silks while others wear rags. We should never admire the women in *Vogue*, because there is something undeniably ugly about women who wear minks while others can't afford shoes—and no amount of $20-an-ounce makeup can hide that brand of ugliness. We must start learning that other people have been victims of this middle-class culture aping the rich. Black and Puerto Rican, Mexican and Indian, Chinese and Japanese people have had their true history concealed and their faces scorned by TV and magazines. We must see that those who share the hardships we share are not the white middle and upper classes, but the black and brown people who work at our sides. As white working-class and poor people we must begin to be proud of ourselves, our histories, and each other; we must unite and support ourselves as a people. Once we respect ourselves, we will find it necessary to struggle with a society and with jobs which tell us we are worthless. In that struggle we will learn that the anger of black and brown people which we have feared for so long has the same direction as our anger, that their enemies are our enemies, and their fight our fight.

Chapter Sixty-Six

The Politics of Housework

Pat Mainardi

> Though women do not complain of the power of husbands,
> each complains of her own husband, or of the husbands of
> her friends. It is the same in all other cases of servitude; at
> least in the commencement of the emancipatory move-
> ment. The serfs did not at first complain of the power of
> the lords, but only of their tyranny.
>
> —John Stuart Mill, *On the Subjection of Women*

Liberated women—very different from women's liberation! The first signals all kinds of goodies, to warm the hearts (not to mention other parts) of the most radical men. The other signals—housework. The first brings sex without marriage, sex before marriage, cozy house-keeping arrangements ("You see, I'm living with this chick") and the self-content of knowing that you're not the kind of man who wants a doormat instead of a woman. That will come later. After all, who wants that old commodity anymore, the Standard American Housewife, all husband, home and kids. The New Commodity, the Liberated Woman, has sex a lot and has a Career, preferably something that can be fitted in with the household chores—like dancing, pottery, or painting.

On the other hand is women's liberation—and housework. What? You say this is all trivial? Wonderful! That's what I thought. It seemed perfectly reasonable. We both had careers, both had to work a couple of days a week to earn enough to live on, so why shouldn't we share the housework? So I suggested it to my mate and he agreed—most men are too hip to turn you down flat. "You're right," he said, "It's only fair."

Then an interesting thing happened. I can only explain it by stating that we women have been brainwashed more than even we can imagine. Probably too many years of seeing television women in ecstasy over their shiny waxed floors or breaking down over their dirty shirt collars. Men have no such conditioning. They recognize the essential fact of housework right from the very beginning. Which is that it stinks. Here's my list of dirty chores: buying groceries, carting them home and putting them away; cooking meals and washing dishes and pots; doing the laundry, digging out the place when things get out of control; washing floors. The list could go on but the sheer necessities are bad enough. All of us have to do these things, or get some one else to do them for us. The longer my husband contemplated these chores the more repulsed he became, and so proceeded the change from the normally sweet considerate Dr. Jekyll into the crafty Mr. Hyde who would stop at nothing to avoid the horrors of—housework. As he felt himself backed into a corner laden with dirty dishes, brooms, mops, and reeking garbage, his front teeth grew longer and pointier, his fingernails haggled and his eyes grew wild. Housework trivial? Not on your life! Just try to share the burden.

So ensued a dialogue that's been going on for several years. Here are some of the high points:

"I don't mind sharing the housework, but I don't do it very well. We should each do the things we're best at."

Meaning: Unfortunately I'm no good at things like washing dishes or cooking. What I do best is a little light carpentry, changing light bulbs, moving furniture (*how often do you move furniture?*).

Also Meaning: Historically the lower classes (black men and us) have had hundreds of years experience doing menial jobs. It would be a waste of manpower to train someone else to do them now.

Also Meaning: I don't like the dull stupid boring jobs, so you should do them.

"I don't mind sharing the work, but you'll have to show me how to do it."

Meaning: I ask a lot of questions and you'll have to show me everything everytime I do it because I don't remember so good. Also don't try to sit down and read while I'm doing my jobs because I'm going to annoy hell out of you until it's easier to do them yourself.

"We used to be so happy!" (Said whenever it was his turn to do something.)
Meaning: I used to be so happy.
Meaning: Life without housework is bliss. (*No quarrel here. Perfect agreement.*)

"We have different standards, and why should I have to work to your standards. That's unfair."

Meaning: If I begin to get bugged by the dirt and crap I will say "This place sure is a sty" or "How can anyone live like this?" and wait for your reaction. I know that all women have a sore called "Guilt over a messy house" or "Household work is ultimately my responsibility." I know that men have caused that sore—if anyone visits and the place *is* a sty, they're not going to leave and say, "He sure is a lousy housekeeper." You'll take the rap in any case. I can outwait you.

Also Meaning: I can provoke innumerable scenes over the housework issue. Eventually doing all the housework yourself will be less painful to you than trying to get me to do half. Or I'll suggest we get a maid. She will do my share of the work. You will do yours. It's women's work.

"I've got nothing against sharing the housework, but you can't make me do it on your schedule."

Meaning: Passive resistance. I'll do it when I damned well please, if at all. If my job is doing dishes, it's easier to do them once a week. If taking out laundry, once a month.

If washing the floors, once a year. If you don't like it, do it yourself oftener, and then I won't do it at all.

"I *hate* it more than you. You don't mind it so much."
Meaning: Housework is garbage work. It's the worst crap I've ever done. It's degrading and humiliating for someone of *my* intelligence to do it. But for someone of *your* intelligence . . .

"Housework is too trivial to even talk about."
Meaning: It's even more trivial to do. Housework is beneath my status. My purpose in life is to deal with matters of significance. Yours is to deal with matters of significance. You should do the housework.

"This problem of housework is not a man-woman problem! In any relationship between two people one is going to have a stronger personality and dominate."
Meaning: That stronger personality had better be *me*.

"In animal societies, wolves, for example, the top animal is usually a male even where he is not chosen for brute strength but on the basis of cunning and intelligence. Isn't that interesting?"
Meaning: I have historical, psychological, anthropological, and biological justification for keeping you down. How can you ask the top wolf to be equal?

"Women's liberation isn't really a political movement."
Meaning: The Revolution is coming too close to home. *Also Meaning:* I am only interested in how *I* am oppressed, not how I oppress others. Therefore the war, the draft, and the university are political. Women's liberation is not.

"Man's accomplishments have always depended on getting help from other people, mostly women. What great man would have accomplished what he did if he had to do his own housework?
Meaning: Oppression is built into the System and I, as the white American male receive the benefits of this System. I don't want to give them up.

Postscript

Participatory democracy begins at home. If you are planning to implement your politics, there are certain things to remember.

1. He *is* feeling it more than you. He's losing some leisure and you're gaining it. The measure of your oppression is his resistance.
2. A great many American men are not accustomed to doing monotonous repetitive work which never ushers in any lasting let alone important achievement. This is why they would rather repair a cabinet than wash dishes. If human endeavors are like a pyramid with man's highest achievements at the top, then keeping oneself alive is at the bottom. Men have always had servants (us) to take care of this bottom strata of life while they have confined their efforts to the rarefied upper regions. It is thus ironic when they ask of women—where

are your great painters, statesmen, etc? Mme. Matisse ran a millinery shop so he could paint. Mrs. Martin Luther King kept his house and raised his babies.

3. It is a traumatizing experience for someone who has always thought of himself as being against any oppression or exploitation of one human being by another to realize that in his daily life he has been accepting and implementing (and benefiting from) this exploitation; that his rationalization is little different from that of the racist who says "Black people don't feel pain" (women don't mind doing the shitwork); and that the oldest form of oppression in history has been the oppression of 50 percent of the population by the other 50 percent.

4. Arm yourself with some knowledge of the psychology of oppressed peoples everywhere, and a few facts about the animal kingdom. I admit playing top wolf or who runs the gorillas is silly but as a last resort men bring it up all the time. Talk about bees. If you feel really hostile bring up the sex life of spiders. They have sex. She bites off his head.

   The psychology of oppressed people is not silly. Jews, immigrants, black men, and all women have employed the same psychological mechanisms to survive: admiring the oppressor, glorifying the oppressor, wanting to be like the oppressor, wanting the oppressor to like them, mostly because the oppressor held all the power.

5. In a sense, all men everywhere are slightly schizoid—divorced from the reality of maintaining life. This makes it easier for them to play games with it. It is almost a cliché that women feel greater grief at sending a son off to war or losing him to that war because they bore him, suckled him, and raised him. The men who foment those wars did none of those things and have a more superficial estimate of the worth of human life. One hour a day is a low estimate of the amount of time one has to spend "keeping" oneself. By foisting this off on others, man gains seven hours a week—one working day more to play with his mind and not his human needs. Over the course of generations it is easy to see whence evolved the horrifying abstractions of modern life.

6. With the death of each form of oppression, life changes and new forms evolve. English aristocrats at the turn of the century were horrified at the idea of enfranchising working men—were sure that it signaled the death of civilization and a return to barbarism. Some working men were even deceived by this line. Similarly with the minimum wage, abolition of slavery, and female suffrage. Life changes but it goes on. Don't fall for any line about the death of everything if men take a turn at the dishes. They will imply that you are holding back the Revolution (their Revolution). But you are advancing it (your Revolution).

7. Keep checking up. Periodically consider who's actually *doing* the jobs. These things have a way of backsliding so that a year later once again the woman is doing everything. After a year make a list of jobs the man has rarely if ever done. You will find cleaning pots, toilets, refrigerators and ovens high on the list. Use time sheets if necessary. He will accuse you of being petty. He is above that sort of thing—(housework). Bear in mind what the worst jobs are, namely the ones that have to be done every day or several times a day. Also the ones that are dirty—it's more pleasant to pick up books, newspapers, etc. than to

wash dishes. Alternate the bad jobs. It's the daily grind that gets you down. Also make sure that you don't have the responsibility for the housework with occasional help from him. "I'll cook dinner for you tonight" implies it's really your job and isn't he a nice guy to do some of it for you.

8. Most men had a rich and rewarding bachelor life during which they did not starve or become encrusted with crud or buried under the litter. There is a taboo that says that women mustn't strain themselves in the presence of men: we haul around 50 pounds of groceries if we have to but aren't allowed to open a jar if there is someone around to do it for us. The reverse side of the coin is that men aren't supposed to be able to take care of themselves without a woman. Both are excuses for making women do the housework.

9. Beware of the double whammy. He won't do the little things he always did because you're now a "Liberated Woman," right? Of course he won't do anything else either . . .

I was just finishing this when my husband came in and asked what I was doing. Writing a paper on housework. Housework? He said, *Housework?* Oh my god how trivial can you get. A paper on housework.

Little Politics of Housework Quiz

The lowest job in the army, used as punishment is: a) working 9–5 b) kitchen duty (K.P.).

When a man lives with his family, his: a) father b) mother does his housework.

When he lives with a woman, a) he b) she does the housework.

a) his son b) his daughter learns in preschool how much fun it is to iron daddy's handkerchief.

From the *New York Times*, 9/21/69: "Former Greek Official George Mylonas pays the penalty for differing with the ruling junta in Athens by performing household chores on the island of Amorgos where he lives in forced exile" (with hilarious photo of a miserable Mylonas carrying his own water). What the *Times* means is that he ought to have a) indoor plumbing b) a maid.

Dr. Spock said (*Redbook* 3/69): "Biologically and temperamentally I believe, women were made to be concerned first and foremost with child care, husband care, and home care." Think about: a) *who* made us b) why? c) what is the effect on their lives d) what is the effect on our lives?

From *Time* 1/5/70, "Like their American counterparts, many housing project housewives are said to suffer from neurosis. And for the first time in Japanese history, many young husbands today complain of being henpecked. Their wives are beginning to demand detailed explanations when they don't come home straight from work and some Japanese males nowadays are even compelled to do housework." According to *Time*, women become neurotic: a) when they are forced to do the maintenance work for the male caste all day every day of their lives or b) when they no longer want to do the maintenance work for the male caste all day every day of their lives.

Chapter Sixty-Seven

Housework

Slavery or Labor of Love

Betsy Warrior

In every period of labor reform, the lot of the houseworker has lain outside the sphere of interest of reformers and radicals alike, and has remained untouched by any improvements accruing to those workers whose jobs are outside the home. This continues to be the case today. Energy is being directed at improving the conditions of migrant workers, minority groups in the labor force, and even women if they happen to be in the "outside" labor force, i.e., in work situations analogous to male workers. No such energy is being directed at the situation of the household worker. The oppression of females who work outside the home is more easily recognizable because general standards that are accepted for male workers can theoretically be applied to females also. Thus their inequality in relation to male workers can be exposed. There are no such standards for houseworkers nor has the labor they perform ever been recognized as such.

The most obvious reason that no attention has been given to the situation of the houseworker is simply the fact that men aren't engaged in this work. As this position is unique to women, men don't see any direct benefit for themselves in the improvement of it; therefore, it remains unchanged. In this respect, as in many others, men constitute an upper caste who have a monopoly on economic and political power and will use it only when it is directly in their interest. Females, on the other hand, although they would benefit from improvements in this area, are relatively powerless and so unable to implement the necessary changes. The failure of men to use their power to improve the situation of the houseworker is also due to the fact that they rightly feel that any major changes in this area would undermine male supremacy. Men now have their domestic work done for them free. If a change occurred in this area it might mean that men would have to share this now low-prestige work and/or pay to have someone else do it.

It has been suggested that women will gain equality only when they are all employed in the "public" labor force and that this step will by some magic free them from the status of unpaid domestic slavery. The solution to this dilemma can't lie in the hope that all women will leave the home and join the outside paid labor force. First of all, women working outside the home receive the lowest wages and fill the lowest positions in the paid labor force. Secondly, even in time of economic expansion when new jobs are created, there aren't enough jobs to go around.

Besides these two factors that deprive women of incentive to join the "outside" labor force, there are other deterrents. One of the main deterrents is the fact that there are no facilities set up by society for child care or home maintenance in the event that a woman decides to work outside the home. The few existing facilities can't even be considered by the majority of women because of their prohibitive cost and their inability to accommodate more than a tiny percentage of those who might have use for them. Someone has to perform the vast amount of labor entailed in raising children and maintaining living quarters. This labor continues to devolve on women even when they have jobs outside the home. Doubly burdened, women are unable to devote their full attention to either job and are effectively kept at the lowest levels of the paid labor force. On top of that they have been used as scapegoats for every ill of society because they are unable to give their full attention to the roles of mother, wife, and housekeeper.

There are other equally discouraging deterrents of a psychological nature such as the belief that it is the duty of a woman to be solely a wife and mother and that she can't overstep these limits except at the risk of losing her "true" identity. Also a woman's education isn't geared to facilitate a successful or fulfilling career outside the home. Indoctrination and tracking take of this. If in spite of this, a woman decides to work outside the home, it can be taken for granted that some of the psychological deterrents have been at least partially overcome. But having decided to work outside the home, she comes up against other obstacles that are impossible to remove by a mere change of thinking.

This brings us back to the problem of child care and housework. In other countries attempts have been made to improve the status of women and release them from their unpaid drudgery by drawing them into the paid labor force. These attempts failed and were doomed to failure from the outset because no adequate provisions were made for housework or the care of children. Because of the reformist nature of the changes in the role of women in these societies, the very basis of woman's oppression remained untouched. Females didn't actively share in the decision-making of these revolutions and in fact weren't equally represented in any important areas of these revolutions.

I don't think the feebleness of these reformist attempts is wholly attributable to innocent error or a faulty analysis on the part of male socialist planners but more likely to the unwillingness of males to share the responsibility for home maintenance and child care and an indifference on their part to something they think need not concern them. To equalize the status of the female would have entailed such major and drastic reorganization of society that, judging by the results of the revolutions, it was something the "revolutionary" leaders were unwilling or afraid to undertake. This attitude led them to attack only a symptom of the problem (i.e., the inequality of women in the paid labor force) rather than its root, woman's primary oppression as unpaid domestic—the underlying reason for this inequality. The revolutionary goal of complete emancipation for the female half of the human race has in all revolutions been a goal of low priority which has later been neglected and finally betrayed. But this is an old story to the woman's movement.

> The reorganization of ordinary home maintenance service is long overdue. Household workers have, historically, been low paid, without standards of hours and working conditions, without collective bargaining, without most of the protections accorded by legislation and accepted as normal by other workers, and without means and opportunity adequately to maintain their homes. (From American Women (1963–1968): Report on the Status of Women—Interdepartmental Committee)

This quote from The Report on the Status of Women gives an understated and inaccurate account of the situation of houseworkers: In fact it is meant only to apply to the tiny minority of houseworkers who actually do get paid! To say that a segment of the labor force is low-paid is quite different from stating that roughly half of the labor force is un-paid—the half that produces and maintains all labor power. Also the quote doesn't recognize that this situation will exist by necessity under the present economy and a real change can be effected only along with a complete change in the sex role system. The situation of the paid houseworker is indelibly tainted by the economic status of the majority of unpaid houseworkers. How much remuneration is society willing to give for a service that is usually provided free?

In another pamphlet put out by the Women's Bureau of the US Department of Labor, this question is posed, "What is Equal Pay?" It goes on to explain that "Equal pay means payment of 'rate for the job' without regard to sex—in the factory, in the office, in the school, in the store—and in all other places where men and women perform work of a comparable character."

In other pamphlets put out by the Department of Labor, it is cited that women on an average work anywhere between 36 and 99.6 hours a week in the home. This a job at which *all* women are employed at one time or another in their lives, if not all their lives. But there is no mention of "rate for the job" for this work, and this oversight holds true for socialist publications as well. The socialist analyses, including those by women, state that woman's oppression arises at the point of production. What production? They mean, of course, the production that men are engaged in— the production of the "public" sector of the economy! The maddening persistence of this oversight lies in the male orientation of all this literature which does not recognize labor except "where men and women perform work of a comparable character."

The phrase "comparable character" betrays the pseudo-equality offered by these analyses. The main function of women, which she is confined to because of sex and which distinguishes her from the male, is just what is responsible for her inferior status in the outside labor force and everywhere. This function is in no way comparable to anything done by males. To offer the illusion that women will be equal by receiving equal pay for work that is also done by males, is a conscious effort to keep women's slavery intact. Women are not just laborers in the male-defined sense of the word. Women are the source of all labor in that they are the producers of all laborers. This is the basic means of production (reproduction) in any society. It creates the first commodity, female and male laborers, who in turn create all other commodities and products. Men as the ruling class profit from this commodity through its labor. These profits come in two sizes: king-size and super. The individual man who is king of his castle (the patrilineal family) has his labor power produced, prepared, and maintained for him free. When he sells his labor power on the market he is selling a commodity he owns but did not produce, thereby profiting from the slave labor that went into the making of this product. The *male* capitalist class makes a super-profit when it buys this labor power and then receives the surplus value of its "outside" economy production.

It is clear to me that women will not be freed from their sexual status (slavery) by being given equal opportunity in the "outside" labor force; it has been tried already and has failed. Rather they will be given the basis for equal opportunity by being freed of their function as domestic slaves and its form, the patrilineal family. If we attempt to improve the situation of the houseworker without attacking the economy and sex role attitudes which make this situation possible, then, in effect, we will be trying to make the slavery of women more palatable.

As it is not possible to make any improvements in the institution of slavery, and this is the only accurate counterpart we can find for housework, we must take housework out of the realm of slavery and thereby change its very nature and social meaning. This means, in effect, the abolition of "housework" and "domestic" service in the sense that it is now known. Once this work has to be paid for, it will be incorporated into the "public" economy. This means that the work that was formerly done in separate, duplicated, single units will be collectivized and industrialized on a large basis with a more efficient use of both time and labor and without the waste, alienation, and duplication now involved in child care and home maintenance. Only when this is accomplished will women be able to fight for their equality on a more nearly equal footing with men.

Appendix 1
Radical Feminist Journals, 1967–1974

This appendix was compiled from a number of sources: the Lesbian Herstory Archives, Wendy Martin, *The American Sisterhood: Writings of the Feminist Movement from Colonial Times to the Present*, New York: Harper & Row, 1972, Roberta L. Salper, (Ed.), *Female Liberation: History and Current Politics*, New York: Alfred A. Knopf, Inc., 1972, Maren Lockwood Carden's, *The New Feminist Movement*, New York: Russel Sage Foundation, 1974, pp. 211–217, and Ginette Castro, *American Feminism: A Contemporary History*, New York: New York University Press, 1990.

A Journal of Female Liberation
Ain't I a Woman
ALAS'S
Amazon Quarterly: A Lesbian-Feminist Arts Journal
Aphra
Aurora: Prism of Feminism
Awake and Move
Battle Acts
Black Maria
Change: A Working Woman's Newspaper (formerly A Change is Gonna Come*)*
Coalition (see Women's Liberation of Michigan Monthly*)*
Common Woman
Do It NOW
Earth's Daughters
Essecondsex
Everywoman
Feelings from Women's Liberation
Female Liberation Newsletter
Female State: A Journal of Female Liberation
The Feminist Bulletin
Feminist Party News
Feminist Studies

The Feminist Voice
FEW's Views and News
The Furies
Goodbye to All That
The Hand (formerly Lysistrata, *and* The Hand that Rocks the Rock*)*
Happening
Happiness of Womanhood (newsletter)
Happiness of Womanhood (men's auxiliary newsletter)
Her-self: Community Woman's Newspaper
Hysteria
It Ain't Me Babe
It Is Not My Baby (formerly It Ain't Me Babe*)*
Just Like A Woman
Kansas City Women's Liberation Union (newsletter)
KNOW News Service
The Ladder
Lancaster Women's Liberation (newsletter)
Lavendar Vision
Lavender Woman
Libera

Lilith

The Link (formerly The Alliance Link*)*

L[os] A[ngeles] Women's Liberation Newsletter (see Sister*)*

Maine Women's Newsletter

Majority Report: A Feminist Newspaper Serving the Women of New York

Matrix: For She of the New Aeon

Momma: The Newspaper Magazine for Single Mothers

The Monthly Extract: An Irregular Periodical

Mother Lode

Moving Out

Ms

Muthah

National Women's Political Caucus (newsletter)

The New Broadside: The Feminist Review of the News

New Broom: A Legislative Newsletter for Massachusetts Women

New Carolina Woman

New Directions for Women

New Woman

New York Radical Feminists (newsletter)

No More Fun and Games: A Journal of Female Liberation

North Dakota Women's Liberation

Notes from the First, Second and Third Year

off our backs

Off the Pedestal

The Opening

Oregon Council for Women's Equality

Pandora

Pedestal

Philadelphia Women's Center (newsletter)

Prime Time: For the Liberation of Women in the Prime of Life

Pro Se

RAT

Real Women

S.P.A.Z.M. (formerly Murra's Maxims*)*

San Francisco Women's Newsletter (formerly Women's Liberation Newsletter*)*

Scarlet Letter

Second Coming

The Second Page

The Second Wave

Sister (formerly L[os] A[ngeles] Women's Liberation Newsletter *and* Women's Center Newsletter*)*

Sister

Sisters in Poverty

Southern Journal of Female Liberation

Spectre

Tell-a-Woman

The Second Wave: A Magazine of New Feminism

The Spokeswoman

Tell-a-Woman

Tooth and Nail

Triple Jeopardy: Racism, Imperialism, Sexism

The Turn of the Screwed

Union WAGE

Up From Under: by, for and about Women

Velvet Glove

Voice of the Women's Liberation Movement

WEAL (national newsletter; formerly WEAL's Word Watcher *and* WEAL's Action*)*

WEAL Washington Report

Whole Woman

Wildflowers

The Woman Activist: An Action Bulletin for Women's Rights

Woman Becoming

Womankind

Woman Power

The Woman's Journal

Woman's World

Women

Women & Art

Women Involved (newsletter)
Women: A Journal of Liberation
Women in Struggle
Women Studies Abstracts
Women Today (formerly Washington
Newsletter for Women*)*
Women Unite NOW
Women West

Women's Legal Defense Fund (newsletter)
*Women's Liberation of Michigan Monthly
(formerly* Coalition*)*
Women's Monthly
The Women's Page
Women's Press: A Women's News Journal
Women's Rights Law Reporter
Women's Studies Newsletter

Appendix 2
List of Archives for Further Research

Barnard College
Barnard College Library
3009 Broadway
New York, NY 10027

Bibliotèque Saint-Jean
Jacqueline Girouard
University of Alberta
8406 Rue Marie-Anne Gaboury, #-12S
Edmonton, Alberta
Canada T6C 4G9

Duke University
Women's Archives
Special Collections Library
Duke University, Box 90185
Durham, NC 27708-0185

Georgia Women's Movement Archives
E. Lee Eltzroth, Women's Collections
    Archivist
Georgia Women's Collections
Special Collections Department
Pullen Library, University Plaza
Georgia State University
Atlanta, GA 30303-3202

Iowa Women's Archives
Karen A. Mason
University of Iowa Libraries
100 Main Library
University of Iowa
Iowa City, IA 52242-1420

Lesbian Herstory Archives
P.O. Box 1258
New York, NY, 10116

Mary McLeod Bethune Council House
    National Historic Site
Susan McElrath
National Park Service
1318 Vermont Avenue N.W.
Washington, DC 20005

Newcomb College
Center for Research on Women
Tulane University
New Orleans, LA 70118

Redstockings Women's Liberation
    Archives
P.O. Box 2625
Gainesville, FL 32602-2625

Sophia Smith Collection
Smith College
Northampton, MA 01063-0001

Tamiment Institute Library
Peter Meyer Filardo, Tamiment
    Archivist
New York University
70 Washington Square South
New York, NY 10012

Women's Educational Center, Inc.
46 Pleasant Street
Cambridge, MA 02139

The Women's Movement Archives and
the Women's Center Library
Libby Bouvier, Archivist

Websites

A Guide to Uncovering Women's History in Archival Collections
University of Texas, San Antonio
http://www.lib.utsa.edu/Archives/links.htm

Women's Collection Roundtable, Directory
http://www.archivists.org/units/home.html

Women's Archives and Special Collections on the world wide web http://scripto-rium.lib.duke.edu/women/article.html

Bibliography

Abbott, Sidney, and Barbara Love. "Is Women's Liberation a Lesbian Plot?" In V. Gornick and B. K. Moran (eds.), *Woman in Sexist Society: Studies in Power and Powerlessness*, 601–621. New York: Basic Books, 1971.

———. *Sappho was a Right-On Woman: A Liberated View of Lesbianism*. Briarcliff Manor, NY: Stein and Day, 1972.

Abcarian, Gilbert. "On the Political Theories of Radical and Socialist Feminism in the USA." *Politico [Italy]* 47 (2) (1982): 417–426.

"Action Committee for Decent Child Care." *Women: A Journal of Liberation* 2 (4) (1970): 7–8.

Adams, Elsie, and Mary Louise Briscoe, eds. *Up against the Wall Mother . . . On Women's Liberation*. Beverly Hills, CA: Glencoe Press, 1971.

Adams, Mary Louise. "There's No Place Like Home: On the Place of Identity in Feminist Politics." *Feminist Review* 31 (1989): 22–33.

Adamson, Nancy, Linda Briskin, and Margaret McPhail. *Feminists Organizing for Change: The Contemporary Canadian Women's Movement*. Toronto: Oxford University Press, 1988.

Alilunas, Kristine. "Women and the Language of Poverty: The Black Analogy in Feminist Language." *Revue Française d'Etudes Américaines [France]* 5 (9) (1980): 47–57.

Allen, Judith. "Contextualising Late-Nineteenth-Century Feminism: Problems and Comparisons." *Journal of the Canadian Historical Association/Revue de la Société Historique du Canada* 1 (1990): 17–36.

Allen, Pamela. "The Small Group Process." In *Free Space: A Perspective on the Small Group in Women's Liberation*, 23–32. New York: Times Change Press, 1970.

———. *Free Space: A Perspective on the Small Groups in Women's Liberation*. New York: Times Change Press, 1970.

Alpert, Jane. *Growing Up Underground*. New York: William Morrow, 1981.

Altbach, Edith Hoshino, ed. *From Feminism to Liberation*. Cambridge, MA: Schenkman Publishing, 1971.

———. "Notes on a Movement." In *From Feminism to Liberation*, 1–18. Cambridge, MA: Schenkman Publishing, 1971.

Arnold, June. "Consciousness-Raising." In Sookie Stambler, compiler, *Women's Liberation: Blueprint for the Future*, 155–161. New York: Ace Books, A Division of Charter Communications, 1970.

Atkinson, Ti-Grace. "Radical Feminism." *The Feminists*, May 1969.

———. "Radical Feminism." In *Notes from the Second Year*, 32–37. New York: Radical Feminism, 1970.

———. *Amazon Odyssey*. New York: Links, 1974.

Babcox, Deborah. "The Liberation of Children." In *Liberation Now! Writings from the Women's Liberation Movement*, 116–123. New York: Dell Publishing, 1971.

Bacchi, Carol. "The Nineteenth Century: Equal But Different." In *Same Difference*, 6–28. Sydney, Australia: Allen and Unwin, 1990.

Baker, Andrea J. "The Problem of Authority in Radical Movement Groups: A Case Study of Lesbian Feminist Organization." *Journal of Applied Behavioral Science* 18 (3) (1982): 323–341.

Baldwin, Janice I. "The Effects of Women's Liberation and Socialization on Delinquency and Crime. Special Issue: The Study of Women: New Challenges, New Directions." *Humboldt Journal of Social Relations* 10 (2) (Spring–Summer 1983): 90–111.

Banks, Olive. *Faces of Feminism*. Oxford: Martin Robertson, 1981.

Barr, Marlene, ed. *Future Females: A Critical Anthology*. Bowling Green, OH: State University Popular Press, 1981.

Barrett, Michele. *Women's Oppression Today: Problems in Marxist Feminist Analysis*. London: Verso, 1980.

Barry, Kathleen. "Feminist Theory: The Meaning of Women's Liberation." *Women's Annual*, 1982–1983, 55–78.

———. *Female Sexual Slavery*. Englewood Cliffs, NJ: Prentice Hall, 1979.

Baxandall, Rosalyn. "Co-operative Nurseries." In Sookie Stambler, compiler, *Women's Liberation: Blueprint for the Future*, 217–223. New York: Ace Books, A Division of Charter Communications, 1970.

———. "Rosalyn Baxandall's Feminist Memoir." Unpublished manuscript, 1994.

Bayes, Marjorie, Lynn Whisnante, and Lynn Anne Wilk. "The Mental Health Center and the Women's Liberation Group: An Intergroup Encounter." *Psychiatry* 40 (1) (Feb 1977): 66–78.

Beal, Frances. "Double Jeopardy: To Be Black and Female." In *Liberation Now! Writings from the Women's Liberation Movement*, 185–197. New York: Dell Publishing, 1971.

———. "Slave of a Slave No More: Black Women in Struggle." *Black Scholar* 6 (6) (1975): 2–10.

Beaman, Arthur L., and Bonnel Klentz. "The Supposed Physical Attractiveness Bias against Supporters of the Women's Movement: A Meta-Analysis." *Personality and Social Psychology Bulletin* 9 (4) (Dec 1983): 544–550.

Bell, Diane, and Renate Klein, eds. *Radically Speaking: Feminism Reclaimed*. North Melbourne: Spinifex Press, 1996.

Benson, Mike, Mariah Evans, and Rita Simon. "Women as Political Terrorists." *Research in Law, Deviance and Social Control* 4 (1982): 121–130.

Benston, Margaret. "The Political Economy of Women's Liberation." *Monthly Review* 21 (4) (Sept 1969): 13–27.

Berlant, Lauren. " '68, or Something." *Critical Inquiry* 21 (Autumn 1994): 124–155.

Bers, Trudy Haffron, and Susan Gluck Mezey. "Support for Feminist Goals among Leaders of Women's Community Groups." *Signs* 6 (4) (Summer 1981): 737–748.

Berson, Ginny Z. "The Furies." *The Furies* 1 (1972a): 2.

———. "Beyond Male Power . . ." *The Furies* 1 (4) (1972b): 13–14.

———. "Only by Association." *The Furies* 1 (5) (1972c): 5–6.

———. "The Furies: Goddesses of Vengeance." *Serials Review* (Winter 1990): 79–85.

Bird, Caroline. "Women's Lib and the Women's Colleges." *Change* 4 (3) (1972): 60–65.

"Black Feminism: A New Mandate." *Ms.* 2 (May 1974): 97–100.

Black, Naomi. "Notes for a Future Historian." *Women's History Review* 1 (1) (1992): 155–160.

Boles, Janet K. "Form Follows Function: The Evolution of Feminist Strategies." *Annals of the American Academy of Political and Social Science* 515 (May 1991): 38–49.

Booth, Heather, Evi Goldfield, and Sue Munaker. *Toward a Radical Movement*. Boston: New England Free Press, 1968.

Borun, M., et al. (The Philadelphia Collective). *Women's Liberation*: An Anthropological View. Pittsburgh: Know Inc., 1971.

Bouchier, David. "The Deradicalisation of Feminism: Ideology and Utopia in Action." *Sociology* 13 (3) (Sept 1979): 387–402.

———. "The Feminist Challenge: The Movement for Women's Liberation in Britain and the United States." *Political Science Quarterly* 99 (Winter 1984–1985): 731–732.

Braidotti, Rosi. *Nomadic Subjects: Embodiment and Sexual Differences in Contemporary Feminist Theory*. New York: Columbia University Press, 1994.

Brown, Rita Mae. "Roxanne Dunbar: How a Female Heterosexual Serves the Interests of Male Supremacy." *The Furies* 1 (1972): 5–6.

———. "The Shape of Things to Come." In Charlotte Bunch and Nancy Myron (eds.), *Lesbianism and the Women's Movement*, 75–80. Baltimore: Diana Press, 1975.

Brown, Jenny. "Women for Peace or Women's Liberation? Signposts from the Feminist Archives."*Vietnam Generation* 1 (3–4) (1989): 246–260.

Brown, Judith. "Origins of Consciousness-Raising in the South." *Mimeograph*, 1968.

Brownmiller, Susan. "The Enemy Within." In Sookie Stambler, compiler, *Women's Liberation: Blueprint for the Future*, 17–23. New York: Ace Books, A Division of the Charter Communications, 1970.

———. *Against Our Will: Men, Women, and Rape*. New York: Simon and Schuster, 1975.

Brunet, Ariane, and Louise Turcotte. "Rapport des Ateliers." *Amazonnes d'hier, Lesbiennes d'aujourd'hui* 1 (2–3): 1982. Rpt. as "Separatism and Radicalism: An Analysis of Similarities and Differences." In *For Lesbians Only*. Trans.

Buechler, Steven M. *Women's Movements in the United States*. New Brunswick, NJ: Rutgers University Press, 1990.

Buhle, Mari Jo, Paul Buhle, and Harvey J. Kaye, eds. *The American Radical*. New York: Routledge, 1994.

Buhle, Paul. "The Eclipse of the New Left: Some Notes." *Radical America* 6 (4) (July–Aug 1972): 1–10.

Bulkin, Elly. "Racism and Writing: Some Implications for White Lesbian Critics." *Sinister Wisdom* 13 (Spring 1980): 3–22.

Bunch, Charlotte. "Lesbians in Revolt: Male Supremacy Quakes and Quivers." *The Furies* 1 (1972): 8–9.

———. "Not for Lesbians Only." In Charlotte Bunch et al. (eds.), *Building Feminist Theory: Essays from Quest, A Feminist Quarterly*, 67–73. New York: Longman, 1981.

———, ed. *Passionate Politics: Feminist Theory in Action*. New York: St. Martin's Press, 1987.

———. "Global Feminism, Human Rights and Sexual Violence." In Institute for Women's Policy Research, (eds.), *Proceedings from the First Annual Women's Policy Research Conference, May, 19, 1989*. Washington, DC: Institute for Women's Policy Research, 1989.

Bunch, Charlotte, et al., eds. *Building Feminist Theory: Essays from Quest, A Feminist Quarterly*. New York: Longman, 1981.

Burris, Barbara. "The Fourth World Manifesto." In A. Koedt, A. Levine, and A. Rapone (eds.), *Radical Feminism*, 322–357. New York: Quadrangle Books, 1973.

Cade (Bambara), Toni, ed. *The Black Woman: An Anthology*. New York: New American Library, 1970.

Cade (Bambara) Toni, ed. "Introduction." In *The Black Woman: An Anthology*, 7–12. New York: New American Library, 1970.

———. "The Pill: Genocide or Liberation." In *The Black Woman: An Anthology*, 162–169. New York: New America Library, 1970.

Camarano, Chris Camarano. "On Cuban Women." In *Liberation Now! Writings from the Women's Liberation Movement*, 364–376. New York: Dell Publishing, 1971.

Campbell, Karlyn Kohrs. "The Rhetoric of Women's Liberation: An Oxymoron." *Quarterly Journal of Speech* 59 (1) (1973): 74–86.

Cantarow, Ellen, and Susan Gushee O'Malley. "Ella Baker: Organizing for Civil Rights." In E. Cantarow (ed.), *Moving the Mountain: Women Working for Social Change*, 52–93. New York: Feminist Press, 1980.

Carby, Hazel V. "White Women Listen! Black Feminism and the Boundaries of Sisterhood." In Contemporary Centre for Cultural Studies (ed.), *The Empire Strikes Back*, 212–235. London: Hutchinson, 1982.

Carden, Maren Lockwood. *The New Feminist Movement*. New York: Russell Sage Foundation, 1974.

———. "The Proliferation of a Social Movement: Ideology and Individual Incentives in the Feminist Movement." *Research in Social Movements, Conflicts and Change* (1978): 179–196.

Cassell, Joan. "Externalities of Change: Deference and Demeanor in Contemporary Feminism." *Human Organization* 33 (1) (1974): 85–94.

———. *A Group Called Women: Sisterhood and Symbolism in the Feminist Movement*. New York: David McKay, 1977.

Castro, Ginette. *American Feminism: A Contemporary History*. New York: New York University Press, 1990.

Chafe, William H. *The American Woman: Her Changing Social, Economic, and Political Roles, 1920–1970*. New York: Oxford University Press, 1972.

———. "Feminism of the 1970s." *Dissent* 21 (Fall 1974): 508–517.

Chalmers, David. "The Struggle for Social Change in 1960s America: A Bibliographic Essay." *American Studies International* 30 (1) (1992): 41–64.

Chasseguet-Smirgel, J. *Female Sexuality*. Ann Arbor: University of Michigan Press, 1970.

Cherniss, Cary. "Personality and Ideology: A Personological Study of Women's Liberation." *Psychiatry* 35 (2) (May 1972): 109–125.

Chesebro, James W., and John F. Cragan. "The Rhetoric of Women's Liberation." *Moments in Contemporary Rhetoric and Communication* 1 (2) (Fall 1971): 1–58.

Chicago, Judy. *Through the Flower: My Struggle as a Woman Artist*. Garden City, NY: Doubleday, 1975.

Chodorow, Nancy. "Family Structure and Feminine Personality." In Michelle Zimbalist Rosaldo and Louise Lamphere (eds.), *Women, Culture, and Society*, 43–66. Stanford, CA: Stanford University Press, 1974.

Cocks, Joan. "Worldless Emotions: Some Critical Reflections on Radical Feminism." *Politics and Society* 13 (1) (1984): 27–57.

Combahee River Collective. "A Black Feminist Statement." In Zillah R. Eisenstein (ed.), *Capitalist Patriarchy and the Case for Socialist Feminism*, 362–372. New York: Monthly Review Press, 1979.

Cook, Elizabeth Adell, and Clyde Wilcox. "A Rose by Any Other Name: Measuring Support for Organized Feminism Using Anes Feeling Thermometers." *Women and Politics* 12 (1) (1992): 35–51.

Cooke, Joanne, Charlotte Bunch-Weeks, and Robin Morgan. *The New Women*. New York: Times Change Press, 1971.

Coote, Anna, and Beatrix Campbell. *Sweet Freedom: The Struggle for Women's Liberation*. London: Picador, 1982.

Cordova, Jeanne. "Radical Feminism?" *Lesbian Tide* (June 1973): 20–21, 25, 27–28.

Cornwell, Anita. "The Black Lesbian in a Malevolent Society" and "The Lesser of the Worst." In *Black Lesbian in White America*, 17–30. Tallahassee, FL: Naiad Press, 1983.

Corrigan, Annette. "Fashion, Beauty and Feminism." *Meanjin* 51 (1) (Autumn 1992): 107–122.

Cott, Nancy. *The Bonds of Womanhood*. New Haven, CT: Yale University Press, 1977.

Cox, Cherise. "Anything Less Is Not Feminism: Racial Difference and the W.M.W.M." *Law and Critique* 1 (2) (Autumn 1990): 237–248.

Crowley, Sharon. "The Semantics of Sexism." *A Review of General Semantics* 30 (4) (1973): 407–411.

Cruikshank, Margaret. *The Gay and Lesbian Liberation Movement*. New York: Routledge, Chapman and Hall, 1992.

———, ed. *Lesbian Studies, Present and Future*. New York: Feminist Press, 1982.

Cummings, Scott. "Class and Racial Divisions in the Female Population: Some Practical and Political Dilemmas for the Women's Movement." *Sociological Symposium* 15 (Spring 1976): 99–119.

Cunningham, F., et al., eds. *Social Movements/Social Change: The Politics and Practice of Organizing*. Toronto: Between the Lines, 1988.

Curran, Daniel J. "The Myth of the 'New' Female Delinquent." *Crime and Delinquency* 30 (3) (July 1984): 386–399.

Cutler, Stephen J. "Aging and Changes in Attitudes about the Women's Liberation Movement." *International Journal of Aging and Human Development* 16 (1) (1983): 43–51.

Dalla Costa, Mariarosa, and Selma James. *The Power of Women and the Subversion of the Community*. Bristol: Falling Wall Press, 1972.

Daly, Mary. *The Church and the Second Sex*. New York: Harper and Row, 1968.

———. "The Spiritual Revolution: Women's Liberation as Theological Re-education." *Andover Newton Quarterly* 12 (4) (March 1972): 163–176.

———. *Beyond God the Father: Toward a Philosophy of Women's Liberation*. Boston: Beacon Press, 1973.

———. *Gyn/Ecology: The Metaethics of Radical Feminism*. Boston: Beacon Press, 1978.

D'Amico, Debby. "To My White Working-Class Sisters." In *Liberation Now! Writings from the Women's Liberation Movement*, 177–181. New York: Dell Publishing, 1971.

Davis, Elizabeth Gould. *The First Sex*. New York: Penguin, 1971.

de Beauvoir, Simone. *The Second Sex*. Trans. H. M. Parshley. New York: Knopf, 1952. Originally published as *Le Deuxième Sexe*. Paris: Gallimard, 1949.

Deckard, Barbara Sinclair. *The Women's Movement: Political, Socioeconomic, and Psychological Issues*. New York: Harper and Row, 1983.

Degler, Carl. *At Odds: Women and Family from the Revolution to the Present*. New York: Oxford University Press, 1984.

dell'Olio, Anselma. "Divisiveness and Self-Destruction in the Women's Movement." Manuscript, n.d.

Densmore, Dana. "Sex Roles and Their Consequences: Research in Female and Male Differences." *No More Fun and Games: Journals of Female Liberation* February 1969.

Didion, Joan. "The Women's Movement." In *The White Album*, 109–19. New York: Simon and Schuster, 1979.

Dietz, Mary G. "Introduction: Debating Simone de Beauvoir." *Signs* 18 (11) (1992): 74–88.

Dixon, Marlene. "Why Women's Liberation." *Ramparts* 8 (6) (1969): 58–63.

———. "On Women's Liberation: Where Are We Going?" *Radical America* 4 (2) (1978): 26–35.

Dobbins, Peggy Powell. "Towards a Theory of the Women's Liberation Movement and Women's Wage-Labor." *Insurgent Sociologist* 7 (3) (Summer 1977): 53–62.

Donovan, Josephine. *Feminist Theory: The Intellectual Traditions of American Feminism*. New York: Frederick Ungar Publishing, 1985.

Douglas, Carol Anne. *Love and Politics: Radical Feminist and Lesbian Theories*. San Francisco: ism press, 1990.

Dreifus, Claudia, ed. *Seizing Our Bodies: The Politics of Women's Health*. New York: Vintage Books, 1978.

Dunbar, Roxanne. "Female Liberation as the Basis for Social Revolution." Boston: New England Free Press February 1969, Cell 16.

Dworkin, Andrea. *Woman Hating*. New York: E. P. Dutton, 1974.

Eastman, Paula Costa. "Consciousness-Raising as a Resocialization Process for Women." *Smith College Studies in Social Work* 43 (3) (June 1973): 153–183.

Easton, Barbara. "The Decline of Patriarchy and the Rise of Feminism: A Critique of Feminist Theory." *Catalyst* 10 (11) (Summer 1977): 104–124.

Echols, Alice. "The Taming of the Id: Feminist Sexual Politics, 1968–83." In Carol Vance (ed.), *Pleasure and Danger*, 50–72. New York: Routledge, 1984.

———. "Feminism and the Contemporary Family." *Socialist Review* 8:3 (39) (May– June 1978): 11–36.

———. *Daring to Be Bad; Radical Feminism in America, 1967–1975*. Minneapolis: University of Minnesota Press, 1989.

———. " 'We Gotta Get Out of This Place': Notes Towards a Remapping of the Sixties." *Socialist Review* 22 (2) (April–June 1992): 9–33.

Edholm, Felicity, Olivia Harris, and Kate Young. "Conceptualizing Women." *Critique of Anthropology* 3 (9/10) (1977): 101–30.

Editorial: "What is Liberation?" *Women: A Journal of Liberation* 1 (2) (Winter 1970): 7–8.

Edwards, Alison. *Rape, Racism, and the White Women's Movement: An Answer to Susan Brownmiller*. Chicago: Sojourner Truth Organization, n.d.

Ehrenreich, Barbara, Barbara Dudley, and Michelle Russel. "The National Conference on Socialist Feminism." *Socialist Revolution* 5:4 (26) (Oct– Dec 1975): 85–93.

Eichler, Margrit. "A Review of Selected Recent Literature on Women." *Canadian Review of Sociology and Anthropology* 9 (1) (1972): 86–96.

———. "Leadership in Social Movements." *Sociological Inquiry* 47 (2) (1977): 99–107.

Eisenstein, Hester. "Lesbianism and the Woman-Identified Woman." In *Contemporary Feminist Thought*, 48–57. Boston: G. K. Hall, 1983.

Epstein, Cynthia Fuchs. "Ten Years Later: Perspectives on the Woman's Movement." *Dissent* 22 (2) (1975): 169–176.

Epstein, Cynthia Fuchs, and Tiger, Lionel. "Will Women's Lib Really Help Women?" *Sexual Behavior* 1 (6) (1971): 56–67.

Evans, Sara M. "The Origins of the Women's Liberation Movement." *Radical America* 9 (2) (March– April 1975): 1–12.

———. *Personal Politics: The Roots of Women's Liberation in the Civil Rights Movement and the New Left*. New York: Knopf, 1979.

————. *Born for Liberty: A History of Women in America.* New York: Free Press, 1989.

Farganis, Sondra. "Liberty: Two Perspectives on the Women's Movement." *Ethics* 88 (1) (Oct 1977): 62–73.

Farrar, Anne. "The Seattle Liberation Front, Women's Liberation, and a New Socialist Politics." *Socialist Revolution* 1 (15) (Sept– Oct 1970): 124–136.

Faunce, Patricia S., and Susan Phipps-Yonas. "Women's Liberation and Human Sexual Relations." *International Journal of Women's Studies* 1 (1) (Jan– Feb 1978): 83–95.

Firestone, Shulamith. *The Dialectic of Sex: The Case for Feminist Revolution.* New York: William Morrow, 1970.

————. "The Dialectic of Sex" and "Racism: The Sexism of the Family of Man." In *The Dialectic of Sex*, 1–14, 105–125. New York: William Morrow, 1970.

————., ed. *Notes from the First Year.* New York, 1968.

————. *Notes from the Second Year: Womens' Liberation—Major Writings of the Radical Feminists.* New York: Radical Feminism, 1970.

Fisher, Elizabeth. *Woman's Creation: Sexual Evolution and the Shaping of Society.* Garden City, NY: Anchor Press-Doubleday, 1979.

Flexner, Eleanor. *Century of Struggle: The Women's Rights Movement in the United States.* Boston: Athenaeum, 1968.

Foner, Philip S., ed. *We, the Other People: Alternative Declarations of Independence by Labor Groups, Farmers, Women's Rights Advocates, Socialists, and Blacks.* Urbana: University of Illinois Press, 1976.

Frances. "The Soul Selects: A New Separate Way." *off our backs* 2 (5) (Jan 1972): 7.

Freeman, Joreen. "The Bitch Manifesto." *Notes from the Second Year*, 1970, 5–9.

————. "Women's Liberation and Its Impact on the Campus." *Liberal Education* 57 (4) (1971): 468–478.

————. "The Tyranny of Structurelessness." In A. Koedt, A. Levine and A. Rapone (eds.), *Radical Feminism*, 285–299. New York: Quadrangle Books, 1973.

————. "The Origins of the Women's Liberation Movement." American Journal of Sociology 78 (4) (Jan 1973): 792–811.

————. *The Politics of Women's Liberation: A Case Study of an Emerging Social Movement and Its Relation to the Policy Process.* New York: David McKay Company, 1975.

French, Laurence. "The Incarcerated Black Female: The Case of Social Double Jeopardy." *Journal of Black Studies.* 8 (3) (March 1978): 321–335.

Frenier, Mariam D. "American Anti-Feminist Women: Comparing the Rhetoric of Opponents of the Equal Rights Amendment with That of Opponents of Women's Suffrage." *Women's Studies International Forum* 7 (6) (1984): 455–465.

Freydberg, Hargret Howe. "Women's Liberation: What Will We Lose?" *American Scholar* 42 (1) (1972–73): 139–147.

Friedan, Betty. *The Feminine Mystique.* New York: Norton, 1963.

————. "Human . . . Not Class." *Social Policy* 3 (1973): 32–38.

————. *The Second Stage.* New York: Summit, 1981.

Friedl, Ernestine. "The Position of Women: Appearance and Reality." *Anthropological Quarterly* 40 (3) (1967): 97–108.

Furies Action. "Day Care." Spring 1971.

Garber, Linda. *Lesbian Sources: A Bibliography of Periodical Articles, 1970–1990.* New York: Garland Publishing, 1993.

Gardiner, Jean. "Political Economy of Female Labor in Capitalist Society." Unpublished manuscript, 1974.

Gerstein, Ira. "Domestic Work and Capitalism." *Radical America* 7 (4/5) (1973): 101–128.

Giordano, Peggy C., and Stephen A. Cernkovich. "On Complicating the Relationship between Liberation and Delinquency." *Social Problems* 26 (4) (April 1979): 467–481.

Gitlin, Todd. *The Sixties: Years of Hope, Days of Rage.* New York: Bantam, 1987.

Gittelsohn, Roland B. "Women's Lib and Judaism." *Midstream* 17 (8) (1971): 51–58.

Goldschmidt, Jean, Mary M. Gergen, and Karen Quigley. "The Women's Liberation Movement: Attitudes and Action." *Journal of Personality* 42 (4) (Dec 1974): 601–617.

Gonzales, Sylvia. "The White Feminist Movement: The Chicana Perspective." *Social Science Journal* 14 (2) (April 1977): 67–76.

Gordon, Linda. *Woman's Body, Woman's Right: Birth Control in America.* Revised and updated ed. New York: Penguin Books, 1990.

Gornick, Vivian. "Consciousness." *New York Times Magazine* 22 (Jan 1971): 72–82.

Gornick, Vivian, and Barbara K. Moran, eds. *Woman in Sexist Society: Studies in Power and Powerlessness.* New York: Basic Books, 1971.

Graskof, Michele Hoffnung, ed. *Roles Women Play: Readings toward Women's Liberation* California: Brooks/Cole, 1971.

Greenberg-lake: The Analysis Group Inc. *Women's Voices: All Women's Frequency Questionnaire.* Washington, DC: Center for Policy Alternatives, 1992.

Greer, Germaine. *The Female Eunuch.* New York: McGraw-Hill, 1971.

Griffin, Susan. "Rape: The All-American Crime." In *Rape: Power of Consciousness*, 3–22. San Francisco: Harper and Row, 1979.

Gyant, LaVerne. "Passing the Torch: African American Women in the Civil Rights Movements." *Journal of Black Studies* 26 (5) (May 1996): 629–647.

Hackett, Amy, and Sarah Pomeroy. "Making History: The First Sex." *Feminist Studies* 1 (2) (1973): 97–108.

Hackleman, Leah. "Plastic Man versus the Sweet Assassin." *Genders* 19 (1994): 125–147.

Haden, Patricia, Donna Middleton, and Patricia Robinson. "A Historical and Critical Essay for Black Women." In E. H. Altbach (ed.), *From Feminism to Liberation*, 125–144. Cambridge, MA: Schenkman Publishing, 1971.

Hamilton, Roberta. "Feminists in the Academy: Intellectuals or Political Subversives?" *Queen's Quarterly* 92 (1) (Spring 1985): 3–20.

Hancock, Brenda Robinson. "Affirmation of Negation in the Women's Liberation Movement." *Quarterly Journal of Speech* 58 (3) (1972): 264–271.

Hanisch, Carol. "The Personal is Political" and "A Critique of the Miss America Protest." In Shulamith Firestone (ed.), *Notes from the Second Year*, 76–78, 85–86. New York: Radical Feminism, 1970.

Hanisch, Carol, and Elizabeth Sutherland [Martinez]. "Women of the World Unite—We Have Nothing to Lose but Our Men!" In Shulamith Firestone (ed.), *Notes from the First Year*, 12–16. New York, 1968.

Hanson, David J. "Women's Liberation: Attitude Extremity and Dogmatism." *International Behavioural Scientist* 8 (4) (Dec 1976): 57–58.

Hanson, Karen. "Women's Unions and the Search for a Political Identity." In *Women, Class and the Feminist Imagination*, Karen Hansen and Ilene Philipson (eds.), 213–238. Philadelphia: Temple University Press, 1990.

Hare, Nathan. "Revolution without a Revolution: The Psychology of Sex and Race." *Black Scholar* 9 (7) (April 1978): 2–7.

Hare, Nathan, and Julia Hare. "Black Women 1970." *Trans-Action* 8 (1–2) (Nov–Dec 1970): 65–68, 90.

Hartmann, Heidi I. "The Unhappy Marriage of Marxism and Feminism: Towards a More Progressive Union." *Capital and Class* 8 (Summer 1979): 1–33.

Hartmann, Heidi, et al. "Bringing Together Feminist Theory and Practice: A Collective Interview." *Signs: Journal of Women in Culture and Society* 21 (4) (1996): 917–951.

Hartmann, Susan M. *From Margin to Mainstream: American Women and Politics since 1960.* New York: Knopf, 1989.

Hayden, Casey, and Mary King. "Sex and Caste: A Kind of Memo." *Liberation* 10 (April 1966): 35–36.

Haymes, Howard J. "Postwar Writing and the Literature of the Women's Liberation Movement." *Psychiatry* 38 (4) (Nov 1975): 328–333.

Heer, David M., and Amyra Grossbard-Scechtmen. "The Impact of the Female Marriage Squeeze and the Contraceptive Revolution on Sex Roles and the Women's Liberation Movement in the United States, 1960–1975." *Journal of Marriage and the Family* 43 (1) (Feb 1981): 49–65.

Heilburn, Alfred B., and David M. Gottfried. "Antisociality and Dangerousness in Women before and after the Women's Movement." *Psychological Reports.* 62 (1) (Feb 1988): 37–38.

Henderson, Elandria V. "The Black Lesbian." *Lavender Woman* 1 (2) (Dec 1971): 4.

Hogeland, Lisa Marie. *Feminism and Its Fictions: The Consciousness-Raising Novel and the Women's Liberation Movements.* Philadelphia: University of Pennsylvania Press, 1998.

Hole, Judith, and Ellen Levine. "Women's Liberation." In *Rebirth of Feminism*, 108–166. New York: Quadrangle Books, 1971.

Hollibaugh, Amber, and Cherrie Moraga. "What We're Rollin around in Bed With—Sexual Silences in Feminism: A Conversation toward Ending Them." *Heresies* 12 (1981): 58–62.

Hood, Elizabeth F. "Black Women, White Women: Separate Paths to Liberation." *Black Scholar* 9 (7) (1978): 45–56.

hooks, bell. *Feminist Theory from Margin to Center.* Boston: South End Press, 1984.

———. *Talking Back: Thinking Feminist, Thinking Black.* Boston: South End Press, 1989.

Hsu, Kwang. "Women's Liberation Is a Component Part of the Proletarian Revolution." *Peking Review* 7 (10) (March 18, 1974): 12–15.

Hubbard, Ruth, et al. *Women Look at Biology Looking at Women: A Collection of Feminist Critiques.* Cambridge, MA: Schenkman Publishing, 1979.

Humm, Maggie. *The Dictionary of Feminist Theory.* Columbus, OH: Ohio State University Press, 1990.

Jacobson, Marsha B. "You Say Potato and I Say Pothato: Attitudes towards Feminism as a Function of Its Subject-Selected Label." *Sex Roles* 7 (4) (April 1981): 349–354.

Jacobson, Marsha B., and Koch, Walter. "Attributed Reasons for Support of the Feminist Movement as a Function of Attractiveness." *Sex Roles* 4 (2) (April 1978): 169–174.

Jaggar, Alison M. *Feminist Politics and Human Nature.* Totowa, NJ: Rowman and Littlefieid, 1983.

Jaggar, Alison M., and Paula S. Rothenberg, eds. *Feminist Frameworks: Alternative Theoretical Accounts of the Relations between Women and Men.* 3d ed. New York: McGraw-Hill, 1993.

James, Selma. "Women, the Unions and Work; or, . . . What Is Not to Be Done." *Radical America* 7 (4/5) (1973): 51–72.

James, Stanlie M. "Mothering: A Possible Black Feminist Link to Social Transformation?" In Stanlie M. James and Abena P. A. Busia (eds.), *Theorizing Black Feminisms*, 44–54. New York: Routledge, 1993.

Jamison, Pollyann H., Franzini, Louis R., and Kaplan, Robert M. "Some Assumed Characteristics of Voluntarily Childfree Women and Men." *Psychology of Women Quarterly* 4 (2) (Winter 1979): 266–273.

Janeway, Elizabeth. *Man's World, Woman's Place: A Study in Social Mythology.* New York: Dell Publishing, 1971.

———, ed. "Radical Feminism." *Women: Their Changing Roles*, 385–457. New York: New York Times, Arno Press, 1973.

———. *Between Myth and Morning: Women Awakening.* New York: William Morrow, 1974.

Jenkins, Julie. "Have You Ever Asked a Black Lesbian to Dance?" *Lesbian Connection* 1 (8) (Nov 1975): 14–15.

Joesting, Joan. "Comparison of Women's Liberation Members with Their November Peers." *Psychological Reports* 29 (3) part 2 (1971): 1291–1294.

Johnson, Ronald W., Denyse Doiron, Garland P. Brooks, and John Dickinson. "Perceived Attractiveness as a Function of Support for the Feminist Movement: Not Necessarily a Put-Down of Women." *Canadian Journal of Behavioural Science* 10 (3) (July 1978): 214–221.

Johnston, Jill. "The Comingest Womanifesto (followed by Resolution of Lesbians International)." In P. Birkby, B. Harris, J. Johnston, E. Newton, and J. O'Wyatt (eds.), *Amazon Expedition: A Lesbianfeminist Anthology*, 89–92. Washington, NJ: Times Change Press, 1973.

———. "The Making of a Lesbian Chauvinist," "The Myth of the Myth of the Vaginal Orgasm," and "The Second Sucks and the Feminine Mystake." In Jill Johnston (ed.), *Lesbian Nation: The Feminist Solution*, 148–164, 164–174, 174, 182. New York: Simon and Schuster, 1973.

Jones, Beverley, and Judith Brown. *Toward a Female Liberation Movement.* Boston: New England Free Press, 1968.

Joseph, Gloria I. "The Incompatible Ménage à Trois: Marxism, Feminism, and Racism." In Lydia Sargent (ed.), *Women and Revolution: A Discussion of the Unhappy Marriage of Marxism and Feminism*, 91–107. Boston: South End Press, 1981.

Joseph, Gloria I., and Jill Lewis. *Common Differences: Conflicts in Black and White Perspectives.* Garden City, NY: Anchor Books, 1981.

Kahn, Karen, ed. *Front Line Feminism, 1975–1995.* San Francisco: Aunt Lute Books, 1995.

Kahn, Kim Fridkin, and Edie N. Goldenberg. "The Media: Obstacle or Ally of Feminists?" *Annals of the American Academy of Political and Social Science* 515 (1991): 104–113.

Kardiner, Abram. "The Social Distress Syndrome of Our Time: II." *Journal of the American Academy of Psychoanalysis* 6 (2) (April 1978): 215–230.

Kenny, Mary. "In the Driver's Seat: On Betty Friedan and Other Women's Libbers." *Encounter* 60 (2) (1983): 25–30.

Kessler, Suzanne, and Wendy McKenna. *Gender: An Ethnomethodological Approach.* New York: John Wiley, 1978.

King, Katie. *Theory in Its Feminist Travels.* Bloomington: Indiana University Press, 1994.

King, Mae C. "The Politics of Sexual Stereotypes." *Black Scholar* 4 (6–7) (March–April 1973): 12–23.

Klagsbrun, Francine, ed. *The First Ms. Reader.* Paperback Library Edition. New York: Warner, 1974.

Koedt, Anne. "The Myth of the Vaginal Orgasm" and "Women and the Radical Movement." In Shulamith Firestone (ed.), *Notes from the First Year*, 11, 26–27. New York, 1968.

———. "Lesbianism and Feminism." In A. Koedt, E. Levine, and A. Rapone (eds.), *Radical Feminism*, 246–58. New York: Quadrangle Books, 1973.

———. "The Myth of the Vaginal Orgasm." In A. Koedt, E. Levine, and A. Rapone (eds.), *Radical Feminism*, 198–207. New York: Quadrangle Books, 1973.

————, ed. *Notes from the Third Year: Women's Liberation*. New York, 1971.

Koedt, Anne, Ellen Levine, and Anita Rapone, eds. *Radical Feminism*. New York: Quadrangle Books, 1973.

Kolodney, Nat. "The Semantics of the Women's Liberation Movement." *Etc.* 35 (3) (Sept 1978): 298–301.

Kreps, Bonnie. "Radical Feminism 1." In *Women Unite!: An Anthology of the Canadian Women's Movement*, 71–75. Toronto, Ont.: Canadian Women's Educational Press, 1972.

Laporte, Rita. "Notes Prompted by the National Black Feminist Organization." *off our backs* 4 (3) (Feb 1974): 2–3.

Larguia, Isabel, and John Dumoulin. "Towards a Science of Women's Liberation." *NACLA Newsletter* 6 (10) (1972): 3–20.

LaRue, Linda J. M. "Black Liberation and Women's Lib." *Trans-Action* 8 (1–2) (Nov–Dec 1970): 59–64.

Laudicina, Eleanor V. "Towards New Forms of Liberation: A Mildly Utopian Proposal." *Social Theory and Practice* 2 (3) (1973): 275–288.

Lavender, Abraham D., and Hannah R. Wartenberg. "Developmental Models of Women's Liberation: Consequences for Men and Women." *Humanity and Society* 7 (3) (Aug 1983): 250–261.

Lavine, T. Z. "Ideas of Revolution in the Women's Movement." *American Behavioral Scientist* 20 (4) (1977): 535–566.

Lee-See, Letha A. "Tensions between Black Women and White Women: A Study." *Affilia* 4 (2) (Summer 1989): 31–45.

Lemann, Nicholas. "Sorting Out the Sixties." *Washington Monthly* 9 (4) (1977): 32–41.

Leone, Vivien. "Domestics." In Sookie Stambler, compiler, *Women's Liberation: Blueprint for the Future*, 39–44. New York: Ace Books, A Division of Charter Communications, 1970.

Lerner, Gerda. "Women's Rights and American Feminism." *American Scholar* 40 (2) (1971): 235–248.

————, ed. *Black Women in White America: A Documentary History*. New York: Pantheon Books, 1972.

————. *The Female Experience: An American Documentary*. Indianapolis: Bobbs-Merrill, 1977.

Levine, Suzanne, et al. *The Decade of Women: A Ms. History of the Seventies in Words and Pictures*. New York: Paragon Books, 1980.

Lewis, Diane K. "A Response to Inequality: Black Women, Racism and Sexism." *Signs* 3 (2) (1977): 339–361.

Lienert, Tania. "On Who Is Calling Radical Feminists 'Cultural Feminists' and Other Historical Sleights of Hand." In Diane Bell and Renate Klein (eds.), *Radically Speaking: Feminism Reclaimed*, 155–168. North Melbourne: Spinifex Press, 1996.

Ling, Susie. "The Mountain Movers: Asian American Women's Movement in Los Angeles." *Amerasia Journal* 15 (1) (1989): 51–67.

Locke, Mamie E. "The Role of African-American Women in the Civil Rights and Women's Movements in Hinds County and Sunflower County, Mississippi." *Journal of Mississippi History* 53 (3) (1991): 229–239.

Long, Priscilla, ed. *The New Left: A Collection of Essays*. Boston: Porter Sargent, 1969.

Lopes, Maureen. "Black Women and the Feminist Movement." *Brown Sister* 4 (1977): 22–33.

Lorde, Audre. "An Open Letter to Mary Daly." In Cherrie Moraga and Gloria Anzaldua (eds.), *This Bridge Called My Back: Writings by Radical Women of Color*, 95–96. Watertown, MA: Persephone Press, 1981.

————. *Sister Outsider*. Freedom, CA: Crossing Press, 1984.

Love, Barbara, and Elizabeth Shanklin. "The Answer Is Matriarchy." In Ginny Vida (ed.), *Our Right to Love*. Englewood Cliffs, NJ: Prentice Hall, 1978.

Maccoby, Eleanor E., ed. *The Development of Sex Difference*. Stanford, CA: Stanford University Press, 1966.

Mainardi, Pat. "The Politics of Housework." In Shulamith Firestone (ed.), *Notes from the First Year*, 28–31. New York, 1968.

Martin, Del, and Phyllis Lyon. "Not Toleration—Lesbian Liberation." *Lesbian/Woman*, 277–283. San Francisco: Glide Publications, 1972.

Martin, Wendy. *The American Sisterhood*. New York: Harper and Row, 1972.

Martin, Biddy, and Chandra Talpade Mohanty. "Feminist Politics: What's Home Got to Do with It?" In Teresa de Lauretis (ed.), *Feminist Studies/Critical Studies*, 191–212. Bloomington: Indiana University Press, 1986.

McDowell, Margaret B. "Reflections on the New Feminism." *Midwest Quarterly* 12 (3) (1971): 309–333.

McPherson, Louise. "Communication Techniques of the Women's Liberation Front." *Today's Speech* 21 (2) (1973): 33–38.

McQuiston, Liz. *Suffragettes to She Devils: Women's Liberation and Beyond*. London: Phaidon Press, 1997.

McWilliams, Nancy. "Contemporary Feminism, Consciousness-Raising, and Changing Views of the Political." In J. S. Jaquette (ed.), *Women in Politics*, 157–170. Los Angeles: John Wiley, 1974.

Meehan, Anita, and Glynis Bean. "Tracking the Civil Rights and Women's Movements in the United States." *International Journal of Intercultural Relations* 5 (2) (1981): 165–173.

Mehrhof, Barbara. "On Class Structure within the Women's Movement." In Shulamith Firestone (ed.), *Notes from the Second Year*, 103–104, 107–108. New York: Radical Feminism, 1970.

Micossi, Anita Lynn. "Conversion to Women's Lib." *Trans-Action* 8 (1–2) (Nov–Dec 1970): 82–90.

Millet, Kate. *Sexual Politics*. New York: Doubleday, 1970.

———. "Theory of Sexual Politics." In *Sexual Politics*, 23–58. New York: Doubleday, 1970.

Mitchell, Juliet. "Women: The Longest Revolution." *New Left Review* 40 (Nov–Dec 1966): 11–37.

———. "Out from Under." *Liberation* 16 (7) (1971): 6–13.

———. "Marxism and Women's Liberation." *Social Praxis* 1 (1) (1973): 23–33.

———. "Female Sexuality." *Journal of Biosocial Science* 5 (1) (Jan 1973): 123–136.

———. *Women's Estate*. New York: Vintage, 1973.

Moraga, Cherrie, and Gloria Anzaldua, eds. *This Bridge Called My Back: Writings by Radical Women of Color*. Watertown, MA: Persephone Press, 1981.

Morgan, Robin, ed. *Sisterhood Is Powerful: An Anthology of Writing from the Women's Liberation Movement*. New York: Random House, 1970.

———. *Going Too Far: The Personal Chronicle of a Feminist*. New York: Random House, 1977.

———. "On Women as Colonized People" and "International Feminism: A Call for Support of the Three Marias." In *Going Too Far: The Personal Chronicle of a Feminist*, 161–162, 202–208. New York: Random House, 1977.

Morris, Monica B. "Definition of a Social Movement: Women's Liberation." *Sociology and Social Research* 57 (4) (1973): 526–543.

———. "Excuses, Justifications and Evasions: How Newspaper Editors Account for Their Coverage of a Social Movement." *Sociolinguistics-Newsletter* 7 (1) (Feb 1976): 20–26.

Morrison, Toni. "What the Black Woman Thinks about Women's Lib." In *New York Times Magazine*, August 22, 1971: 15–16, 63–64, 66.

Morton, Peggy. "*A Woman's Work Is Never Done*." In E. H. Altbach (ed.), *From Feminism to Liberation*, 211–229. Cambridge, MA: Schenkman Publishing, 1971:

Morton, Nelle. "The Rising Woman Consciousness in a Male Language Structure." *Andover Newton Quarterly* 12 (4) (March 1972) : 177–190.

Ms. Foundation for Women and Center for Policy Alternatives. *A Polling Report—Women's Voices: A Joint Project*. New York and Washington, DC: Ms. Foundation for Women and Center for Policy Alternatives, September 1992.

Mueller, Carol. "In Search of a Constituency for the 'New Religious Right.' " *Public Opinion Quarterly* 47 (2) (Summer 1983) : 213–229.

Mueller, Kate Hevner. "The Women's Liberation Movement: What Delayed Its Impact?" *Journal of the NAWDAC* 40 (2) (1977): 43–45.

Murphy, Marilyn. "Sisterhood Is Painful, or What's All the Fuss about the Lesbian Issue." *University of Michigan Papers in Women's Studies* 2 (4) (1978): 55–65.

Myron, Nancy. "Class Beginnings." *The Furies* 1 (3) (1972): 2–3.

Myron, Nancy, and Charlotte Bunch, eds. *Lesbianism and the Women's Movement*. Baltimore: Diana Press, 1975.

Negrin, Su. *A Graphic Notebook on Feminism*. New York: Times Change Press, 1971.

North, Gary. "The Feminine Mistake: The Economics of Women's Liberation." *Freeman* 21 (1) (1971): 3–14.

O'Connor, Lynn. "Male Supremacy." Mimeograph, n.d.

O'Connor, Lynn, Pam Allen, and Liz Bunding. *The Small Group, Three Articles by Lynn O'Connor, Pam Allen, Liz Bunding*. Berkeley: Women's Liberation Basement Press, n.d.

Oakley, Ann. *Sex, Gender, and Society*. New York: Harper and Row, 1973.

Okoth, Sonya. "Liberation Must Include the Women of Africa." In *Liberation Now! Writings from the Women's Liberation Movement*, 337–342. New York: Dell Publishing, 1971.

O'Neil, Harold F., Mary Teague, and Robert E. Lushene. "Personality Characteristics of Women's Liberation Activists as Measured by the MMPI." *Psychological Reports* 37 (2) (Oct 1975): 355–361.

O'Sullivan, Sue. "Passionate Beginnings: Ideological Politics, 1969–1972." *Feminist Review* 11 (June 1982): 70–86.

Painter, Edith G. "Women's Lib Is Dead." *Journal of the National Association of Women Deans and Counselors* 36 (2) (1973): 68–69.

Papachristou, Judith. "The Revival of the Women's Movement: 1960's and 1970's." *Women Together*, 216–255. New York: Knopf, 1976.

Pawlicki, Robert E., and Carol Almquist. "Authoritarianism, Locus of Control, and Tolerance of Ambiguity as Reflected in Membership and Nonmembership in a Women's Liberation Group." *Pychological Reports* 32 (3), part 2 (June 1973): 1331–1337.

Penn, Barbara P. and Penn, Nolan E. "The Women's Movement: Historical Perspectives and Current Trends." *Psychiatric Annals* 6 (2) (Feb 1976): 12–21.

Polatnick, Rivka. "The Wave and the Movement: Doing Justice to the Feminist Activism of Women of Color." Unpublished manuscript. San Jose, CA: San Jose State University, 1994.

———. "Poor Sisters Decided for Themselves: A Case Study of '60's Women's Liberation Activism." In K. Vaz (ed.), *Black Women in America*, 110–130. Thousand Oaks, CA: Sage, 1995.

———. "Diversity in Women's Liberation Ideology: How a Black and a White Group of the

1960s Viewed Motherhood." *Signs: Journal of Women in Culture and Society* 21 (3) (1996): 679–706.

Pompei, Giuliana. "Wages for Housework." *Women: A Journal of Liberation* 3 (3) (1973): 60–62.

Popkin, Annie. "An Early Moment in Women's Liberation: The Social Experience within Bread and Roses." *Radical America*, Jan–Feb 1988, 19–34.

———. "An Early Moment in Women's Liberation: The Social Experience within Bread and Roses." *Radical America* 22 (1) (1988): 19–34.

———. "The Social Experience of Bread and Roses, Building a Community and Creating a Culture." In Karen Hansen and Ilene Philipson (eds.), *Women, Class, and the Feminist Imagination*, 182–212. Philadelphia: Temple University Press, 1990.

Powers, Ann. "Class Conflicts: A Vindication of the Rights of Women's Studies." *Village Voice Literary Supplement* 119 (Oct 1993): 10–12.

Radicalesbians. "The Woman-Identified Woman." In Anne Koedt (ed.), *Notes from the Third Year*. New York, 1971.

Radical Women Manifesto, Seattle, *Women: A Journal of Liberation* 3 (4) (1974): 56–57.

Red Apple Collective. "Socialist Feminist Women's Unions: Past and Present." *Socialist Reviews* 8 (2) (March–April 1978): 37–57.

Redstockings Manifesto, 1969.

Redstockings West Manifesto, 1969.

Reed, Evelyn. "Women: Caste, Class or Oppressed Sex?" *International Socialist Review*, Sept 1970, 14–17, 40–42.

Reid, Susan. "Growth and Guilt: The Aftermath of the Women's Movement." *Journal of Social Welfare* 3 (3) (Winter 1976): 27–34.

Reisman, David. "Liberation and Stalemate." *Massachusetts Review* 17 (4) (1976): 767–776.

Reiter, Rayna R., ed. *Toward an Anthropology of Women*. New York: Monthly Review Press, 1975.

Renik, Owen. "Some Observations on 'Sisterhood' in the Feminist Movement." *Bulletin of the Menninger Clinic* 39 (4) (July 1975): 345–356.

Rich, B. Ruby. "Feminism and Sexuality in the 1980s." *Feminist Review* 12 (3) (Fall 1986): 508.

Riley, Denise. *"Am I That Name?" Feminism and the Category of "Women" in History*. London: Macmillan, 1988.

Rivet, Monique. "Sisters." *Esprit* 4 (1975): 511–529.

Robins, Joan, ed. *Handbook of Women's Liberation*. North Hollywood, CA: Now Library Press, 1970.

Robnett, Belinda. "African-American Women in the Civil Rights Movement, 1954–1965: Gender, Leadership, and Micromobilization." *American Journal of Sociology* 101 (6) (May 1996): 1661–1693.

Rosenberg, Rosalind. *Beyond Separate Spheres: Intellectual Roots of Modern Feminism*. New Haven, CT: Yale University Press, 1982.

Rosenfelt, Deborah, and Judith Stacey. "Review Essay: Second Thoughts on the Second Wave." *Feminist Studies* 13 (2) (Summer 1987): 341–361.

Ross, Becki. *The House That Jill Built: A Lesbian Nation in Formation*. Toronto: University of Toronto Press, 1995.

Rossi, Alice S. "Women—Terms of Liberation." *Dissent* 17 (6) (1970): 531–541.

———. *The Feminist Papers: From Adams to de Beauvoir*. New York: Bantam Books, 1973.

———. "Equality between the Sexes: An Immodest Proposal." *Daedalus* 117 (3) (Summer 1988): 25–71.

Rowbotham, Shelia. *Women's Liberation and the New Politics*. Bertrand Russell Foundation and The May Day Manifesto, 1970.

———. *Woman's Consciousness, Man's World*. London: Penguin, 1973.

———. *The Past Is before Us: Feminism in Action since the 1960s*. Winchester, MA: Unwin and Hyman, 1989.

Rothman, Sheila M. "The Carrot, the Stick, and the Movement." *Radical America* 7 (4/5) (1973): 73–79.

———. "Other People's Children: The Day Care Experience In America." *Public Interest* (30) (1973): 11–27.

———. "Family Life as Zero-Sum Game." *Dissent* 25 (4) (Fall 1978): 392–397.

———. "The Women's Movement and Organizing for Socialism." *Radical America* 13 (5) (1979): 9–28.

Rowland, Robyn. "Women Who Do and Women Who Don't, Join the Women's Movement: Issues for Conflict and Collaboration. Special Issue: Sex, Gender, and Social Change." *Sex Roles* 14 (11–12) (1986): 679–692.

Rowland, Robyn, and Renate Klein. "Radical Feminism: History, Politics, Action." In Diane Bell and Renate Klein (eds.), *Radically Speaking: Feminism Reclaimed*, 9–36. North Melbourne: Spinifex Press, 1996.

Rowntree, M., and J. Rowntree. "More on the Political Economy of Women's Liberation." *Monthly Review* 21 (8) (1970): 26–32.

Rubin, Gayle. " 'The Traffic in Women': Notes on the 'Political Economy' of Sex." In Rayna R. Reiter (ed.), *Toward an Anthropology of Women*, 157–210. New York: Monthly Review Press, 1975.

Rule, Jane. *Lesbian Images*. Feminist Series. Trumansburg, NY: Crossing Press, 1982.

Rupp, Leila J., and Verta Taylor. *Survival in the Doldrums: The American Women's Rights Movement, 1945 to the 1960s*. New York: Oxford University Press, 1987.

Russ, Joanna. "The New Misandry." In P. Birkby, J. Johnston, E. Newton, and J. O'Wyatt (eds.), *A Lesbian Feminist Anthology: Amazon Expedition*, 27–32. Washington, DC: Times Change Press, 1973.

Russell, Diana E. H. "Pornography and the Women's Liberation Movement." In Laura Lederer (ed.), *Take Back the Night: Women on Pornography*, 301–306. New York: William Morrow, 1980.

Ruth, Sheila. "A Serious Look at Consciousness-Raising." *Social Theory and Practice* 2 (3) (1973): 289–300.

———, ed. *Issues in Feminism: A First Course in Women's Studies*. Boston: Houghton Mifflin, 1980.

Ryan, Barbara. "Ideological Purity and Feminism: The U.S. Women's Movement from 1966 to 1975." *Gender and Society* 3 (2) (1989): 239–257.

Salper, Roberta L., ed. *Female Liberation: History and Current Politics*. New York: Knopf, 1972.

Sandage, Diane, and Polly F. Radosh. "The Women's Movement and the Rebirth of Feminism: Conflicts and Contradictions." *Humanity and Society* 16 (3) (Aug 1992): 277–296.

Sanday, Peggy R. "Toward a Theory of the Status of Women." *American Anthropologist* 75 (1973): 1682–1700.

Sanger, Susan Phipps, and Henry A. Alker. "Dimensions of Internal-External Locus of Control and the Women's Liberation Movement." *Journal of Social Issues* 28 (4) (1972): 115–130.

Sarachild, Kathie. "Funeral Oration for the Burial of Traditional Womanhood." In *NYRW*, 20–22. New York: Redstocking's Women's Liberation Archives, 1968.

———. "A Program for Feminist Consciousness-Raising." November 27, 1968.

Sarachild, Kathie. "The Power of History." In Kathie Sarachild (ed.), *Feminist Revolution*, 7–29. New Paltz, NY: Redstockings, 1975.

———. "The Civil Rights Movement: Lessons from Women's Liberation," 1–10. Paper presented at University of Massachusetts at Amherst, 1983.

———. "Taking in the Images: A Record in Graphics of the Vietnam Era Soil for Feminism." *Vietnam Generation* 1 (3–4) (1989): 235–245.

Sarachild, Kathie, Faye Levine, Barbara Leon, and Colette Price, eds. *Feminist Revolution*. Abridged edition with additional writings. New York: Random House, 1979.

Sargent, Linda, ed. *Women and Revolution: A Discussion of the Unhappy Marriage of Marxism and Feminism*. Boston: South End Press, 1981.

Sayers, Sohnya, Anders Stephanson, Stanley Arnowitz, and Fredric Jameson, eds. *The 60s without Apology*. Minneapolis: University of Minnesota Press, 1984.

Schaeffer, Alice. "Women's Liberation: A Non-Print Media Compilation." *Previews* 2 (6) (1974): 5–9.

Schmelz, Jerome. "Rising Aspirations of American Women and the Declining Birth Rate." *International Journal of Sociology of the Family* 6 (2) (1976): 179–196.

Schulder, Diane, and Florynce Kennedy. *Abortion Rap*. New York: McGraw-Hill, 1971.

Sealander, Judith, and Dorothy Smith. "The Rise and Fall of Feminist Organizations in the 1970s: Dayton as a Case Study." *Feminist Studies* 12 (2) (Summer 1986): 321–341.

Segal, Lynne. *Is the Future Female?* London: Virago, 1987.

Shapiro, Fred R. "Historical Notes on the Vocabulary of the Women's Movement." *American Speech* 60 (1) (Spring 1985): 1–16.

Shea, Gail Anne. "Voluntary Childlessness and the Women's Liberation Movement." *Population and Environment* 6 (1) (Spring 1983): 17–26.

Shelley, Martha. "Lesbianism and the Women's Liberation Movement." In Sookie Stambler, compiler, *Women's Liberation: Blueprint for the Future*, 123–129. New York: Ace Books, A Division of Charter Communications, 1970.

Shelley, Martha. "Notes of a Radical Lesbian." In Robin Morgan (ed.), *Sisterhood Is Powerful: An Anthology of Writings from the Women's Liberation Movement*, 333–348. New York: Vintage Books, 1970.

Sherfey, Mary Jane. "A Theory on Female Sexuality." In Robin Morgan (ed.), *Sisterhood Is Powerful: An Anthology of Writings from the Women's Liberation Movement*, 220–230. New York: Vintage Books, 1970.

Shibles, Warren. "Radical Feminism, Humanism and Women's Studies." *Innovative Higher Education* 14 (1) (Fall–Winter 1989): 35–47.

Shostak, Arthur B. "The Women's Liberation Movement and Its Various Impacts on American Men." *Journal of Sociology and Social Welfare* 4 (6) (July 1977): 897–907.

Showalter, Elaine. *Women's Liberation: A Sourcebook of Feminism and Literature*. New York: Harcourt Brace Jonavich, 1971.

Shulman, Alix Kates. "A Marriage Agreement." In Sookie Stambler, compiler, *Women's Liberation: Blueprint for the Future*, 211–217. New York: Ace Books, A Division of Charter Communications, 1970.

———. "Sex and Power: Sexual Bases of Radical Feminism." *Signs* 5 (4) (Summer 1980): 590–604.

Siassi, Iradj, and Wesner, David O. "Women's Liberation and the Two Adolescent Movements." *International Journal of Social Psychiatry* 20 (1–2) (Spring–Summer 1974): 99–108.

———. "Women's Liberation and the Radical Faction." *International Review of Psychoanalysis* 2 (4) (1975): 487–499.

Simons, Margaret A. "Racism and Feminism: A Schism in the Sisterhood." *Feminist Studies* 5 (2) (Summer 1979): 384–401.

———. "The Silencing of Simone de Beauvoir: Guess What's Missing from *The Second Sex?*" *Women's Studies International Forum* 6 (5) (1983): 559–564.

Singh, Nikhil. "Rethinking Politics and Culture: Social Movements and Liberation Politics in the United States, 1960–1976." *Radical History Review* (57) (1993): 197–201.

Sloan, Margaret. "Black and Blacklesbian." *Lavender Woman* 1 (1) (Nov 1971): 4.

Smiley, Virginia. "The Chicago Women's Liberation School." *Change* 6 (3) (1974): 18–20.

Smith, Dorothy E. "A Sociology for Women." In Julia A. Sherman and Evelyn Torton Beck (eds.), *The Prism of Sex: Essays in the Sociology of Knowledge*, 135–187. Madison: University of Wisconsin Press, 1979.

Snitow, Ann. "Mass Market Romance: Pornography for Women Is Different." *Radical History Review* 20 (Spring–Summer 1979): 141–161.

———. "The Front Line: Notes on Sex in Novels by Women, 1969–79." *Signs* 5 (4) (Summer 1980): 702–718.

———. "Gender Diary." *Dissent* (Spring 1989): 205–224.

Snitow, Ann, and Rachel Blau DuPlessis, eds. *The Feminist Memoir Project: Voices from Women's Liberation*. New York: Three Rivers Press, 1998.

Snowden, Elizabeth. "*Collecting Women's Serials.*" *Serials Librarian* 2 (1) (1977): 21–30.

Solanas, Valerie. S.C.U.M. *Society for Cutting up Men Manifesto*. New York: Olympia Press, 1968.

Sontag, Susan. "The Third World of Women." *Partisan Review* 40 (2) (1973): 180–206.

Spelman, Elizabeth V. *Inessential Woman: Problems of Exclusion in Feminist Thought*. Boston: Beacon Press, 1988.

Spender, Dale. "Women's Studies: Notes on the Organization of Women's Studies." *Women's Studies International Quarterly* 1 (3) (1978): 255–275.

Spilman, M. A. "Feminist Ideology in the United States: Its Development from 1966–70 as the Indicator of a General Social Movement." *Contemporary Crises* 2 (April 1978): 195–208.

Stage, Sarah. "Women's History and 'Women's Sphere': Major Works of the 1970s." *Socialist Review* 50/51 (March–June 1980): 245–253.

Staggenborg, Suzanne. "Stability and Innovation in the Women's Movement: A Comparison of Two Movement Organizations." *Social Problems* 36 (1) (Feb 1989): 75–92.

Stambler, Sookie, compiler. *Women's Liberation: Blueprint for the Future*. New York: Ace Books. A Division of Charter Communications. 1970.

Stein, Arlene. "Sisters and Queers: The Decentering of Lesbian Feminism." *Socialist Review* 22 (1) (Jan–Mar 1992): 33–55.

Stimpson, Catharine R. "Neither Dominant nor Subordinate: The Women's Movement and Contemporary American Culture." *Dissent* 27 (3) (1980): 299–307.

Stimpson, Catharine R., and Ethel Spector Person, eds. *Women: Sex and Sexuality*. Chicago: University of Chicago Press, 1980.

Stollof, Carolyn. "Who Joins Women's Liberation?" *Psychiatry* 36 (3) (Aug 1973): 325–340.

Suelzle, Marijean. *What Every Woman Should Know about the Women's Liberation Movement*. N.p.: Amazon Graphics, 1971.

Sutherland, Elizabeth. "Colonized Women: The Chicana." In Deborah Babcox and Madeline Belkin (compilers) *Liberation Now! Writings from the Women's Liberation Movement*, 197–204. New York: Dell Publishing, 1971.

Taleporos, Elizabeth. "Motivational Patterns in Attitudes Towards the Women's Liberation Movement." *Journal of Personality* 45 (4) (Dec 1977): 484–500.

Tanner, Leslie B., ed. *Voices from Women's Liberation*. New York: Signet Books, 1970.

Tax, Meredith. "Women and Her Mind: The Story of Daily Life." Bread and Roses Publication, 1970. Cell 16.

———. "The United Front of Women." *Monthly Review* 32 (5) (1980): 30–48.

———. "The Sound of One Hand Clapping: Women's Liberation and the Left." *Dissent* (Fall 1988): 457–462.

Taylor, Verta. "Social Movement Continuity: The Women's Movement in Abeyance." *American Sociological Review* 54 (5) (1989): 761–775.

Terry, Robert M. "Trends in Female Crime: A Comparison of Adler, Simon, and Steffensmeier." *California Sociologist* 2 (2) (Summer 1979): 200–212.

Third World Women's Alliance. "Women." *Triple Jeopardy* 1 (1) (Sept–Oct 1971): 8–9.

Thompson, Mary Lou, ed. *Voices of the New Feminism*. Boston: Beacon Press, 1970.

Tong, Rosemary. *Feminist Thought*. Boulder, CO: Westview Press, 1994.

Torrey, Jane W. "Racism and Feminism: Is Women's Liberation for Whites Only." *Psychology of Women Quarterly* 4 (2) (Winter 1979): 281–293.

Travis, Carol. "Who Likes Women's Liberation and Why: The Case of the Unliberated Liberals." *Journal of Social Issues* 29 (4) (1973): 175–198.

Travis, Cheryl Brown. "Women's Liberation among Two Samples of Young Women." *Psychology of Women Quarterly* 1 (2) (1976): 189–198.

Tuttle, Lisa. *Encyclopedia Of Feminism*. New York: Facts on File Publications, 1986.

Ulmschneider, Loretta. "Bisexuality." *The Furies* 2 (1) (1973): 2.

Unsigned. "Fight against Women's Oppression Parallels Struggle Against Racism." *Progressive Labor* 9 (3) (1973): 24–29.

Van Gelder, Lindsay. "The Truth about Bra-Burners." *Ms.* 3 (Sept–Oct 1992): 80–81.

Vickers, Jill, Pauline Rankin, and Christine Appelle. *Politics as if Women Mattered: A Political Analysis of the National Action Committee on the Status of Women*. Toronto: University of Toronto Press, 1993.

Vogel, Lise. "The Earthly Family." *Radical America* 7 (4/5) (1973): 9–50.

———. "Questions on the Woman Question." *Monthly Review* 31 (2) (June 1979): 39–59.

Wall, Cheryl, ed. *Changing Our Own Words: Essays on Criticism, Theory, and Writing by Black Women*. New Brunswick, NJ: Rutgers University Press, 1989.

Wallace, Michele. *Black Macho and the Myth of the Super-Woman*. New York: Dial Press, 1979.

Ware, Cellestine. *Woman Power: The Movement for Women's Liberation*. New York: Tower Publications, 1970.

———. "The Relationship of Black Women to WLM." and "The Politics of Women's Liberation." In *Woman Power: The Movement for Women's Liberation*, 75–99, 16–74. New York: Tower Publications, 1970.

Warrior, Betsy. "Housework: Slavery or Labor of Love." In A. Koedt, A. Levine, and A. Rapone (eds.), *Radical Feminism*, 208–212. New York: Quadrangle Books, 1973.

Watson, G. Llewellyn. *Feminism and Women's Issues: An Annotated Bibliography and Research Guide*. Vol. 1. New York: Garland Publishing, 1990.

Weathers, Maryanne. "An Argument for Black Women's Liberation as a Revolutionary Force." In Sookie Stambler (complier) *Women's Liberation: Blueprint for the Future*, 161–165. New York: Ace Books, A Division of Charter Communications, 1970:

Weber, Shirley N. "Black Power in the 1960s: A Study of Its Impact on Women's Liberation." *Journal of Black Studies* 11 (4) (June 1981): 483–497.

Weil, Mildred. "The Rise and Fall of Women's Liberation: The New Feminism Emerges." *Social Studies* 66 (4) (1975): 164–167.

Weisstein, Naomi. "Psychology Constructs the Female or the Fantasy Life of the Male Psychologist (with some attention to the fantasies of his friends, the male biologist, and the male anthropologist)." In A. Koedt, A. Levine, and A. Rapone, *Radical Feminism* (eds.), 178–197. New York: Quadrangle Books, 1973.

Welch, Susan. "Support among Women for the Issues of the Women's Movement." *Sociological Quarterly* 16 (2) (Spring 1975): 216–227.

Whelehan, Imelda. *Modern Feminist Thought: From the Second Wave to "Post-Feminism."* New York: New York University Press, 1995.

White, Judy. "Women Divided?" *off our backs* 1 (5) (May 1970): 5.

Whitney, Ruth. "Is Women's Liberation a Religious Movement?" *Religion in Life* 45 (4) (1976): 411–426.

———. "American Women's Responses to Women's Liberation." *Counseling and Values* 22 (3) (1978): 151–165.

Whittier, Nancy. *Feminist Generations: The Persistence of the Radical Women's Movement.* Philadelphia: Temple University Press, 1995.

Williams, Patricia. *The Alchemy of Race and Rights.* Cambridge, MA: Harvard University Press, 1991.

Willis, Ellen. "Up from Radicalism: A Feminist Journal." *US* 2 (October 1969): 102–122.

———. "Women and the Left." In Shulamith Firestone (ed.), *Notes from the Second Year*, 55–56. New York: Radical Feminism, 1970.

———. *Beginning to See the Light: Pieces of a Decade.* New York: Wideview Books, 1981.

———. "Sisters under the Skin? Confronting Race and Sex." *Village Voice Literary Supplement* 8 (June 1982): ff1.

———. "Radical Feminism and Feminist Radicalism." In Sohnya Sayres, Anders Stephanson, Stanley Aronowitz, and Fredric Jameson (eds.), *The 60s without Apology*, 91–118. Minneapolis: University of Minnesota Press, 1984.

Wilson, Elizabeth, and Angela Weir. *Hidden Agendas.* London: Tavistock, 1986.

Wisse, Ruth R. "Living with Women's Lib." *Commentary* 86 (2) (1988): 40–45.

Wittig, Monique. *Les Guerillieres* (1969). Trans. David LeVay. New York: Viking, 1971.

———. *The Straight Mind.* Boston: Beacon Press, 1992.

"Women's Liberation and the Black Panther Party." YAWK Women's Caucus, New York, August 26, 1970. (YAWK-Youth Against War and Fascism [*sic*].)

Worell, Judith, and Leonard Worell. "Support and Opposition to the Women's Liberation Movement: Some Personality and Parental Correlates." *Journal of Research in Personality* 11 (1) (1977): 10–20.

Yates, Gayle Graham. *What Women Want: The Ideas of the Movement.* Cambridge, MA: Harvard University Press, 1975.

Zimmerman, Bonnie. "The Politics of Separatism." *Lavender Woman* 3 (March 1974): 11.

Permissions

"Toward a Female Liberation Movement" was written by Beverly Jones and Judith Brown in Gainesville, Florida, and was published as a pamphlet and distributed by Gainesville Women's Liberation in 1968. It is reprinted by permission of Gainesville Women's Liberation. This article, as well as other writings from the 1960s rebirth years of feminism and by current women's liberation organizers, is available from Redstockings Women's Liberation Archives Distribution Project, P.O. Box 2625, Gainesville, FL 32602-2625. Please enclose a self-addressed stamped envelope with inquiries.

Heather Booth, Evi Goldfield, and Sue Munaker. *Toward a Radical Movement*. Boston: New England Free Press, 1968.

Anne Koedt. "Women and the Radical Movement." In A. Koedt, A. Levine, and A. Rapone (eds.), *Radical Feminism*, pp. 318–321. New York: Quadrangle Books, 1973.

"What is Liberation?" Editorial, *Women: A Journal of Liberation* 1 (2) (Winter 1970).

Marlene Dixon. "Why Women's Liberation?" *Ramparts* 8 (6) (1969): 58–63.

Ti-Grace Atkinson. "Radical Feminism." *The Feminists*, May 1969.

Shulamith Firestone. "The Dialectic of Sex." In *The Dialectic of Sex*, pp. 11–22. New York: Bantam Books, 1970. Copyright © 1970 by Shulamith Firestone. By permission of William Morrow & Company, Inc.

Cellestine Ware. "The Relationship of Black Women to the Women's Liberation Movement." In *Woman Power: The Movement for Women's Liberation*, pp. 75–99. New York: Tower Publications, 1970.

Carol Hanisch. "The Personal is Political." In Shulamith Firestone (ed.), *Notes from the Second Year*, pp. 85–86. New York: Radical Feminism, 1970.

Susan Brownmiller. "The Enemy Within." In Sookie Stambler (compiler), *Women's Liberation: Blueprint for the Future*, pp. 17–23. New York: Ace Books, A Division of Charter Communications, 1970.

Kate Millet. "Theory of Sexual Politics." In *Sexual Politics*, pp. 23–58. New York: Doubleday, 1970.

Frances Beal. "Double Jeopardy: To Be Black and Female." In *Liberation Now! Writings from the Women's Liberation Movement*, pp. 185–197. New York: Dell Publishing, 1971.

Ginny Berson for the Furies. "Beyond Male Power . . ." *The Furies* 1 (4) (1972): 13–14.

Joanna Russ. "The New Misandry." In Phyllis Birkby, Jill Johnston, Esther Newton, and Jane O'Wyatt (eds.), *A Lesbian Feminist Anthology: Amazon Expedition*, pp. 27–32. Washington, DC:

Times Change Press, 1973. Reprinted by permission of Ellen Levine Literary Agency. Copyright © 1973 by Joanna Russ.

Lynn O'Connor. "Male Supremacy." Np., n.d.

Naomi Weisstein. "Psychology Constructs the Female; or, The Fantasy Life of the Male Psychologist (with Some Attention to the Fantasies of His Friends, the Male Biologist and the Male Anthropologist). In A. Koedt, A. Levine, and A. Rapone (eds.), *Radical Feminism*, pp. 178–197. New York: Quadrangle Books, 1973.

Valerie Solanas. *S.C.U.M. (Society for Cutting Up Men) Manifesto*. New York: Olympia Press, 1968.

The "Redstockings Manifesto" was launched by Redstockings of the Women's Liberation Movement on July 7, 1969. Reprinted by permission. A catalog to order this and other documents from the 1960s rebirth years of feminism, as well as material by current women's liberation organizers, is available from the Redstockings Women's Liberation Archives Distribution Project, P.O. Box 2625, Gainesville, FL 32602-2625. Please enclose a self-addressed stamped envelope with inquiries.

Joreen Freeman. "The Bitch Manifesto." In Shulamith Firestone (ed.), *Notes from the Second Year*, pp. 5–9. New York: Radical Feminism, 1970.

Radicalesbians. "The Woman-Identified Woman." In Anne Koedt (ed.), *Notes from the Third Year*. New York, 1971. (25 cent publication, copyright 1970, March Hoffman, Elen Bedoz, Cythnia Funk, Rita Mae Brown, Lois Hart, Barbara XX with other Radicalesbians.)

Barbara Burris, in agreement with Kathy Barry, Terry Moore, Joann DeLor, Joann Parent and Caté Stadelman. "The Fourth World Manifesto." In A. Koedt, A. Levine, and A. Rapone (eds.), *Radical Feminism*, pp. 322–357. New York: Quadrangle Books, 1973.

Jill Johnston. "The Comingest Womanifesto (followed by Resolution of Lesbians International." In Phyllis Birkby, Bertha Harris, Jill Johnston, Esther Newton, and Jane O'Wyatt (eds.), *Amazon Expedition: A Lesbianfeminist Anthology*, pp. 89–92. Washington, NJ: Times Change Press, 1973.

Radical Women Manifesto, Seattle, *Women: A Journal of Liberation* 3 (4) (1974): 56–57.

"A Program for Feminist Consciousness-Raising," by Kathie Sarachild is reprinted by permission. The program was prepared for the First National Women's Liberation Conference, Lake Villa, Illinois, November 27, 1968. It is also published in Redstockings (ed.), *Feminist Revolution* (New York: Redstockings, 1975; abridged ed. with additional writings, New York: Random House, 1978). This book, as well as other writings from the 1960s rebirth years of feminism and by current women's liberation organizers, is available from Redstockings Women's Liberation Archives Distribution Project, P.O. Box 2625, Gainesville, FL 32602-2625. Please enclose a self-addressed stamped envelope with inquiries.

Pamela Allen. "The Small Group Process." In *Free Space: A Perspective on the Small Group in Women's Liberation*, pp. 23–32. New York: Times Change Press, 1970.

June Arnold. "Consciousness-Raising." In Sookie Stambler (compiler), *Women's Liberation: Blueprint for the Future*, pp. 150–161. New York: Ace Books, A Division of Charter Communications, 1970.

Vivian Gornick. "Consciousness." *New York Times Magazine*, January 10, 1971, pp. 22, 72–82.

Martha Shelley. "Lesbianism and the Women's Liberation Movement." In Sookie Stambler (compiler), *Women's Liberation: Blueprint for the Future*, pp. 123–129. New York: Ace Books, A Division of Charter Communications, 1970.

Sidney Abbott and Barbara Love. "Is Women's Liberation a Lesbian Plot?" In Vivian Gornick and Barbara K. Moran (eds.), *Woman in Sexist Society: Studies in Power and Powerlessness*, pp. 601–621. New York: Basic Books, 1971. Copyright © 1971 by Basic Books, Inc. Reprinted by permission of Basic Books, a subsidiary of Perseus Books Group, LLC.

Elandria V. Henderson. "The Black Lesbian." *Lavender Woman* 1 (2) (Dec. 1971): 4.

Margaret Sloan. "Black and Blacklesbian." *Lavender Woman* 1 (1) (Nov. 1971): 4.

Frances. "The Soul Selects: A New Separate Way." *off our backs*, 2 (5) (Jan. 1972): 7.

Charlotte Bunch. "Lesbians in Revolt: Male Supremacy Quakes and Quivers." *The Furies* 1 (1972): 8–9.

Jill Johnston. "The Making of a Lesbian Chauvinist," "The Myth of the Myth of the Vaginal Orgasm," and "The Second Sucks and the Feminine Mystake." In *Lesbian Nation: The Feminist Solution*, pp. 148–164, 164–174, 174–182. New York: Simon and Schuster, 1973.

Jeanne Cordova. "Radical Feminism?" *Lesbian Tide*, June 1973, pp. 20–21, 25, 27–28.

Judy White. "Women Divided?" *off our backs* 1 (5) (May 1970): 5.

Julie Jenkins. "Have You Ever Asked a Black Lesbian to Dance?" *Lesbian Connection* 1 (8) (Nov. 1975): 14–15.

Anne Koedt. "The Myth of the Vaginal Orgasm." In A. Koedt, A. Levine, and A. Rapone (eds.), *Radical Feminism*, pp. 198–207. New York: Quadrangle Books, 1973.

Carol Hanisch. "A Critique of the Miss America Protest." In Shulamith Firestone (ed.), *Notes from the Second Year*, pp. 85–86. New York: Radical Feminism, 1970.

Toni Cade. "The Pill: Genocide or Liberation." In *The Black Woman: An Anthology*, pp. 162–169. New York: New American Library, 1970.

Dana Densmore. "On the Temptation to Be a Beautiful Object." In Sookie Stambler (compiler), *Women's Liberation: Blueprint for the Future*, pp. 13–17. New York: Ace Books, A Division of Charter Communications, 1970.

Alix Shulman. "A Marriage Agreement." In Sookie Stambler (compiler), *Women's Liberation: Blueprint for the Future*, pp. 211–217. New York: Ace Books, A Division of Charter Communications, 1970.

Rita Mae Brown. "Roxanne Dunbar: How a Female Heterosexual Serves the Interests of Male Supremacy." *The Furies* 1 (1972): 5–6.

Rosalyn Baxandall. "Cooperative Nurseries." In Sookie Stambler (compiler), *Women's Liberation: Blueprint for the Future*, pp. 217–223. New York: Ace Books, A Division of Charter Communications, 1970.

Day Creamer and Heather Booth. "Action Committee for Decent Child Care." *Women: A Journal of Liberation* 2 (4) (1970): 7–8.

Debby D'Amico. "To My White Working-Class Sisters." In *Liberation Now! Writings from the Women's Liberation Movement*, pp. 177–181. New York: Dell Publishing, 1971.

Pat Mainardi. "The Politics of Housework." In Shulamith Firestone (ed.), *Notes from the Second Year*, pp. 28–31. New York: Radical Feminism, 1970.

Betsy Warrior. "Housework: Slavery or Labor of Love." In A. Koedt, A. Levine, and A. Rapone (eds.), *Radical Feminism*, pp. 208–212. New York: Quadrangle Books, 1973.

Index

About the Editor

Barbara A. Crow is Assistant Professor of Women's Studies at the University of Calgary and writes on feminist politics and technology.